THE COMPLETE MISSION: IMPOSSIBLE™ DOSSIER

PATRICK J. WHITE

AVON BOOKS ◆ NEW YORK

Passages on pages 353—354 from ACTRESS by Elizabeth Ashley and Ross Firestone. Copyright © 1978 by Elizabeth Ashley and Ross Firestone. Reprinted by permission of the publisher, M. Evans and Company, Inc., New York.

THE COMPLETE MISSION: IMPOSSIBLE DOSSIER is an original publication of Avon Books. This work has never before appeared in book form.

AVON BOOKS
A division of
The Hearst Corporation
1350 Avenue of the Americas
New York, New York 10019

First Avon Books Trade Printing: December 1991

AVON TRADEMARK REG. U.S. PAT. OFF. AND IN OTHER COUNTRIES, MARCA REGISTRADA, HECHO EN U.S.A.

Printed in the U.S.A.

ARC   10   9   8   7   6   5   4   3   2   1

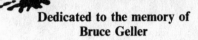

Dedicated to the memory of
Bruce Geller

To Olga Simon,
who proved that
nothing is impossible.

Acknowledgments

JIM PHELPS NEEDED ONLY three or four experts to save the world, bend time, and do the impossible. But they were never foolhardy enough to attempt to write a nonfiction book.

For their time and patience in granting interviews and answering questions, I am indebted to Robert Altman, Barbara Anderson, Arthur R. Ashe, Jr., Luke Askew, Ron Austin, Reza S. Badiyi, Nicholas E. Baehr, Robert Guy Barrows, Julian Barry, Frank Barton, William M. Bates, Eric Bercovici, John D. F. Black, Antoinette Bower, Howard Browne, James D. Buchanan, Jonnie Burke, Robert Butler, Joanna Cassidy, Joel Cohen, Margarita Cordova, Douglas S. Cramer, Marc Daniels, Michael Dann, Bradford Dillman, Philip Fehrle, Edward Feldman, John Florea, Joseph Gantman, Jeannette Geller, Lynda Day George, Jackson Gillis, Tony Giorgio, Ivan Goff, Murray Golden, Peter Graves, Allan and Joyce Greedy, Olga Griffin, James F. Griffith, Robert Hamner, Orville H. Hampton, Alf Harris, Laurence Heath, Shirl Hendryx, Max Hodge, Carolyn Horn, Buck Houghton, Jack Hunsaker, Rick Husky, Donald James, Robert H. Justman, Austin "Rocky" Kalish, Stanley Kallis, Stephen Kandel, Norman Katkov, Lee H. Katzin, Terry Keegan, Paul King, Christopher Knopf, Bernard L. Kowalski, Paul Krasny, Chester Krumholz, Perry Lafferty, Martin Landau, Bruce Lansbury, Robert Lewin, Abbey Lincoln, Harold Livingston, Jerry Ludwig, Barbara Luna, Peter Lupus, Ellis Marcus, Leslie H. Martinson, Gerald Mayer, Barbara McNair, Lee Meriwether, Mina Mittelman, Greg Morris, Gary Morton, Leonard Nimoy, Marc Norman, Carroll O'Connor, Michael O'Herlihy, Albert Paulsen, Joan D. Pearce, Arnold and Lois Peyser, Robert Phillips, Paul Playdon, Stefanie Powers, Brad Radnitz, Robert O. Richards, Don Richardson, Peter Mark Richman, Sam Roeca, Sutton Roley, Charles R. Rondeau, Jerome Ross, Mann Rubin, Sy Salkowitz, Alden Schwimmer, Ralph Senensky, Mike Severeid, Dodie Shepard, Alexander Singer, George F. Slavin, Peter Sloman, Ron Soble, Herbert F. Solow, Sheldon Stark, Beatrice Straight, Dan Striepeke, George Takei, Adele Taylor, Robert E. Thompson, Robert Totten, Guerdon Trueblood, Leigh Vance, John Van Dreelen, Virgil W. Vogel, the late Herb Wallerstein, Jessica Walter, Lesley Ann Warren, Robert and Phyllis White, William Read Woodfield and Robert Malcolm Young.

Also: Charles Aidman, Claude Akins, Val Avery, Barbara Babcock, Jane Badler, Barbara Bain, Diane Baker, Dirk Benedict, Theodore Bikel, Lloyd Bochner, Eric Braeden, Lloyd Bridges, Peter Brown, Michele Carey, Joan Collins, Robert Conrad, Lawrence Dane, Peter Donat, Sam Elliott, Greg Evigan, Bruce Glover, Tony Hamilton, Noel Harrison, Terry Markwell, Mary Ann Mobley, Ricardo Montalban, Phil Morris, David Opatoshu, Thaao Penghlis, George Peppard, Nehemiah Persoff, Joseph Reale, William Shatner, William Smithers, Fritz Weaver, H.M. Wynant, and Anthony Zerbe.

To the following my heartfelt appreciation for their assistance: Allan Asherman, Drew and

THE COMPLETE MISSION: IMPOSSIBLE DOSSIER

Mark Bishop, Lester Borden, Elliott and Sandra Camaren, Esme Chandlee, Charmaine Chester, Diane Chin, Alison Clark, Jerry Cohn, Darlene and Debbie Coyne, Robert Dockery, John Douglas, Joel Eisner, John Ficarra of *Mad* Magazine, Michael Fisher, John Javna, Michael Larkin, Claudia Menza, Doug and Pam Murray, Douglas Olsen, Carol Ossandon, Raymond Pence, Jody Revenson, Lourdes Rivera, Tom Sciacca, Ori Seron, Linda Simeone, Olga Simon, Leslie Solow, Jeff Sorensen, Lois White, and Claire Wolf.

This book would not have existed without the assistance of Paramount Pictures' Paula Block, Cindy Collins, Diane Isaacs, Mary Jane McKinney, Shayne Sherer, John Symes, John Wentworth, Anthony Williams, and especially Kathleen Dunker, who truly made this mission possible.

Contents

Introduction 1

Backstory 2

Writing *Mission: Impossible* 8
Origins 8
Structure and Approach 9
Ethics and Morality 21

Making the Pilot 23
Casting *Mission: Impossible* 23
Directing *Mission: Impossible* 35
Props and Special Effects 39
Mission: Impossible Makeup 40
Postproduction: Editing, Sound, and Music 47

Year One: September 1966–April 1967 53

Year Two: September 1967–April 1968 111

Year Three: September 1968–April 1969 159

Year Four: September 1969–April 1970 211

Year Five: September 1970–April 1971 273

Year Six: September 1971–April 1972 335

Year Seven: September 1972–April 1973 379

Mission: Accomplished 425

Encore 433

Year One: 1988–1989 439

Year Two: 1989–1990 445

"The reader may be able to get a better view of the situation if he will imagine for a moment what would happen if, say, fifteen of his friends decided to play a prank on him. They get together without his knowledge and write the script for a play which will last for an entire week. There are parts for all of them. The victim of the prank is isolated from everyone except the friends who have parts. His every probable reaction has been calculated in advance and the script prepared to meet these reactions. Furthermore, this drama is motivated by some fundamental weakness of the victim—liquor, money, women, or even some harmless personal crotchet. The victim is forced to go along with the play, speaking approximately the lines which are demanded of him; they spring unconsciously to his lips. He has no choice but to go along, because most of the probable objections he can raise have been charted, and logical reactions to them have been provided in the script. Very shortly the victim's feet are quite off the ground. He is living in a play world which he cannot distinguish from the real world. His natural but latent motives are called forth in perfectly contrived situations; actions which, under other circumstances, he would never perform seem natural and logical. He is living in a fantastic, grotesque world which resembles the real one so closely that he cannot distinguish the difference. He is the victim of a confidence game."

—DAVID W. MAURER, *The Big Con*

Introduction

ON THE EVENING OF September 17, 1966, over the CBS television network, a hand struck a match and lit a fuse to a series that was like no other before it.

At the expense of characterization, it presented plots so complex and sophisticated that audiences were challenged to follow them. Propelling these plots were treacherous saboteurs who would lie, cheat, steal, kidnap, subvert the media, destroy the property of innocent people, and break any civil and legal code that stood in their way. They were the *heroes*. The series broke with traditional TV techniques and helped expand and change the way television looked—and was looked upon.

The fuse was lit by a man named Bruce Geller, and the story of *Mission: Impossible* starts with him.

Backstory

*"I don't like the way television program-
ming is going. There is too much sameness,
too much repeating of the old formulas.
There is no real exploring of new avenues
for entertainment. . . . The public deserves
more creativity from TV."*
—LUCILLE BALL, PRESIDENT,
DESILU PRODUCTIONS, 1965

"Nothing is new except in how it's done."
—BRUCE GELLER, 1967

ONE OF THE MOST frequent observations made of *Mission: Impossible* was that each episode looked more like a little movie than a television show. There were two very good reasons for this. The first was that *Mission* was originally planned as a movie; the other was the man behind it.

"The first thing anybody thinks of when he thinks of Bruce Geller is *brilliant,*" says writer-producer Sy Salkowitz. Bruce was born on October 13, 1930, in New York City, the son of Dorothy Friedlander and Justice Abraham N. Geller of the New York State Supreme Court. Judge Geller had always hoped that Bruce, his only son, would become a lawyer. But Bruce had other ideas—he wanted to be a writer. "His father never understood why Bruce threw his life away," Bruce's friend, writer Christopher Knopf, wryly recalls. "Judge Geller was a very imposing man, very strong and forceful. Bruce was always courting his respect and approval, no matter what he was doing. For years he could never get it." Throughout his career, Bruce seemed obsessed with doing a show about a judge and tried three times to film pilots (episodes designed to launch a series). "I don't know whether he was trying to prove something to his father," his friend Salkowitz speculates, "or trying to make up for something. Who knows what lurks in the hearts of men?" It wasn't until Bruce won his first Emmy that the judge learned to appreciate what his son was doing. "In the last several years," says Chris Knopf, "when he saw the big house and all the awards, I think Judge Geller really began to believe that maybe there's more to the world besides the law."

Bruce attended Yale University where, besides excelling in varsity basketball, he wrote for the school paper, theater, and radio station while studying psychology and sociology. After

graduating in 1952 with a BA, Bruce landed a Hollywood job as a reader in Warner Brothers' story department. Fourteen months later, the studio dismissed the entire department to cut costs. "He was fired the day after we were engaged," notes the former Jeannette Marx, who married Bruce in September 1953. Geller returned to New York and made his first script sale by watching television. Without an agent, he wrote and mailed in a script for *Jimmy Hughes, Rookie Cop* (1953), a live show over the Dumont network. The script was accepted and Bruce was paid three hundred dollars.

Bruce's early writing career was a varied one. In addition to scripts for *Flash Gordon* (1953) and *Rocky King, Detective* (1954), he wrote gags for a TV weather girl (three for fifty dollars), bits for nightclub acts, comedy (*The Red Buttons Show*, 1952–54), and quiz shows like *The Big Payoff* and *Strike It Rich*. One of his great interests was musical comedy, and he was a very talented lyricist. Bruce, Jacques (Jack) Urbont, and Dale Wasserman (who later wrote *Man of La Mancha*) collaborated on a musical version of Mark Twain's *Tom Sawyer* called *Livin' the Life*, which opened in New York in 1957. Bruce followed it up with the book and lyrics for *All in Love*, based on Richard Brinsley Sheridan's *The Rivals*, which had a five month Broadway run in 1961–62 and a London production in 1964. Says Knopf, "In *All in Love*, he had a lyric that went, 'Since a rib told a fib to the first foolish man . . .' His lyrics were at times so intricate and brilliant that you couldn't listen to it and appreciate it. They were so clever that you would miss the next few lines trying to figure each one out." Knopf still remembers the lyrics Geller wrote for Writers Guild roasts, including those written in 1963, when Twentieth Century-Fox's production of *Cleopatra* was threatening to bankrupt the studio: " 'Fox you grossest dragon, look at the cost/If Cleo doesn't make it, then one century is lost/Better face the fact, now you know it's true/She did it to Marc Antony and she's doing it to you.' " Says Knopf, "That's Bruce Geller, very bright, very quick, loved words and what he could do with them."

With sales to *The Kaiser Aluminum Hour* and *Have Gun Will Travel*, Bruce and Jinny returned to Hollywood, where his career began to take off with scripts for *The Rifleman* and *The Rebel*. At the end of the decade he moved to Four Star Television, a thriving production company run by Dick Powell. "There never were four stars at Four Star," notes Knopf, who worked there. "People think it was Ida Lupino, but it wasn't. It was Dick Powell, David Niven, and Charles Boyer. They never found a fourth, but they still called it Four Star." In 1960, Geller, Knopf, and Gene Roddenberry were contracted to write nine scripts in ten weeks for *The June Allyson Show* before an impending Writers Guild strike. One of Bruce's was called "Trenchcoat," a comedy for David Niven. Knopf recalls Bruce's behavior during the making of the show. "Bruce could not stay away from the production. He had a way of dramatizing that he was dying when he was seeing something gone wrong. It was not quite a grunt, but it was driving everyone crazy. Finally David Niven said, 'Get that nasty little boy off the set.' " It would not be the last time Bruce was barred from a set. Increasingly unhappy with the way his work was handled, Bruce was already determined to produce and direct his own work. "Bruce would never compromise and he would never back off," Knopf says, "and I never knew him to be wrong, that was the amazing thing. He was brilliant, and had the most amazing damned mind."

Four Star was populated by up-and-coming writers and directors who would soon make their mark in television. Thanks to Powell, many got their start as producers. "It was because they were good directors and writers that Dick offered them their own producing arrangements," says Stan Kallis, producer of *The Dick Powell Show*. "Powell was a man who believed

3

in you," Geller once noted. It was at Four Star that Geller blossomed, with scripts for *Zane Grey Theater* and others. Most of Bruce's work was directed by Bernard L. Kowalski, who became a close friend. Joining them on occasion was writer-producer-director Sam Peckinpah. "Bruce, Sam, and Bernie were a unit in *The Dick Powell Show*," says Kallis. "Aaron Spelling did the standard action melodrama, then there was a group that Dick assembled for the prestigious work." Eventually Geller and Kowalski became partners who developed their own projects.

In 1960 Bruce worked on a series which many old-timers still consider television's finest western. Created and produced by Peckinpah, *The Westerner* was set along the Mexican border and told of wandering cowboy Dave Blassingame (Brian Keith) and his dog, Brown. Geller's main contribution to the show was the character of Burgundy Smith (John Dehner), a cynical, would-be scoundrel who invariably wound up doing the right thing. *The Westerner*'s arch humor, improvisational feel, and gritty realism were fresh air in a genre rapidly becoming exhausted. Perhaps because it was such a departure, *The Westerner* was short-lived. "It was sold and time-slotted for thirteen episodes," says Bernie Kowalski. "Before it was even viewed, *The Nanette Fabray Show* was booked into that time slot after the first thirteen *Westerner*s. I never understood why. To my mind, it stands out as a classic western series." Within the industry, *The Westerner* helped make the reputations of Peckinpah, Kowalski, and Geller. "Bruce did the best scripts he ever wrote in his life for *The Westerner*," says Chris Knopf. "He had a classic line, when Keith is sitting with his dog on a curb and he looks at the dog and says, 'Man's best friend is his mother.' That's a Bruce Geller line." Bruce got his first directing credit on the series and once proudly said of his seven scripts for the show, "I couldn't wait to see them shot." Continuing with Four Star, Geller became producer of *The Dick Powell Show* in 1961, wrote four episodes, and was nominated for a Producers Guild award.

In 1963 Geller and Kowalski embarked upon *The Robert Taylor Show*, in which the veteran actor would portray an investigator for the Department of Health, Education, and Welfare, assisted by a younger officer (George Segal). "We flew to Washington and had the cooperation of the HEW," says Kowalski. The scripts, based on HEW case files, addressed modern American problems. "We had a pickup for thirteen episodes, and were doing shows that were quite meaningful," Kowalski feels. Says Chris Knopf, who wrote one, "Several scripts were ordered and they really got into sensitive areas. Bruce was taking very liberal positions about what was wrong in this country in social areas of deprivation and ignorance. And before the show ever got on the air, NBC panicked and said, 'Well, we just can't put this thing on.'" Five scripts were written before the series was killed. "It was about the time that HEW was coming out with their bans on cigarettes and various other products," says Kowalski. "To the best of my knowledge, big business stepped in and said, 'We don't want to create an image for HEW so that when it speaks, someone of the stature and integrity of Robert Taylor is gonna give it all the more meaning.' So we made four of them, they were never shown, and we were all paid off."

Dick Powell died in 1963, and Four Star faltered. "We were all trying to get out of our contracts," Chris Knopf states. "When Dick Powell died they had thirteen shows on the air. Two years later they had two. He was Four Star and he was magnificent." Knopf negotiated his way out of his contract, but Geller and Kowalski weren't so lucky and waited out their time. "The two of them and director Charlie Rondeau would sit around playing hearts all day long," says Knopf.

While under contract to Four Star, Geller and Kowalski produced *Rawhide*'s sixth season

for CBS in 1964–65. They decided to shake up the series, concentrating less on cattle drives and more on characters and departures like a two-part musical segment. The title of one script, "The Lost Herd," sums up the attitude. Another, Sy Salkowitz's "Nobody Calls Me Mister," was positively surrealistic. "There was a semiretarded character who was assistant to the cook and he washed the dishes," Salkowitz explains. "He was big, rugged looking, but very childlike. They wanted me to get inside his head. We would do a flip, and this character would be playing the lead roles, the Eric Fleming and Clint Eastwood parts, and they would be him, washing the dishes."

Kowalski and Geller won several Western Heritage awards for their *Rawhide* work, but CBS was unhappy. "We were told that Mr. Paley (CBS chairman of the board) wanted more cows back in the episodes," Kowalski relates, "and he didn't like the dark photography we were affecting. We knew that we were making good shows and felt that it wasn't Paley who was watching *Rawhide,* that it was someone else at the network. It ends up that it was his *favorite* show, he *was* watching, and the orders handed down to us came directly from him! We had ignored them for a season, so they took us off the show."

After their firing, Geller and Kowalski split up. "We were such good friends and respected each other that after approximately five years we felt that we would rather maintain the personal relationship than the professional one," says Bernie. Four Star Television was sinking at the same time. Out of four new series for the 1965–66 season, only one (*The Big Valley*) survived.

Four Star wasn't the only TV studio in trouble. Desilu Productions was founded in 1951 by Desi Arnaz and Lucille Ball to produce their TV series, *I Love Lucy.* The rest truly is history and by 1956, Desilu was a TV factory, producing or renting facilities to shows like *Our Miss Brooks, December Bride* and *The Whirlybirds.* In 1957 Desi bought the former RKO lot from General Tire for over six million dollars, acquiring thirty-five stages and a forty-acre backlot among four separate locations. Five years later Lucy bought out Arnaz's interests in the studio for three million dollars and replaced him as company president.

Desilu, never a TV giant, was reasonably successful in the fifties. By the mid sixties, however, the only Desilu show on the air was Lucille Ball's top-rated *The Lucy Show,* and the studio was functioning mainly as a rental facility for companies like Bing Crosby Productions. *Ben Casey, Lassie, My Favorite Martian,* and *My Three Sons* were just a few of the series filmed at Desilu. The company was consistently unable to sell another series to any of the networks, despite many pilots. CBS had a separate development deal with Desilu, but Mike Dann, the network's top programmer, and Perry Lafferty, the west coast vice president, remained unimpressed with everything the studio pitched.

"Every year we would make maybe five pilots," Desilu music supervisor Jack Hunsaker recalls, "and none of them sold." In 1965, all of the studio's five pilots failed, and in the fall, as in the previous year, all Desilu had was *The Lucy Show.* "The management was not strong," Hunsaker feels. "Lucy owned the studio but she was not really a management person." At Desilu's August stockholders meeting there were grumblings about the company's drop in net profits, from $800,000 in 1964 to $455,000. Desilu's lack of dividends also spurred criticism. "Our money is being used to support the company," Lucille Ball explained. Clearly, big changes were necessary.

Desperate, Desilu approached the talent agency of Ashley-Steiner to work with CBS's development funds and try to get more series sold. The agency put one of its top men, Alden Schwimmer, on the project. Schwimmer did what any self-respecting agent would do: He

5

assigned his own clients to the job. "It wasn't as simple as that," observes Schwimmer, who knew he was walking a tightrope. "There was a giant conflict of interest which had to be handled very delicately. If you represent one side of the deal (the writer), you want to get the best deal for him; if you also represent the buyer, you want to buy for as cheap as you can. You had to be a diplomat and know how to make everyone content that it was a fair deal for all parties." Schwimmer was in a unique position. "It is very rare that an agent has the power to *give* his clients wonderful deals. That's what I had, this Desilu money to spend on my clients. Obviously, the ultimate responsibility was to make something good come out of it, which it did, but it was a hell of a thing which I had going."

Schwimmer's power extended to picking a new Desilu chief: former CBS executive Oscar Katz. "We needed a figurehead," says Schwimmer. "We never expected Oscar Katz to be a creative genius and he wasn't. He was a decent, honorable, intelligent man who knew what he could and could not do. We brought Oscar in because we wanted a free hand there. I didn't want anybody as the head of Desilu who was going to give me trouble and tell me he didn't like the project." Katz brought in as vice president Herbert F. Solow, a former NBC daytime programmer and talent agent who eventually replaced Katz when he returned to CBS after a year at Desilu.

Among Schwimmer's clients were Gene Roddenberry, who sold *Star Trek* to Desilu, and Bruce Geller, who was busy developing an idea he hoped would get him out of TV and into motion pictures. Inspired by the popular 1964 caper movie *Topkapi, Briggs' Squad* was conceived during his days with Kowalski. "He had a lot of research on it," says Kowalski. "He must have had a lot of approaches, because there were a lot of papers." Geller, unaccustomed to writing mechanical and complicated scripts, had great difficulty plotting *Briggs' Squad,* but remained excited by its potential. When Alden Schwimmer saw an outline, he surprised Bruce by suggesting that he write it as a pilot script for Desilu. Bruce wasn't crazy about the idea; this was his breakthrough script, and besides, if *one* plot was giving him such trouble, how could he do a *series* of them? Ultimately he reconsidered and submitted a thirty-minute version of *Briggs' Squad* as one of three scripts in his development deal with Desilu (the others were a western and a comedy).

Lucille Ball's husband, Gary Morton, recalls sitting up with Lucy until 3 A.M. trying to decide which of a handful of scripts would be produced with CBS's development funds. According to Morton, he recommended *Briggs' Squad* (now retitled *Mission: Impossible*) to Lucy, who responded, "I read it, but I don't understand it."* Like Schwimmer, Morton believed the show could sell, and Lucy went with the decision.

According to Schwimmer, "When we brought the script into CBS as part of Lucy's development deal, we had a meeting with Mike Dann. Mike said, 'You can make this if you want to, I can't stop you. I will never put it on the air.' That is a direct, absolute quote. He didn't like it; it wasn't his type of program.

"That put a tremendous pressure on us. Here is the head of programming at CBS telling us that we're gonna throw the money down the sewer because even if we make it, he isn't gonna put it on the air." Schwimmer met with Lucy's attorney, Mickey Rudin. "Mickey had the ultimate say with Lucille Ball," Schwimmer claims. "Mickey was the real brains behind Desilu in an administration, financial, and Lucy sense. He asked, 'What should we do?' I said, 'Make the pilot.' See, he could get Lucy to do just about anything, and we had a wonderful

---

* Lucy always maintained that she never understood *Mission: Impossible,* even after she saw it.

relationship. So we made *Mission: Impossible* in the face of Mike Dann's statement that he would never put it on the air."

Soon afterward, Dann threw Desilu yet another curve. "I was much opposed to the half-hour dramatic form," he explains. "It was a carryover from radio, and I was convinced that you had to have hour dramas." The network informed Desilu that they were no longer interested in half-hour dramas, and Bruce had to expand his thirty-minute script. Fortunately, he was blessed with enormous powers of concentration. "He had the ability," says producer-writer Leigh Vance, "to sit in the middle of a room with his two little daughters and his wife and the radio and the television on, and do his writing." Over a weekend, Geller enlarged the script to an hour.

From the start, Bruce Geller considered the pilot a calling card for movie work. "He said there was no possible way it could sell," Jinny Geller recalls. There were other reasons besides Mike Dann's dictate. "The audience would have to change its viewing habits," Jinny adds. "They couldn't get up for a can of beer or go to the bathroom. If they did they would miss an important point." The idea was too complex for TV and far too expensive to produce on a weekly basis. Worst of all, how could you write one every week? Logically, there was no way it could sell.

So, of course, it did.

Writing *Mission: Impossible*

"Mission isn't a what, it's a how."
—BRUCE GELLER, 1967

"It's not exactly writing. It's building Rube Goldberg crossword puzzles."
—WRITER STEPHEN KANDEL

Origins

"I HAVE ALWAYS admired movies such as *Rififi, Topkapi,* and *League of Gentlemen,* enjoyed the elaborate working out of a criminal thing," Bruce Geller once remarked. Says *Mission* star Greg Morris of Bruce's inspiration, "We discussed it. It was a straight rip-off of two pictures, *Rififi* and *Topkapi."* Indeed, *Mission*'s pilot features many scenes without dialogue (à la *Rififi*), and a scene in which a safecracker's hands are broken (right out of *Topkapi*). But what *Mission* resembled most was an obscure TV show called *21 Beacon Street.*

This intelligent half-hour series, produced by Filmways in 1959 for NBC (and later rerun by ABC) centered around the Dennis Chase Detective Agency at the title address. Brilliant planner Chase (Dennis Morgan) is assisted by a beautiful Phi Beta Kappa (Joanna Barnes), a law school graduate and ex-Marine (Brian Kelly), and a dialectician and inventive genius (James Maloney). Although he always urged his clients to go to the law, Chase took on cases that the police couldn't or wouldn't solve, like proving that an accident was murder, recovering a kidnap victim, ending a murder-for-insurance racket, and outswindling swindlers. The team, which rarely used violence, operated as con artists, intercepted and replaced criminals as a means of infiltration, and were well equipped with hidden tape recorders, bugs, and a pair of radio-transmitter eyeglasses.

21 Beacon Street ran for thirteen weeks and was forgotten—until 1968, when Filmways brought suit against *Mission.* According to Laurence Heath, one of *Mission*'s best writers (and coincidentally, *Beacon Street*'s script consultant), "Bruce claimed, 'I never saw *21 Beacon Street,* I didn't even know it existed.' I believed him, but the evidence was so overwhelming. . . ." *Beacon Street*'s pilot, written by Heath, required Chase's team to steal a letter from a bank's safe deposit box; *Mission*'s involved the theft of nuclear bombs from a hotel vault. Another *Beacon Street* segment, "The Payoff," is nearly identical to a *Mission* two-part episode, "The Contender." Both series featured an apartment scene, in which the impending caper was discussed. The lawsuit was settled out of court for "very little," Heath

8

claims, "just an acknowledgment that there was merit in the case." *21 Beacon Street* then returned to television limbo, an unjust fate for a show ahead of its time.

Structure and Approach

In an early treatment, Geller wrote that Briggs' Squad was formerly a Special Forces group that performed wartime missions "often incredibly hazardous and totally without reward because the government of the United States must disavow any knowledge of these particular activities. Once, in a country in a crisis, the group of men . . . were pulled together to do a job. . . . It was only the first job of five years work under the leadership of Lt. Col. David Briggs, for what had come to be known, unofficially, to the few men who knew of its existence, as Briggs' Squad."

The team consisted of Albert Ney, a wheeler-dealer "who never owns anything longer than it takes to turn it over at a profit"; Jack Smith, who "does not know what a woman means by the word 'no,' never—not once in his life—ever having heard it"; Barney Collier, "expert in ballistics, demolition, submarine vessels," and possessor of a "graduate degree in bioelectric chemical engineering, permutative mathematics, microphysics"; Willy "the Arm" Armitage, "ugly, ill-educated, inept," and "probably the strongest man in the world"; Little Terry Targo, a mild-mannered martial arts expert, "three-time felony offender," and professional killer; and Martin Land, "a master of disguise, quick change, a superb pickpocket, fluent in fifteen languages, able to hold his breath for six or seven minutes," and above all a master magician. Ironically, peacetime transformed these daredevils into crooks. "The criminals have all the fun," Geller once observed. "Psychologically, when you watch a film where a group of people get together to rob a bank, even though you know they're on the wrong side of the law, you find yourself rooting for them."

Their leader is David Briggs* who, in Geller's treatment, explains his team: "I once led them, and, for better or for worse, I turned them into what they are. . . . In each case I have made them unfit to live like normal human beings. Call it because of a death wish, a compulsion, a streak of larceny, competitive instinct, a desire for adventure, or just the lure of life, one way or another, each of them seems destined to end up in the electric chair or serving a long term in prison—unless—unless I, the responsible party, can channel all this that I have made . . . I am a PhD in analytical psychology and highly paid as a behavioral analyst. All this means is that I am an expert in human beings, i.e., one of the world's greatest guessers."

Briggs reunites the team for "a crime that men of good will may admire," one which takes two million dollars just to finance. "In six weeks . . . three powerful men will meet aboard a yacht. Surrounding that yacht will be three heavily armed, full complemented destroyer escorts. Aboard that yacht will be the fabled wealth of the Indies." The men on the yacht are evil dictators, bent on dividing the treasure. The job of Briggs' Squad is to steal it, using a World War II Japanese five-man submarine, a helium-filled balloon, a gold-plated gun and bullets, a dozen canaries, an electric train set, a case of liquor, a bulletproof suit, and a dozen fresh roses! "This crime will not be unfolded in detailed sequence—now," the treatment concluded. "There is much more to be said . . . particularly Briggs' real reason for leading them again. Enough for the moment to say—this robbery on the high seas is the crime of the century. There is only one group of men who could do it. Briggs' Squad."

---

* Later changed to Dan Briggs.

Bruce ran into trouble as soon as he started scripting the movie. "When I wrote the pilot," he later admitted, "I didn't quite know what I was doing. I made mistakes." According to *Mission* writer Paul Playdon, "He told me he had to work it out with index cards. It was the only way he could come to grips with the timing and how the different story threads would interweave. He explained that after working it all out with the cards, he still couldn't straighten out all the threads."

Bruce was undecided over how to open it: launch right into the caper and introduce each character via expository flashbacks or begin with Briggs tracking down each member of the squad? He jettisoned the high seas robbery and plotted another caper: the theft of two nuclear warheads from a guarded hotel safe before a Latin American dictator can deploy them. Albert Ney and Jack Smith disappeared from the team, replaced by "an absolutely stunning girl in her twenties" named Cinnamon. What did *not* change was the morality of the squad: Barney is a cheating 21 dealer and compulsive gambler; Cinnamon "a total waste of a woman" hooked on alcohol and narcotics; Terry Targo a hit man who enjoys his work; Willy "the Arm" Armitage a woman-beating strip joint bouncer; Martin Land a top magician—and thief. "I made you unfit to live as normal human beings," Briggs reminds them. "We did too much that was too fascinating too often. I led you, so I feel responsible for what you all are . . . bored, as I am. Bored by an honest life, a life without excitement . . . or danger."

With the possibility of a TV sale, Bruce added a one-paragraph forecast. "The series based on *Briggs' Squad* is obvious," he wrote. "This group of men may attempt anything. It is probable that some of the characterizations will have to be altered to fit the Television Code. *Briggs' Squad* may have to be given a semiofficial status (unknown to any of them but Briggs) by which they are actually performing their services for the United States government without any official aegis and with Briggs' full awareness that if they are caught they will have to take the full rap as the government will not acknowledge any awareness of their existence. Thus, constantly pursued by the law and the forces of society, always in pursuit of the unattainable, *Briggs' Squad* is a series about fascinating men in motion—both physically—and kinetically."

The sale of the pilot (retitled *IMF,** then *Mission: Impossible*) forced Bruce to develop a series concept. He made his unsavory crooks palatable for TV by turning them into secret agents. Sparked by the early James Bond films starring Sean Connery, spies and secret agents were everywhere in 1965—in movies, best-selling books, and TV shows like *The Man from U.N.C.L.E., The Wild Wild West, Get Smart, I Spy,* and Britain's *The Avengers* and *Secret Agent.* While the early scripts were being written, Geller spoke about his IMF, which he called "a private group, not a government group. It always works on the right side. It takes on delicate assignments for the government or anyone. Such as if the CIA doesn't want to be directly involved in a case. . . . Sometimes, because of circumstances, the FBI, New York police, or California sheriffs can't enter into a situation—then they hire this group. The impossibility of the challenge enters into it. . . . It's very difficult to define what they are because their missions have a broad scope—sometimes it's spying, sometimes detective work."

The show was designed for only three regular characters: Briggs, Cinnamon, and Barney. "Some missions require skills they don't have," Bruce told a reporter, "so they go outside, and that's when a guest star comes in." A variety of "guest spies," like those in the pilot, were to be used when necessary. Some would even be killed in action to generate suspense.

Geller designed *Mission* to stand out from similar shows. "The story was what always

---

* Impossible Missions Force.

pushed the program forward, not the characters," Herb Solow notes. In fact, Geller dispensed with characterization altogether. Our heroes' personalities and backgrounds were never referred to or explored, and the only reference to the past is uttered by a mysterious recorded voice who, after offering Briggs his pilot assignment, says with some warmth, "I hope it's welcome back, Dan, it's been a while." Nothing more was ever made of it. Until now, television was populated by likable characters whom viewers could care about. *Mission* offered characters the audience would never get to know, characters who, five minutes into the show, are playing a role within the story and aren't who they really are.

The complete absence of characterization made the IMF seem more like machine parts than people, which was precisely what Geller wanted. "They are what they do," he said more than once, and the strategy was invaluable: The IMF could more credibly be who they pretended to be because they weren't contrasted against any "real" personalities. As a result, said series star Barbara Bain, "There are some interesting points made. The willingness to accept externals. The way people react to a person simply because he wears a uniform."

Nevertheless, audiences learned to like these ciphers, thanks to the charm of the actors portraying them and the show's underlying message of teamwork, loyalty, mutual respect, and absolute mutual dependency. Because their schemes were so complex, the agents had to be in sync with each other. When Willy was hit with a villain's shotgun blast, he was fully confident that Barney had earlier replaced the bullets with blanks. Says Greg Morris, "The audience knew that if one of the characters was in trouble, the other four would carry out the mission and come back and get the fifth one." There was never any doubt.

Geller also considered serializing the show. "The theory," Herb Solow explains, "was to do a cliff-hanger each week. A story could take two episodes to tell, or three or four. We would do a highly stylized cliff-hanger each week." In 1966, only *Batman,* which aired in two weekly installments, and *Peyton Place,* a prime-time serial, had such a format. Geller envisioned plots too complex to tell in a single sitting. Says Sy Salkowitz, who wrote two episodes, "Bruce's concept was *Topkapi:* Get in there, establish the fact that one misstep and you're dead, and thereafter it's nothing but suspense." Each show would contain a "random element" to threaten the IMF plot and force them to find another solution. "The idea was that no story would look like what it started out to be," says Robert Lewin. "In other words there would always be a reverse twist, a switch, or a switch on a switch. You could never be ahead of the story, you were always to be surprised, yet it would always be logical and ingenious."

An inevitable consequence of such mechanical plots was *Mission*'s ever-increasing reliance on electronic devices—a direction which surprised Geller. "A lot of writers are very much influenced by *The Man from U.N.C.L.E.* and James Bond," he noticed in 1966. "They go overboard on gimmicks." Similarly, fictitious "magic drugs" which provided whatever effects the IMF needed (scramble a man's memory, simulate heart attacks and death, provide immunity from nerve gas and narcotics, etc.) become more predominant.

Although many of Geller's ideas for the show went unrealized, he was able to develop concepts that helped individualize the show. The most innovative was a three-scene opening which became classic: the tape, dossier, and apartment scenes.

In the tape scene, Briggs enters a nondescript locale like a rooftop, elevator, pawnshop, or penny arcade. Sometimes exchanging a seemingly innocuous code phrase with a contact, he is left alone to uncover and activate a tape, record, or other playback device. A tape voice explains an imminent crisis beyond the means of conventional solutions, offers it to Briggs with the words, "Your mission, should you decide to accept it," and warns him, "should you

The IMF leader (in this case Peter Graves as Jim Phelps) received his instructions in out-of-the-way locales.

or any of your IM Force be caught or killed, the secretary will disavow any knowledge of your actions." The recorded instructions then either self-destruct in a matter of seconds, or Briggs disposes of them in a furnace, acid bath, or other irrevocable process. The audience never learned who the mysterious tape voice belonged to or who the secretary was. Indeed, there were indications that even Briggs didn't know, but considering the type of assignments offered, he was certainly a high US government official.

In the pilot, Briggs's instructions are on a hermetically sealed record album which decomposes one minute after exposure to the air. During the first season, Dan found messages on records, reel-to-reel tapes, dictaphones, and nickelodeons. Geller wanted the information destroyed differently in each episode. When that became impractical, the process was standardized, and a self-destructing reel-to-reel tape most commonly utilized. Making the tapes self-destruct was easy: special effects man Jonnie Burke piped smoke from the bottom of the tape machine up through the reels. The scene became *Mission*'s most popular trademark.

The tape scene was usually filmed long before the rest of the episode. After the first year, the tape scenes were filmed en masse by a special unit over a two-day period at the start of each season. Says director Gerald Mayer, "We were always interested in seeing the shows on the air, just to see what the opening scene was gonna be!"

In the next scene, Dan returns to his elegant black-and-white high-rise apartment in (unspecified) New York and consults a large portfolio marked, Impossible Missions Force. From the portfolio he examines an assortment of dossiers (visually represented by photographs) and picks the agents for his assignment by tossing the dossiers on his coffee table.

Dan Briggs (top, Steven Hill) and Jim Phelps choose their operatives from the IMF portfolio.

THE COMPLETE MISSION: IMPOSSIBLE DOSSIER

It was via this dossier scene that we learned all we would ever know about the operatives. A magazine clipping showed Willy Armitage lifting an enormous barbell; Barney Collier's dossier was a brochure for Collier Electronics and a close-up of its president; Cinnamon Carter graced the cover of *Elite* magazine, where she reigned as model of the year; Rollin Hand (originally Martin Land) was seen on a theatrical flyer. To keep things fresh over the years, the photos would change. The dossiers Dan rejected were usually pictures of crewmen and their wives, among them Bruce and Jinny Geller, writer Allan Balter, property man Bill Bates, associate producers Bob Justman and Barry Crane, hairstylist Adele Taylor, and producer Joseph Gantman. The dossier scene lasted through the first four seasons and, like the tape scene, was frequently lampooned. In an episode of *Get Smart,* agent Maxwell Smart consulted his own portfolio which included photos of TV personality David Susskind, da Vinci's *Mona Lisa, Mad* magazine's Alfred E. Neuman, and singer Tiny Tim (whose picture Max tears to pieces!)

Following the dossier scene is the apartment scene, in which the IMF cryptically discuss their impending mission, presenting intriguing bits and pieces of their plan and demonstrating devices to be used later in the show, all to whet the audience's appetite. "They never told you what they were planning," writer Laurence Heath recalls. "You knew that they had had a meeting or two before this scene, and this was just like a teaser." In keeping with the apartment's black-and-white decor, the actors wore only black, white, and gray during this scene. "There's nothing quite as arresting in color as black and white," Geller told *TV Guide.* "It brings out the colors in the faces and it's a contrast. Then when you cut to something in color, the effect is startling." Geller, who hoped to make a color feature using only black and white, was rigid about this stylized touch and vetoed any suggestion that would change it, including one from actor Steven Hill (Briggs) to put an American flag in the apartment.

After the apartment scene, the show literally jumped into the next scene—the mission

WILLY ARMITAGE
SETS NEW W...

14

ELITE

JANUARY • ONE DOLLAR

MODEL OF
THE YEAR

CINNAMON
CARTER

PRESENTING

ROLLIN
HAND

MAN OF A MILLION FACES

WORLD'S GREATEST IMPERSONATOR · QUICK CHANGE · ILLUSION

The dossiers of the IMF: Peter Lupus as Willy (opposite page), Greg Morris as Barney (top), Barbara Bain as Cinnamon (left), and Martin Landau as Rollin (right).

The Apartment scene offered tantalizing glimpses of the IMF plan.

already underway. Bruce had devised television's most original way of presenting awkward story exposition, and the effect was breathless. Says writer Sam Roeca, "You could get on that tape what would take ten pages of standard dialogue to make palatable." In a sense, it eliminated the story's act one. As writer Jerry Ludwig explains, "In terms of the classic three-act structure, normally there's a problem, the characters muse upon it and decide what their alternatives are, then they make a decision and decide to act. *Mission* would begin in the second act. As if you've lost a reel of the picture, you just leap forward and start telling the story."

Of course, the notion of a spy receiving his secret orders on a tape anyone could activate made about as much sense as the existence of Briggs's labeled IMF portfolio. But it never seemed to matter; these were great visual scenes that hooked the audience.

Another Geller touch was the series' total lack of humor. "The key to the show is that it's played for real," he said, "as opposed to *U.N.C.L.E.* and Bond. We try to make the audience feel that what they see is plausible." The fact that there was no comic relief and that the IMF almost never joked among themselves, distinguished *Mission* and had a beneficial side effect. Similar shows (notably *The Man from U.N.C.L.E.*) degenerated into self-parody and exhausted themselves after only a few seasons. *Mission* outlasted them all. Bruce may have purposely chosen not to encourage the audience. As he told one writer, "I don't want to start them laughing, because we may have trouble stopping them!"

There *was* humor in *Mission,* but it was subliminal—for example, "Gellerese," the vaguely European language seen in the series' many fictitious locales. Gellerese was developed largely by Bruce, Peter Sloman, and Joan Pearce of deForest Research, the company that checked the accuracy of the scripts. "Bruce's idea was that it should be intelligible to anyone who speaks

only English," says Sloman, "but it should look like German, Hungarian, whatever." What he usually did was change the letters in a familiar word to make it look strange, "but if you said it you could generally understand what was being said." He and Joan Pearce spent Friday afternoons laughing themselves silly, creating terms like "machina werke" (machine repair), "zöna restrik" (restricted area), and the ever-popular "gäz" (gas).

Like the pilot, *Mission*'s early episodes pose physical puzzles to be solved: break someone out of prison, smuggle someone *into* prison, uncover a hidden message, lure a crook onto American soil for extradition. But as Laurence Heath (who'd write more *Mission*s than anyone else) points out, "If you took that approach, you would have had four episodes and that would have been the end of it." It was the writing team of William Read Woodfield and Allan Balter who opened up and defined the show. In their first script, episode 5, "Odds on Evil," the IMF must bankrupt a prince before he can buy an arms shipment. They don't crack his safe and steal the cash—they maneuver him into *giving* them the money.

They con him.

As a boy, Woodfield read *The Big Con* (Bobbs-Merrill Co., New York, 1940), a marvelous study of American confidence men and their methods, written by English professor David W. Maurer. "Everybody in Hollywood has read *The Big Con* and over the years has incorporated various ideas and thoughts," claims writer-producer James Buchanan. In fact, Maurer sued the makers of the hit film *The Sting* (1973) because it so closely followed his book (the character played by Paul Newman was called Gondorff, the name of three brother cons whose exploits Maurer described). Billy Woodfield, a con devotee and self-described "apprentice cheat," was the prime mover behind the IMF's transformation into con artists. The approach had great story potential, gave the series its own identity, and helped make *Mission* a hit.

The confidence man's motto, "You can't cheat an honest man," could well have been the IMF's. "A confidence man prospers only because of the fundamental dishonesty of his victim," wrote Maurer. "He allows the victims to make large sums of money by means of dealings which are explained to him as being dishonest and hence a 'sure thing.' . . . The mark puts all his scruples behind him. He closes out his bank account, embezzles from his employer or his clients. In the mad frenzy of cheating someone else, he is unaware of the fact that he is the real victim, carefully selected and fattened for the kill."

The Big Con tells of the "grifter" (a nonviolent con man) who, aided by "ropers" (who lure victims into the con), sets up a "big store"—a phony (but fully-equipped) betting hall, telegraph office, or brokerage firm operated solely for the benefit of the "mark" or victim. The Impossible Missions Force created their own big stores in the form of artificial prison cells, hospital rooms, airplane cabins, penthouse apartments, submarines, trains, ocean freighters, or military offices, all to make the mark say or do what they wanted him to. Having succeeded, the team would sometimes wheel away the "store's" phony walls, bringing the dumbfounded mark face-to-face with his downfall.

When they couldn't create the proper setting, the IMF adapted to a genuine environment, even if it meant penetrating a palace and impersonating a prince. "They took reality and went beyond it," says actor Tony Giorgio, an expert in magic and cons. Perennial *Mission* scams include the "time warp," in which the mark believes he's had amnesia for months or years, and the "dream machines," with which the team convinced their adversaries that they could produce diamonds, heroin, counterfeit cash, eternal youth, mind-controlling drugs, and various computer setups to rig card and billiard games.

Jerry Ludwig, who wrote only four episodes but truly understood the show, explains that "essentially it was manipulation. Pernell Roberts has all that gold in his vault. How do you get it out? You can't, but he can get it out for you! Balter talked about the idea of manipulating someone, say a guy like me, so that I would want to, more than anything in the world, kiss Victor Buono* on the lips!"

The most commonly expressed "secret" behind *Mission* was that it was "written backwards," that the writer had to know what the last scene was before he could accurately plot out a suitably complicated story line. Woodfield and Balter, *Mission*'s consummate masters, *"never* wrote it backwards. I've heard that," says Woodfield. "I don't understand that." The Woodfield–Balter system was a four-page outline based partially on the principles of Lajos Egri, writing instructor and author of *The Art of Dramatic Writing* (Simon & Schuster, New York, 1946).

On their "idea" page Woodfield and Balter listed story elements like **world** (the story's setting, as in "the world of diamonds," or "the world of railroads"); **incidents** (events which take place in that world); **shtick** (visual material or "gags" applicable to that world); and most important, **characters,** upon which the entire Woodfield-Balter system was built.

"Egri took a very sensible position," says Woodfield, "that you take a guy's fatal flaw, such as dishonesty, and tie it to a statement that must be true, like 'dishonesty leads to destruction.' Every villain we ever used *obsessively* had one of these fatal flaws, and it was precisely that fatal flaw that every show was engineered around." The writers hoisted the villain on his own petard. If he was obsessively greedy, the IMF fed that greed by offering him an irresistible, dishonest way to profit. "We made the guy reach for something," Woodfield stresses, "and the method always had to appear very logical."

The writers avoided making the villain gullible. Also, says Woodfield, "We always made the villain stronger than any member of the team. We also backed him up and made him vicious

---

* The obese character actor.

Writers William Read Woodfield (left) and Allan Balter (right) defined the series and were *Mission: Impossible*'s consummate masters.

Three recurring bad guys (from left to right): John Vernon ("The Exchange"), Anthony Zerbe ("The Photographer"), and Albert Paulsen, who appeared in five episodes.

and mean. When you send a team in after a guy, they've got to go for a really *bad* person. It had to be a contest in which everything is in favor of the bad guy. If you don't have a worthy adversary dedicated to doing something that you must stop, something that you cannot walk away from, then you don't have an episode. A worthy adversary is the key to the whole thing. James Bond had worthy adversaries, crackpot though they were. But Bond didn't make them reach out for something. No traps were ever set, even in the books. Goldfinger was interested in gold and wanted to rob Fort Knox, but Bond didn't set that for him. The psychology of *how* you get the sucker (in our case, the villain) to go for it is all explained in *The Big Con.*"

To avoid engendering audience sympathy, the villains were always portrayed as wholly evil, deserving the devious fate the IMF prepared for them. In the show's later years, this "sympathy dilemma" was an occasional problem, with some opponents so overwhelmed by the IMF assault that they seemed pitiable. *Mission*'s most effective bad guys—John Vernon, Fritz Weaver, Anthony Zerbe, Albert Paulsen, and others—projected a formidable strength and intelligence and were called back again and again.

Woodfield and Balter's Egri page listed other plot elements like **premise** (good triumphs over evil, jealousy leads to destruction, etc.); **thesis** (for example, a man whose father was killed by the US government for treason decides to avenge him by destroying the USA); **antithesis** (the IMF must stop him); **synthesis** (the IMF stops him by making him think that he *has* destroyed America, at which point they get the information they need to prevent it). The **handcuff** was usually the mission itself, presenting a villain or crisis so dire that the IMF, being good Americans, *must* accept the job. **Point of attack** was the point at which the audience (and the IMF) enter the plot, usually a critical moment with time running out. The **transition** is the villain's eventual shift from threat to victim. **Growth**, the changes made in the characters over the course of the story, was rarely explored in *Mission*. "When those things fell into place," says Woodfield, "then you know you've got a show." The final step was a two-page story plan made of twenty-four separate scenes in which the four "act curtains" or "cliff-hangers" were developed. "It would usually take us two days to block out a show," Woodfield says, "and four to five days to write one. It was not easy." *Mission* was one of the few series to effectively use the four-act TV format by presenting exciting act breaks which left an IMFer in danger of exposure. When the show resumed after the commercial break, the viewer invariably learned that the agent was *deliberately* exposed as part of the plan!

THE COMPLETE MISSION: IMPOSSIBLE DOSSIER

Sometimes the scams went to extremes. Although IMFers would often shoot each other with blanks for the mark's benefit, in one case an agent purposely took a rifle shot to the arm as part of the plot. In another segment, an operative impersonates a powerful gangster and even approves a contract murder! "That was where the fun lay," says actor Martin Landau, "the absolutely insane fanning out and bringing it back together, creating such a web to accomplish one little act. In actuality, there'd be an assassination. What an easy way to get rid of that dictator. Get a sharpshooter in there to pull the trigger, and we'd have a three-minute show."

Although the idea of the con opened up the show, writers still found *Mission* extremely difficult to script because of its strange structure and unconventional story lines. Geller's dovetailed structure, in which seemingly unconnected subplots meshed at the climax to accomplish the mission, was daunting. It meant interweaving a "visible" IMF approach (usually headed by Rollin and Cinnamon), an "invisible" approach (Barney and Willy performing the technical-mechanical aspects of the plan), and the actions of the villains. "There are many fine writers in TV," Bruce said, "but they can't do our show. They're used to well-drawn characters and we have no use for this kind of script. . . . We never try to explain anything before it happens. While this goes against the grain of some writers, it has a residual effect, we discovered. People like to discuss the show long after it's over." Says veteran Guerdon Trueblood, who was unable to write the show, "I don't think there has ever been a more difficult show to write in the history of American television. It had nothing to do with what kind of writer you were. You either clicked into the format or you didn't." Partners Ron Austin and James Buchanan went into a story meeting with a *Mission* producer and admitted, "We don't understand the show. There's no first act." The producer responded, "Good! You're the perfect people to write it!" Alf Harris, who wrote one episode, explains that "it was not a who-done-it but a how-done-it. How were they going to do it? You had to come up with very clever ways, and that was the trouble. You can tell the same love story again and again, but you can't tell the same how-done-it again and again. It was almost impossible to come up with a really good how-done-it that hasn't been done a million times."

The actual writing was the easy part, says Jerry Ludwig; it was the plotting that took all the time. "You would spend weeks into months getting the story right. The actual writing would take maybe four days because it was so detailed by that point. By God, it had to make sense by the time it was done. This was before home video recorders, so the audience couldn't roll it back and look at it again. But if there was a detail that didn't seem to make sense, you'd hear about it."

"Getting through the first script was the hardest part," remembers Paul Playdon, who worked on the show for two years, "as hard as what Bruce had to do (for the pilot). It wasn't just a case of working out different characters—he was establishing a very ritualistic pattern which would have to be continued in each show and became trademarks and catchphrases. In effect, you had to write your own pilot to that show. Once you had, you understood how you could do it. The whole show tended to be a bit of a puzzle to the audience. People knew that somehow you would explain just what these little threads were leading to. It wasn't all just going to evaporate. They knew it was all going to wind up somehow and the poor heavy was going to have his pants dropped, but how it was going to happen, in the very best *Mission*s, was like blindsiding the audience at the very last minute. Then they began to realize, 'Oh, that's why it was done!' When you got the scripts to work that way, it was a real joy.

"I got the sense that there were two or three threads, and you had to understand the chronological unfoldment and how, by interweaving them at certain moments, you could heighten suspense. You could create geographical distance between our people which would make communication difficult, but they were all on a schedule with a plan that had been very well worked out. They tended to operate as isolated islands which you could follow. Then suddenly something would happen and you could see that it was going to affect some other part. Now how to get that information to that party and alert them of the danger? You had to figure out what the whole plot was. When you understood that, then you knew how to lay it out and where to cut for maximum tension."

Playdon specialized in developing prolonged suspense scenes. "They were always interfacing with some system that they were penetrating which had built-in rules and procedures regarding penetration. If they were very good, then that would only give them about two to three hours before that system would start throwing up red flags and send out a general alert which worked well with *Mission*. The show worked best when they had only four or five hours to get something done." Most of Playdon's shows set such a clock at the beginning of the show. "Although the writing was very difficult, in some ways it was easy because you had that clock set and just packed the scripts with a lot of energy and tension, which most shows can't get through.

"Part of the problem on every show was validation: How were they gonna get in? You had to validate them somehow, and you could play wrinkles on that. We'll get one to invalidate the other and when that invalidation proves true, that validates the other one. It means you've blown one of your agents, but they're gonna take her to the very prison where they house the person you want to get out!"

Perhaps because of the overemphasis on structure, the show's weakest element was verbal. "Some of the dialogue is terrible, isn't it?" muses William Read Woodfield of his own work. Fortunately, *Mission* relied almost entirely on visuals, which seemed to please CBS. Ellis Marcus, the network's liaison for the show, never once made a suggestion or criticism in his three years on the job. When story editor Laurence Heath asked about his seeming lack of interest, Marcus replied, "I never read the scripts. I never understand them. I figure you guys know what you're doing!" Adds Heath, "They literally didn't understand some of the scripts. But the audience loved them."

Those who *did* write *Mission* found that the show seemed to follow them around, and still does. "Whenever people learn that I was identified with the show," says Sam Roeca, "an immediate interest and curiosity is uncorked." Sy Salkowitz remembers a woman who proceeded to tell him, scene by scene, the story line of his own script. "She had to tell it," he says, "because she relished the telling of it." Another writer recalls an attractive young lady offering herself to him when she learned what show he wrote for!

Ethics and Morality

Mission: Impossible rarely employed violence, especially after its first season. The advent of the con usually made physical force unnecessary. When it was unavoidable, the IMF preferred to use a quick chop to the neck or a small "slap needle" which, when applied, "zapped" their opponents to sleep. The villain's demise (usually at the hands of his own people via IMF instigation) was generally performed off-camera, the sound of a gunshot telling us that our heroes had maneuvered the enemy into killing their own man.

THE COMPLETE MISSION: IMPOSSIBLE DOSSIER

CBS's censorship wing, the Standards and Practices Department, never complained, even when the industry was reeling from an antiviolence backlash. Says Woodfield, "After Bobby Kennedy was assassinated in 1968, Mike Dann called a meeting of all the people who had programs on CBS. It was a big antiviolence discussion. Then he said, 'By the way, I want to meet the *Mission: Impossible* people in Perry's office.' Mike said, 'I want you to know that what we're saying does not apply to you people. We're not really talking about you guys.' " Woodfield briefed Dann about their latest plot, which took place largely in a gas chamber. "Mike said, 'Oh, that's fine.' It was pretend violence, you see? We weren't doing violence." Unlike other TV spies, however, there was still something very sinister about the Impossible Missions Force.

Mission: Impossible matter-of-factly offered the premise that the United States government sponsored a group of saboteurs who were answerable to no one. In the course of their duties, the IMF could—and did—lie, cheat, steal, falsify media, hold persons illegally, falsely incriminate, destroy the property of innocent people, kidnap, plot (though never personally execute) assassinations, and break any civil and criminal rule that stood in their way. Individual rights were ignored. To get a professional killer to incriminate his mob boss, the killer is abducted, made to think he's on death row, dragged into Woodfield's gas chamber, and strapped into the chair. When the gas starts seeping into the chamber, the killer breaks down and babbles a confession, naming his employer. Geller switched Briggs' Squad to the right side of the law, but they were as ruthless and deceitful as their opponents. "In *Mission*," Bruce said, "we do all the things the heavies do, but we've made them the good guys." It was a curious format to spring from a judge's son. When Ellis Marcus asked Geller if his father was proud of *Mission*, Bruce answered, "Well, he has problems with it, because the theme of the show is contrary to his philosophy." In *Mission: Impossible*, the end always justified the means.

The IMF framed and entrapped opponents with no qualms, regrets, or remorse. If they couldn't nail him for something he did, they'd see to it that he was punished for something he didn't do, or something they made him do. "It was a frame," Jerry Ludwig explains. "The trick was to make it so clever and enjoyable that the audience would want this villain to get his comeuppance. He couldn't say, 'Well, they made me,' because most of the time they were getting in the van and driving away. He couldn't prove it, couldn't prove that they even knew each other or virtually that they'd ever even been there!"

There were those who found the show offensive. One of the most eloquent was Robert Lewis Shayon, writing for *Saturday Review* in 1966. Calling *Mission* "my candidate for the season's most harmful program," he pointed out that the IMF, "for pay and at government instigation, interfere directly in the affairs of foreign nations with whom we are at peace and from whom no direct threat to our safety emanates. They break the laws of these nations, yet are never brought before any bar of justice. . . . Abroad, this series certainly will not win us friends." Shayon's fears were unfounded, for *Mission* was more popular overseas than at home, most viewers seeing the program as an entertaining television show and nothing more.

The show certainly was cold and emotionless, but it did have some redeeming social value. "Films can make you feel," muses Jerry Ludwig, "be they *On the Waterfront* or *Terms of Endearment*. That's not what *Mission: Impossible* did. It didn't make you feel, but in a way it made you think. *Mission* made you feel smarter, if only for having followed the damn story! Having figured out what they were doing, you *were* smarter, and it encouraged people to look at things another way."

Making the Pilot

"The script was very complex and people said, 'Aw, what the hell, it's Lucy, we'll just have to put up with it.' It was the film that bowled everyone over."
—CBS EXECUTIVE PAUL KING

SIGNING WITH LITTLE DESILU allowed Bruce Geller a freedom which would have been impossible at larger studios. He took advantage first by insisting that CBS not see an inch of *Mission* until the final cut was ready—a remarkable demand that could have been backed up only by someone as important to CBS as Lucille Ball. Says then-CBS executive Stanley Kallis, "Lucille Ball had absolute autonomy. She laid down the rule to the network. Lucy didn't want anyone to look at *Mission: Impossible* because *Bruce* didn't want anyone to look at it." Assured of minimal network interference, Geller proceeded to cast his pilot.

Casting *Mission: Impossible*

Three guest roles were written into the pilot—safecracker Terry Targo, actor Martin Land, and strongman Willy Armitage. Since Terry Targo was written for a small man, Wally Cox was signed. It was a rare dramatic role for an actor well known for comedy parts, and Cox was effective in the part.

There was never any doubt who would play Martin Land. Brooklyn-born Martin Landau spent four years as a cartoonist for *The New York Daily News* before deciding to become an actor in 1951. After some off-Broadway and summer stock experience, he was one of two thousand actors who auditioned for the prestigious Actors Studio, and was one of only three accepted. In 1956 he landed his first Broadway role in Paddy Chayefsky's *Middle of the Night,* with which he toured. The play closed in Los Angeles, where Landau began his film career. One of his earliest screen roles was in Hitchcock's *North by Northwest* (1959).

The first people Landau met in Hollywood were director Monte Hellman and Bruce Geller. At the time Hellman was operating the Doll Theatre and asked Landau to teach an acting workshop. He agreed on the condition that he pick the students. Among the chosen: Warren Oates, Robert Blake and his wife Sondra (who appears in the pilot's opening scene), Harry Dean Stanton, and Jack Nicholson. "Bruce was a young writer who wanted to learn about actors," says Landau, "so he came into my class." Geller was fascinated by Landau's dexterity with accents and characters, and wrote Martin Land specifically for him. By the time *Mission*

23

had gone from movie to TV script, Landau was one of Hollywood's busiest character actors in films and television, with credits including *Cleopatra* (1963) and *The Greatest Story Ever Told* (1965). He signed to appear in the pilot, but turned down a series option deal. Because he felt it would hurt his motion picture career, Martin didn't want to be tied down and regularly refused series offers, including *Star Trek* (Gene Roddenberry wanted him for Mr. Spock before Leonard Nimoy was cast). "There's no sense in doing a series," the actor maintains. "There *is* sense in doing a special kind of series." Evidently, Landau was not convinced that *Mission* would be sufficiently special. Determined to have him in the pilot, Geller hired Landau without signing him for the series—a decision which would have serious repercussions.

The day before production began, Martin Land was rechristened Rollin Hand. Landau describes the character: "He was a nightclub performer who was liked, was loyal, was an adventurer, a soldier of fortune in a sense. He wanted to enliven his life and was basically willing to take on any challenge with a certain panache and style. He was a guy who liked performing, actually enjoyed it. So the ultimate performance would be when your life was on the line. Rollin is basically that kind of animal; he likes the moment when the crunch is on and he's being tested.

"More than most characters on series television," Landau feels, "we had to fatten the characters that we played. You had to make the audience believe that this guy was all the things that were said about him." One way he made Rollin "fatter" was his behavior in crises. Rollin was a supreme master of the bluff, often blustering his way out of tight spots and exhaling in relief when the performance was over. "People use the word 'cool' in relation to my character," he says. "Well, the character was cool, but he was also scared from time to time. You learn the most about a character when he's alone, and it's those moments alone when you saw the real Rollin, his vulnerability."

Landau was so popular in audience tests of the pilot that he was to be one of several recurring IMF "guest spies" to appear when needed. In addition to his frequently seen acting, voice, makeup, and magic talents, Rollin was skilled in cheating, picking pockets, quick changes, and escape, all of which made him the IMF's star performer. *Mission* was a perfect vehicle for Landau's performance skills and in three years he would play quite an assortment of roles, from clergymen to Adolf Hitler.

For the part of silent strongman Willy Armitage, Geller, Solow, and casting agent Joe D'Agosta saw dozens of musclemen-actors and weren't satisfied. Solow's assistant Morris Chapnick remembered Peter Lupus, a card-playing pal who seemed perfect for the role. Unfortunately, Lupus was in Europe, making movies.

Peter Lupus was born in Indianapolis, Indiana, of Greek-Lebanese-French-Irish ancestry. Dramatics and physical fitness were major enthusiasms from the start. As an actor he took part in the Indianapolis Starlight Musical series and did summer stock in Milwaukee, Detroit, and Pennsylvania. He was more successful as a bodybuilder and has held titles as diverse as Mr. Indiana, Mr. Indianapolis, Mr. Hercules, and the world title of Mr. International Health Physique.

By the time he moved to Hollywood, Peter was a six-foot four-inch 250-pound mass of muscle with a thirty-three-inch waist and fifty-inch chest. His health regimen included 150 organic vitamin and mineral pills a day, and the actor could down thirty-eight pills in one swallow. Lupus managed a gym while waiting for his first break, which turned out to be a part in AIP's *Muscle Beach Party* (1964), in which he executed chin-ups and leg raises while

Martin Landau as Rollin Hand, master of disguise and illusion (clockwise from lower left) at work in the "Pilot," as an Arabian beggar in "The Slave," as Nazi criminal Martin Bormann in "The Legend," and as the Man of a Million Faces.

hanging from a helicopter. Studio chief Sam Arkoff signed him to a contract but insisted that Peter change his name. "We want you to have an American name," said Arkoff, "and make you a star in body pictures." An assortment of names were considered, from Rocky Road to Chuck Steak. Finally, it was as Rock Stevens that Lupus was billed in *Muscle Beach* and five European features, including *Hercules and the Tyrants of Babylon* and *Goliath at the Conquest of Damascus.* He vividly recalls returning from Italy to meet with Geller, Solow, and D'Agosta. "You know how everybody starts looking at each other when they know, 'That's what we want'? That's the expression they all had. We talked for a little while. When I left, Bruce followed me into the hall and offered me the part."

Geller liked Lupus; he did *not* like the name Rock Stevens, and tried to talk Lupus out of it. "Nobody's gonna take you seriously with that name," Bruce said. "Use your own name and stick with it." Lupus didn't want to change his name every time he got a part, but eventually agreed. "Thank goodness I did," says Lupus. "Bruce never gave me bad advice." Apart from an occasional trivia quiz, Rock Stevens was never heard of again.

Since Willy would have very little dialogue, the actor portraying him had to project a strong likability, and Peter Lupus certainly did that. "I was looking for a human quality," said Geller of his choice. In Lupus he found "a sort of Ferdinand sweetness. People just *like* him." Contrary to what some believed, Lupus was not simply playing himself. "The strong silent type like Willy is so unlike me," he says, "because I'm a talker. It's just a character that I did, but people see you that way. They expect me to be like that, to walk through walls and pick up cars." Lupus found Geller's concept interesting and recalls Bruce's thumbnail sketch of Willy Armitage. "Willy is not dumb. He is an intelligent strong man who uses his strength to accomplish these very intricate missions." A shrewd and intelligent businessman in real life, Lupus added his own contribution: "Willy was very highly paid. All of us were, you know."

"At the first meeting, Bruce asked me if it was possible to carry a man in a suitcase and make it look easy." On the set, Lupus found that the cases he was required to lift weighed forty pounds each—empty. The man inside one of the cases, Wally Cox, weighed approximately 135 pounds, and Lupus had to weigh the other case with an equal amount of lead weights for proper balance, which meant that he'd be carrying about 300 pounds at a time. "I had to make it look easy," Lupus says. "Well, we did about twelve takes, and that night I felt like my back was attached to my heel!"

Lupus tested well with pilot audiences and was signed as a series regular. But the large role he played in the first episode was deceptive. As the series evolved, *Mission* veered more and more from the physical action that was Willy's stock in trade. Consequently, he became less and less important to the plots. Willy's strength was rarely needed, so he tended to act more as a utility man, carrying unconscious bodies or working as Barney's assistant. Very often he seemed to be literally along for the ride, driving the IMF van. "Supposedly," says Lupus, "I can drive anything with wheels, because that's all I used to do!" Willy was given even shorter shrift when it came to dialogue. In many episodes he had no more than a line or two, and even then was usually kept to one-word responses like, "Right" or "Yes."

He may have been *Mission*'s least important regular player, but Loop (as he was known among the company) was popular with audiences. "I had a lot of fan clubs out there that kept pushing the network. They wanted to see more of Willy. Whole groups and fraternities were Willy Fan Clubs. They used to sit around and count Willy's words! They'd make bets and have a ball. The Hollywood club had Willy campaigns, wrote a couple of songs, and made Willy bumper stickers—HONK IF YOU LOVE WILLY!" Lupus's early fan mail came largely from

Peter Lupus as strongman Willy Armitage provided the IMF muscle and was adept at moving about undetected.

women, some of whom said they'd prefer him a bit slimmer. When Loop trimmed down, Herb Solow complained. "Don't cut down your weight," he ordered. "I hired you big!" Claims Peter, "He threatened to pay me by the pound!"

Lupus's diminished duties never affected his enthusiasm for the show. "Can you imagine getting up at four or five in the morning and looking forward to going to work? To me it was a real learning experience, and it was because of the people. It was like we all picked each other as people we wanted to work with, yet we didn't. It just worked out that way."

Geller was just as careful casting the *core* Briggs' Squad and had a specific actor in mind for its leader. Steven Hill was born Solomon Krakovsky in Seattle, Washington, of Russian immigrant parents. An avid moviegoer as a child, his lifelong ambition was to be an actor. After a stint in the Marines he did radio work in Chicago and spent two tough years in New York before joining the first class of the Actors Studio alongside Kim Stanley, Julie Harris, Montgomery Clift, and Marlon Brando. There he developed a reputation for being difficult and unpredictable, prone to outbursts and stubbornness. "I felt I had to be brash to make my mark," he later said. "In this business you don't make out application forms—you have to make an instant impression. I had to do it over and over again before I was finally recognized." Actor Albert Paulsen, Hill's friend from the Studio days, claims that "there were always problems. Steve is a terrific guy, but he intensifies problems that are always there for actors. But you work it out, you don't stop everything. He stops and ruminates and changes things. It's not a vicious thing, it's just a problem with how he sees the truth and what it means to him."

Among his peers Hill was considered nothing short of brilliant. Lee Strasberg, founder of the Studio, once called Hill one of America's finest actors. "When I first became an actor," Martin Landau recollects, "there were two young actors in New York: Marlon Brando and Steven Hill. A lot of people said that Steven would have been the one, not Marlon. He was legendary. Nuts, volatile, mad, and his work was exciting." Hill's earliest successes were on Broadway in *Mister Roberts, The Country Girl* and *A Far Country,* in which he played Sigmund Freud. He worked constantly in television and appeared in movies like *The Goddess* (1958) and *A Child is Waiting* (1963).

Hill guest-starred in a Geller-Kowalski *Rawhide.* Says Paul Krasny, who edited the episode, "It was a very introverted, introspective kind of thing, and Steve was excellent in it. Bruce really got to like him from that." Geller was delighted when Hill agreed to play Briggs in the pilot. Why Steven Hill? "Because," says Herb Solow, "we wanted to get the kind of guy you'd think would do these kind of things." Says Bernie Kowalski, "Steve was a very thinking, cerebral type of actor, and Bruce wanted that kind of man, the brain behind the action. Although he was not physical, he was physical-looking enough, and was good."

Not everyone agreed. Many CBS and Desilu executives saw Hill as a liability. Despite a long and prolific career, he was largely unknown to the general public and considered too low-key to carry a series. His fiery reputation within the industry didn't help. The most discouraging factor, however, had nothing to do with his acting skill or style.

A scene in Broadway's *A Far Country* (1961) required actress Kim Stanley to shout at Hill (as Freud), "You're a Jew!" As Hill explained in 1983, "When she would let loose this blast, I would take it. And in the pause that followed, I would think, 'What about this?' . . . I slowly became aware that there was something more profound going on in the world than just plays and movies and TV shows . . . I was provoked to explore my religion." By 1965 Hill was a devout Orthodox Jew, following traditions that have not changed in 3,500 years. He ate only

Steven Hill as Dan Briggs, the IMF's original leader.

kosher food, wore specially lined clothing, and, to enable him to attend prayer services, left the set before sundown every Friday.

Orthodox living had serious ramifications for an actor. Since he could no longer perform on Friday evenings or at Saturday matinees, Hill's theatrical career was virtually over. He turned down a major role in a feature, *The Sand Pebbles* (1966), because it required him to work late Fridays. Even TV work became troublesome since Friday, the last day of the work week, is always a late night.

Geller fought for and finally signed Hill, whose contract specified that he not work on Jewish holidays and that he leave the set before sundown Fridays. These stipulations caused little trouble during the pilot's production but would be a major headache during *Mission*'s first season.

Partially due to his brief tenure, Dan Briggs remains one of *Mission*'s most mysterious characters. With his flat delivery and strange, cold smile, Hill was wholly believable as a plotter of complex, treacherous counterstrategies, a man as ruthless as events warranted. Good-looking in a John Garfieldish way, he also had an amazing facility to shift from center of attention to total anonymity, sometimes in the same scene. It was the latter quality which most bothered the anti-Hill factions at Desilu and CBS: facelessness might be a wonderful trait in a secret agent, but not in a TV star.

Barney Collier, the IMF's mechanical and electronics genius, played a minor role in the pilot, jamming a television transmission and setting a diversionary fireworks display. Few could have guessed how important he'd be to the series or that he'd appear in more episodes than any other character. For the role Geller chose another actor he'd worked with before. Cleveland-born Gregory Allan Williams was the product of a broken home, son of a trumpet player who separated from wife Iona Morris when Greg was three. After an Army stint he entered Ohio State and later the University of Iowa, where his interests shifted from basketball to drama. Before he could graduate, he drove to Seattle and won the lead in a local production of *A Raisin in the Sun.* He reprised the role in Long Beach, California, then starred in a Los Angeles production of *Purlie Victorious.* Film and TV work followed, including *The New Interns* (1964), *The Dick Van Dyke Show,* and an episode of Geller's aborted HEW series. When Greg tried for the Barney Collier part, Bruce remembered him.

"We considered at least two dozen actors for the role," said Bruce, "and we decided on Greg for two reasons. First, we were familiar with his work and knew he could act. And second, he was physically qualified for the part. He is tall and athletic, and he can scale a wall and throw a punch, which is what is required of Barney Collier in many situations." That Greg was black had no bearing on the decision. In fact, while accepting an Image Award from the National Association for the Advancement of Colored People, Geller admitted, "If Greg Morris turned down the role of Barney, my next choice was a blue-eyed, blond Scandinavian." Race was never a factor; Geller just wanted the best man for the part.

Greg's career was launched by a combination of talent, luck, and good timing. "I got into Hollywood during the age of realization," he once said. "It was a time when casting directors and producers were thinking about how to cast Negroes. So I personally have not had a hard time in the industry." A handsome six foot two inches, he was the second black actor (behind Bill Cosby of *I Spy*) to portray an intelligent, successful character in an American television series.

After the pilot sold, Geller and Morris discussed the future of Barney Collier, and how they would handle the concept of a black man operating in certain areas of the world that were

Greg Morris (clockwise from top left) as IMF genius Barney Collier, as a circus clown in "Old Man Out," with a detonation device in "The Falcon," and attempting a risky prison break-in in "Memory."

essentially all white. "If it becomes necessary," Greg offered, "that as part of the plot I am a chauffeur or a doorman, it doesn't bother me one iota." At times it was necessary, but the subject was usually avoided by never acknowledging the fact that Barney was black. The topic was so studiously ignored that Greg's mother was often told by viewers, "You know, there are times that I forget that he's black." Barney Collier was as much a cipher as any other character in the series. As a result, he could go anywhere in the world and not arouse suspicion. Peter Sloman of deForest Research explains: "One of the things we always found fascinating was that the presence of a black East European peoples republic security guard never caused any questions. We brought it up to them once or twice, and decided that the idea of a Hollywood production team being so absolutely color blind was such a great idea that who cares?"

Curiously, some blacks were offended that Barney's race was *not* an issue. An intellectual black woman once asked Greg to justify Barney's presence in Eastern bloc countries. His answer: "Have you seen African students in Russia?" The woman's reply: "You win." Says Greg, "Her question was an honest one, which I answered honestly. On the other hand, a very famous black musician once told me, 'Now my son's got a show he can watch'; someone else said that I had turned his son around; on another occasion a boy told me, 'Before that show I didn't know what I wanted to be. Now I want to be an engineer.' Before he started watching the show he was about to flunk out of school." Over the years Morris has met dozens of people to whom Barney Collier was a positive role model. "It's probably difficult for some people, including some black people, to understand, but when you have a young person or a parent come up and simply say, 'Thank you,' you must have done something right. That's one of the fringe benefits."

Greg wasn't popular with everyone. After the series was over, Greg learned that Geller had had his fan mail presorted to remove the inevitable racist letters before Greg could see them. "Some people wrote resenting my relationship to Barbara Bain on the show. It was funny, because our relationship was like brother and sister!" An early network memo suggested that Greg and Barbara not stand near each other, ostensibly because of a makeup contrast. It was clear to everyone what was really being implied and from that point on, says Martin Landau, "we would find all the *more* reason to stand them together."

According to Greg Morris, Barney "came from a middle or upper-class background. His parents were teachers and he was an only child.* He was exposed to cultural things, but never so much that he was not aware of life. All these things made Barney a thinking person. He was president of Collier Electronics, bright enough to have multiple contracts, was independently wealthy, as all of us were.

"Why were we involved? I'll only speak for Barney: There were things that nobody else could do better than Barney. He received a quiet satisfaction from being part of the fall of someone corrupt or on the wrong side of society." In many ways Barney was the most invaluable IMF member. His expertise extended beyond electronics to include demolition, construction, counterfeiting, metallurgy, special effects, puzzle solving, safecracking, lock picking, computers, robot technology, criminology, and codes. He was a pilot, singer, boxer, and by the end of the series a vocal mimic and accomplished con man. As the IMF's "inside man," he usually worked unseen in tunnels, elevator shafts, walls, rafters, and basements, often secreted in false filing cabinets, packing cases, limousines, trucks—just about anything that could conceal a human being. Because his job was the most dangerous, he was constantly

---

* An older brother appears in episode 116, "Cat's Paw."

exposed to peril. In seven years Barney was shot (three times), beaten, blinded, poisoned, brainwashed, left stranded in a live mine field, and caught in a firetrap. He survived it all unfazed. "The one thing Barney never did was show fear," Greg explains. Forced to endure a game of Russian roulette in one show, Barney remains impassive as the gun barrel is pressed against his head and the trigger pulled. "Barney was never afraid. If that's the way he had to die, then that's the way he was gonna die."

The role required someone who looked like he knew what he was doing while using complex machinery and tools. "Greg is one of the few actors I've worked with who handles props well," says special effects man Jonnie Burke. "He doesn't have to spend a lot of time rehearsing with them." Despite the image *Mission* bestowed upon him, Greg has never been mechanically inclined. When he called a TV repairman to have his set fixed, the man took one look at the actor and laughed, believing himself the victim of a practical joke!

In fact Morris *was* an incorrigible prankster and general cutup. "To this day I don't think I can look Greg in the eye without laughing," says Peter Lupus, who shared many scenes with him. Propman Bob Richards agrees. "There was a lot of tension and hard work on the set and there had to be some comic relief. Greg was good at breaking it up when it got too serious."

The part of femme fatale Cinnamon Carter, the last and most difficult role to cast, went to an actress who once wanted to be a dancer. Born in Chicago, Barbara Bain graduated from the University of Illinois with a sociology degree, then moved to New York to study dance with Martha Graham. With her green eyes and photogenic features, she paid the bills by modeling. Attending her first acting class, she met Martin Landau, whom she married in 1957. They continued concurrent acting careers and worked together in the production of *Middle of the Night* which brought the couple to Los Angeles. It was as a member of Landau's acting workshop that Barbara first met Bruce Geller.

Bruce once claimed that Cinnamon was written specifically for Bain. "I wanted a sexy broad who was still very much a lady. Barbara was perfect for that character." It really wasn't that simple. "We had a difficult time finding someone who had the class and style," Herb Solow recalls. "We spoke to various women and went through a great many people." Conceived primarily as a visual distraction, Cinnamon possessed a certain élan and a certain sizzle. "It's a very difficult role," says Martin Landau, "because you want Marilyn Monroe and Grace Kelly in the same person, a sexy woman who is also dignified. What Bruce needed was a movie star who could act. I think Bruce somehow *did* write it for Barbara, knowing her, coming to my classes and watching her onstage, seeing her look a certain way and yet be something else, which is what *Mission* is." Barbara was cast as Cinnamon.

In 1965 Barbara was a working actress, but was best known as Mrs. Martin Landau. When word reached Desilu's upper echelons that "someone's wife" had been hired for the role, Lucille Ball finally put her foot down. "Barbara was the only person Lucy wanted to meet before we hired her," Solow reveals. "Lucy always felt that I was doing things without consulting her, but she was always busy with her show. We tried to make her a part as best we could, but you have to get on with things." Solow took Lucy down to Stage 12 and introduced her to Barbara who, as always, radiated charm and self-assurance. "Lucy spent some time with her and liked her," Solow adds. Barbara Bain was in.

On the set, Barbara was generally considered everyone's favorite, and not just because she was the only lady in the cast. "Barbara was so unaffected by stardom," recalls Peter Lupus. "If she had a 5:00 A.M. makeup call, she would get there a half hour early on her own, unpaid, so she wouldn't hold anybody up. And she smiled all day long, no matter how long she was there. She put up with things I would have raised my voice over." Carefully coiffed by Adele

WANTED:
CINNAMON

Barbara Bain as femme fatale Cinnamon Carter was *Mission Impossible*'s most popular leading lady.

Taylor and made up by Dan Striepeke or Bob Dawn, she was one of television's most glamorous stars and made what was essentially a "man's show" a crossover hit with female audiences. Women loved Cinnamon, enjoyed her wry insouciance, and undoubtedly reveled in the way she wrapped unsuspecting men around her finger. "If the script gives me just ten lines to catch a man," Barbara quipped, "I try to get him by the second."

Barbara frequently called Cinnamon "the most wonderful series role for a woman on television." She defined her as "pretty cheeky and contemporary. There is no polite apology in relation to her position to the men, where they are, how they travel." Contrary to most TV ladies of the time, she was quick witted and moved effortlessly through a man's world without losing her femininity.

In episodes 2, 35, and 52 she demonstrated excellent memory skills, but Cinnamon's main gift was always obvious. "She is specifically valuable to the Impossible Missions Force in her womanly wiles. In other words, I can be helpful in many situations where a man just wouldn't be as effective," Barbara said, laughing. "My job's only doing what comes naturally," Cinnamon explains in the pilot. In the series she turned up in many guises: cabaret singer, repressed career woman, shill, princess, floozy, fashion model, astrologer, plastic surgeon, stewardess, drug addict, mind reader. She walked a very thin line, at times posing as a virtual whore yet never losing the essential class that was Cinnamon. The audience knew that Cinnamon was acting, but the performance's artificiality was so subtle that the audience could *also* believe that Cinnamon's victims were genuinely fooled. It was a remarkable, hairsplitting kind of acting and in that respect, Barbara Bain was inimitable. "I don't think that anyone could have done it better," says Martin Landau, one of her biggest fans. "I don't think anyone did it as well." Most *Mission* fans agree.

To direct the pilot, Geller called upon old pal and former partner Bernie Kowalski, one of TV's most successful directors. He'd just finished the pilot for *The Monroes* when he met with Bruce and Herb Solow, who explained that they wanted *Mission* shot in a style similar to *The Ipcress File,* a spy movie then in release. Kowalski saw *Ipcress* and liked its urgent, absorbing manner. "I based my style on that film," he says, "combined with Bruce's intent in the script."

Directing *Mission: Impossible*

"I think *Mission: Impossible* is one of the milestones in television film," says Michael O'Herlihy, who directed three episodes. "It changed the whole style of film." That it did, but the style that made *Mission* so entertaining to watch gave directors headaches and ulcers. The series was known around town as the "director killer." Directors had one week to prepare (developing a camera plan, casting the guests, checking the special effects) and seven work days to shoot. There seemed to be twice as many cuts and shots in a one-hour *Mission* as there were in any other hour show, and the challenge was to film, on schedule, three (or more) separate plots: the "outside" con (usually Rollin and Cinnamon setting up the sting), the "inside" men (Barney and Willy doing the dirty work), and the villains. *"Mission* was not fun," states Gerald Mayer, who shot four episodes. "You were behind schedule from the first minute you started shooting."

Most TV directors were used to dialogue scenes with actors or action that could be easily condensed if the company fell behind schedule. "I've been on shows where they threw out

three or four pages of dialogue to alleviate problems," said script supervisor-director Allan Greedy. "If you tried that on *Mission,* you were in a lot of trouble." Because every shot was so closely tied to what would happen in the next, abridgment was out of the question. Says Reza S. Badiyi, who directed more *Mission*s (eighteen) than anyone else, "New directors who'd done wonderfully with other shows couldn't do it. It was a jigsaw puzzle with a different kind of timing."

Veterans had trouble as well. Greedy recalls an older director losing time on an early episode. "At the time I laughed at the mistakes he was making," he admits. "With the experience I now have, I realize that he was shooting in a legitimate way. He just wasn't shooting it in the way that *Mission* should be shot." Greedy directed a *Mission* after four years experience as script supervisor and even *he* fell behind! "Whenever I get into a tough situation I always say to myself, 'You did *Mission: Impossible.* Nothing you ever do could be as tough as that.' I always say that and it always gets me through." Another cause for bewilderment was the character impersonations. As Greedy elaborates, "Sometimes the guest villain wasn't really the guest villain but Rollin Hand in a mask. Under pressure you can forget that. You forgot that they would dub in Landau's voice later, and it screwed up many a director."

Those who fell behind had to answer to Barry Crane, production manager-hatchet man. Constantly trying to cut costs and stay on schedule, production managers are often looked upon as the enemy on the set. "A production manager is not a contributor," feels Joseph Gantman, who produced *Mission*'s first two seasons. "They have a way of coming up with terrible solutions without offering anything better."

Crane's responsibilities encompassed every physical aspect of the production: breaking

Reza S. Badiyi directs Diane Baker in this scene from "The Falcon."

down the script into a shooting schedule, budgeting the show, controlling the show once it started shooting, supervising assistant directors, arranging location scouts and caterers, overseeing the construction department, and more, including acting as link between production and studio. Crane was perfect for an executive producer like Geller who never hesitated to spend money, especially on *Mission.* "Barry never saw himself as the guy whose job it was to say no," claims Phil Fehrle, Crane's assistant during *Mission*'s first season. "He saw himself as the guy whose job it was to find a solution that would please everyone." Crane did his best to accomplish what Geller wanted and still keep him from bankrupting the studio. It was an arduous job, but he was phenomenally adept at it.

Born Barry Cohen in Detroit, Crane attended the University of Michigan and moved to Hollywood to become an actor. After two years at the Pasadena Playhouse he realized that performing was not his forte and became a production assistant at Four Star Television, where he met Geller. The word most often used to describe Crane (who died in 1985) is "genius." Says producer Stan Kallis, "I don't think anyone in the business ever had a production brain equal to Barry Crane ever. Anyplace, anytime. To make it simple, he was a walking computer. He had perfect recall and could juggle in his mind eighty facts at any moment. He didn't have to check his scripts on a production board. He'd move the schedule around after he'd already solved the problem mentally. That's how good he was." Effects man Jonnie Burke remembers how Crane handled questions at production meetings. "He'd say, 'We did pretty much the same thing on this episode X years ago by that director, and it cost this much.' He had a computer in his head and he never forgot anything." Many believe that he could have run a studio. "When I left *Mission* I went over to Universal," Allan Greedy explains. "I was always told how efficient Universal was, how every dime counted. I was shocked to discover how indecisive, time- and money-consuming they were compared to *Mission.* Barry Crane planned everything, and it made a big difference." Crane was also a contract bridge expert with more awards than anyone else in the history of the game. In twenty-five years he had amassed thirty-five thousand master points, more than anyone else in the world (his nearest competitor was eleven thousand points behind). Asked when he had time to break down *Mission*'s intensely complex scripts, he answered that they were done during bridge games while waiting for his opponents to bid. Nobody doubted it.

"The first couple of years Barry would suggest how to save money," Allan Greedy says. "Often we wouldn't do it, because it was such a cheap thing to do. It would work, but it wouldn't have the quality that *Mission* should have. Joe Gantman would insist, and we would go right on working late hours." Crane's influence and power on the show increased in direct proportion to the studio's mounting pressure over high costs. In the series' final years, Crane, by then a producer, was effective at designing good-looking shows on a practical basis.

Mission's celebrated directorial style consisted mainly of then-unusual and arresting camera acrobatics, especially in the middle and later years of the series. The emphasis was on keeping the camera moving as much as possible, and directors had an assortment of tricks to do so. The zoom lens, which allows a scene to go from long or medium shot to close up without moving the camera, has often been called the visual equivalent of an exclamation point. It came into use early in *Mission*'s history and was one of its most frequent (and ultimately overused) camera devices. An optical zoom, in which a static shot was made to zoom in to a face or object, was accomplished in the lab and was also commonly seen. Another was rack focusing, in which a foreground object blurs when the camera refocuses upon a background object. Directors would often meet with the set decorator just to find interesting foreground props to shoot!

The crew prepares for a climactic shot of Greg Morris for "A Snowball in Hell." Director Lee Katzin is at right.

Mission's single most important element was the insert, a shot which does not require the presence of a specific performer. *Mission*'s most common inserts were of fingers pushing buttons, hands holding photos or tools, and of course, watch and clock faces ticking away.

"Directorially," says Robert Totten, who worked on two *Mission*s, "a show like *Mission* will never work unless you shoot many shots, many inserts. There are certain rules in filmmaking. If a tree falls or a building caves in, many camera setups must be made, otherwise there would be no pace. It happens too quick, and you need a lot of shots to slow it down so the audience has the chance to enjoy it. For *Mission,* you just can't have a guy climb up an air vent from the basement to the third floor. You have to have a lot of stuff in the middle, otherwise it won't play. You never felt that you had enough, but that's what made the show work. You could never say, 'Well, this is just a case of taking four bolts out of a faceplate so we'll just do two shots.' You'd better insert *all four bolts,* and then you have inserts which go inside the inserts! And every time you move the camera it's gonna take thirty minutes."

Inserts for the first few shows were actually filmed during principal production, and a full crew would wait while the cameraman lined up a shot of say, a hand holding a wallet. Production fell drastically behind and the insert crew (explained in the upcoming Postproduction category) was created to lessen the directors' burden.

Mission's best directors—Reza Badiyi, Paul Krasny, Lee Katzin, John Moxey, Alexander Singer, Sutton Roley, Stuart Hagmann among others—had a highly developed visual sense and a great deal of patience, because directing *Mission* was a slow ordeal which offered little satisfaction until the entire piece was edited, with inserts, weeks later. Badiyi once likened himself to an Eastern artist who assembled tiles to form a mosaic. *Mission: Impossible* was a

mosaic of shots. Each shot by itself was a bore. But in its proper place, it helped make a beautiful picture.

Associate producer Robert Justman had to find a suitable "Santa Costa" in Los Angeles in the middle of winter. After Malibu's palatial Serra Retreat (a later *Mission* locale) refused, Justman found sprawling Mount St. Mary's College in the hills above Brentwood. "Bruce and I said, 'We can make this work,' " says Justman, and they did, despite a sudden snowfall in Geller's banana republic—one of many production delays.

Justman was also responsible for assembling a crew. Finding a good cameraman wasn't easy. "Everyone was filming at the same time," he says, "and people were not available." He remembered John Alton, an excellent director of photography, author of a book on the subject, *Painting with Light,* and Academy Award winner for *An American in Paris* (he shot the film's ballet). Alton, sixty-five years old and retired, was excited by Justman's description of the pilot and signed on despite the wishes of his wife, who wanted him to stay retired. Mrs. Alton wasn't thrilled when, near the end of production, Alton somehow collided with a camera crane and was knocked cold. Fortunately, the injury wasn't serious. "He was able to do things with very little light that no one else could do," Justman points out. "He always said, 'It's not what you light, it's what you *don't* light.' An absolutely wonderful man, a genius." Alton's style is especially evident in the vault sequences and those with Barbara Bain, who looks radiant.

In the meantime the Desilu property department was getting their first taste of Bruce Geller. "He wanted suitcases that could hold two atomic bombs," says Chris Knopf, "and they turned up with a couple of pieces of cardboard junk. Bruce went through the roof! They weren't used to doing it that way, they were used to doing it cheap." Two appropriately strong and heavy cases (which gave Peter Lupus such a hard time) were eventually secured.

Props and Special Effects

"Bruce made it very plain that any gadgets, gimmicks, or instruments to be used had to be already in use somewhere or on a drawing board somewhere," says Bill Bates, property master for years two and three. Mechanical feasibility would distinguish *Mission* from most TV spy shows. It was discovered, however, that what is real does not always look real and was sometimes difficult to reproduce, even if the item was only supposed to *look* as if it worked. Props and special effects people worked weeks in advance, trying to create what the writers imagined.

"Mission: Impossible was not 100 percent accurate in terms of gadgetry," says deForest Research's Peter Sloman, whose job was to verify such matters. "They wanted not so much a gadget that existed, but if the technology existed, if such a device *could* be built, we assumed that Barney could build it even if it didn't exist. If the principle was valid, we'd allow them to have it. The *Mission: Impossible* gadget I want most is the one that changes streetlights from red to green when you're going in that direction. You would have to install a receiver device in every control box along the way, but we assume that Barney and Willy had already done that weeks before!"

Since so many props had to be specially built, special effects played a much more important role than in most series. Heading the crew was the remarkable Jonnie Burke who, while working on the spy film *The Silencers* (1966) at Desilu, fell in love with the tiny lot. After the

39

film, Desilu's production manager offered Burke three scripts: a western, *Mission,* and *Star Trek.* He picked the western, which was soon dropped. Burke's next choice was *Mission* because *"Star Trek* looked like too much work. Well, after the first few months, *Star Trek* settled down and all they had to do was basically repair the stuff the actors broke. *Mission* went the other way, and each show got heavier and heavier." Burke had a solid engineering background, was experienced in construction, and had worked in the aircraft, custom auto, and racecar industries. It all served him in good stead during *Mission.* Geller's insistence on realism meant lots of research for Burke, who pored over medical, scientific, and electronics journals. He found that much of the technology in *Mission* was available. "If I took one item I saw in a medical journal and tied it to another guy's research in electronics and tied them both with a hydraulic drive . . . you know, if somebody wanted to spend a billion dollars they could have built the damned things. The principle was right there, but the two people hadn't gotten together." Burke's crew consisted of five to ten people during the first season. By the following season it was up to twelve, split between *Mission* and *Mannix.* By the third season, Burke was in charge of the entire special effects department and had between eighteen and twenty-four people working fulltime on seventeen shows. All were experts in their field: "One was a top gunsmith and a good all-around machinist; another came from Fairchild Camera Company; we had top plastics people, you name it." Burke's squad had a backstage skill worthy of Briggs' Squad, and over the course of the series were *Mission*'s unsung heroes.

In mid November, makeup tests were made with Martin Landau for his role of General Rio Dominguez, evil ruler of Santa Costa. "That was a two hour job with two guys," the actor remembers. "I had Dan Striepeke working on one side, Johnny Chambers on the other side, and with *that* it was two hours!" Landau had worked in makeup before, notably in an *Outer Limits* episode, but he'd never been subjected to anything so detailed. "They were all separate appliances which had to be put on and then joined with latex so it became one piece. The first day, I felt like I was in a tomb, wondering, 'Is anything coming through?' It was monstrous and uncomfortable."

Mission: Impossible Makeup

Commercial artist-sculptor John Chambers was Hollywood's resident expert in appliances and prosthetic work, with credits including *The Munsters, The Outer Limits,* and the disguises which hid Frank Sinatra, Tony Curtis, and others in *The List of Adrian Messenger* (1963). Chambers did the pilot's preliminary lab work and called makeup man Dan Striepeke to assist him. "John and I discussed how to do the appliances for that character," says Dan, "and I did the makeup for a test."

For the role of Dominguez, Landau endured a bald cap, receding hair wig, upper and lower eye bags, chin wadding, mustache, false teeth, and rubber grease, *plus* four foam-rubber appliances for his forehead, nose, chin, and cheekbones. The actor was unrecognizable in the disguise, and Geller, Kowalski, and Solow liked what they saw.

Striepeke was *Mission*'s *sole* makeup artist during the first season (although Chambers joined him for the two-parter "Old Man Out"). The preponderance of work forced Dan to switch from the time-consuming appliances to "blank" latex masks. "We developed that cheat and it worked quite well," he feels. Of course, he was also in charge of standard makeup requirements. He worked closely with Barbara Bain to develop the "Cinnamon look," a cool pale style that accentuated the actress's cheekbones.

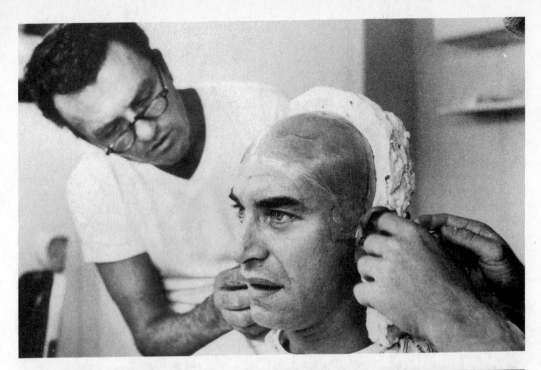

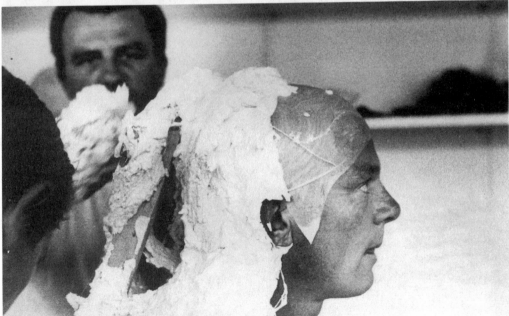

Makeup man Bob Dawn works on Landau (top) and Graves (bottom) for "The Council."

For the "Pilot," makeup man Dan Striepeke buried Martin Landau's features to turn him into General Rio Dominguez.

General Dominguez was the first of many makeup ordeals for Landau.

At the end of the first season, an exhausted Striepeke left to take over Twentieth Century-Fox's makeup department. His replacement, Bob Dawn, had enough assistants to take actual face molds of the guest stars whom Rollin would be impersonating.

Making a life mask is a far more complicated and tedious process than Rollin made it seem on-screen. An hour is spent just making a mold of the actor's face. First a bald cap is applied, then gooey dental alginate (normally used for teeth impressions) backed with a plaster matrix to keep its shape. "Contrary to what most people believe, you don't put straws up the actor's nose so he can breathe," Dan says. "You just work around the nostrils very carefully so you don't get any distortion." Once the mold has hardened and been removed from the actor, a plaster positive is made from the alginate negative. Then a negative mold, made from the plaster positive, is oven dried, sprayed with vinegar, and filled with liquid latex. When the latex solidifies it is peeled out of the mold and placed back on the positive, where it is airbrushed for the proper coloring. The entire process takes three long days, but the masks' realistic look immensely helped the show's credibility.

The masks were used for the "peel-off," a famous bit of business in which the guest villain—supposedly Rollin in disguise—reaches for his neck (covering his face with his arm in the process). After a cutaway to whoever is watching him, the scene resumes, this time with *Landau,* in clothing identical to the guests', already peeling off the latex mask and hairpiece. It looked so perfect that "we had plastic surgeons call and want to know how that was done," according to hairstylist Adele Taylor. The peel-off continues to be spoofed and copied in movies, TV shows, and commercials.

Production began on the pilot on Wednesday, December 8, 1965, at Mount St. Mary's College, which doubled as the Hotel Nacionale, headquarters of General Dominguez and hiding place of the nuclear warheads the IMF must steal. As filming continued, it became evident that the script's complexity had been seriously underestimated, and the show fell behind after only a few days. There were unexpected delays, like a soundstage fuse blowing and causing an expensive twenty-minute wait. One mistake was almost deadly. For the climax the IMF speed toward the airport in two vehicles, then transfer to an ambulance Barney is driving. Greg Morris remembers all too well what happened. "Bernie wanted me to swing by in the ambulance and shine the lights in the limo that Lupus and Marty were in—I had everyone else in the ambulance. Fortunately I had the good sense to test the ambulance that I had to drive. I made Steve, Wally, and Barbara get out because I wanted to get a feel of this. So I drive in and just before I make the turn I hear this incredible *POW!* I figured we'd just blown a tire. I got out and found that the front axle had popped. If it had popped while I was turning, I'd have had no control over the car and I'd have run into the limo. I got out and Steve came over to me and very quietly said, 'If you hadn't made us get out, we'd be dead, wouldn't we?' I said yeah, and he walked away."

An additional annoyance for director Kowalski was the ever-present Bruce Geller. "It was the first time I was working for Bruce in a sense," Bernie says. "He was very nervous and about a foot and a half away from me through the whole thing. John Alton and I speak Spanish fluently, so when Bruce was driving me crazy, I would only speak to John in Spanish. Bruce and I drove each other nuts during the making of it, just out of wanting and caring and collaborating together." Herb Solow would venture onto the set, size up the situation, and ask Kowalski, "How much will you give me if I take him away for thirty minutes?"

Bob Justman lightened things up by making sure that everyone had a director's chair on the set—except Bruce. When an embarrassed Bruce awkwardly asked for his own chair, Justman

44

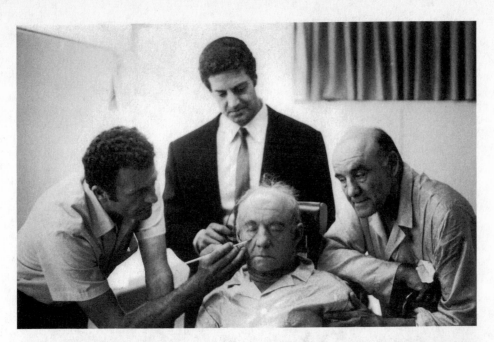

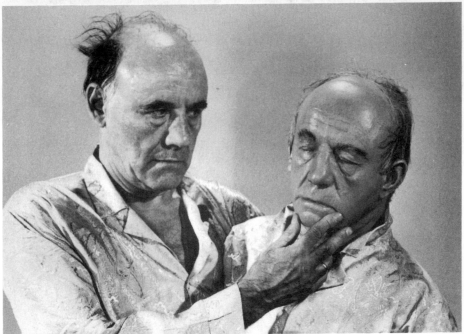

Bob Dawn prepares an inflatable replica of guest Torin Thatcher for "The Numbers Game."

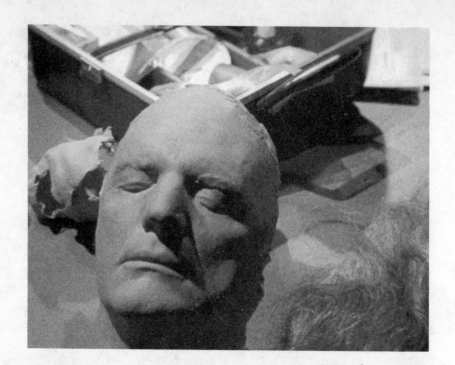

Rollin's handiwork from the "Pilot" (top). Rollin demonstrates the "peel-off" in "Echo of Yesterday" (bottom).

apologized profusely. The next day Bruce had a chair—the most worn, battered chair Justman could find. Again, Bruce was too polite to complain. After a few more days, he mentioned to Justman that everyone's chair had a name on it—except his. Again Justman apologized and remedied the situation by scrawling "Bruce *Gellor"* on a piece of electrician's tape and attaching it to the arm!

What was planned as a thirteen-day shoot budgeted at $440,346 wound up going nineteen days (plus one for inserts), at a cost of over $575,744. Much of that money went for cast and crew overtime. "The studio was going crazy," says Dan Striepeke, "because we were going so far over. We worked until about 10 P.M. Christmas Eve and to at least 8 or 9 on New Year's Eve." Long hours would become a *Mission* tradition.

"The Desilu owners felt that too much money was being spent," recalls Solow, who disagreed. "I think the investment was well worth it. Bruce was spectacular at style, and everything in that show had a style that came from Bruce. He was not the kind of guy to sit back and let something wrong go by and I admired him for that, even though it ran up the bills. It was the first time that Desilu had done something this ambitious. It meant foreign-looking locations, foreign automobiles, uniforms, a lot of things that were very costly for a small studio." Despite the front office pressure, Solow would visit the set and act as cheer-leader. According to Kowalski, "Herb would see the dailies and say, 'You know, they're screaming and yelling about the money, and if there's any way for you to do it faster, it's my job to tell you. But don't mess up the look—the look is great!' " Kowalski stayed with the show through a first cut, then moved on to another pilot. In fact the director worked on four consecutive pilots, all of which sold—*The Monroes, Mission, N.Y.P.D.,* and *The Rat Patrol.*

Postproduction was only slightly easier than actual shooting. Geller's perfectionism and endless reediting meant a lot of work, and it infuriated some Desilu department heads. Says Bob Justman, "Instead of joining in, trying to help us and making it easier, they would fight us at every turn." The studio's editing chief was particularly uncooperative. "Building E was where we were cutting," adds Justman. "The head of the department looked at me with icy cold eyes, trembling with rage and said, 'Stay out of Building E!' " Justman told Bruce, who responded by returning to Building E and continuing his work.

Postproduction: Editing, Sound, and Music

Bruce was proud of *Mission*'s rapid pace and loved to get letters from viewers who com-plained, "It's too tense." One woman wrote, "Slow it down, I get stomach cramps!" Editing gave *Mission* a sense of momentum unique to TV at the time, and the key to that momentum was intercutting. Simultaneously crosscutting two or more separate sequences, "jumps the story forward," Geller once explained. Unlike other shows, *Mission* never used fade-ins or fade-outs, and rarely used dissolves, montages, or any technique to show time lapses or slow down the film's staccato rhythm.

The large amount of inserts made cutting the show an even bigger chore, but *Mission* wouldn't have been *Mission* without them. "It was too intricate," says head editor Paul Krasny, "and intricacies don't work in wide master shots because they're just too slow. It was always pacing that made *Mission,* and without cuts you can't pace. It was imperative."

Inserts were originally filmed during principal production. When that became impractical, the editors and assistant directors generally took over during postproduction, which had advantages other than saving money. "We didn't know until we cut the picture together

For his IMF portfolio photo, Bruce Geller donned dark glasses to look as sinister as possible.

exactly what we needed," says Phil Fehrle, who handled the work in years two and three. Second unit work, like shots of car "drive bys" and establishing shots of office buildings or ocean liners, were done at the same time. "In the third season, Paul and I would shoot either a one- or two-day second unit on each show," Fehrle adds, "and we'd do fifty to seventy-five setups a day." In later years it became a three-day system, as prop man Bob Richards explains. "The first day we had a meeting with someone from the prop shop, wardrobe, effects, and usually Barry Crane. We would discuss all the inserts we'd need for two or three shows on the first day, shoot them the second day, then return the material we used in the shots on the third day." Although the insert crew wasn't encumbered by a large company and cast (they were shot without sound), it was never easy. "We once shot ninety-six inserts in one day," says Richards, "ninety-six different camera setups which took almost the same technique and amount of time to move the camera and match the lighting in the film you've already shot. It was a horrendous job."

The crew had its own cast which stood in for the stars, for it was simply too expensive to pull Greg Morris or Barbara Bain off the principal unit just to shoot inserts of their hands. At times Jonnie Burke, his hands and forearms covered in "black" makeup, doubled as Barney Collier—until the dailies revealed blond hairs on "Barney's" arm!

Adding to the film cutters' burden was the assembly of each episode's main title, which, because it included clips of that particular show, was always different. "The editing crews never went home," states Desilu's music supervisor Jack Hunsaker. "They were there night and day and I think there were six divorces because of it."

Postproduction also involved sound effects and "looping," the process of rerecording sound and dialogue in the studio. "Very often we were at noisy locations," notes Fehrle, "or we had to replace a voice for story reasons."

One of *Mission*'s most important stars was never seen on screen, only heard. The strong, no-nonsense taped voice which sent the IMF on their assignments belonged to Robert Johnson, an accountant whom Robert Justman knew from Daystar Productions, where Johnson did some voice-overs for *The Outer Limits.* "He'd been a singer and had a great voice," Justman says. "When it came time to do *Mission: Impossible,* I brought Bob in." A one-shot job for $125 became a seven-year annuity for Johnson, who'd come in every few weeks and read several episodes' worth of taped messages at a time. "We paid him for years for that," Justman laughs.

From the start Geller knew that *Mission,* with its many scenes without dialogue, would rely heavily upon music. But even he must have been surprised at just *how* crucial music became to the show.

Boris "Lalo" Schifrin was born in Argentina in 1932, son of the Buenos Aires Symphony Orchestra's concert master. He started composing at fourteen, then discovered American jazz at sixteen and was instantly hooked. He studied at the Paris Conservatory, returned to Argentina at twenty and began to write film music. In 1957 Lalo met one of his heroes, jazz trumpeter Dizzy Gillespie, who was impressed by the young man's work and hired him as a pianist-arranger. By 1964 Schifrin was known as an innovative composer-producer-arranger, mainly for Gillespie. He settled in Hollywood and worked for Universal TV and MGM where, in addition to a few low-budget features, he scored shows like *The Man from U.N.C.L.E.*

Lalo was a busy, in-demand composer when Geller hired him for the pilot. "He was new to most of us," says Hunsaker, who noticed that Lalo's score sounded very much like *Jericho,* another Schifrin pilot that season. In fact the music was reminiscent of an even earlier Schifrin

score for a *Man from U.N.C.L.E.* episode, "The Fiddlesticks Affair," (1965) which detailed another vault break-in. Whatever its origins, the score worked superbly for *Mission,* especially after Geller and Hunsaker extensively reedited or retracked it. Geller was particularly taken with an oddly scored, compelling selection in 5/4 time which was originally written for the end chase. Bruce found it so exciting that he made it the series' main title theme, the visuals of which were designed specifically for that music.

Mission's theme became one of television's most popular pieces of music, launched two soundtrack LPs, and set the tone for the entire series. One subtheme became almost as famous as the main title. The *Mission* March, with its snare drum and precise military tempo, "was used when we wanted to identify the *Mission* team," Hunsaker says. The tune appears on the first *Mission* soundtrack album as "The Plot."

Schifrin, a student of film, instinctively understood *Mission*'s visual rhythm and found a way to translate it musically. "We went through a lot of composers," says Hunsaker. "The problem was always to try to emulate Lalo, and no one was successful. There was no composer in town who could do what Lalo did. None of them understood. A lot of them didn't agree with what Lalo did, thought that his music was repetitious, and that his arrangements disturbed people. They would come in and do their own thing, and we would throw out anything that did not have to do with *Mission.* A lot of composers didn't understand the style, but we were always able to reach back (and retrack Schifrin melodies). No matter who wrote what, Lalo's music always dominated every episode, and that went on for almost the entire series. Of all the composers who worked on the show in subsequent years, only Jerry Fielding came close to creating the suspense which worked so well for the show."

Lalo Schifrin became one of the screen's great dramatic composers, but was never too busy to return and score an episode or two each season. The difference was always discernible.

Because of Bruce's endless tinkering, the pilot missed its delivery date to CBS. According to Chris Knopf, who was at CBS, "Mike Dann told Geller, 'If that pilot isn't turned in on time, you won't be on the schedule.' " The day came, the show was not turned in, and the network decided to buy another pilot. *Nightwatch,* a dark, stylish hour about a Chicago cop (Carroll O'Connor), was the network's choice, and its sale seemed a certainty. "We were moving back to Chicago," says *Nightwatch* director Robert Altman, "we'd secured real estate there and had many scripts in the works."

Then *Mission: Impossible* was delivered to CBS.

"When I saw the pilot I went crazy," says Mike Dann. "It was smashing, a good, well-done *Topkapi* caper. I knew I had a winner." He confidently screened the show for CBS's founder and chairman of the board, William Paley. As Dann explains, "Paley was sitting next to me, engrossed. The lights went on and I said, 'Well, Bill, what do you think?' I saw this look of depression on his face, and I knew I was gonna get bad news. I said, 'What's wrong with it?' He said, 'Dammit, there's nothing wrong with it! But you can't do it every week. You can't keep up that quality of production.' " CBS was undecided between *Mission* and *Nightwatch,* and Desilu's high asking price of $170,000 per episode did not help swing CBS in *Mission*'s direction. "It was certainly the highest license fee in CBS's history," Paul King maintains. It was Lucille Ball who turned the tide. According to Gary Morton, Lucy, angered by CBS's indecision, personally phoned Paley and exclaimed, "It's the best pilot of the season."

Another, far more common version of the story is that *Mission* sold because Ball threatened to quit *The Lucy Show.* As one of the few performers with a year-to-year television contract,

she was in a unique position and, as the story goes, launched an annual event called "the Lucy game" which never failed to scare CBS. The network was willing to do almost anything to keep TV's most popular star happy—and at CBS. "Desilu was putting a lot of pressure on us via Lucille Ball to try to get something on the air," admits Perry Lafferty. On January 17, 1966—before a decision on *Mission* had been rendered—Lucille publicly considered leaving CBS. "I have things I want to do," she said, "specials and pictures." On March 1, 1966—about the time that *Mission* was bought—it was announced that Desilu and CBS had signed a twelve-million-dollar contract, the largest television deal of its time.

Just how much pressure Lucy exerted has always been a matter of speculation. She and Gary Morton maintained that it amounted to one phone call to Paley; others, like *Nightwatch*'s Robert Altman, were told that Lucy forced the network to take *Mission*. "I don't know if it's the truth or not," says Altman, "but that's the way we heard it and that's what we thought." No matter how powerful Ball was, however, *Mission* would never have sold had it not been an excellent pilot—Desilu's past record is ample proof of that. "We went on the air not because Lucy pushed or yelled," says Herb Solow, "but because it happened to be a very good pilot. I *would* say that if our pilot and another were as good, I think that because of Lucy, CBS would lean our way."

"There was no question in anyone's mind that *Mission* was clearly the show of the year," Mike Dann insists. "The question was whether you could keep it up or control costs. I showed it to the CBS affiliates and there was simultaneous applause. I never felt better in my life." Other factors appealed to the network as well. "It wasn't controversial like *The Defenders*," Dann continues, "it wasn't built around a star that you had to pay a fortune to. There was no leading man in the traditional sense and that was very rare for television drama—it later proved to be very valuable. It was just a Bruce Geller drama well done, by God. It could run forever if you made it work."

Whatever the reasons, *Mission* was in and *Nightwatch* out. Robert Altman threw a huge party in his Westwood offices and called it a wake. "We put Lucille Ball's picture up all over the place and threw darts at it," he recalls. Among those in attendance: Mike Dann, Perry Lafferty, and CBS's liaison for the project, Stanley Kallis, who'd seen both shows and couldn't believe that *Nightwatch* lost. "It was disappointing at the time," Robert Altman explains. "But in retrospect, it's just as well that it didn't go." Altman, of course, went on to become one of America's most admired filmmakers.

Stan Kallis wasn't the only one surprised to hear of *Mission*'s sale—so was Bruce Geller. "Bruce never thought it would sell," says his secretary Olga Griffin, "because it was too costly at that time. He really wanted to go into motion pictures and he thought that this pilot would be his entry." Bruce was in Las Vegas with his wife, Jinny, when Oscar Katz called with the fateful news. Geller immediately called Stan Kallis and admitted, 'Jesus, am I in trouble!' Kallis refused Bruce's offer to produce the series. "I thought *Mission: Impossible* was immoral," he explains, "that it would have dangerous consequences because it was basically a neo-Fascist concept. It's no different from an elitist CIA or worse, the SS." Ironically, Kallis eventually produced the series, under less pleasant circumstances.

To round up prospective writers for the series, the pilot was frequently screened. Almost everyone who saw it was impressed. "It was slickly produced and beautifully done," says writer Ellis Marcus. "Sam Rolfe, who did *Have Gun Will Travel* and *The Man from U.N.C.L.E.*, said it was the best pilot he'd ever seen and I blinked, because I thought that his pilot for *U.N.C.L.E.* was the best *I'd* ever seen!" Some writers were *too* impressed and felt incapable of writing such a show. "You're crazy," Sy Salkowitz told his friend Geller. "How can we top the theft of atom bombs? We can only go straight downhill!" Bruce laughed and answered, "That's why it's good to write pilots. I wouldn't want your job. You have to come in and think of something better than I thought of, and in far less time!" Others who couldn't or wouldn't included thriller master William McGivern, author of *The Big Heat* and *Odds Against Tomorrow,* and legendary short story writer John Collier. The show's suspense seemed to work on just about everyone. When Greg Morris watched it with his wife, Lee, she grabbed his arm during the chase climax and exclaimed, "I know you're here, but I wish you'd get the hell out of *there!*"

Year One

September 1966 – April 1967

Production Credits*

Starring: Steven Hill
Also Starring: Barbara Bain, Greg Morris, Peter Lupus
Special Appearances by:
Martin Landau as Rollin Hand
Executive Producer: Bruce Geller
Produced by: Joseph Gantman
Associate Producer: Barry Crane
Story Consultants: William Read Woodfield and Allan Balter
Theme Music by: Lalo Schifrin
Directors of Photography: Charles Straumer, ASC (episodes 2 through 7), Gert Andersen, ASC (episodes 8 through 24), Jerry Finnerman (episodes 25 through 27)
Art Directors: J. M. Van Tamelen; Rolland M. Brooks
Supervising Art Director: Rolland M. Brooks
Film Editors: Paul Krasny; Robert Watts, ACE; Mike Pozen, ACE; Stanley Rabjohn; Neil MacDonald; Robert L. Swanson
Set Decorator: Lucien Hafley
Script Supervisor: Allan Greedy
Property Master: Arthur Wasson
Makeup Artist: Dan Striepeke, SMA
Special Effects: Jonnie Burke

Hairstylist: Adele Taylor
Postproduction Executive: Bill Heath
Production Supervisor: William Eatherly
Production Assistant: Philip Fehrle
Key Grip: Ross Cannon
Assistant Directors: John W. Rogers, Wilbur Mosier, Major Roup, Ric Rondell, Mark Sandrich, Jr., David Hawks
Costume Supervisors: Forrest T. Butler, Robert Spencer
Costumers (Women): Sabine Manela, Grace Kuhn
Gaffers: Joe Edesa, Bobby Jones, Joe Wharton, George H. Merhoff
Casting: Joseph D'Agosta
Music Consultant: Wilbur Hatch
Music Editors: Ted Whitfield, Jerry MacDonald
Sound Engineers: Thomas N. Thompson, Carl W. Daniels
Sound Editors: Joseph G. Sorokin, John Post, Marvin Walowitz
Steven Hill's Wardrobe Furnished by: Promenade Fashions for Men
Sound: Glen Glenn Sound
Executive in Charge of Production: Herbert F. Solow

---

* Differing credits listed by episode.

Joseph Gantman produced the series' first two seasons.

"Nobody knew what to do. Nobody."
—PRODUCER JOSEPH GANTMAN

THE SUMMER OF 1966 was chaotic for Desilu. After years of relative inactivity as a production company, the lot suddenly had two intensely difficult, innovative, and costly series: *Mission* and *Star Trek,* which had been sold to NBC. Both series would demonstrate the kind of expansive adventure shows that could be made for television.

"We had tremendous confidence," Herb Solow recalls. "I was young, we all were. Bruce, Gene Roddenberry, Bob Justman, Barry Crane. I don't think Desilu's old guard was particularly happy with us. But the bottom line was, we put the pilots together, put them on the air, and made them successful, so we must have done something right." Solow ran the studio like a family. "The *Star Trek* people related to the *Mission* people, and it was really nice." The atmosphere created a warm, close-knit feeling which Solow believes comes through in the shows.

With the sale of the pilot, Bruce Geller's next responsibility was to assemble a crew. Not surprisingly, Geller went after people he'd worked with before. Associate producer Barry Crane came over from Four Star and brought assistant Phil Fehrle and script supervisor Allan Greedy with him; editor Paul Krasny worked on *Rawhide.* Many of this season's directors were old pals: Bernie Kowalski of course, Charlie Rondeau, Leonard Horn, Michael O'Herlihy, Tom Gries, and Lee Katzin, an assistant director on *Rawhide* who'd become one of *Mission*'s best. Some of the pilot's crew (makeup man Dan Striepeke, costumer Sabine Manela, and property master Art Wasson) were retained. Newcomers like hairstylist Adele Taylor and special effects man Jonnie Burke would be important contributors to the show's style. The one thing this diverse group had in common was that none of them expected to work quite so long or hard as they would this season. "We were all young and eager and trying to do something new, really good television that the audience would have to pay attention to," says Lee Katzin.

Geller had a difficult time finding someone to produce the show. The final choice was a man Geller had never worked with and never even met. Joseph Gantman was associate producer on *The Man from U.N.C.L.E.*'s pilot, but what impressed Bruce even more was *Separate Lives,* a half-hour CBS comedy pilot Gantman produced for Norman Felton at MGM. Written by Christopher Knopf, the story involved a Denver designer sharing a New York apartment with an actor from the Bronx. "It was done with a lot of style, was well paced, and was cute like a television comedy was supposed to be," says Gantman, whose credits include work as associate producer on the feature *The Vikings* (1958). After screening the pilot, he accepted the job. "I always think I can make something work," he explains. *Mission: Impossible* would be his ultimate test.

When Gantman signed on, there were no scripts and only a few ideas in the works. Most shows prepare a "bible," a description of the series concept and characters. "For whatever reasons, Bruce Geller never prepared such a bible," states Gantman. "He never satisfactorily explained to me why he didn't have something on paper about these characters. If there was

55

one, he didn't show it to me." In time Gantman realized that Geller had no intention of working on *Mission* in anything but a supervisory way. Bruce contributed heavily to the postproduction process of editing and music and would rewrite scripts, but never initiate them. "Once I was on the show and we were in trouble, Bruce stayed out. He did not participate. When it came to story, he was at arm's length." Gantman acted as producer *and* story editor, trying to navigate a course for a series which so far was aimless.

Unhappy with the writers and stories coming in, Gantman quickly called a couple of friends, writers William Read Woodfield and Allan Balter. Born in Detroit, Balter had been a World War II paratrooper. During the fifties he worked in the casting departments of Twentieth Century-Fox and MGM. A job editing Fox's house magazine led to a position in the studio's publicity department, where he stayed in various functions through 1962. From Fox he moved to Daystar Productions as publicity director, then associate producer on *The Outer Limits* (1963–65). He cowrote two episodes before moving back to Fox for Irwin Allen's *Voyage to the Bottom of the Sea* (he and Gantman were associate producers). There Balter met Billy Woodfield, whose career and exploits would make an interesting book of its own.

San Francisco–born Woodfield rose to prominence in the late fifties and sixties as a film and magazine photographer. His credits include the famous nudes of Marilyn Monroe from her last, unfinished film. Tiring of photography, he turned to writing. In addition to scripts for *Death Valley Days* (1952–64) and *Sea Hunt* (1957–61), he coauthored a book on death row prisoner Caryl Chessman and got Jack Ruby's autobiography by smuggling a secret tape recorder into Ruby's jail cell. Balter talked Woodfield into writing a *Voyage,* which he claims he wrote in a day. Irwin Allen gave him a contract for multiple episodes, and after the show's first season, Woodfield and Balter became writing partners. Physically at least, they were an odd couple: Balter was soft-spoken and smiling, Woodfield outspoken and boisterous. They made a formidable team.

Woodfield was considered a Renaissance man around Hollywood, known for his wide range of knowledge and expertise in varied fields (he was, among other things, a magician). Joe Gantman knew that, "If anyone could make this thing work in a reasonable way, Billy Woodfield and Allan Balter were the ones to key in on it. I don't know how their collaboration worked, but my guess would be that a lot of the mind-set that we used had to come from Billy. That kind of thinking comes with being a magician: You think you see it but you don't see it."

Free-lancers Balter and Woodfield saw three pilots in one day: *The Big Valley, Mission: Impossible,* and *Star Trek.* The only one they were *not* interested in was *Mission.* "Oh it was a joke," says Woodfield, "guys in trunks and all that." Gantman suggested they write a *Mission* anyway, using a gambling theme (another Woodfield specialty). Woodfield was so disappointed with the result, "Odds on Evil," that he was reluctant to send it in. He was persuaded otherwise, and as he recalls, "Joe called with the highest praise he ever gives anything: 'I think it will work. We wanna shoot it and give you a multiple.' " "Odds on Evil" was fast, sophisticated, different, and above all, promising—it was the first story to portray the IMF as classic confidence artists. Without knowing it, Woodfield and Balter had set the mold for the series.

The pair were instantly hired as story consultants, but unlike most staff writers did not meet with prospective writers. They were so busy on their own scripts (ultimately writing ten of the first twenty-eight shows) that Gantman commissioned the rest of the scripts. "Balter and Woodfield got involved when rewrites were necessary," he says. The team took their job very seriously and did not like their work changed by as much as a word. It was a source of consternation to some of the directors and crew, but the writers' concern was justified—considering their intricacy, the plots could well have been drastically altered by any changes, however minor.

By the time *Mission* began filming, a personality conflict had already developed between Woodfield and Geller. Like Gantman, Woodfield was surprised by Geller's aloofness and began to suspect that Bruce had no idea where the show was going. "There was always an antipathy between Bruce and Bill," says actor Tony Giorgio, a friend of both. "You hear the word 'genius' bantered about, but I think they were both geniuses. What's gonna happen when you have two geniuses with tremendous egos?" The reasons behind the conflict are difficult to understand fully. Both men had strong egos to be sure, but there may have been other causes. "I don't know that Bruce had an appreciation for Balter and Woodfield," Gantman wonders, "how they worked and what went into it. Their contribution was so immense, and you've got to give people credit for that." In fact, Geller often acknowledged the pair in press interviews but face-to-face, he remained curiously silent. "I don't think that Billy walked in the door wanting to hate him," Gantman adds, "but they sure didn't like each other." This conflict would come to a boil two seasons later, with near-disastrous results.

Script problems seemed minor when compared to *Mission*'s production difficulties. In its first year, the show may have set a record for horrendous overages. Because each show required so many camera setups, *Mission had* to run over—each episode's *main title* was different. "They were always in a state of disarray that first year," says Bob Justman, *Star Trek*'s associate producer. "They could never seem to complete a show, and the studio executives couldn't understand why you couldn't complete the show in six days if that was the schedule. But there were too many shots for the amount of hours in the day." As each show took more time and money to complete, the costs became enormous and to a studio like Desilu used to three-camera situation comedies, incomprehensible. *Mission*'s first year series budget was $186,865 per episode; because of the complexity of the scripts, every hour was budgeted higher than that. Even so, at least twenty-two of the twenty-eight hours still exceeded their budget. Some, like episode 24, "Shock," went over by only about $820. Others were much higher: the two-parter show number two, "Old Man Out" cost $84,000 more than planned! Since CBS was paying no more than $170,000 per hour initially, it was clear that *Mission* was digging a very deep financial hole. Not everyone was upset by the overages—Peter Lupus has only happy memories of that period. "I almost got rich on the overtime! Those checks were amazing, thousands of dollars for going over. And we *always* went over."

The show began to fall behind. "Because we had fifty to seventy-five more setups than any other show on the air, we were taking too long to shoot shows," Martin Landau explains. "Most shows had a six-day schedule; we had a seven-day schedule. With a six-day schedule, you can shoot four shows a month; with a seven-day schedule, you can only shoot three. We'd air four shows a month but only shoot three, and we were losing ground." Since at least eleven episodes went over *seven* days, *Mission* fell even further behind. Shows would go eight days or more and still be unfinished, with inserts and second unit work (like the tape and dossier scenes) postponed to a later date. This necessitated the development of *Mission*'s insert crew, which became increasingly important to the series. Originally, the editing staff was in charge of shooting the "leftovers"; but when they were too busy to leave their moviolas, others got a chance, from Geller and Gantman to Barry Crane and special effects man Jonnie Burke.

"It was impossible. Whatever we were doing was impossible," Gantman says. "The budget

A cast pose from "A Snowball in Hell."

was very low, and they sold it for too little money." The *Mission* company virtually lived at Desilu from June 1966 through March 1967. "We worked tremendous hours," editor Paul Krasny explains, "but we loved it, absolutely loved it. I couldn't wait to go to work. I don't ever remember going home; I just remember always being at the studio. Consequently, my marriage didn't survive that. I don't think anyone knew what it would take to do it every week." Says Jonnie Burke, "We were all so tied into the show that we hated to go home, get some sleep, a bath and a shave and change clothes. You just hated to take the time out." Makeup man Dan Striepeke was logging seventy-two-hour weeks, and Geller and others spent Thanksgiving in a restaurant going over the next day's schedule. Christmas Eve was no better.

Gantman's perfectionism didn't expedite matters. "They called Jo, the lintpicker," says Olga Griffin, Geller's secretary. "If he wanted a foreign-looking gentleman, he wanted a foreign-looking gentleman. He didn't want a Mexican to look like he came from Scandinavia!" Gantman's workaholism helped make the first two seasons *Mission*'s best. "It's an impossible way to work, but that's the fun I get out of it," he says. Even a back ailment couldn't stop him: Gantman attended story meetings and editing sessions lying on the floor!

"We had no idea what we were doing," says production assistant Phil Fehrle, who this season worked as Barry Crane's right hand. "Bruce had sold a show that had a format like no other show on the air, ever. Everyone who saw it loved it and no one understood it, least of all those of us making it. It was an exciting time. Every week we were reinventing the wheel and we didn't even know if it was rolling, because of the lag time between the making of the shows and the airing of them. My own father said, 'Phil, I'm sorry but you have to understand, I watch *Bonanza*. I don't understand your show.' A lot of people didn't understand our show, but it was thrilling to work on."

In addition to *Mission,* Geller wrote and produced another pilot this season. *Mannix* was a private-eye concept by Richard Levinson and William Link, two then-obscure clients of Alden Schwimmer, who felt that Bruce's participation would make the show saleable. He was correct: *Mannix,* starring Mike Connors, was promptly bought by CBS for the 1967–68 season.

In a sign of good faith, the network scheduled *Mission* for Saturday nights from 9 to 10 against strong competition like *The Lawrence Welk Show* and *The Hollywood Palace* on ABC, and NBC's *Saturday Night Movie.* The network even kicked in additional funds to help defray Desilu's enormous deficit. "We had to come up with some monies to help them out," Mike Dann acknowledges. "No matter what your licensing cost is, you have the problem of them saying, 'OK, we'll do the next four shows in one room,' which they can, legally. So we did have to come up with extra monies." It wasn't nearly enough to keep *Mission* out of the red—but that was *Desilu's* problem.

CBS's main concern about *Mission*—perhaps its only one—was Steven Hill, who was perceived as bland and not commercial as a lead. Early in the season CBS vice president Perry Lafferty held a luncheon for more than a dozen CBS and Desilu executives. The purpose of the lunch, says Lafferty, "was to try to get Steven Hill off the show. Lucille Ball was expected but didn't come. She had put down this ultimatum that he would stay." Evidently, Lucy—and Desilu—were still behind Geller and Solow.

"Bruce thought that Steven Hill was a very good actor with interesting, offbeat elements," according to Gantman. "Bruce would often try to go offbeat, but he resisted for a long time from saying he made a mistake." Hill's contract put forth very specific requirements. "Everything that we had to do for him, including his shoes and hose, had to be kosher and sent from New York," says Olga Griffin. Those prerequisites were a mere annoyance compared to the clause which allowed Hill to leave the set before sundown every Friday, in accordance with his religion. It was so important that Hill would walk off the stage in the middle of a scene as Friday night approached. Friday is the last workday for television productions, a day when most companies work late to complete the show. *Mission* would often shoot to midnight and *still* be behind schedule. The disappearance of the leading man every Friday afternoon was yet another production hindrance. "Bruce's main beef was that Steve Hill would not work past sundown and he wouldn't break that rule," says director Charles Rondeau. "That was the agreement and it drove Bruce crazy. He wanted more out of Steven Hill."

"The production problems were unfortunate," says Gantman, who recalls the trouble intensifying as the season went on. "They developed; it became more to the letter of his contract. Being an Orthodox Jew, he'd insist on being at prayers at a certain time. He then begins to say, 'But I have to leave here in order to get where I have to pray. I can't work up until that time, you don't expect me to . . .' It was like that. What will happen is that people will disagree amiably, but then over a period of time it becomes very disagreeable. If someone understands your problems and says he understands them, you feel better about it. But if he doesn't care about your problems, then you begin to really resent him. And I think that's what happened." Steven Hill may have felt exactly the same way.

At times Hill lived up to his reputation for being unpredictable. At times he was hypersensitive: Dust from the soundstage rafters would fall on him and he would become infuriated and threaten to complain to the Screen Actors Guild. At other times he could be insensitive, calling Barbara Bain unprofessional for humming prior to a close-up during which she was to make a lighthearted comment. "Geller would come down and say, 'Why are you causing so much

damned trouble?' " Charles Rondeau recalls. Most of the time, however, Hill was preoccupied with his spiritual calling, trying to arrange prayer meetings among Desilu's Jews, or attempting to persuade Mr. and Mrs. Landau to have a kosher home. Landau remembers Hill (who always called him "Landau") testing him on Jewish history, or pointing out how the Jewish people have been persecuted throughout history.

"As is the case with any convert, Steve was very involved," says Greg Morris, who was probably closest to him. "Steve was a very intense, nice man. He was not treated very well." Hill had to phone *Greg* to learn if the pilot had sold. "I was surprised that they did not inform Steven Hill," says Morris, who believes that Hill may have had a misconception regarding the amount of work expected of him. "Whether someone gave him the wrong information or not I don't know, but what he wanted to do was just deal with the apartment scene, and the four of us would deal with the rest."

The main beneficiary of Hill's absences was Martin Landau, whose contract for the pilot granted Desilu an option "to render services for (three or four) additional episodes" for a fee "no less than $5000 for a one-hour episode." To fill the void left by Hill, Landau was called more and more often and always as an expensive guest star. Studio chief Solow remembers that "when it came time to negotiate he and I walked around the lot and came to terms, always on the basis that he could leave on two weeks' notice." Ultimately Landau agreed to do all the shows for the remainder of the season, but always as a guest star. "That way I wouldn't cause them any grief if I left on the two-week clause to do a feature," says the actor. When the show was renewed at the end of the first year, Landau and Solow again walked around the lot, and Landau become a series regular—on a year-to-year basis only, in contrast to the long-term contracts preferred by the studio.

Hill's absence was partially responsible for Landau's emergence as year one's star performer. "I knew I was getting stuff that Steve could have been doing," Landau says, "but I wasn't about to say, 'No, don't give me the good part!' Steve could have done 'A Spool There Was,' or 'Elena.' There was no reason why he couldn't, there was no makeup involved. I think the intention was to give some of that stuff to Steve." The other reason for Landau's rise was that the character of Rollin Hand and his unique talents made him much more exploitable than Briggs, whose function was essentially that of leader. Writers found it more logical and exciting to send Rollin on perilous adventures and keep Briggs, the mastermind, home.

Landau's semiregular status killed the possibility of other IMF guest spies, Geller's original intention. It turned out that having one guest IMFer was more interesting than a retinue of them. "With Landau they had a gimmick they could use every week," says Robert Justman. "In Television Land, people want to see what's familiar. They wanna see it happen again and see how they get out of it this time. They don't tune in to see something different. They want to see something different, done the same way."

The reasons behind the shift in emphasis became moot during the filming of episode 22, "Action!," when Steven Hill cost the company two days' work by suddenly refusing to play a scene, retreating to his dressing room, and locking the door, forcing Bruce Geller and Herb Solow to come down to the set and ultimately suspend him. This apparently was the last straw even for Geller, Hill's staunchest supporter. Dan Briggs was then written out of the scripts whenever possible, his duties confined mainly to the tape, dossier, and apartment scenes. Even so, Hill was costing Desilu money, drawing a star's salary for what usually amounted to three short scenes, and forcing the hiring of an additional actor to play what would have been Hill's role in the rest of the episode.

"I felt that he was digging his own grave," says Marty Landau. "There was always something self-destructive, always a part of him that didn't want success, along with this very special talent. When he wanted to work he was exceptional; when he didn't want to work, for whatever reasons, he was destructive *to himself.* I must say that he was troublesome at times, but basically he wasn't. Most of the time he was professional, he learned his lines and was there. But Bruce, who wanted him very badly, was fed up."

Evidently, Hill had no inkling that his days were numbered. Script supervisor Allan Greedy recalls the actor asking about rumors of his impending dismissal. "He was not expecting it to occur," says Allan. "I was amazed, because it was such common knowledge that even *I* knew it for at least a week previous."

Hill learned about his departure in a most unfortunate way. During the filming of episode 26, "The Traitor," *Daily Variety* ran the following blurb in its March 6, 1967 issue: "In an attempt to soup up its Nielsens, CBS-TV is switching the series to 10 P.M. Sundays next semester and plans are also underway to change leads, with Steven Hill to depart and Peter Graves taking over his spot. These changes should help *Mission.*" That is how Steven Hill learned he had been fired. Greg Morris relates what happened on the set that day. "Bruce came down with this Rock of Gibraltar face on to apologize to Steve. He went over to Steve and Steve said, 'Look, I don't want to talk to you.' He walked away. And Bruce said, 'I can understand.' It was one of those distasteful moments that you don't wish to remember because Steve was a friend of mine, and I know how I'd feel if I'd found out that way." The secondhand manner in which Hill learned of the sale of the series *and* his dismissal from it was cruelly ironic. "He forced them to fire him, that's what happened," says Hill's friend Albert Paulsen. "He threw away millions of dollars. Millions."

Setting the precedent for all future cast departures, Mr. Briggs's exit was never explained on-screen. Was he killed during a mission? Did he retire from the IMF? The questions were never answered, Briggs disappeared as mysteriously as he arrived, and was never mentioned again.

Mission's first season went largely unnoticed in 1966–67. By the time it was rerun in syndication the series was a classic with a large following, most of whom had never seen year one. Many viewers were surprised by the elements found in *Mission*'s first semester. Here was a dark, anonymous IMF leader who only occasionally participated in missions and did *not* always choose the same four operatives. In contrast to the breathtakingly researched strategies to come, the IMF often enters a situation blind and is forced to improvise a plan along the way. Our heroes are a bit more human, and even joke between themselves to alleviate the tension triggered by frequent fistfights and gun battles. Like most series, *Mission*'s first season was one of slow coalescence. As the show grew, much of what appears this season would be revised or phased out, including the use of violence; the sense of humor, characterization, and spontaneity; the eclectic choice of protagonists; and even the leading man.

THE COMPLETE MISSION: IMPOSSIBLE DOSSIER

Note: Episodes are numbered as scripts are accepted. Episodes are not always aired in production order.

1: PILOT

Written and Produced by: Bruce Geller
Directed by: Bernard L. Kowalski
Music by: Lalo Schifrin

First Aired: 9/17/66

TEAM: Briggs; Rollin; Cinnamon; Barney; Willy; Terry Targo, convicted safecracker

Good morning, Mr. Briggs. General Rio Dominguez, the dictator of Santa Costa, makes his headquarters in the Hotel Nacionale. We've learned that two nuclear warheads furnished to Santa Costa by an enemy power are contained in the hotel vault. Their use is imminent. Mr. Briggs, your mission, should you decide to accept it, would be to remove both nuclear devices from Santa Costa. As always, you have carte blanche as to method and personnel, but of course should you or any member of your IM Force be caught or killed, the secretary will disavow any knowledge of your actions. As usual, this recording will decompose one minute after the breaking of the seal. I hope it's welcome back, Dan. It's been a while.

Jewelry salesman Briggs and assistant Willy check into the Army-guarded Hotel Nacionale and deposit two large sample cases in the hotel vault, which is guarded at all times and opened only twice a day. Inside, Terry emerges from one of the sample cases. Armed with safecracking gear, flashlight, and oxygen, he finds a way to open the vault from inside, then returns to the sample case. Willy and Dan remove their cases from the vault, meet "Dominguez" (a disguised Rollin), and enter the real general's quarters, overpowering him. In the attempt, however, Terry's fingers are broken, making it impossible for him to return to the vault and take the warheads. His replacement: Briggs.

Willy redeposits the cases in the vault. Briggs emerges from one case and releases a bound and gagged Dominguez from the other. Because the warheads are color coded, Briggs must get the proper code from the general if he is to safely remove them from their container. When Briggs threatens to randomly pick colors, Dominguez panics and divulges the correct code. Briggs removes the warheads and places them in the sample cases, then stows Dominguez and himself in the warheads' empty container. Willy and "Briggs" (Rollin) remove the cases from the vault. Briggs opens the vault from inside and escapes, leaving Dominguez locked in the container. Briggs joins the team in a race to the airport. Eluding the militia, they take the warheads and themselves onto a jet and fly off.

GUEST CAST: Wally Cox (Terry Targo), Harry Davis (Alicio), Paul Micale (Desk Clerk), Patrick Campbell (Day Vault Clerk), Frederic Villani (Night Vault Clerk), Joe Breen (Loft Manager). *Unbilled:* Martin Walker (Lobby Guard), Josh Adams (New Guard), Victor Dunlap (Head Waiter), David Renard (TV Floorman), Sondra Kerr (Girl Clerk)

Terry Targo (Wally Cox) opens a vault from the inside in the "Pilot."

Pilot Credits

Associate Producer: Robert H. Justman
Director of Photography: John Alton
Art Director: Matt Jefferies
Set Director: Art Parker
Film Editors: Mike Pozen; John Foley, ACE; Axel Hubert
Property Master: Art Wasson
Makeup Artists: Dan Striepeke, SMA; John Chambers
Special Effects: John Erickson
Postproduction Supervisor: Bill Heath
Production Supervisor: James A. Paisley

Sound: Glen Glenn Co.
Photographic Effects: Howard Anderson Co.
Assistant Director: Gregg Peters
Costumer (Men): Clark Ross
Costumer (Women): Sabine Manela
Hairstylist: Sylvia Setzler
Sound Engineer: Walter Goss
Sound Editor: Joseph G. Sorokin
Music Supervisor: Wilbur Hatch
Music Editor: Jack Hunsaker
Executive in Charge of Production: Herbert F. Solow

With its intricate plotting, sophisticated derring-do, elaborate masquerades, and exotic locale, episode 1 seems to exemplify the series in general and year one particularly. Yet it has elements which set it apart from the series it spawned. The script is not as sophisticated as later episodes and includes a flaw other than the illogic of storing nuclear bombs in a hotel safe: just before Briggs, "Dominguez," and Willy break into the general's quarters, Cinnamon is seen wheeling her invalid husband around the hotel lobby. Since Barney is crawling around the hotel,* and Terry is in the storage case, who is the old man in the wheelchair?

The unexplained appearance of Dan Briggs set the precedent for all future regulars. He reveals not a single personality trait until his vault scenes with Dominguez show him to be tough, hard, and utterly uncompromising. When Dominguez gives Briggs his word that the bombs won't be used against the US, Dan is unfazed.

BRIGGS: I'll give you the same guarantee, General. You read my meaning? Those things might go off, but it won't be in *my* country.

We meet the rest of the team in Dan's apartment, where they are cheating at penny poker. Rollin is flamboyant, Cinnamon mock-narcissistic, Barney self-assured, Terry soft-spoken, and Willy virtually mute (since he is squeezed into a suit through most of the show, his physique does his talking for him). We don't learn anything more and have no time to dwell on it, for we are plunged directly into the adventure.

Apart from Terry's safecracking equipment and some electronic gear used by Barney to prevent "Dominguez" from making a televised speech, the gadgetry is kept to a minimum, in contrast to later *Mission*s. There are also some obligatory spy set pieces: a fistfight with Dominguez's guards; a car chase finale during which Briggs uses a smoke machine to lose his pursuers; the gunfire punctuating the chase (it is significant that *Briggs,* not the militia, fires the first shot). Clichés like these were phased out of the series by the end of its first year.

Who would watch a show like this? It lacked the charm of *I Spy* and the camp of *The Man from U.N.C.L.E. Variety*'s review of the pilot made valid points. "This was no show for anyone to come in at the middle of," wrote "Les." "Too much happened by too many people—and the worst of it was that the viewer didn't get to know anyone well enough to care

---

* Posing as an exterminator, he rigs a fireworks display to cover the IMF's exit.

Written and Produced by

BRUCE GELLER

The IMF is first seen cheating at penny poker (top)—guest star Wally Cox is center. (Bottom) Mission Accomplished!

anything about them. It's elementary that character involvement is a weighty factor with the Nielsen homes, and this effort seems astonishingly barren in that department." Prophetically, the episode ends not on a shot of our triumphant heroes, but on a freeze-frame of Rollin's discarded Briggs mask. *Variety* also noted that the performances were of necessity undistinguished and that the script lacked suspense, since, "the viewer always knew they'd make it."

The New York Times's Jack Gould realized that the suspense stemmed not from whether or not the good guys would succeed—this was, after all, 1966 American TV, and there was no question that they would. "What made the episode attractive," wrote Gould, "was the intricacy of planning for the penetration of the safe and the circumvention of the elaborate dictatorial bureaucracy designed to thwart just such an intrusion." He liked Steven Hill and Barbara Bain best among the cast, noting, "Their skills were integrated into a frequently fast-moving suspense show that was noteworthy for its unusually imaginative and varied photography and for a series of technical gimmicks that succeeded in diverting attention from Bruce Geller's script, which was more of a cue sheet than a repository for dialogue. . . . CBS may have found its *U.N.C.L.E.*"

In fact, they had found a series that would outlast NBC's spy show by years.

2: OLD MAN OUT (in two parts)

First Aired: 10/8/66; 10/15/66

Written by: Ellis Marcus
Directed by: Charles R. Rondeau
Music Composed and Conducted by:
    Walter Scharf

TEAM: Briggs, Rollin, Cinnamon, Barney, Willy, trapeze artist Crystal Walker

Good evening, Mr. Briggs. This is Anton Cardinal Vossek, who, despite being eighty years of age and physically infirm, is nonetheless the acknowledged leader of his country's freedom movement. The government towards whose overthrow Cardinal Vossek is working has arrested him preparatory to a trial before a people's court which is certain to convict him. He's being held for interrogation on the top floor of this building, Seravno Prison, which is located immediately adjacent to the city's main park. Seravno Prison is considered the most impregnable in Eastern Europe; no escape has ever been made from it. Mr. Briggs, your mission, should you decide to accept it, would be to rescue Cardinal Vossek. As always, should you or any of your IM Force be caught or killed, the secretary will disavow any knowledge of your actions. In any event, please dispose of this tape recording as directed.

A traveling carnival troupe sets up camp in the park adjoining Seravno Prison. The performers include mind reader Dan, his assistant Cinnamon, strongman Willy, clown Barney, and trapeze expert Crystal.

Carnival rigger Rollin, caught pick-pocketing, is jailed inside Seravno. He sneaks out of his cell, frees Vossek, and gets him to the roof undetected. This is merely a test run for the actual escape, scheduled for the next day. But Vossek is suddenly transferred to a guarded, solitary confinement cell, killing the IMF plan and forcing Dan to plot another course and somehow relay it to the imprisoned Rollin.

GUEST CAST: Mary Ann Mobley (Crystal Walker), Cyril Delevanti (Anton Cardinal Vossek), Joseph Ruskin (Colonel Jovann Scutari), Oscar Beregi (Commandant), William Wintersole (Captain), Monte Markham (Tosk). *Unbilled:* Eddie Durkin (Maintenance Man), Chris Anders (Special Guard), Chuck Couch (double, Rollin), Fred Krone (double, Briggs), George Margo (Sergeant), Norbert Siegfried (Officer), Jon Cedar (Second Guard), Jon Silo (Victim), Sunny Woods, Patty Elder (doubles, Crystal), Marilyn Moe (double, Cinnamon), Alan Gibbs (double, Vossek)

Ellis Marcus's first version of the script, "The Vossek Rescue," used a roguish circus character named Bellini in Rollin's place. With the show rewritten to accommodate Landau, Rollin adds yet another talent to his repertoire: stealth, as he makes his way in, around, and over the prison without detection. This facility would be used again in episode 6, "A Spool There Was," also written by Ellis Marcus. This *Mission* is a good rewrite of the pilot, detailing the penetration of and escape from an impregnable locale. According to Geller, the script's strengths were, "A solid story, well executed, a role in depth for Steve Hill, strong human interest in Vossek, pictorial as well as practical functions for team, sustained suspense, extraordinary production values." Its flaws: "Lack of clarity in both identity and function of MIF [sic]. Who are they? Why are they risking their lives? Why is Briggs forced to take his assignments in such a bizarre fashion?" Obviously, there were some series points that even its creator could not answer!

Marcus's script was too long and too expensive, so Geller rewrote it as a two-parter. To flesh it out, he was forced to give his characters some *character*. Geller added two sequences: one in which Vossek gives confession to a guilt-ridden prison officer, and another, more interesting one, Crystal's recruitment. Briggs visits her backstage at a circus, where she is a headliner. She is delighted to see him—at first. Then she realizes why he must be there. Crystal, it turns out, is in love with Dan, who never calls her except for business. Despite her vehement insistence that she will not participate, Crystal soon melts.

In this show more than any other, the IMF seems composed of human beings. The agents talk casually and joke with one another. Barney, that expert in mechanical devices, watches Cinnamon use a torturous eyelash curler and declares, "That's the most diabolical looking piece of equipment I've ever seen!" Applying his clown whiteface, he asks Dan, "What comedian thought of this makeup?" In a revealing scene, Cinnamon eyes Crystal mooning over Dan and says, "He's all wrapped up in his work. Forget it." Crystal replies by commenting, "You worry about Rollin, right?" Cinnamon gives her a look; "I worry about earthquakes," she answers, fooling no one. Other moments showcase efficient but friendly *people,* not robots or unfeeling chameleons. Was the extended time of a two-parter the reason behind this? Upcoming installments indicate that the same results could be achieved within an hour episode—if desired.

Considering the spacious location work, it is surprising to note that "Old Man Out" was filmed in downtown LA near the Los Angeles County Museum, not far from the slums of Watts. It's a colorful, extremely visual show with lively performances, especially from Mary Ann Mobley who shines as Crystal (doubled on the trapeze by Sunny Woods, a remarkable look-alike). Walter Scharf's exciting score is heightened by the cheerful tooting of a circus calliope. Bad weather, the complexity of the story, and the sheer density of production sent the show three days over schedule to seventeen, with a final budget of over $490,000, a whopping overage from the already large $406,770 projected. CBS was pleased enough with the show to pay Desilu an additional $50,000 to help finance a feature release of the show to Europe, which never transpired. Producer Joseph Gantman had mixed feelings about the episode. "In execution, it turned out fine. But it's a pretty straightforward escape story that I'd seen before. That was the problem." Gantman was already looking for a way to make *Mission* something more than a string of vault and prison escapes. He'd soon find it.

3: MEMORY

Written by: Robert Lewin
Directed by: Charles R. Rondeau
Music by: Lalo Schifrin

First Aired: 9/24/66

TEAM: Briggs, Cinnamon, Barney, Willy, memory expert Joseph Baresh, and an unexpected assist from Rollin Hand

Instead of a taped message, Briggs is handed the following information on a small card by a street photographer:

LUBJANKA MILITARY PRISON
Headquarters of Dimitri Soska
Our investigations are to begin immediately. Proceed
as per our previous instructions and report as soon as
possible. Alternate plan X59.

Briggs reads the card, then destroys it.

"Behind the Iron Curtain there's a man we've got to remove from power within two weeks," Briggs explains. Janos Karq, "the Butcher of the Balkans," is a warmonger who has systematically eliminated his opposition. "We're going to destroy Karq politically by making him appear to be a traitor." Dimitri Soska, Karq's head of intelligence, will capture a long-elusive enemy agent named Sparrow who, under torture, will confess that his orders came from Karq. To validate this unlikely story, an elaborate—and deliberately unsuccessful—attempt to rescue Sparrow will be performed. With luck, Sparrow's eventual release would be negotiated. Dan briefs Joseph Baresh, whose amazing photographic memory makes him the only person capable of "becoming" Sparrow in so short a time.

"Sparrow" is caught, taken to Lubjanka Prison, and brutally questioned by Soska before naming Karq as his superior. An IMF smoke bomb wreaks havoc inside the prison. During the confusion, Ba-resh, alone in Soska's office, reads (and memorizes) Soska's list of agents before being sent back to his cell. Firemen Willy and Dan leave axe marks in Baresh's cell door to fake an aborted rescue. But when Dan learns that Baresh knows the identity of every one of Soska's agents, Briggs must find a way to get Baresh out.

GUEST CAST: Albert Paulsen (Joseph Baresh), Leonard Stone (Dimitri Soska), Eddie Carroll (Street Photographer), William Keene (Janos Karq), Heinz Brinkman (First Guard), Gene Dynarski (Sergeant Of Guard). *Unbilled:* Donald Journeaux (Passport Clerk), John Magnusson (Policeman), Paul Busch (Jeep Guard), William Foster (Fireman), Forrest Burns (First Security), Max Kleven (Second Security), Howard Curtis (double, Briggs), Chuck Couch (double, Baresh)

Geller's rewrite of "Old Man Out" made "Memory" the first *Mission* filmed after the pilot. This time the objective is not to free a prisoner or steal weapons. Briggs's job, indirectly, is to kill Janos Karq. "As usual," he tells the IMF, "assassination has been ruled out as a matter of policy." The only alternative is to get Karq's own people to kill him. The IMF do some killing of their own during Baresh's real escape. Barney electrocutes two tower guards, and he and Willy shoot two more before they leave.

The star of "Memory" is IMF recruit Joseph Baresh, who can instantly memorize anything (the sequence of a deck of cards, a telephone directory page). The gift hasn't done him much good: Baresh is a drunk whose IMF dossier consists of a carnival flyer boasting him as the

67

main attraction. Baresh is played by Albert Paulsen, who would become one of *Mission*'s most frequent guest stars. "Memory" is the only show in which he appears as a hero, and his liquor-soaked, world-weary performance is a good counterpoint to his sharp young colleagues. " 'Memory' was the best part I ever had on the show," the actor says. "A drunk, but not a villain." The night before the apartment scene was filmed, Paulsen, himself a recovering alcoholic, deliberately drank. "In the morning I got up with red eyes and pretty groggy," he remembers proudly. "You can see it. I'd go to any length to get it done right."

Interestingly, there actually was a "Butcher of the Balkans." Andrija Artukovic, interior minister in the Nazi puppet state of Croatia during World War II, was responsible for the murder of 700,000 Jews, Gypsies, and others. Artukovic used phony papers to emigrate to the US after the war, was arrested in 1984, and sent to Yugoslavia two years later to be executed at the age of eighty-six for his war crimes.

4: OPERATION ROGOSH

Written by: Jerome Ross
Directed by: Leonard J. Horn
Music by: Lalo Schifrin

First Aired: 10/1/66

TEAM: Briggs, Rollin, Cinnamon, Barney, Willy, Dr. Ira Green, M.D., The Horizon Repertory Players, stunt driver Sonny Allison

Good morning, Mr. Briggs. This man is Imry Rogosh, known to us as "the monster." His specialty is mass murder, in order to create political anarchy. Here are some samples of his work: North Africa, Bombay, Rio de Janiero. Yesterday Rogosh was discovered to have been in Los Angeles for a week. He has bought airline tickets home for tomorrow night. Considering Rogosh's history, the secretary believes that thousands in the Los Angeles area might die unless Rogosh's plan is discovered and countered. Dan, our experts consider Rogosh unbreakable by any known means. Nevertheless, your mission, should you decide to accept, would be to break Rogosh—fast. Please destroy this recording by the usual method.

Rogosh is hit by a car driven by Sonny and rushed away in an IMF ambulance. He awakens in a rat-infested cell in his own country—he thinks. In fact he is still in Los Angeles, in a building resembling his country's Stefan Castle Prison. Rogosh is told that three years have passed and that he is about to be executed as an American agent.

Desperate to prove his loyalty at his slanted trial, Rogosh details his plot to murder thousands of Americans—a plot he has been led to believe was successful. But before he can reveal the full operation, Rogosh accidentally uncovers the IMF charade, forcing Briggs to find another way to break "the monster."

GUEST CAST: Fritz Weaver (Imry Rogosh), Allan Joseph (Dr. Ira Green, M.D.), Charles Maxwell (Lazloff), James Lanphier (Colonel Klimi), Svea Grunfeld (Woman Judge). *Unbilled:* Dina Harmson (Matron), Howard Curtis (Stunt Driver), Dick Dial (Stunt Double)

In Jerome Ross's first draft of May 27, 1966, the tape-dossier-apartment sequence is not used. Briggs is briefed by a counterintelligence officer, who explains that Rogosh has recently suffered an auto "accident."

BRIGGS: Did you arrange for this accident?

C. I. OFFICER *(shocked):* Deliberately?

BRIGGS *(hastily):* Forgive me. I forgot, we never do things like that, do we?

"They asked me to come up with a story in which there'd be a time element involved," says Ross, "a transposition of time." The concept certainly didn't originate here; an MGM feature, *36 Hours* (1964), based upon a Roald Dahl story, told the same type of tale, set during World War II. "Rogosh" was probably the first time, however, that such a story was ever presented within the confines of a television series, and Ross's script was good enough to win the Edgar Award that year from the Mystery Writers of America. "The transposition of time is something that's been done before, God knows, and it's very good," Ross says. "Chiefly, I think it works because your audience is more aware of the deception than that of, say, a man in a maze. The mistaken concept of time is much more dramatic than the mistaken concept of place. Identity is the strongest, really." Within seven years, *Mission* would exhaust all three concepts.

The first *Mission* to concentrate on psychological rather than physical manipulation, "Rogosh" is a good indication of where the series was headed. Careful detail is needed to fool Rogosh and entertain the viewer. Futuristic dates are scrawled on the walls of Rogosh's cell;

tape recordings of screaming "prisoners" are played for his benefit; and Rogosh's hair is grayed to complete the illusion that years have passed. Rogosh's cell has an excellent view of the prison gallows, where he sees his superior (Rollin in disguise) hanged. When he finds that his lawyer is a stooped, mumbling Briggs, who has lost similar cases, it is incumbent upon Rogosh to redeem himself by detailing his "prior" Los Angeles operation.

Dazzlingly effective editing by Paul Krasny enhances the show. By using dozens of angles, optical zooming, and very quick cuts, Krasny gives Rogosh's solo scenes in his cell a feeling of tension and confusion. The actors are very good, especially Fritz Weaver as the befuddled Rogosh, Steven Hill as the miserable lawyer, Barbara Bain as Rogosh's supposed secretary-girlfriend (also jailed), and Greg Morris as a Caribbean student agitator.

"Rogosh" and its eccentric plot attracted the attention of several critics who had heretofore ignored the series. *The New Yorker* called "Rogosh" "fine stuff," while *The New York Times* speculated that *Mission*, "May turn out to be the most interesting of the regular new shows. . . . The simulated kangaroo court trial and the brainwashing in reverse were cleverly done, and Leonard J. Horn's direction was unusually good." "Rogosh" was such an unqualified success that it was considered the jewel of *Mission*'s crown for many years, and its time warp idea became a series perennial.

5: ODDS ON EVIL

Written by: William Read Woodfield and
   Allan Balter
Directed by: Charles R. Rondeau
Music Composed and Conducted by:
   Gerald Fried

First Aired: 10/22/66

TEAM: Rollin, Cinnamon, Barney, Willy,
   André Malif

Good evening, Mr. Briggs. This is Prince Iben Kostas, absolute ruler of a tiny principality whose sole income derives from its famous gambling casino. It's Kostas's intention to declare war on the oil-rich nation that borders his. He's accumulated a million and a half dollars to purchase arms from a man named Borgman. The munitions ship is already on its way. Mr. Briggs, your mission, should you decide to accept it, would be to prevent the delivery of those arms, and make sure that Kostas cannot buy any more. As always, should you or any of your IM Force be caught or killed, the secretary will disavow any knowledge of your actions. This material will decompose in five seconds.

The IMF set up headquarters in Kostas's hotel casino. Cinnamon flirts outrageously with ladies' man Kostas, enraging her husband, André, who breaks the bank at the roulette table but loses everything to Rollin at baccarat. Eager to retrieve the casino's money, Kostas engages a "reluctant" Rollin in a game. Although Kostas wears tinted contact lenses to read the marked cards, a series of bad hands (dealt by Rollin, wearing similar lenses) frustrates the prince. Kostas antes up the $1.5 million meant for the arms deal, certain that his "edge" will win the game for him. Rollin matches the cash with certified checks, then beats Kostas by cheating the cheater. Despite the efforts of Kostas's men, our heroes get out of the country with the cash and their lives intact.

GUEST CAST: Nico Minardos (André Malif),
   Nehemiah Persoff (Prince Iben Kostas),
   Vincent Van Lynn (Oliver Borgman),
   Lawrence Montaigne (Kostas's Aide), Joey
   Tata (Roulette Croupier), Roger Til

(Baccarat Croupier), Alex Bookston (Man in Arcade), Greg Benedict (Karl). *Unbilled:* George Sawaya, Paul Nuckles, Marilyn Moe, Howard Curtis (Stunts)

Cinnamon seems to be on the side of Prince Kostas (Nehemiah Persoff) in "Odds On Evil."

In Woodfield and Balter's original outline, the target was Ben-Jack Turner, a millionaire paramilitary hatemonger operating his own casino in his own city. Armed with tips from card cheats, Briggs enters as a Texas high roller and wins big. When Dan outcheats Turner at chemin de fer, Turner closes the casino and holds Dan at gunpoint until a gas bomb from Willy allows Briggs to flee. The IMF escape in a van, chased by Turner and his goons. Barney takes to the air in a one-man helicopter and drops a bomb on a bridge as Turner's car crosses it, killing Turner and his goons. Briggs expresses regret over the loss of the bridge, but notes that his winnings can build a new one!

Balter and Woodfield's opening episode introduces several firsts which would become commonplace. Briggs masterminds but doesn't participate in the mission; the hiring of Nico

Minardos in the role meant for Briggs suggests that Steven Hill's scheduling dictates were already causing production problems. Cinnamon graduates from minor distraction to major player and demonstrates her skill by wrapping Kostas around her finger. Most importantly, this is the first show to rely upon elaborate electronic hardware. To bankrupt the roulette table, three pieces of equipment are used: a sensor in Cinnamon's purse which calculates the speed of the roulette wheel and ball, a ninety-pound computer system in Willy's tuxedo vest which receives the sensor's data and projects the winning number, and André's wristwatch, which displays that number in its date window seconds before the spinning ball stops.

The gaming sequences required an inordinate amount of insert shots of the trick IMF watch, the spinning roulette wheel, the marked baccarat cards, and more. Because of this, production went one-and-one-half days over schedule and was still incomplete. Three weeks later, an insert crew of editors Paul Krasny, Robert Watts, and Mike Pozen were filling in the blanks on this and the previous show, while Joe Gantman directed pickups for episode 2, "Old Man Out" *and* "Odds on Evil." On that same day, July 28, Bruce Geller went before the camera, picked up a match and struck it against a black backdrop, kicking off one of television's most famous main titles.

"When Bruce and I saw the rough cut of 'Odds on Evil,'" says Gantman, "we were scared. It was a shambles. The gambling scenes had no rhythm and it didn't make any sense. Bruce said, 'You've got to do something. You've just got to recut the picture.' That was one of the things that keyed me into how this thing was going to work! I fired the first editor and hired another guy. The new editor did a totally new first cut that turned out so well, in terms of building excitement, that from then on Bruce pulled away from the area of editing."

According to cowriter William Read Woodfield, the story was not built around the baccarat scene, as might be imagined, but around the antagonistic couple played by André and Cinnamon. "It was *Who's Afraid of Virginia Woolf?* in a gambling casino," he explains. "We played out a little subdrama and we got a Writers Guild nomination for that, but never won it. Harlan Ellison beat us out for a *Star Trek,* which crushed us." Woodfield, expert in gaming and cheating, recalls stories of old-time gamblers called section players, the only people who could actually beat the game. "A guy would come in, look at the wheel, and be able to measure where the ball was going to stop and in what section. He would then make a bet, and his confederates would then make bets on all sides of it so they'd cover about ten numbers. They figured that the ball is going to land in one of those ten numbers, and since they're getting maybe thirty-six to one odds for it, they've got a profit. We set 'Odds on Evil' in Europe instead of Vegas because there's only one zero on the European roulette wheel, it's green (a different color), and it could be measured. The IMF were really playing sections, although it worked on just one number and was done with computerized sophistication. That much of it was untrue, it would have had to be played in a section."

Woodfield admits that such a computerized setup is anachronistic for 1966, but he has heard and read of professors and professionals who have extrapolated upon the system seen in this episode. "Recently," says the writer, "some graduate students put together, laminated in their shoes, some microcomputers which they operated with their toes, measuring the speed of the ball and the speed of the wheel, and registered the number. They took it to Vegas. It worked. It didn't work very well, because they kept sweating and shorting out the machines. But that method of beating roulette developed from this episode." This was only the first example of life imitating *Mission: Impossible.*

6: A SPOOL THERE WAS

Written by: Ellis Marcus
Directed by: Bernard L. Kowalski
Music Composed and Conducted by:
 Lalo Schifrin

First Aired: 11/12/66

TEAM: Rollin, Cinnamon

Good afternoon, Mr. Briggs. Please put on the red light, then remove the cover from the developing trays. * *There is in existence a reel of recording wire with details of a chemical warfare project being developed for use against the free world. One of our agents carrying the reel made his way to the lake shown. We assume his intention was to appropriate a boat and row across to neutral territory. But he was seen by secret police and forced to hide. Shortly thereafter he was discovered and killed resisting capture. However, in that brief period of time before being discovered, he managed to hide the reel so ingeniously that the secret police, with every resource at their disposal, have still not been able to find it, despite the limited area they have to search. Other, unfriendly nations also have agents working in the area. Your mission, Mr. Briggs, should you accept it, would be to find the reel and bring it out of the country. As always, should you or any of the IM Force be caught or killed, the secretary would disavow any knowledge of your actions. This recording will decompose in sixty seconds after the breaking of the seal. Good luck, Dan.*

Dock worker Rollin and photographer Cinnamon join the lakeside's uniformed officers, secret police, and enemy agents, all of whom are frantically searching for the reel. The IMF pair feign a lovers' reunion and adjourn that night to Rollin's room, which is wired by the police. As Rollin slips out a window, Cinnamon plays a long, prerecorded dialogue for the benefit of the listening police. At the lake, Rollin lets his presence be known to the night guards, then reenacts the last desperate moments of the courier's life. Under that pressure he finds the wire—so openly displayed that no one has noticed it. Barely eluding capture, Rollin returns to Cinnamon and plans to take the wire the next day, "openly and conspicuously, right under their noses."

Before Rollin can complete the mission, he must counter two enemy agents who'll stop at nothing to get the wire, and retrieve the recording when a young boy takes it for fishing wire.

GUEST CAST: Richard Devon (Inspector Gulik), Warren Vanders (Holbeck), Michael Shea (Pieter Stakovar), Curt Lowens (Lt. Daglieri), Eric Lord (Concessionaire), Lynn Wood (Mrs. Stakovar), Todd Martin (Mr.

Stakovar). *Unbilled:* Horst Ebersberg (Rissko), Ben Astar (Diplomat), Harry Basch (Konya), Louie Elias (Stunt), Gene LeBell (Sudow)

Rollin retraces the steps of a murdered courier in "A Spool There Was."

---

* This week's drop is a darkroom.

73

Originally called "The Czernik Wire," this story went through various incarnations, first involving photographer Rollin, model Cinnamon, and journalist Barney. It was revised as a solo mission for Briggs, and after a Bruce Geller polish it became "A Spool There Was." Geller may have decided that it was inappropriate IMF casting for Briggs to embark on this extremely hazardous, almost suicidal mission. Writer Ellis Marcus was given the premise of a lost wire recording. "In those days before tape recordings were popular, it was wire recordings. That shows you how long ago that was!"

This is the only show to feature just Rollin and Cinnamon, and their cover offers a delightful last chance for the spies to flirt with each other. From now on there would be no hint of an attraction between the two. The series would later avoid any sign of emotion—but not yet.

7: FAKEOUT

Written by: Leigh Chapman
Directed by: Bernard L. Kowalski
Music Composed and Conducted by:
   Lalo Schifrin

First Aired: 12/3/66

TEAM: Briggs, Cinnamon, Barney

Good morning, Mr. Briggs. Anastas Poltroni, head of the International Narcotics Syndicate, now resides as Ted Carson in a country with which we have no extradition treaty. Your mission, should you decide to accept it, would be to get Poltroni out of that country so that he may be legally arrested and brought back to the United States to face trial. Unfortunately, kidnapping has been ruled out as too embarrassing politically. As always, should you or any of your IM Force be caught or killed, the secretary will disavow any knowledge of your actions. Please dispose of this recording by the nearest means. Good luck, Dan.

Cinnamon woos Carson until her "husband," Briggs, intrudes and suggests that Carson bribe him to forget this indiscretion. Carson sees through this con game and exits. Barney stashes a large supply of Carson's heroin in Carson's hotel room and tips the police, who arrest him.

The IMF ambush Carson and the police and steal the heroin. Carson escapes, grabs Cinnamon, and chases Briggs to a deserted lodge, where he retrieves the drugs. Pursued by the police and with Cinnamon as hostage, he flees via the confusing mountain roads, made more confusing by the IMF, who have altered the road signs. Following the misleading directions, Carson unwittingly drives across the border into Chagueo, which has extradition ties with America. A horde of officers descend upon Carson (still carrying the heroin) and deport him back to the US.

GUEST CAST: Lloyd Bridges (Anastas Poltroni, aka Ted Carson), Sid Haig (Hidalgo), Alberto Monte (Attendant), Ken Renard (Assistant Manager), Richard Angarola (Policeman). *Unbilled:* Kathleen O'Malley (Researcher), Gary Lasdun (Zack), Lee Delano (First Cop), Dehl Berti (Young Zookeeper), Mike Steele (Holloway), Monte Mansfield (Paolo), Eli Behar (Aniso), Dante Orgolini (Old Zookeeper), Cal Brown (double, Barney)

This very simple *Mission* ironically went through many different drafts before the final version. "Fakeout" originally employed Rollin, who was jettisoned by Geller in favor of Briggs. In future episodes, however, the situation would usually be reversed.

Director Kowalski, with other commitments, left the episode before it was finished (it was one-and-one-half days behind), leaving the show to Bruce Geller, who directed the apartment scene and portions of the bribe sequence with Briggs, Cinnamon, and Carson. The show, overbudgeted at $204,896, ran over to more than $235,000 before it was completed. According to special effects man Jonnie Burke, Carson's Lincoln convertible, a key participant in the hectic chase finale, actually belonged to Lucille Ball. "It was brand-new. We borrowed it, drove it off the road and into the dirt, and wracked the whole car!"

8: WHEELS

First Aired: 10/29/66

Written by: Laurence Heath
Directed by: Tom Gries
Music Composed and Conducted by: Jack Urbont

TEAM: Briggs, Rollin, Cinnamon, Barney, Willy

Good afternoon, Mr. Briggs. A critical election is about to take place in Valeria. Should the police-controlled Nationalists win over the Liberty party, the country will become a terrorist dictatorship. We have information that, to ensure their victory, the Nationalists have fixed the voting machines in the key twelfth district. Mr. Briggs, your mission, should you decide to accept it, would be to unfix the election so that the result will honestly reflect the vote of the people. The secretary instructs you that no citizen of Valeria may be directly employed, and, as always, should you or any of your IM Force be caught or killed, he will disavow any knowledge of your actions. Please dispose of this recording as usual.

Cops Briggs and Willy arrest Barney during a protest and jail him in the twelfth district police station, where the rigged voting machines are stored. While Cinnamon distracts the desk officers, Barney examines the machines and determines what tools he'll need to realign them that night. But during his escape Barney is shot in the back and hustled by his teammates to an IMF hotel room. As the result of the jailbreak, an around-the-clock guard is posted at the voting machines.

Cinnamon, supposedly on the run from the police, preoccupies Miguel Cordova, a conscientious citizen whom Rollin impersonates at the twelfth district polls. "Cordova" enters the voting booth and collapses, evidently the victim of a stroke. Medics Willy and Dan wheel a stretcher into the booth and draw the curtains. Barney, barely conscious from his wound, emerges from below the stretcher and unfixes the machine while Rollin is placed on the stretcher and moved just outside the booth. Briggs stalls manfully until Barney finishes

his job and returns to the stretcher. The "patient" is removed; the Liberty party wins; and Cinnamon bids an emotional good-bye to good Samaritan Cordova, who lost his chance to vote by saving a lady in distress.

GUEST CAST: Percy Rodriguez (Captain Trez), Mark Lenard (Felipe Mora), Jonathan Kidd (Registrar), David Fresco (Libertadist), Edmund Tontini (Nationalist), Tom Hernandez (Desk Sergeant). *Unbilled:* George Sawaya (Weapons Guard), Mario Badolati (Dr. Brosa), Paul Bertoya (Young Man), Diana Denning (Young Woman), Larry Gelman (Voter), Joe Lo Presti (Mechanic), Perry Lopez (Priest), Ray Martell (Policeman), Ernesto S. Cervera (Radio Voice), Jimmy Casino (Plainclothesman), Roy Sickner (Guard), Bob Herron (Stunt Guard), Carey Loftin (Stunt Double)

"Wheels" is the first of twenty-three remarkable scripts from Laurence Heath who, with Balter and Woodfield, would become the series' preeminent writer. " 'Wheels' had an interesting premise," says Heath. "I'd found a book in the Los Angeles library that an ex-policeman had printed himself. The purpose of the book was to prove why they should not use voting machines but should go back to the ballot box." In the original outline, Dan recruits Tony Leica, "a fortyish ex-racketeer and pinball machine expert" to unfix the machines. Leica is killed attempting to escape, forcing the IMF to reevaluate their strategy. By the time "Wheels" reached the soundstage, Barney had assumed Leica's role. His wounding comes as quite a shock, adding extra tension to an already tough assignment.

Composer Jack Urbont, Geller's collaborator on the musical *All in Love,* contributes one of *Mission*'s ripest scores, loaded with explosive horns and "hearts and flowers" melodies for Cinnamon and her near-romance with Cordova. One wonders if her attraction to him is due, at least partially, to his resemblance to Rollin. This is the first (but not the last) time that Rollin perfectly impersonates a man whose voice he has never heard.

Paralleling the script, the production of "Wheels" did not go as smoothly as planned. What was supposed to be a seven-day shoot, budgeted at $208,000, went two days longer and cost over $234,791, while pickups were being shot for episodes 5 through 8 at the same time. The insert stage, like overbudgeting, was becoming a *Mission* tradition and would stay that way for years to come.

9: THE RANSOM

Written by: William Read Woodfield and
   Allan Balter
Directed by: Harry Harris
Music Composed and Conducted by:
   Walter Scharf

First Aired: 11/5/66

TEAM: Briggs; Rollin; Cinnamon; Barney; Willy;
Dr. Ira Green, M.D.; Steve, who resembles
Augie Gorman

In a departure from the series format, mobster Frank Egan, facing a grand jury indictment, forces Briggs to kidnap the key witness, Augie Gorman, by holding the daughter of Dan's friend hostage.

Gorman is guarded in a hotel room surrounded by police on every side. Three officers cover the hall outside, and a detective stays with Gorman at all times.

In the room two floors above Gorman's, Barney cuts into the waterpipe and lowers an incapacitating drug into the faucet of Gorman's bathroom sink. Gorman takes a drink of water, collapses, and is rushed to a hospital where nurse Cinnamon, using a rotating lab table, switches Steve for Gorman. Doctor Hand wheels Gorman out of the hospital to Briggs's apartment.

At the hostage exchange, Egan tries to double-cross and kill Briggs, but Dan hatches a scheme to save the girl, keep Gorman alive, *and* capture Egan.

GUEST CAST: Lin McCarthy (George Forrester), William Smithers (Frank Egan), Joe Mantell (Augie Gorman), Allen Joseph (Dr. Ira Green), Cheryl Callaway (Sandy Forrester), Walter Mathews (Detective), Don Marshall (Police Officer), Michael Barrier (Intern). *Unbilled:* Vic Tayback (Man in Car), Jack Donner (Driver), Eddie Paskey (Steve), Ted Jordan (Gunman), Richard Mansfield (Intern), Chuck Courtney (double, Gorman)

"The Ransom" is the first of a handful of "personal" episodes which find the IMF working on their own time, albeit in a crisis as tense as any assigned mission. It's a fine show, thanks to Steven Hill's performance and an astoundingly crafty script (although how gangster Egan knows Dan is unexplained). Briggs's personal motivation, plus the obstacles he must overcome, push the IMF leader to new levels of resourcefulness.

How can you snatch someone away from dozens of police? Briggs knows that you cannot; you get the cops to give him to you. It takes three strategies before Gorman is made to drink the tainted water and is sent to the hospital, where the Gorman-Steve switch is made literally under the nose of a wary detective.

"The Ransom" gives us more insight into the character of Dan Briggs and the ruthlessness required of him. In a warehouse district, where the hostage exchange is to occur, Dan lets himself walk into an Egan trap: "Gorman" is shot by an Egan gunman, who prepares to do the same to Dan. But Briggs suggests that Egan examine the corpse, which turns out to be a dummy. Now *Briggs* takes over—and so does Steve Hill.

BRIGGS: We'll exchange Gorman for the girl *my* way. . . . And one more little thing, Egan. If anything happens to that girl—anything—I'll finish you. Wherever you are, whatever you're doing, I'll find you and I'll kill you. And you know I can do it.

Hill's flat, chilling delivery makes the threat believable. Later, when Gorman refuses to cooperate, Briggs implies that a dead Gorman would be just as good to Egan as a live one. "You're not the type to shoot a man down in cold blood," Gorman scoffs. "Really," says Dan, as he pulls a gun and calmly presses it to Gorman's head. One look at Briggs's face makes Gorman reconsider. "I think you would," he admits. "You know I would," Briggs tells him. So do we.

10: ELENA

Written by: Ellis Marcus
Directed by: Marc Daniels
Music by: Lalo Schifrin

First Aired: 12/10/66

TEAM: Rollin, psychiatrist Dr. Carlos Enero

Good afternoon, Mr. Briggs. Elena Del Barra has been acting as an agent for us. Her important assignment deals with enemy plans to infiltrate her country, which is friendly to our government. Recently she began behaving in a bizarre manner, indicating a severe emotional disturbance. Last week she sent us a strip of microfilm not of enemy plans, but one which details defense secrets of her own country. Mr. Briggs, your mission, should you decide to accept it, would be to find out why Elena Del Barra is behaving so strangely and whether or not this key agent will continue to be a dangerous threat to our organization. As always, should you or any of your IM Force be caught or killed, the secretary will disclaim any knowledge of your actions. Please destroy this tape by the usual means.

Rollin must learn how Elena got the microfilm, and return it without causing an international incident. Compounding the problem is Callao, an assassin working "independently" with orders to kill Elena if Rollin cannot redeem her within two days.

Elena's late father, the country's former president, was deposed after he was unable to prevent terrorists from infiltrating the government. She and her family are on friendly terms with current President Fortuna. Rollin befriends Elena and witnesses her behavior, which shifts suddenly from rational to wildly unstable. He induces her to see Dr. Enero, who hypnotizes her and learns only that she is suffering from a posthypnotic suggestion which is forcing her to do something against her will.

As time runs out, Rollin reveals his identity to Elena and uses all his powers of persuasion to make her remember that she has been pro-grammed to denounce President Fortuna. But she cannot recall who is controlling her, and is unable to stop herself from going through with the plan, despite her awareness of it.

That evening, Rollin manages to solve the mystery, ingeniously return the microfilm, uncover the true traitor, and save Elena.

GUEST CAST: Barry Atwater (Dr. Carlos Enero), Barbara Luna (Elena Maria Del Barra), Abraham Sofaer (Tomas de Cuarto), Ben Hammer (Callao), Renzo Cesana (Presidente Gustavo Alfredo Fortuna), Ann Ayers (Consuelo Del Barra), Valentin De Vargas (Miguel de Ramos). *Unbilled:* Blaisdell Makee (Morrito); Paul Kent (Frederico); David Perna, Troy Melton, Patty Elder (Stunts)

Ellis Marcus's script originally featured Briggs in Rollin's role. But it seems that Steven Hill was already being written out of the show, for in the apartment scene Briggs mentions that since he knows Elena, he cannot participate, making this another strong Rollin story.

Psychological coercion, an IMF staple, is employed by the other side in "Elena," one of the last *Mission*s to present characters that are more than just cardboard. Director Marc Daniels (brother of this episode's writer) concentrates on the performances of Landau and Barbara Luna, the latter in a memorable and most demanding role as the tormented Elena. "That show was unlike *Mission: Impossible*," notes Barbara, who still names *Mission* as her favorite television series. " 'Elena' was more like a regular episodic drama, which was really quite boring. Not boring to do, but the format was like old television. Elena was rather interesting, actually. It was the only time I played a somewhat intelligent human being. It was well thought

out. I was surprised that they took a lot of rehearsal time. Marc Daniels is a director who loves to rehearse and so did Marty Landau." Landau feels that the show was a good departure. "The series was finding itself, and I was interested in that show. It was different." The show's densely psychological plot was a further indication that this series would demand total attention from its viewers.

11: ZUBROVNIK'S GHOST

Written by: Robert Lewin
Directed by: Leonard J. Horn
Music by: Lalo Schifrin

First Aired: 11/26/66

TEAM: Rollin, Barney, "psychic consultant" Ariana Domi

Good morning, Mr. Briggs. You remember Dr. Martha Richards. Two years ago while on vacation in Austria, she met and married Dr. Kurt Zubrovnik. She never returned to America, continuing her extremely important research work with her husband in Austria. About a year ago, Kurt Zubrovnik was burned to death in a laboratory fire in their home. Martha went on working after her husband's death, but recently stopped sending us the results of her experiments. We have reason to believe it is because this man, Sigismund Poljac, is pressuring her to work behind the Iron Curtain. If it were an ordinary pressure we could fight it, but Poljac is a medium, and Martha Zubrovnik is being asked to defect by the ghost of her dead husband. Mr. Briggs, your mission, should you decide to accept it, would be to keep her from going behind the Iron Curtain, and get her to working for us again. As always, should you or any of your IM Force be caught or killed, the secretary will disavow any knowledge of your actions. Please dispose of this recording in the usual manner.

The IMF trio pose as a psychic research team visiting Dr. Zubrovnik and the ever-present Poljac.

Poljac conducts a séance during which he claims that Kurt will return to Martha only after she completes her work. He also reveals the combination of a locked box and reads the note inside—information known only to Kurt and Martha. Using her "powers," Ariana discovers that a spirit does inhabit the house—not Kurt's, but a vengeful one which "will kill." She receives another impulse which tells her that Kurt is indeed dead—but that he has died only moments ago. Her findings are correct: Poljac has been torturing Kurt for the information he divulges during the séances. With

Kurt's death, Poljac realizes that his hold on Martha will weaken, and he persuades her to leave immediately for an Iron Curtain country.

Rollin decides to hold a final séance, during which the "spirit" of Kurt (via Barney's trickery) will expose Poljac as a fraud. A blackout renders Barney's equipment useless, but Ariana's powers, plus some genuinely unexplainable occurrences, help to accomplish the mission.

GUEST CAST: Martine Bartlett (Ariana Domi), Donald Davis (Sigismund Poljac), Beatrice Straight (Dr. Martha Richards Zubrovnik), Frank Oberschall (Kroger)

Amusing, intriguing, offbeat, and ultimately unsatisfying—all these describe "Zubrovnik's Ghost," the first of several "spook" episodes and the only one to showcase genuinely supernatural elements instead of the artificially created IMF brand.

The amusing aspect is Rollin's and Barney's attitude toward Ariana, their strange teammate. "For Martha Zubrovnik," Briggs explains, "the spirit of her dead husband exists. You can't fight that belief with logic." Barney makes no secret of his skepticism; he's a man who has based his life on mechanical explainables. Rollin, a magician and expert faker in his own right, is somewhat more open-minded (though in an early draft, he demonstrates his cynicism by producing a blinking bulb in midair during the apartment scene). Is Ariana a fake as they suspect, or the the genuine article, as Briggs suggests? The truth is told at the end of the show.

Director Lenny Horn uses all the standard "haunted house" trappings, including thunder and lightning at dramatically proper moments. The supernatural denouement is ill-suited to *Mission,* which demanded more prosaic elements to seem realistic. In this coalescing period of the series, however, it certainly makes an interesting show.

12: THE TRIAL

First Aired: 1/28/67

Written by: Laurence Heath
Directed by: Lewis Allen

TEAM: Briggs, Rollin, Willy

Good morning, Mr. Briggs. Josef Varsh, public prosecutor and head of his country's secret police, is one of the most dangerous men in Eastern Europe. He heads the political faction which wants to heat up the Cold War. Opposed to him are those who favor coexistence, led by Anton Kudnov, a deputy premier. Varsh now plans to stir up feeling against the United States by arresting and charging some innocent American with a serious crime, and then staging a propaganda show trial for the world. He plans to use this to gain absolute power for himself. Should Varsh succeed, not only will the victim lose his freedom and possibly his life, but the international peace will be threatened. Your mission, should you decide to accept it, is to stop Varsh and to so discredit him that he will never again be a political threat. As always, should you or any of your IM Force be caught or killed, the secretary will disavow any knowledge of your actions. This recording will decompose in five seconds. Good luck, Dan.

Lisa Goren, who betrayed her Western-operative husband to her boyfriend Varsh, gets a call from an American anxious to see her late husband. Rollin, disguised as Briggs, visits Lisa while at the same time Dan meets with Deputy Premier Kudnov for business. "Briggs" escapes from Lisa's apartment before Varsh can arrest him, but leaves behind enough evidence of sabotage that Varsh is certain he is a true spy. Briggs is arrested and brought to trial for espionage.

Before the world press (and a judge predisposed to find Briggs guilty), Varsh prosecutes Dan and demands the death penalty. Briggs's lawyer Rollin can do little more than suggest that the explosives found among Dan's belongings may have been manufactured by the state, and to confirm that "Dan" met Lisa at exactly 9:00. Kudnov, who knows that Dan was with *him* at 9:00, demands that Varsh drop the charges. To save his reputation, Varsh orders Kudnov's death.

While Varsh wonders if Kudnov's abrupt disappearance is good or bad news, Rollin must discredit Lisa and Varsh *and* get Kudnov into the courtroom past Varsh's men (who have orders to kill him) if he is to save Dan and keep the Cold War cold.

GUEST CAST: Carroll O'Connor (Josef Varsh), David Opatoshu (Deputy Premier Anton Kudnov), Michael Strong (Barsky), Gail Kobe (Lisa Goren), Don Keefer (Zubin), Ivan Triesault (Platinov), Paul Lukather (Moisev). *Unbilled:* Chuck Couch (double, Rollin)

Impossible assignments sometimes call for impossible solutions, so this time Briggs simply arranges to be in two places at once, thanks to Rollin's cosmetic magic!

Guest Carroll O'Connor remembers "The Trial" chiefly "because all the actors were personal friends of mine. They were all splendid actors and I had worked with them previously, so the job was a particular pleasure. The episode itself was not informed fiction but fantasy fiction and rather trivial. The series on the whole was fundamentally trivial, though very well acted and photographed."

"The Trial" brought some rare good news to the Desilu accounting department: The show stayed on budget at $211,339—minus inserts, of course.

David Opatoshu, with Martin Landau from "The Trial," was a frequent guest star.

13: THE CARRIERS

Written by: William Read Woodfield and
Allan Balter
Directed by: Sherman Marks
Music by: Lalo Schifrin

First Aired: 11/19/66

TEAM: Briggs; Rollin; Cinnamon; Barney; Willy; Roger Lee, bacteriologist

Good morning, Mr. Briggs. This is Janos Passik, an enemy expert on American traditions, slang, and customs. Passik is gathering some two hundred agents who are in final training, learning to act as Americans for a special operation. All we know about the plan is that it will be some form of bacteriological warfare against the United States. Your mission, should you decide to accept it, is to get into that training center and stop Passik. Make certain his plan fails—put him permanently out of business. As usual, should you or any of your IM Force be caught or killed, the secretary will disavow any knowledge of your actions. This tape will destroy itself in five seconds. Good luck, Dan.

Barbara Bain in "The Carriers."

Passik operates behind the Iron Curtain in an amazing replica of a typical American small town, where his agents complete their training. Briggs knows that beneath the movie theater is a lab where the germ warfare project is being prepared.

Rollin, Cinnamon, Barney, and Roger intercept and impersonate Passik's latest recruits and are escorted into "town." Passik gives them American names and their future occupations in the US, but no details of the impending mission. From a sample of the lab's wastewater, Roger diagnoses the bacteria as septicemic plague—the deadliest type in existence. "The carrier just has to touch you and you've got it."

Rollin deduces that Passik's "Americans" will be infected with the disease and sent to the US, where they will spread the plague and kill millions. Together, the IMF conceive and execute a counterplan to eradicate the threat and leave the enemy unable to determine the cause of the failure.

GUEST CAST: George Takei (Roger Lee), Arthur Hill (Janos Passik), Phil Posner (Tigran Portisch), Barry Cahill (Guard), Rick Traeger (Instructor), Barry Russo (Tiso Kastner). *Unbilled:* Rick Richards (Trainee), Josh Adams (Guard), Beatriz Monteil (Dancer)

"The Carriers" is inaccurate in certain areas. Septicemic plague requires vectors, such as rats or fleas, to spread from person to person. It can be controlled by antibiotics and vaccine. It would be difficult for Roger to identify the bacteria after it has been pumped, via wastewater, out of the lab: Cultures are usually destroyed in an autoclave, the heat of which breaks down the cell structure, making identification impossible.

Year One: 1966–1967

It is difficult to find a more exciting, fascinating, or brilliantly plotted *Mission* than this one. The idea of a phony American town is magnificently presented. Communist instructors teach Cinnamon how to go-go dance, and Rollin the rudiments of ballpark vending. Movie buffs will notice a familiar poster outside the movie theater. Look closely for MAX O'HARA'S EARTHQUAKE BALLET, a prop from RKO's classic *Mighty Joe Young* (1949), undoubtedly found somewhere in the Desilu property room.

Less amusing are the murders Barney and Rollin commit inside the theater-lab. Barney engages in an awkward struggle with a guard, strangling him, while Rollin simply shoots another guard, who falls slowly and painfully to his death. The IMF must get into the lab, spoil the bacteria culture, and get out, making it look like they were unsuccessful in their attempt to break in. Things don't go entirely as planned in the lab, however: Rollin breaks a culture dish and is infected with the plague!

George Takei (center) appeared as an IMF agent in "The Carriers."

85

14: THE SHORT TAIL SPY

Written by: Julian Barry
Directed by: Leonard J. Horn
Music by: Lalo Schifrin

First Aired: 12/17/66

TEAM: Briggs, Cinnamon, Barney

Good afternoon, Mr. Briggs. Two espionage groups from an enemy country are engaged in a power struggle—which has focused on the problem of which group will assassinate this man, Professor Napolsky, who recently defected to us. In six days, the professor must appear at a scientific conference where he will be an open target. This is Andrei Fetyukov, the number one assassin for the new young civilian group, which the secretary considers far more dangerous than the old-line military intelligence service, represented by this man, Colonel Shtemenko. Mr. Briggs, your mission, should you decide to accept it, would be to stop the assassination in such a way as to totally discredit Fetyukov and his organization so that the old group, which we find easier to handle, will remain in power. As always, should you or any of your IM Force be caught or killed, the secretary will disavow any knowledge of your actions. Please dispose of this recording in the usual manner. Good luck, Dan.

Dan, who does not underestimate Fetyukov, gives him a foolproof way to get to the professor: by seducing American agent Cinnamon, who is assigned to protect Napolsky. Fetyukov recognizes the trap but finds the challenge—and Cinnamon—difficult to resist.

Cinnamon and Fetyukov begin a whirlwind romance, both playfully ignoring the real reason behind their blossoming relationship. Briggs tells Shtemenko that he has seen through his cover, and the old man believes that Fetyukov exposed him out of fear that Shtemenko's assassination plot is the better one. Shtemenko traces Dan to the professor's room. He enters, attempts to kill Napolsky, and is photographed by the IMF. To his surprise, he is given a plane ticket home and Briggs's word that the photos will be destroyed if he leaves. Shtemenko, certain that Fetyukov is behind this obvious attempt to get rid of him, tries to

kill Fetyukov; Cinnamon foils the attempt. Impressed that she "ruined" a clever American attempt to eliminate him, Fetyukov takes advantage of Cinnamon's feelings for him and spends the night with her.

The next morning, Fetyukov convinces Cinnamon that he has fallen for her and wants to defect. She asks him to wait while she tells Dan. Fetyukov follows her to Napolsky's hotel room. Intending to kill the professor, he holds everyone at gunpoint. With even Briggs unable to act, Cinnamon saves the day.

GUEST CAST: Albert Dekker (Colonel Shtemenko), Hans Gudegast (Andrei Fetyukov), Joe Sirola (Suverin), Edward Colmans (Professor Napolsky). *Unbilled:* Joe Breen (Projectionist)

The show's title refers to Fetyukov's alleged status in his native country: "No children, no mother, no relatives, no one that they can threaten me with," making his supposed defection that much simpler. The script allows for vulnerability from Briggs (who wonders if Cinnamon has lost control in her relationship with the killer) and of course, Cinnamon, who goes beyond the call of duty by spending the night with Fetyukov. It doesn't happen on-screen: Act three ends with his seduction of her, and act four begins with Cinnamon wearing a different dress as she and Fetyukov watch the dawn.

A potent combination of unusually literate script, direction, acting, and sheer novelty make this one of *Mission*'s most distinctive installments, and it is not difficult to see why similar stories were not filmed. Geller's insistence on cipher characters had to be upheld, and besides,

you can't have the regulars fall in love and sleep with the enemy each week. It is astonishing that any 1966 American TV heroine was permitted such an action. The network Standards and Practices people either didn't catch on (very likely) or figured that anyone who stuck with such a complex story deserved a little shock near the end!

Guest Hans Gudegast, formerly of *The Rat Patrol,* would soon change his name to Eric Braeden and continue a successful career. Writer Julian Barry, a friend of Geller's from New York, was a novice TV writer struggling to become a playwright; before long he succeeded with a play called *Lenny. "Mission* was the last thing I ever wrote for television," says Barry, who was asked to write a story for Barbara Bain. "The hardest writing I've ever had to do in my entire life was that one paragraph in the beginning, the taped message," Barry admits. "There was no embellishment, no opportunity for fantasy, you had to say, 'Your mission, should you decide to accept it—,' and I never worked so hard on a page in my life. It was so convoluted, and one of the greatest writing lessons in my life. It was terrifying."

15: THE LEGACY

First Aired: 1/7/67

Written by: William Read Woodfield and
Allan Balter
Directed by: Michael O'Herlihy

TEAM: Briggs, Rollin, Cinnamon, Barney, Willy

Good morning, Mr. Briggs. You're probably aware that since late in 1945 the Allied command has been trying to track down Adolf Hitler's personal fortune. Now it looks like we've finally gotten a break. Four young men, sons of Hitler's most trusted officers, are gathering in Zurich, Switzerland. We believe they have knowledge which will lead them to the Hitler treasure. They plan to use it to launch the Fourth Reich. We've been able to identify one of the young heirs. His name is Paul von Schneer. He'll be coming to Zurich from Argentina. Dan, your mission, should you decide to accept it, is to get that money, believed to be over three hundred million dollars, before they do. As always, should you or any of your IM Force be caught or killed, the secretary will disavow any knowledge of your actions. Please dispose of this recording in the usual manner.

Rollin replaces von Schneer and meets the three heirs. He learns that each of them knows part of an account number which is the first part of the puzzle. Rollin must get "his" numbers by the following morning. Cinnamon poses as a rich countess and charms the bank officer into attending her party that night, where he is drugged, hypnotized, and fooled into revealing the account number, which is discreetly passed to Rollin.

At the bank, the quartet present their numbers and are given an envelope containing a microdot. Then, each man removes from his pocketwatch a tiny transparency which, when overlaid on the microdot, begins to resemble a map. Rollin feigns the loss of his watch and calls hotel manager Briggs, who escorts Rollin to the Lost and Found. Rollin uses his transparency to complete the map,

which leads the IMF to a cemetery crypt. A thorough search of the crypt yields nothing.

The Nazis trace Rollin to the graveyard and a gunfight erupts, leaving Briggs shot in the chest. The IMF prevail, and Dan notices that bullets have chipped away the crypt's false front, revealing gleaming gold underneath. "It wasn't in the crypt," he notes, "it *is* the crypt!"

GUEST CAST: Donald Harron (Ernst Graff), Lee Bergere (Alfred Kuderlee), Bill Fletcher (Max Brucker), Claude Woolman (Paul von Schneer), Patrick Horgan (Erich Wolfe), John Crawford (Professor Franz Lubell), Walter Friedel (Lieutenant Eiler), Richard Peel (Guide). *Unbilled:* Troy Melton (double, Rollin), Dick Geery (double, Graff), Karl Bruck (Attendant)

Like "The Carriers," this Balter and Woodfield effort forces the IMF to really push, with almost none of the customary data which usually helps them succeed. The show is filled with suspenseful moments and interesting touches. Steven Hill's remarkable ability to become totally anonymous is well utilized. At Cinnamon's party he is an innocuous waiter; later, as the hotel manager, he is the image of pedestrian efficiency, all smiles and politeness. Yet, in other scenes he is clearly the man in charge. When Rollin informs him that he'll need the account number, Briggs begins to walk across the room. He almost immediately slows down and by the fourth step, it is obvious that he has his plan.

Running throughout the show is a deep and developing hatred between Rollin and Graff, the self-appointed leader of the Nazi quartet. After Graff has shot Briggs and runs out of bullets, Rollin jumps and throttles him until Willy pulls him away. For the only time, the main villain escapes retribution and runs while he has the chance.

Michael O'Herlihy was a rarity among *Mission* directors. "He wouldn't let an actor, producer, or anybody change the way he had a show laid out," effects man Jonnie Burke remembers. "He never shot any excess footage, so you could not change his shows. He shot a lot of *Mannix*es too. Actors would come over wanting to change something and he'd just sit there in his chair ignoring them." O'Herlihy's method, contrary to series style, worked: His three *Mission*s are good. This famous and effective episode was remade when *Mission* was reincarnated in 1988.

Rollin provides the final piece of the solution in "The Legacy."

16: THE RELUCTANT DRAGON

Written by: Chester Krumholz
Directed by: Leonard J. Horn

First Aired: 1/14/67

TEAM: Rollin, Barney

Good morning, Mr. Briggs. The man you're looking at is Helmut Cherlotov, the Iron Curtain's expert in rocket control. A year ago, his wife, Karen, defected to the West. He was supposed to follow but never made it. Since then, Cherlotov has been under suspicion by Taal Jankowski, the head of security. On his own, Cherlotov has developed the key to a simple yet extremely effective antiballistic missile system. A system of that sort, in the wrong hands, could completely destroy the balance of power in the world. Your mission, should you decide to accept it, is to get Cherlotov out before his government discovers what he's achieved. As always, should you or any of your IM Force be caught or killed, the secretary will disavow any knowledge of your actions. Please destroy this recording in the usual manner. Good luck, Dan.

Cherlotov, a security risk since Karen's defection, has been transferred to a research position on a university campus.

African student Barney arrives on campus, and Rollin enters as part of a quartet of visiting offi-

Rollin must persuade a loyal enemy scientist (Joseph Campanella) to defect in "The Reluctant Dragon."

cials on a tour guided by Jankowski. Rollin contrives a rendezvous with Cherlotov and learns that he has no intention of defecting. All he wants is to convince Jankowski that he is loyal and should be reinstated to his former duties.

Back home, Briggs realizes that only one person can convince Cherlotov to defect: his wife. Disguised and under an assumed name, a nervous Karen Cherlotov returns to her country. Jankowski, angered by the doctor's pleas, takes Rollin's suggestion and places Cherlotov in a cell with other political prisoners, some of whom were his college professors. Cherlotov finally realizes what his country is actually doing. Upon his release, Barney escorts him back to his lab, where Karen persuades him to leave with her. But Jankowski learns that Rollin is an imposter and apprehends them all, forcing the IMF to make a drastic escape attempt.

GUEST CAST: Joseph Campanella (Dr. Helmut Cherlotov), John Colicos (Commissioner Taal Jankowski), Mala Powers (Dr. Karen Cherlotov), Michael Forest (Lupesh), Elisa Ingram (Sofia), Alex Rodine (Duchinoff), Norbert Schiller (Lauchek), Norbert Meisel (Berkov), Allen Bleiweiss (Lukowski), Robert Boon (Kravetsky), Felix Lucher (Yablonski). *Unbilled:* Howard Curtis (Man), Chuck Couch (double, Rollin), Fred Carson (double, Lupesh), Maria Schroeder (Carla), Frank Kreig (Bartender), Liz Bronte (Anya), Judy Levitt (Girl), Fred Krone (double, Jankowski)

More blatantly political than most, this hour presents unusual challenges. As Barney states in an early version of the script, "This is impossible. No gimmicks. No electronic devices. It isn't a matter of nerve. This is a man's mind. And we can't break in." A mission of retrieval becomes one of persuasion, since Briggs has been given erroneous information from the start: Cherlotov does not want to defect, and Karen had hoped that he would follow her. In the script, Dan opts to pull his two agents. "I'm not going to risk their necks for someone who doesn't want out," he tells Karen. It is Rollin who persuades Barney that the mission is not only possible, but worthwhile.

BARNEY: Things here stink. It's sickening. But it's his privilege to be as nearsighted as he wants to be.

ROLLIN *(looking at Barney):* That's it. That's the way to go. We *find* a way to make him see.

Cherlotov is thrown in a filthy cell with a collection of sad, old intellectuals who have lost their dignity. One has a hearing aid but is refused batteries. In a pathetic attempt to keep busy, he spends his days sweeping dirt back and forth. By the time he is released, Cherlotov is a shattered man.

Offsetting the show's grim tone is a party scene in which Rollin delights everyone by making coins and drinking glasses disappear, and steals a wristwatch and belt. The victims never realize that Rollin is actually frisking them for their passports!

17: THE FRAME

First Aired: 1/21/67

Written by: William Read Woodfield and
Allan Balter
Directed by: Allen Miner

TEAM: Briggs; Rollin; Cinnamon; Barney; Willy;
Tino, Wellman's favorite restauranteur

*Good morning, Mr. Briggs. In each of the accidents you're looking at, an important elected official
was killed: two congressmen and two state attorney generals. Their deaths had one thing in common:
Their successors were, in every case, known to be favorably disposed toward organized crime. The
Syndicate has a finger in every other legitimate business. Now they're moving into government. This
move is the brainchild of Jack Wellman, acknowledged head of the Syndicate in the United States.
He must be stopped. Officially, he's beyond the reach of the law. Your mission, Dan, should you
choose to accept it, is to stop Wellman. As always, should you or any of your IM Force be caught or
killed, the secretary will disavow any knowledge of your actions. This filmstrip will self-destruct when
you stop the machine. Good luck, Dan.*

The four million dollar profit from Wellman's
murderous activities sits in a bank-style vault encased in concrete in Wellman's basement.

Wellman arranges a private dinner with three
fellow mobsters with whom he will split the cash.
Tino caters the affair, with chef Briggs, waiter Rollin, and assistant Willy. Barney sneaks into the
basement and Cinnamon into Wellman's bedroom. Tino and Rollin serve dinner while upstairs,
Cinnamon drills a large, deep hole in the bedroom
wall and inserts a wall safe.

Willy and Barney blast through the vault's concrete shell, blow-torch their way into the vault, and
take the money. After dinner, the caterers (and
Barney) leave. The vault is opened and the theft

discovered. Wellman swears that no one has been
in the house and is shocked when Cinnamon, clad
in a black camisole and high heels, is found in his
bedroom. "I told you it wouldn't work," she tells
Wellman, who asks, "Who are you?" She is forced
to reveal the wall safe, and is allowed to escape.
When Wellman is ordered to open "his" safe, he
plaintively answers, "I can't! That's not my safe. I
never saw it before!" In moments, a gunshot ends
the threat of Jack Wellman.

GUEST CAST: Simon Oakland (Jack Wellman),
Arthur Batanides (Tino), Joe Maross
(Frank Bates), Joe DeSantis (Vito Scalesi),
Mort Mills (Al Souchek)

"The Frame" is an auspicious episode. It's the first appearance of the perfect frame, a
Woodfield and Balter device which would prove very popular with audiences. There is a
special emphasis placed on characterizations, notably Arthur Batanides's agitated, nervous
Tino; Rollin's deaf waiter; and Dan's Italian cook. When Wellman finds Dan where he
shouldn't be, Briggs becomes a simpleminded man. After talking his way out of trouble, the
slow cook disappears and Dan Briggs instantly returns.

18: THE DIAMOND

Written by: William Read Woodfield and
    Allan Balter
Directed by: Robert Douglas

First Aired: 2/4/67

TEAM: Briggs; Rollin; Cinnamon; Barney; Willy;
diamond expert Hans Van Meer; Ian
McCloud, formerly of Scotland Yard

Good morning, Mr. Briggs. The man you're looking at is Henrik Durvard. He seized power in Lombuanda, a small country on the Gulf of Guinea, and has given himself the title of prime minister. He is in fact a dictator who rules with an iron hand, keeping two million natives half starved, with no schools, hospitals, or any voice in government. Recently, native tribesmen in the northern part of the country discovered a natural diamond that is rumored to be the largest ever found: nearly twenty-seven thousand karats, worth about thirty million dollars. Durvard has confiscated the stone and intends to sell it, using the proceeds to take over other independent tribal areas. Your mission, Dan, should you decide to accept it, is to stop Durvard and return the diamond to its rightful owners. As always, should you or any of your IM Force be caught or killed, the secretary will disavow any knowledge of your actions. Please dispose of this tape by the usual means. Good luck, Dan.

In London to auction the diamond, Durvard meets Rollin, Cinnamon, and Dan, who offer to top any bids for the diamond in exchange for exclusive rights to all future gems which might be found in Lombuanda. Since everyone knows that Lombuanda is not a diamond-producing country, Durvard is suspicious until he uncovers the trio's real scheme: to use Lombuanda as an official source for the gems Dan creates in his diamond synthesizing machine. Durvard pushes his way into the racket and is convinced of the device's practicality when it fashions a perfect "duplicate" of the only stone cut from the mother diamond. Durvard invites his new partners to set up shop in his country, plotting to liquidate them once he has learned to operate the elaborate invention.

In Lombuanda, an attempt is made to duplicate the enormous diamond, but the strain is apparently too much, and the machine malfunctions severely. The IMF sneak off, thirty million dollar rock in hand, as Durvard and the machine are blown to bits.

GUEST CAST: John van Dreelen (Prime Minister Henrik Durvard), Harry Davis (Hans Van Meer), Woodrow Parfrey (Henks), Peter Bourne (Peters), Ivor Barry (Ian McCloud). *Unbilled:* Gil Stuart (Man), Jason Johnson (Proprietor)

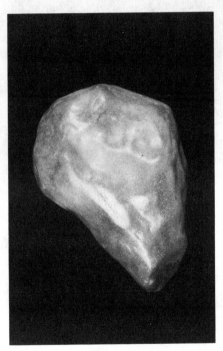

The world's largest stone is the quarry in "The Diamond."

Jerome Ross, author of episode 4, "Operation Rogosh," submitted a fourteen-page outline called "The Diamond," in which Dan, Willy, Cinnamon, and a renowned diamond cutter must keep two powerful gangsters from splitting the take from a multimillion-dollar diamond cutting. After a complex series of feints and unexpected perils, the IMF persuade the crooks to kill each other, and the diamond is crushed under a sidewalk steamroller. This plot wasn't filmed, but Woodfield and Balter wrote their own version, a classic con involving an IMF "dream machine."

The IMF's switch of the real gem cut from the diamond for an exact replica is accomplished by Barney. In the hotel room next to Durvard's, he removes the electrical outlet from the wall separating the rooms and inserts a long, metal extending arm and claw to carefully remove the stone from a jewelry case and replace it with the bogus gem. The real stone is used as the product of the IMF's diamond machine, a large device resembling a vertical compactor, complete with hydraulic compressors. "I did a lot of research on that," effects man Jonnie Burke explains, "and got descriptive literature from two or three companies that make commercial diamonds, principally for cutting tools. So we designed and built this unit based on the principle we got from them. Technically, what we did they were actually doing at the time, on a smaller scale." The machine turned out to be one of the series' most expensive props.

"The Diamond" is also noteworthy for the glee with which our heroes undo Durvard, who is so utterly doomed that Dan, Cinnamon, and Rollin use their real names when dealing with him—proof positive that his days are numbered.

19: THE LEGEND

Written by: Mann Rubin
Directed by: Richard Benedict

First Aired: 2/11/67

TEAM: Briggs, Rollin, Cinnamon, Barney

Good afternoon, Mr. Briggs. The man you're looking at is Dr. Herbert Raynor, a dedicated official in Hitler's National Socialist Party. For the last twenty years, he has been in Spandau Prison outside of Berlin. On Tuesday of next week, Dr. Raynor finishes his sentence and, with his daughter, flies immediately to Puerto Huberra in South America, thanks to the generosity of an anonymous benefactor who has sent him a round-trip ticket. Our informants tell us other of Hitler's top Nazis are also at this moment on their way to Puerto Huberra. Whoever is bringing them together seems to be well financed and determined to sow the seeds of Nazism across the world again. Your mission, Dan, should you decide to accept it, is to put these Nazis out of business. As always, should you or any of your IM Force be caught or killed, the secretary will disavow any knowledge of your actions. This tape will self-destruct in ten seconds. Good luck, Dan.

"Four countries have sent agents down," Briggs tells his team. "They've gotten as far as a huge château in the jungle . . . and no further."

"Raynor" (Dan) and daughter Cinnamon arrive at the château and meet Frederick Rudd, secretary to the man who has summoned them. They and the other guests are introduced to their benefactor: Nazi war criminal Martin Bormann who, owing to injuries received in a plane crash, is bedridden and hidden in shadows. Bormann orders his comrades to follow the instructions he will deliver via Rudd.

After an initial attempt nearly kills him, Dan breaks into Bormann's room, gun in hand, and sees that Bormann is merely a mannequin dressed in a Nazi uniform. His "voice" has been provided by audio tapes made by Rudd, the last of which will bestow upon Rudd the leadership of the new reich.

Realizing that Rudd is his target, Briggs hatches a devastatingly neat solution to make the power-mad Nazi a victim of his own trickery.

GUEST CAST: Gunnar Hellstrom (Frederick Rudd), Gene Roth (General von Cramm), Ben Wright (Kleister), Paul Genge (Frick), Larry Blake (Eckhart). *Unbilled:* Lou Robb (Guard 2), Chuck Couch (Stunt Double)

Employing a plot devoid of the gimmickry which would soon characterize the series and utilizing only a few sets, "The Legend" is a splendid example of economical television scripting. Writer Mann Rubin's first of three *Mission*s forces Briggs to come up with three different plans, each more ingenious than the last, and perfect cliff-hangers for the first three acts.

Act four is sensational, with the appearance of Rollin as "Bormann" ruining Rudd's plan to reveal himself as the brains behind the operation. Rollin is reverently *heiled* by everyone, except Rudd, who is thunderstruck—but cannot expose Rollin without revealing his own deception. "If you realize what Rollin's doing," says Martin Landau with a laugh, "it's hilarious! Now my Martin Bormann, there was a gentleness in that guy, he's old and sick. But there's a little steel in him, too. As old and feeble and weak as he was, there was still a bit of the animal in this guy, and I use the word *animal.*" "Bormann" is the catalyst for a delicious finale which eliminates both Rudd and the threat of the Nazi resurgence.

20: THE CONFESSION

First Aired: 2/25/67

Written by: William Read Woodfield and Allan Balter
Directed by: Herschel Daugherty

TEAM: Briggs, Rollin, Cinnamon, Barney, Willy

Good morning, Mr. Briggs. The man in the photo on your right is Andreas Solowiechek, a member of a Communist trade delegation to the US. Yesterday, Solowiechek was arrested and charged with the assassination of Senator William Townsend. Already, Townsend's extremist supporters, led by his principal backer, R. J. McMillan, are demanding that we break relations with the Communist bloc. With the end of diplomatic relations, the Cold War will immediately start to heat up. Even though Solowiechek won't admit it, we're convinced that he was not acting on orders of his government. Your mission, Dan, if you decide to accept it, is to prove it. As always, should you or any of your IM Force be caught or killed, the secretary will disavow any knowledge of your actions. Please dispose of this recording in the usual manner. Good luck, Dan.

Solowiechek's prison cellmate is tough guy Rollin, whose lawyer (Barney) smuggles him a gun. Rollin's plot to escape is "ruined" when he is handcuffed to Solowiechek en route to court. Rollin escapes anyway, taking an unwilling Solowiechek with him. Rollin severs the cuffs, then decides to kill Solowiechek to keep him quiet. Solowiechek tells Rollin that he can get money from the man who hired him to kill the Senator—McMillan. That night they steal into McMillan's study and confront him. Across the room is a hidden IMF television camera which broadcasts the mission's solution to an audience of millions.

GUEST CAST: Pat Hingle (R. J. McMillan), David Sheiner (Andreas Solowiechek), Kent Smith (Senator William Townsend), James Gavin (Deputy), Biff Elliot (Guard), Robert B. Williams (Proprietor). *Unbilled:* Buzz Henry, Chuck Wilcox (Stunts)

Guest Kent Smith has Rollin on the wrong side of the trigger in "The Confession."

"The Confession" features an excellent example of Balter and Woodfield shtick. During his guise as a magazine's portrait artist, Briggs brings into McMillan's study a prepainted canvas covered in white paint. By having McMillan pose in a specific way and by slowly removing the white paint, Briggs seems to be creating a work of art. Dan leaves his unfinished work in the study, ostensibly to return the next morning (the camera is hidden in Dan's paintbox.)

Actor David Sheiner, *Mission*'s most often used heavy, appears for the first time as the hapless Solowiechek, who is so bullied by despicable con Rollin throughout the show that he is almost sympathetic. The name Solowiechek stems from mock pressure placed upon the show's writers by Herb Solow to see his name in a script!

21: SNOWBALL IN HELL

First Aired: 2/18/67

Written by: Judith and Robert Guy Barrows
Directed by: Lee Katzin

TEAM: Briggs, Rollin, Cinnamon, Barney, Willy

Good evening, Mr. Briggs. This is Boradur, for two hundred years the most infamous penal colony on earth. Until five years ago when it was closed down, Boradur was run by this man, Gerard Sefra, who still remains there with a small group of former guards. Sefra has come into possession of a sample of cesium 138 and its formula, which he memorized and destroyed. He has offered these for sale to the highest bidder. Dan, cesium 138 is the key to a low-cost, nuclear arsenal. Your mission, should you decide to accept it, would be to make sure no one gets the cesium or learns the formula. As always, should you or any of your IM Force be caught or killed, the secretary will disavow any knowledge of your actions. This tape will automatically destruct in five seconds. Good luck, Dan.

Cesium 138 explodes in temperatures higher than 70°F. In the tropical climate of Boradur, Sefra must keep the liquid refrigerated.

Photographer Rollin and model Barney enter Boradur to shoot a photo session. Sefra learns that Barney is an ex-prisoner who had escaped years earlier. When Rollin leaves, Sefra holds Barney to beat the "truth" out of him: that he has returned to kill Sefra.

Boradur's generator "suddenly" breaks down, and Sefra panics when the air-conditioning gives out. He locks Barney up and frantically transports the cesium to a nearby hospital's cold storage room. While Sefra's guard stands outside, Rollin, hiding inside, empties the cesium jar. The genera-tor is repaired; Sefra removes the empty jar and returns to the prison. When he learns that the ce-sium has been stolen and the generator sabotaged, he adds things up. Barney leads him to an escape tunnel in one of the cells. Climbing inside, Sefra comes face-to-face with the cesium, now stored in an IMF minitank heading his way. The cesium heats to the exploding point, sealing the tunnel and Sefra's fate.

GUEST CAST: Ricardo Montalban (Gerard Sefra), Warren Kemmerling (Raff), Emile Genest (Dr. Kronen), Steven Marlo (Faud). *Unbilled:* John Garwood (Guard)

In an early outline, "The Honeymoon Pirates," the action took place on an enemy freighter, where the IMF had to recover and destroy a container of volatile secret fuel. Within a month the story became "Return to Hell's Last Bastion," with its Boradur-Devil's Island concept. Reluctantly joining the IMF is the ex-con who built the escape tunnel, and he becomes the story's random element, always on the verge of cracking or making a fatal error. Joe Gantman liked the explosive liquid idea, and kept retooling the plot until it became "Snowball in Hell."

Greg Morris enjoys a large amount of time on screen, mostly with guest Ricardo Montalban, a perfect mix of charm and menace as Sefra. Barney takes quite a beating from sadist Sefra, and Greg Morris feels, "that was the scariest piece I ever did, and such fun. In this particular episode Barney was scared, but he was not gonna convey that to anyone else, including himself."

"Snowball" includes one of those personal interludes which occasionally pop up this season, when Rollin impulsively gives off-the-cuff acting tips to Barney, who quips, "Everybody's a critic." Moments like these would soon disappear completely and, within the concept of the later seasons, seem as jarring as a pie in the face.

22: ACTION!

First Aired: 3/4/67

Written by: Robert Lewin
Directed by: Leonard J. Horn

TEAM: Rollin, Cinnamon, Barney, Willy,
cameraman David Day

Good morning, Miss Carter.* This is Miklos Klaar, the head of Cinefot Studios, one of the largest behind the Iron Curtain. Klaar has political ambitions, and to further them has turned captured American newsreel footage into an atrocity film portraying our soldiers as wanton murderers. He's planning to show this to representatives of the world press. If this film is shown it will seriously damage the United States and our future peace talks. The mission, should it be accepted, would be to stop Klaar and in such a way that he can never repeat this technique. As always, should any of the IM Force be caught or killed, the secretary will disavow any knowledge of your actions. This tape recording will decompose immediately. Good luck.

Klaar's film begins with genuine footage of American soldiers prowling through a Southeast Asia jungle. Klaar has cleverly spliced on his own, perfectly matched continuation in which the "soldiers" (actors) in the "jungle" (soundstage) machine-gun a Vietnamese medical camp, ignoring the doctors and wounded who beg for mercy. Only one print of the film exists, and the negative is stored in a vault on the Cinefot lot.

Using a small razor attached to a moviola projector, Ministry of Propaganda officer Rollin sees to it that the one print is destroyed. Barney, operating from the studio cellar, floods the negative vault, rendering Klaar's footage useless and forcing him to reshoot the atrocity scene.

On the set, crewman Willy wheels in a dollyful of "corpses" for background atmosphere. Amid the dummies, his face painted a ghastly white, is David, who sneaks into the rafters above the stage with a movie camera and microphone. Klaar refilms the "murders"—as does David, from his own vantage point. Barney, hiding on the lot, processes the film.

The world press gathers to view the film. Before

the IMF can replace his reel with theirs, Klaar places two guards in the projection room and personally watches David thread his film into the projector. Rollin watches helplessly as Klaar's footage is screened for the horrified journalists. The lights go up and they question a smug Klaar. Suddenly they are interrupted by another sight on-screen: David's film, showing Klaar rehearsing his actors, shooting the phony massacre, and congratulating cast and crew for a job well done. David and Willy have overcome the projection room guards, and Klaar is made a laughing stock.

GUEST CAST: Tom Troupe (David Day), J. D. Cannon (Miklos Klaar), Julian Burton (Petyov), Eric Feldary (Assistant Director), Alfred Shelly (Guard), Arline Anderson (Receptionist). *Unbilled:* Helen Boll (First Floor Guard), Harold Dyrenforth (Sokoloff), Frederic Villani (George Bengst), Jerry Sommers (double, David), Peter Tenen (Third Floor Guard), Marilyn Moe (double, Cinnamon), Mark DeVries (Messenger)

The first draft of "Action!" cast Briggs in the role Rollin would ultimately play; less than a week later, Briggs was written out and Barney assumed his chores. But before shooting began on January 23, Briggs was back, this time as the hidden photographer. Two days worth of film was shot of Steven Hill in and around the studio streets and the jungle set. Late in the second day, Hill brought production to a halt by refusing to play the scene in which Dan runs up the soundstage staircase and into the rafters. He gave no explanations to anyone, not even Geller and Herb Solow, who were called onto the set. Solow finally suspended Hill, who was replaced the next day by actor Tom Troupe, as David Day. Two days' shooting was now unusable and would have to be reshot. So "Action!", which, because of its movie set locale

---

* Briggs does not appear in this episode.

should have been inexpensive to film, went two days over schedule and almost $40,000 over budget.

"Steve acted up," Landau says. "He was suspended from that show for something so silly . . ." This escapade was the last straw in terms of Steven Hill's future on the show. In the episode prior to this one, Hill had crawled through dirt tunnels and climbed rope ladders without a complaint. Now he refused to ascend a staircase flanked with railings. For the rest of the season, the character of Briggs would be eliminated from the scripts whenever possible, his place taken by a series of one-shot IMF agents. Luckily, *Mission*'s concept made even its leading man expendable—a fact which Geller and others in charge realized and would soon act upon.

The day after Hill's suspension, Geller rewrote the tape scene to feature Cinnamon, picking up her instructions in a beauty salon. The dossier scene remains: The camera pans along an anonymous coffee table, where the chosen IMF dossiers lie (Geller cryptically identifies the location as "Limbo"!). The next scene, presided over by Rollin, takes place in Cinnamon's apartment. No mention is made of Briggs, not even an explanation of his absence.

"Action!" remains one of the cleverest and most suspenseful *Mission*s, carried largely by Rollin, who plays the staunch colleague of the understandably paranoid Klaar. When Klaar is humiliated at the end of the show, Rollin faces him, removes his glasses with a theatrical flourish, and smiles at Klaar, who in that instant begins to understand everything.

23: THE TRAIN

First Aired: 3/18/67

Written by: William Read Woodfield and
Allan Balter
Directed by: Ralph Senensky

TEAM: Rollin; Cinnamon; Barney; Willy;
Dr. Harrison Selby, heart surgeon;
Art Director Oliver Donovan and crew

Good morning, Mr. Briggs. The man you're looking at is Ferenc Larya, the prime minister of Svardia, who has long fought to establish democracy and freedom for his people. Larya is now gravely ill and hasn't long to live. He has groomed Deputy Premier Pavel to succeed him and carry on his policies. We know, however, that once in power, Pavel would set up a dictatorship and then purge the country of all opposition. But Larya will not hear anything against Pavel. The mission, if you decide to accept, is to keep Pavel from becoming prime minister. As always, should you or any of your IM Force be caught or killed, the secretary will disavow any knowledge of your actions. This tape will self-destruct in ten seconds. Good luck, Dan.

Dr. Selby and nurse Cinnamon convince Larya that special surgery is required in far-off Switzerland. Larya, accompanied by Pavel and his sinister aide Androv, boards the overnight express in Svardia. Instead of going to Bern, Larya's railroad car makes an unnoticed detour into a railway warehouse, where IMF hydraulic rockers and a complex projection system simulate the voyage to Bern. In reality, the train remains stationary in the warehouse. When the train loses its brakes and "crashes," Pavel and Androv are rendered unconscious.

Androv and Pavel awaken in a hospital and learn that Prime Minister Larya didn't survive the crash. Pavel is quickly sworn in as prime minister and issues decrees designed to erase the memory of his predecessor, whom he calls "a pathetic old fool." At Larya's funeral there will be "no monuments, no mementos, no memories. They will soon

forget that he ever existed." Pavel then orders all political prisoners and opponents put to death. Before he can go further, the "hospital's" wall is removed; behind it stand the IMF and Larya, who has heard it all. "I accept your resignation," he tells a stunned Pavel. Larya then thanks the Force. "You have given me a gift even greater than life. You have permitted me to see beyond my death. Now I must choose my new successor."

GUEST CAST: William Windom (Deputy Premier Milos Pavel), Rhys Williams (Prime Minister Ferenc Larya), William Schallert (Dr. Harrison Selby), Noah Keen (Androv), Richard Bull (Oliver Donovan), Booth Colman (Dr. Huss). *Unbilled:* Ray Baxter (Conductor), Kris Tel (Girl), Paul Prokop (Guard), Don Sherman (Technician)

The show's script originally had Dr. Ira Green and Rollin fulfilling Dr. Selby's functions, and Briggs in Rollin's eventual role as the train conductor. Steven Hill's conduct during episode 22, "Action!" resulted in his role being reduced in all remaining year one scripts, starting with this one.

"The Train" is the first segment to employ the false journey, a famous *Mission* trademark, in which a subject is led to believe he is in transit when in fact he isn't moving at all. Later episodes would vary the vehicle, from truck to airplane to submarine, but the technique was probably never better used than here, where it is fresh, well detailed, and convincing. We get a good look at every element of the deception, from the rear-screen projection to the battery of audio tapes operated by Barney. The extensive location work, shot at Los Angeles's Union Pacific yards, was completed, amazingly, in *one* day by director Ralph Senensky. "The whole script was built on a fallacy," says Senensky. "It is impossible to look at a projection screen and not know that it's a projection screen. So you don't even try to explain it, you just go along. I remember Bruce chuckling as we were leaving the dailies and saying, 'It's all so real,'

which was the essence of doing the caper, to make it believable. Not to play it for its outlandishness but to make it so that you believe it." Cowriter Bill Woodfield qualifies the illusion. Years ago while researching the concept of 3-D, he and a partner discovered a patent by Adelbert Ames, a psychologist at the Dartmouth Eye Institute. "Ames had a way of seeing 3-D on a screen without glasses. It involved cutting the screen into a shape that matched the tracking of the eye horizontally and vertically. We could have done that in "The Train," use special screens which would have cost a lot of money." The phony train voyage takes place at night, says Woodfield, because "depth perception at night is very different. You don't get overlapping shadows and so forth. So the bottom line is, you're right, it wouldn't work but you're wrong, it could be made to work by cutting the screen into the Adelbert Ames screen. There is such a patent for that screen. You would have needed very good, sharp film and the plates would have had to have been well made, but it would have given a perfect illusion."

Pavel is the only *Mission* opponent to ever express any qualms over his dastardly plans. "If there were any other way to rid my country of her enemies . . ." he says of his plan to murder his political adversaries, "but the decay goes too deep. It must be cut away." As IMF strategies grew more and more ruthless, it became obvious that to present the heavies as anything less than 100 percent evil was a sympathy-engendering mistake. Pavel's musings were the first and last of their kind.

"The Train" was chosen to represent *Mission* in the Emmy nominations that year. It was a good choice: *Mission* won.

24: SHOCK

Written by: Laurence Heath
Directed by: Lee H. Katzin

First Aired: 3/25/67

TEAM: Briggs; Rollin; Cinnamon; Barney; Willy; Dr. Ira Drake, neuropsychologist

Good evening, Mr. Briggs. This is Carl Wilson, a special US envoy who is about to succeed in effecting a vital exchange agreement between our government and a neutral country important to us. This man, Peter Kiri, a notorious enemy agent, has kidnapped Wilson and replaced him with an imposter. Kiri's purpose must be to discredit Wilson and so prevent the exchange agreement from being ratified. Wilson is still alive and being held prisoner, so any move against the imposter would bring Wilson's instantaneous death. Your mission, should you decide to accept it, is to save Wilson and to put Kiri out of action. As always, should you or any member of your IM Force be caught or killed, the secretary will disavow any knowledge of your actions. This recording will self-destruct in five seconds. Good luck, Dan.

Wilson is being impersonated by actor Josef Gort in Wilson's house. Gort is surprised by Wilson's visiting niece, Cinnamon. During their meeting, Willy kidnaps Gort while Briggs, also disguised as Wilson, takes his place. Dan learns that the enemy plan will occur that evening at a reception in Wilson's home.

Gort is taken to an IMF mental hospital mock-up, where Dr. Drake administers enough electro-shock treatment to blot out his recent memory and leave him severely confused. Psychiatrist Rollin tells Gort that he is really Georgi Kroll, an accountant suffering from the delusion that he is an imaginary secret agent named Josef Gort.

ROLLIN: Last time, you told us that Gort was working with a special team of agents in a foreign country. They'd kidnapped the American envoy, a man named Wilson, and that you took his place.

GORT: I told you all that?!?

ROLLIN: Yes, many times.

Gort is told that since he cannot remember any details of his "real" life, he must endure more shock therapy. Gort is terrified, but can remember only the Gort "delusion," which he explains totally to Rollin: Gort will kill American official Davis after accusing the US of subverting the country's neutrality. Then he will run into the

study, kill "himself" (the real Wilson), and disappear.

At the reception, Barney and Willy remove the unconscious Wilson from the study and replace him with the drugged Gort, still disguised as Wilson. Dan, as Wilson, incriminates the American government, argues with Davis, then "shoots" him before rushing into the study. Dan fires a shot, then places the gun in Gort's hand before escaping. Kiri and the others find "Wilson," apparently a suicide.

KIRI: Poor man . . . He brooded a great deal about what he thought he was being made to be a party to. I suppose his conscience just couldn't stand it any longer.

Briggs reenters, minus his disguise, rips the face mask off Gort, and exposes Kiri as an enemy agent. As Kiri is arrested, Willy and Barney bring in Carl Wilson, dazed but alive.

GUEST CAST: James Daly (Carl Wilson), Sorrell Booke (Peter Kiri), Stanley Waxman (Jonathan Davis), Patrick Michenaud (Duv), Gerald Michenaud (Fydor), Vic Perrin (Dr. Ira Drake). *Unbilled:* Mike Kopcha (Droka), Donald Ein (Waiter)

In Laurence Heath's story outline, "Imposter," Rollin and Dan's roles are reversed. After extensive replotting of act four, the final version is a tighter and more exciting story with a memorable finale involving three "Wilsons." "Shock" cleverly uses Briggs as the story's main character without requiring the presence of Steven Hill, since Dan is disguised during most of the show. Rollin turns Briggs into Wilson by pasting patently false latex patches all over Briggs's face. One cut later, it is not Hill but James Daly ("Wilson") sitting in the makeup

chair, with a patch of latex on his cheek to tell us exactly who he's supposed to be. There is no reference to Briggs's mastery of Wilson's voice, which he performs like a pro.

Gort's electroshock sequences and his subsequent frightening hallucinations are disturbing and may be the most sadistic moments in the series. It's easy to forget that the victim is in fact a villain and his stone-faced torturers are the heroes. "I think the shock sequences were very well done," says director Katzin, who notes that it was Geller's idea not to use music during these scenes. This sort of physical abuse, an extension of the type seen in episode 4, "Operation Rogosh," was disliked by head writers Woodfield and Balter, who tried to steer *Mission* away from it whenever possible.

25: A CUBE OF SUGAR

First Aired: 4/1/67

Written by: William Read Woodfield and
Allan Balter
Directed by: Joseph Pevney
Music Composed and Conducted by: Don Ellis

TEAM: Briggs, Rollin, Cinnamon, Barney, Willy

Good morning, Mr. Briggs. The man you're looking at is Vincent Deane, a jazz musician who is also one of our best agents. While on a concert tour behind the Iron Curtain, Deane came into possession of a computer microcircuit and its code, which will tell us their entire second-strike potential. Deane has memorized the code, but before he could reach his contact point he was caught. Senko Brobin, director of counterintelligence for all of Eastern Europe, so far has not been able to break Deane or find the microcircuit. Your mission, should you decide to accept it, is to get Deane and the microcircuit out—before he breaks. As always, should you or any of your IM Force be caught or killed, the secretary will disavow any knowledge of your actions. This tape will self-destruct in five seconds. Good luck, Dan.

Drugged and psychotic, Deane is locked in a medical center's padded cell block in a windowless room which is guarded around the clock. Brobin has hooked him on narcotics, hoping that an agonizing withdrawal will break him. The microcircuit is hidden in one of a handful of drug-laced sugar cubes Deane was carrying when he was caught. Brobin has crushed the cubes, but hasn't found the chip because Deane had it coated to avoid detection.

Deane's "wife," Cinnamon, tells Brobin that Deane is no agent, just an acidhead delivering material for someone else—Rollin. Brobin arrests Rollin, who is straitjacketed and thrown into a padded cell near Deane's. He frees himself, tampers with Deane's drug compound, and returns to his cell unnoticed. When Deane gets his next injection, he "dies."

Brobin learns that Cinnamon, like Deane, is an addict. He gives her the remains of Deane's drugged sugar cubes. The magnetized ring on her finger picks up the microcircuit, which she pockets.

Brobin learns of Deane's death. When US representative Briggs demands the body, Brobin, fearing the repercussions of an autopsy, hastily arranges for the body to be cremated—immediately. Deane is sent to the mortuary and placed in the crematorium, which is ignited. But the flames are courtesy of Barney and Willy, who have broken through two walls to enter the furnace and cut off the gas. They take Deane out through tunnels and a manhole to safety. Rollin, in his cell, agrees to tell Brobin where the microcircuit is hidden, then knocks him out. With the help of two masks, they switch identities, and "Brobin" exits.

GUEST CAST: Francis Lederer (Senko Brobin), Jacques Denbeaux (Vincent Deane), Lou Robb (Doctor), Max Kleven (Attendant), Joyce Easton (Clerk), Kurt Kreuger (Polya). *Unbilled:* Eric Forst (Policeman); Ivan Ivarson (Maintenance Man); Rico Cattani (Workman); Jill Gordon, Sharon Garrett (Dancers)

This hour introduces one of several IMF magic drugs, although they were never referred to as such. Since the mission requires Rollin and Cinnamon to ingest dangerous drugs, Rollin tells Dan during the apartment scene that an off-screen visit with Dr. Green has rendered them both immune to narcotics for seven to ten days!

Rollin's dandy escape sequence begins after he squirms out of his straitjacket and uncovers a small metal cylinder from the wall of his padded cell (smuggled in earlier by Briggs). This package, slightly larger than a cutting blade, has everything Rollin needs: a knife to cut through his padded wall; a bar bender, which, when wedged between two cell bars and twisted, bends them wide enough for Rollin to crawl through; a slingshot to create a diversion across the room; and, most improbably, the two masks needed for Rollin's escape.

26: THE TRAITOR

Written by: Edward J. Lakso
Directed by: Lee H. Katzin

First Aired: 4/15/67

TEAM: Briggs, Rollin, Cinnamon, Barney, Willy, Tina Mara

Good morning, Mr. Briggs. Edward Hughes, an American intelligence officer, has defected to the enemy and taken refuge in their embassy here. Hughes took with him a top-secret message before we had a chance to decode it. We believe the information in that message to be vital. The sender of the message has died. Hughes himself does not know the code, so Victor Belson, one of the enemy's best cryptographers, is on his way to the embassy now. Belson is unknown to the personnel there. The mission, Dan, should you decide to accept it, would be to get the message back before the enemy deciphers it, and get Hughes out of the embassy in such a way as to discredit any other information he may have given them. As always, should you or any of your IM Force be caught or killed, the secretary will disavow any knowledge of your actions. This recording will self-destruct in five seconds. Good luck, Dan.

Belson (Rollin) enters the embassy and "discovers" a coded message in a recently delivered magazine, obviously meant for someone inside the embassy. The message tells of a Mr. Beaumont in a nearby hotel. Ambassador Brazneck has Beaumont's room bugged and hears him (Dan) assuring an American government official (Cinnamon) that he can retrieve stolen papers from the embassy once he pays off an accomplice.

Rollin and Hughes work on the decoded message. Hughes is discreetly drugged, puts the data in a vault, then falls asleep in his room. Furnace repairman Willy installs a new duct for the vent system containing petite Tina, who, via the vents, enters Hughes's room. By throwing a false bed top over Hughes and inflating it, she makes him seem to vanish from his room. Then she enters the vault room, penetrates the security, takes the coded message, and replaces it with a phony before exiting.

Dan is seen passing an envelope to a man in a car, which Brazneck assumes to be the "missing" Hughes. Checking the vault, he sees that the original message has been taken and concludes that Hughes has sold it back to the Americans. Tina returns to Hughes's room, removes the bed top, and plants an envelope full of cash on Hughes. Brazneck finds the money on Hughes and is convinced that the American is a double agent. Hughes, fearing for his life, runs out of the embassy and is arrested by US authorities.

GUEST CAST: Eartha Kitt (Tina Mara), Malachi Throne (Ambassador Brazneck), Lonny Chapman (Edward Hughes), Frank Marth (Koler), Paul Sorensen (First Floor Guard), Socrates Ballis (Maintenance Man), Ed McCready (Telegraph Clerk), Michael Rye (Victor Belson). *Unbilled:* Walter Alzmann (Foyer Guard), Buzz Henry (Officer)

Eartha Kitt assisted the team in "The Traitor."

In the first draft script, titled "Run, Rat, Run," Tina Mara was not included. Fulfilling her function was John Tate, a "small, intense little man expert in locks, etc." Eartha Kitt's Tina is one of the IMF's more intriguing agents. Her dossier suggests that she is a contortionist, and she is used here because the embassy vent system is too small to accommodate anyone else. Tina might have made an effective regular addition had not future assignments taken place in buildings with air ducts large enough for Barney to crawl through!

Visual highlights include the false, inflatable bed top which in effect buries Hughes in his bed and Tina's agile evasion of the vault security system, using a series of mounted, circular mirrors to avoid electric eyes, and an audio reader which lights up when the vault tumblers fall. Making its first of several appearances is a strangely built screwdriver which allows Tina (and, in later shows, Barney) to open a duct grating from *inside* the vent.

"The thing I remember most about 'The Traitor,'" director Lee Katzin says, "is that the day after I finished shooting, I had a tapeworm eliminated. I remember trying to keep my energy up and it was a little difficult towards the end—no pun intended."

27: THE PSYCHIC

First Aired: 4/22/67

Written by: William Read Woodfield and
    Allan Balter
Directed by: Charles R. Rondeau

TEAM: Rollin, Cinnamon, Barney, Willy, Judge
Wilson Chase, actor Byron Miller

Good morning, Mr. Briggs. The man you're looking at is Alex Lowell, a promoter of several large investment trusts. A few weeks ago Lowell's trusts gained control of a majority of the shares in Sud-Aero, a foreign company which manufactures some of NATO's top-secret defense hardware. Lowell immediately transferred the stock into his own name and with it, left for South America—out of our reach. We believe he intends to put Sud-Aero's secret patents up for sale to the highest bidder. Jan Vornitz, an agent for an unfriendly country, is the most interested and most likely customer. Your mission, Dan, should you decide to accept it, is to stop Lowell before he has a chance to sell the patents, and make sure he does not remain in control of the company. As always, should you or any of your IM Force be caught or killed, the secretary will disavow any knowledge of your actions. This recording will self-destruct five seconds after the speaker has been replaced. Good luck, Dan.

Miller, representing a group of "businessmen," offers to buy Lowell's Sud-Aero stock for eighty million dollars, which Lowell refuses. Judge Chase (whom Lowell knows) attends a party on Lowell's estate, accompanied by famous psychic Cinnamon. After several accurate predictions, she warns Lowell that his life is in danger. When Lowell finds his car booby-trapped, he takes Cinnamon seriously. Gangster Rollin, Miller's boss, arranges to meet Lowell that night. Cinnamon predicts that Lowell and Rollin will play poker for the Sud-Aero stock. "He intends to cheat and assure he'll win," says Cinnamon of Rollin, "but he won't." Lowell learns that his cards have been tampered with, decides to play Rollin's game and "cheat a cheater."

Lowell and Rollin play their eighty million dollar poker game. Rollin loses quickly and is thrown out. A triumphant Lowell discovers too late that Rollin has cleverly switched phony stock documents for the real ones, leaving behind an unendorsed eighty million dollar check.

GUEST CAST: Barry Sullivan (Alex Lowell), Milton Selzer (Jan Vornitz), Richard Anderson (Judge Wilson Chase), Paul Mantee (Byron Miller), Michael Pataki (Ed), Rita D'Amico (Girl at Party), Eric Mason (Man at Party), Shep Sanders (Politician). *Unbilled:* Jay Ose (Dealer)

Cinnamon makes studies of Lowell's guests to forecast extremely believable "predictions." Barney wires Lowell's car with explosives, switches his playing cards with obviously marked ones, and hides literally under Lowell's nose beneath an end table in Lowell's card room. How? By crouching behind a magician's mirror, angled toward the floor to reflect the carpet. When he emerges from behind the mirror, Barney seems to materialize out of thin air.

The show's best prop is an automated feeder arm rooted on a circular base, installed by Barney under Lowell's card table. When Rollin loses the game, he "impulsively" grabs his eighty million dollar check and the signed stock certificates, and places them on his lap. Then he activates the "arm," which thrusts the counterfeit stocks and the unendorsed check at him. Rollin places the real stocks in the arm, which feeds them to Cinnamon, standing nearby. She picks up her purse from the table, discreetly snatches the stocks, and exits. Lowell forces Rollin to return "his" stocks. "That was one of the cutest little gadgets we made," says Jonnie Burke. "Two weeks after that show went on the air I got a call from a guy who wanted to know if it was available. He wanted to use it!"

Watch closely for an in-joke during the tape scene, when Dan pulls into a drive-in for his instructions. The theater marquee reads, "Geller and Solow in *Spend The Money*," a tongue-in-cheek reference to a serious concern among Desilu executives.

Wrap

By January 1967, twenty-five of the thirty-four series introduced the prior September had already been canceled. Since *Mission* ended the season at 51 in the Nielsen ratings with a 29 share, many felt that its days were numbered. Luckily, the show's greatest ally was CBS. Despite audience reaction that could be called lukewarm at best, the network renewed the show almost immediately. Says Perry Lafferty, "It was such a classy show and so well done that you just didn't have the heart to kill it. It was a superior piece of work and that's what kept it alive." The fact that the founder and chairman of the company liked the show didn't hurt: It was William Paley's faith that kept it on the air. "His taste was extraordinary," adds Lafferty, "and his commercial sense was very good, too." For its second season, CBS would move *Mission* to Sundays at 10 P.M. It turned out to be an ideal time slot for the show, and *Mission* would stay there for three years.

The 1966 holidays were bountiful. Since both Christmas and New Year's Eve (traditionally low-rated TV nights) fell on Saturdays that year, programming was dominated by specials and reruns. *Mission*'s pilot was rebroadcast December 24, and episode 4, "Operation Rogosh" on December 31. The repeats attracted a larger audience than usual, and the series' ratings increased from that point on.

For *Mission*'s cast and crew, all the hard work paid off on the evening of March 25, 1967, at the annual Emmy awards presentation. *Mission* was up for six trophies: Individual Achievements in Film and Sound Editing (Paul Krasny and Robert Watts), Individual Achievements in Music Composition (Lalo Schifrin), Outstanding Writing Achievement in Drama (Bruce Geller for the pilot), Outstanding Continued Performance by an Actress in a Leading Role in a Dramatic Series (Barbara Bain), Outstanding Continued Performance by an Actor in a Leading Role in a Dramatic Series (Martin Landau), and Outstanding Dramatic Series.

It was a sweet night for *Mission,* which won four of the six Emmies it was nominated for: Dramatic Series, Actress, Writing, and Editing.* The awards certainly helped widen the series' audience during the spring reruns. Few viewers knew that they were seeing the last of Steven Hill in the series. After his firing from the show, Hill left acting and devoted more time to religion. In addition to living in a community of Jews in New York, Hill dabbled in writing and selling real estate. In the mid seventies the urge to perform returned. "They say you can't quit show business," he told a reporter in 1977, "and it took ten years, but I couldn't get it out of my system. So I called an agent and put him to work." By the mid eighties, Hill was in great demand as one of the screen's busiest character actors, with plum roles in features like *Eyewitness* (1981), *Rich and Famous* (1981), *Yentl* (1983), *Legal Eagles* (1986), *Heartburn* (1986) and many more, including a supporting role in the television series *Law & Order* (1990). One of the most interesting facets of Hill's later career is his success in comedic roles, a shock to anyone who knows him only from *Mission: Impossible.* Despite his high regard within the industry, he is still largely unknown to the general public. Hill remains as devoutly Orthodox as he was in 1966, but there are no reports of strange, paranoid behavior

---

* More awards followed, including two Grammies for Lalo Schifrin, and Golden Globes for Best Television Show and Best Television Star, Male (Martin Landau).

anymore. "Twenty years ago, people in the business thought I was off on some religious kick," he has said. "Well, that kick has gone on for twenty years.

"I don't think an actor should act every single day. I don't think it's good for the so-called creative process. You must have periods when you leave the land fallow, let it revitalize itself . . . I think probably because of all the years and time that have gone by, I enjoy my work more than I ever did before—certainly more than I did in my early years when it took a lot of effort to do the best job I wanted to do. Now it is more of a joy and much more exciting." And, apparently for Steven Hill, more rewarding than ever.

Bruce Geller's "Pilot" script won him an Emmy Award in 1967. The show garnered a total of four Emmy Awards that year.

The series cast for Years Two and Three.

Year Two

September 1967 – April 1968

Production Credits

Starring: Peter Graves
Also Starring: Martin Landau as Rollin Hand, Barbara Bain, Greg Morris, Peter Lupus
Executive Producer: Bruce Geller
Produced by: Joseph Gantman
Associate Producers: John W. Rogers and Robert F. O'Neill
Script Consultants: William Read Woodfield and Allan Balter
Theme Music by: Lalo Schifrin
Director of Photography: Michel Hugo
Art Director: Bill Ross
Film Editors: Robert L. Swanson; David Wages, ACE; Paul Krasny; Neil MacDonald; Robert Watts, ACE; John Loeffler
Assistant Directors: Bill Schwartz, Jack P. Cunningham, Victor Vallejo, Dale Coleman, Jerome M. Siegel, Al Kraus
Set Decorator: Lucien Hafley
Supervising Property Master: Arthur Wasson

Property Master: William M. Bates
Production Coordinator: Philip Fehrle
Special Effects: Jonnie Burke
Makeup Artist: Bob Dawn
Hairstylist: Adele Taylor
Script Supervisor: Allan Greedy
Casting: Joseph D'Agosta
Supervising Film Editor: Paul Krasny
Supervising Sound Editor: Joseph G. Sorokin
Music Editor: Dan Carlin
Production Mixer: Dominick Gaffey
Rerecording Mixers: Elden E. Ruberg, CAS; Gordon L. Day, CAS
Sound: Glen Glenn Sound
Supervising Costumer: Forrest T. Butler
Costume Supervisor (Women): Sabine Manela
Men's Clothing Furnished by: Promenade Fashions for Men
Executive in Charge of Production: Herbert F. Solow (through episode 44)

Peter Graves's performance in the *Call To Danger* pilot (with co-star James Gregory) won him the lead in *Mission: Impossible*.

> *"I must say that I went into that show with
> a lot of confidence. I just had the feeling that
> it was right for me."*
>
> —PETER GRAVES

BUOYED BY ITS EMMIES, CBS's good faith, and a growing audience, *Mission* embarked upon a second semester of "one-hour movies." Martin Landau was so satisfied with year one that he signed on as an official series regular—but only for one season. "It's hard to see what will happen," he told *Daily Variety*'s Dave Kaufman. "If the series and scripts continue to maintain quality, I will continue."

The search was on for a new leading man, and everyone had ideas. Gary Morton wanted Stuart Whitman, but the actor wasn't interested. Also asked: John Forsythe, who wasn't ready for another series after *The John Forsythe Show* (1965–66) fizzled. CBS, which had fought to oust Steven Hill and had renewed *Mission* before a new lead was chosen, had its own suggestion.

In 1961 Perry Lafferty directed and produced a half-hour pilot titled "Call to Danger," starring Larry Blyden. "I think the idea is still sensational," Lafferty insists, "that there exists in Washington a government agency that has computer files on anyone who had unusual talents and abilities. If you had perfect pitch, could speak Spanish, and ride a unicycle, you'd be in this computer bank. When there was some kind of situation they couldn't solve with their own personnel, they would go to this computer agency and see if any of these people could match their plan." The idea was viable enough to be refilmed as an hour pilot in 1966, produced by Paul King and directed by Lamont Johnson. The remake had the same story but a different cast: Albert Paulsen as the villain; Daniel Travanti as the recruit, a barber-locksmith-stamp collector; and, as the government agent, Peter Graves.

" 'Call to Danger' was a pretty good concept," says Graves. "We made a good pilot, it went into the market, and got penciled in and penciled out, the usual game." Ultimately it didn't sell. "In those days," says Lafferty, "they didn't believe that you could do an hour show where the lead was not pushing the action. They said, 'It's too anthological.' " *Mission* was operating in exactly the same way—but no one wanted it to. Among those who saw "Call to Danger" were Herb Solow and Bruce Geller. As Solow recalls, "We looked at the pilot and said, 'Peter Graves!' "

Born Peter Aurness in Minneapolis, Graves is the younger brother of actor James Arness, who preceded Peter to Hollywood. Although music was a childhood ambition, Peter caught the acting bug early and majored in drama at college. After moving to Hollywood, times were lean until he landed a major role in Billy Wilder's *Stalag 17* (1951). Many less auspicious films followed. Graves was more successful on television, in the series *Fury* (1955), followed by *Whiplash* (1961), shot in Australia, and *Court-Martial* (1966), filmed in London. He kept busy in films and TV until offered what would be his fourth, and most successful series.

"They said that Steve Hill was going out of it, and they wanted me to do it," says Graves. "I had seen it a couple of times and knew it was good. I really don't think it took me much time to make a decision. I don't think I said anything right then except, 'Gulp.' But I thought

Peter Graves joined the series in 1967 as IMF mastermind Jim Phelps. . .

Sorgfältig aufzubewahren, da diese Bescheinigung nur einmal ausgefertigt wird.

Standesamt [illegible]

Familienbuch-Nr. [illegible]

STAATSPOLIZEI

(Nur gültig für die Entgegennahme des Ehestandsdarlehns)

Vor- und Zuname sowie Geburtstag und -jahr und Stand des Ehemannes: [illegible]

Vor- und Geburtsname sowie Geburtstag und -jahr der Ehefrau: [illegible]

Tag der Eheschließung:

[illegible], den [illegible] 1964

(Siegel) [illegible]

Der Standesbeamte

[illegible]

(Unterschrift)

. . . who could turn up anywhere, in any guise.

about it, and within a day or so I knew it was the right thing for me." Graves met with Bruce Geller, whom he knew from an earlier project. "We talked about this Mr. Phelps, although we didn't even have a name yet. He was kicking around several names. One of them was Phillips. At the time there was a CBS executive named Jim Phillips, so Bruce said, 'Oh no, we can't have that name.' Eventually we decided on Jim Phelps." Graves wrote a backstory which depicted Phelps coming out of college, serving in the Korean War, then on to a career with Pan Am Airways. One day Jim returned to his New York apartment and found a message on his record player. "I read this background to Bruce and Joe Gantman. Bruce listened and then said, 'Very nice. Why don't you keep going?' " Evidently, Geller was willing to search for story ideas anywhere he could!

Hiring Graves was a shrewd move. He was a more conventionally attractive leading man than Hill and a veteran used to the long hours of a television series. The differences between Dan Briggs and Jim Phelps were negligible, drawn solely by the actors portraying them. Clearly, they both liked black and white apartments and were partial to picking the same four agents for every mission. "Briggs was an expert in behavioral psychology—cerebral, a brilliant manipulator," said Geller at the time, trying to rationalize the change. "He liked to devise an ingenious plot, set the stage, then watch the performers play out the parts he had designed for them. Jim Phelps, in addition to being brilliant and cerebral, is a strong, rugged, athletic man. Not only can he outwit his adversaries, he can outfight them." And he didn't mind working late on Fridays.

Despite the fact that he was a replacement and not the series' most frequently used actor, Peter Graves, more than anyone else, became irrevocably linked to *Mission: Impossible*. His impact upon the show was so profound that some find it unimaginable to think of one without the other, and many people are not aware that *Mission* ever existed without him. To this day, *Mission*'s first season is not rerun as often as the later shows in some markets, presumably because Graves is not in it. Although he has had a long and prolific career before and after the series, *Mission* shadows Graves wherever he goes. In a 1985 *People* magazine survey, Jim Phelps placed second (behind Maxwell Smart!) as TV's best secret agent. *Mission* made Graves a major television star, and to most of the world he will always be Jim Phelps.

"You play Phelps as a very cool, calculating, intellectual thinker, planning to achieve a certain end," says the actor. "He also has to be a good enough performer or con artist." Phelps would play a vital part in the schemes he concocted. And while having the mastermind along on such perilous missions may not be a sensible strategy in real life, it was fine on television. "I think each of us did some very fine work in encapsuled miniversions," says Graves. Over the course of six years, Phelps appeared in a variety of guises, most often as authority figures like doctors, scientists, and investigators. But he also portrayed hustlers, assassins, gangsters, spies, and an interesting assortment of rugged tough guys. One of his most successful recurring characters was what writer Bill Woodfield calls "the Rotarian," the typically unctuous, middle-class American salesman-manufacturer.

Perhaps Graves's greatest asset was a straightforward vocal delivery which made paralyzingly bad dialogue sound natural. Consider lines like, "I can't freeze you while you're alive, it's not legal!"; "Is the comb ready?"; or "Then we're all set except for the typhoid. Who's got it?"

"The show had a looseness that it hadn't had the first year," says hairstylist Adele Taylor. "Peter brought a lot of that. Although he was a very reserved man, he made you feel very much

at home." Graves was the type of professional who got along with virtually everyone, and he became the linchpin of one of Hollywood's friendliest sets.

Mannix, Geller's private eye project for CBS, went into production this season. With associate producer Barry Crane getting that series off the ground, Robert F. O'Neill and assistant director John W. Rogers filled in on *Mission.* Other staff changes included camera operator Michel Hugo's promotion to director of photography; a new property master, William Bates; and Bob Dawn, replacing Dan Striepeke in the makeup room. Following Striepeke's lead, Dawn (son of MGM's Jack Dawn, whose many credits include *The Wizard of Oz*) would successfully meet *Mission*'s innovative and ever more elaborate makeup effects. Striepeke moved to Twentieth Century-Fox to play a major role creating the remarkable prosthetic techniques in *Planet of the Apes* (1968) and its sequels.

The lessons learned in year one prompted Geller to move Paul Krasny out of the editing pool and into the position of postproduction head for the entire series. "I did what Gantman was doing," says Krasny, "sit with each editor, then show it to Bruce, make his changes, and get it done." Aiding Krasny in dubbing was Phil Fehrle, who eventually took over that department. Together they created S&S Films which, as far as the studio was concerned, was a film library. Its real purpose was quite different: It was a disguised second unit. "It's absolutely against union rules and we could have gotten busted and fined for this," Phil Fehrle notes, "but we were concerned about having the absolute best show that we could for the money that we had. Bruce approved this, but the studio didn't know." The crew of S&S (which stood for Saturday and Sunday) spent the weekends shooting sequences or pieces of sequences (a car chase, traveling shots) that "probably would have cost the studio ten thousand dollars if they'd done it with an official crew. We'd charge twelve hundred dollars, bill the studio for stock footage, and pay our crew out of that. But the bottom line is that the pictures were opened up and improved immeasurably. We'd never have been able to get the approval."

At about this time, changes were about to take place concerning Desilu. Lucille Ball was being courted by Charles Bluhdorn, a vastly successful financier who in eight years had amalgamated sixty-five companies into a conglomerate called Gulf + Western Industries. Bluhdorn had just acquired Paramount Pictures and saw commercial possibilities in making Desilu Paramount's TV division and consolidating the two adjoining studio lots. Lucy, who saw that the days of the television independent were drawing to a close, carefully considered Bluhdorn's offer, and finally sold the studio for approximately seventeen million dollars.

In July 1967, Desilu Productions officially became Paramount Television, and the walls dividing the two lots were torn down. *Star Trek*'s George Takei remembers "a lot of sprucing up being done. It was a more spacious feeling to be able to expand out to the Paramount side. When Paramount took over, they repainted the buildings and repaved." Not everyone was happy with the change; some felt that Desilu had lost its mom and pop feeling.

The new management was less than thrilled over *Mission*'s operating expenses. "They became very angry about the costs involved and I was told that [Paramount's executive vice president] Martin Davis wanted my head," states Joseph Gantman, who was not worried. "Nobody could have done it for less. And everyone knew, because no one came around and said, 'This is your last week.' Desilu sold the show for too little and promised what they promised. It was very easy to prove on paper that it couldn't be done for less. You are faced with making a series a success. That doesn't happen by trying to save money. You want people to watch and start talking." That was beginning to happen, but more conflicts between show and studio were in the offing.

Herbert F. Solow, who was vice president in charge of production for Desilu one day and vice president in charge of television for Paramount the next, became disenchanted. "I spent about a month in meetings and said, 'That's that.'" he claims. "It wasn't the same, so I asked out of my contract and said, 'I don't like it here because it's changed.'" It didn't take him long to realize that the president of Paramount Television, John T. Reynolds, was not about to grant Solow the free rein and extravagant budgets Desilu did. "Paramount was entitled to run it the way they wanted to run it," Solow explains. "They'd paid a lot of money, they could have burned it all if they wanted to. They bring in the management that they think is good for their way of doing business and that's fine, but I chose not to be a part of it." Solow moved to MGM, where he became vice president in charge of television (and eventually motion pictures). He was the first of many Desilu personnel to leave.

The management change would have serious effects on the show as time went on. For now, however, *Mission*'s award-winning team and popular new star concentrated upon another season of sophisticated entertainment, backed by all that a major studio like Paramount could provide.

Phelps relies on his pool skills—and some electronic help from Barney—in "Break!" (left), and appears as a U-boat commander in "Submarine" (right).

28: THE SURVIVORS

Written by: William Read Woodfield and
Allan Balter
Directed by: Paul Stanley
Music Composed and Conducted by:
Walter Scharf

First Aired: 9/24/67

TEAM: Jim Phelps, Rollin, Cinnamon, Barney,
Willy

Good morning, Mr. Phelps. These men are Edward Stoner and Wilson Cardel, two of the three key scientists vital to the development of the United States' Project Twelve. They have been kidnapped along with their wives by this agent, Eric Stavak. The Wilsons [sic] and Cardels are in great danger as they are useless to Stavak without the third scientist on the project, Dr. Robert Webster. But should Stavak succeed in getting all three men and forcing them to talk, the solution to what has been described as "the ultimate weapon" will be in enemy hands. The mission, Jim, should you decide to accept it, is to prevent that at all costs and get those two scientists and their wives back—alive. As always, should you or any of your IM Force be caught or killed, the secretary will disavow any knowledge of your actions. This tape will self-destruct in five seconds. Good luck, Jim.

"Stoner and Cardel and their wives will be killed immediately if any rescue attempt is made," Phelps tells his crew. "Either Stavak gets the Project Twelve equations or nobody does."

Stavak's henchmen abduct Phelps and Cinnamon, believing them to be the Websters, and lock them up with the Cardels and Stoners in a warehouse cellar in San Francisco's Chinatown.

Jim seems ready to give Stavak the equations when a tremendous "earthquake" occurs, isolating the basement from the rest of the world. The quake is an illusion created by Barney's sonic-vibration apparatus, Rollin's false radio broadcasts, and some well-placed debris from Willy. After Phelps laboriously digs an exit from the basement into a storm drain, Stavak and his hoods escape through it and strand their victims. Jim then easily leads the captives out via an elevator shaft which isn't as inaccessible as it seemed. Stavak and company are arrested when they emerge onto a perfectly intact San Francisco street.

GUEST CAST: Albert Paulsen (Eric Stavak),
Lawrence Dane (Dr. Anton Yubov), John
McLiam (Dr. Edward Stoner), Angela
Clarke (Nancy Stoner), Nancy Jeris (Emily
Cardel), Robert Homel (Kopik), Marc
Adams (Minister), Bill Sargent (Dr. Wilson
Cardel). *Unbilled:* Jack Carol (Driver #1),
Brett Dunham (Driver #2), Winston de
Lugo (Policeman)

Mr. Jim Phelps is ushered in with a typically stylish, assured hour, setting the pace for the rest of the season. Albert Paulsen, laying the foundation for the smooth villain persona he would perfect in later episodes, has a fine moment at the end of the show when he emerges from a manhole onto a normal, undamaged street and sees his associates being arrested by gun-toting IMFers. The beaten look as he glares at Rollin and Cinnamon defies description.

29: TREK

Written by: Laurence Heath
Directed by: Leonard J. Horn
Music Composed and Conducted by:
  Gerald Fried

First Aired: 9/17/67

TEAM: Phelps, Rollin, Cinnamon, Barney,
  puppeteer Robert Field

Good afternoon, Mr. Phelps. Recently, in a desperate attempt to save its economy, the government of the tiny democracy of Santales sold its priceless collection of Incan gold artifacts. Before the treasure could be delivered it was hijacked by this man, Jack Cole. Cole's accomplices were all killed. He was captured and is being held at the provincial prison where a Colonel Cardoza is trying to "persuade" him to reveal where the treasure is hidden. We know Cardoza to be a traitor who intends to take the treasure for himself and flee, bankrupting the country. Your mission, should you decide to accept it, is to recover the treasure and expose Cardoza. As always, should you or any member of your IM Force be caught or killed, the secretary will disavow any knowledge of your actions. This tape will self-destruct in five seconds. Good luck, Jim.

Phelps, supposedly sent by Cardoza's "fence" for the treasure, plots with Cardoza to get Cole to lead them to the treasure. Jim is jailed, then he and Cole "overpower" Cardoza and, using him as hostage, escape into the desert, ostensibly heading for the border. When their car breaks down, Jim "kills" Indian Rollin for his horses. They find archaelogist Cinnamon with what seems to be part of the loot, making Cole fear that the treasure has been uncovered. Rollin, meanwhile, reports the theft of his horses to Cardoza's superior, General Diaz, and tells him that *Cardoza* is leading the trio.

Cole takes Jim and Cardoza to the cavern where the treasure is hidden. Cardoza kills Cole and helps Jim drag the chests outside, to be loaded onto the approaching helicopter piloted by Barney. Diaz and his men catch up to the pair. Jim grabs the copter ladder and flies off, leaving Cardoza to be arrested and the treasure recovered.

GUEST CAST: Daniel O'Herlihy (Jack Cole), Mark Lenard (Colonel Luis Cardoza), Michael Pate (General Diaz), Jack Donner (Robert Field), Ralph Maurer (Sergeant). *Unbilled:* Alfred Shelly (Guard #1)

Peter Graves remembers "Trek" well; not only was it his first episode (it was shot before episode 28, "The Survivors" for production reasons), but filming took place during the Middle East's Six Day War. "We shot it in the desert," says Graves. "I was thrilled about going on this classy, wonderful series and spending weeks in wardrobe with beautiful, tailor-made suits, and this wonderful black and white apartment. Then, in the first episode here I am in grubby khakis with a four-day growth of beard, crawling around in the desert!" The end of the show called for Graves to be picked up and dropped off by a helicopter dangling a rope ladder. He was told that a dummy would be placed on the ladder for the long shots. "Lenny Horn said, 'Gee, if we could get you stepping on the ladder as the thing goes up, it would help us so much. You step on, we take you three feet up, you jump off, and we edit it.' So I said okay, and we did it and he took me up fifteen feet instead of three, and back down. I said, 'Why don't we just do it?' They said okay, so I spent a couple of hours flying around the desert hanging from a helicopter and I loved it, sailing through the air with no straps or restraints or safety harness. That was my first experience on this wonderful, classy, well-dressed show!"

30: THE BANK

Written by: Brad Radnitz
Directed by: Alf Kjellin
Music Composed and Conducted by:
  Walter Scharf

First Aired: 10/1/67

TEAM: Phelps, Rollin, Cinnamon, Barney, Willy, convicted bank robber Paul Lebarre

Good morning, Mr. Phelps. The man you're looking at is Alfred Belzig, director of the Socialist People's Bank in the East Zone, but secretly a fanatic who has never given up working for a supreme fascist state. Using his position, Belzig offers to help anyone who has money and wishes to escape to the West. He "helps" them and they're never heard from again, and Belzig appropriates their bank accounts. The mission, should you decide to accept it, is to stop Belzig and prevent the over three million dollars which he has "appropriated" from falling into the hands of his new Nazi party. As always, should you or any member of your IM Force be caught or killed, the secretary will disavow any knowledge of your actions. This record will self-destruct when it reaches the final groove. Good luck, Jim.

At the bank, suspicious loiterers Barney and Lebarre attract the attention of federal officers Phelps, Cinnamon, and Willy. Belzig's latest victim, Rollin, hands over his life savings to Belzig, who puts the cash in his personal safety deposit box in the bank vault, then "disposes" of Rollin.

Barney and Lebarre reenter the bank, where Barney heads for the vault. Despite heavy surveillance and the presence of a huge amount of foreign currency, Barney steals only Belzig's deposit box while Lebarre robs the bank customers. Willy interrupts and arrests the pair. When the real police arrive, they wonder why the thieves attempted to steal the one particular box. Before the box can be opened, Belzig grabs it and tries, unsuccessfully, to escape.

GUEST CAST: James Daly (Alfred Belzig), Pierre Jalbert (Paul Lebarre), Gene Dynarski (Kutler), Ray Baxter (Professor Henks), Julian Burton (Captain Heindorf), Kurt Landen (Vitter), Sasha Berger (Secretary). *Unbilled:* Kris Tel (Vault Clerk), Richard Anders (Bank Guard)

"Bruce Geller asked me to come up with a new way to rob a bank," says Brad Radnitz, at that time an already established comedy writer *(The Lucy Show, Family Affair)* making his first foray into dramatic television. Radnitz opted to split up the team: one half robbed the bank while the other half passed as the police who arrested them.

"At the end," Peter Graves relates, "walking past the camera, I gave a small sly grin, as if to say, We got the bastards. The next day Bruce was down on the set, having just seen the dailies, and said, 'Don't comment. I don't want you to editorialize. Play it straight, do the guys in, walk off with nothing on your face. Nothing.' Bruce and Gantman had a great dedication to their idea of the show and watched it like hawks."

31: OPERATION—"HEART"

First Aired: 10/22/67

Written by: John O'Dea and Arthur Rowe
Directed by: Leonard J. Horn
Music Composed and Conducted by:
   Gerald Fried

TEAM: Phelps, Rollin, Cinnamon, Barney, Willy, Dr. Owen Siebert

Good afternoon, Mr. Phelps. This is Professor William Bennett, the Nobel Prize–winning archaeologist who has become the innocent pawn in a political coup being staged by this man, Stephan Gomalk. The chief of security police, Gomalk, plans to overthrow the pro-Western government of his closest friend, Beyron Rurich. The plan to assassinate Rurich has been code-named Anniversary. Professor Bennett has a chronically weak heart. When he was arrested by mistake and intensively interrogated by Gomalk, Bennett's heart failed. He is now in a hospital maximum security ward. Your mission, Jim, should you decide to accept it, is to get Bennett out alive and prevent Rurich's assassination by Gomalk. As always, if you or any of your IM Force are caught or killed, the secretary will disavow any knowledge of your actions. This recording will self-destruct in five seconds. Good luck, Jim.

An "unsuccessful" IMF assassination "attempt" on President Rurich the day before Anniversary effectively spoils Gomalk's element of surprise. Just as Gomalk becomes convinced that Bennett is not an American agent and prepares to let him die, Mrs. Bennett (Cinnamon) is caught trying to poison her husband. Gomalk then finds a hidden message concerning Anniversary (planted by Cinnamon) among Bennett's belongings. Gomalk knows that Bennett is being framed for some reason, but wants Rurich kept unaware of it to avoid having his own treacherous plans uncovered. Magazine writer Phelps informs Rurich that Bennett is indeed an American spy.

Rurich wants to question the unconscious Bennett personally and orders a life-saving operation. During surgery, Doctor Hand discovers a bomb in the operating room and calls a bomb disposal unit consisting of Barney, Willy, and Dr. Siebert, who pull guns and try to remove Bennett, who subsequently begins to "die," thanks to Rollin's remote control of Bennett's oscillometer. The doctors are locked in an adjoining room and Bennett (hidden in a bomb disposal gantry) is secreted, with the "bomb," in a truck equipped to treat him medically. Rurich and Gomalk walk into the operating room to find "Bennett" (Rollin) dying. His last words, spoken to Gomalk as Rurich listens, are, "Stephan . . . Anniversary . . . has it started? . . . Is Rurich dead?" Rurich, betrayed, shoots an absolutely defenseless Gomalk.

GUEST CAST: Pernell Roberts (President Beyron Rurich), Michael Strong (Stephan Gomalk), Michael Fox (Dr. Levya), Peter Coe (Kramer), Aaron Fletcher (Professor William Bennett), Robert Karnes (Dr. Owen Siebert). *Unbilled:* Helen Boll (Nurse), Joe Ryan (Policeman), Alan Bleiweiss (Employee), Svea Grunfeld (Doctor), Arline Anderson (Clerk)

Pernell Roberts makes his first of several *Mission* appearances in "Operation—'Heart,'" his only sympathetic role. Another series stalwart, Michael Strong (Gomalk), would reappear later this season, in episode 43, "The Emerald." But it is Martin Landau who steals the show with three different impersonations, including a very funny masquerade as an uncontrollable, nasty old man in Bennett's hospital. Chased by a gaggle of flustered nurses, old man Hand terrorizes the hospital halls in his wheelchair, brandishing a cane and yelling, "No respect! No respect for the old! I demand a private room!" This pest does get a room of his own, where he becomes Doctor Hand, who leaves the room, warning his "patient" inside to behave as he emerges into the hallway.

32: THE SLAVE
(in two parts)

Written by: William Read Woodfield and
Allan Balter
Directed by: Lee H. Katzin
Music Composed and Conducted by:
Robert Drasnin

First Aired: 10/8/67; 10/15/67

TEAM: Phelps, Rollin, Cinnamon, Barney, Willy,
Akim Hadramut

Good morning, Mr. Phelps. As you know, for the past twenty years the United Nations has worked throughout the Near East to abolish slave markets. These efforts have been successful except in Elkabar, a small country on the Persian Gulf whose ruler, Ibn Borca, an absolute monarch, continues to auction thousands of human beings into slavery each year. Borca's principal source of slaves is this man, Karl de Groot. His raids into nearby nations to abduct free men and women into slavery could aggravate the tense situation in the Near East. Your mission, Jim, should you decide to accept it, is to stop this traffic in slaves and rid Elkabar of de Groot and Borca. As always, should you or any of your IM Force be caught or killed, the secretary will disavow any knowledge of your actions. This recording will self-destruct in five seconds. Good luck, Jim.

Barney, abducted in one of de Groot's raids, is jailed, photographs his cell, then escapes so the IMF can reconstruct an exact duplicate of the cell. Jim sells Cinnamon to de Groot and his partner, Jara, for Borca. Willy retrieves Cinnamon and apprehends de Groot. Jim tells Jara that he killed the cheating de Groot and will replace him as Jara's partner.

Willy abducts Amara, wife of the king's brother Fasar, who refuses to believe that slave trading exists in Elkabar. She is thrown into the IMF cell, where "Borca" (Rollin) tells her that she'll be sold at the next auction. Amara is sedated and made up to resemble Cinnamon. Jim delivers Cinnamon to Borca, who places her in a cell. Guards Barney and Willy ingeniously switch the unconscious Amara for Cinnamon. Interpol agent Rollin convinces Fasar that slavery still thrives in his country. They attend an auction, where a disguised Fasar sees his brother put Amara on the block. Fasar reveals himself, and Amara tells of the "king's" visit to her cell. Borca is killed, and Fasar takes over, declaring, "Slavery is abolished in Elkabar."

GUEST CAST: Joseph Ruskin (King Ibn Borca), Percy Rodriguez (Jara), Warren Stevens (Karl de Groot), Antoinette Bower (Amara), Steve Franken (Akim Hadramut), David Mauro (Prince Fasar), Sid Haig (Musha), Peter Lorre, Jr. (Kadi), Michael St. Clair (Shah). *Unbilled:* Socrates Ballis

(Sheikh), Jan Arvan (Auctioneer), Kanan Awni, George Sawaya, John Arndt, Josh Adams (Guards); Lee Duncan (Stunt); Dale Van Sickle, Stephanie Epper, Cary Loftin (Stunt Drivers)

Joseph Ruskin plays an oddly named trader in "The Slave."

123

"The Slave" is an entertaining and effective show but is rife with inaccuracies. Ibn Borca (translation: "son of a lady's veil"), Fasar ("to examine a urine specimen"), Jara, Musha, and Akim are not Arabic names. Barney, a jailed slave, is loaded with camera equipment beneath his robe, which evidently hasn't been searched. The biggest flaw concerns the way in which Willy abducts Amara from her bedroom one evening: bats, "frozen" in an airtight cylinder (!) are lowered into the bedroom fireplace. Once they thaw out, the bats disperse across the room, causing chaos and allowing Willy to break in and steal Amara away.

However illogical the scene may be, it certainly is compellingly done. Lee Katzin was Hitchcock's assistant director on *The Birds* (1963), and his experience came in handy on this show. "How do you shoot a bat attack? It was a challenge. I had three 'bats' on monofilament strings, and used an unusual lens to make them look as if they were flying into Antoinette Bower's face." At least, that's how it started. "We used parakeets," effects man Jonnie Burke reveals. "That's the closest I ever came to quitting. I was so mad that day. They clipped their tail feathers so they'd fly erratically. The trainer would dip the birds in a bucket of dye and put them in a cage. Parakeets are like canaries, one-lung animals, and they'd go into shock. None of them died, but I was so goddamn mad that I went to Bruce and Barry and said, 'Shove it, I didn't hire on to torture birds and animals. If this is the way the show is going, I don't want anything to do with it anymore.' " Antoinette Bower also complained. To keep the birds safe and easily wrangled, a chute and fan were placed behind the fireplace, and the set surrounded by nets to catch them. "They worked well as bats," Burke admits, "but those little boogers were just mad as hell at everything and everybody that day." An unpleasant experience to be sure, but an effective scene, as even the director admits. "The bat sequence is still as good a piece of film as any I've ever done, and as good an editing job as Paul Krasny ever did. He was the best editor I ever worked with."

One scene provided Barbara Bain with a challenge of her own. To make the switch between Cinnamon and Amara in the cell, Amara is stowed in the hollow bottom of a food carriage. In the cell, Amara is taken out and Cinnamon climbs in. Unfortunately, Barbara Bain is very claustrophobic, and it was quite an ordeal for her to climb into that tiny carriage and let the lid shut her in, even for the second or two the scene required. "She did it," says Katzin, "but she didn't want to. She couldn't stand being in phone booths or anything enclosed."

33: THE WIDOW

First Aired: 9/10/67

Written by: Barney Slater
Directed by: Lee H. Katzin
Music Composed and Conducted by:
   Gerald Fried

TEAM: Phelps, Rollin, Cinnamon, Barney, Willy, Dr. Premel

Good morning, Mr. Phelps. The man you're looking at is Alex Cresnic, one of the world's largest dealers in heroin. Recently, Cresnic made his biggest deal: He bought the entire heroin crop of an Asiatic country and smuggled it into Marseilles, where he plans to wholesale it to his major buyers. In order to get enough financing for such a big operation, Cresnic took in a partner. His name is Mark Walters, head of the numbers bank in Miami. The mission, Jim, should you decide to accept it, is to prevent Cresnic and Walters from selling their heroin, and put them out of business permanently. As always, should you or any of your IM Force be caught or killed, the secretary will disavow any knowledge of your actions. This recording will self-destruct in five seconds. Good luck, Jim.

Walters enters an elevator containing Phelps and Barney. At the thirteenth floor, the elevator suddenly stops and shudders. Then, as indicated by the digital counter and accompanying noises, it "plummets" toward the ground. Just before "impact," Walters is rendered unconscious and Barney shuts off the special effects which made the stationary elevator seem to fall. Walters awakens "blind" in a hospital and is told by Dr. Premel that his sightlessness is temporary. Rollin, mimicking Cresnic's voice, tells Walters that someone is out to get them. "Cresnic" gives him specific instructions to follow upon his release from the hospital.

Cresnic meets Walters's "widow," Cinnamon, whose talk of incriminating papers persuades him to accept her as his new partner. Just before his death, she claims, he was approached by a competitor—Rollin. Cresnic and his thugs burst in on Rollin's setup, which involves chemist Jim dyeing processed heroin to pass as bath crystals for easy exporting. Cresnic returns, "kills" guard Willy, and takes the drugs and Jim to process *his* heroin in the same clever manner. Hidden in the lining of Jim's jacket is a silent vacuum pump that sucks the heroin up one sleeve; out the other sleeve pours powdered milk identical in appearance to the heroin.

At the sale, Cresnic is paid, puts the money in his strongbox, and places it in the bottom of his desk (which has been secretly opened by the IMF from the basement). As per "Cresnic's" instructions, Walters, in the basement, takes the strongbox. Rollin breaks in and advises the buyers to check their merchandise; when they learn they've bought powdered milk, they demand repayment from Cresnic. Walters is discovered counting the cash and is shot; a moment later another shot is heard. Outside, Jim cracks to Cinnamon, "There aren't too many women who can claim to being widowed twice by the same man."

GUEST CAST: William Windom (Alex Cresnic), Joe Maross (Mark Walters), George Tyne (Dr. Premel), John Orchard (Maharis), Britt Lomond (Thornton). *Unbilled:* George Sawaya (Simms), Walt Davis (Beatty), Howard Beckler (Heroin Buyer)

Although not a superb episode, "The Widow" premiered the new season, most likely because it introduced new leader Phelps in as unobtrusive a way as possible: Like the final Briggs episodes, "The Widow" offers the head man little to do.

The heroin buyer faintly resembling Tony Bennett is director Katzin's lawyer Howard Beckler, now a well-known criminal attorney in Los Angeles. He's there just for fun. More inexplicable is the inclusion of a short scene from episode 14, "The Short Tail Spy" in which Cinnamon pensively paces her room, wondering whether to make a phone call. By the time of "The Widow," Barbara Bain's hair color was more platinum blonde than in the earlier show, so the sequence not only has no real purpose, it actually looks out of place.

Daily Variety's review for this opener was fairly inconclusive, noting that the show "was not up to the high standard set last season." Graves was considered "highly competent," however, so maybe "The Widow" accomplished its mission.

34: THE MONEY MACHINE

First Aired: 10/29/67

Written by: Richard M. Sakal
Directed by: Paul Stanley

TEAM: Phelps, Rollin, Cinnamon, Barney

Good afternoon, Mr. Phelps. The man you're looking at is Walter DuBruis, the most unscrupulous financier in Africa. DuBruis's brokerage firm is in Ghalea, a small African nation whose pro-Western government is the key to stability in the area. Last week, a shipment of paper used to make Ghalean currency was hijacked by this man, a counterfeiter, Raf Tagoor. We believe Tagoor has made a deal with DuBruis to pass the counterfeit money, which would wreck the Ghalean economy. Because DuBruis is powerful and influential, he cannot be arrested on suspicion alone. Your mission, Jim, should you decide to accept it, is to recover the paper and put DuBruis out of business . . . permanently. As always, should you or any of your IM Force be caught or killed, the secretary will disavow any knowledge of your actions. Please destroy this tape in the usual manner. Good luck, Jim.

DuBruis is intrigued when Cinnamon walks into his brokerage firm and tried to corner the market on Ambuli Copper, a heretofore dormant property. Desperate to get DuBruis to relax the margin required on stock purchases, Cinnamon admits that her husband, an Ambuli mining engineer, has found a fabulous new copper vein. When this news is reported in two days, Ambuli Copper will be worth millions. A teletype (patched in via Barney) confirms her story, and DuBruis decides to start buying Ambuli Copper not for Cinnamon but for *himself*.

Rollin buys fifty-seven thousand dollars worth of unrelated stock through DuBruis, pays him in cash, then suffers an epiletic seizure. Searching his pockets for an address, DuBruis finds that Rollin entered the country with less than five hundred dollars, and that the fifty-seven thousand dollars is phony. Rollin leads DuBruis to his source: a high-speed computer copier located in a truck and manned by Phelps. DuBruis, who needs eight million dollars to buy out Ambuli, finds a way to come up with the cash: "Three million of my own, and five million I make today!" DuBruis provides the paper and watches the money machine produce "perfect" Ghalean currency. He is unaware of the machine's secret ingredient: Barney, who, hidden inside, takes DuBruis's paper and feeds out "special" currency.

DuBruis greedily buys out Ambuli Copper, a fact which does not escape the notice of Finance Minister Giroux, who demands to see DuBruis's cash. DuBruis smugly reaches into his suitcase, but instead of removing crisp new currency, he removes handfuls of smeared, useless paper. DuBruis is left with eight million dollars worth of stock he cannot pay for, and the IMF drives off with the real Ghalean paper.

GUEST CAST: Brock Peters (Walter DuBruis), Michael Shillo (Raf Tagoor), Davis Roberts (Anton Bouchet), Rockne Tarkington (Paul Giroux). *Unbilled:* John Copage (Valet), Lee Duncan (Stunt), Tom Steel (Epileptic Stunt)

DuBruis falls for one of the oldest cons in the book, "the money box," jazzed up computer-style by the IMF.

Curiously enough, in early 1988, several American banks accepted checks coated with a chemical which, like DuBruis's money, made the paper deteriorate in a matter of hours. "In a few days," reported *Time* magazine, "they were little more than confetti." Said a Chicago police captain investigating the case, "It's like something out of a James Bond movie."

Almost.

35: THE SEAL

Written by: William Read Woodfield and Allan Balter
Directed by: Alexander Singer
Set Decorator: Steve Potter

First Aired: 11/5/67

TEAM: Phelps, Rollin, Cinnamon, Barney, Willy

Good morning, Mr. Phelps. For the past twenty-five years this country has depended on the friendship of Kuala Rokat, a small but strategic nation on the China-India border. This is the imperial seal of Kuala Rokat: a priceless, two-thousand-year-old jade figure on a golden rope. Two weeks ago it turned up in the art collection of the famous American industrialist J. Richard Taggart. Yesterday our government, on behalf of Kuala Rokat, requested that Taggart return the stolen jade to its rightful owners, who regard the seal as sacred. Taggart has refused and there appears to be no legal way he can be compelled to do so, despite the fact that his refusal will undo years of diplomacy and drive Kuala Rokat into the Communist camp. Your mission, Jim, should you decide to accept it, is to get the imperial seal so that it may be returned to Kuala Rokat. As always, should you or any of your IM Force be caught or killed, the secretary will disavow any knowledge of your actions. Please destroy this tape in the usual manner. Good luck, Jim.

The seal is in a display case in Taggart's private penthouse gallery. The entrance is charged with 500 volts of electricity; its interior equipped with highly sensitive sonic detectors and pressure alarms beneath the floor.

Phelps fouls a Taggart Industries computer, requiring Willy to deliver a replacement containing

Rusty the cat burglar steals "The Seal," literally and figuratively.

Barney and a trained cat named Rusty. Jim, Barney, and the cat enter Taggart's offices via the elevator shaft. TV reporter Cinnamon interviews Taggart and examines the jade. She tells him something he doesn't know about the treasure: "Anyone who keeps the jade seal from its holy place in Kuala Rokat will die within a fortnight, which means that you have about six hours to live." Taggart laughs it off, but Cinnamon decides to stay until Taggart's time is up. She invites a professor from Kuala Rokat (Rollin), who confirms the curse.

Using magic as a distraction, Rollin enters the gallery and is "electrocuted." To save his life, Security Chief Conway must shut down the system—long enough for Barney to carve a hole in the gallery wall and install a miniature catwalk for Rusty, who strolls down the walkway, opens the display case, steals the jade, and brings it to Barney. Taggart, having survived his two weeks of ownership, is smug. But Cinnamon advises him to check the jade, then quickly exits as Taggart discovers the theft.

GUEST CAST: Darren McGavin (J. Richard Taggart), Mort Mills (William Conway), Joan Tompkins (Miss Putnam), Russ Bender (Duty Guard), Pete Kellett (Guard). *Unbilled:* Eric Cooper (Attendant)

"The Seal" may be the only *Mission* ever built around a specific star: Rhubarb, a remarkable feline owned by animal trainer Frank Inn. "On command the cat opened a lady's purse and removed a string of pearls, turned on the television set, and did other stunts," said Allan Balter at the time. "So our problem was to write a story using the cat's skill logically—that is, having him help our stars by doing things that humans could not do." Says William Read Woodfield, "The Seal of Koala Rokat was made with a little handle exactly like the string of pearls. That was that."

Well, not exactly. "When I read the script," director Alex Singer relates, "I observed that it would take at least one day of work with the cat. It took *three* days of second unit work and *four* cats, who were very very hungry! It was the hardest thing that I was ever involved in shooting. The scene was pasted together with some sequences that were one second long."

"We made cards for every cut," says Joe Gantman of the editing, "and we started shuffling the cards around, moving them because it was just too much to move the film, even for an editor like Bob Swanson, who was very fast with a moviola. It was not easy to put together." The scene works beautifully, in the oddly compelling way that the best *Mission* sequences have. It might sound or read silly, but *seeing* the cat open the display case, grab the seal's handle in his mouth, and drag it down the metal walkway to Barney is the convincer. Shot from various angles and intercut with anxious reaction shots of Phelps and Barney, the scene works like a charm and is one of *Mission*'s most famous moments. *Daily Variety* raved about the show in its review of November 7, 1967, calling it, "loaded with suspense and tension," and "executed with finesse and intelligence."

"The Seal" of Kuala Rokat.

36: CHARITY

First Aired: 11/12/67

Written by: Barney Slater
Directed by: Marc Daniels

TEAM: Phelps, Rollin, Cinnamon, Barney, Willy

Good morning, Mr. Phelps. The man you're looking at is Erik Hagar who for years has collected vast sums of money supposedly for charity, most of which he keeps for himself. He steals from the sick, the hungry, the destitute. Hagar's partner in these despicable activities is his wife, Catherine. The latest fraud of the Hagars is the collection of one million dollars which is supposed to build a new hospital wing. To get this money, the Hagars have invited a group of millionaires to spend the weekend on the estate in Montaigne on the French-Italian border. The mission, should you decide to accept it, is to recover the millions which Hagar and his wife have stolen from the needy, and put a stop to their charity racket for good. As always, should you or any of your IM Force be caught or killed, the secretary will disavow any knowledge of your actions. This recording will self-destruct in ten seconds. Good luck, Jim.

The Hagars employ a blind child in their attempt to wring donations from their houseful of millionaires. The Hagar fortune, almost two million dollars, is in the form of platinum bricks hidden in the base of a pool table on the estate.

Jim poses as a gigolo supposedly hired by Hagar to keep Catherine occupied for the weekend, while wealthy invalid Cinnamon does the same with Hagar. From the basement, Barney tunnels into the pool table and steals the platinum, replacing the bricks with an inflatable facsimile.

Hit man Rollin tries to kill Hagar, ostensibly on orders from Catherine, but makes a deal with Hagar to kill her instead. When Rollin's "attempt" fails, Jim suggests to Catherine that Hagar was behind it. She decides to flee with the "platinum," which Phelps graciously places in his car trunk. Hagar spots them leaving and chases them to the

border. Jim and Catherine leave the country successfully, but Erik Hagar isn't so lucky: Unknown to him, his platinum has been melted down by Barney and Willy and attached to his car as the front grill and fender. Hagar is arrested attempting to smuggle the precious metal out of the country while Catherine learns she's been duped by Jim. "I believed you," she tells Phelps. "Those little blind children believed you," says Jim.

GUEST CAST: Fritz Weaver (Erik Hagar), Hazel Court (Catherine Hagar), J. P. Burns (Mr. Beruch), Lilyan Chauvan (Mrs. Beruch), Jean Del Val (Mr. Wolf), Linda Sue Risk (Renee). *Unbilled:* Arline Anderson (Mrs. Kreuger), Roger Til (Butler), Don Gazzaniga (Guard)

"Charity" has more of a human touch than usual and is leisurely paced. The Hagars are not threats to the free world, but are totally devoid of ethics. Their racket is so abhorrent that it's easy to dislike them.

"Charity" is a satisfying, lightweight show—a milk run compared to upcoming episodes.

37: THE COUNCIL
   (in two parts)

Written by: William Read Woodfield and
   Allan Balter
Directed by: Paul Stanley
Music Composed and Conducted by:
   Jerry Fielding

First Aired: 11/19/67; 11/26/67

TEAM: Phelps; Rollin; Cinnamon; Barney; Willy;
   Dr. Emerson Reese, plastic surgeon

Good morning, Mr. Phelps. The man you're looking at is Frank Wayne, head of the Syndicate, number one man in the vast criminal empire that is corrupting our nation's economy. Wayne has not been content with merely running the rackets and controlling vice and gambling, but has taken over dozens of other heretofore honest businesses. Recently, Wayne launched a system whereby the Syndicate's annual income, now over ten billion dollars, is being deposited in Swiss banks, causing an intolerable drain on US gold reserves. Your mission, should you decide to accept it, is to get the Syndicate's records, which are kept at Wayne's country estate, and see that they are turned over to the proper authorities, and put an end to Frank Wayne and his organization. As always, if you or any of your IM Force should be caught or killed, the secretary will disavow any knowledge of your actions. This recording will self-destruct in five seconds. Good luck, Jim.

Harassment from special investigator Phelps forces Wayne to move his records to the Syndicate's office headquarters. Jim and Barney subpoena Wayne and brutally grill him in a hotel room while Rollin studies Wayne in a two-way mirror. Jim takes a break, Wayne "overpowers" Barney and calls his partners for help. Rollin, as Wayne, drops the crook and replaces him. When Wayne's hoods arrive, "Wayne" "kills" Barney and returns to his office, where he is pressured to leave the country. But "Wayne" has a better idea: He calls plastic surgeon Cinnamon, who performs a total facelift, giving "Wayne" a new face—that of Rollin Hand.

"Wayne" takes it upon himself to order Phelps's murder, an act strictly forbidden unless approved by the council, the Syndicate's ruling members. As Jim is "killed" across town, Rollin cracks the office

safe and photographs the Syndicate's financial records.

Phelps's "death" makes headlines. The council, fearing severe federal reprisal, confronts "Wayne," who becomes arrogant and power mad. "Wayne" is condemned to death, and Rollin runs. A mob killer catches him and does his job, killing the *real* Frank Wayne, who has been surgically altered to resemble Rollin.

GUEST CAST: Paul Stevens (Frank Wayne), Vincent Gardenia (Vito Lugana), Nick Colasanto (Jimmy Bibo), Paul Lambert (Al Morgan), Vic Perrin (Cheever), Joan Staley (Ginny), Stuart Nisbet (Dr. Emerson Reese), Robert Phillips (Johnny), Eduardo Ciannelli (Jack Rycher). *Unbilled:* Nelson Olmstead (Janitor)

" 'The Council' was a one-parter that started to get out of hand," says writer Bill Woodfield. "It got a little long." It was expanded by adding scenes involving Jimmy Bibo (Nick Colasanto), a disloyal mob courier who is given a death penalty by Wayne and his council. The sentence is carried out by Johnny, a hit man who makes Bibo literally dig his own grave. When Bibo pleads for mercy, Johnny viciously slams him in the midsection with the shovel, tosses him into the hole, and buries him alive, an act so cold that even the IMF, spying on the scene, react in shock. Jim and company are there to retrieve Bibo, who grew up with Wayne and can help Rollin impersonate him.

Rollin assembles a safecracking unit in "The Council" . . .

. . . while Phelps uses a false back to elude an assassin.

The first of *Mission*'s few backstage accidents occurred during the filming of "The Council." While setting up for the sequence in which Jim's car is dynamited on Paramount's New York street, something went wrong and the car exploded early. "The trunk lid of the car, cabled down so it wouldn't fly too far away, snapped the cable and landed next to the camera, half a block away," prop man Bill Bates vividly remembers. Says Peter Graves, "Boom! The fender went sailing past my ear and landed about fifty yards away. How nobody was hurt or killed, I don't know." As a result, the actual explosion isn't seen on screen. Responsibility for the blast was bounced around: from Barry Crane, who was pressuring the effects assistant to wire the car quickly so the shot could be filmed before lunch, to head effects man Jonnie Burke, who finally took the blame. "If you're running the crew, you can't blame everybody," Burke admits. "You're getting the glory for doing the job, and you're responsible." The effects assistant who did the actual wiring, an alcoholic, was reassigned, ultimately fired, and was killed rigging another exploding car for a commercial a few years later.

Taking the clichés of the gangster genre and serving it up series style, Woodfield and Balter create the quintessential *Mission* mob story in "The Council," one of their best scripts. Frank Wayne (played by Paul Stevens but dubbed by Landau in a low, sinister voice throughout) is the archetypical mob boss, aided by two monosyllabic icebergs named Vito and Al. Freshening up the story is a wonderful variety of Woodfield and Balter shtick: Rollin's cracking of Wayne's safe, using a winchlike device which, mounted onto the safe door, pries the dial off the door; Jim's escape from the booby-trapped car (wearing a bracelike "false back," Jim enters the car, removes the phony back and slips into a manhole beneath the car!); Cinnamon's transformation of "Wayne" into Rollin by carefully removing Rollin's Wayne mask in segments; the final switch of Wayne for Rollin in parallel, moving elevators; and a half dozen other surprises.

The performances are perfectly suited to the show, the most striking of which is Robert Phillips's terrifying killer, Johnny. With a minimum of dialogue, Phillips infuses this secondary role with such malevolence and menace that his abrupt demise at the finale (dispatched by a cop) is somewhat disappointing. Before becoming an actor, Phillips was an undercover cop whose career was the basis of a TV series (*Tightrope,* starring Mike Connors). A friend of Balter and Woodfield, the part of Johnny was written for him and he made the most of it. Phillips, whose name was on the preliminary Emmy nomination ballot for Best Supporting Actor for "The Council," would make other *Mission* appearances, but would never be more hateful or frightening than he is here.

"The Council" was an unqualified success. Paul Stanley was nominated for a Directors Guild award for his work, and the two-parter was released as a movie in Europe, titled *Mission: Impossible vs. The Mob.*

38: ECHO OF YESTERDAY

First Aired: 12/10/67

Written by: Mann Rubin
Directed by: Leonard J. Horn

TEAM: Phelps, Rollin, Cinnamon, Willy, two movers

Good morning, Mr. Phelps. The man you're looking at is Colonel Marcus von Frank, who has led the recent resurgence of the neo-Nazis. Otto Kelmann, head of the largest munitions plant in all Europe, is preparing to turn over to von Frank complete control of his vast industrial empire. With such a huge financial base, there's no question that von Frank could become a second Adolf Hitler, fanatically dedicated to the overthrow of democracy wherever it exists. Your mission, Jim, should you decide to accept it, is to stop Kelmann and von Frank. As always, should you or any of your IM Force be caught or killed, the secretary will disavow any knowledge of your actions. This recording will self-destruct in five seconds. Good luck, Jim.

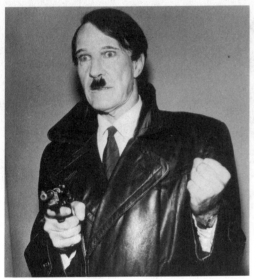

Martin Landau captures Adolf Hitler's madness in "Echo of Yesterday."

American Nazi leader Phelps arrives to learn from von Frank, while Cinnamon befriends the elderly Kelmann. The rich industrialist is beguiled by her resemblance to his late wife, who was murdered in 1932 by Adolf Hitler. Goaded by Jim, the paranoid von Frank distrusts and hates Cinnamon, despite Kelmann's assurances that she means no harm. Phelps uncovers evidence that Cinnamon is not what she claims to be, and convinces von Frank that she will destroy him.

In a drugged state, Kelmann vividly relives the murder of Mrs. Kelmann (Cinnamon) by Hitler (Rollin). When von Frank bursts in and "slays" Cinnamon in the same manner, Kelmann fatally shoots the new führer.

GUEST CAST: Wilfrid Hyde-White (Otto Kelmann), Hans Gudegast (Colonel Marcus von Frank), Richard Morrison (Karl), Gregory Mullavy (Heinz). *Unbilled:* George Weber (Stunt)

Mann Rubin's early preproduction draft did not involve the Hitler charade, and it is Kelmann who dies at the hand of von Frank, who then falls prey to a booby-trap while searching Kelmann's safe for the old man's will. It was Joe Gantman who, with the writer, developed the Hitler bit to make the show more visually dramatic. Martin Landau adds to his collection of Nazi villains the most horrendous of them all. "Physically I'm very different in terms of size," Landau notes. "I wanted that insanity, so I figured I'd play it in extremis. This woman [Cinnamon] was standing in the way of my cause, and had to be eliminated. It's logical. Now, taking that to the point of absurd fanaticism makes the guy nuts, and I wanted him to be nuts and yet to be totally sold on something so crazy, going way beyond the point of reasonableness." My Hitler wasn't a bad guy, he was just overzealous to the point where you

135

say, 'Wait a minute!' Just like the real guy, actually, who had to be passionate enough to convince sixty million Germans. If they saw the insanity in him, they never would have gone for it. The terrifying thing is that he was a good actor."

Peter Lupus, who played "Hitler's" bodyguard, recalls an unpleasant lunchtime incident. "We were in the first shot after lunch, and since it took a long time to get out of the boots and costume, Marty and I went to lunch in costume. We walked ten steps into the commissary and heard bloodcurdling screams!" The actors were unaware that some of the commissary staff were concentration camp survivors who'd lost family members to the Nazis. "The next day we covered the uniforms," says Lupus, "but that was the realism we had on the show. Every detail, right down to the pin, was right."

Director Leonard Horn adds interesting black-and-white subliminal cuts of "Mrs. Kelmann" (Barbara) during Cinnamon's scenes with Kelmann to foreshadow her eventual pose as the dead woman at the finale.

Desilu chief Herb Solow (center) visits Bain and Landau on the set of "Echo of Yesterday."

39: THE ASTROLOGER

First Aired: 12/3/67

Written by: James F. Griffith
Directed by: Lee H. Katzin

TEAM: Phelps, Rollin, Cinnamon, Barney, Willy

Good morning, Mr. Phelps. Nikolai Kurzon, in spite of his exile from Veyska by the military junta that took over the country, has continued to lead a popular movement to overthrow this dictatorship. We know that two days ago, Colonel Alex Stahl, head of the Veyskian secret police, seized Kurzon outside the country, but we don't know where. Kurzon had in his possession a frame of microfilm containing the names of Veyskian officials and leading citizens who support him. If Kurzon and the microfilm are returned to Veyska, it will result in the murder of these patriots and kill their chance to liberate the country. Your mission, Jim, should you decide to accept it, is to rescue Nikolai Kurzon and make sure that microfilm does not get to Veyska. As always, if you or any of your IM Force should be caught or killed, the secretary will disavow any knowledge of your actions. Please destroy this tape in the usual manner. Good luck, Jim.

On his way back to Veyska by air, Deputy Chancellor Grigov is to pick up rival Stahl and the unconscious Kurzon. Before boarding, Grigov meets world-famous astrologer Cinnamon, who warns him that Veyska's chancellor is in dire peril. Grigov speaks to the chancellor (Rollin) over the phone just as an assassination attempt is made. Thanks to Cinnamon's warning, the "chancellor" survives, and Rollin requests her to accompany Grigov back to Veyska.

Rollin and Barney stow away in the baggage room of the plane, just below the conference room. The plane lands to pick up Stahl and Kurzon. Stahl places an envelope containing the microfilm into the conference room's wall safe, and Kurzon is placed in a separate compartment, guarded by Grigov's assistant Trubner. During takeoff, while the passengers remain seated, Rollin cracks the safe, takes the microfilm, and replaces it with a bogus list naming Grigov as one of the state's enemies. Cinnamon's astrology charts convince Gri-

gov that Stahl is plotting against him, and vice versa. Grigov finds his name on the microfilm and accuses Stahl of framing him. Stahl, believing the list to be real, places both Grigov and Trubner under arrest, leaving Kurzon unattended.

As the plane approaches Veyska, Barney and Rollin take Kurzon and put him in a storage trunk. They replace him with an automated double, which they place by the emergency door. On cue, the dummy triggers an alarm and, before Stahl's eyes, opens the door to be sucked out to his "death." Landing in Veyska, Official Phelps takes Cinnamon to meet the chancellor, while Willy and Rollin remove two large trunks: one containing Barney, the other Nikolai Kurzon.

GUEST CAST: Steve Ihnat (Colonel Alex Stahl), David Hurst (Victor Grigov), Bob Tiedemann (Nikolai Kurzon), Ed McCready (Steward), Barbara Bishop (Hostess), Don Hanmer (Trubner)

"The Astrologer" proves that *Mission* need not be exorbitantly expensive in order to be entertaining. Seventy-five percent of the show takes place in a cramped airliner, which offers our heroes no way to escape should something go wrong and actually intensifies the suspense.

Writer Griffith consulted with noted astrologer Sydney Omarr on the technical end of the script. "I determined the personality traits," says Griffith, "and he determined the astrological signs that would match those traits. He was intrigued by the show. The first time we sat down together, he asked me my astrological sign. Then he did a trip on me about my career background, and what I was going to be doing in the future. It blew my mind because he was right on about the past, and the future turned out to be pretty accurate, too. I always thought that astrology was a lot of bunk, but he did astound me with the things he told me about myself. I gained a new respect for astrology through my interaction with him."

Rollin uses a complex phone-tapper in "The Astrologer."

40: THE PHOTOGRAPHER

First Aired: 12/17/67

Written by: William Read Woodfield and Allan Balter
Directed by: Lee H. Katzin
Special Still Photography by: Bob Willoughby

TEAM: Phelps, Rollin, Cinnamon, Barney, Willy

Good morning, Mr. Phelps. The man you're looking at is David Redding, one of the top photographers in the country. He is also the contact for a spy apparatus that has secretly brought 150 agents into the United States over the past few months. Yesterday one of the agents was picked up. We have not been able to get any information from him, except that they carry deadly pneumonic plague bacillus which is to be released on our population within seventy-two hours. We have dozens of coded messages in and out of Redding's headquarters which we are certain locate and identify the agents. However, we have so far been unable to break Redding's code. Your mission, should you decide to accept it, is to get the key to the code so we can pick up those agents before it's too late. As always, if you or any of your IM Force should be caught or killed, the secretary will disavow any knowledge of your actions. This recording will self-destruct in five seconds. Good luck, Jim.

Redding and his assistant Morley operate from a bomb shelter beneath Redding's estate, located about twenty-five miles from New York City.

Elite magazine hires Redding to do a layout on former cover girl Cinnamon Carter Crawford, now a biochemist working for the government. Redding manages to photograph one of Cinnamon's formulas—for eosin methylthionine chloride, the culture medium supporting the deadly bacillus. Redding tortures Cinnamon's "husband," Phelps, until she admits that the US is planning a nuclear strike against Redding's country. Redding and Morley reason that if New York were wiped out by a missile before the US strike, Washington would retaliate against the Russians or Chinese, leaving *their* country as a surviving power. Jim and Cinnamon are "killed," and the news radioed (but blocked by Barney's parabolic antennae).

Expecting an attack on New York within an hour, Redding and Morley's attempt to leave is thwarted by federal agents Rollin and Willy, who arrest them for espionage and plan to take them to New York's Court Building. Frantic, the pair lead the agents to the bomb shelter, where Willy is "killed" and Rollin held at gunpoint. Redding's radio blares emergency warnings, the shelter shudders violently, and the air gets searingly hot for a few moments. Through the shelter's periscope, Redding views the nuclear wasteland above, then telegraphs another coded message to his country (again, blocked by the IMF). Awaiting a response, Redding lays out the complex code system, not bothering to hide it from Rollin, who watches every step. Rollin grabs the paperwork, opens the door, and exits, ignoring the "bullets" fired at him. Following him out, Redding and Morley are shocked to learn that their firearms have been loaded with blanks; that contact with their country has been jammed; and that the nuclear devastation they witnessed is in fact a 360-degree cyclorama built around the periscope by the IMF.

GUEST CAST: Anthony Zerbe (David Redding), John Randolph (Alex Morley), Kathleen Hughes (Fran Williams), Ludmila (Mandy). *Unbilled:* Josh Adams (Young Man)

The germ behind "The Photographer" wasn't the apocalypse con, rendered here for the first time, but rather the search for a new kind of villain, one "that hasn't been done to death," says Woodfield. He and partner Balter decided upon the child of Julius and Ethel Rosenberg, who were convicted of treason and executed in this country in 1953. David Redding (played masterfully by Anthony Zerbe in his first of five *Mission*s) is the son of an American scientist

139

similarly executed for treason, and he has vowed to make the US pay. At the end of the show he learns, from Phelps, that if his father was indeed wrongfully executed, it was because he was framed by his best friend, Redding's partner, Morley.

The end-of-the-world con proved to be so irresistible that it was repeated often, with minor variations, in later seasons. As Woodfield points out, *"We* never did it again."

No one survived more "shootings" than the IMF, as exemplified in "The Photographer."

Year Two: 1967–1968

41: THE SPY

Written by: Barney Slater
Directed by: Paul Stanley

First Aired: 1/7/68

TEAM: Phelps, Rollin, Cinnamon, Barney, Willy

Good morning, Mr. Phelps. A secret detailed map of NATO's missile defense system was recently prepared on two overlays, neither of which is complete without the other. They were sent by separate couriers to a meeting between NATO and one of Europe's small, uncommitted nations. Felicia Vabar, a member of an enemy spy apparatus, had one of the couriers intercepted, and the overlay he was carrying stolen. To get the other, she has recruited Captain Miklos Cherno, an internal security officer of the country where the conference was being held. Your mission, should you decide to accept it, is to prevent Miss Vabar from getting the second overlay, without which the first is useless. As always, should you or any of your IM Force be caught or killed, the secretary will disavow any knowledge of your actions. This recording will self-destruct in five seconds. Good luck, Jim.

The remaining overlay is locked in a special vault room at military headquarters. With Cherno's help, Felicia will penetrate the room during an air raid drill and steal the overlay at exactly 10:35 A.M.

Ten minutes before Felicia's scheduled raid, Barney sets off an air raid siren. Jim enters the vault room, cracks the safe, photographs the overlay, and fires it in a projectile out a window to Rollin, who comandeers Felicia's car to escape. Phelps is captured by Cherno, whose attempts to get him to talk are useless (Jim has been given a posthypnotic suggestion by Rollin to keep him silent until an attempt is made to kill him). Rollin deliberately drops the film cartridge out the car window. Cinnamon retrieves it and forges a phony overlay from it.

Felicia offers to buy the film from Rollin, who arranges to meet her at a deserted warehouse.

American embassy official Cinnamon visits Colonel Dubov with data concerning the location of the stolen overlay. Meanwhile, Cherno's attempt to kill Phelps finally forces Jim to "cooperate."

Hidden in the warehouse shadows, Cinnamon and Dubov watch as Jim and Cherno enter. Cherno takes the overlay from Rollin, who escapes. On schedule, Felicia enters and buys the overlay from Cherno. She then shoots him in the back before *she* is killed by Dubov.

GUEST CAST: Joseph Campanella (Captain Miklos Cherno), Kate Woodville (Felicia Vabar), Karl Swenson (Colonel Dubov), Edward Knight (Nikos), Dehl Berti (Makar), Walter Alzman (Arno), Nikita Knatz (Sergeant), George Sperdakos (Lieutenant Dreis). *Unbilled:* George Wilbur (Stunt)

Phelps employs an unusual technique to crack the vault. Two *V* belt drive wheels, one attached to a tiny motor, are applied to the vault door, one wheel fitting over the combination dial. By hooking a belt between the wheels and turning on the motor, he sets the dial spinning to a very high rpm. Then, he uses a pointed tool to cut through the spinning dial.

Much of the show concerns the interplay between Rollin and the treacherous Felicia, who tries unsuccessfully to use her considerable sex appeal to get him to hand over the overlay. At the finale, when the heavies have been liquidated and almost everyone has gone, Rollin stares down at the fallen Felicia ambiguously. Is it a look of regret or sorrow? It's impossible to tell, but according to Landau, "There was a lot going on there. It could even be Rollin thinking, 'That could be me down there.'"

"The Spy" introduces two significant firsts for the series. Barney appears quite nonchalantly as a military officer in this episode's obviously East European country and attracts absolutely no suspicion whatsoever. The second detail appears at the very end of the show and would have profound effects on *Mission* within a very short time: the logo of Paramount Television, replacing Desilu forever.

141

42: A GAME OF CHESS

First Aired: 1/14/68

Written by: Richard M. Sakal
Directed by: Alf Kjellin

TEAM: Phelps, Rollin, Cinnamon, Barney, Willy

Good morning, Mr. Phelps. Two weeks ago, one million dollars in gold bullion intended for the underground in one of the anti-western satellites was intercepted by that government's military police. Preparations are now being made to ship the gold behind the Iron Curtain. This loss to the resistance movement will set back for years any chance for liberty in that country. The man you're looking at is Nicholas Groat, whose reputation as a brilliant chess master has given him entry and enabled him to con and steal on an international scale. Groat has organized a group which plans to steal the gold for itself before it is shipped out of the country. Your mission, Jim, should you decide to accept it, is to stop Groat, get the gold, and turn it over to the underground. As always, should you or any of your IM Force be caught or killed, the secretary will disavow any knowledge of your actions. This tape will self-destruct in ten seconds. Good luck, Jim.

Groat guts the bank in which the gold was to be stored, forcing it to be placed in a vault at the hotel where a chess tournament, attended by Groat and Rollin, is held.

Groat has the combination to the vault door but is distressed to learn that, for extra security, a time lock has been installed. He loses his match to Rollin, then learns that his opponent is using a computer and hearing aid to win. Groat gets Rollin to demonstrate the computer, which wildly accelerates Groat's watch, giving him an idea: He can use the computer to cancel out the time lock. Groat makes a deal with Rollin and his four aides to steal the gold and get it past the scores of soldiers protecting it. Rollin agrees on the condition that *he* call the shots.

Barney saturates the hotel water supply with a drug, then "collapses" in the lobby, a victim of what Dr. Phelps diagnoses as typhoid. Jim quarantines the hotel and calls the health department. Others in the hotel fall ill. Dr. Hand "inoculates" everyone, starting with the soldiers. Soon the entire hotel is immobilized, its inhabitants asleep from the shots.

The IMF computer speeds up the clock in the time lock, and Groat opens the door, at which point the Force takes the gold at gunpoint, locking Groat in the vault.

GUEST CAST: Don Francks (Nicholas Groat), Curt Lowens (Captain Stevya), Lou Robb (Clerk), Jason Johnson (Referee), Will J. White (Sergeant), Michael Guarini (Opponent), William Wintersole (Mueller)

With its emphasis on small rooms, a hotel lobby, and backlot streets, "A Game of Chess" was one of the season's more economical outings, with a simplistic story and execution.

Barney's dream machine this time is an "unbeatable" computer. Of course, a computer is only as good as its programmer, and even if the world's greatest chess master programmed the computer, it could still lose because the chess master can lose. Other, even more omnipotent devices would follow in later seasons.

43: THE EMERALD

Written by: William Read Woodfield and
Allan Balter
Directed by: Michael O'Herlihy

First Aired: 1/21/68

TEAM: Phelps, Rollin, Cinnamon, Barney, Willy

Good morning, Mr. Phelps. Details of a plan by an unfriendly country to force devaluation of US currency were concealed by one of our agents on this forty-one-karat emerald for transit to us. This is Victor Tomar, an international arms dealer who sells to anyone. By mistake the emerald has fallen into his possession. Without question, if he becomes aware of the information on the stone, he will use it to his own advantage. The day after tomorrow Tomar, with the emerald, will board the S.S. Queen of Suez at Beicosia, en route to Tangiers. Also aboard the ship will be Yorgi Petrosian, a totally ruthless Red agent. His orders are to get the details of the plan any way he can. Your mission, Jim, should you decide to accept it, is to get the emerald and dispose of Petrosian. As always, should you or any of your IM Force be caught or killed, the secretary will disavow any knowledge of your actions. This tape will self-destruct in ten seconds. Good luck, Jim.

The IMF board the *Queen of Suez*, armed with a duplicate emerald and a computerized gaming tabletop with built-in sensors to "read" playing cards and identify them via a transmitter hidden in Phelps's eyeglasses.

Card shark Rollin engages Petrosian's interest, and together they plot to sting Tomar. "I take the gem," says Petrosian, "the cash is yours." Rollin, whose expertise is helped by a card feeder attached to his arm, agrees.

That night at the tables, Cinnamon becomes suicidal over the loss of her expensive bracelet to Phelps. Tomar offers to win back the bracelet in return for later favors. In the ensuing game, Tomar, holding four aces, antes up the gem and promptly loses it to Petrosian (as prearranged with Rollin). Then Rollin double-crosses Petrosian by beating him, leaving the table with the cash *and* the emerald.

Petrosian attempts to shoot Rollin on the ship's empty deck but is overwhelmed by Willy, then

made to believe he's been thrown overboard. Willy kayos Petrosian and drags him away as Rollin yells, "Man overboard!"

Petrosian comes to in Rollin's room (disguised as a trawler) and "wires" a message to his aide Williams, on the *Suez*, telling him to get the gem and kill Rollin. Petrosian passes out again and Rollin applies a Rollin mask to Petrosian. Then the team clears out as Williams sneaks into Rollin's room, steals the (duplicate) gem and shoots "Rollin," dumping the body overboard.

GUEST CAST: William Smithers (Victor Tomar), Michael Strong (Yorgi Petrosian), Claude Woolman (Williams), Francisco Ortego (Joshu), Jacques Denbeaux (Steward), A. G. Vitanza (Purser), Albert Carrier (Captain). *Unbilled:* Robert Ondean (Porter); George Sawaya, Walter Linden, Tom Curtis, Josh Adams, Albert d'Arno, Phillip de Firmian (Poker Players)

Variations on old themes abound in "The Emerald," which is basically an extension of episode 5, "Odds on Evil." Joe Gantman felt it was time for another gambling show, and writers Balter and Woodfield chose poker as the game. Says Woodfield, "How do you make a poker game interesting? You need a guy [Petrosian] who's willing to take an edge. How do you get rid of a body on a boat? It seemed that throwing one of our people [Petrosian as Rollin] into the ocean was an interesting idea. So you throw him over the side. See, you start filling in shtick." Unfortunately, the script is so meticulously well planned that there is never an element of danger to concern the IMF (or us).

The close-ups of Rollin's hands during his card trickery feature the hands of actor-magician Tony Giorgio, who was often called in as special consultant for the show. Giorgio also appeared in several episodes, most notably episodes 65, "The System," and 107, "My Friend, My Enemy."

Cinnamon's necklace is the bait in "The Emerald."

44: THE CONDEMNED

Written by: Laurence Heath
Directed by: Alf Kjellin

First Aired: 1/28/68

TEAM: Phelps, Rollin, Barney, Willy

In a departure from the series format, Phelps calls upon the IMF to save the life of a friend, sentenced to death for a murder he didn't commit.

David Webster is the victim of a perfect frame. Lured by girlfriend Louisa to the home of a George Corley, he finds an unrecognizable corpse. Louisa plants the murder weapon in Webster's car, and he is convicted of Corley's murder. With less than a day to prevent his friend's execution and uncover the real murderer, Jim summons the IMF.

Priests Rollin and Willy visit Webster in his cell. Under Willy's robe is a collapsible, lightweight metal wall. Webster hides behind this facade, which exactly matches the actual cell wall. After the clergymen leave, it seems that Webster has vanished into thin air when in fact he hasn't left his cell.

Searching Corley's home for clues, Jim encounters a man named Constantine who financed Corley's theft of a ten million dollar crown from a Greek museum. Jim, posing as a private eye hired by Webster, agrees to "finger" Webster for Constantine, who assumes that Webster killed Corley for the crown.

"Webster" (Rollin) breaks in on Louisa and demands the identity of her partner in the frame. "Police sirens" chase "Webster" away, and Louisa runs to her partner's hideout, tailed by Jim and Willy. Louisa's partner, Arthur Warner, shoots her, but in attempting to kill Phelps, he falls from a staircase and is killed. Before dying, Louisa reveals that Warner is really George Corley, after preliminary plastic surgery. Corley killed the unrecognizable man found in his home and framed Webster for the murder of "Corley."

Insurance man Phelps informs the police officer in charge of the case that he is offering one million dollars for the return of the crown, in the hopes of smoking out Webster and the crown (already discovered by the IMF in Corley's hideout). Monitored by the police and Constantine, Jim gets a call from "Corley" (Rollin) and arranges to buy the crown on a lonely mountain road. Constantine goes to the meeting instead of Jim to retrieve the crown and kill "Corley."

At the meeting, "Corley" slugs Constantine and speeds off. As the police follow, Rollin stops his car at a blind curve, places Corley's corpse behind the wheel, and joins Barney who, by remote control, sends the car over a cliff, where it bursts into flames. The police recover the crown from the car, hidden in a crushproof, fireproof IMF sphere. Police Captain Barrera, having seen "Corley" "die" in the crash, realizes that Webster is innocent. Jim then "beeps" Webster, who emerges from the false wall in his cell and astounds the duty guard by asking for a pack of cigarettes, adding, "I seem to have . . . run out."

GUEST CAST: Marianna Hill (Louisa Rojas), Peter Donat (Arthur Warner), Kevin Hagen (David Webster), Nate Esformes (Captain Vicente Barrera), Will Kuluva (Edmund Constantine), Steve Marlo (Diego), Jon Cedar (George Corley), Phil Donati (Officer), Keith McConnell (Tom). *Unbilled:* Tom Steel, Robert Hoy (Stunts)

Neat and efficient, "The Condemned" offers a different sort of *Mission* puzzle. In addition to the usual, How-will-they-pull-it-off mystery, we wonder how the IMF can thwart what seems to be a foolproof setup. We also get a rare look at Jim Phelps's vulnerable side. Gathering his three operatives, he seems insecure.

PHELPS: The only thing at stake here is one man's life. He happens to be a friend of mine. We'll be improvising all along the way, according to what—

WILLY: Jim, I—

PHELPS: No, Willy, let me finish, please. This problem is purely personal. It's mine. None of you has to get involved at all.

BARNEY: Are you finished now?

PHELPS: Yes.

ROLLIN: Good. Jim, not often, but sometimes you talk too much.

As usual, there are implausibles. The crew convenes in Spain in a very short span of time, and one does wonder where Willy found that collapsible wall so quickly. Minor discrepancies like these, however, never seriously detract from a good *Mission* with an irregular approach and nice personal touches. "The Condemned" fits the bill.

45: THE COUNTERFEITER

Written by: William Read Woodfield and
  Allan Balter
Directed by: Lee H. Katzin

First Aired: 2/4/68

TEAM: Phelps, Rollin, Cinnamon, Barney, Willy,
laser surgeon Dr. McConnell

Good afternoon, Mr. Phelps. Raymond Halder, owner of a chain of clinics, is also the head of the largest drug counterfeiting ring in the US. He is behind the sale of millions of dollars worth of drugs that not only are useless, but often kill. A new drug, Dilatrin, developed by Gant Pharmaceuticals, which could have saved thousands of victims of primary vascular disease, has been ineffective because Halder has flooded the market with worthless fakes. Gant is about to reissue the drug in a different form, in an attempt to beat the counterfeit problem. Your mission, should you decide to accept it, is to stop Halder before the new Dilatrin is put on the market. As always, should you or any of your IM Force be caught or killed, the secretary will disavow any knowledge of your actions. This tape will self-destruct in five seconds. Good luck, Jim.

Federal agent Phelps, detective Rollin, and cop Willy shut down Halder's drug factory, but Halder avoids arrest. Attending a Gant Pharmaceuticals meeting, Halder arranges a date with Cinnamon, a Gant employee in charge of preventing further Dilatrin imitations. Halder bribes Rollin to frame Cinnamon, then offers to save her if she reveals Gant's anticounterfeiting strategy.

An ultrasonic laser system operated by Willy makes Halder suffer symptoms of primary vascular disease. He ends up in one of his own clinics, where Dr. Barney prescribes Dilatrin—Halder's

version, that is. A terrified Halder admits to producing and selling the deadly fakes.

GUEST CAST: Edmond O'Brien (Raymond Halder), Frank Campanella (Eddie Burke), Noah Keen (Dr. McConnell), Roy Engel (Foreman), Joe Breen (Chauffeur), Jon Lormer (Charles Gant), Dave Armstrong (Patrolman), Aaron Fletcher (Doctor). *Unbilled:* Bob Board (Artist); Ron Rondell, Cal Brown (Stunts)

"The Counterfeiter" was based on a story by William Read Woodfield's wife, Lily, who'd wanted to write a *Mission* and had read about drug counterfeiting. Most of the story elements were worked out by Mrs. Woodfield and Gantman. To expedite matters, the story was scripted by Balter and Woodfield.

Director Lee Katzin remembers this episode as the one bad experience he had on *Mission,* due to guest star Edmund O'Brien, who was quite ill during shooting. "There was a problem with his eyes," says Katzin. "He couldn't remember more than one line at a time and he became very testy. It was very difficult, because he was one of my all-time favorite actors." Luckily, since Halder is supposed to be ill during much of the show (thanks to an IMF laser which distorts his sense of gravity and causes headaches), the actor's problems are not readily evident. Nevertheless, this relatively inexpensive episode went a day over schedule.

147

46: THE TOWN

Written by: Sy Salkowitz
Directed by: Michael O'Herlihy

First Aired: 2/18/68

TEAM: Rollin, Cinnamon, Barney, Willy

In a departure from the series format, Phelps uncovers a townful of assassins who immobilize and plot to kill him.

On holiday and en route to meet Rollin at a mountain lodge, Jim stops in a quiet little town to have his car checked. While he enjoys a drink in the local drug store, a couple enter to pick up a package. The woman drops the package, activating a gas gun inside. Jim helps evacuate the place, and is taken at gunpoint to an old man named Doc, who runs the townful of enemy agents posing as small-town dwellers. Jim learns the details of their plot to murder a Soviet defector in Los Angeles. Doc shoots Jim with curare, leaving him conscious but unable to speak or move. The young couple head for Los Angeles, intent on murdering the defector Mosnyevov.

Rollin, searching the area for Phelps, learns from Doc that Jim has suffered a massive stroke, is too weak to be moved, and may have another, fatal attack. At Jim's bedside, Rollin notices that Phelps is sending an SOS by blinking his eyes. Rollin calls "Mrs. Phelps" (Cinnamon), who arrives in a limousine driven by Barney. When trucker Willy pulls into town, the IMF mobilize and attempt not only to stop the assassination, but escape from the town with Jim—and their lives.

GUEST CAST: Will Geer (Doc), Eddie Ryder (Williams), Brioni Farrell (Jan), Robert Pickering (Marty), Robyn Millan (Gina), William O'Connell (Instructor), Dee Carroll (Liz), Gregg Palmer (Deputy), George Perina (Mosnyevov), Glen C. Gordon (Desk Clerk)

"I think I have a terrific idea," writer Sy Salkowitz told Bruce Geller. After telling him the idea behind "The Town," Geller's immediate response was, "Go tell Joe right away." The original inspiration behind the story was a bizarre set, a huge mock-up of the inside of Phelps's head. Salkowitz's conception was, "That we saw the inside of his face in large proportions, and Phelps was in this 'room,' yelling out of his own mouth, running up and peering out of his eyes to see what was going on. Outside that mask he was drugged, with all the semblance of a stroke and he couldn't make a sound. I wanted to go inside that mask, I envisioned him yelling so the audience can hear him say, 'Rollin, I didn't have a stroke, I've been drugged, can't you hear me?' Yet nothing's coming out of his mouth, which I felt would be highly dramatic. Jim is not just caught, but caught inside his own brain." The first draft was written just this way, but the idea was vetoed on the grounds that it would be too expensive. "So what sparked the whole idea got lifted out, and we just did the show," says the writer, who was disappointed "because we had to depend upon old-fashioned techniques like getting close to his face and hearing his voice-over, but without that frenzied action on the inside, which I think would have been magnificent."

Because of its radical departure from type, this episode is one of *Mission*'s most famous "personal" episodes, with Phelps in genuine peril, and a concerned IMF, led by Rollin, improvising a way out. " 'The Town' is the nearest I ever got to getting people in *Mission: Impossible*," says director O'Herlihy of his final *Mission*. "I began to get bored with it, frankly, because you couldn't put humanity into it. I said, 'Bruce, do you mind if I don't do any more of these? There are no people in them!' He said, 'Well, that's how the show is.' I said, 'Why

the hell don't you round out the characters or something?' He said, 'Look, they are what they do.' And he was so right."

"The Town" posed little challenge to Peter Graves, who spends much of the show flat on his back, unable to move or speak. He remembers having a big lunch one day, returning to the set and climbing into bed for the next scene, involving Landau and guest Will Geer (Doc) at Phelps's bedside. It wasn't until after the scene was filmed that it was noticed that Graves had fallen asleep. "Sound asleep," Graves emphasizes. "I don't know if it was the chuckling I heard that woke me up, but there was Marty doubled up, and the whole crew behind the camera, laughing like hell!" Only in *Mission* could a leading man sleep through a scene without causing a disruption.

47: THE KILLING

Written by: William Read Woodfield and
   Allan Balter
Directed by: Lee H. Katzin

First Aired: 2/28/68

TEAM: Phelps, Rollin, Cinnamon, Barney, Willy

Good morning, Mr. Phelps. We recently learned that, in order to carry out the underworld's policy of enforcement, this man, Burt Gordon, has set up an organization similar to the old Murder, Inc. Gordon will arrange for the disposal of anyone, anywhere for a price. The victims always disappear with no evidence of foul play and the body is never recovered. Although we are sure Gordon is the man behind this murder ring, he has kept himself so far removed from the actual killings, we are unable to pin anything on him. Your mission, should you decide to accept it, is to prove Gordon is in fact a killer, and put him away for good. As always, should you or any of your IM Force be caught or killed, the secretary will disavow any knowledge of your actions. Please destroy this recording in the usual manner. Good luck, Jim.

Gordon accepts a dinner invitation from new neighbors Phelps and Cinnamon. Mysterious psychic phenomena disrupt the meal, which Jim's brother Rollin attributes to the ghost of a long-dead sibling. Later that evening, Cinnamon seduces Gordon and asks him to kill her "husband," Jim. He angrily refuses and goes home. Jim, aware of his wife's intentions, attacks Gordon, whose hit man Connie "fatally" stabs Jim, then disposes of the "corpse" in an incinerator.

The next evening Cinnamon rants to Gordon that Jim has returned from the dead. Gordon's house undergoes a series of "psychic" disturbances, and Jim's "ghost" appears in a mist to vow vengeance upon his killers. Cinnamon is struck "dead," and Gordon, terrified, grabs a shotgun. He follows Jim's eerily accusing voice to Phelps's body and fires. Gordon then watches in amazement as Jim's face miraculously dissolves, revealing *Connie* underneath. The police arrive and arrest Gordon for murder.

GUEST CAST: Gerald S. O'Laughlin (Burt Gordon), Roy Jenson (Connie). *Unbilled:* Walter Mathews (Lew); Lee Duncan, Stephanie Epper, Chuck Hicks (Stunts)

By far the best of *Mission*'s sporadic forays into the supernatural, "The Killing" works at maximum efficiency using the barest of material. Although the technical gadgetry is quite involved, the script is Balter and Woodfield's simplest, the cast the smallest ever required, and the reliance on performance heavier than normal. It is also one of the finest hours of the series.

The show's shtick includes a wealth of "spook" effects: the rigging of Gordon's home inside (cut electricity, flickering candles, hidden speakers for disembodied voices, etc.) and out (thunder and lightning machines hidden in the bushes); Jim's stabbing "murder" (he's wearing an IMF turtleneck, lined with eight layers of laminated nylon and backed by a fine chain mail, plus the obligatory fake blood); and Phelps's disposal in a lumber yard furnace (where Barney and Willy await outside the furnace's back door).

"'The Killing' was the best one I did," Lee Katzin feels, "the best story. A really black *Mission: Impossible*." It is a classically conceived and well-executed episode, and one of the most honored, with Emmy nominations for director Katzin and cameraman Michel Hugo.

"The Killing" garnered Emmy nominations for (from left) writer Woodfield, producer Gantman, writer Balter, actors Bain and Landau, and director Lee H. Katzin.

48: THE PHOENIX

Teleplay by: John D.F. Black
Story by: Edward DeBlasio and
    John D.F. Black
Directed by: Robert Totten

First Aired: 3/3/68

TEAM: Phelps, Rollin, Cinnamon, Barney, Willy

Good afternoon, Mr. Phelps. The party chairman of a small Iron Curtain country recently demoted this man, the infamous Stefan Prohosh, from his post as head of internal security and relegated him to the unimportant position of director of the People's Art Museum. In an attempt to regain power, Prohosh has had a sample of a highly secret alloy stolen from an experimental laboratory in Western Europe. The sample has been cleverly hidden in this massive modern sculpture, which arrives at the museum tomorrow. Prohosh hopes to trade this invaluable metal sample to one of the major Red nations for their support in his bid for power. Your mission, Jim, should you decide to accept it, is to recover the alloy and stop Prohosh. As always, should you or any of your IM Force be caught or killed, the secretary will disavow any knowledge of your actions. This tape will self-destruct in five seconds. Good luck, Jim.

Prohosh is directing the installation of the sculpture into the museum when a "bullet" nearly fells him. Rollin is arrested as culprit, and Prohosh calls the Internal Security Bureau (Barney), who dispatch Inspector Phelps and aides Willy and Barney. Jim deduces that Rollin had an accomplice, and a search yields Cinnamon hiding in the museum basement. After a long interrogation designed to keep Prohosh occupied, Cinnamon and Rollin explain that they wanted to kill Prohosh to avenge his slaughter of their entire village years ago.

Barney and Willy, "inspecting" the museum, dismantle the sculpture and find the metal alloy hidden inside. Barney takes it and plants an explosive inside the rebuilt piece just as the chairman arrives to view it. Jim discreetly detonates the explosive, and the chairman is unharmed. Amid the wreckage Jim "uncovers" a remote control device, the detonator of which is found in Prohosh's pocket. Our heroes exit immediately as Prohosh is dragged away.

GUEST CAST: Alf Kjellin (Stefan Prohosh), Scott Hale (Janos), Charles H. Radilac (Chairman), Peggy Rea (Cleaning Woman), Mills Watson (Guard #3). *Unbilled:* Charles Hovarth (Guard #1), Louis Massad (Relief Guard), Max Klevin (Guard #4), Norbert Siegfried (Guard #5)

In "The Phoenix," execution takes precedence over plotline. After the phony assassination attempt, the main goal is to keep Prohosh busy so he cannot interfere with Barney and Willy's dismantling job.

The sculpture, a stark modern piece consisting of long steel bars crisscrossing in a frenzy of directions, was "just a bunch of tubing all soldered together," director Bob Totten remembers. It's a perfect place in which to hide the cylindrical metal alloy.

Actor Alf Kjellin, who directed three *Mission*s this year, portrays Stefan Prohosh. Referring to himself by surname and uttering lines like, "It is much easier to explain too much caution than to bleed from not enough," and, "At a distance, be courageous; up close, be practical," he is one notch above a raving lunatic. His eye-popping paranoid antics easily rate him as the broadest acted and most obviously dangerous heavy on Phelps's hit list.

49: TRIAL BY FURY

Written by: Sy Salkowitz
Directed by: Leonard J. Horn
Director of Photography:
  Fred Koenekamp, ASC

First Aired: 3/10/68

TEAM: Phelps; Rollin; Cinnamon; Barney; Juan
  Mario Valesquez, Red Cross officer

Good afternoon, Mr. Phelps. Manuel Delgado, the patron saint of his country's freedom party, recently was sent to prison by the totalitarian regime now in power. To help Delgado continue to lead the resistance movement from behind bars, this man, Santos Cardoza, had himself arrested and imprisoned. Needing freedom of action in order to act as liaison, Cardoza managed to become a trustee. This has led to great danger for him, because the other convicts believe he is an informer, and Cardoza cannot reveal the true reason for his actions. Your mission, Jim, should you decide to accept it, is to expose the real informer and keep Cardoza alive so that he may continue to aid Delgado. As always, should you or any of your IM Force be caught or killed, the secretary will disavow any knowledge of your actions. This recording will self-destruct in five seconds. Good luck, Jim.

New prisoners Jim and Barney provoke a court-yard riot, and are deposited in Barracks G, which houses the meanest of the convicts. When a prisoner is killed during an escape attempt, the cons are convinced that Cardoza tipped off the *comandante*. Barney worries aloud that Cardoza may jeopardize *his* impending escape plan.

Red Cross officials Cinnamon and Valesquez examine the camp. They see a guard hand the *comandante* a tiny ball of tinfoil which, coded with strategically placed pinholes, informs the *comandante* that an escape is imminent. Unseen, Valesquez retrieves the foil from the trash and passes it to guard Rollin.

Cardoza is smuggled into Barracks G, where he is beaten and humiliated before he is to be hanged. Rollin enters to search for a stolen watch and drops the foil into Jim's pocket. Cardoza is about to be strung up when Jim reveals the foil that he "pick-pocketed" from Rollin. The prisoners trace the foil to the genuine informer, and Cardoza is spared. The next morning, Barney and Jim use Rollin, Cinnamon, and Valesquez as hostages in their successful escape.

GUEST CAST: Michael Tolan (Santos Cardoza); Victor French (Leduc); Sid Haig (Sperizzi); Paul Winfield (Klaus); Joseph Bernard *(Comandante);* Edmund Hashim (Valesquez); Ernest Sarracino (Manuel Delgado); Don Paulin, Jay Della, Gil Galvano, Shep Sanders (Convicts). *Unbilled:* George Wilbur, Jerry Catron, Lee Duncan, Jerry Summers, Bob Hoy, Stephanie Epper, George Sawaya, Fred Carson, Buzz Henry (Stunts)

Shot at Culver City's "40 Acres" concentration camp set where *Hogan's Heroes* was filmed, this adventure is low on intricacy and high on brutality, with lots of physical abuse and violence. "The most violent thing in it," says writer Salkowitz, "was not when the prisoners were beating Cardoza up and hurting him." He feels the most violent scene was the one in which the prisoners force Cardoza to relentlessly walk the length of the prison cabin back and forth to the point of exhaustion, and he is not allowed to stop.

The show's tense and claustrophobic direction echoes the classic *Stalag 17* (1951), which also involved the search for an informer among prisoners, in which one of the suspects was a young actor making his first splash in motion pictures—Peter Graves.

153

50: RECOVERY

First Aired: 3/17/68

Written by: William Read Woodfield and
   Allan Balter
Directed by: Robert Totten
Director of Photography:
   Fred Koenekamp, ASC

TEAM: Phelps, Rollin, Cinnamon, Barney, Willy

Good morning, Mr. Phelps. Last night, one of our SAC bombers crashed behind the Iron Curtain. The plane's fail-safe mechanism did not destruct and has been taken to the Vatzia Institute, which is headed by the brilliant American scientist Paul Shipherd, who defected several years ago. If Shipherd succeeds in disassembling the mechanism, he will learn the key to our entire fail-safe system. Your mission, Jim, should you decide to accept it, is to recover the fail-safe before Shipherd can take it apart, and bring Shipherd back. As always, should you or any of your IM Force be caught or killed, the secretary will disavow any knowledge of your actions. Please dispose of this recording in the usual manner. Good luck, Jim.

Shipherd has already opened the fail-safe's outer mechanism. To proceed further, he must remove the unit's restraining bolts in their proper sequence. If he pulls the wrong bolt at the wrong time, the device will explode.

The pilot of the downed bomber (Phelps) is questioned by Shipherd. Jim angrily suggests that Shipherd "write a long letter to Duluth where they make" the fail-safe. Amazingly, Shipherd has just met wheelchair-bound Rollin and "wife," Cinnamon, who manufacture a top-secret mechanism for the US government *in Duluth*. Jim is released to the American embassy.

Shipherd invites Rollin on a tour of the Vatzia Institute. Embassy official Barney accompanies Rollin and waits while he examines the classified section. Shipherd confronts Rollin with the fail-safe—and Cinnamon, seated beside it. By threatening to randomly remove the bolts and risk an explosion, Shipherd forces Rollin to slowly, laboriously open the fail-safe. But before he can finish, Rollin suffers a "heart attack" and is taken to the

infirmary, accompanied by Cinnamon (a doctor) and Shipherd.

Barney fouls the building's disposal-vent system which leads to a shredder in the subbasement. Repairman Phelps enters the shredder from the subbasement, climbs up the vent to the room where the fail-safe is held, and takes it.

In the infirmary, Barney knocks Shipherd out and drops a rope down the shredder duct to Jim, who sends the fail-safe to him. Barney hides the unit in the rear of Rollin's wheelchair. With the help of masks, Rollin and Shipherd exchange identities. Barney wheels out a "dead" "Rollin," and "Shipherd" offers to escort Cinnamon back to her hotel. The team regroup not far away with their prizes: the fail-safe and Paul Shipherd.

GUEST CAST: Bradford Dillman (Paul Shipherd), Emile Genest (Technician), Peter Coe (Laso), Peter Hellman (Guard), Gregory Gay (Minister), Judy Levitt (Nurse), Art Stewart (Attendant)

"We said, 'Let's do a show that takes place in a think tank,' " Billy Woodfield recalls. "We decided to go to the Rand Corporation. The head of security there took us through the joint. He was a fan of the show. He said, 'Do you find any deficiencies?' I said 'Yes.' He said, 'What?' I said, 'These chutes that go down to the shredder. They're on every floor. It seems to me that even though the offices are locked, you could move from office to office through the chutes.' He said, 'That'll be corrected.' "

Disassembling the fail-safe required the use of remote-controlled metal manipulator arms

154

and a lot of inserts, which meant that special effects man Jonnie Burke had to move quickly. "We worked Saturday, Sunday, Monday all day," says Burke. "By Tuesday afternoon we were carrying the arms out, and I'm walking alongside them with a can of silver spray paint, painting them."

"Even when they were installed, they were still working on it," says director Robert Totten, "and I was shooting around them." The arms were delivered to second unit director Paul Krasny, and Burke was certain that something would go wrong. To his surprise, "It worked perfectly. Not a thing broke." Burke's manipulators, based on an existing pair used by a major corporation for handling radioactive materials, turned out to be more effective than the prototype. "Their arms had an offset wrist, so if you were going to turn a knob, you could only turn about thirty or forty degrees before the fingers would fall off," claims Burke. "Well, our arms, which cost about $3600, did more than theirs did, which cost $36,000!" "That Jonnie Burke was always building things better," says Woodfield, matter-of-factly. "He drove us crazy."

Guest star Bradford Dillman's strongest memory of the episode concerns a friend of his mother's who had a low opinion of his talent. "Because the lady was close to the family she worried each acting appearance could be my last, that sooner or later I'd be exposed as an imposter, thereby starving a wife and six innocent children." Her alarm intensified after seeing the finale of "Recovery," in which Dillman was playing the masked Rollin playing Shipherd. "I was acting my heart out," says Dillman, "impersonating Martin Landau, who was impersonating me. What did it get me? My mother's friend, ever supportive, observed, 'Boy, that Martin Landau is a great actor. I sure hope you were studying him, because you could've learned a lot. He was more like you than you!'"

Wrap

Mission: Impossible made an impressive jump in the Nielsens to an average number 32, with a 34.9 share of the viewing audience, surpassing its competition, ABC's *Sunday Night Movie* and NBC's *The High Chaparral.* "Whether our ratings are up this year because of the time change or Peter Graves joining our series, I don't know," Bruce Geller told a reporter. He was aware, however, that CBS's faith was largely responsible. "Had we been on ABC, we would have been on thirteen weeks and off."

The show was beginning to attract more attention. *Time* magazine devoted an article to *Mission* toward the end of the season, calling it, "TV's hottest suspense series." The British series *The Avengers* dubbed one of their wild adventures, "Mission—Highly Improbable." Perhaps the highest form of flattery was one of the first episodes of Lucille Ball's new series, *Here's Lucy* (1968) titled, "Lucy's Impossible Mission." Lucy blunders into a phone booth, where a taped voice (Bob Johnson) issues mysterious instructions before self-destructing. The tall, white-haired man the message was meant for, a Commander Geller, recruits Lucy and her family to thwart an enemy agent—played by *Mission* familiar Joseph Ruskin. The show even included reorchestrated versions of famous *Mission* melodies. In *Daily Variety*'s issue of November 8, 1967, Paramount TV reported, "record foreign sales of pix and TV product, with sales to Japan of *The Lucy Show, Mission: Impossible, Star Trek,* [and] *Mannix.*"

Although only five episodes officially went over budget (episodes 28, 30, 31, 32, 47), costs barely diminished, for more and more had been left to *Mission*'s insert stage this year. Paul Krasny and his postproduction crew were becoming so important that Krasny was able to squeeze a directing assignment out of Geller for the upcoming season. "He wanted to keep me in postproduction because he didn't have anyone else," says Krasny. "I directed only the first episode because once the season started, I could never have gotten away to do any more. I was loaded with work!"

Mission's Emmy nominations increased to eleven this year, tops for any series. Among those recognized: actors Bain and Landau; writers Woodfield and Balter for episode 35, "The Seal"; director Lee Katzin and cinematographer Michel Hugo for episode 47, "The Killing"; Lalo Schifrin for Musical Composition ("The Seal"); David Wages for editing episode 40, "The Photographer" and Robert Watts for episode 26, "The Traitor"*; Bill Ross and Lou Hafley for Art Direction and Scenic Design for episode 38, "Echo of Yesterday"; Joseph Sorokin for Sound Editing for episode 28, "The Survivors"; and, again, producer Joe Gantman for Outstanding Dramatic Series. The winners: Barbara Bain and Joseph Gantman, who had already decided to leave the show. "I think his wife had a lot to do with it," Peter Lupus suspects. "She said that for those two years, they hardly ever saw Joe. It was terrible, the guy was putting in eighteen, twenty hours a day. After a while it was just too much."

"After two years," Gantman elaborates, "it was not just that it was hard work, but, 'Well, I've done this.' I wasn't in an ownership position; I was a lot younger then, and foolish enough to say, 'I got into all this because I thought it would be fun, not because I wanted to keep a job.' So I've never worried about that, and I'm not giving that advice

---

* Although a first season episode, "The Traitor" aired after that year's Emmy nominations had been made.

to anyone, by the way! The most fun in any show, unless it's an anthology, is the first year or two." There was no doubt who *Mission*'s new producers would be, and William Read Woodfield and Allan Balter enthusiastically accepted the job.

"Everyone said I was crazy," says Gantman about leaving, "because the third year of a series is the one where people relax. You've got writers, you've had enough time to get ahead for that season and so on."

Gantman's theory sounds tried and true. But *Mission*'s year three would not be a typical one. Instead of relaxing and getting ahead, *Mission: Impossible* nearly fell apart.

Mission: Impossible's **most popular line-up.**

Year Three
September 1968 – April 1969

Production Credits

Starring: Peter Graves, Martin Landau as Rollin Hand
Also Starring: Barbara Bain, Greg Morris, Peter Lupus
Executive Producer: Bruce Geller
Produced by: William Read Woodfield and Allan Balter
Associate Producer: Barry Crane
Script Consultants: Robert E. Thompson (episodes 51 through 61); Paul Playdon
In Charge of Postproduction: Paul Krasny
Production Manager: Edward Haldeman
Assistant to the Executive Producer: Philip Fehrle
Theme Music by: Lalo Schifrin
Directors of Photography: Andrew J. McIntyre (episodes 52 and 53); Gert Andersen, ASC (episode 67), Keith C. Smith
Art Director: Bill Ross
Film Editors: Robert L. Swanson; David Wages, ACE; John Loeffler; William Cairncross; Jodie Copelan, ACE; Jerry Taylor
Assistant Directors: Victor Vallejo, Ted Butcher, Rowe Wallerstein, Jim Myers, Al Kraus, Michael P. Schoenbrun

Set Decorator: Lucien Hafley
Supervising Property Master: Arthur Wasson
Property Master: William M. Bates
Vehicles: Ed Chamey
Special Effects: Jonnie Burke
Makeup Artist: Bob Dawn
Hairstylist: Adele Taylor
Script Supervisor: Allan Greedy
Production Coordinator: Alan Godfrey
Casting: Joseph D'Agosta, William J. Kenney
Music Editor: Dan Carlin
Supervising Sound Editor: Joseph G. Sorokin
Editorial Coordinator: Jerry Taylor
Production Mixer: Dominick Gaffey
Rerecording Mixer: Gordon L. Day, CAS
Recorded by: Glen Glenn Sound
Chrysler Vehicles Furnished by: Chrysler Corporation
Supervising Costumer: Forrest T. Butler
Costume Supervisor (Women): Sabine Manela
Wardrobe Furnished by: Worsted-Tex
Executive Vice President in Charge of Production: Douglas S. Cramer

> *"Bruce Geller, in my opinion, was a mad genius."*
>
> —DOUGLAS S. CRAMER,
> PARAMOUNT TELEVISION'S
> EXECUTIVE VICE PRESIDENT IN
> CHARGE OF PRODUCTION

*M*ISSION CAUGHT ON in a big way during its third season. "It became a social necessity," says William Read Woodfield. "People would stay home Sunday night to watch it, and would talk about it the next day." Bruce Geller was amused by the sudden popularity. "The things they used to damn the show, they now use to praise it. Only the inflections have changed. They used to berate it—'It's so fast!' Now they praise it—'It's so fast!' " Viewership was increasing everywhere. A 1968 *TV Guide* study found *Mission* the number one series for viewers with one or more years of college; overseas, Nigeria and Sweden were just two countries where *Mission* found a loyal, large audience. All indications pointed to year three as being *Mission*'s best yet.

Martin Landau was an immediate beneficiary of the show's growing success. A new contract netted him $6500 per show, an increase in residual payments, and sixty thousand dollars in "development" money. Barbara Bain too saw some recompense, her salary raised to $2500 per show, plus a golf cart to get her around the recently expanded Paramount lot. Unfortunately, and despite a new paint job, the ancient cart quickly self-destructed.

Barbara's transportation was one of the early skirmishes between the *Mission* unit and Herb Solow's replacement, Douglas S. Cramer. After starting his career as a television supervisor for Procter and Gamble's daytime serials, Cramer moved to the Ogilvy and Mather ad agency. In 1965 he was hired as ABC's vice president of program development, where he oversaw the debut of *Peyton Place* and *Batman*. While in the number two position at Twentieth Century-Fox, Cramer was asked by Paramount president John Reynolds to join Paramount Television. The requirements of the position were made very clear. "My job," says Cramer, "was to control costs on the three shows then on the air, and also to get new shows on the air.

"The people doing *Star Trek,* Gene Roddenberry and his people, were open to conversations about budgets and weren't impractical; *Mannix* was not as complicated, and the producers, Ivan Goff and Ben Roberts, knew how to do the show and could handle the scripts and budgets." Cramer soon learned which of the Desilu holdovers would be his primary concern.

"Bruce had a wonderful concept of the show," Cramer feels, "put it together beautifully, but paid no attention to budget. Secondly, he traditionally wrote bigger shows than we could afford to do. They had a wonderful look, but once he decided on a location, there was no stopping him. Bruce was a madman about scripts and there would be layer after layer of writers working on them. He also left vast portions of the picture undone, even though he would go over the regular schedule. In those days Universal did hours in six days. He was doing them in eight, nine, ten, eleven days and then he would do another two days of inserts on a separate stage, and would never think of using an insert from another show. He would never use an insert again!"

Bruce Geller's initial reaction to Cramer was to ignore him. When Cramer installed his own production managers on the set and devised an elaborate requisition form to keep track of production expenditures, "Bruce would find ways to run around the guys in the accounting department and my form. He had his own little empire and was going off and doing things on his own." Eventually, confrontations arose. "We came head-to-head on a number of occasions," says Cramer, "and he would always run to the network. The network would then call Charley Bluhdorn or Marty Davis at Gulf + Western and say, 'We are never gonna speak to you unless you leave this man alone. These are our hit shows.' The costs were astronomical and the network loved it, because the show was a hit and they paid us a flat price and couldn't care less."

Studio pressure made Geller angrier and more intractable. Says Olga Griffin, Geller's secretary, "Bruce didn't want anyone saying a word. It was his thought and his dream." He refused to look at the dailies when Cramer did, and unsuccessfully tried to have Cramer's name removed from *Mission*'s end titles. Before long, there was a state of undeclared war between Doug Cramer and Bruce Geller. "Geller's stages were Geller's territory," adds Cramer, "and it was as though there were two armed camps, my side and his side."

Paramount's concern over extravagant television budgets seems odd in view of what was happening in the studio's feature division. No one explains the situation better than Peter Graves: "Charley Bluhdorn bought the studio and thought he could produce pictures. He was a big executive who knew how to run businesses but didn't know anything about the picture business, and he produced some of the great all-time hits, like *Darling Lili, Paint Your Wagon, Catch-22, On a Clear Day You Can See Forever . . .*" These features were enormously expensive productions; when released in 1969–70, their box-office results ranged from disappointing to disastrous. "He had two hundred fifty million dollars worth of negative tied up that nobody wanted," Graves exclaims. "Nobody in the world! That's why they were cutting costs on *Mission: Impossible* and *Star Trek,* because Bluhdorn spent all the money elsewhere. So Charley said, 'Yeah, we gotta cut costs here.' "

"At the start of the third season," Woodfield explains, "Cramer said, 'We're gonna have to stop spending money here, we're spending too much money.' Bruce said, 'We'll spend all the money we can.' Once we wrote a show that could be shot on budget. Bruce said, 'You've got to add more stuff to it. I don't ever want to bring in a show on budget. If we do, they're always gonna want them on budget.' Keeping total independence was something that Bruce instigated."

"Obviously, they were unhappy with the overages," says Martin Landau. "Bruce was concerned with making the show good, feeling very confident that the show would make much money back in reruns (which it has). Bruce was concerned with the quality of the show. His name was on it; all our names were.

"For some reason, there was an adversary position created, though we're all in it together. Somehow the studio thought, 'They're trying to take advantage of us, we have to keep them in their place.' Like we were unstable." The conflict between Geller and Cramer would grow even worse as time progressed.

Woodfield and Balter's appointment to producers was met with mixed reactions. "They were two of the best writers," Jonnie Burke says, "but I had run-ins with them all the time. They were terrible producers. They didn't want anything changed one iota from what they wrote, and a lot of their ideas were wrong." In the season's first show, a Laurence Heath script required a heater powerful enough to melt gold. Burke was told to build the apparatus as

written, even though it could not possibly do the job. "If it wasn't technically right I didn't want to do it. You could talk to them as writers, but as producers they became too dictatorial and it became a clash of temperaments all the way down the line."

"Woodfield and Balter were dictators, very tough," says Max Hodge, who wrote one *Mission* this semester. "I got along with them very well, and I don't know why." The pair had little trouble with writers and the cast, who loved them. They did have trouble with members of the crew, and were far less amiable with Bruce Geller. Woodfield's resentment of Geller, which stemmed from year one, had intensified, and apparently Allan Balter agreed with his partner that Geller should retire from the series and leave *Mission* to them. "We kept saying to him, 'Go write a script, Bruce.' He never wrote one other than the pilot, and doesn't that tell us something?" Billy Woodfield wonders. "Believe me when I say that the man had no idea of how that show worked."

According to Woodfield, Geller would pick on Balter's work. "He didn't do this much, maybe three or four times when we were producers. He'd know which acts were Balter's because they'd come in on different paper from different typewriters. He'd go to Balter and say, 'What are these words? I don't understand these words.' Balter would say, 'Well, I understand them, Bruce.' Balter was a nebbisher guy with a very weak heart which ultimately killed him. Sure, we all pick bad words and don't always say what we mean when we write but, boy, if Bruce could find it, he would go for Balter's. Finally we said, 'We're not interested in your notes, we're not interested in your opinion, we're not interested in talking to you and from now on we're not talking to you, and don't talk to us. We'll do our job and shoot our show, and you look at the rough cuts and the dailies.' He said, 'You can't talk to me that way.' I said, 'I just did.'"

On July 22, with less than eight shows in the can, the final battle occurred. Woodfield claims that Geller instigated it by walking into their office and telling Allan Balter, 'I want this inserted into the script.' Woodfield recognized the dialogue as an Ambrose Bierce quotation. "'This is gonna come out of the mouth of the villain without saying, 'As Ambrose Bierce once said'? He said 'Yeah.'" What happened next was a royal screamfest complete with threats and profanity. "We got up and walked out and never came back," recalls Woodfield. "Bruce said, 'Wait wait wait,' so now we're in the hall and I went for him. I yelled at him and called him every name in the book. I said, 'Come on, I'll give you the first punch.' I'd have killed him. I would have killed him without a second's hesitation." It was a shouting match so brutal that although virtually everyone in the building heard it, no one had the temerity to interfere. Woodfield and Balter were gone within five minutes.

Word spread quickly that the producers had been *fired*. While some rejoiced at the news, *Mission*'s cast was taken by surprise. "We were all shocked by it," claims Peter Graves. "I never knew there was that much strife." In an unprecedented move, the five stars banded together and requested a meeting with Geller. "It wasn't, 'Let's go challenge Bruce,' because Geller you did not challenge," Greg Morris says. "The five of us were sitting there and we voiced our opinion. I don't remember Bruce's exact words, but I remember the attitude: 'They're fired.' He was not going to be pressed against the wall. So we all went to our respective accommodations and faced the fact that Woodfield and Balter had been fired. There wasn't a damn thing we could say about it."

Whether Woodfield and Balter quit or were fired was hardly the issue. What mattered was that the pair, who many felt understood the show better than Geller, were gone. For all the backstage angst, the seven Woodfield- and Balter-produced hours show no sign of strain: three

163

of them (episodes 51, 52, and 56) are outstanding. Had they stayed, it is possible that this season would have been *Mission*'s finest. Bill Woodfield is not certain. "The show was in the top ten when we left," he explains, "and we knew that we could not keep that up forever. We'd have to start doing the same show over and over and so to some extent, the blowup with Bruce was motivated by that. This was just a good time to get out." Some blame Geller's attitude for the trouble. "The producers were bothered," Laurence Heath says. "One of the things that rankled them: He was the boss and they felt they were doing all the work. That was rampant. That's a prescription for annoyance and resentment. That's why Gantman left, that's what was behind the trouble with Woodfield and Balter." According to script supervisor Allan Greedy, Geller was, "a person you could depend on for his word but one who showed almost no emotion. If you did something well he was not likely to gush over it. He was a person you could absolutely depend on to stick with you, something I didn't appreciate until years later when producers would not stick by me. For all their drawbacks, Woodfield and Balter dreamed up good *Mission*s, and it was a mistake for him to have had that falling out with them."

The pair's abrupt exit had disastrous consequences. "When Billy and Allan went out, there were almost no scripts," says their script consultant, Robert E. Thompson. "They *were* the scripts. They were doing one this week to shoot next week." Thompson had been hired on the basis of one story (episode 52, "The Heir Apparent"), and took the job because it was easy. "Billy and Allan did all the work," he admits. "I wasn't wildly desirous of sitting there until twelve at night rewriting scripts, and they were. They wanted to put their imprint on everything, and in the end they did and they did it fairly well. I don't know what they needed a story editor for. It was really their show. I commissioned a few scripts and mildly rewrote a couple, but in the end they rewrote those." Suddenly, *Mission* had no producer and worse, no scripts. "There was nothing there," Thompson states, "only one first draft." Geller talked Thompson (who'd produced *Rawhide* and *The Travels of Jaimie McPheeters*) into taking over. "I agreed to stay for only the most minimum amount of time," Thompson says, "and only if he agreed to try to find someone else immediately."

Thompson was faced with the choice of having to write *Mission*s himself (which he felt incapable of doing), or interviewing new writers. "Bruce was not about to sit down and write, although he said, 'All right, maybe I'll write two or three.' And that's the last I ever heard of him," says Thompson, laughing. In the end Thompson did both, writing episode 61, "The Bargain" in four days, and meeting with as many as twenty writers a day. "I'm not sure I wouldn't have done better had I sat down and started writing. There was an awful lot of wasted time going through fifteen or twenty writers a day with no ideas. I was gonna get out one way or another, even if it meant alienating the network. Bruce would be stuck, and it would be the absolute worst thing that could happen to him. That was his terror, that he would be stuck doing it." The day before he left, Thompson found the writer *Mission* needed.

From the outline which would become his first *Mission* (episode 62, "The Mind of Stefan Miklos"), it was obvious to Thompson that Paul Playdon was perfect for the series. The British-born writer, just in his mid-twenties, had worked on the last season of *Combat!*, and was free-lancing when he walked into Thompson's office. By the time Playdon had a first draft ready, *Mission* had yet a new producer, an unexpected choice.

Stanley Kallis, the CBS executive behind Robert Altman's *Nightwatch* pilot, had left the network to work on pilots at Paramount, and was walking across the lot on the fateful day that Balter and Woodfield made their noisy exit, "hurling invectives at Bruce Geller as they

were walking down the street. It was a very angry moment, and Bruce was livid and upset." But not too upset to ask Kallis if he wanted to take over. Kallis had declined the job back in 1966 for ethical reasons. But now, *"Mission* had been on the air long enough that the world didn't think it was the worst thing ever perpetrated, so my questions about the morality of the show were not being asked widely." Kallis thought about the job, then accepted. "I couldn't lose. The show was on the way to shutdown. If I couldn't get it started again, I would not be judged, the world was not going to say, 'Well, he screwed up *Mission: Impossible.'* " His first move was to make Paul Playdon script consultant. "That's right," says Kallis with a smile, "I really fixed him! I saw a home run hitter who could hit right-handed and left-handed." Says Playdon, "It was really a surprise when Stan said, 'I'd like you to come on the show— tomorrow.' I did, and the next day I had to start writing the next script. They had nothing. The shelf was completely bare."

It is difficult to imagine the situation Kallis and Playdon walked into that summer of 1968. *Mission* was peaking, and regularly placing in the Nielsen top ten. Its fame was spreading far and wide and the show's trademarks, music, and catchphrases were being repeated and spoofed all over the country. Behind the scenes, however, *Mission* had a new producer, new head writer, and for a time no executive producer, for in the middle of it all, Bruce Geller flew to Hawaii with his wife. "I was not good casting for *Mission,"* Kallis feels, "unlike Larry Heath, who was, and liked doing it. I didn't know *Mission.* It was like riding a tiger by the tail. That damned thing whacked me, it whacked Playdon, whacked us all over the place." With Geller off the continent, the show's destiny was being charted by two strangers. "I don't think we could have done the show without a clear understanding that it was going to take a massive commitment to get through this," Playdon says. To him fell the burden of coming up with the rest of the season's scripts, and rewriting the few usable ones coming in from other writers. "Something had to be done and it had to look like this thing called *Mission: Impossible.* There was no way to keep the show going unless I was writing twelve to fifteen pages a day. There was no time to go through a story outline. I look back and cannot quite think how I put some of those scripts together. Sometimes I winced and wished that I had two or three more days, but they were shooting first drafts. That was the best that I could do." Playdon was a prodigious writer who turned out a script a week until he collapsed from exhaustion in his office one late evening. In those frantic weeks, he somehow contributed the series' most intellectually brilliant and densely plotted mindbenders, notably episodes 62, "The Mind of Stefan Miklos" and 67, "Live Bait," which he heavily rewrote. Some of the Kallis-Playdon shows are in fact too complex for a one-hour television show. "I wanted *Mission* to be worth the time of an intelligent man," Kallis says. "I may have gone too far. I didn't know how many complications you could have without driving an audience crazy." Kallis believes that Playdon could have joined Len Deighton and John le Carré as masters of the spy form. "Paul was a very original writer; he never approached *Mission* as a formula."

Things were becoming more complex for Doug Cramer too. As the season progressed, each *Mission* seemed to get more and more expensive, culminating in the construction of a three-story working elevator on one of the stages (needed to complete a show). "The building of that elevator triggered a massive row on the lot," recalls Paul Playdon who, like Kallis, had already been called in by Cramer. "Doug had his job to do," Playdon continues, "but I think that he really did try to understand that it was not just personal whim that was making the show expensive."

"Doug didn't come at me," says Kallis. "He said, 'Isn't there something you can do to help

us, Stan?' The studio tried to find a way to make me behave, but I never misbehaved. I didn't set out to make that show costly. The show by its very nature was costly. If they didn't want to do *Mission: Impossible* and they wanted to do something else, we could make it cheaper. Paramount's arguments about the money were always spurious. They could always talk to Barry Crane, who used all of his genius to try to do it as cheap as possible. Whenever it was possible, we would rewrite to Barry's specifications. I wouldn't know how to go back and do it better, and I am now how many years older? I don't think I could bring more experience to the solutions of those problems."

For the remainder of the season, work continued without a break for Playdon, Kallis, and the entire crew. Eighteen-hour production meetings and impromptu hallway gatherings were normal. "Many times I was writing the script as we were having the meeting," Playdon comments, "so you had the rare case in television of everyone in the office getting it at the same moment the writer is. Only with that kind of timing did we have a ghost of a chance of getting most of those shows on the air."

Inevitably, even Paul Playdon ran out of ideas. There is a famous story told about the night Kallis and Playdon arrived at Bruce Geller's home to inform him that, "There are no more *Mission: Impossible*s. We've used them all up." Geller's reaction? "Welcome to the club. We've been here before. You're welcome to take as much time as you want to get the next script. If it doesn't happen next week or the week after, sooner or later you'll get it started again." When Kallis pointed out the expensive prospect of shutting down in mid-season, Geller replied, "That's not your problem, that's not my problem."

"I tell that as one of the great stories of my life," marvels Kallis. "He was quite wonderful. Paul and I arrived at the office the next morning after a good night's sleep and came up with a story. I went down to the production office and told them what the story would be, scene for scene. Paul was delivering pages to the set each day and we were shooting. We'd lost one scene. It was the only time we'd built a set and never used it; it turned out to be an unnecessary scene." Somehow, the series never missed an airdate. "A lot of shows today can't say that," says Paul Krasny. "I did a *Moonlighting* that finished on Friday and aired the following Tuesday!"

"A crazy elitism did happen," Kallis remembers. "In a way you were proud of the fact that you were on a very small team, because not everyone could do it." The Kallis-Playdon shows of year three suffer only from an abundance of East European locales, hardly a new handicap. Considering the time factor, the results were better than expected. "Being good was to a large extent not knowing how to hit the target every time," Kallis suspects. "We didn't have a great confidence in hitting it, just getting it so that it wasn't going to embarrass anybody! So it would work." An Impossible Missions Force, indeed.

Most of these catastrophes were undreamed of on May 7, 1968, when Bruce Geller directed Peter Graves and a small crew in a handful of tape scenes shot in and around Hollywood locations like the interior of the Pantages Theater, the roof of the Knickerbocker Hotel, and a kiddie amusement park at the corner of La Cienega and Beverly Boulevard. At that point, things couldn't have seemed better.

51: THE MERCENARIES

Written by: Laurence Heath
Directed by: Paul Krasny
Music Composed and Conducted by:
Robert Drasnin

First Aired: 10/20/68

TEAM: Phelps, Rollin, Cinnamon, Barney, Willy

Good afternoon, Mr. Phelps. You're looking at Colonel Hans Krim, the leader of a mercenary army currently ravaging equatorial Africa. Ostensibly, Krim fights for the cause of emerging nations, but in reality he is nothing but a military gangster who plunders ally and enemy alike. Krim and his mercenaries have converted their loot into gold bars which are kept within the enclave used as headquarters. Your mission, Jim, should you decide to accept it, is to destroy Krim and return the gold. As always, should you or any of your IM Force be caught or killed, the secretary will disavow any knowledge of your actions. This tape will self-destruct in five seconds. Good luck, Jim

Impenetrable jungle and high mountains make Krim's enclave accessible by only one road, which is sentry guarded at all times.

Rollin enlists in Krim's army and enters the enclave. Gunrunners Jim and Cinnamon follow, in a truck which conceals Willy and Barney. Krim suspects that Rollin has uncovered a large cache of bullion long rumored to have been hidden in the area. Rollin is tortured until he agrees to take Krim to the gold, stashed in a deserted section of the installation. Krim, who plans to keep this gold for himself, "kills" Rollin and hires Phelps to smuggle it past the sentry and into a Tangiers bank. Krim holds Cinnamon hostage to make sure that Phelps returns with a bank deposit receipt.

Krim's aide Gruner listens suspiciously as Krim orders the sentry not to search Jim's truck. Then Rollin, mimicking the sentry, tells Gruner that the truck *was* searched and a huge supply of gold found. Gruner accuses Krim of stealing the army's gold. Krim feigns ignorance of the gold in the truck and, to prove his innocence, takes Gruner to the guarded vault where the army's gold bars are stored. He is amazed to find the vault empty, with no signs of forced entry. The bullion has been miraculously stolen by the IMF and Krim unwittingly maneuvered into stealing *that* gold. Gruner, furious, stabs and kills Krim. Phelps smilingly drives his truckful of gold (and IMFers) past the sentry who, following Krim's orders, passes it through without a search.

GUEST CAST: Pernell Roberts (Colonel Hans Krim), Skip Homeier (Major Jan Gruner), Victor Tayback (Sergeant Gorte), Bo

Svenson (Karl). *Unbilled:* William Lucking (Corporal Stolman), Boyd Santell (Corporal Verte), Beatriz Montiel (Camp Follower), Chuck Couch (double, Rollin)

Pernell Roberts is a greedy IMF target in "The Mercenaries."

"The Mercenaries" is a favorite *Mission* not only of many series fans, but also of many who worked on it. It is part of the strongest opening of any season of the series, ironically the same season which would see the show come close to shutdown and face much turmoil and change.

Paul Krasny makes his episodic directorial debut, handling one of the most technically daunting segments. The key challenge was the IMF gold heist from the vault, one of *Mission*'s most unforgettable gambits. Unknown to Krim, an old escape tunnel runs below his compound, including the area just below the vault. Barney and Willy enter the tunnel and drill a hole in the vault floor at its lowest slope. Into the vault is placed an extremely powerful heater which, once inside, unfolds like an umbrella, its coiled spires heated to 2200°F. The gold bars slowly soften and melt into liquid which oozes down the sloping floor, down a pipe and into metal molds, where the gold is recast once again into bars to be deposited on the other side of the enclave. When the gold has been completely drained, Barney pumps into the vault liquid concrete which hardens, creating a new vault floor and leaving no sign of the theft.

The mechanics behind this scene were extremely tough. In their first outing as producers, Woodfield and Balter expanded upon the intractability they had cultivated as writers. Despite Jonnie Burke's insistence that the "umbrella heater" could not possibly achieve heat levels to feasibly melt gold, he was forced to build the unit anyway. There were difficulties in getting the heater to work, or even look like it was working. "There just was not enough space in the hole in that floor for all the voltage and amperes we were putting through it." As soon as the mechanism began to glow, the heater shorted out and caused a long production delay. Burke rebuilt the prop, but didn't make the same mistake: "It got red hot, then white hot, then we shut it off and used fluorescent paint to make it look like it was hot."

The "gold" was in fact a specially blended molded ice cream, spray-painted with gold. "By using color filters, the melting ice cream looked like molten gold," says Burke. "The paint became a crust that looked like the kind you'd get on molten metals." The sequence works perfectly and has an eerie sort of beauty to it. Only Jonnie Burke could turn ice cream into gold.

The gold scene is only one highlight of this show, one of the greatest of all *Mission*s. After twenty years, Paul Krasny still points to "The Mercenaries" as, "my favorite of all of them. It really was a terrific show. When you can make an audience believe this stuff, you've gotta be doing something right!"

52: THE HEIR APPARENT

Written by: Robert E. Thompson
Directed by: Alexander Singer
Music Composed and Conducted by:
Lalo Schifrin

First Aired: 9/29/68

TEAM: Phelps, Rollin, Cinnamon, Barney, Willy

Good morning, Mr. Phelps. In exactly five days Archbishop Djelvas, the ecclesiastic patriarch of Povia, must name a regent to succeed the king who died recently, leaving no heir. This man, General Envir Qaisette, has vowed that unless he is named regent he will seize the throne in a bloody coup d'etat. If Qaisette succeeds, Povia, a free constitutional monarchy, will become a military dictatorship. Your mission, Jim, should you decide to accept it, is to stop Qaisette. As always, should you or any of your IM Force be caught or killed, the secretary will disavow any knowledge of your actions. This tape will self-destruct in five seconds. Good luck, Jim.

Rumors spread throughout Povia that the legendary Princess Celine, a genuine heiress to the throne who disappeared as a child, is still alive. Meanwhile, Cinnamon studies all that is known about Celine.

Barney and Willy, caught stealing relics from the royal cathedral, lead Qaisette to Phelps, who accompanies an old, blind woman (Cinnamon) who claims she is Celine. Qaisette knows she is a fake: Elderly doctor Rollin has proof that the real Celine's arm would be crippled. "She could fool anyone but me," Qaisette muses. He opts to give the archbishop this "Celine," then discredit him by exposing her as a fraud.

During her authentication in the royal cathedral, Cinnamon correctly answers every question, opens a complex puzzle box only Celine could open, and delivers proof that Qaisette is a murdering traitor. Qaisette is arrested and Cinnamon abdicates the throne to the archbishop's choice. "Celine" and her retinue drive off, never to be seen again.

GUEST CAST: Charles Aidman (General Envir Qaisette), Torin Thatcher (Archbishop Djelvas), Rudy Solari (Zageb), Leonidas Ossetynski (Grand Duke), Diana Bourbon (Mme. Pollan), Fred Villani (Tour Guide),

Alphonse Martell (Dr. Vachtel), Peter Hellman (Police Captain). *Unbilled:* Max Kleven (Secret Policeman), Brian Wood (Priest), Joseph Tornatore (Dungeon Guard), George Sawaya (Stunt Guard)

Povia's Archbishop (Torin Thatcher) watches as Cinnamon is rigorously tested in "The Heir Apparent."

Writer Brad Radnitz submitted a story outline during year two involving an Anastasia-like princess who must journey by train to reclaim her kingdom. The IMF is assigned to protect her, and by the end of the show her car has vanished off the tracks. This story was never filmed, but *Mission* newcomer Robert E. Thompson's version made it to the soundstage. Woodfield

169

and Balter were so happy with Thompson's first draft that they offered him the job of *Mission* story consultant, which he accepted.

"It was plagiarism, essentially," Thompson explains. "The genesis of it was purely *Anastasia.* I thought it fit the mold and it did, but Allan and Billy put in a half dozen little pieces of business that made it better. I could see that they had a knack for it that not only Bruce didn't have but I didn't have, and essentially no one else had."

Picked as the season's premiere episode, "The Heir Apparent" was a smashing way to open year three. Aided by Bob Dawn's makeup, Barbara Bain's portrayal of an ailing, sightless old woman may be the pinnacle of her work in the series. The plot is typically clever, using the dovetail effect Geller loved. This time the IMF has an amazing wealth of data on hand. Considering how much Cinnamon memorizes, the Celine dossier must be enormous. She knows everything from her childhood name for Qaisette to the nervous habits of her adult companions. In addition, Jim knows that catacombs linking the jail's solitary confinement cell to the royal vault are still open. That avenue is used by prisoners Barney and Willy to break into the vault, where Barney frantically works to solve the solution to Celine's puzzle box. Learning the sequence, he "marks" the box for Cinnamon, who is actually blind, thanks to special eyedrops.

The climax in the cathedral is one of the most enjoyable. Qaisette knows that Cinnamon is a fake who will eventually humiliate the archbishop, but should she double-cross him, Qaisette has several options. First, he blackmails several officials into confirming Cinnamon as Celine. More importantly, he knows that Cinnamon won't be able to open the puzzle box. Finally, Qaisette has old doctor Rollin as his insurance policy, sitting in the church should he need to testify. But of course, Qaisette is outsmarted. In a superbly intercut sequence, Cinnamon slowly opens the puzzle box while Rollin, unnoticed by all, discreetly sheds every element of his disguise without ever leaving his seat. Cinnamon opens the box and reveals her father's diary, which indicts Qaisette, who looks for the elderly physician to prove his claim that the real Celine would be crippled. But the old doctor has vanished. Sitting in his place is Rollin, who faces Qaisette with a marvelously innocent Who, me? look.

Mention should also be made of Lalo Schifrin's lovely score, especially Celine's theme, rendered on harpsichord. The score earned him another Emmy nomination and the music would surface again in later episodes.

Reviews for "The Heir Apparent" were favorable. *Daily Variety*'s critic called Bain "excellent," and commented dryly on Barney and Willy's tunnel adventure: "For all the subterranean burrowing carried out on blueprints provided off-camera by unchallenged sources, not a grain of mortar was left out of place in the IMF's wake. Man, that's professionalism."

Year three was off to a great start.

53: THE DIPLOMAT

Written by: Jerry Ludwig
Directed by: Don Richardson
Music Composed and Conducted by:
  Gerald Fried

First Aired: 12/1/68

TEAM: Phelps, Rollin, Barney, Willy, Dr. David
  Walters, Presidential aide Everett Buchanan
  and wife, Susan

---

*Good morning, Mr. Phelps. The day before yesterday, information pinpointing the locations of
America's four missile-control centers was stolen. A Major Barrett and several other enemy agents
involved were arrested but not before the information was delivered to this man, Valentin Yetkoff,
military attaché at the embassy in Washington. As usual with vital information, it must be verified
before it can be acted upon. Yetkoff has given that assignment to Roger Toland, his top agent in
diplomatic circles. Jim, if the information is confirmed, this country will be vulnerable to a
preemptive missile attack. Your mission, should you decide to accept it, is to prevent this. As always,
if you or any of your IM Force should be caught or killed, the secretary will disavow any knowledge
of your actions. This tape will self-destruct in five seconds. Good luck, Jim.*

The stolen data is irretrievable, so the IMF must
convince Yetkoff that the information is false.

Toland, a staple of Washington society, sets
about wooing the attractive and neglected Mrs.
Buchanan and soon spots a top-secret booklet in
her wall safe which he knows can verify the control
sites.

When he learns that blackmailer Rollin has incriminating photos of Susan, Toland acquires the
photos and presents them to Susan, claiming to
have paid a high price for them. She opens the wall
safe to reimburse him. Toland overpowers her and
feeds her a deadly overdose of pills. As she sinks
into unconsciousness, he photographs the required
data from the booklet and leaves Susan for dead.
Her life is saved by Dr. Walters, who has been
anxiously awaiting Toland's exit.

Phelps introduces himself to Yetkoff as one of
the arrested Major Barrett's underlings. Yetkoff
learns that Jim is really an American agent, but
feigns acceptance of his proof that the stolen information is *accurate*. When Toland delivers the identical data to him, Yetkoff explains, "We can be
absolutely certain that these are *not* the locations.
The Americans think they have put one over on us.
They somehow planted this ["false"] information
for Major Barrett and then made certain that their
own agents verified it for us." "But I too verified
it," Toland protests. "Then you too are an American agent," says Yetkoff. "You are loyal to whoever pays you the most. Obviously, it is the
Americans." Toland is killed, and Yetkoff informs
his superiors that the sites are *inaccurate*.

GUEST CAST: Fernando Lamas (Roger Toland),
  Alfred Ryder (Colonel Valentin Yetkoff),
  Lee Grant (Susan Buchanan), Sid Haig
  (Grigor), Don Randolph (Everett
  Buchanan), Russ Conway (Dr. David
  Walters), Harry Basch (Nicolai), Allen
  Bleiweiss (Courier). *Unbilled:* Lou Robb
  (Harry Nielsen), Larry Barton (General),
  Alan Pinson (double, Rollin)

A salary dispute kept Barbara Bain home for "The Diplomat," forcing producers Woodfield and Balter to find a replacement. "We wanted Greer Garson," claims Woodfield, "because 'The Diplomat' had Fernando Lamas in it and it would have looked like an MGM
movie. Greer Garson wouldn't do it. Lee Grant was next." Ms. Grant was expensive, but as
Woodfield says, "We were told to cast it and we cast it. I phoned Barbara, who said, 'Oh my
God, Lee Grant's *perfect* for that part. You had to get *Lee Grant*?'" Woodfield's strategy
worked well, for Barbara and the studio came to terms shortly thereafter. "Lee Grant was
costing them a fortune," he chuckles.

Grant's participation makes the overdose in the final act more suspenseful than if it had been Bain, who we know would be back for the next show. Barbara's absence, however, did not make it the most comfortable of sets. According to director Don Richardson, the producers didn't help, and photographer Andrew McIntyre was their first victim. "They seemed to be on his tail from the start." By noon the first day, McIntyre had quit. "Then," says Richardson, "he came back and worked for the rest of the day. Woodfield and Balter saw the dailies and there was something they didn't like, and he quit again." Richardson, a friend of Woodfield's from the Irwin Allen days, felt that the pair were inept producers. "They didn't understand creative people. They wrote very good scripts, but movies are a collaborative art. Woodfield and Balter thought that they were the towering intelligence behind it all, so I felt nullified, the cameraman felt nullified, Lee Grant didn't feel any great enthusiasm from them. The crew were delightful, the cinematographer was excellent, the editor was excellent. Everyone knew what they were doing except for Woodfield and Balter, who didn't know how to use other people's talent."

In "The Diplomat," the regulars work strictly in support of guests Grant and Lamas, the latter steely and menacing when forcing Rollin to hand over the photos of Mrs. Buchanan in a romantic dalliance. After knocking Rollin down and threatening him with a broken bottle, Toland gets the photos. Then Rollin runs, trips, and falls onto an open light stand, the tip of which juts through his back! Toland smiles, having saved himself a bullet. Later, Jim helps Rollin out of the ingenious back brace which, on cue, thrusts the stand's tip through the back of Rollin's coat!

54/55: THE CONTENDER
(in two parts)

Written and Produced by: William Read
Woodfield and Allan Balter
Directed by: Paul Stanley
Music Composed and Conducted by:
Lalo Schifrin

First Aired: 10/6/68; 10/13/68

TEAM: Phelps, Rollin, Cinnamon, Barney, Willy,
former contender Richy Lemoine, Rena

Good morning, Mr. Phelps. The man you're looking at is Charles Buckman, who is attempting to obtain a strangehold on all forms of professional and amateur sports. If he succeeds, the US will be ostracized from the world community of athletics and our enemies handed a propaganda weapon of immeasurable value. Buckman's main financing comes from boxing. He works in association with this man, Dan Whelan, whose syndicate controls the betting on the fights Buckman rigs. Your mission, Jim, should you decide to accept it, is to eliminate Buckman and his plan once and for all. As always, should you or any of your IM Force be caught or killed, the secretary will disavow any knowledge of your actions. Please dispose of this recording in the usual manner. Good luck, Jim.

Barney (a former Navy champ) takes a crash course in boxing from Lemoine, a top contender before a war injury damaged his hands. Since Barney resembles Richy, Rollin adds a few touches to perfect the impersonation.

"Richy" announces a comeback attempt, arousing Buckman's interest. Buckman forces manager Rollin to sign Barney over to him, while Phelps gets a job in Whelan's gambling headquarters and gains access to a complete list of Whelan's bookies.

Barney fights his way through a series of matches, finally facing Buckman's champ Staczek in a bout Barney is supposed to lose. Barney sends Staczek to the canvas, and Buckman is caught in a perfect IMF frame.

GUEST CAST: Ron Randell (Charles Buckman), John Dehner (Dan Whelan), Sugar Ray Robinson (Wesley), Robert Phillips (Ernie Staczek), Ron Rich (Richy Lemoine), Wayne McLaren (Artie Calvitos), Thomas Geas (Vince), Joey Giambra (Stevens), James Gambina (Trainer), Jimmy Lennon (Announcer), Lee Grossman (Referee), Biff Elliott (Kid Wilson), Angus Duncan (Stan), Robert Conrad (Bobby). *Unbilled:* Alex Daoud, Tony Cortez, Vince Barbi, George Washburn, Arthur Eisner (Reporters); Red West (Sparring Partner); Lee Duncan, Cisco Andrade, Tom Huff (Boxers); Dick Clancy (Calabasos)

Owing much to last year's episode 37, "The Council," "The Contender" is unquestionably the series' most physical segment. Like the earlier two-parter, an insider is recruited to help dismantle a racket too widespread to allow (although why Jim has a dossier on Lemoine in his IMF file, and *then* goes to recruit him, is a mystery). Clinching the similarity is Robert Phillips, who had also appeared in "The Council"; this time he plays a vicious boxer.

One key difference is the extent to which Barney carries the plot. "Greg assured us he could fight," says Billy Woodfield. "Turned out he didn't know how to fight at all. Our mistake was that we didn't use Peter Lupus, but we asked him and he told us he really didn't fight." Interestingly, Lupus played a boxer in a segment of *The Joey Bishop Show* (1961–65).

Greg trained for two weeks under the tutelage of Phillips, who staged all the fights, and Phillips's pal Robert Conrad, who makes a cameo as Barney's trainer. Conrad even doubled for one of Barney's opponents when the boxer hired for the part could not be found. To help Barney in this scene, the IMF installs a devious little device below the ring which emits an invisible gas in the opponent's corner to slow him down.

During his training Greg suffered what he calls a traumatic experience. While sparring with Lee Duncan, a misunderstanding in cues nearly knocked Lee out. "I did not want to hurt anyone," Greg explains, "but it was clear in the rushes that I was pulling my punches." In the ring with ex-boxer Dick Cangey, Greg had to throw a knockout punch. "It had to look real," says Greg. "I don't know what came over me but when the moment came I just walked out of the ring. Cangey, Bobby Phillips, and Paul Stanley didn't know what had happened. They came over and I said, 'Paul, I can't hit him. I know him, I like him, and I'm afraid I'll hurt him.' Cangey put his arms around me and said, 'Don't worry about it.' They got me some oxygen and I was fine. I did it and it was one of the best fight scenes we did. He and Phillips kept goading me, and we had a good fight." Even so, the show was plagued by delays and injuries. Bob Phillips pulled an arm muscle, and both Greg and boxer Joey Giambra suffered hand injuries. One unexpected problem was encountered when an office set was lit for day scenes instead of night, as required by the script. The scene had to be completely reshot.

Barney's procession through the boxing ranks is shown in a montage, one of the few times the device was ever used in the series. The mission itself takes an unusually long time, in contrast to the typical hair-raising deadlines the IMF is accustomed to. Barney and Richy don't really look much alike, but after Rollin adds a mustache, fake nose bridge, and pomaded hairdo, Barney's pose fools everyone. Oddly, the only character who notices the change in "Richy's" looks is Staczek, the show's least intelligent figure, who attributes the differences to Richy's war injuries.

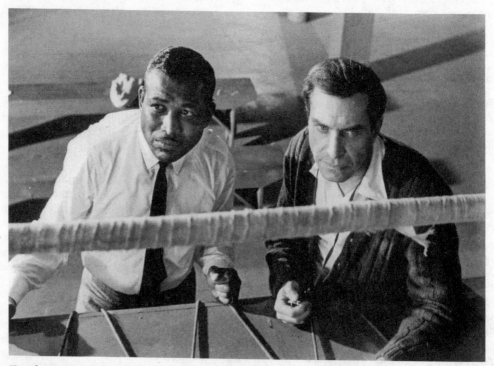

Boxing great Sugar Ray Robinson appeared in "The Contender."

56: THE EXECUTION

First Aired: 11/10/68

Written and Produced by: William Read
Woodfield and Allan Balter
Directed by: Alexander Singer
Music Composed and Conducted by:
Jerry Fielding

TEAM: Phelps, Rollin, Cinnamon, Barney, Willy,
clinical psychologist Dr. Henry Loomis

Good morning, Mr. Phelps. The man you're looking at is Lewis Parma, who by extortion, kidnapping, and murder, is coming close to taking control of the food distribution industry for the entire United States. Using his control of food prices as leverage, Parma is now moving toward positions of power in other important areas of business, labor, and government. Your mission, Jim, should you decide to accept it, is to put Lewis Parma out of business. As always, should you or any of your IM Force be caught or killed, the secretary will disavow any knowledge of your actions. This tape will self-destruct in five seconds. Good luck, Jim.

Parma's men bully resistant produce distributor Phelps and ruin his stock. When Jim barges into Parma's office, slaps him around, and threatens to kill him, Parma calls assassin Vic Duchell, who firebombs Jim's apartment but is cornered and rendered unconscious.

Duchell awakens "years" later on death row, his execution for Jim's murder mere hours away. He refuses to believe that the powerful Parma has suddenly abandoned him and ignores lawyer Cinnamon's urging to take the governor's offer of a life sentence in exchange for testimony indicting Parma. Finally, strapped in a gas chamber and watching the fumes spread, Duchell snaps and confesses, providing enough data to send Parma to a *real* gas chamber.

GUEST CAST: Luke Askew (Victor Pietro Duchell), Vincent Gardenia (Lewis George Parma), Val Avery (Al Ross), Byron Keith (Dr. Henry Loomis). *Unbilled:* Kay Kimberly (Secretary), Alex Sharp (Big Man)

"The Execution" is considered by many to be the greatest *Mission: Impossible* of all. For William Woodfield, it was a personal episode: he co-authored a book, *Ninth Life* (1961), which told of the final hours of Caryl Chessman, a prisoner who died in the gas chamber. Despite accusations that *Mission* was an amoral show, Billy Woodfield is a moral man with definite values (as *Mission* story editor, he refused to work on episode 38, "Echo of Yesterday," in which Marty Landau plays Hitler). Woodfield found death row hideous, and "The Execution" was written as a protest against capital punishment. "The whole idea was to show that horror within the context of a *Mission: Impossible,*" says guest star Luke Askew. They did it by carefully detailing the ritual which preceded every inmate's final moments: the preparation of the chamber, the rolling of the floor carpet, the dressing of the prisoner—dozens of factual touches which grimly add suspense to the story.

The show brought out a bit more from everyone, particularly actors Askew and Landau as the denizens of death row. Rollin is locked in the next cell, awaiting death for the accidental killing of his wife. Landau built an elaborate backstory for a character which, even in the confines of *Mission,* did not exist. "I said, 'Let's make this an absolutely unbearable experience for the viewer,' " says Landau, tallying with Woodfield's original intention. "I made this guy a poor innocent schlemiel. He lost his head in an act of passion, hit his wife, and she died. Not that he isn't guilty, but he didn't mean to kill her, and an hour later he wouldn't even have hit her. And here he is on death row with this hardened killer." For this portrayal, Landau

is at his most nakedly dramatic, almost hyperdramatic, first breaking down helplessly in sobs, then moaning and weeping as he is dragged by guards Barney and Willy into the death chamber. It is a purely pathetic performance and unforgettable, despite the blatant superficiality of the plot within the plot. Landau told director Alex Singer that there would be much emotion in the scene. "Alex saw where I was going, and let me go."

The whole sham, of course, is meant to break down the iron reserve of Duchell, who resolutely refuses to sign the testimony against Parma (who has gotten Duchell out of this situation once before). Nothing works—until it is *his* time to walk the last mile. In contrast to Rollin's exit, Duchell's is angry and full of hatred as he, too, goes kicking and screaming to the chamber. "There was actually a feeling of tension on that set, an edge of uncontrollability," Askew recalls. "Landau and I assiduously avoided comparing notes. We didn't relate to each other because I was supposed to be full of scorn for him because he cracked up."

It is not until he is strapped into the gas chamber, the observation windows closed, and the cyanide capsules finally dipped into the acid, that Duchell finally breaks and manically shouts out a confession. "It was the only time in television where I got to do a scene twice, to go back the next day and do it again," says Askew. Director Singer wasn't satisfied with Askew's confession, and told the actor that he believed he could do better. The next day, he did. Singer says, "Occasionally in television you get a marvelous actor out of what's usually available for the villain parts. And that's what happened. Luke was so wonderful, a superb professional."

"I can't speak for the whole series," Luke Askew adds, "but that particular episode was done like a feature. It looked to me as if they shot a show until they were satisfied with the results." In this case the extra time and expense paid off thoroughly. Askew's range of emotions and expressions, from indifference to worry to disbelief to hysteria, are glorious to behold, and his half-mad ravings in the chamber abnormally satisfying.

"The Execution" remains an unusually strong and memorable *Mission*. Appropriately, it was the last segment Woodfield and Balter saw to completion.

57: THE PLAY

First Aired: 12/8/68

Produced by: Robert E. Thompson
Written by: Lou Shaw
Directed by: Lee H. Katzin
Music Composed and Conducted by:
Robert Drasnin

TEAM: Phelps, Rollin, Cinnamon, Barney

Good morning, Mr. Phelps. The man you're looking at is Milos Kuro, minister of culture and director of the National Theater of the UCR. Kuro has been bombarding his people with vicious anti-American propaganda in order to discredit the UCR's premier, Leon Vados. Considered a progressive behind the Iron Curtain, Vados is attempting to negotiate a nonaggression pact between his country and ours. Your mission, Jim, should you decide to accept it, is to stop Kuro before he destroys all hopes for peace between our two countries. As always, should you or any of your IM Force be caught or killed, the secretary will disavow any knowledge of your actions. Please dispose of this recording in the usual manner. Good luck, Jim.

While visiting America, Kuro attends a controversial play written by Cinnamon, depicting Premier Vados and the president of the United States. American reaction to the play seems so negative that Kuro considers it a strong propaganda weapon and arranges to have it staged in the UCR.

Rehearsals progress smoothly under Kuro's direction. But when Cinnamon and actor Rollin tell Premier Vados that Kuro is changing the play to portray him as a corrupt fool, Vados attends a rehearsal. The premier sits directly below an IMF radar disk which creates a sound envelope. Through the disk and heard only by those under the disk, Barney plays a tape recording of the play's dialogue designed to humiliate Vados. Enraged, the premier has Kuro arrested.

GUEST CAST: John Colicos (Milos Kuro), Michael Tolan (Vitol Enzor), John McLiam (Anton Usakos), Barry Atwater (Premier Leon Vados), Charles Maxwell (Bok), Jason Wingreen (Official), Clete Roberts (Announcer), Ed McCready (Inspector), Socrates Ballis (Driver). *Unbilled:* Essence Alexander (Woman), Bruno VeSota (Heckler #1), Dave Armstrong (Heckler #2), Charles Napier (First Guard), Joe Prete (Second Guard)

This enjoyable and colorful show is built around the sound disk, a conceivable device but one not involving radar, as described in the show. In theory, air molecules between the disk and Vados are ultrasonically agitated to prevent passage of sound waves. Radar, electromagnetic radiation of radio wavelengths used for detection, is an unrelated system.

The disk adds a new dimension to the IMF play, all for the premier's benefit. Note the way the dialogue changes in the following chart. On the left is the text as performed on the stage, on the right, the taped lines Vados hears via the disk:

I understand. But when one is with one's advisers, one must keep track of time.
Especially at this stage.
Yet, just pressures can make our responsibilities bearable.
Not in my country. And it comforts me to know there is no paper like this to count.
A defense fund is still the same thing.
Especially in these troubled times. After all, a leader's first duty is to resist.

I understand. But when one is with one's mistress, one loses all track of time.
Especially at our age.
It's such pleasures that make our responsibilities bearable.
Not in my country. But it comforts me to know it is safe in my Swiss bank account.
A retirement fund is always a good thing.
Especially in these troubled times. After all, a leader's first duty is to himself.

58: THE CARDINAL

Produced by: William Read Woodfield and
   Allan Balter
Written by: John T. Dugan
Directed by: Sutton Roley
Music Composed and Conducted by:
   Jerry Fielding

First Aired: 11/17/68

TEAM: Phelps, Rollin, Cinnamon, Barney, Willy

Good morning, Mr. Phelps. The man you're looking at is General Casimir Zepke, who is plotting to make himself a dictator. Only one man stands between Zepke and absolute power—Stanislaus Cardinal Souchek, whose influence with the people has kept his country free. We have learned that Zepke imprisoned the cardinal six weeks ago when he entered Zolnar Monastery for his annual retreat. Zepke intends to replace him with an exact double who will politically endorse Zepke, guaranteeing his final seizure of power. Your mission, Jim, should you decide to accept it, is to save Cardinal Souchek and stop Zepke. As always, should you or any of your IM Force be caught or killed, the secretary will disavow any knowledge of your actions. This tape will self-destruct in five seconds. Good luck, Jim.

Thanks to an infected IMF mosquito, imposter Anton Nagorski develops an extremely high fever on the day he, as "Cardinal Souchek," is to endorse Zepke. Under Zepke's watchful eye, Dr. Phelps and nurse Cinnamon attend to the sick man. Cardinal Ortoloni (Rollin), an old friend of Souchek's, sees through Nagorski's impersonation, but is buried alive in an airtight sarcophagus. He escapes to help Barney and Willy enter the monastery. Together they proceed to the room adjoining Nagorski's, where the real cardinal is held.

Phelps places Nagorski in an oxygen tent. When the tent mists, Willy and Barney open up the wall behind the sleeping Nagorski, pull him out of bed, and replace him with the cardinal. Before the world press, Zepke introduces the man he believes is Nagorski. Expecting a glowing endorsement, he is stunned to hear Cardinal Souchek condemn him.

GUEST CAST: Theodore Bikel (General Casimir Zepke), Paul Stevens (Stanislaus Cardinal Souchek/Anton Nagorski), Barbara Babcock (Major Maria Felder). *Unbilled:* Mike Masters, Gary Pagett (Monks), Allen Bleiweiss (double, Souchek/Nagorski)

"The Cardinal," which *Daily Variety* dubbed, "one of the best in the series," is a first-rate rendition of the old doppelganger warhorse. The show is so smoothly produced that it is difficult to believe the segment was worked on by *three* producing teams. Director Sutton Roley handles the proceedings well, including one scene where three Soucheks (Nagorski, Souchek, and the disguised Rollin) are in one room.

One of the oddest props ever seen in *Mission* appears here. It's a STEM, or storage tubular extendable member. About the size of a musical metronome, the STEM is a box which, when activated by small motors, extends a metal cone or horn fifty feet long, with enough tensile strength not to bend. "A fella at Fairchild Aircraft loved the show," Jonnie Burke recalls, "and he brought down a STEM. It was basically like a measuring tape which rolls up on a reel inside. It all went into this little box!" Barney and Willy utilize the STEM below the window of Nagorski's room at the monastery. By attaching a boxful of mosquitoes to the STEM's mouth and activating a fan in the unit, the infected insects are blown up the tube and through the window. The tube is then retracted into its tiny box. The STEM, although phony-looking, is a genuine apparatus, used more commonly as the body for aerospace

Barney and Willy employ a space-age device to penetrate a monastery in "The Cardinal."

antennae on space satellites and lunar vehicles. Anyone doubting the STEM's authenticity should ask Greg Morris—he cut his finger on the tubing!

The mosquitoes used in the STEM were an example of what prop man Bill Bates calls, "one of those little things that can happen." On location at Mount St. Mary's College (where the pilot was filmed), Bates had no luck coming up with the insects. "One of the nuns at the college told me, 'Oh, the biology department has lots of mosquitoes; they're doing some experiments.' She gave me a jarful." On the set and about to shoot the scene requiring the mosquitoes, Bates got a frantic call from the college, urging him *not* to use the mosquitoes. "They'd given us the wrong bunch," Bates says, "and we had a jarful of *malarial* mosquitoes! She caught us just before we released them."

How does Cardinal Rollin escape from the sarcophagus? On a chain around his neck is a pectoral cross with two crossbars. Inside the tomb he opens the crossbars and removes two small, very strong metal rollers, then uses the cross as a jack to imperceptibly lift the lid, allowing air to filter in. Placing the rollers in the space between the sarcophagus and the lid, he slides the top off the coffin.

59: THE ELIXIR

First Aired: 11/24/68

Produced by: Robert E. Thompson
Written by: Max Hodge
Directed by: John Florea

TEAM: Phelps, Rollin, Cinnamon, Barney, Willy, plastic surgeon Dr. Paul van Bergner

Good morning, Mr. Phelps. The woman you're looking at is Riva Santel, widow of the late president of San Cordova. Riva has always been the actual power behind the throne and she arranged to make herself the focus of an intense personality cult. The people of San Cordova have been systematically propagandized into revering her face and name. In seventy-two hours this man, Deputy Premier Tomas Avilla, plans to announce free elections. Before then, however, Riva intends to make a televised speech in which she will announce her takeover as dictator of San Cordova. Your mission, Jim, should you decide to accept it, is to stop the coup planned by Riva Santel, and to make possible free elections in San Cordova. As always, if you or any of your IM Force should be caught or killed, the secretary will disavow any knowledge of your actions. This tape will self-destruct in ten seconds. Good luck, Jim.

A TV crew (Jim, Barney, Willy, and host Cinnamon) arrive at the palace to tape a documentary hosted by Riva, who is eager to use them to cover her own impending broadcast from Deputy Premier Avilla. Cinnamon falters during the broadcast, and Riva hears the crew make sarcastic remarks about Cinnamon's age. Mysterious specialist Rollin is called in. Riva learns that Rollin is a plastic surgeon and that Cinnamon is *seventy years old.* Rollin quickly restores Cinnamon to youth. Longing for eternal beauty, Riva persuades Rollin and his "assistant" Dr. van Bergner to operate on her. Rollin can schedule the operation only on the evening that Riva is to make her live TV speech. Riva accepts Cinnamon's suggestion to videotape her speech, but uses her own camera and crew to record it.

Barney and Willy patch their "dormant" cameras into Riva's and secretly tape the speech. Barney carefully reedits the tape and switches it for the real one. Riva undergoes surgery but remains sedated, forcing the tape to air. Her face in bandages, she awakens. Instead of announcing her takeover, Riva is aghast to see—and hear—herself announce her retirement from public life. Cinnamon, disguised as Riva, makes a conspicuous final exit from San Cordova, while Riva removes her bandages and comes face to face with the IMF's devastating coup de grace.

GUEST CAST: Ruth Roman (Riva Santel), Morgan Sterne (Raoul Lenz), George Gaynes (Dr. Paul van Bergner), Ivor Barry (Deputy Premier Tomas Avilla), Richard Angarola (Colonel Diaz), Arthur Eisner (Salesman), Cosmo Sardo (Official), Marco Lopez (Cameraman), Charles Picerni (Border Guard), Irene Kelly (the Young Riva). *Unbilled:* Victor Paul (Guard), Al Shelly (Guard #1)

"The Elixir" is another script commissioned by Woodfield and Balter, but ultimately produced by Bob Thompson. According to writer Max Hodge, Woodfield and Balter liked the Eva Peron aspects of the story, and felt that a female villain would be a good change of pace (it was). The story itself is simpler than usual which, considering the tense time in which it was produced, was probably a relief.

Embodied by the elegant Ruth Roman, Riva is quite a contrast from the IMF's usual, pockmarked antagonists. A female adversary makes little difference to the Force. In the climax, Riva gets what she wanted: a facelift which makes her look years younger. She takes off her bandages and finds in the mirror a young, attractive woman—who looks nothing like Riva Sentel. In an almost sadistic triumph, Riva's plans, power, even her identity have been taken away by the Impossible Missions Force.

60: THE EXCHANGE

First Aired: 1/4/69

Produced by: Stanley Kallis
Written by: Laurence Heath
Directed by: Alexander Singer
Music Composed and Conducted by:
    Jerry Fielding

TEAM: Phelps, Rollin, Barney, Willy

In a departure from the series format, Cinnamon is captured while completing a mission in the Eastern Zone of a divided country.

Through no fault of her own, Cinnamon is caught and arrested seconds after delivering top secret information to Jim and Rollin, who flee. Questioned by chief of intelligence Colonel Strom, she is seated in a chair which records her physiological reactions. Cinnamon is immune to bribery and to threats of physical torture, disfigurement, and death. But when she unwittingly reveals that she is claustrophobic, Strom locks her in a tiny, narrow cell where, drugged and under tremendous psychological pressure, she comes ever closer to identifying herself and the IMF.

An anguished Phelps concludes that the only way to save Cinnamon is to trade her for Rudolf Kurtz, an extremely valuable Eastern spy currently imprisoned in the West Zone. Kurtz, jailed for more than a year, hasn't divulged his vital information to Western officials. The IMF must spring Kurtz from prison, get him past Western police, and somehow break him before Strom breaks and kills Cinnamon.

GUEST CAST: John Vernon (Colonel Josef Strom), Will Kuluva (Rudolf Kurtz), Curt Lowens (Major Mecklin), Michael Bell (Captain Anders), Robert Ellenstein (Dr. Emil Gorin). *Unbilled:* Bob Homel (Guard), Dick Ziker (West Gate Guard), Kenneth Karols (East Gate Guard), Katey Barrett (Matron)

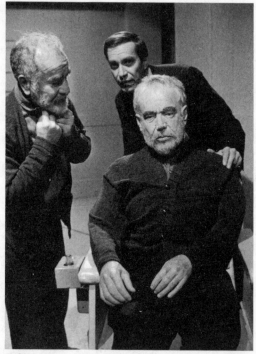

Will the real Rudolf Kurtz (Will Kuluva) please stand up?

"We don't do stories about our people getting caught," Geller told writer Laurence Heath regarding "The Exchange." Nevertheless, Geller didn't stand in Heath's way and a good thing too, since "The Exchange" is one of *Mission*'s best hours and would become one of Geller's favorites.

The obvious distress on Jim's face after the slipup makes it clear that this is the first time an IMFer has been caught. In addition to getting Kurtz out of jail and breaking him, Jim must also wrestle with his guilt over Cinnamon's capture. The added tension makes for a fine show.

In an example of art imitating life, Cinnamon's great weakness, claustrophobia, was also Barbara Bain's. Cinnamon is held captive in a cubicle with no windows or doors. "Even

leaving the roof off to shoot from above was not enough to make Barbara comfortable," says prop man Bill Bates. "We could only keep her in there for a very short time. She was very frightened." In the show's most harrowing scene, Cinnamon labors to open her cell's air vent. But as soon as she crawls into the vent tunnel, steel doors slam shut around her, trapping her in an even smaller box than before. The shock sends her into unconsciousness.

Rescuing Cinnamon involves some of the team's most elaborate and frantic ruses, starting with an inflatable Kurtz dummy left in the spy's jail cell by wheelchair-bound Rollin (the real Kurtz crawls into the rear of the chair to escape). Kurtz is told he's going home, and from a warehouse hideout, is placed in a storage box and trucked across the border—he thinks. In fact, he is moved onto a bouncing hydraulic platform which, along with additional sound effects, convinces Kurtz that he is crossing the border. Kurtz emerges from the box to find himself in Colonel Strom's office (an exact IMF replica), now occupied by Colonel Phelps, who has replaced the "traitorous" Strom. After some hesitation, Kurtz tapes his report. Jim tosses the tape to Rollin, who astounds Kurtz by bounding from his wheelchair to exit. Kurtz now realizes that he has been tricked. "When they find out I've been debriefed, they'll kill me," he cries. "We would be fools to tell them," Jim replies. "I assume you won't."

Strom has brought Cinnamon to the edge of breaking, but has now run out of time, and must trade her for Kurtz in no-man's-land between East and West. The exchange goes well—until Strom pulls out a machine gun and shoots Jim and Cinnamon, then speeds off. "Whoever they were, it doesn't matter now," he tells Kurtz. Fortunately, the spies' bulletproof trenchcoats save their lives.

Laurence Heath's first draft was more drastic than the final version: Originally, Cinnamon does break and reveals her name and Jim's to the enemy! This shock would have been neutralized at the finale when Strom "kills" the pair and considers the case closed. It was undoubtedly Geller who nixed the confession, but what a shocking scene it would have been had he granted Cinnamon more vulnerability.

61: THE BARGAIN

Produced by: Stanley Kallis
Written by: Robert E. Thompson
Directed by: Richard Benedict

First Aired: 12/15/68

TEAM: Phelps, Rollin, Cinnamon, Barney, Willy

Good morning, Mr. Phelps. The man you're looking at is General Ernesto Neyron, the former dictator of Surananka who now lives in exile at his closely guarded Miami estate. In order to finance a military coup which will return him to power, Neyron is about to conclude a deal with this man, Frank Layton, a top Syndicate leader. In exchange for several million dollars, Neyron has agreed to legalize gambling in Surananka and give all rights to the Syndicate. Your mission, Jim, should you decide to accept it, is to stop Neyron and the Syndicate. As always, should you or any of your IM Force be caught or killed, the secretary will disavow any knowledge of your actions. This tape will self-destruct in five seconds. Good luck, Jim.

The IMF operation begins only hours before Layton is to give Neyron the cash he needs to reconquer his country. Jim, as aide to billionaire financier Rollin, tries to buy the Syndicate hotel Layton works out of, but Layton learns that this is a ploy meant to divert Layton from Rollin's real plan: to swipe the Surananka gambling rights from the Syndicate, with the cooperation of Neyron.

Neyron, of course, is unaware of all this. On his estate, chef Barney, with the help of kitchen staff Willy and Cinnamon, uses a mixture of drugs, electronic tricks, and projections to convince Neyron that he is suffering from a rare illness which allows him to make uncommonly accurate predictions.

Neyron foresees his own murder by Layton moments before Layton angrily arrives to confront him. Neyron takes the first opportunity to shoot Layton just as the police, summoned not so clairvoyantly by Phelps, drive onto the estate.

GUEST CAST: Albert Paulsen (General Ernesto Neyron), Warren Stevens (Frank Layton), Nate Esformes (Colonel Santagura), Phillip Pine (Arnold Grasnik), Phil Posner (Bodyguard), James Wellman (Hotel Manager), Gregg Martell (Eddie), Jay Jostyn (Dr. Brandt), Richard Karie (Bell Boy). *Unbilled:* Ken Strange (Maintenance Man)

Combining the "international" and "gangster" formulas, "The Bargain" is swamped by an overabundance of gadgets, at least one of which is inaccurate. The scheme involves the projection of a film in which Rollin, as Layton, "shoots" Neyron, which prompts Neyron to shoot Layton first. Barney explains the illusion's principle: "A concave surface [Neyron's mirror] reflecting an image into space, much like the well-known oasis in a desert mirage. Ours is better focused." But in real life the resulting image would be upside-down. Also, mirages are almost never caused by reflection, but by *refraction* due to the unequal indices of cool and hot air. We can only assume that the IMF projector or film was inverted to compensate!

In addition to the trick film, "The Bargain" offers a battery of devices that would turn James Bond's Q Branch green with envy: a black light to enable Neyron to read cards facedown; a rub-on forgery kit Cinnamon uses to apply Neyron's signature onto Rollin's fake contract; Jim's inflatable black bag, suggesting a parcelful of cash to Layton's spies; a gadget to snap open Neyron's wall safe at will; and the usual drugs and taped messages to convince Neyron he is hallucinating.

The show has bright spots, like Rollin's quick change in an elevator, turning from a rich old man to himself in twenty-seven seconds. But the hardware does all the work in "The Bargain," which was written in four days by Bob Thompson at a time when there were *no* scripts on the shelf. Luckily, the next show was provided by a writer who'd solve the script crisis.

62: THE MIND OF STEFAN MILKOS

First Aired: 1/12/69

TEAM: Phelps, Rollin, Cinnamon, Barney, Willy

Produced by: Stanley Kallis
Written by: Paul Playdon
Directed by: Robert Butler
Music Composed and Conducted by:
Richard Markowitz

Good morning, Mr. Phelps. The man you are looking at is Walter Townsend, one of our high-ranking intelligence officers, whom we recently discovered is a top enemy agent. Upon learning this, we allowed Townsend access to false information which will cause his country severe embarrassment if believed and acted upon. Unfortunately, this man, George Simpson, Townsend's only contact in America, discovered the information was false and reported to his superiors that Townsend had defected. However, his superiors are aware Simpson is jealous of Townsend. The truth or falsity of this information is so important that they are sending their most brilliant intelligence officer, Stefan Miklos, to investigate. Your mission, Jim, should you decide to accept it, is to make Stefan believe Townsend's information. As always, should you or any of your IM Force be caught or killed, the secretary will disavow any knowledge of your actions. This tape will self-destruct in five seconds. Good luck, Jim.

Calculating, ruthless, and possessing a photographic memory, Stefan Miklos has no flaws and is invulnerable to everyone—except himself. So Jim invents a painstakingly intricate plot designed to be uncovered by Stefan.

Stefan (Rollin) visits Simpson, who delivers proof that Townsend is relaying false information. Phelps, as "Stefan's" aide, announces that they are under American surveillance and hustles Simpson out. The real Stefan arrives, and is told by Simpson (Rollin) that proof of Townsend's disloyalty is forthcoming.

Searching Townsend's apartment, Stefan finds a photo of Cinnamon (planted earlier by Rollin) hidden away. He breaks into her hotel room to find her bags packed and two mysterious keys. He also finds a nearly burned matchbook cover containing the phone number of a brokerage firm. Broker Barney tells Stefan that Cinnamon has recently sold $200,000 in stocks. Cinnamon is spotted depositing items in two airport lockers.

"Stefan" (Rollin) gives Simpson special orders: Simpson tells Townsend that he has been called back home and that Townsend will be getting a new contact and new codes that night at an airport locker. Simpson gives him the key to the locker. Townsend (his watch discreetly set back thirty minutes by the IMF) goes to the airport, opens the locker, and is grabbed by Stefan, who finds a passport and ticket to Rio in the locker.

Townsend pleads his innocence to Stefan, who plans to kill him. "It was Simpson who sent me to the airport," he insists. "He told me to go to the airport at 4:30." "But you didn't get there until five," Stefan notes. "No," Townsend insists, "I got there at 4:30." Checking Townsend's watch and finding it thirty minutes slow, Stefan stops and thinks. He remembers that a matchbook belonging to left-handed "Simpson" (Rollin) had matches missing on its left side. But right-handed Cinnamon had a matchbook used in an identical manner. "It could be a link," he muses. Comparing notes, he and Townsend learn that Townsend's report to his country regarding a US arms treaty was altered in transit—presumably by "Simpson."

Stefan returns to the art gallery drop point where he first received his information about Simpson, and checks videotapes which show Cinnamon, Barney, and Jim in the place moments before he arrived. Convinced that these American agents have tried to trick him, Stefan returns to "Simpson" (Rollin), who delivers proof of Townsend's treachery via fellow agent Phelps, whom Stefan recognizes from the tapes. Feigning acceptance of their data, Stefan returns to Townsend. "I allowed them to think they fooled me," says Stefan. "His proof authenticated the document concerning the arms treaty as being false. Therefore it must be true. Our immediate concern now is to get word back that the document is valid."

GUEST CAST: Steve Ihnat (Stefan Miklos), Jason Evers (Walter Townsend), Edward Asner (George Simpson), Vic Perrin (Owner), Joe Breen (Vincent), Arland Schubert (Cooper*)

Peter Graves believes "Stefan Miklos" to be, "intellectually, the best one we ever did." Paul Playdon's first *Mission* is easily the most complicated ever, with plotting so sophisticated and detailed that prior labyrinthian *Mission*s seem like clothesline plots by comparison. An excellent and amazingly logical tale, the show suffers terribly when aired by many local stations, which cut anywhere from two to ten minutes out of the episodes. Editing is harmful enough to any *Mission,* but to cut a minute of "Stefan" can render it impossible to follow.

" 'The Mind of Stefan Miklos' was an attempt on Paul's part, with my backing, to find something else besides the magic tricks," says producer Kallis. "We weren't satisfied to just take the Balter-Woodfield formula, measure it out, and scoop. We were looking for another avenue to break the formula. Our hope was to look for a larger frame, and then invite more writers to come and play." It didn't quite turn out that way, but shows like "Stefan," "had some fun in them," Kallis feels. And suspense too, for the show actually has a scene near the end in which Phelps worries that his scheme may in fact have been too subtle for Stefan to uncover. Some, like Paul Krasny in postproduction, believed that a television audience, even *Mission*'s, would be unable to follow such a dense plot. Perhaps he was right. Playdon concedes "Stefan" was, "very ambitious and perhaps too complex," but it did point the series in a new direction when it was most necessary.

Dominating "Stefan" are the performances of Landau and, in the title role, Steve Ihnat. Landau is excellent, playing two different characters intermittently (sans masks): as Stefan he is brusque, disdainful, and as intimidating as the real thing; and as Simpson, slow, halting, and unintelligent. Ihnat is perfectly cast, with a penetrating stare, precise physical movements, and contempt for those around him. Not until the finale do we notice any emotion from him, and what he does express is surprising. "I wish I could meet the man that masterminded their operation," Stefan tells Townsend. "He was brilliant. I feel sorry for him. He played the game well, but he lost. And it'll destroy him." The real irony, however, didn't make it into the finished show.

CINNAMON: What do you think will happen to Stefan and Townsend?
PHELPS: I'm certain their country will reward them suitably.

---

* Inexplicably called Willoughby throughout the show.

63: THE FREEZE

Produced by: Stanley Kallis
Written by: Paul Playdon
Directed by: Alexander Singer

First Aired: 12/23/68

TEAM: Phelps, Rollin, Cinnamon, Barney, Willy, Dr. Jacob Bowman

Good morning, Mr. Phelps. The man you're looking at is Raymond Barret, who is currently serving a five-year sentence in the state penitentiary. We have just learned through his cellmate Max Davis that Barret is actually Albert Jenkins, who masterminded the Oakdale armored car robbery five years ago, double-crossed his associates, and hid the ten million dollar take. By cleverly allowing himself to be caught and convicted as Raymond Barret of a burglary charge he did not commit, he hoped to wait out the statute of limitations on the robbery. That statute expires in two days. When Barret is released from prison in a few months, he will be able to collect the ten million dollars scot-free. Your mission, Jim, should you decide to accept it, is to bring Barret to justice and recover the money. As always, should you or any of your IM Force be caught or killed, the secretary will disavow any knowledge of your actions. This tape will self-destruct in five seconds. Good luck, Jim.

Dr. Bowman tells Barret that he may be suffering from a potentially fatal disease, and arranges an early release for the prisoner. Specialist Rollin confirms the diagnosis and tells Barret that his case is incurable. Desperate, Barret blackmails cryogenic pioneer Phelps into "freezing" his body until a cure for his ailment is found. Phelps reluctantly does so.

Barret awakens in a futuristic hospital room attended to by a graying Rollin, who tells him that he has been thawed out in the year 1980. Barret panics when Rollin informs him that currency has been eliminated from society, and that the police are waiting to question him. With less than three hours before the statute actually expires, Barret escapes and learns that the "real" date is August 18, 1968—one day *past* the statute of limitations.

Convinced that the statute has expired (in fact it has not), Barret leads the IMF and the police to a cemetery where the stolen money is located, just as his two accomplices, baited by the Force, arrive. The ten million dollars is recovered and the three crooks arrested.

GUEST CAST: Donnelly Rhodes (Raymond Barret), John Zaremba (Dr. Jacob Bowman), Lucetta Jenison (First Receptionist), Milt Kogan (David Singleton), Vince Howard (Max Davis), Walter Mathews (Sammy Gilbert), Carol Andreson (Phonovision Girl). *Unbilled:* Pat Newby (Second Receptionist), Bill Couch (Stunt)

Cryonics, the practice of freezing the terminally ill until science can cure them, first made headlines when a seventy-three-year-old psychologist became the first "frozen man." The premise was outrageous enough to fit *Mission,* and Paul Playdon wove a simple plot line around this far-out hook.

"The Freeze" uses the same MO as "Stefan Miklos": the elaborate plan designed to be seen through and cover the real scheme. Since writer Playdon was forced to write "The Freeze" in a very short time, the result is not as tight or as smooth as the earlier show, and everyone seemed aware of it. Director Alex Singer, who had previously helmed some of the best *Mission*s, was disappointed by the quality of the script, although he was aware of the reasons behind it and got along well with Playdon and Kallis. Singer was also suffering from the early stages of pneumonia during filming, which didn't help matters at all.

64: THE TEST CASE

First Aired: 1/19/69

Produced by: Stanley Kallis
Written by: Laurence Heath
Directed by: Sutton Roley

TEAM: Phelps, Rollin, Cinnamon, Barney, Willy

Good morning, Mr. Phelps. This man, Dr. Oswald Beck, has succeeded in developing a mutation of the bacteria which causes cerebral spinal meningitis. A spray of this mutant strain produces death within minutes, yet becomes harmless in a few hours, making it practical for our enemies to use as a battlefield weapon. Your mission, Jim, should you decide to accept it, is to destroy the bacteria culture and stop Beck. As always, should you or any of your IM Force be caught or killed, the secretary will disavow any knowledge of your actions. This recording will self-destruct in five seconds. Good luck, Jim.

Rollin replaces the political prisoner chosen as guinea pig for Beck's bacteria tests. Barney switches the lethal gas cylinder for one filled with knockout gas and attaches a balloon to its nozzle, preventing Rollin from inhaling it. Rollin "dies," presumably from the gas, and is wheeled into the autopsy room, where military medic Phelps "discovers" that the prisoner has not died from the gas—a fact which shocks Beck.

The balloonful of knockout gas seeps into the observation room by IMF remote control, felling security chief Olni and military representative Kirsch. When Jim and Beck find the pair evidently dying from the virulent gas, Beck, afraid he'll be thought a traitor, tries to run but is shot. Jim then destroys the bacteria forever.

GUEST CAST: David Hurst (Dr. Oswald Beck), Noah Keen (Captain Rudolf Olni), Richard Bull (Lorkner), Paul Carr (Dr. Zeped), Laurence Haddon (Lieutenant Marlov), Bart LaRue (General Kirsch), Larry Vincent (Prisoner Stoltz), Mike Masters (Gate Guard). *Unbilled:* Robert Bralver (Driver Guard)

"The Test Case" concerns itself with the issue of germ warfare, a theme which writer Heath would expand upon in next season's two-parter, episode 76, "The Controllers."

"That was a very claustrophobic show," says director Sutton Roley. "It was very tight, never opened up, and most of it was all interior. I remember Bruce Geller saying to me, 'Fascinating style, Sutton, fascinating. But I don't know where the hell I am! But I guess it doesn't matter.'"

Perhaps the episode's strongest feature is the work by art director Bill Ross. His sparse, gloomy, utilitarian sets add a menacing feel to an already dark and sinister plot.

65: THE SYSTEM

Produced by: Stanley Kallis
Written by: Robert Hamner
Directed by: Robert Gist

First Aired: 1/26/69

TEAM: Phelps, Rollin, Cinnamon, Barney, Willy

Good morning, Mr. Phelps. The man you're looking at is Constantine Victor, the Syndicate's boss contractor, known to his associates as Mr. V. Recently a grand jury indicted Victor for murder, and he has been out on bail, awaiting trial. Then yesterday the prosecution's star witness was killed, and it appears the case will be dropped. Only one other man, Johnny Costa, Victor's close friend for over ten years, knows enough to convict Mr. V. Costa himself seems invulnerable, as he currently runs the Syndicate's gambling operation in an area where gambling is legal. Your mission, Jim, should you decide to accept it, is to get Costa to talk and make sure that Mr. V is convicted. As always, should you or any of your IM Force be caught or killed, the secretary will disavow any knowledge of your actions. Please dispose of this tape in the usual manner. Good luck, Jim.

Syndicate killer Phelps tells Costa that someone has put a contract out on the casino head. At the tables, Cinnamon charms Costa into endorsing minor credit slips which Rollin forges into major ones. Syndicate bookkeeper Rollin arrives to audit the books. When he discovers an unlisted twenty-five thousand dollars (planted by Barney) and the flurry of credit slips which Costa claims are fake, Rollin angrily calls "Victor" in New York. Before witnesses, "Victor" (prerecorded Rollin) relieves Costa of his duties and places Rollin in charge.

Thinking he's in big trouble, Costa forces Cinnamon to admit that Victor has paid her to compromise him. When hit man Willy tries to kill him, Costa locks himself in the casino vault and shouts to Rollin, "Tell Mr. Victor I'll see him in court."

GUEST CAST: James Patterson (Johnny Costa), Robert Yuro (Arnie), Peter Marko (Markos), Art Lewis (Cashier), Tony Giorgio (Dealer), Joel Lawrence (Wilson), Val Avery (Constantine Victor). *Unbilled:* George Washburn (Stickman), Joseph D'Angelo (Dealer #2), Jerry Wills (Stunt double, Costa)

Another mission of persuasion, "The System" utilizes an impressive device called the "snorkel camera," developed by cameraman-director Paul Kenworthy which, by moving across a gaming table, transforms the tabletop's dimensions into those of a football field. The device, introduced in commercials, makes its episodic debut here. The most memorable use of the snorkel occurs when Barney, in an air vent twelve feet away, uses a metal arm and claw to open Costa's vault safe and plant the twenty-five thousand dollars. In one remarkable shot, the snorkel moves into the tiny wall safe, then turns around inside the safe to face Greg Morris.

"The System" placed eighth in the Nielsen ratings of that week, demonstrating *Mission*'s dramatically rising popularity. The show's audience had no way of knowing that creatively, *Mission* had already peaked and was in fact on a slow downward curve.

66: THE GLASS CAGE

First Aired: 2/2/69

Produced by: Stanley Kallis
Teleplay by: Paul Playdon
Story by: Alf Harris
Directed by: John Moxey

TEAM: Phelps, Rollin, Cinnamon, Barney, Willy

Good morning, Mr. Phelps. The man you're looking at is Anton Reisner, the much-beloved leader of the resistance against his country's tyrannical government. Three weeks ago, he was incarcerated in the automated Trast Prison, from which no escape has ever been made. The prison is currently commanded by this man, Major Nicholas Zelinko, who is torturing Reisner in order to get the names of other resistance leaders. Your mission, Jim, should you decide to accept it, is to get Reisner out of Trast Prison. As always, should you or any of your IM Force be caught or killed, the secretary will disavow any knowledge of your actions. This message will self-destruct in five seconds. Good luck, Jim.

An escape-proof glass cubicle holds Reisner, video monitored at all times. Whenever the cell door is opened, it is electronically registered on a digital counter in the master control room *and* numbered manually in a code book.

Barney and Willy are jailed at Trast while Cinnamon, as head of the country's prison system, arrives for an inspection. Cinnamon lures Zelinko away from the prison long enough for the master control room to be filled with gas and Barney and Willy to free themselves from their cell. They wreck the video monitor, overcome an electrified hallway, and open Reisner's cell door. Barney tells Reisner to stay in the cage and to behave differently from now on.

Zelinko returns to a chaotic prison, where Willy and Barney have been rejailed. He notices that the

digital counter to Reisner's door has been advanced by one number, but *no matching entry* has been made in the code book. Observing Reisner's odd behavior in the cell, Zelinko assumes that his prisoner has somehow been replaced by a double. Cinnamon and a prison lieutenant overhear Zelinko and his aide Gulka conspire to keep the switch from her. Zelinko is arrested; Cinnamon takes Barney, Willy, and the "imposter" to "headquarters" for further questioning.

GUEST CAST: Lloyd Bochner (Major Nicholas Zelinko), Larry Linville (Captain Gulka), Richard Garland (Anton Reisner), Lou Robb (Lieutenant Vasney), George Perina (Szabo), Al Shelly (Guard #1), Max Klevin (Guard #2)

"The Glass Cage" stems from a story Alf Harris wrote in the early days of Canadian television about a man escaping from prison. Harris remembered the idea and saw Paul Playdon, who rewrote it to fit the *Mission* confines. "When we started 'The Glass Cage,'" Playdon remembers, "I actually did not know the ending to the script! That was the most nightmarish of all the shows in its own way because I didn't have a clear idea of how it would all come together." Apart from a suspicious gadget which creates images on the prison's monitoring tapes, there are no major story holes.

The subplot which gets Zelinko out of the prison offers Barbara Bain one of her better roles this season. As a hand-twisting, neurotic woman infatuated with fellow official Rollin (a cad competing with Zelinko for a promotion), she underplays beautifully.

GRENZ - PASS

Vor- und Zuname: IGOR DRAGA

Staatsangehörigkeit: COLONEL

Gewerbe _____ Tag der Ankunft 14592

Ständiger Wohnort mit Strasse u. Hs. Nr.:
14 DIV. INTELLIGENCE

Reisezweck _____

GRENZ - PASS

Vor- und Zuname: IVAN BRINOV

Staatsangehörigkeit: MAJOR

Gewerbe _____ Tag der Ankunft 15942

Ständiger Wohnort mit Strasse u. Hs. Nr.:
14 DIV. INTELLIGENCE

Reisezweck _____

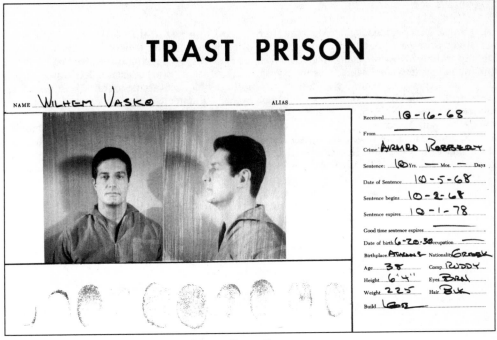

TRAST PRISON

NAME WILHEM VASKO   ALIAS _____

Received 10-16-68

From _____

Crime ARMED ROBBERY

Sentence: 10 Yrs. ___ Mos. ___ Days

Date of Sentence 10-5-68

Sentence begins 10-2-68

Sentence expires 10-1-78

Good time sentence expires _____

Date of birth 6-20-30 Occupation _____

Birthplace ATHENS Nationality GREEK

Age 38 Comp. RUDDY

Height 6'4" Eyes BRN

Weight 225 Hair BLK

Build LGE

Phoney ID cards from "The Glass Cage."

67: LIVE BAIT

Produced by: Stanley Kallis
Teleplay by: James D. Buchanan and
    Ronald Austin and Michael Adams
Story by: Michael Adams
Directed by: Stuart Hagmann
Music Composed and Conducted by:
    Richard Markowitz
Director of Photography: Gert Andersen, ASC

First Aired: 2/23/69

TEAM: Phelps, Rollin, Cinnamon, Barney

Good morning, Mr. Phelps. The man you are looking at is Orin Selby, one of our agents who has managed to become a high-ranking member of the enemy's intelligence service. But this man, Helmut Kellerman, the enemy's chief of internal security, has begun to suspect Selby. Then recently Kellerman captured a courier, code-named Marceau, who knows that Selby is an American agent. Your mission, Jim, should you decide to accept it, is to protect Selby and put an end to the threat posed by Kellerman. As always, should you or any of your IM Force be caught or killed, the secretary will disavow any knowledge of your actions. This tape will self-destruct in five seconds. Good luck, Jim.

Angry that Kellerman has taken Marceau from his custody, Selby calls "headquarters," who send Rollin to investigate Selby's claim that *Kellerman* is a double agent whom Marceau can expose. Alone with Kellerman, Rollin gives him twenty-four hours to break Marceau or the courier will be returned to Selby. Kellerman, knowing Selby would either kill Marceau to protect himself or allow the Americans to retrieve him, devises a plan with Rollin to trap the Americans, using Kellerman's man Brocke, who officially works for Selby.

Kellerman gives Brocke fraudulent blueprints of the building where Marceau is held and tells him to plant them in Selby's office. Kellerman learns that American agent Jim has kidnapped Brocke's girlfriend Stephanie to force Brocke to hand over the blueprints revealing Marceau's location. What is actually happening, however, is far different: The captive Stephanie sees and hears "Kellerman" plotting with American agent Jim to frame Selby by using the "expendable" Brocke. She escapes and informs Brocke that Kellerman plans to kill him. Brocke's chance meeting with American agent Cinnamon leads Kellerman to believe that Brocke has delivered the phony blueprints to the Americans in exchange for Stephanie's freedom.

Rollin, interrogating Marceau in the basement of the security building, sees that the prisoner is wired to a powerful explosive to prevent any attempt to free him. Brocke and Stephanie are arrested fleeing the country. Based on Stephanie's information, Brocke accuses Kellerman of being the double agent trying to frame Selby. But Stephanie, intimidated by Kellerman, retracts her claims.

Rollin triggers a nerve gas which immobilizes the entire security building, then leads the rest of the IMF (disguised as medics) to Marceau's cell. Barney uses liquid nitrogen to freeze the bomb and free Marceau. The unconscious Kellerman is placed near Marceau's empty cell, then Rollin revives Brocke. Together they discover Kellerman at the empty cell, "convincing" Rollin of Brocke's claim that Kellerman is indeed the double agent. Rollin assures Brocke that he will be reinstated with Selby, and Brocke kills the "traitorous" Kellerman.

GUEST CAST: Anthony Zerbe (Colonel Helmut
    Kellerman), Martin Sheen (Lieutenant
    Albert Brocke), Diana Ewing (Stephanie),
    Edmund Gilbert (Marceau), Bert Holland
    (Doctor), Dick Dial (Bauer), John
    Crawford (Orin Selby). *Unbilled:* Dick Ziker
    (double, Brocke), Stephanie Epper (double,
    Cinnamon)

The "Michael Adams" who supplied the original story of "Live Bait" was in fact veteran TV writer Meyer Dolinsky, but by the time it was rewritten by Buchanan and Austin and further revamped by the fine hand of Paul Playdon, it bore little resemblance to the first draft. Rollin and Cinnamon switched parts as the investigator and Brocke's supposed American contact, and Willy was along as Cinnamon's military chauffeur. In addition to saving Selby, the IMF also had to learn just *who* Kellerman had captured and to silence the mystery man if rescue was impossible. Lost was a delicious moment when Brocke and Stephanie, running for the border, are shocked when police discover American agent Rollin in the trunk of their car, apparently trying to leave the country with his "cohort," Brocke. Dragged out of the car by the secret police, Rollin offers stunned Brocke a sheepish shrug, adding, "Well, we tried"! Another unfilmed scene involved Cinnamon's quick visit to the security building's decoding room to photograph the enemy's decoding manual while the rest of the team are with Marceau.

A memorable scene which did stay in was Phelps's way to convince the kidnapped Stephanie that Kellerman is dealing with the Americans. This would normally be accomplished by having Rollin don a Kellerman mask, but since Rollin is busy with the real Kellerman, another solution is found. Barney, shooting through a two-way mirror, films Rollin's initial conversation with Kellerman in which they devise the plan to ruin Selby by using Brocke. Rollin makes sure that Kellerman stays to one side of the room. Next, Barney films footage of Jim sitting in Rollin's position in the same room, spouting dialogue which suggests that Kellerman is working with the Americans. Using an optical printer, Barney then creates a split-screen film in which Jim and Kellerman, who have never met, are seen and heard plotting together. Stephanie is allowed a peek at this film before being allowed to escape and inform Brocke.

Keeping "Live Bait" moving *and* coherent was the chore of twenty-eight-year-old director Stuart Hagmann, whose style perfectly suited *Mission*. Winner of a Screen Producers award while a student at Northwestern University, Hagmann was a veteran of Kodak commercials when he was invited on to *Mission* and *Mannix* by Bruce Geller. Although he would direct just three *Mission*s, he made an indelible impression. "He did brilliant things with nothing," says script supervisor Allan Greedy. "All he had for an airplane was the stairs that come off the plane [episode 78, "The Code"] but with that, and by painting the streets in a certain way, he made it look as though you were really at an airport. On 'Nicole' [episode 73] we were shooting inside a car on a soundstage and he decided that he was going to have it rain. It was a little extra expense, because they had to sprinkle rain on the windshield, but it was very effective. One time he had just a couple of pillars and a doorway and you felt that you were in a room." This economical director not only made the front office happy, but also shot diverting shows.

"Live Bait" is a tortuously involved story, too complicated even for a *Mission: Impossible*. Everyone seems to be using or trying to double-cross everyone else. Along with episode 62, "The Mind of Stefan Miklos," it is the most densely plotted show in the series.

68: DOOMSDAY

Produced by: Stanley Kallis
Written by: Laurence Heath
Directed by: John Moxey

First Aired: 2/16/69

TEAM: Phelps, Rollin, Cinnamon, Barney, Willy

Good morning, Jim. The man you're looking at is Carl Vandaam, the European tycoon whose overextended industrial empire is on the verge of financial collapse. In order to raise ready cash, Vandaam has masterminded the theft of enough plutonium 240 to manufacture a hydrogen bomb, which he intends to sell to the highest bidder. If an aggressive small nation should purchase and use this weapon, it could lead to World War III. Your mission, Jim, should you decide to accept it, is to recover the plutonium and put Vandaam out of business. As always, should you or any of your IM Force be caught or killed, the secretary will disavow any knowledge of your actions. This tape will self-destruct in five seconds. Good luck, Jim.

Jim and Cinnamon meet Kura, one of Vandaam's prospective bidders, and offer him three million dollars to make sure that his country gets the bomb. "We own very valuable oil rights in your country," Phelps claims. "In case there's a war in your part of the world, we want to be sure who is the winner." Kura agrees, and physicist Cinnamon accompanies him to the auction.

Vandaam assembles his bidders and demonstrates the bomb's lethal dose of plutonium, unaware that Barney watches from a ceiling conduit. When they leave, Barney perilously lowers himself via a pulley onto the bomb, takes the plutonium casing, and replaces it with an empty cylinder. Vandaam's aide Thorgen unexpectedly discovers the theft, seals the building, and informs Vandaam, who continues the bidding, hoping to capture the thief and retrieve the plutonium before the bidding is over.

Kura and Cinnamon are high bidders and their money is put into Vandaam's wall safe. Vandaam is thrown when Cinnamon demands to see the plutonium again, forcing him to reveal the theft. Kura demands his money back, at which point Cinnamon activates a device which destroys the cash in the safe. Unable to produce the plutonium or return the money, Vandaam is shot. Cinnamon makes a hasty exit, and the IMF summon the authorities.

GUEST CAST: Alf Kjellin (Carl Vandaam), Arthur Batanides (Kura), Wesley Lau (Dr. Thorgen), Philip Ahn (Dr. Liu), Khigh Dhiegh (General Wo), Arthur Peterson (Helm), Scott Walker (Chief Guard), Josh Adams (Reception Guard), Sid Haig (Marko). *Unbilled:* Tony Mancini (Hall Guard); Craig Chudy, Chuck Couch (Stunt Guards); Lee Duncan (double, Barney); George Wilbur (double, Phelps)

Much of "Doomsday" occurs in and around the Vandaam building elevator shaft, via which cable-climbing Barney gains access to the bomb. The company had just one day at CalTech's new science building in Pasadena to shoot the extensive footage needed. Time ran out, and another location day was out of the question. To complete the show, a working elevator was built on a soundstage over a weekend, perfectly matching CalTech's. "We cut a hole in the stage floor and went from the basement clear to the grid," Jonnie Burke explains. "They'd shot so much of the CalTech elevator that everything had to match: the top of the cap, the pull wheels at the top, all the cables." Burke called one of southern California's biggest metal supplies salesmen while art director Bill Ross speedily made sketches. "We cut all the stuff out of aluminum instead of steel," says Burke. "I put a double shift on it, and ran each shift thirteen hours so they'd overlap each other. It was real frantic, but we had it ready."

The huge expense was probably tagged to the following two parter, which also utilized the elevator. Even so, the budget of "Doomsday" jumped from the planned $239,951 to over $256,000, making it one of *Mission*'s costliest. "Eventually they began renting that elevator out to pay back its production cost," says Paul Playdon.

This episode was costly for Greg Morris, too: While descending from the ceiling to straddle the bomb, he had trouble maintaining his balance, slammed into the bomb, and tore knee ligaments.

THE COMPLETE MISSION: IMPOSSIBLE DOSSIER

69/70: THE BUNKER
(in two parts)

Produced by: Stanley Kallis
Written by: Paul Playdon
Directed by: John Moxey
Music Composed and Conducted by:
Richard Markowitz

First Aired: 3/2/69; 3/9/69

TEAM: Phelps, Rollin, Cinnamon, Barney, Willy

Good afternoon, Mr. Phelps. The man you're looking at is Dr. Erich Rojak, the brilliant scientist who is being held in an underground laboratory by a totalitarian enemy government. Because of his fear that they will kill his wife, Anna, Rojak has been forced to work on a small but extremely powerful long-range missile which, if successful, could dangerously affect the balance of world power. Another unfriendly government fears this even more than we do, and has sent this professional killer, Alexander Ventlos, to make certain that Rojak never completes his work. Your mission, Jim, should you decide to accept it, is to rescue Rojak and his wife and destroy the test missile. As always, should you or any of your IM Force be caught or killed, the secretary will disavow any knowledge of your actions. This tape will self-destruct in five seconds. Good luck, Jim.

One hundred meters below an anonymous cavern is a huge military base housing the missile project. Rojak is watched constantly through the glass wall of his sealed lab, the door of which can be opened only by a voice code spoken by project head Colonel Ziegler and his assistants, Strat and Dromm. Anna is held in the nearby State Security Headquarters Building.

Security officer Jim arrives to introduce a new hand-stamp device designed expressly to keep Ventlos out. But unknown to all (including the IMF), Ventlos, a master of disguise, has already replaced the bunker's security chief, and is the first man stamped by Phelps.

Jim exposes security officer Cinnamon as a phony. She is jailed in Security Headquarters near Anna's cell. High atop the building, workman Willy uses a motorized pulley to descend into the furnace. Inside, he freezes the alarm system, knocks out the duty guard, frees Cinnamon from her cell, and smuggles Anna out. Cinnamon enters Anna's cell, pulls off the Cinnamon mask she wears and reveals an Anna Rojak mask beneath it, then takes her place as Anna.

Pressured to finish his work, Rojak refuses to continue, forcing "Anna" to be threatened at gunpoint. In a brief moment together, Cinnamon reveals herself to Rojak and tells him to be near his lab's air vent at a specific time. Rojak agrees to resume his work.

Jim stows a small flying disk in the bunker's air vent system. Attached to the saucer is a drug-filled hypo. Operating the disk remotely, Barney steers it through the vent corridors to Rojak's vent. Rojak discreetly pockets and follows the enclosed instructions. He soon collapses from a "heart attack," and calls for Anna. Jim summons heart specialist Rollin who advises immediate open-heart surgery and suggests that "Anna" be at her husband's side to sustain his will to live. But Ventlos has no intention of seeing Rojak recover. Before the IMF ambulance can arrive, he wreaks havoc and destroys not only Jim's rescue plan but the entire installation.

GUEST CAST: David Sheiner (Colonel Ziegler), Lee Meriwether (Anna Rojak), Milton Selzer (Dr. Erich Rojak), George Fisher (Major Strat), Jack Donner (Captain Praedo), George Sperdakos (Dr. Dromm), Ray Baxter (Alexander Ventlos), Gene Benton (Dr. Taber), Paul Lukather (Lieutenant), Martin Kosleck (General), Jacques Denbeaux (Reporter #1), Walter Alzman (Elevator Guard), Bruce Mars (Sergeant). *Unbilled:* Red Morgan, Donna Garrett, Dick Farnsworth, Tom Steel, Stephanie Epper, Craig Chudy (Stunt Doubles); Burt Kramer (Routine Guard); Jason Heller (Gate Guard); David Frank (Reporter #2)

Following a string of dark, austere mind twisters comes "The Bunker," a Playdon pulp adventure fraught with danger, peril, and trouble—on both sides of the camera.

The script was inspired by a remote-controlled toy helicopter Playdon had seen. To his disappointment, Playdon's helicopter was reworked by Jonnie Burke into a small flying saucer-hydrofoil which supposedly floated on a self-created cushion of air. The principle was not new: In 1961 a flying saucer ride was introduced in Disneyland which worked the same way. *Mission* took the theory but not the working apparatus, which explains the painfully apparent wires adorning the disk during its trip through the vents.

The show literally crashed to a halt on its second day of production, November 29, one day after Thanksgiving. Following the script, Willy smuggles Anna (Lee Meriwether, cast against type) out of prison via the basement furnace, where a motorized rope and pulley awaits to take them to the roof. "Lee went first," Peter Lupus recalls, "then I jumped on. Halfway up the chimney I felt a snap, and the rope broke." Dropping fifteen feet, the actors bounced against a side wall before hitting the furnace floor. "I fell onto Peter," Lee Meriwether says. "He was so well built that he cushioned my fall." Lee was unconscious, and Lupus thought he'd broken his neck. "They took us to be x-rayed," Lupus adds. "The doctor said that because I worked out, my trapezius and neck were strong enough to absorb the fall and the blow." Lee suffered a twisted ankle, torn leg ligaments, and a bruised cheek from landing on Lupus. "Nobody felt worse than Jonnie Burke," says Lupus. Burke was terribly upset, because the rope had been tested for 900 pounds. It had a weak point, however, and the actors had found it.

Lee and Lupus recuperated over the Thanksgiving weekend, and Lee had a nightmare in which she saw Peter Lupus slipping out of her hands and falling. The impact of this dream was felt when she returned to work to complete her scenes on a painter's scaffolding (the IMF means of escape from the prison). Filming on a soundstage mock-up of the scaffolding, Lee saw that, "it was just like my dream, and I began to cry." "She was terrified because she was reliving that whole terrible experience," says Lupus. Greg Morris took her off the set and back to her dressing room, where she begged Greg not to let Peter on the rigging. "One of the crewmen then came in," Lee recalls, "and said that it was good that I said this because it was not really all that secure."

If the Cinnamon and Anna masks which Rollin applies to Cinnamon look exceedingly real, it's because they are not masks but the actual faces of actresses Bain and Meriwether, protruding through holes in Rollin's makeup kit. Barbara's claustrophobia made the mask-making procedure out of the question. "The Bunker" kept makeup man Bob Dawn quite busy. Besides the IMF face masks, the story also involves killer Ventlos, Rollin's opposite number who, at the end of the show, overtakes and assumes Rollin's identity!

The expense of running three days over schedule pushed the budget for "The Bunker" into the stratosphere, exceeding $511,000. "At that time it was an incredible sum," says Paul Playdon. The bunker set alone, a two-story affair including a lab, observation foyer and working elevator, seems worth the budget. "The Bunker" was the highest rated show of the season, according to Playdon, but some viewers were not happy with what they saw. "The people at Hughes [Aircraft] asked for an investigation," says producer Stan Kallis. "Apparently Hughes had been working on a miniaturized hydrofoil, and we had accidentally designed our fictitious system to match, function for function, what they were doing, even to the extent of turning a corner with it. We told them that none of our stuff worked, that ours is just movie magic. We showed them exactly how we did what we did." How the Hughes people failed to see the hydrofoil's blatant wires is a mystery.

71: NITRO

Produced by: Stanley Kallis
Written by: Laurence Heath
Directed by: Bruce Kessler

First Aired: 3/23/69

TEAM: Phelps; Rollin; Cinnamon; Barney; Willy;
General Tamaar, assistant to King Said

Good morning, Mr. Phelps. The man you're looking at is General Zek of the Karakian Army. Zek is so bitterly opposed to the peace treaty between the Kingdom of Karak and the Republic of Agir that he has conspired with this man, Ismir Najiid, a munitions maker, to provoke war between the two countries instead of peace. His plan is to destroy the Government House of Karak while the young and progressive head of that country, King Said, makes a public announcement of the peace treaty. Your mission, Jim, should you decide to accept it, is to stop Zek and Najiid in such a way that they never again threaten the peace. As always, should you or any of your IM Force be caught or killed, the secretary will disavow any knowledge of your actions. This recording will self-destruct in five seconds. Good luck, Jim.

Zek and Najiid employ terrorist Skora to plant explosives (and evidence incriminating the Agirian government) in Karak's Government House.

Systems analyst Barney arrives at Najiid, Ltd. to increase production. He programs specific instructions into the munitions factory's alarm system and vault door. Journalist Jim identifies Cinnamon to Zek as the confrere of notorious Agirian terrorist Colonel Hakim. Zek has her watched. That night "Hakim" (Rollin) sneaks into Najiid, Ltd. and makes sure a guard sees him before knocking him out. He heads for the vault which, thanks to Barney's programming, opens for him. He steals three large jars of nitroglycerine and carefully delivers them to Willy.

Rollin and Willy take Skora out. "Skora" (Rollin) informs Zek that his plan to destroy Government House will not work. Zek traces Cinnamon to a warehouse where the body of heart-attack victim Hakim (really a drugged and masked Skora) is found near a radio-controlled truck containing the nitro. Zek reasons that Hakim had planned to destroy the Government House with the nitro. "His plan is perfect—for us," explains the supposed Skora.

In Government House, King Said begins his televised speech before an audience of reporters, including Phelps and Willy. Cleverly drugged by the IMF, Najiid suddenly becomes weak and unable to move. From a window he watches "Skora" (Rollin) place "Hakim" behind the wheel of the truck for a suicide run. Rollin, imitating the voice of Zek's aide, describes the truck's approach to Zek over the phone while in fact the truck hasn't moved. At the precise "point of impact," Jim shorts out the television transmission, leading Zek to believe that Government House has been razed.

Waiting for transmission to be restored, King Said watches Zek broadcast a special report claiming that Hakim and the Agirian government have just killed the king. Barney then starts the truck toward the building and Najiid, unable to leave, confesses and implicates Zek. Barney stops the truck at the curb; "Hakim" is removed from the truck and unmasked as Skora. He, Najiid, and Zek are arrested.

GUEST CAST: Titos Vandis (General Zek), Mark Lenard (Aristo Skora), Sandor Szabo (Ismir Najiid), Joe E. Tata (King Said), Dick Latessa (General Tamaar), Peter Coe (Major Abdul-al-Tarek). *Unbilled:* Larry Anthony (Gate Guard); Louis Neervoort (Voice-over), Tom Steel, Robert Bralver (doubles, Rollin), Frank Arno (Guard #1)

"Nitro" was an example of a seasoned director becoming completely lost. "I didn't find Bruce Kessler well prepared," says Stan Kallis, who believes "Nitro" is a better script than

episode. Kessler fell behind quickly and by the time the nitro theft was filmed one evening on the lot, he was in "terrible trouble," says Paul Krasny. "He does very good work, but on that particular night he didn't know how to get out of all that he had to do." Krasny shot much of the sequence later in the insert stage. The scene, which takes up most of act two, is the best in "Nitro." Rollin places the nitro jars on a forklift whose battery abruptly dies, forcing him to remove a battery from another vehicle. This eats up precious time which Rollin needs to elude the factory guards and deliver the nitro to Willy. Rollin's slow and steady exit concludes the scene. It was Krasny who filmed the inserts of the jiggling bottles, the forklift wheels inching over the ground's speed bumps and, of course, the inevitable cuts to the wristwatch. It's an extended visual sequence, almost devoid of dialogue but heavy on music. In other words, pure *Mission*. As for Bruce Kessler, the director continued a long and successful career, but never returned to *Mission*.

Perhaps the time problems were responsible for a blooper at the finale, when blue-eyed Martin Landau (Skora disguised as Hakim) is unmasked, revealing *brown-eyed* Mark Lenard.

72: THE VAULT

Produced by: Stanley Kallis
Teleplay by: Judy Burns
Story by: Judy Burns and John Kingsbridge
Directed by: Richard Benedict

First Aired: 4/6/69

TEAM: Phelps, Rollin, Cinnamon, Barney, Willy, KDF International Auditors

Good morning, Mr. Phelps. The man you're looking at is Miguel De Varo, the liberal president of Costa Mateo. Recently, De Varo announced a forty million dollar industrialization program for his country. This program is to be financed solely from funds in the presidential vault. However, this man, Phillipe Pereda, Costa Mateo's finance minister, secretly removed the money and deposited it in a Swiss bank. Since it is reputed that the presidential vault can only be opened by De Varo, it is Pereda's plan to frame the president for embezzlement and take over the country. De Varo considers Pereda to be his closest friend and would not believe that his minister of finance was planning such a move. Your mission, Jim, should you decide to accept it, would be to stop Pereda. As always, should you or any of your IM Force be caught or killed, the secretary will disavow any knowledge of your actions. This tape will self-destruct in five seconds. Good luck, Jim.

Unknown to De Varo, whose perfect pitch makes him uniquely capable of opening the sonic-combination presidential vault, Pereda used an audio tape of the correct pitch to remove the forty million dollars.

Eastern representatives Jim and Cinnamon offer to buy land in Costa Mateo for military bases. De Varo refuses the offer, but Pereda is quietly intrigued. He tells the pair that De Varo will be out of office within twelve hours and that, as new head of state, he would accept their offer.

While Rollin and the KDF auditors conduct a thorough accounting of the treasury vaults, janitor Willy smuggles Barney into a security office next to the vault room. Barney locates the vault's emergency exit passageway in the wall common to the vault, lasers it open, and crawls into the passageway until he reaches the steel door leading into the main vault. Using a small magnetic disk to open the combination lock from the rear, Barney enters the vault. He cracks a deposit box, throws its contents around the room, then opens the vault door from the inside and leaves it ajar before deliberately triggering the alarm.

A security guard enters the vault, followed by Rollin, who allows him a fleeting glimpse of Barney's shadowy figure before knocking him out. Barney returns to the emergency passageway, closes the door, and waits. Finding the guard and Rollin "unconscious," Pereda realizes that the missing presidential funds will be attributed to this new theft, dashing his plan for conquest. Jim and Cinnamon suggest that before De Varo inspects the scene, Pereda temporarily replace the stolen money with Treasury cash.

CINNAMON: Once it is officially established that the presidential vault was not looted in the robbery . . .

PEREDA: . . . . I could remove the money again and proceed with the original plan!

Using his recording, Pereda opens the presidential vault while Barney, hiding in the passageway, records the proper frequency pitch. Pereda then puts forty million dollars worth of Treasury money inside De Varo's vault.

Rollin informs De Varo of the robbery. He then makes himself up as De Varo and arrives to inspect "his" vault. Inside, he leaves an electronic device on the door of the presidential vault. "De Varo" tells a smiling Pereda that his money is still safe, then leaves. Pereda hurriedly reopens the vault and starts removing the cash, at which point Barney electronically shuts the door, locking Pereda inside. When the *real* President De Varo arrives to check his vault, he finds Pereda inside and has him arrested.

GUEST CAST: Nehemiah Persoff (Phillipe Pereda), Rodolfo Acosta (Presidente Miguel De Varo), Ray Martell (Security Guard), Taldo Kenyon (Paulo), Nick Benedict (Corporal), Jerry Riggio (Ortega)

Barney's vault break-in is probably the most lengthy, complex, and elaborate to date. The small disk which opens the main vault is nearly identical to the one Briggs used in the pilot but the rest of the procedure is new, requiring the increasingly familiar laser gun.

During his stay in the secret passageway, Barney has an exceptional camouflage: He hides behind a false-front screen which looks exactly like the access door at the other end of the passageway!

73: NICOLE

Produced by: Stanley Kallis
Written by: Paul Playdon
Directed by: Stuart Hagmann

First Aired: 3/30/69

TEAM: Phelps, Rollin

Good afternoon, Mr. Phelps. The man you're looking at is Anton Valdas, the enemy's highest ranking intelligence minister. We have just been informed by a friendly nation that Valdas has in his possession a master list of all the Allied agents who have defected to him. Knowing the identities of these double agents is of the utmost importance to our allies and to us. Your mission, Jim, should you decide to accept it, is to get that list. As always, should you or any of your IM Force be caught or killed, the secretary will disavow any knowledge of your actions. This tape will self-destruct in five seconds. Good luck, Jim.

Jim and Rollin's contact, an allied agent named Sparrow, explains that Valdas's secretary, Nicole Vedette, is on their side but Phelps, unwilling to endanger her cover, decides not to utilize her.

The IMF plan is to steal the list out of Valdas's wall safe during a party at his château, where Jim and Nicole enjoy an unexpectedly romantic first meeting. Rollin seems to get drunk, so Jim takes him to a room near Valdas's guarded office. Rollin knocks out the guard, cracks the safe, and takes the list. A secret alarm sounds, trapping Rollin in the office. Phelps holds Valdas at gunpoint to get Rollin out, but is shot and collapses. Rollin escapes with the list.

Jim is jailed. Nicole's attempt to free him is foiled by Valdas, who claims to have suspected her all along. Locked up with Jim, Nicole mentions that no search party has been sent after Rollin. Jim is puzzled.

PHELPS: Valdas said he suspected you for some time, and yet he let you see the list. Nobody's been sent to catch Rollin. Now that doesn't figure, unless Valdas *wants* us to have the list. Which means it's a phony.

Nicole tells him that *Sparrow* is a double agent, leading Phelps to believe he's been set up. Meanwhile, Rollin delivers the list and determines to retrieve Jim.

Jim and Nicole escape and head for the border, chased by armed search parties. Phelps passes out in a hayloft, allowing Nicole to report to Valdas that Jim has bought their charade and thinks the list, which has her name on it, is false. Attracted to Jim and sick of her double life, she blackmails Valdas into allowing her to leave the country with Jim.

Alone, Jim finds a transmitter among Nicole's belongings and realizes he's being deceived. Continuing their frantic race to the border, Nicole breaks down and confesses that Valdas wants Jim to escape and report that the list is false when in fact it is genuine. "You don't know, do you?" he asks, then shows her the hidden bug. Now that

In "Nicole," Phelps falls in love with a double agent (Joan Collins).

Valdas is *really* after them, they forge ahead but Jim, exhausted from his wound, slows them down. They are finally cornered by Valdas and his soldiers. Valdas informs Nicole that her blackmail is useless. Before he can kill the pair, he is stopped by one of the guards—Rollin. Valdas pretends to disarm, then fires at Nicole. Rollin machine-guns Valdas to the ground, but too late: Nicole dies in Jim's arms, and Rollin drives a shattered Phelps away.

GUEST CAST: Joan Collins (Nicole Vedette), Logan Ramsey (Anton Valdas), Ann Shoemaker (Madame Prokov), Dal Jenkins (Razoff), James McCallion (Sparrow), Jon Lormer (Minister), Anita Mann (Ilsa), Rena Horton (Helga). *Unbilled:* Joseph Reale (Guard), Jacques Denbeaux (Man), George Wilbur (double, Phelps), Carole Ferguson (double, Nicole), Fred Krone (Cell Guard #1), Robert Bralver (Cell Guard #2)

Director Hagmann wanted to shoot the lengthy chase scene in the Hollywood hills and had constructed a typically complex camera plan. But the show was shot in late January when daylight is scarce and rain in Los Angeles can be plentiful. During that season, it was torrential. Location work was put off until it became necessary to build a "green set" on the stage. Hagmann was upset, feeling a giant compromise was made. Oddly enough, the set's artificiality makes the moonlit chase more nightmarish, with the uncharacteristic use (for *Mission*) of dissolves and superimpositions to indicate the passage of time.

Peter Graves was dismayed by the way his big scene, Nicole's death, turned out. "Marty had caught up with us, and as she dies in my arms I figured it's about time to shed a tear or two. So I'm trying to squeeze out a tear, I look up at Marty, and there are tears streaming down his face! I said, 'What are you doing, crying in my goddam scene?!'" Landau explains plaintively, "Well, I was moved! Tears were just flowing. I don't think I was on camera, however."

As originally written, Rollin wounds but doesn't kill Valdas after Nicole is shot. Following her death, Jim levels a gun at Valdas with hate in his eyes. Valdas says, "In your country you would have played the same game with me." Either because of the validity of the statement or an inability to kill in cold blood, Phelps cannot pull the trigger.

74: ILLUSION

First Aired: 4/13/69

Produced by: Stanley Kallis
Written by: Laurence Heath
Directed by: Gerald Mayer
Songs: "Buy My Glass of Wine" and "The Lady
  'Bove the Bar": Lyrics by Bruce Geller,
  Music by Lalo Schifrin; "Ten Tiny Toes":
  Lyric by Bruce Geller, Music by Herschel
  Burke Gilbert and Rudy Schrager.
  Arrangements by Marl Young

TEAM: Phelps, Rollin, Cinnamon, Barney, Willy

Good afternoon, Mr. Phelps. These two men, Emil Skarbeck and Kurt Lom, are bitter rivals for the vacant post of chief of secret police for the East European Peoples Republic. Both are hard-liners determined to turn their country into one vast concentration camp. Your mission, Jim, should you decide to accept it, is to eliminate both from contention so that this third candidate, Paul Trock, who is friendly to the West, becomes the new chief. As always, should you or any of your IM Force be caught or killed, the secretary will disavow any knowledge of your actions. This tape will self-destruct in five seconds. Good luck, Jim.

Years ago Emil Skarbeck found his lover, cabaret singer Carlotta Kleve with another man (who escaped before Skarbeck could identify him). When she taunted and humiliated him, Skarbeck murdered Carlotta, framed her costar Fritz Mueller for the crime, and killed him in a car crash before suffering a total mental collapse. Skarbeck's psychosexual disturbance will explode when triggered by jealousy, and this is what Jim Phelps has in mind.

At the popular Traumerie Café, a flood of recognition hits Skarbeck while watching a cabaret act featuring comic Rollin and sultry Cinnamon: The act is identical to Carlotta Kleve's. Cinnamon admits to Skarbeck that his rival Lom is paying her to seduce him for unspecified reasons. Skarbeck, intrigued, gives her a tiny tape recorder to tape Lom's further instructions. Meanwhile Jim, posing as the brother of a man Skarbeck killed, shows Lom a letter which incriminates Skarbeck in Carlotta's murder. He urges Lom to use Cinnamon to bring about another mental collapse in Skarbeck, but Lom has a better scheme: to nail Skarbeck for Cinnamon's murder.

Skarbeck swallows a hypnotic drug. Under its influence, he is instructed by Jim to think of Cinnamon exactly as he thought of Carlotta, and to kill her if he learns she has been unfaithful to him. Tricked into thinking that Cinnamon is having an affair with Rollin, Skarbeck becomes unhinged

and threatens Rollin with a pistol. Rollin then admits to being Fritz Mueller, Carlotta's former co-

In "Illusion," Rollin takes on the guise of a dead cabaret performer.

star, and tells him that, like Carlotta, Cinnamon is involved with Lom. Skarbeck confronts Cinnamon, who taunts and humiliates him as Carlotta did. He goes berserk and strangles Cinnamon, who zaps him with a knockout needle hidden in her ring. Before passing out, Skarbeck sees her slump to the floor, "dead."

Skarbeck comes to at the café, where Jim and "Lom" accuse him of killing Cinnamon. "We made you kill her," Jim gloats, "because this time we have the proof." "You made me do it," says Skarbeck, reaching for his gun. "You made me kill her." Willy dims the café lights, allowing Jim and "Lom" to vanish in the darkness. The lights go up as the real Lom (lured to the café by Trock) enters. Skarbeck sees him and kills him before a roomful of witnesses. Backstage, Rollin pulls off his Lom mask and the IMF exit.

GUEST CAST: Fritz Weaver (Emil Skarbeck), Martin E. Brooks (Paul Trock), Kevin Hagen (Kurt Lom), Horst Ebersberg (Otto), Jack Baker (Cabaret Spectator), Ethel Wolfson (Wife), Robert Wolfson (Husband)

Completely dominating "Illusion" is Barbara Bain in perhaps her most memorable characterization as the sexually arrogant Mona Bern, a role perfectly suited to Cinnamon's man-killing talents. Clad in black, tossing her garters into the audience as she struts across the stage singing wry Bruce Geller lyrics in her own smoky voice, she is Marlene Dietrich and then some. Barbara is no singer* and was very anxious about recording her three songs. Even with Geller on hand to cheer her on, the recording sessions were a disappointment. "It was passable," says Jack Hunsaker, head of Paramount's music department. "It wasn't what they hoped it would be. We worked quite a long time until it got to the point where she wasn't improving. So we settled for what we had and doctored it as much as we could." Vocal limitations aside, the numbers are a delight to watch, and as one Barbara Bain fan so succinctly put it, "Well, Dietrich was no great singer, either."

Backing Barbara all the way is Landau as Fritz, his most fascinating role. Using dancelike moves and the flamboyant, stylized phrasings of a cabaret master of ceremonies, his introduction of Cinnamon dazzles one and all.

A heavy air of sexuality distinguishes "Illusion" from other *Mission*s, particularly in the way Skarbeck's fears of emotional involvement and sexual inadequacy are exploited. As Skarbeck, Fritz Weaver etches a portrait of what Jim calls, "an emotional time bomb" whose fuse runs out when Cinnamon humiliates him, as per the IMF plan. "You don't know how to make a woman happy," she sneers at him. "You're clumsy, you're stupid, I despise you. Yes, I made love to [Lom] and we laughed. We laughed while we made love. We laughed at you!" History repeats itself, and Skarbeck "kills" Cinnamon.

Fabulous performances from Bain, Landau, and Weaver, the ominous sexual overtones and gloomy Germanic flavor of the show, and an especially neat finale (in which Barney plays a key part disguised as Rollin!) combine to make "Illusion" a classic *Mission: Impossible*.

---

* Although Lee Meriwether, a student with Barbara in Curt Conway's class in New York, remembers Barbara's knockout rendition of "Diamonds Are a Girl's Best Friend."

75: THE INTERROGATOR

Produced by: Stanley Kallis
Written by: Paul Playdon
Directed by: Reza S. Badiyi

First Aired: 4/20/69

TEAM: Phelps, Rollin, Cinnamon, Barney, Willy, Hartford Repertory Company

Good afternoon, Mr. Phelps. The man you're looking at is Norvan Kruger, an agent who knows the details of his country's plan for an act of aggression so cataclysmic it will affect the entire world. We know nothing about the plan except that it triggers in two days at four o'clock. Two weeks ago Kruger was captured by a government unfriendly to us and has been under interrogation by this man, Friedrich Spindler, who has not succeeded in breaking Kruger. Even if he does, we are certain his government will not inform us. Your mission, Jim, should you decide to accept it, is to find out exactly what Kruger's country intends to do. As usual, should you or any of your IM Force be caught or killed, the secretary will disavow any knowledge of your actions. This tape will self-destruct in five seconds. Good luck, Jim.

Spindler is transporting the unbreakable Kruger to a General Kutzof for execution when the vehicle is gassed by Barney. Spindler awakens in a jail cell. His claim to be state interrogator is dismissed by psychiatrist Rollin and Major Phelps as the ravings of a demented man. Anxious to get out and recover his missing captive, Spindler gives Jim half of the puzzle.

SPINDLER: Kruger must be found before tomorrow or it will be too late. Only he can tell us where his country has placed submarines that are going to launch nuclear missiles against the United States.

Jim must get the rest—the location of the subs— from Norvan Kruger.

Kruger is injected with a drug inducing partial amnesia, scrambling whatever memories remain. He awakens in an exact duplicate of his home and finds papers identifying him as *state interrogator* Norvan Kruger. He finds this somewhat familiar (having actually been an interrogator at one time). He has fleeting memories of interrogation rooms, but sees himself as both interrogator and prisoner. Cinnamon enters, wearing a red wig, and informs him that she is his wife, prompting Kruger to recall spotty memories of a red-headed wife whose face he cannot remember. Kruger learns that his superior, a General Kutzof, will kill him if he does not break resistant prisoner Rollin within three hours.

Kruger finds an oddly familiar statement in Rollin's file: "He has admitted to the fact that his country intends to launch missiles from submarines." But he remembers *himself* being questioned by a nameless man (Spindler). When he learns that

Cinnamon is going to run off with a man who is the image of Kruger's imagined interrogator (Rollin in a Spindler mask), Kruger explains his confusion to staff psychiatrist Phelps, who offers a hypothesis.

PHELPS: When you felt you could not hold your wife you felt rejected, a failure. You wanted to be punished, tortured, persecuted. So you invented a persecutor.

Minutes before Kutzof is to arrive, Kruger grills Rollin to get the submarine sites. After an intense interrogation, Rollin breaks. But to Kruger's horror, he is unable to hear the words Rollin mouths. Jim explains this temporary deafness:

PHELPS: You wanted to fail. You needed an excuse for Kutzof to kill you. . . . When [Rollin] broke you did not want to hear that and so you did not. But it is there in your memory, Colonel. You can't throw your life away like this. No!

"Kutzof" arrives and demands answers which Kruger, despite his efforts to remember, can't give. When Cinnamon is taken to be shot, Kruger concentrates and remembers what he believes Rollin told him: the location of the submarines. After divulging the data, Kruger is zapped and returned with Spindler to the truck from which they were abducted.

GUEST CAST: Henry Silva (Norvan Kruger), Gunnar Hellstrom (Friedrich Spindler), Erik Holland (Rostov), Vincent Van Lynn ("Kutzof"), Anne Newman (Kruger's Wife), John Rose (Prisoner). *Unbilled:* Lee Duncan (double, Barney); Jerry Randle, Joe Hooker (stunts)

Iranian director Reza S. Badiyi began his career as a cameraman and won an award for a documentary film, *Flood in Kurdistan,* which brought him much attention and led to his arrival in the US as an exchange student in 1955. He shot industrial films for Robert Altman and worked with Sam Peckinpah before joining NBC as a journalist cameraman, where he shot a staggering 1065 episodes of a religious program, *Daily World.* More work with Altman followed (Reza shot the *Nightwatch* pilot) before moving to Talent Associates in New York. Reza developed a reputation as a designer of series main titles and is proud of the fact that at one point, twelve of his titles were on the air. Some of his more enduring work in the field includes *That Girl, Hawaii Five-O,* and *The Mary Tyler Moore Show.* Geller saw Badiyi's work on *N.Y.P.D.* and hired him. His approach to main titles work makes it clear why Geller picked him for *Mission* and why Badiyi ultimately became the series' most frequent director. "You have to capture the audience and keep them from going to another channel," he explains. "That was the trick. You create the concept, go out and shoot the elements, then put them together with a certain music and a certain rhythm. By the time the titles are over, they're hooked. It's like doing a wonderful commercial without showing what the product is." It was exactly the style Geller wanted, and it was *Mission* which greatly enhanced Reza's reputation as a fast, flashy, and extremely visual filmmaker.

As fast and furious as Badiyi was, "The Interrogator" still fell behind schedule. It was finished in seven days, only after much overtime. On the final day of shooting, the strain began to show in Martin Landau's performance. During the final, heated interrogation scene with Henry Silva, Landau had difficulties with his lines. Some of the crew felt the actor's mind was more on next season's salary negotiations than the script, but this was the last day of an especially grueling season for Landau, who had contributed energetic and explosive performances throughout the year. The lapse is forgivable when one learns that he was on stage that February 18 from 10:00 A.M. to 10:55 P.M., not including a forty-five-minute makeup session.*

"He wasn't really prepared," says Badiyi of Landau, "and apologized. I told him, 'Just let it happen.' So in reality Marty just went off the cuff and babbled, and Henry handled it nicely." The scene is effective, with Landau (at his most manic) cracking as the prisoner, losing his mind, and finally believing himself to be the interrogator, screaming back the questions he has been relentlessly asked. Landau's former student Jack Nicholson was at Paramount filming *On a Clear Day You Can See Forever,* and stopped by the *Mission* stage while this scene was filmed. "We did it first as a master shot," Marty Landau recalls. "Jack watched the scene where I suddenly switch over and become the interrogator. He thought I'd flipped! I started barking and taking over and Jack thought something weird had happened to me. The predictable way the scene seemed to be going was obviously not where it went!" The ad libs added spontaneity and everyone was happy with the end result except, of course, the hapless script supervisor Allan Greedy, who got angry at Landau for not following the script.

Despite the exhausting hours, "The Interrogator" turned out well and was a good first show for Badiyi. "Little did I know it would be *my* last," says Martin Landau years later. But that's another story, to be told in the following chapter.

---

* Peter Graves had it worst of all that day, arriving at 7:30 A.M. and not finishing until 11:15 P.M.

Wrap

Somehow, year three had been salvaged and the *Mission* machine kept moving. The series had hit its all time high in the annual Nielsens, number 11 with a 41 share, easily beating NBC's *The Beautiful Phyllis Diller Show* and ABC's *Sunday Night Movie,* which shared its time slot.

To Paramount's accounting department, things looked worse than ever. Instead of cutting costs, *Mission* was becoming more expensive. Every episode of the season had been budgeted higher than the $185,000 unit price; and every one (except episode 53, "The Diplomat") exceeded its budget. "The Bunker," even with a $370,000 budget to play with, went over by $142,600. This hit series had actually cost Paramount over $830,000 this season alone.

Douglas Cramer decided that things would never get this far out of hand again. "It was crazy almost every day, and at the end of the week it was madness. Bruce and his refusal to pay any attention to budget had permeated all the people that worked for him. Stan Kallis was a rubber stamper and did what Bruce told him to do. Barry Crane, out of all this, remained the one person who could talk to me and Tom Tannenbaum [who replaced Cramer in 1971]." To use a curiously appropriate analogy, Cramer saw Bruce Geller as a "mad dictator" whose excesses had to be stopped, while Geller was watching his series slowly strangled just as it was finally beginning to blossom.

Paramount's problem was that CBS fully supported Geller and his system. "The general attitude," explains Cramer, "was that all of this just wasn't worth the trouble, that CBS was not putting any more shows on the air for Paramount, that they never thought they'd get the cost back from syndication. Our attitude was, 'There are two other networks. They may not be CBS, but we'll manage somehow to handle it. We'll do business with the other networks.' And in rapid order, we did." Paramount had already sold *Love, American Style* and *The Brady Bunch* to ABC for the upcoming season, and *The Odd Couple* would appear the season after that. "So CBS didn't seem quite so important," Cramer continues, "and it gave us the courage to take on Bruce and say, 'We're not gonna spend that kind of money.' I gave great credit to Martin Davis for supporting me in those days." Bruce Geller was losing ground.

As usual, *Mission* was well represented at the annual Emmy Awards that June 8 evening, with eight nominations, third behind *Rowan & Martin's Laugh-In* (eleven nominations) and *Hallmark Hall of Fame* (nine). The nominations: Outstanding Dramatic Series; Outstanding Dramatic Program (episode 56, "The Execution"); Outstanding Performance by an Actor in a Leading Role in a Dramatic Series (Graves and Landau); Outstanding Performance, Supporting Role (Greg Morris); Music Composition (Schifrin for episode 52, "The Heir Apparent"); Art Direction and Scenic Design (episode 69, "The Bunker"); and, as usual, Leading Dramatic Actress (Barbara Bain).

Surprisingly, *Mission* won just two awards this time, in the last categories listed. "Barbara and I were sitting across the aisle from each other when I lost," Greg Morris recalls. "Barbara leaned over, pointed to Marty and said, 'Look what you've done to my husband.' Marty was sitting there crying!"

Barbara's victory came as no great surprise. But her acceptance speech certainly did. Clutching her third consecutive Best Actress Emmy (unprecedented at the time), she said, "As the girl who *used* to be on *Mission: Impossible,* this is a bittersweet moment. *Mission* has been a very special kind of thing for me. . . . There are a lot of people who worked with me on *Mission: Impossible* whom I'd like to thank. There are a couple of people I'd like *not* to thank, but seeing as that they each know their names, I won't call them. Thank you."

Barbara—and her husband—had already announced their decision to leave *Mission: Impossible.*

Mission: Impossible, Year Four.

Year Four
September 1969 – April 1970

Production Credits

Starring: Peter Graves, Leonard Nimoy as Paris
Also Starring: Greg Morris, Peter Lupus
Executive Producer: Bruce Geller
Produced by: Stanley Kallis
Associate Producer: Barry Crane
Script Consultant: Paul Playdon
In Charge of Postproduction: Paul Krasny
Production Manager: Bill Derwin
Postproduction Supervisors: Robert L. Swanson, William Cairncross
Theme Music by: Lalo Schifrin
Director of Photography: Keith C. Smith
Art Director: Gibson Holley
Film Editors: Donald R. Rode; William Cairncross; David Wages, ACE, John Loeffler; Arthur D. Hilton; John A. Fegan, Jr.
Assistant Directors: Gordon A. Webb, Michael P. Schoenbrun, Gene H. DeRuelle, Neil T. Maffeo
Supervising Property Masters: Arthur Wasson, Robert O. Richards
Special Effects: Jonnie Burke

Set Decorator: Lucien Hafley
Supervising Costumer: Forrest T. Butler
Costume Supervisor (Women): Dodie Shepard
Casting: Jim Merrick
Makeup Artist: Bob Dawn
Hairstylist: Adele Taylor
Script Supervisor: Allan Greedy
Production Coordinator: Dale Tarter
Vehicles: Ed Chamey
Music Editor: Dan Carlin
Supervising Sound Editor: Douglas H. Grindstaff
Sound Editor: Michael Colgan, MPSE
Editorial Coordinator: Mike Vejar
Production Mixer: Dominick Gaffey
Rerecording Mixer: Gordon L. Day, CAS
Wardrobe Furnished by: Worsted-Tex
Recorded by: Glen Glenn Sound
Chrysler Vehicles Furnished by: Chrysler Corporation
Executive Vice President in Charge of Production: Douglas S. Cramer

> *"Nobody at Paramount understood the mystique of Mission: Impossible. Douglas Cramer didn't understand the show."*
> —MUSIC SUPERVISOR JACK HUNSAKER

> *"Our research said that the audience buys the show itself, rather than those who populate it."*
> —DOUGLAS S. CRAMER, 1969

> *"We were sacrificial lambs in a sense."*
> —MARTIN LANDAU

HIATUS 1969 MEANT relaxation for some of the *Mission* family, while others simply found more work. The Landaus, for instance, vacationed in Yosemite National Park, while Peter Graves made a feature in Italy, *The Five Man Army*. Alas, Stan Kallis and Paul Playdon did not have the luxury of choice: The producer and head writer enjoyed a few weeks of rest, then geared up for the new season.

As ever, preproduction consisted mainly of developing scripts. Playdon and Kallis spent much of the spring and summer interviewing dozens of hopefuls who proved incapable of writing the show. The only finds were veterans Ken Pettus and Howard Berk, both of whom would contribute rewrites and stories throughout the series' remaining years. Otherwise, the horizon was as barren as ever. "The first time we got a substantial amount of relief was when Jerry Ludwig did a script," Kallis maintains. "Jerry didn't want to do a lot of them but he was a relief hitter until Larry Heath, who was on other assignments, came home." One Ludwig script, "Show Trial," challenges the IMF to free the jailed premier of Svardia (remember that country from episode 23, "The Train"?) before he can be put through a kangaroo court and executed by the ambitious state prosecutor. Encased in a glass booth supposedly for his own protection, Premier Pavel is tried in public court. By electronically feeding Pavel questions contrary to those heard by the rest of the court, the prosecutor hopes to twist Pavel's truthful replies into an apparent confession of treason. For unknown reasons, this intriguing plot was never filmed.

Writing problems on the home front compelled Geller to look overseas for help. On Bruce's behalf, producer Cedric Francis (*Maverick*), who'd settled in England, and Ivan Goff contacted British TV agents. Several writers attended a briefing session in Mayfair but by the time Geller arrived to commission scripts, only two writers, Donald James and Leigh Vance, were still standing. Vance remembers Goff pitching the Geller unit to him as the happiest in Hollywood. "When I arrived," he adds, "Geller was in the middle of a screaming match with Doug Cramer over money! Bruce's attitude was, 'I will spend whatever money it takes to make this show work.' And he did, but it was a constant struggle."

The battles grew longer and more heated this year. On April 14 Cramer sent Geller a five-page memo which not only caused a further deterioration in the Geller-Paramount relationship but also became the talk of the lot. Cramer's memo seemed to be issuing Geller an ultimatum. "None of us can deny, forget, or allow a repetition of the past season's financial disaster. . . . Paramount's loss position at the current time is probably the worst a studio has ever had on a single television series in the history of the business. . . . Some of the production personnel on *Mission* have been with the show since [it] began and through various factors unfortunately have reached salary levels in excess of that paid comparable positions on other shows about town. . . . There eventually comes a point when people have out-priced themselves for TV, be they Steve McQueen or a hairdresser."

Bruce Geller took these comments personally. "Doug saw me as the enemy," he told *TV Guide*'s Richard Warren Lewis months later. "I cannot give you a logic, nor do I know anybody who can." Again, he repeated his justification for *Mission*'s expense. "I may not be making Paramount as much as they would like, but I'm not costing the studio money. To some degree, *Mission* and *Mannix* put the studio back in the television business. And they will do quite nicely, in time. *In time* is the key to any television situation. Nobody makes money right away."

"It was expensive," admits Greg Morris. "Barry Crane was always on top of the budget, but because of Bruce Geller's perfectionism and that of the people he surrounded himself with, we didn't want to give the audience a second-rate product. And that costs money. Collectively, and each in our own way, we felt dismayed that the titular factions felt it necessary to fool with success. It made us angry." Martin Landau has his own opinion of Cramer's criticism of the series' salaried employees. "The bottom line is that a hairdresser who makes people feel good in the morning will ultimately *save* you thousands of dollars. If a guest actor comes on who's nervous, it's important that the first people he sees [usually the assistant directors, hairdresser, or makeup artist] are nice. Conceivably, by the end of the year the crewman's salary will save you $150,000. We had nice people; Adele was wonderful. Danny Striepeke, John Chambers, Bob Dawn, all good people. We went out of our way to make the actors who came on the *Mission* set feel welcome, and it was a nice show to work on."

Explanations and excuses made no impact on Cramer, who was doing his job. Although the series had achieved its highest rating, a survey among viewers suggested that *Mission: Impossible* had fallen into a rut at the end of the third year. The episodes cited were the ones broadcast after February—the hurried, frantically written shows which Kallis and Playdon had barely produced on schedule. Evidently, Cramer did not attribute the slump to the backstage shakeup which had taken place at that time. He ordered another survey to learn what made *Mission* click with its audience, and which elements were the most popular. According to the poll, *Mission*'s key ingredients were its concept, execution, production value, and Peter Graves. Reluctant to tamper with this recipe, Cramer found an obvious target to concentrate upon.

"Bruce had allowed a situation with Martin Landau which no responsible producer or production company should allow," says Cramer. "They permitted Marty to play a major role in the pilot without having a series deal. Marty was brilliant in the pilot, and they had to make a deal with him for the series. Replacing Steven Hill gave him even more negotiating strength. At the end of every year the network said, 'We've gotta have him.' I was of the opinion, backed by Bluhdorn and [Paramount's executive vice president] Marty Davis, that he was not essential to the show."

When he returned from Yosemite on April 4, Landau knew that it was time to negotiate for

another season. But this session would be a far cry from the days when he and Herb Solow strolled around the Desilu lot, giving and taking. In fact Landau and Cramer had not yet been introduced to each other, never met during the ensuing negotiations, and would not come face-to-face until much dust had settled.

"My year-to-year contract disturbed Cramer," Landau explains, "and he wanted me to sign for five years. When *Bruce* was in charge I would never do that." Paramount offered the actor $7000 per episode for the coming season (up from year three's $6500), matching Peter Graves's salary. Landau's counteroffer: $11,000 per show, and $12,500 for each year five episode. Aside from the fact that this was an exorbitant figure for TV at this time, there was another obstacle in Landau's way: a "favored nations" clause in Graves's contract which specified that no series regular be paid more than Graves. "If they had given that to Martin," Graves points out, "they would have to give it to me."

The studio wasn't about to give either actor that much money, but CBS *was* willing to chip in to keep Landau in the series. Commercial time on *Mission* had risen to $65,000 per minute, an all-time industry high, and the network knew that *Mission* was attracting an audience which didn't watch much television. CBS offered to pay Landau the additional $4000 per week for year four and $5500 per week the following season, matching his demands. This would not resolve the Graves situation, however, and Doug Cramer had no intention of setting such an expensive and dangerous precedent. Said Cramer at the time, "We asked CBS if they would undertake to be responsible for everything that bringing Martin back on his terms would obligate us to." Obviously, CBS could not.

Aware that Landau was slightly more valuable to the show than his "hairdresser memo" implied, Cramer offered him a compromise in which the actor would appear in half of the new season's twenty-six episodes. "He would phase me out, is what it meant," says Landau. "Why should I lend my name to that?" Negotiations lumbered on through April and May. When it became clear that the matter would not be settled by year four's May 23 start date, Geller and Kallis had to find a replacement for Landau in the opening two-part episode. It was hoped that with a little luck, Marty would miss only a few episodes. Among the actors Paramount considered as part of a string of substitutes were former TV spies Robert Vaughn (*The Man from U.N.C.L.E.*) and Ross Martin (*The Wild Wild West*). The first performer hired, however, had been literally next door to *Mission* for the last three years.

Boston born Leonard Nimoy had developed a moderately successful acting career during the fifties and sixties in TV and features, mostly in minor roles. He had also forged a solid reputation as an acting instructor. It was his costarring role as Mr. Spock, the half-human science officer in *Star Trek,* which made him a star and cult figure of the late sixties. "When *Star Trek* went off the air, Leonard was really the star of the show and a personality," says Doug Cramer. "I always felt that he was a wonderful actor, that he had a range as Marty did."

The careers of Landau and Nimoy share interesting parallels. Both were acting teachers, deadly serious about their art; both spent much of their careers playing villainous roles until hired by Desilu as series second leads who ultimately overshadowed the shows' official stars. Both were accustomed to long hours in the makeup chair and knew how to project through whatever appliances concealed their facial features. And of course, Landau's refusal of the *Star Trek* pilot in 1964 enabled Nimoy to take the role which would make him famous.

Mr. Spock was a muted character, an emotional man who refused to acknowledge his emotions. Carefully written scripts and Nimoy's deft underplaying added many layers to this potentially dull role. As a result it was Nimoy more than anyone else who gained notoriety

Leonard Nimoy as actor/magician Paris (top left). Zastro the Magician, from "The Falcon," was one of Nimoy's favorite *Mission* roles (top right). Paris poses as a Kabuki artist in "Butterfly" (bottom left), and impersonates a notorious guerrilla leader in "The Code" (bottom right).

from *Star Trek*. During its original run the series was a failure, never climbing higher than number 52 in the Nielsens. Despite this, people who'd never seen *Star Trek* somehow knew who Leonard Nimoy was, or at least recognized his pointy-eared alter ego.

Like *Mission, Star Trek* had its problems; it too had been undersold budget-wise by Desilu. Unlike *Mission,* however, *Star Trek* was not a success and was dying a slow death. It was never really taken seriously by Desilu, Paramount, or NBC, even after it was clear that the show had developed a loyal following. After two seasons *Star Trek*'s creator and executive producer Gene Roddenberry left and the quality of the show dropped during its third and final season. Despite a strong letter-writing campaign from fans who'd helped save the show the season before, *Star Trek* was canceled. Nimoy, who'd grown dissatisfied with the show's quality and the handling of Spock during the final season, wasn't all that sorry to see *Star Trek* die. He was eager to find new work and was already starting to wonder if Spock had become a Vulcan albatross he'd carry for the rest of his career. He had in fact recently vacated his Paramount office when he was asked to return and replace his friend, Marty Landau. A quick phone call to Landau assured Nimoy that he was not jeopardizing Landau's position on *Mission*. "I'm not going back," Landau told him.

Paramount offered Nimoy a deal for the first eight shows of the season at the same salary Landau would have received: $7000 per show, parity with Peter Graves. "Theoretically," says the actor, "it was an opportunity for me to spread out from the Spock character and broaden my base as a character actor." The scripts were quickly rewritten to eliminate Rollin Hand and replace him with Nimoy's character, the Great Paris. Since there was no need, and certainly no time, to make distinctions, Paris's functions were identical to Rollin's, and the only difference was the way in which Nimoy played it. In contrast to Landau's flashy, energetic style, Nimoy chose a quieter, low-key portrayal, unless of course the script called for a flamboyant performance. In this respect Paris was probably the more realistic of the two characters. It was Bruce Geller who provided the new character's unusual monicker. "It was a favorite name of his," says Stan Kallis.

On Friday, May 30, as production was winding down on *Mission*'s third hour with Nimoy, *The New York Times* reported that Martin Landau would not be returning to *Mission: Impossible*. Paramount then offered Nimoy a standard five-year contract. Happy with the episodes he had already filmed, he accepted only on the condition that Bruce Geller remained. "I'd had that terrible experience on *Star Trek* where Gene Roddenberry left and I had a lousy relationship with the new producers. I felt that they didn't know what the show was about. I felt twisted and distorted during that third season, and I did not want to go into *Mission: Impossible* if it wasn't gonna be the *Mission: Impossible* that I admired. I assumed Bruce was the focal point of the series, and I was guaranteed that he would stay during that first year." To his credit, Nimoy made a smooth and easy entry into the show. "It really was a fun series to work on," the actor remembers. "It didn't have anywhere near the sense of tension and pressure that we had on *Star Trek.*" A familiar face from his *Star Trek* days on the lot, he was well liked by the crew and the rest of the cast. "I thought Leonard would be superserious, like he is on camera," says Peter Lupus. "But he's a very funny guy with a dry sense of humor, and he was terrific to work with." Like Landau, Nimoy would play a wide variety of parts, including a Latin-American revolutionary, Chinese general, Middle Eastern cop, Japanese kabuki dancer, Gypsy, even a robot. His portrayals lean toward the roguish, due more to the scripts than the actor.

During the Landau conflict, another casting dispute arose. Barbara Bain received her

official year four pickup notice from the studio on April 9. Her pay had been renegotiated at $3000 per show. During the Paramount-Landau haggling she heard nothing from the studio, but had read blind items in the trade papers which hinted that she might not be back for the new season. On Friday, May 16, Barry Crane informed Barbara that wardrobe meetings for the new season were scheduled for the following Monday, May 19. Barbara asked for a script to the opening show, and for a postponement. Monday was her maid's day off, and the following day she and Landau were to shoot promos for the American Cancer Society and the Heart Association. She asked to have the wardrobe meeting rescheduled for Wednesday, May 21, two full days before filming was to begin. Barbara got the script she requested, but never got an answer regarding the rescheduling.

Paramount *did* contact her representatives, the William Morris Agency. In a notification reminding the agency of "all rights and remedies" should she default, Barbara was ordered to report on Monday, May 19. Barbara Bain did not report on May 19. Nor did she appear on Wednesday, May 21. With shooting just two days away, the studio asked William Morris if their client intended to report for work. "She has given me no reason to believe otherwise," a Morris spokesman replied. Later that day, Paramount informed the agency that Barbara had been replaced in the opening two-parter by actress Dina Merrill. The next day William Morris sent Paramount a letter asking for Bain's release from her contract, since it seemed that her services were no longer required. "She would have reported for wardrobe May 21 had she been requested to do so, but was never so advised," an agency spokesman told the press. On June 2, William Morris once again asked for Bain's release. Once more Paramount refused. A studio spokesman explained that the actress had not yet been officially suspended; another wardrobe meeting would have to be scheduled. Should she then fail to appear, the suspension would become official. By now, nobody seemed to understand what was going on, including Barbara Bain. "I'll know definitely what my position is at the end of the week," she told the media. Three days later and true to her word, Barbara announced that she would not be returning to *Mission,* and proceeded to sue Paramount for breaching her contract. "I feel that I have been seriously maligned and harassed in the press by Paramount TV and that they, in fact, have broken my contract and my heart as well," she explained. Meanwhile, the studio accused her of breaking her pact. Barbara capped this tumultuous week by winning her third consecutive Emmy and making that controversial acceptance speech.

That is the generally accepted version of the events leading to Barbara Bain's departure, and the one she has resolutely held to for over twenty years. But clearly, a two-day wardrobe postponement was insufficient reason for a triple Emmy winner to leave a hit series. In this case, each participant has his own story. Douglas Cramer's version: "The network was always afraid that if Marty walked, Barbara would walk," he says. "We said to him, 'We're going to have to replace you. But, Barbara, you have a contract and we expect you to return.' Her response was first, 'I want X amount of dollars more to return' (which we moved toward), and then came, 'But I'm not coming back unless Martin comes back.' She actually said it; she refused to come back because he wasn't."

According to Bruce Geller, Barbara's departure was engineered by the studio. In December 1969, he explained the front-office attitude concerning Martin Landau and Barbara Bain. Cramer told Geller that the *Mission* audience survey revealed that the role of Rollin Hand was more attractive to the audience than the actor playing it. "I had no interest or belief in this kind of material," Geller recalled, "and I didn't really want to see any more of it." He noted that "Mr. Cramer's viewpoint was that Mr. Landau was not necessary to the show. . . . Mr.

Cramer said quite clearly he didn't want Marty back. . . . I think if [Landau] would have done the show for a dollar an episode, Mr. Cramer wouldn't have objected.

"I or someone else brought up the obvious . . . fact that Marty and Barbara were married, that this might have a strong effect on Barbara, and Mr. Cramer's attitude was, in effect, a shrug."* That reaction so disturbed Geller that he and Jinny visited the Landaus one evening. "I have a long-term friendship with Marty and Barbara," stated Geller, "and I thought I should tell them of these developments, and I did." The actors were shocked and upset by the news, and Jinny Geller recalls Barbara exclaiming, "They're ruining me." Bruce, in an awkward spot, preferred to stay out of negotiations altogether, other than advising Paramount to retain the couple and suggesting that Landau, "for his own sake," accept the thirteen-episode offer.

Barbara's departure has always seemed harder to explain than her husband's. As Cramer acknowledges, "If they didn't notify her and she didn't show up that one day, then you work around it. All Barbara had to do during any of this was to come back and fulfill her contract for the money she was getting." Perhaps Barbara deliberately used the wardrobe excuse as a convenient way to exit *Mission,* whatever her reasons; perhaps her "unofficial" suspension was Paramount's idea of a reprimand, an easy way to show Barbara Bain who was boss. Either way, the dispute was costly to both parties.

Peter Graves, who'd heard about the Landau-Bain issue while filming in Italy, recalls bumping into the couple at a charity function during the fourth season. He remembers asking, "Is there anything I can do to help put it back together again?" But according to Graves, the damage had already been done. "By that time, pride was such a big, huge factor there. They felt terribly injured by Cramer and/or Paramount, who were standing firm."

CBS, upset by Cramer's handling of Landau, was enraged when Barbara walked out. At the time Mike Dann railed against Cramer, whom he called "crazy. The real truth of the matter is that he wants to show he's bigger than anybody involved in the show." Says Cramer, "Dann never forgave me. I wasn't allowed in CBS for at least three years." Says Dann today, "I insisted that we couldn't take the loss of Barbara Bain. Not only was she the only woman; she was the glue, more than any of the other characters." But Cramer was unshakable, as he related in a memo to Martin Davis in 1969: "It is all of our opinion here, as well as many people at CBS who are hesitant to fully express it in the face of Dann's strong position, that neither Landau nor his wife are essential to the series but rather that Peter Graves and Greg Morris are the positive forces in the show's appeal and the glue that holds it together." One year later, even Bruce Geller would be considered dispensable.

Perry Lafferty's final attempt to lure the couple back took on an almost surreal flavor. Dressed as a cowboy and on his way to a costume benefit, CBS's vice president stopped by the Landaus' home. "I attempted to cajole them back into the show," he describes. "I was not successful, and I remember being very uncomfortable and disappointed because there wasn't very much I could say. I couldn't give them any more money. I could only say how much we hoped they'd both come back and how important they were to the show. That didn't convince them."

Landau too recalls the meeting. "I told Perry, 'I don't wanna be there.' Lenny [Nimoy] was already set but they were saying in essence, we can get rid of Lenny if you come back. I said,

---

* It was common knowledge around the studio that Cramer never cared for Bain in the series. "Barbara was no Streisand," he maintains. "She has had very little career since [*Mission*]."

'Too late. I don't wanna be there.' " And so the cowboy walked dejectedly out of the Beverly Hills mansion and into the sunset, providing a strange climax to a very strange story.

Twenty years after his departure from *Mission,* Martin Landau brushes aside questions of salary and concentrates instead on what he claims were the real motives behind his exit. "It wasn't going to be the same show," he says. "The elevator had gone to the top floor and it couldn't go any higher. Woodfield and Balter were gone; Geller was basically a figurehead at this point and his hands were tied. So what was I going to do, sign for *five years?* They couldn't have paid me enough. When Bruce was in charge prior to that and it was *logical* for me to sign, I kept a year-to-year arrangement whereby I had the option. I wanted to hold on to that and after the third year I was glad I had it. Had I forsaken it I would have gone down with that show. There was no reason for me to continue with what they were going to do with that show and I knew it beforehand. It's important that you're attached to something that you can be proud of. I don't like being in a place that's not exciting and creative. Desilu had been sold, a new group had already moved in, and the pressures began to filter down. I didn't know that group but I just felt the differences and there was no sense in going on.

"See, I really felt that I was valuable to *Mission* and that was the thing that really bothered me, the lack of regard for the value and kind of commitment I had to it. On *Mission* I worked harder on the weaker scripts; I went on the public relations tours in the beginning because Bruce *asked* me to. My feeling is that Cramer wanted to make a name for himself. He came out of an ad agency and wanted to make some noise."

Landau's recollections may well be true, but it is a fact that after two decades, nearly everyone connected with *Mission* believes that *both* Landaus left over one reason. "Pure and simply, they wanted more money," says actor Tony Giorgio, who claims that Geller told them, "You're making a mistake. They'll dump you." Peter Graves thinks the couple was badly advised and points to his favored nations clause as a good example. "The lawyer handling that for Martin certainly should have known that I had a clause that no one could get more money than me. Actors should not always be left to their own business devices and mostly they're not. But I think they had bad advice. It was a damn shame, their losing four years of the show. That's the pity."

"Barbara and Marty wanted a lot of money," says Stan Kallis, who had no part in the negotiations. He does not adhere to the theory that the couple's demands were just an excuse to get out of a series on the wane. "They asked for the money to get the money. I believed they were going to get it, although Bruce was sure that Paramount wouldn't stand still for it."

The Landaus' absence marked a significant change on the *Mission* set, one which belied the show's status as an ensemble. "That was a well-oiled acting company and a bunch of wonderfully defined characters," says Peter Graves. "With the loss of two of those, I was certainly apprehensive." The Landaus (and in particular, Barbara) had been favorites, and it wasn't uncommon for the couple to buy lunch for some of the crew. Peter Sloman, delivering pages from deForest Research, recalls Martin treating him more like a friend than a messenger. Jonnie Burke considers them "the two nicest actors I've ever known. They're lovely people. Landau was a nice guy and very safety conscious. He'd go anywhere and do anything, but if he saw something wrong, he'd report it to the office and walk off the set until it was corrected. When we had Martin and Barbara it was a whole family." Frequent guest Antoinette Bower feels "it was a nice atmosphere with Barbara and Marty, and on the days they weren't working so much the whole atmosphere would change." Even Geller's secretary Olga Griffin, who rarely visited the set, felt it. "When we had the complete composition they were a marvelous

team. But once the composition had changed, it was like letting the air out of the balloon." Hairstylist Adele Taylor agrees. "I could never put my finger on it, but there was a magic with Barbara and Marty. They left and were missed. Something was not quite the same."

Paramount quickly learned that Barbara Bain would not be as easy to replace as her husband. There was no telling when or if Bain would legally be forced to return and fulfill her contract, so another actress could not be hired on a permanent basis. With Barbara AWOL, Geller was forced to compose a list of prospective actresses for the two-part opener, "The Controllers." From a list which included Dina Merrill, Gena Rowlands, Jessica Walter, Laura Devon, and Janice Rule, Bruce chose Lee Meriwether, guest star of last season's "The Bunker." While shooting an assortment of tape scenes for the new season, Geller got a call from Doug Cramer, who suggested that Dina Merrill be hired for the show. "I said we had discussed Miss Merrill," Bruce later related, "and we had decided that we would prefer Miss Meriwether. Mr. Cramer said Miss Merrill was a star. I disputed this fact. He told me it was all right by Mr. Kallis. My working procedure is not to overrule my producers unless I think it is a hideous error. I said, 'On that basis, all right.' When I got back to the studio, I discovered that what Mr. Kallis said was that it was all right by him if it was all right by me." For once, Bruce had been conned!

Lee Meriwether recalls that the initial deal was for the entire season. Excited by the prospect, her hopes were dashed when Merrill was signed for the opener. Lee was called for the next show, and nothing more was said about a regular spot on the series. "We were hoping for Lee Meriwether," Greg Morris reveals. "She was our first choice. With her sophistication and carriage, we felt that she could handle it very comfortably. She was looking forward to it, and I could tell that she was disappointed when she didn't get it."

"Not getting that role was one of the biggest disappointments of my life," Lee admits. "I wanted it so desperately, and I never found out why." Years later, Lee ran into Bruce Geller in the Twentieth Century-Fox commissary. "He was short on change and borrowed fifty cents from me. I said 'Sure, but I want that back and I want to talk.' He said okay, but I wasn't on the lot the next day, and the day after that *he* was gone." She never saw Geller again.

There was some consolation for Lee Meriwether: She was the only actress called back, eventually appearing in six segments this season, including the three-parter "The Falcon." She kept returning, says producer Kallis, simply "because we could not find any better. What she had was better than what was around at the moment." He believes that what *Mission* needed was an actress with "a protean quality. The essence of that role is that you *don't* have a personality. Off-screen, Barbara Bain is no more like the fifty roles she played in *Mission* than the man in the moon. But if you say to her, 'You are Olga Rostopovitch, a Soviet scientist in the Q section of an atomic laboratory,' she'll give you that character. The transformation is quick and clean. That is what I'm talking about, and many of the girls who attempted to do it just became incredible by trying. They were pressing, and the very act of pressing kills the credibility." The producer wasn't totally satisfied with any of the twelve actresses recruited. "Looking at who was acting in television at that time, it wasn't rich," says Kallis, who can name one actress who'd have made the grade. "Jane Seymour would have instantly become the regular," he declares. In 1969, however, Jane Seymour was nowhere to be found.

Lee Meriwether has fond memories of her stint on *Mission: Impossible*. "I loved the show because you played different characters all the time, unlike other series where you play the same character week after week. It was a wonderful working atmosphere where I was given the chance to do characters that no one would let me do anywhere except in a theater or a

workshop situation. I was able to grow as an actress, and the friendships that were created on that show are ongoing and lasting. My daughters Kyle and Lesley grew up on that set. They particularly loved Greg and Peter Lupus because those two paid attention to them. They would take them off and play with them, and come back with candy bars." When Lee chided health specialist Lupus over those sugary goodies, Pete innocently replied, "Greg got them the candy bars. *I* gave them the sugarless gum!"

During the height of the Landaus versus Paramount battle, yet another *Mission* star pressed the front office. Greg Morris knew the time was right to hit the studio for a raise, especially after dropping hints in certain circles that he too was considering a permanent departure from the show. "I held out," he explains. "Marty and Barbara were having their contractual fights at the same time and the simple fact was that they got more media coverage than I did. It was fine with me because I didn't want it in the press, anyway." The handling Greg's agent received from Paramount was indicative of the attitude the studio was developing about series regulars in general and *Mission* stars in particular. "My agent went in to renegotiate and was verbally mistreated," says Greg. "So I called my attorney." The situation grew serious enough for Bruce Geller to pay Greg a visit. "We discussed it," the actor remembers. "I told him exactly how I felt. I told Bruce I'd send my agent back in.

"In the meantime the trades had printed that Arthur Ashe [the black tennis champion] was on the lot. Now I get a hand-delivered message from Doug Cramer, whom I had not met prior to this, saying that Arthur Ashe was *not* on the lot for *Mission,* but that they did have a hold on Robert Hooks. I started laughing and never answered Doug's message."* The sore points were healed and Greg got a $500 raise. "After the problems were solved," he adds, "a friend said, 'You could have gotten a hell of a lot more.' But I didn't care. I wasn't interested in going through a lot of fighting. Neither was the public. All they were interested in was their hit show continuing, that's all."

Midway through the season, Stanley Kallis at last saw a light at the end of the tunnel that was *Mission: Impossible.* CBS's *Hawaii Five-O* was experiencing growing pains during its second season, and executive producer Leonard Freeman asked Kallis if he'd be interested in taking over. Kallis jumped at the idea, but got a typical reaction from Geller when he broke the news. "You can't do this," said Bruce. "I can't let you go. I don't know what to do if you go. Write yourself a new deal and whatever you want you can have." The last thing Geller wanted right now was another disruption, and he was as terrified as ever at the possibility of producing *Mission* himself. But Kallis would not place himself in further bondage. "This show is not my natural way of life," he told Bruce. "I found out that I could stretch, but now I'm stretched out of shape. This just isn't my work." Geller's reply was typically to the point: "Whose work is it?"

"His point," Kallis elaborates, "was that the show had never produced enough people to make choices possible. I responded that we had gone a little ways: We had Playdon and Heath, and we had found Jerry Ludwig for a couple of shows." When it became clear that nothing in the world could make Stan Kallis stay, the search was on for another producer. The new man would have to handle what was in the best of times a mind-bending, intensely difficult

---

* "I was on the Paramount studio lot," Arthur Ashe relates, "but I was never offered a spot on the show. There was never an offer either verbally or in writing concerning this particular show, so it seems that Paramount must have been playing some games with Greg."

Lee Meriwether as recurring IMF agent Tracey.

show. And this was hardly the best of times. The demise of another CBS series provided such a man.

Bruce Lansbury stems from a strongly theatrical family. His uncle, Ralph Mantell of Ireland, was a popular performer at the turn of the century; Bruce's mother, Moyna Macgill, an actress. Angela Lansbury is his sister, and his twin brother Edgar a Broadway producer. Born in London on January 12, 1930, Bruce and family migrated to New York in 1940, following the death of Bruce's father. After a UCLA education, Bruce became a stage manager in New York and spent much of 1958 writing an ABC daytime show, *Day in Court*. His first producing experience was CBS's *Great Adventure* (1963–64), a historical anthology (Lansbury produced a two-parter starring Peter Graves as Daniel Boone). After a stint as CBS's vice president in charge of programming and some Broadway work with his brother, Bruce returned to Hollywood in 1966 to salvage CBS's *The Wild Wild West*. "They had about six or eight producers before me," he says. "It was an incredible turnover." Among those who had come and gone were John Mantley (*Gunsmoke*) and Gene L. Coon, one of the creative forces behind *Star Trek*.

Lansbury succeeded where others had failed on a series that required a special touch and a peculiar story sense. The show, which took place in post–Civil War America, followed secret service agents James West (Robert Conrad) and Artemus Gordon (Ross Martin) and their battles against bizarre supervillains and outlandish strategies. *West*'s creator and executive producer Michael Garrison sold the show as "James Bond in the west," and *Wild Wild West* lived up to its premise and title, soon exceeding 007 himself in terms of farfetched ideas, futuristic gadgets, and some of the most vigorous fight scenes in television history.

"The structure of *Wild Wild West*," says Lansbury, "was two guys going off in two different directions and meeting up at the end to mutually contribute to the solution. You had to combine one flamboyant character [Martin] who did disguises and accents to a fare-thee-well, with a guy who went straight through the door and knocked people around [Conrad]. You had to have plenty of action for Bob, and that character for Ross. Surprise was the key to that show. You always had to do something that the audience did not expect. The key was in one line of dialogue which I put up on my office wall to remind the writers: 'Nothing, Artemus, is ever what it seems.'" Lansbury produced *Wild Wild West* for three years until it was abruptly canceled during the antiviolence pressure that swept the industry following the 1968 assassinations of Dr. Martin Luther King, Jr., and Senator Robert F. Kennedy. "It was a sacrificial lamb," Lansbury feels. "It went off with a thirty-two or thirty-three share which in those days was virtually break-even, but it always won its time period."

Many of the elements Lansbury had mastered so adroitly on *Wild Wild West*—the multilevel story lines, gadgetry, wild plots, and sense of surprise—were also essential to *Mission*. Lansbury, who'd already moved to Paramount to produce pilots and TV movies, got the nod as new *Mission* producer. Explains Doug Cramer, "I thought he would have a background and understanding for the show. He was wonderful and a very strong talent." Lansbury soon learned that producing *Mission* was much like producing *Wild Wild West,* only more so: *more* multilevel story lines, *more* gadgetry, *more* surprises. More of everything, of course, except scripts. "That was a major problem," he confirms. "I think you could say that *Mission* was the most difficult show in the history of television to write. It was such a strict, rigorously formatted concept show and that's what made it new and exciting. It was difficult to try to repeat the uniqueness of the concept. There were very few writers who could come in with that structure."

Bruce Lansbury was Paramount's choice to take over the series.

"I couldn't wait for Bruce to take it over," says Stan Kallis with a smile. "It was the happiest occasion for me." He gladly saw Lansbury through the changeover period, but the new producer had to make do without a head writer. After his eighteen-month trial by fire, Paul Playdon finally lost his grip on the series. It happened while he was writing episode 90, "Time Bomb," which greatly disappointed him and led him to feel that he'd completely lost touch with what *Mission* was all about. There were other motivating factors for his exit as well. "Bruce Lansbury had been brought to Paramount," he explains, "and they started to develop a Bruce Lansbury wing to write and produce the show. What happened is that everybody became their own little island. Everyone had a certain professional admiration for each other, but I just felt that there was a real disintegration occurring." There was no doubt in anyone's mind that Bruce Lansbury was part of the Cramer camp, not the Geller one. The "war" was coming to an end.

Playdon also admits that brighter opportunities beckoned. "At the time I was twenty-six, so there had been quite a catapult in my own personal career. I was being approached to write pilots, and to have people court you that way when you're that young is a little seductive, but it was also an opportunity I wanted. A lot of television is concerned with making a reputation, developing a rapport with people, and understanding how television works. The education that I acquired in that year and a half on *Mission* would have been a ten-year education anywhere else. A lot of hard work was put in, but a lot of rewards came out of it." Playdon's only regret is his hasty departure before the season was even over. Upon reflection, however, he sums up his situation and that of others in the *Mission* family: "It seemed that everyone who left that show left very suddenly."

For each departure, of course, there is a replacement. Laurence Heath came into his own at the end of the year, filling the void left by Playdon. His move to story consultant the following season was good casting, for there seemed to be no one left who could write *Mission* as consistently or as well. In addition to Robert O. Richards, the new property master replacing Bill Bates, year four marked the *Mission* debut of former *Mannix* wardrobe mistress Dodie Shepard, taking over for Sabine Manela, who had succumbed to cancer. Among the mourners at Sabine's funeral was someone who had visited her frequently in the hospital and who grieved visibly at the burial. Her name—Barbara Bain.

Bruce Geller directs a Year Four tape scene.

76/77: THE CONTROLLERS
(in two parts)

First Aired: 10/12/69; 10/17/69

Written by: Laurence Heath
Directed by: Paul Krasny
Music Composed and Conducted by:
Jerry Fielding

TEAM: Phelps, The Great Paris, Barney, Willy, Meredyth

Good morning, Mr. Phelps. The people you're looking at have become useless catatonics from being used as guinea pigs in experiments with a compound called B-230. It is a superhypnotic, mind-controlling drug being developed by this man, Dr. Karl Turek. The solution to Turek's problem of B-230's catatonic side effects is in the hands of two disloyal American scientists, Dr. Arthur Jarvis and his wife, Vera, who have undergone plastic surgery. Their defection in Geneva is now being arranged by this man, Colonel Borodin. Once they're working together, Turek's country will soon have the power to enslave the free world. Your mission, Jim, should you decide to accept it, is to stop Turek and B-230. As always, should you or any of your IM Force be caught or killed, the secretary will disavow any knowledge of your actions. This tape will self-destruct in five seconds. Good luck, Jim.

Jim and Meredyth pass themselves off as the Jarvises, postplastic surgery. To his distress, Turek learns that Phelps has developed Voliticon, an effective mind-control drug which, unlike B-230, has no side effects. A demonstration for the deputy premier in which Jim controls prisoner Willy goes off perfectly, and government funding is switched to Phelps, leaving Turek in the lurch.

Turek gets a call from Meredyth. She frantically tells him that Jim has destroyed her solution to B-230's side effects, that she has been forced to remain silent, and that she believes that Jim and Borodin intend to kill her. Turek, understanding that his days are also numbered, gets an idea.

Meredyth "drugs" Jim with Voliticon. Obeying Turek's command, he "fatally" shoots Borodin (with a tranquilizer bullet). Turek tells Jim to put the body in his car and drive it and himself off a cliff. As Jim motors out of the base, an abortive escape attempt by prisoners seals off the camp. Since his plan doesn't allow him to stop, Phelps crashes through the barricades. A gate guard fires, hitting the trunk and killing Borodin inside. The IMF strategy, which depended upon Borodin as a surprise witness during Jim's murder trial, is ruined. Unless Jim can plot another course, Turek will prevail.

GUEST CAST: Dina Merrill (Meredyth), David Sheiner (Dr. Karl Turek), Alfred Ryder (Colonel Borodin), Brooke Bundy

Willy rescues a damsel in distress (Brooke Bundy) from the sadistic scientist (H.M. Wynant) in "The Controllers."

228

(Katherine), H.M. Wynant (Lorkner), Robert Ellenstein (Deputy Premier Voss), Harry Davis (General Zagin), Leonard Stone (Major Alud), Jonathan Brooks (Martyn), Michael Stefani (Jailhouse Guard). *Unbilled:* Ralph Leabow (Corridor Guard); Lee Duncan (double, Barney); Bill Couch (double, Guard); Ben Dobbins (double, Lorkner); Hubie Kerns, Jim Burke (Stuntmen)

Little of *Mission*'s backstage calamity is evident in "The Controllers." The cast is larger than usual, our heroes are kept quite busy, and the disastrous turn midway through the story is a great hook. On the minus side, the studio's Administration Building doubles as State Security Headquarters. The building would appear more and more often on-screen under a variety of guises.

Desilu's huge water tower was the spark behind Larry Heath's plot, and figures prominently in the story when Barney boldly climbs the tower in broad daylight amid heavy patrols, and pours the B-230 into the water supply to immobilize the base and allow the IMF to escape safely. The tower, of course, is carefully photographed so the Desilu logo is never seen.

"I can't even remember 'The Controllers,' " Paul Krasny admits years later. Confronted by the usual pressures of a new season, the company seemed equally preoccupied by the cast's two notable absentees who had not yet officially left the series. "That was real strange," says Krasny. "I guess we were all still figuring that they were gonna come back and we were just going to fill in this two-parter. But we kept shooting and shooting, and we realized that they were gone and were not coming back. That was it."

78: THE CODE

Written by: Ken Pettus
Directed by: Stuart Hagmann
Music Composed and Conducted by:
    Gerald Fried

First Aired: 9/28/69

TEAM: Phelps, Paris, Barney, Willy, Lynn

Good evening, Mr. Phelps. This man, Vincente Bravo, the dictator of Nueva Tierra, intends to launch an invasion against the neighboring democracy of San Cristobal. Within forty-eight hours, vital details of the invasion plan will arrive in code from the UPR, the United Peoples' Republic, which has sent this man, Nikor Janos, to Nueva Tierra. Janos is to supervise the invasion and the installation of Bravo as president of a puppet regime in San Cristobal. Your mission, Jim, should you decide to accept it, is to break the code, get the details of the invasion plan, and shatter the alliance between Nueva Tierra and the United Peoples' Republic. As always, should you or any of your IM Force be caught or killed, the secretary will disavow any knowledge of your actions. This tape will self-destruct in five seconds. Good luck, Jim.

Paris, as notorious guerrilla "El Líder," self-proclaimed leader of all revolutionary forces in San Cristobal, hijacks a plane leaving that country and forces it to land in Nueva Tierra. His aim: to meet with Bravo and Janos and take for himself the presidency of the soon-to-be-conquered San Cristobal. He warns that if he is refused, his forces will unite with the government to oppose the invaders. While Bravo is out of the room, Janos, unwilling to battle El Líder, offers Paris a high position in the new government.

Among the hijacked plane's passengers is Lynn, whom Bravo's agents suspect is a courier carrying San Cristobal military data to the U.S. A thorough search of Lynn reveals microdots which seem to detail the entire deployment of San Cristobal's armed forces. This information is coded and sent to the UPR via Bravo's communications room, which Barney has ingeniously tapped into. Since Lynn's data is IMF created, Jim and Willy, in a computer-equipped van, can decode the message and thus decipher Bravo's code.

Paris stalls Bravo and Janos until the approved invasion plans arrive from the UPR. The IMF alerts San Cristobal of Bravo's precise battle plans. Bravo and Janos, the *only* ones to know where the invading divisions will strike, are astonished when their assault divisions are met with overwhelming resistance at every point. Recognizing a leak, Bravo and Janos accuse each other. The IMF listens as the argument ends with a gunshot.

PHELPS: The alliance is broken.
BARNEY: Who fired?
PHELPS: What difference does it make?

GUEST CAST: Alexandra Hay (Lynn), Michael Constantine (Janos), Harold Gould (Vincente Bravo), Nate Esformes (Lacerda), Roberto Contreras (Captain Avila), Art Lewis (Janitor), A. Martinez (Young Man), Joaquin Martinez (Desk Guard), Joany Playdon (Stewardess), Jay Tavars (Technician). *Unbilled:* Victor Campos (Mansion Guard)

In retrospect, it seems amazing that "The Code" opened the new season on CBS. By series standards the plot is static, the staging desperate, the budget small, and the heroine virtually nonexistent. It's an unexceptional hour and certainly not the type of segment a series in transition should use as a season premiere.

Why was it chosen? There can be only one reason, and that is the performance of Leonard Nimoy. Based upon Che Guevera, El Líder (originally "El Guerrero") is sly, colorful, and very threatening to the plans of Janos and Bravo. Taking advantage of one of his best roles, Nimoy plays it expertly and carries the hour. Yet that is the very problem with "The Code": There

is little else to recommend the show. An apparent demonstration that *Mission* could survive without Martin Landau was undoubtedly the reason why this episode led off the new season, but other series elements are neglected and it shows.

"The Code" seems to ignore the fact that the series ever had a leading lady. Alexandra Hay, a sexy young blonde with large brown eyes, is the season's first Cinnamon surrogate and she has the most thankless role of all. Used in just two scenes, her main purpose is to be undressed during a police search to find the microdots. The only help she gets from the heavies (or the story) is a towel after her clothes have been torn to shreds. This may have disappointed or insulted many female fans of the series. To some it seemed a deliberate, if indirect slap at Barbara Bain and her former importance to the show (although the script was originally intended for her). It was a big mistake.

The biggest problem is the show's leaden pace. After act one, the bulk of the story occurs in two or three sets, and almost all of it is talk. Director Hagmann, evidently aware of the problem, does all he can to keep the show moving: pans, dollies, zooms, rack focus, and tilts abound, but to little avail. The cracking of the code, a complex procedure involving the transmission of a photograph, doesn't go over well at all.

Besides Nimoy's performance, the only visual treat is a remarkable invention used by Barney to spy on the decoding apparatus in the communications room. A tiny robot, complete with wheels, drill, and video camera, makes its way through a ceiling pipe until Barney stops it precisely over the communications table. The unit's drill bores a tiny hole in the bottom of the pipe, then advances a few inches so the camera lens can peer down through the hole and tape the encoding of the message. Another of the show's more successful features is Gerald Fried's energetic score, which employs a flavorful and unexpected harpsichord.

Predictably, critical reaction to "The Code" was less than favorable. Leonard Nimoy received universally good reviews, but few had anything positive to say about the show in general. *Daily Variety* called it, "static," "tiresome," and "incoherent," and correctly diagnosed the trouble as, "lack of action and movement." The same review noted the absence of Landau and Bain but remarked, "Their absence is not missed nearly so much as a story." Jack Gould of *The New York Times* was similarly unimpressed, commenting that the gimmickry was, "a trifle wearing and baffling. This, chiefly because it is never explained how complicated devices can be designed to micrometer measurements before they are utilized." *Mission,* he concluded, "runs the risk of becoming so impersonal and complex as to invite diminished interest in what up to now has been the most serviceable espionage series."

Mission quickly regained some of its luster and made it through a more than commendable season. But opening with "The Code" was an error which seemed to confirm the fears, however inaccurate, that the defection of Marty and Barbara would ruin the series.

79: MASTERMIND

Teleplay by: Jerry Ludwig
Story by: Jerry Ludwig and
Richard Neil Morgan
Directed by: Georg Fenady

First Aired: 11/23/69

TEAM: Phelps, Paris, Barney, Willy, Dr. Irving
Berman, pharmaceutical man Thomas Galvin,
Phillip's Maintenance Service

Good afternoon, Mr. Phelps. Blackmail evidence which will provide organized crime with an unprecedented hold on high government officials has been engineered by this ambitious man, Lou Merrick, who plans to turn it over to the Syndicate when they hold their national convention here next week. Merrick's blackmail file is now being held for safekeeping under close guard by Merrick's boss Jonas Stone, the aging local Syndicate chief who has been grooming Merrick as his successor. Your mission, Jim, should you decide to accept it, is to destroy Merrick and his blackmail file. As always, if you or any of your IM Force should be caught or killed, the secretary will disavow any knowledge of your actions. This tape will self-destruct in five seconds. Good luck, Jim.

Stone abruptly collapses from an IMF delayed-action drug and is taken, by Dr. Phelps, to a hospital. In Stone's absence, Willy and Galvin lead Merrick to believe that they are involved in a profitable, secret drug deal with Stone.

At the hospital, Merrick finds Phelps using Stone (unconscious in an iron lung) in a brainwave transference experiment, with clairvoyant Paris speaking "Stone's" thoughts. Using a wealth of information about Stone, Paris convinces Merrick that Stone is indeed speaking through him, then explains his deal with Galvin and Willy: Galvin supplies morphine to chemist Willy, for which Galvin is paid one million dollars in Syndicate cash which Stone is accountable for. Willy then processes and distributes the drugs so quickly that the million is returned—with a nine million dollar profit for Stone. Merrick, planning to muscle into the deal, takes Paris to Stone's office, where Paris withdraws the cash for Galvin.

Stone awakens in the hospital, learns from Dr. Berman that *Merrick* was responsible for his unnecessary hospitalization, and heads for his office with a vengeance.

Merrick pays Galvin the one million dollars, then sends Paris away with a hit man (whom Jim zaps). Unknown to Merrick, Barney has looted Stone's wall safe from the rear. Stone finds Merrick and the empty safe—no blackmail, no Syndicate cash. A moment later, there is no Merrick.

GUEST CAST: Donnelly Rhodes (Lou Merrick), Paul Stewart (Jonas Stone), William Bryant (Nicholson), Gerald Hiken (Thomas Galvin), Ben Wright (Dr. Irving Berman), Joel Lawrence (Carter), Lucas White (Flynn), Alice Reinheart (Nurse Larkin). *Unbilled:* Lee Duncan (double, Barney)

"Mastermind" was hatched during one of the bleakest periods of the show's history. Stanley Kallis vividly recalls his difficult search for *Mission: Impossible* writers. At a time when Paul Playdon was nearing exhaustion, both he and Kallis had banked on three stories from three different writers. Says Kallis: "We'd had this massive number of failures already and we reached the point where we said, 'Well, *one* of these next three has got to work.' *None* of them worked. We had three extraordinary failures in a row; we couldn't repair them, we couldn't shoot them." Kallis contacted Jerry Ludwig, who had provided the well-received episode 53, "The Diplomat" for Woodfield and Balter. Ludwig had no more ideas for the series, so Kallis gave him one. "He started talking about a thought transference thing involving a man in an iron lung," says Ludwig. "The idea tickled me—it was a kind of reverse ventriloquist act. I

thought, 'Gee, these guys are real clever to come up with something like this,' and I felt lucky that they handed it to me." It wasn't until the script was nearly complete that Kallis admitted that the idea had been on the shelf for years and was considered unworkable. "Nobody could figure out what to do with it, but you did," said Kallis, who promptly gave Ludwig another nugget which evolved into episode 84, "The Double Circle."

In Ludwig's script the blackmail is fabricated, making Merrick seem quite despicable. However, in the actual show the legitimacy of the data is never questioned, casting a pall over the show's climax: Merrick is routed, but those corrupt politicians remain safely at their posts—and this in pre-Watergate 1969! The IMF drives off with the blackmail and the Syndicate's one million dollars and as usual, we are not told what will become of either.* "I guess that's their annuity," cracks Jerry Ludwig before nobly adding, "I think they burned the blackmail."

But what of the money?

---

* In the script, Jim mentions that the cash will be donated anonymously to charity.

80: THE NUMBERS GAME
  (formerly THE KEY)

Written by: Leigh Vance
Directed by: Reza S. Badiyi
Music Composed and Conducted by:
  Richard Markowitz

First Aired: 10/5/69

TEAM: Phelps, Paris, Barney, Willy, Tracey, Dr.
  Ziegler, the Hartford Repertory Company

Good morning, Mr. Phelps. After five years in exile, General Rados Gollan, the deposed dictator of Luxania, is ready to launch the invasion which will return him to power. Such an invasion would succeed in overthrowing the present democratic regime and lead to general war in the area. Gollan intends to pay his mercenary army with funds from the six hundred million dollars he stole during his tenure of office. Your mission, Jim, should you decide to accept it, is to stop Gollan. As always, should you or any of your IM Force be caught or killed, the secretary will disavow any knowledge of your actions. This recording will self-destruct in five seconds. Good luck, Jim.

Thanks to Dr. Ziegler, Gollan contracts what appears to be pneumonia. Ziegler and nurse Tracey sedate him while the rest of the team burrows into Gollan's bunker beneath his estate. Gollan is brought down to the bunker, an inflatable replica replacing him upstairs. He awakens to find his bunker overrun by "frontier soldiers," and learns that World War III is underway, his current country of residence one of the first atomic casualties. He sees tank divisions mobilize on television and hears radio broadcasts tell of massive worldwide destruction.

Gollan is told that he needs penicillin to survive. But the medicine is in short supply, and Captain Phelps plans to use it on a wounded enemy officer to learn military information. Gollan bribes soldier Paris to kill Jim, but Paris won't hand over the penicillin until he is paid something other than paper currency, which is now "worthless." Desperate, Gollan provides his Zurich account number as payment (having heard earlier that Zurich was destroyed in the war). Jim then abruptly rises from the dead and leaves with the others before the disbelieving eyes of General Gollan.

GUEST CAST: Lee Meriwether (Tracey), May Britt (Eva Gollan), Don Francks (Major Alex Denesch), Torin Thatcher (General Rados Adolph Gollan), Karl Swenson (Dr. Ziegler), Than Wyenn ("Dr. Wessell"), Gil Perkins ("Russian Colonel"), Vincent Deadrick ("Private"), Erik Holland (Announcer). *Unbilled:* Robert Bralver (Driver); Lew Palter (Lawyer)

Using 20/20 hindsight, it seems obvious that this episode should have opened up the new season. It's the first year four segment to really score, and is a more typical *Mission* than the one chosen, "The Code."

The bunker charade offers the usual fine audio-visuals from Barney. Phelps and Paris introduce the antagonistic act they would use often this season, pitted against each other strictly for the benefit of the mark. Nimoy, outfitted with a nasty facial scar, is good as the soldier cracking from the "war" and Captain Phelps's relentless orders. The acting honors, however, go to Torin Thatcher as wheezing, grasping old Gollan, who'll do anything to cling to life. "If I do not have penicillin I will die," he cries to Jim, who blithely responds, "Yes, this is a time of great personal sacrifice for us all."

"The Numbers Game" marks the second appearance of the redoubtable Hartford Players and the postponed debut of the season's most frequent Cinnamon substitute, Tracey, played by Lee Meriwether. Setting the tone for the rest of her appearances this year, she has a minor role as Gollan's nurse. Because of the IMF-induced "pneumonia," Gollan is placed in an

oxygen tent. The plastic figure which replaces him is extremely realistic. Lee Meriwether recalls it looking just as real onstage. "One day we were filming Torin in the tent. We broke for lunch and forgot all about him—he'd fallen asleep." The actor had been mistaken for the dummy!

Leigh Vance was the one writer found in England who would contribute more than one *Mission.* Vance, who'd written films and series like *The Saint* and *The Avengers,* became a *Mission* fan after the English broadcast of episode 4, "Operation Rogosh." He would work on four more *Mission*s, and wove interesting variations on the same basic plot of the target believing himself so deathly ill that he virtually invites the IMF to fleece him. Within a few years Vance had become a top "action series" regular. He was story editor, producer, or executive producer on programs like *Cannon, Switch, Hart to Hart,* and *Bronk,* the latter for executive producer Bruce Geller.

81: COMMANDANTE

First Aired: 11/2/69

Written by: Laurence Heath
Directed by: Barry Crane
Music Composed and Conducted by:
  Richard Hazard
Director of Photography: Paul Uhl
  (and Keith C. Smith)

TEAM: Phelps, Paris, Barney, Willy

Good morning, Jim. Until recently, Father Paolo Dominguin has led a democratic revolution against the cruel dictatorship that rules his country. Now our far eastern enemies are taking over Father Dominguin's movement. Their agents are Carlos Martillo, a local insurgent, and the legendary international revolutionary, Juan Acero. They're holding Father Dominguin prisoner in the mountain village of Lagonas, and Acero plans to murder him as soon as he can find a way to do so without arousing the hatred of the local population. Your mission, Jim, should you decide to accept it, is to rescue Dominguin and restore his control of the revolution. As always, should you or any of your IM Force be caught or killed, the secretary will disavow any knowledge of your actions. This tape will self-destruct in five seconds. Good luck, Jim.

Acero and Martillo are bitter rivals. Acero keeps Lagonas's skeptical townspeople at bay by accusing Dominguin of working with the US to keep the country's dictator in power.

Acero meets with Jim, representing a charitable organization whom Acero suspects is an American intelligence front. Acero agrees to release Dominguin for a cache of arms, which Willy delivers in a truck. Willy first deposits Barney and several large crates in a quiet canyon. There Barney unpacks the crates and proceeds to assemble a US intelligence helicopter. Acero adds the new weapons to his large arsenal and locks up Phelps and Willy.

Paris enters, representing the Far Eastern People's Republic which sponsors the country's dictatorship. He demands the immediate execution of Dominguin. But when Acero learns of the chopper in the canyon, he devises a plan to kill the priest without implicating himself.

Acero sabotages the helicopter, then frees Dominguin, Willy, and Jim. Instead of motoring out of the country as they had promised, the trio meet Barney and prepare to fly out in the chopper. Acero, Lagonas's mayor, and others watch the vehicle take off amid a cloud of dust, then promptly

crash and burn. "If only he had trusted us," Acero tells the grieving mayor, "if only he'd gone out by the road as he said he would, no harm would have ever come to him. We would have protected him. We wanted him to live because he meant so much to your people." Acero is sure that Dominguin's revolution is dead. But when no bodies are found amid the wreckage of the helicopter, it is learned that the priest and the Americans ingeniously used another way to escape. Paris angrily strips Acero of power. When Acero tries to shoot Paris, Martillo kills him and takes over. Paris concludes the mission by detonating the IMF weapons in the armory, rendering Dominguin's opponents powerless.

GUEST CAST: Lawrence Dane (Commandante Juan Acero), Arthur Batanides (Father Paolo Dominguin), Sid Haig (Major Carlos Martillo), Rodolfo Hoyos (Mayor Esbarto), Pepe Callahan (Colonel Ortiz), David Sachs (Pedro Sanchez), Anne Morell (Louisa), Robert Padilla (First Guard). *Unbilled:* Victor Leona (Prison Guard)

Associate producer Barry Crane finally gets his chance to direct in "Commandante." Like most of the fifteen *Mission*s he'd helm, the show's direction is largely uninspired. Unless he had an exceptional cast or script, Crane the director was not able to match the brilliance and precision of Crane the production manager, who could predict budgets nearly to the penny

or realign complex shooting schedules within minutes. Crane was a perfect example of a front office man trying to be creative in a job whose requirements were utterly different, says Stephen Kandel, writer and story editor for *Mission* during its seventh and final year. "Barry's strength was that he had a meticulously organized mind," Kandel explains, "but God, he was cautious. He worked out all of the possible moves and stayed within the parameters of the structure he'd worked out. It made him a wonderful associate producer, and a limited but valuable director. He never created on the set, never took a chance. He demanded a lot of specificity in his scripts. When he went over a script he'd say, 'It says the villain enters the square right here. But from what direction? I've worked it out and he has to enter from the northwest in order to intersect with what's coming in from here.' He wanted it all down there on the page."

Apart from Nimoy's impersonation of a Chinese general, the most impressive part of "Commandante" is Barney's single-handed assembly of a full-size working helicopter from the contents of a few packing crates. Writer Laurence Heath contends, with *almost* a straight face, that such a stunt is feasible. Special effects man Jonnie Burke wasn't so sure. "The way the script was originally written," he says, "they made a helicopter out of three overnight bags! I said, 'Barry, a seven-year-old kid isn't gonna believe this.'" Burke took Crane to his storeroom and showed him a large collection of odd helicopter parts, described the most compact way to pack them and found that it all worked within the limits of budget. Crane said, "Well, Jon, I know we've got a director that's happy, and I think we've got an effects man who's happy." Jonnie Burke remembers his reply: "'Yeah, Barry, but that goddamned production manager is gonna be livid when I tell him just how much of the budget this thing is gonna eat up.' Barry's chin fell practically to his chest," says Burke, exploding into laughter.

Villains (left to right) Sid Haig, Pepe Callahan, and Lawrence Dane are outwitted in "Commandante."

82: ROBOT

Produced by: Bruce Lansbury
Written by: Howard Berk
Directed by: Reza S. Badiyi
Music Composed and Conducted by:
    Richard Markowitz

First Aired: 11/30/69

TEAM: Phelps, Paris, Barney, Willy, Tracey

Good morning, Mr. Phelps. You're looking at a picture of Premier Pavel Zagov, taken yesterday—but Zagov died a month ago. His death was kept a secret by this man, Deputy Premier Gregor Kamirov, who substituted this double, called "Gemini." Kamirov is forcing Gemini to keep posing as Premier Zagov until a television address two days from now, when the double will announce his retirement because of failing health and name Kamirov as his successor. Kamirov then plans to kill Gemini, abandon his country's policy of strict neutrality, and ally with the Iron Curtain bloc. Your mission, Jim, should you decide to accept it, is to stop Kamirov. As always, should you or any of your IM Force be caught or killed, the secretary will disavow any knowledge of your actions. This tape will self-destruct in five seconds. Good luck, Jim.

Jim hopes to have Anton Massick, neutral head of the ministry of information, appointed as the next premier of Lucarno.

Tracey, supposedly working for Massick, allows entertainers Phelps and Willy (carrying large metal cases) into the country, bypassing customs. Kamirov and security chief Silensky learn that Jim has smuggled in a lifelike robot which resembles the premier. Deducing that Massick plans to replace Gemini with the robot for the televised speech and have himself designated premier, Kamirov forces Jim to reprogram the robot and name Kamirov as successor. Barney rescues the imprisoned Gemini, who replaces "robot" Paris and announces, on the air, that free elections will be held. Outraged, Kamirov interrupts the speech to expose the mechanical man, but is shocked to discover Gemini in its place.

GUEST CAST: Lee Meriwether (Tracey), Malachi Throne (Deputy Premier Gregor Kamirov), Lawrence Linville (Alexi Silensky), Jan Merlin (Captain Danko), Vic Perrin (Anton Massik), Richard Anders (Lieutenant), Socrates Ballis (Customs Man), Ken Delo (Mr. Mechanico), Sergei Tschernisch (TV Director)

Leonard Nimoy is unrecognizable in this disguise from "Robot."

Lee Meriwether remembers an incident during "Robot" which demonstrates how much postproduction can improve a show. During the scene in which Barney rescues Gemini from his prison cell and replaces him with an inflatable dummy, Tracey is in a nearby cell. She must distract Captain Danko while Barney does his job. In the script, Tracey is supposed to seem

terrified to the point of tears. The night before the scene was filmed, Lee's husband suffered a serious injury, and she spent the entire night at the hospital with him. "So when the script called for me to be hysterical," she relates, "I said, 'It's a snap, no problem, I'm already red-eyed and everything.' When I was ready to go, Reza Badiyi stopped me and said, 'I want you to be sexy with [Danko], play with him.' I said, *'What?* Reza, look at me. These are up-all-night eyes, red and baggy.' But after some repairs from Bob Dawn and his magic pencil, I was in there trying. I did a terrible job and thought it was just awful. The next day I went to the dailies and saw how bad it was. I was no sexier than a limp fish. It was dreadful."

When she saw the finished show on the air, however, Lee was pleasantly surprised. "It was edited to within an inch of its life," she feels. "I called Paul Playdon and asked him if I could meet the editor* because he did such a great job. 'Thank you for saving me,' I told him!"

In a riot of deceptions, doubles, and double-crosses, Leonard Nimoy plays *five* different characters in "Robot": Paris, the late premier (in stills), Gemini the double, the "robot," and even security chief Silensky in an IMF gambit to eliminate the latter. Nimoy goes to some lengths to differentiate his guises, using a low, slurred voice for Gemini, a wavering, raspy tone for Gemini's impersonation of the premier, and halting, effective movements as the robot. The concept of a robot con is shaky. Kamirov, who depends upon the automaton to win the premiership for him, never bothers to carefully inspect the "machine," simply accepting a phoney articulated arm Paris wears as proof enough.

"Robot" is helped in no small way by the astonishing makeup worn by Nimoy during most of the show. Crafted by Bob Dawn, the cosmetics manage to bury all traces of the actor's familiar visage. It also provides a *Mission* first when, at the end of the show, Paris rips off the disguise in one complete take—no cutaways or other tricks. It's a dramatic sight and immeasurably helps the show's credibility.

---

* David Wages, ACE.

83: FOOL'S GOLD

First Aired: 10/26/69

Written by: Ken Pettus
Directed by: Murray Golden
Music by: Lalo Schifrin

TEAM: Phelps, Paris, Barney, Willy, Beth

Good morning, Mr. Phelps. One of these hundred drona notes is the legitimate currency of the Kingdom of Bahkan. The other is a perfect counterfeit. One hundred million of these counterfeit drona have been printed by Igor Stravos, finance minister of the Federated Peoples' Republic. Stravos has demanded that Bahkan redeem its currency in gold. If Bahkan cannot prove the notes are counterfeit, it must meet the demand. Stravos knows this will exhaust Bahkan's gold reserve and precipitate the overthrow of Bahkan's pro-Western government. Your mission, Jim, should you decide to accept it, is to destroy the counterfeit drona, get the plates, and make certain that Stravos never again presents a threat. As always, should you or any of your IM Force be caught or killed, the secretary will disavow any knowledge of your actions. This tape will self-destruct in five seconds. Good luck, Jim.

The government of Bahkan agrees to redeem, in gold, the hundred million drona held by Stravos. Stuffy Bahkan envoy Phelps sends his associate, ex-counterfeiter Paris, to confirm that the cash is genuine. Paris tells Stravos that the counterfeit cash won't bankrupt Bahkan because the country actually has *two* hundred million in gold, not one. If Bahkan is to be ruined, Stravos must get Jim to redeem the *entire* gold supply of Bahkan.

Stravos films a tryst between Paris and Phelps's wife Beth, which he shows to a scandalized Phelps. Jim agrees to deliver the extra hundred million in gold at a prearranged site. Paris breaks into Stravos's vault, takes his fake drona plates, and leaves imperfect replicas.

Stravos removes "his" plates from the vault so Paris's assistants Barney and Willy can print the extra hundred million. The original bogus cash is ruined by an acid bath which Barney pipes in to the sprinkler system. The new money is used for Stravos's legitimate deal with Phelps, which is witnessed by a member of the World Monetary Commission. The money, printed off the IMF plates, is deemed quite fraudulent, and Stravos's co-conspirator, the premier, disavows any knowledge of his actions.

GUEST CAST: Sally Ann Howes (Beth), Nehemiah Persoff (Igor Stravos), David Opatoshu (Premier Roshkoff), Ronald Long (Sir Malcolm Forrester), Paul Marin (Clerk), Arline Anderson (Secretary), Jak Brami (Guard)

A surface problem of "Fool's Gold" is its similarity to last season's "The Vault." The casting of Nehemiah Persoff and the heavy involvement with vaults and cash make the confusion even more acute. In fact the plot lines are different, this one relying more on detail than the earlier one.

This show presents Peter Graves in one of his favorite roles, as an incredibly Victorian nobleman contemptuous of his associate Paris and crushed by his wife Beth's dalliance with the criminal. Paris's duties include his nocturnal entry into Stravos's vault, which is shielded by a lethal system of sound. As Jim explains, "Ultrasonic waves operating at a million cycles a second can cook an egg. The sound frequency in that [vault] corridor is *three* million cycles. You won't be able to hear it, but in two minutes it can turn you into a vegetable." Paris, in his driest tone, notes, "I will try to remember that." Barney provides him with a set of protective headphones which shield him long enough for him to penetrate the vault and switch

240

the plates. Then the headphones give out and Paris suffers searing head pains. He barely escapes, crawling out of the vault on his hands and knees.

This episode's oddest distinction is an unexpected leaning toward comedy, making it a unique installment. Director Murray Golden makes the most of a droll Ken Pettus script, helped by Nimoy and Nehemiah Persoff. As fellow schemers working each other, they all but wink conspiratorially and elbow each other in their scenes together. Consider the following dialogue, when Paris demands a full partnership in Stravos's plan to blackmail Phelps.

STRAVOS: No, you can't be serious.

PARIS: I am very serious when it comes to risking my life. I don't know what I would do without it.

Or this, when Stravos forces Jim to submit to his plot.

PHELPS: The house of Rakozny dates from the fourteenth century without a breath of scandal. Now, to protect it, you would ask me to become a thief and a traitor to my country.

STRAVOS: We all have to make little compromises.

These sequences are perfectly played and don't detract from the plot's required somberness. Everyone was pleased by the dailies, including Bruce Geller, who bought an ad in a trade paper congratulating Golden. "Sometimes you would break your ass trying to get a specific effect," says Golden, who would direct five *Mission*s. "If it was a nice shot Geller kept it in, whereas a show like *Medical Center* would cut the whole thing out and you had a run-of-the-mill show. I liked Geller because he would say, 'Gee, that's beautiful,' and I would stretch my muscles and look for things that were interesting and eccentric. That's very pleasing to a director."

Paris must infiltrate a vault protected by lethal soundwaves in "Fool's Gold."

84: THE DOUBLE CIRCLE

Written by: Jerry Ludwig
Directed by: Barry Crane

First Aired: 12/7/69

TEAM: Phelps, Paris, Barney, Willy, Gillian Colbee, Ericson

Good afternoon, Mr. Phelps. The man you're looking at is the eccentric art collector Victor Laszlo, who recently arranged the theft of a new fuel formula vital to America's missile defense. The theft was executed by Laszlo's partner Ray Dunson, who also killed the one American scientist capable of duplicating the formula. Enemy scientists have recently solved the same problem, so they do not need our copy of the formula. But they will pay Laszlo handsomely for the privilege of destroying it, and thereby putting us years behind in military capability. Your mission, Jim, should you decide to accept it, is to recover the formula. As always, should you or any of your IM Force be caught or killed, the secretary will disavow any knowledge of your actions. This tape will self-destruct in five seconds. Good luck, Jim.

Operating from a plush penthouse suite, Laszlo will sell the formula (hidden in his wall safe) to the United Peoples' Republic.

The IMF recreates Laszlo's offices on the floor directly below and rigs the private penthouse elevator to stop when desired at their suite instead. While government intermediary Gillian tempts Laszlo with a priceless artifact in exchange for the formula, Barney penetrates the room containing the safe. On the roof, Willy and Ericson use a laser to burn a narrow furrow across the roof, and drop a false wall (identical to the one containing the safe) in front of Barney, shielding him from sight.

UPR agent Phelps tells Dunson that Laszlo intends to sell the formula to Gillian and the Americans. He shows Dunson a film of "Laszlo" hiding the formula in a secret room in "his" office. Dunson examines "Laszlo's" office, where he not only discovers that Laszlo has made a deal with Gillian,

but also hears "Laszlo" (Paris) plot to frame Dunson for the "theft" of the formula when the UPR men arrive. Dunson informs Jim, who explains that the UPR buyers will be aware of Dunson's "cooperation."

At the buy, Laszlo opens the dummy safe anchored in the false wall and finds it empty. Dunson discloses Laszlo's supposed double-cross and shoots him. When Dunson fails to open the "secret room" where he insists the formula is hidden, he too is killed. Barney, hiding behind the false wall, opens the real safe and takes the formula.

GUEST CAST: Anne Francis (Gillian Colbee), James Patterson (Victor Laszlo), Jason Evers (Ray Dunson), Albert Sklar (Markoff), Thom Barr (Dick Miller), Robert Ritchee (Ericson)

"If you had a seventh floor apartment that was identical to a sixth floor apartment, and you fixed the elevator so that when you pressed seven you got six, you'd get off on six but think you were on seven, wouldn't you?" That's how Stanley Kallis explained to Jerry Ludwig the nebulous idea which ultimately became "The Double Circle." "It was an intriguing item," Ludwig agrees, "but no one could figure out what to do with it. Not knowing that it couldn't be licked, I went and figured it out." Ludwig worked wonders with the idea and added a better one: the secret room gag, which triggers one of *Mission*'s funniest climaxes. While Laszlo opens the phony IMF wall safe, Dunson casts knowing glances at the UPR agents who, of course, have no idea what is about to happen. After the safe is opened and Laszlo killed, Dunson attempts to open the secret room that doesn't exist. He *knows* it must be there: He's

seen it and was even inside it. He wrecks the room trying to trigger the sliding panel which is, of course, in the office replica one floor below. One can imagine an elderly Phelps and Barney chuckling over this one at the secret agents' retirement home someday.

If "Victor Laszlo" sounds familiar, it was the name of Paul Henreid's character in *Casablanca* (1942). "I went through a period when I was doing that," Jerry Ludwig confesses. "The operative word is *homage*." Dunson was John Wayne's name in one of Ludwig's favorite films, *Red River* (1948); Nicholson, which the writer used in "Mastermind," was Alex Guinness in *The Bridge on the River Kwai* (1957). As for Victor Laszlo, Ludwig believes, "the name worked. It was a better name for my character than it was for Henreid's."

243

THE COMPLETE MISSION: IMPOSSIBLE DOSSIER

85: SUBMARINE

Produced by: Bruce Lansbury
Written by: Donald James
Directed by: Paul Krasny
Music Composed and Conducted by:
    Lalo Schifrin

First Aired: 1/16/70

TEAM: Phelps, Paris, Barney, Willy, Tracey,
    Carella and Somers of the Hartford Repertory
    Company

Good morning, Mr. Phelps. You are looking at Kruger Schtelman, who is due to be released in three days from a prison in the East European Republic, after serving a twenty-five-year sentence for war crimes. Schtelman is the only man alive who knows the whereabouts of the funds stolen by the SS from the countries occupied by the Nazis in World War II. This enormous sum is intended to finance a neo-Nazi coup in Europe which is set to trigger as soon as they get the money. Your mission, Jim, should you decide to accept it, is to learn where this vast horde of cash is hidden before the neo-Nazis do. As always, should you or any of your IM Force be caught or killed, the secretary will disavow any knowledge of your actions. This tape will self-destruct in five seconds. Good luck, Jim.

The East European Republic wants the same information the IMF does, and to this end have assigned to Schtelman a brilliant interrogator, Colonel Sardner. Despite Sardner's best efforts, Schtelman has not broken and gives no indications that he will weaken during his last few days as a prisoner. Schtelman is ingeniously drugged and liberated by the Force. He awakens in a cramped submarine bunk near a delirious woman (Tracey). Captain Phelps and the crew treat him with contempt. Through SS officer Paris, Schtelman learns that this U-boat (actually an IMF warehouse mock-up) is bound for SS headquarters in Scandinavia, where both Schtelman and Tracey will be tried as traitors for divulging vital data to Sardner. Schtelman, knowing he hasn't broken, plans to reveal the location of the hidden money to his superiors when he arrives at headquarters, thereby proving his loyalty.

The "sub" is set upon by an "enemy destroyer" whose "depth charges" force the sub to the "ocean floor." When heavy damage is suffered, Phelps drowns the crew and jettisons a screaming Paris through the escape hatch. "There is only one form of evidence a destroyer commander will accept," he tells an admiring Schtelman. Jim and Schtelman don buoyancy jackets and masks to leave the sub. Schtelman, afraid he won't survive the trip to the surface, insists on giving Phelps the account number of the stolen loot to relay to headquarters. "Take the account number," he begs, "prove to them I never cracked!" But regular navy Phelps doesn't care. He crawls into the escape hatch and vanishes as Schtelman screams the account number at him.

GUEST CAST: Lee Meriwether (Tracey), Stephen McNally (Kruger Schtelman), Ramon Bieri (Colonel Jaroslav Sardner), William Wintersole (Raskov), Albert Kramer (Carella), Steve London (Somers), Gene Tyburn (Sergeant)

If one were to feed all the classic components of *Mission: Impossible* into a computer and ask it to fashion a script for the series, the result would undoubtedly be "Submarine," Bruce Lansbury's second episode as *Mission: Impossible* producer. To note that it is largely a combination of earlier shows—episode 4, "Operation Rogosh" and episode 23, "The Train"—takes nothing away from this excellently produced hour. "Submarine" is so typical of the series that when CBS included *Mission* as part of its 1978 gala special *On the Air: A Celebration of 50 Years,* excerpts from this episode were used.

The IMF's greatest weapon is Schtelman's own ego. "Schtelman has survived for twenty-five years on pride," says Phelps, "pride that he hasn't broken. If Schtelman isn't as proud as

Director Paul Krasny shares a laugh during "Submarine."

I think he is, our plan won't work." By the end, of course, Schtelman is begging Jim to take the information he's kept secret for a quarter of a century.

Schtelman's hijacking is shot and edited with the utmost precision. While in transit from prison to police headquarters, his vehicle is flanked at all times by two radio-linked police cars. When the convoy turns a corner it is interrupted: Monks Phelps and Paris isolate Schtelman's car from the police vehicles by blocking the road with identical trucks. Each police car believes Schtelman to be on the other side of the truck and in view of the *other* police car. Tracey fires a gas missile into the car, rendering Schtelman unconscious. The Nazi is hustled into a warehouse one block from the ambush point. Of course, it all takes place on the deserted Paramount side streets and as director Paul Krasny remembers with a smile, "We drove the guy right in through the open stage door! 'Submarine' was shot entirely on the lot."

The show features some of the false alarms *Mission* was famous for. When Paris introduces himself to Schtelman as SS, the old man challenges him. "If you are SS, you have one of these," he says, revealing a numbered tattoo on his shoulder. Paris anxiously glances at Jim—then unbuttons his shirt to show his own numbered tattoo. Earlier, Tracey is declared dead by Jim, but Schtelman unexpectedly checks her pulse and finds that she is indeed still alive. Phelps does the only thing he can: He ignores Schtelman. "I say she is dead," he barks. Lee Meriwether considers her exit from this scene one of the unique opportunities *Mission* offered her. "After all," she wonders, "how many actresses have been shoved into a torpedo tube? That was not a dummy, that was me. Oh, my back!" Her guise during the show called for a remarkable makeover from Bob Dawn, turning the beautiful actress into a beaten, tortured, and exhausted casualty. "The makeup took only fifteen minutes," says Lee. "I asked Bob why it took him three hours to make me up normally. Then I realized what I was saying!"

British television writer Donald James *(The Champions, The Persuaders)* was one of only two authors found in England by producers Cedric Francis and Ivan Goff. James wrote his first draft in England based on his outline and comments from Geller, and finished the second draft after consulting with Bruce Lansbury by phone and correspondence. "It was one of those rare scripts that ran smoothly from beginning to end," says James. Unfortunately, the problem of writing for a show 6,000 miles and several time zones away made it impossible for James to write another *Mission*. It's fascinating to speculate what James would have contributed after "Submarine," which could be called the ultimate, distilled *Mission: Impossible* story, and one which is well remembered.

A World War I submarine mock-up was brought out of storage for the show and placed on wooden platforms so Jonnie Burke's hydraulic cylinders could move the sub up and down and simulate its movement in water. While hot and extremely cramped, the set had its advantages, according to director Krasny. "If you can confine an intricate show to one stage, you have a better chance than if you're in a jungle or someplace where you don't have much control." The claustrophobic feeling certainly enhances the show's tension, as does the creative work of the sound department.* It all adds up to an unforgettable hour and a feather in newcomer Lansbury's cap. As he admits, "That was really a good show. I liked 'Submarine' because it worked."

---

* Mixers Gordon Day and Nick Gaffey won *Mission*'s only Emmy this season for their work on this episode.

86: THE BROTHERS

Produced by: Bruce Lansbury
Teleplay by: Leigh Vance
Story by: Robert C. Dennis
Directed by: Murray Golden

First Aired: 12/14/69

TEAM: Phelps, Paris, Barney, Willy, Lisa,
Hartford Repertory Company

Good morning, Mr. Phelps. The man you're looking at is King Selim III of Qamadan, a good friend of the West. Unknown to the world, the king has been imprisoned somewhere for over six months by his younger brother, Prince Samandal. With the king in his power, Samandal now controls the huge oil royalties which are Qamadan's main source of revenue. To suppress those opposing him, the prince resorts to inhuman torture and murder carried out by this man, Colonel Hatafis, who heads one of the most brutal and feared police forces in the Middle East. Your mission, Jim, should you decide to accept it, is to rescue King Selim and restore him to his throne. As always, should you or any of your IM Force be caught or killed, the secretary will disavow any knowledge of your actions. This tape will self-destruct in five seconds. Good luck, Jim.

Oil magnate Paris, traveling with physician Phelps and actress Lisa, arrives for a long-standing meeting with the king, only to find that he must deal instead with Prince Samandal while the king is "on retreat." Dining with Lisa, Samandal collapses and specialist Jim diagnoses severe uremia. He recommends an immediate kidney transplant using a "close relative" as donor. With no choice and in severe pain, the prince has his unconscious brother brought back to the palace where, to avoid publicity, the operation will take place.

Thanks to Barney and Willy, the prince and king change places during the operation despite the careful scrutiny of power-hungry Hatafis. The "transplant" is a success.

While the patients recuperate, Lisa convinces Hatafis that Samandal will align with Paris, who has insisted that Hatafis be removed. Hatafis kills "King Selim," but before he can blame "Samandal" for the murder and assume power, he is stopped by the real king who, disguised as his brother, is quite alive.

GUEST CAST: Michele Carey (Lisa), Lloyd Battista (King Selim/Prince Samandal), Joseph Ruskin (Colonel Hatafis), Lee Bergere (Dr. Labashi), David Fresco (Ahmed), Noel De Souza (Behram), Henry Brandon (Farid), Elizabeth Perry (First Nurse), Fred Villani (First Reporter), Lee Duncan (Second Reporter)

A hokey idea undergoes a *Mission: Impossible* transfusion and emerges as a felicitous switcheroo with an exceptional bogus operation scene.

The operation is performed in the palace's largest room, its gymnasium. Jim begins with a full staff (the Hartford Repertory), assisted by Samandal's private consultant, Dr. Labashi (Paris). As Hatafis watches from an adjoining observation room, the IMF block his view of the "patients." A dish of blood is used to soil the instruments Jim "uses." Actually, all he does is wait for Willy and Barney who, from the basement, cut through the gym floor and set up a scaffold-type rigging which lowers the tabletops on which the king and prince lie (the table frames remain stationary upstairs). Jim fixes metal cords covered by the bed sheets to simulate the contours of the missing patient, and a dummy head is placed at the head of the table to complete the illusion. The prince and king are disguised to resemble each other, then returned upstairs. Lisa plants the seed of doubt in Hatafis's mind, prompting him to kill Samandal (disguised as his brother).

The IMF operation ran smoother than did the crew's attempt to film it, mainly because the

elaborate mechanism needed to lower the tabletops took hours to work properly. "You start sweating," says director Murray Golden, "because the one thing you do not want to spend time on is *that*. You've got too many other things that are more important." With many hours of *Medical Center* to his credit, Golden jokingly considers himself a surgical authority. But even he had never filmed a *phony* kidney transplant before. "I never thought of hanging out a shingle," he claims, "but a kidney transplant is nothing to me. In case you know anybody who needs a kidney transplant, send him to Murray Golden. I'll do it cheap!"

Highlights include Lloyd Battista's standout job as the brothers and a memorable trick bottle used to sicken and drug the prince. It looks like a regular brandy bottle. But when triggered by remote control, the bottle itself secretes the drug into the liquid it holds.

87/88/89: THE FALCON
(in three parts)

Written by: Paul Playdon
Directed by: Reza S. Badiyi
Music Composed and Conducted by: Richard Markowitz

First Aired: 1/4/70; 1/11/70; 1/18/70

TEAM: Phelps; Paris; Barney; Willy; Tracey; Sebastian; Lucifer, a falcon

Good morning, Mr. Phelps. The man you are looking at, Prince Stephan, was his country's rightful ruler until he was reported killed two weeks ago in an automobile accident. However, we have learned that Stephan is alive and being held by this man, General Ramon Sabattini. Sabattini has imprisoned Stephan in order to force Stephan's fiancée, Francesca, to marry him. This marriage would make Sabattini a legitimate heir to the throne, currently occupied by Francesca's cousin Nicolai. We believe it is Sabattini's plan to kill all three of the royal family, take the throne, and ally with our enemies. Your mission, Jim, should you decide to accept it, is to stop Sabattini and rescue Stephan, Francesca, and Nicolai. As always, should you or any of your IM Force be caught or killed, the secretary will disavow any knowledge of your actions. This tape will self-destruct in five seconds. Good luck, Jim.

On the day of the wedding, Zastro the Magician (Paris), his mind-reading assistant (Tracey) and manservant (Willy) appear at the palace to entertain at the invitation of Nicolai, a simpleton infatuated with magic. Hidden within Zastro's equipment boxes are Sebastian, who is disguised as Paris, and Barney. Barney cuts into the palace floor and crawls to the heavily guarded jewel room, where he replaces the crown jewels with replicas. Paris reveals himself to Francesca, giving her a gun and very specific instructions.

During the magic show, Paris deftly assumes the identity of Nicolai while Sebastian replaces Paris as Zastro. Tracey predicts a catastrophe which comes true when Francesca, using the gun Paris gave her, "fatally" shoots herself at the altar, ruining Sabattini's plans for conquest. "Nicolai" orders her immediate entombment in the palace crypt, where she is rescued from inside by Barney. Together they return to Zastro's prop boxes. Willy packs up and leaves, taking Barney, Francesca, and the sleeping Nicolai with him.

Jim alerts Sabattini to the theft of the jewels and identifies himself as a fence, claiming that Prince Stephan, who stole the jewels, is the only one who knows their whereabouts. Jim is taken to Stephan's prison cell to sweat the needed information from him. There, Jim (with Barney's unseen help) blocks the guard's view of the cell with a projected film showing Jim interrogating "Stephan." Hiding behind the movie screen, Jim frees Stephan and flees with Barney to join the rest of the Force and the liberated royal family.

GUEST CAST: Lee Meriwether (Tracey), Noel Harrison (Nicolai), Diane Baker (Francesca), John Vernon (General Ramon Sabattini), Logan Ramsey (Colonel Vargas), Marcel Hillaire (Bishop), Joseph Reale (Prince Stephan), Dal Jenkins (Rousek), Tony Giorgio (Foyer Guard), Josh Adams (Tour Officer), Majorie Bennett (Woman), Jason Heller (Man), Jack Donner (Buccaro), William Visteen (Maintenance Room Officer), John Rose (Upstairs Officer), Peter Kilman (Stephan's Guard), Arline Anderson (Receptionist)

Tracey with Nicolai (Noel Harrison) in "The Falcon" . . . or is that Paris in disguise?

249

THE COMPLETE MISSION: IMPOSSIBLE DOSSIER

Mission's only three-parter began as a simple story which kept growing. "The Falcon" gives us a glimpse of what the series may have been like had Geller's original plan for a serialized *Mission* come to pass. The script relies less on Playdon's typical mind benders and more on the type of outrageous mechanical stunts which were Woodfield and Balter's hallmarks. The show's punchline, the movie decoy, is a vintage Woodfield and Balter gag. Playdon liked to collect odd story elements which could be dropped into any script to add tension. Several of these turn up here: Barney is blinded, Tracey uncovered, and Paris caught in an explosion meant to kill Nicolai (it shreds his Nicolai mask and nearly finishes him). "Even though *Mission* had a very definite construct," says Playdon, "it was still a construct made of many bits and pieces, and to some degree they were interchangeable.

" 'The Falcon' was classic genre stuff, the beautiful princess forced to marry the evil general. What ennobled the mission is that they were saving sweethearts, Stephan and Francesca, as well as a European country from falling into the hands of a ruthless usurper. It too was written under pressure, but I enjoyed writing it because it had a certain brand of make-believe and a certain theatricality to it." Indeed, "The Falcon" has a fairy tale quality and a feeling of great romance. Of course, there are plenty of new twists provided by the IMF.

For the most ambitious *Mission* to date, Reza Badiyi had two weeks to "prep" (it was filmed in nineteen days). He provided his usual creativity, but in an unusual way. While art director Gibson Holley was out sick and Badiyi waited for the sets, the director spotted some impressive flats which were about to be stored away on the lot. Reza, who thought they'd be perfect for "The Falcon," learned that the sets were made for the Paramount feature *On a Clear Day You Can See Forever* (1969), which had been completed but not yet released. After some haggling with the front office, the sets were repainted, altered, and finally used as the palace interiors. In a typical ending to such a story, *Mission*'s art department received an Emmy nomination for the sets. "They should have gotten an award for the series, anyway," the director declares.

The title character, a trained Asian falcon, is part of Paris's magic show, but his real purpose is to furnish diversions for several IMF gambits. "The bird was awful," Badiyi remembers. "It would just stand around posing and wouldn't do anything." When it did move, it was prone to disappear into the soundstage rafters, forcing its trainers to lure it down with live animals as bait—a scene Lee Meriwether chose not to witness. In the end the falcon was used only in close-ups and a lowly buzzard, made up to look like a falcon, did the flying—when *it* felt like flying. "The trainer told me that this bird would go where it was supposed to go," claims the director, "but it wouldn't take off. When it finally did, it fell! The trainer told me there wasn't enough wind while we were on location. I asked, 'Is that a bird or a kite?' He got so insulted he took his bird and was ready to go home. At last the bird got up, flew away . . . and never came back! The trainer accused me of insulting the bird. So we lost that bird. Finally we found another one, an awful bird who made noise and lost feathers every time it flew. We filmed him during the action scenes, then cut to the falcon looking like he had just arrived."

Greg Morris was also having trouble. Barney is wheeled into the palace in a property box, then removes the bottom of the box and cuts into the floor with a square, four-way saw whose dimensions exactly fit the tile he is cutting through. Barney must hold the saw in place as it works, and it wasn't easy. "I hated that saw," Greg yells. "I had to crawl between floors and take out tiles with this damn saw that weighed seventy pounds, at times lying on my back!"

The movie trick was based on a Las Vegas nightclub act Playdon had seen years earlier. The routine opened with a film of the star who, by standing behind the screen and jumping through

it at the right moment, seemed to leap off the screen. "It was really amazing, and I never forgot it," Playdon relates. His version of the setup is nimble. Stephan is chained to a wall at the end of a long, windowless corridor; two guards watch him from the other end of the corridor. In the middle of the ceiling is a low-hanging beam. While Jim questions Stephan, Barney's drill quietly emerges from a side wall. He inserts a long metal cylinder which eventually runs the entire length of the corridor and suctions itself to the opposite wall, hidden from view of the guards by the ceiling beam. Jim distracts the guards long enough for a movie screen to drop from the cylinder and a projector, hidden in Jim's briefcase, to activate. The film depicts exactly what the guards were watching a moment ago: Phelps interrogating "Stephan." The effect is striking, but Badiyi wasn't convinced it would work, and numerous tests were made. "Every time we tried it, it just didn't work out the way we wanted it to. We brought in a specialist from Disney, who'd done it; still, I wasn't totally convinced that it would pay off." Since a real projection effect could not register effectively enough on film, a matte was used. Naturally, it looks perfect.

The performances in "The Falcon" are fine, particularly from villains John Vernon and Logan Ramsey, and would-be victims Diane Baker and Noel Harrison. Lee Meriwether finally has some fun in her last *Mission* as know-it-all seer Madame Vinsky. Leonard Nimoy is afforded his flashiest guise as the florid, temperamental Zastro. It is the only episode in which Paris uses magic, and Nimoy enjoyed it. The actor does a good job conjuring gold eggs and rare coins from thin air and demonstrating a floating ball trick, all taught to him by magician-actor Tony Giorgio, who appears in the show as the palace's foyer guard.

With a budget equal to three episodes, "The Falcon" is lavish, especially in this season of diminished production values. Cost cutting occurs only in the final hour: Footage of Barney climbing an elevator shaft is lifted from episode 68, "Doomsday," and Stephan's prison is all too clearly Paramount Studios, its arched gates unmistakable. These are small complaints regarding a show which proved to be a grand send-off to the *Mission: Impossible* the public had come to know. Physically at least, the series would never look this good again.

This test matte (left) illustrates the principle behind the IMF illusion (right) in "The Falcon."

251

90: TIME BOMB

Written by: Paul Playdon
Directed by: Murray Golden

First Aired: 12/21/69

TEAM: Phelps, Paris, Barney, Willy, Wai Lee, Globe Repertory Company

Good morning, Mr. Phelps. Twelve years ago, this man, Anton Malek, was planted in the Federated People's Republic to infiltrate their atomic research program. Now suffering from an incurable disease, Malek is acting independently against his country's orders. At four o'clock the day after tomorrow, Malek is going to turn a nuclear reactor into an atomic bomb, which will wipe out the capital and bring on an atomic war. Any attempt to expose Malek will only result in his setting off the blast ahead of schedule. Your mission, Jim, should you decide to accept it, is to stop Malek. As always, should you or any of your IM Force be caught or killed, the secretary will disavow any knowledge of your actions. This tape will self-destruct in five seconds. Good luck, Jim.

The Federated People's Republic's premier has decreed that all government installations include a culturally satisfying environment. He commissions an artist to install a huge stained glass window of his ladyfriend, Miasmin, in the nuclear complex. Jim detours and replaces the artist. An "accident" shatters the window, which is to be viewed shortly by the visiting premier. A devastated Phelps calls the premier (Paris), who reluctantly agrees to send Miasmin (Wai Lee) to the complex so the damage can be repaired.

Upon meeting Malek, Wai Lee "senses" that he is a very sick man. Despite his denials, she offers to cure him through her unorthodox "gift." Paris switches Malek's medication for a serum which makes him ill and unable to leave the country before four o'clock, when the bomb will blow.

Barney's sabotage cracks a wall in the nuclear reactor room. Engineer Barney is called in and evacuates the building. Malek, unconscious, leaves with Wai Lee.

Malek awakens to find the building in a state of

partial collapse. Tempted by Wai Lee's promise to cure him, Malek enters the reactor room to disarm the bomb. He is in fact in an exact replica of the room, disarming a bogus bomb while Jim, watching him on a monitor, relays each step of the process to Barney, who works on the real bomb in the genuine reactor room. All goes well until Malek realizes, two minutes before detonation, that he is being tricked, forcing Phelps and Barney to do something—fast.

GUEST CAST: Barbara Luna (Wai Lee), Bert Freed (General Brenner), Morgan Sterne (Anton Malek), William Hansen (Dr. Wimmel), Michael Mikler (Lt. Reigler), Jacques Denbeaux (IMF Captain), John Aniston (First IMF Captain), Art Koulias (Doctor), Mario Machado (Technician), Lucetta Jenison (Nurse), Robert Bralver (Foreman), Allen Bleiweiss (Orderly). *Unbilled:* Peter Church (Engineer)

After a year of intensive, exhaustive work, Paul Playdon was beginning to fear that time was running out. During the writing of "Time Bomb," he finally lost his confidence. "I was so unhappy with 'Time Bomb,' " he relates. "It was written in a couple of days and I just couldn't focus on it. Something about the way it was thrown together told me that I had lost touch with what the show was all about. I felt that my ability to write *Mission* was gone and I was in a vacuum. I had suddenly hit this blank wall." The script was the first casualty of an episode which many still look back on with embarrassment.

Considering some of the scripts to follow, this one isn't so bad. Jim's pose as an eccentric glass artist, complete with red beard and wig, was a serious error in judgment. Originally a genuine artist named Kirk was utilized, but budgetary pressure eliminated him from the story.

Even so, the role is tailor-made for Paris, not Phelps, and Peter Graves knew it. "Peter begged us not to use him as the artist," says Stan Kallis. According to Graves, "that was one of those mistakes that you want to forget about." The disguise bothered the actor more than the character did: "He could have been a wild character *without* that red beard and wig." It was an attempt to freshen things up which didn't work and was never repeated.

On the set, criticism was being leveled by nearly everyone, including Geller, Kallis, Playdon, and director Murray Golden. "Stan and Paul both admitted that I would not emerge a hero out of 'Time Bomb' and I sure didn't," says Golden. "It was a bum show and I should have turned it down. We were talking about it on the last day of shooting, and everything that could have possibly gone wrong went wrong." The show's claustrophobic interiors and bland backlot exteriors complete the picture of an uninspired show.

Still, there are consolations. Beautiful Barbara Luna returns, this time as IMFer Wai Lee. With the help of drugs, she first makes Malek sick, then miraculously well, giving Malek hope that his end may not be at hand. The key feature of "Time Bomb" is probably Jonnie Burke's elaborate nuclear bomb, with manipulator arms and steel pins which must be removed in a special sequence if the bomb is to be successfully disarmed. It earned Burke an Emmy nomination.

What went wrong with "Time Bomb"? Stan Kallis rules out exhaustion as an excuse. "We were always exhausted, and did some of our best work in total exhaustion." Perhaps the main problem after all was the script, which ultimately cost the show its resident story genius. After one more episode, Paul Playdon left, convinced that he could no longer write *Mission: Impossible.** "Looking back," says Playdon, "I can see that I overreacted momentarily. If I'd stayed, I probably could have broken through a little more in terms of my approach to the show and overcome the lack of fix that I suddenly had on it." One of the most revealing moments in the story was rewritten early on and it's too bad, because it says much about Playdon and his feelings about *Mission*. The Malek character is found sitting alone in the reactor room after setting the bomb. "This will sound strange," he tells his superior, General Brenner, "but I believe there is more of myself in here than in me . . . this room has been [my] life for the last two years." Playdon couldn't have summed up his own experience on *Mission: Impossible* any better.

---

* He would contribute another story and script in later seasons.

91: THE AMNESIAC

First Aired: 12/28/69

Produced by: Bruce Lansbury
Teleplay by: Robert Malcolm Young and
  Ken Pettus
Story by: Robert Malcolm Young
Directed by: Reza S. Badiyi
Director of Photography: Al Francis

TEAM: Phelps, Paris, Barney, Willy, Monique, stunt driver Jack Ashbough, Globe Repertory Company

Good morning, Mr. Phelps. Two years ago, a sphere of a rare isotope known as trivanium was stolen from us. Trivanium is invaluable as it could lead to development of nuclear weapons so inexpensive that any nation in the world could afford them. Three men engineered the actual theft of the trivanium. One was Otto Silff. The second, Major Paul Johan. The third, the leader, Colonel Alex Vorda, security chief of their country. Your mission, Jim, should you decide to accept it, is to find out where the trivanium is hidden and get it back. As always, should you or any of your IM Force be caught or killed, the secretary will disavow any knowledge of your actions. This tape will self-destruct in five seconds. Good luck, Jim.

Johan killed Silff after the theft, hid the trivanium, and blamed its disappearance on Silff, thwarting Vorda's plot to exchange the isotope for the United People's Republic's support of his impending coup. Johan is scheduled to sell the trivanium to the North Asia People's Republic in forty-eight hours.

Silff's ex-girlfriend Alena and Johan meet Paris and Monique, the former dropping hints which suggest that he is somehow Otto Silff. Alena informs Vorda, who has Paris questioned. Paris's fingerprints match the ones in Silff's file, at which point Paris admits to a memory loss of his entire existence prior to a disfiguring accident two years ago. Vorda calls in amnesia specialist Phelps, who attempts to restore Paris's memory within twenty-four hours.

Monique tells Johan that she has uncovered him as Silff's secret partner in the trivanium heist. They become partners in the sale, then spot what seem to be Vorda's men following them. "If Vorda is having us followed," says Monique, "they must have already gotten something out of Otto." To

save himself from Vorda's wrath, Johan tells Monique the location of the isotope and demands that she somehow relay the data to Paris so *he* can tell Vorda. Willy and Barney take the trivanium and replace it with a worthless facsimile.

Between grueling memory sessions, Paris demands to see his friend Monique, who tells him, in code, the location of the trivanium. At the next session, Paris "recalls" not only the isotope's whereabouts, but also the fact that it was Johan who tried to kill him. Vorda kills Johan, then barters a useless container to an unsuspecting representative of the United People's Republic.

GUEST CAST: Julie Gregg (Monique), Anthony Zerbe (Colonel Alex Vorda), Steve Ihnat (Major Paul Johan), Lisabeth Hush (Alena Ober), Tony Van Bridge (Erhard Poltzin), Bruce Kirby (TV Newsman), Kurt Grayson (First Guard), Philippe Nemonn (Second Guard), Victor Paul (Jack Ashbough), Jerry Spicer (Black)

"The Amnesiac" was an important episode for camera operator Ronnie Browne. Because of previous disagreements with director Reza Badiyi, regular director of photography Keith Smith stayed home. Cinematographer Al Francis (whose credits include *Star Trek*) was called in, essentially to supervise while Browne actually shot the show. Browne was fast and effective and his work on "The Amnesiac" earned an Emmy nomination—ironically enough, for Al Francis!

The crux of the plot involves Paris's obvious allusions that he is the late Silff. A dossier on

the dead man gives him everything he needs: vocal and physical mannerisms, a flair for caricatures, a penchant for quoting Edmund Burke. In a show which relies heavily on his performance skills, Leonard Nimoy has a field day during the memory sessions. His stream of consciousness recollections take him from a happy boy cradled in his mother's arms to a terrified victim pursued along winding mountain roads by Major Johan. While Paris makes his final revelation, Barney and Willy enter the army warehouse where the trivanium is hidden (in reality, the distressingly familiar Paramount lumber yard). The trivanium is kept in a huge sphere, taller than Willy and three times as wide. Barney and Willy take the sphere and leave a ringer in its place, filled with water. Before exiting, Barney uses a cobweb and dust gun to cover their tracks and restore the warehouse to its original, untouched look. So all is settled but for one question: How does the IMF smuggle that huge globe out of the country, and how did they get the phony sphere in?

Lalo Schifrin fans will recognize Otto and Alena's love song (played by nightclub pianist Monique) as "Beyond the Shadow of Today," a lovely Schifrin melody from the *Mannix* LP soundtrack.

92: CHICO (formerly THE CHIHUAHUA)

First Aired: 1/25/70

Produced by: Bruce Lansbury
Written by: Ken Pettus
Directed by: Herb Wallerstein

TEAM: Phelps, Paris, Barney, Willy, Chico (a terrier)

Good morning, Mr. Phelps. Six months ago, Ramon Prado, one of the largest narcotics dealers in Latin America, bribed a courier for the Pan-American Narcotics Agency into giving him half of a microfilm containing the names of sixteen agency undercover men. Prado's half is useless by itself, but two weeks ago his bitter underworld enemy, Arturo Sandoval, contacted Prado and announced that he has the other half. The two have been attempting to arrange a truce and thereby combine both halves of the microfilm. Your mission, Jim, should you choose to accept it, is to gain possession of the microfilm before Prado and Sandoval can work out the terms of their truce—one that would mean certain death to the sixteen PANA undercover agents whose names are listed on the film. As always, should you or any of your IM Force be caught or killed, the secretary will disavow any knowledge of your actions. This tape will self-destruct in five seconds. Good luck, Jim.

Sandoval's high price for his half of the microfilm prevents the two kingpins from getting together. Stamp and coin collector Prado has hidden his microdot on one of the many framed pieces which adorn his guarded bomb shelter museum. Paris, who must find the key piece, offers to trade Prado a very rare coin in exchange for some of his stamps. Prado offers any of them—except one. Onto the frame of that stamp Paris places a tiny oscillator that radiates sound waves no human can hear. Then he leaves to get his coin and consummate the deal.

Syndicate courier Jim tells Sandoval that, because Prado has been hit hard by PANA and Sandoval has not, the mob suspects Sandoval of dealing with PANA. Jim pointedly suggests that Sandoval cooperate with Prado and combine the microfilm. Sandoval reluctantly calls Prado and makes an appointment to do just that.

Paris trades Prado a counterfeit coin and is forced to confess that he wanted to steal Prado's stamp because *he* has the other half of the microfilm. He insists that anyone else claiming to have it is trying to set Prado up.

Barney, Willy, and Chico climb Prado's roof. Chico is lowered in a basket into an air vent leading to Prado's museum. Lured by the oscillator inside, Chico grabs the framed stamp in his mouth and returns to Barney, who replaces Prado's microdot with one which will match Paris's. Chico then returns the stamp.

Sandoval arrives. His dot is meshed with "Prado's," but the result is an unintelligible mess. Paris arrives with *his* microdot, which not only meshes with "Prado's" but also lists Sandoval as one of the PANA agents. Prado has his rival shot, and the IMF call the police.

Fernando Lamas guest stars in "Chico."

GUEST CAST: Fernando Lamas (Ramon Prado), Percy Rodrigues (Arturo Sandoval), Tom Geas (Sanchez), Jock Gaynor (Rafael), Gregory Sierra (Butler), Jay Tavars (Desk Clerk). *Unbilled:* Chuck Hicks (Guard)

Casting problems are probably the reason why this hour's title was changed from "The Chihuahua" to "Chico." Although the animal gimmick is straight from episode 35, "The Seal," the story itself owes little to the earlier adventure and in fact plucky little Chico is a more sympathetic hero than the indifferent, cool pussycat of "The Seal."

Veteran Herb Wallerstein, directing his only *Mission,* had surprisingly few difficulties with guest star Chico, who was provided by animal trainer Frank Inn and was most cooperative. "Luckily," says Wallerstein, "the dog couldn't talk back." Since he was trained to fetch, getting the dog to take the framed stamp in his mouth was easy. Returning it was even simpler: The footage was reversed. Incidentally, many of the stamps in Prado's museum were provided by the director's younger brother, *Mission* assistant director and longtime collector Rowe Wallerstein.

93: TERROR

Written by: Laurence Heath
Directed by: Marvin Chomsky

First Aired: 2/15/70

TEAM: Phelps, Paris, Barney, Willy

Good morning, Mr. Phelps. The Middle East's most ruthless terrorist, Ismet El Kabir, who has been sentenced to die for mass murder, is about to be pardoned and released. A proclamation by his secret supporter Ahmed Vassier, the propaganda minister of Suroq, will declare that El Kabir committed his crimes only out of concern for his people. El Kabir's release would signal a terrorist uprising that could engulf the whole region in war. Your mission, Jim, should you decide to accept it, is to see that El Kabir is never released. As always, should you or any member of your IM Force be caught or killed, the secretary will disavow any knowledge of your actions. This tape will self-destruct in five seconds. Good luck, Jim.

Barney and Willy steal a truckful of government dynamite and sell it to El Kabir's fanatical girlfriend Atheda. Intelligence officers Phelps and Paris question Kabir about the missing truck. During this, Paris plants a bug in Kabir's cell. Paris frightens Vassier by suggesting that Kabir plans to escape in order to humiliate the government. Vassier asks Kabir to promise not to escape but the arrogant terrorist refuses, even though there is no way he *can* escape. Unknown to Vassier, the prison's *commandante* allows Phelps to be placed in a cell near Kabir's to learn more about the "escape."

"Vassier" (Paris) tells Atheda that the government will double-cross them by hanging Kabir. He gives her a map of the ancient water system below the jail and urges her to free Kabir. Atheda has Barney boil down the stolen dynamite sticks to their most volatile element, nitroglycerine, which will do the job.

Jim identifies himself to Kabir as *Vassier*'s man, alerts him to the bug in his cell, tells him that the government has sent Paris to kill Kabir, and that a rescue attempt is in progress. Atheda visits Kabir and confirms Jim's news. She, Barney, Willy, and other terrorists enter the water tunnels, reach Kabir's cell, and trigger the nitro.

Kabir escapes with his comrades. Jim tells the authorities that Kabir mentioned a specific location to him, and when the criminals emerge from the tunnels they are trapped by the militia. Kabir grabs one of Barney's nitro bottles and threatens to hurl it at his adversaries, but an IMF trick succeeds and leads to Kabir's ignominious end.

GUEST CAST: David Opatoshu (Ahmed Vassier), Joe DeSantis (Marak), Arlene Martel (Atheda), Michael Tolan (Ismet El Kabir), Ronald Feinberg (Jenab), Blaizdell MaKee (Guard), Leland Murray (Rafik)

In the first of four consecutive and diverse plots, Laurence Heath rewrites last season's "Nitro." The mission and strategy are the same: Eliminate terrorists by first giving, then taking away the explosives they need to achieve their ends. This time, however, the web of IMF lies and deceptions is much more complicated, and each pawn is made to believe something completely different.

Phelps's alias, originally a Suroq citizen like Paris, was rewritten as a British mercenary. Evidently, not even Paris could turn blond, blue-eyed Phelps into a Middle Eastern native!

94: GITANO
(formerly TOYS)

Written by: Laurence Heath
Directed by: Barry Crane

First Aired: 2/1/70

TEAM: Phelps, Paris, Barney, Willy, Gypsy entertainer Zorka Banat, Captain Luis Serra of Sardia

Good morning, Mr. Phelps. General Aragas, regent of the Kingdom of Sardia, plans to murder young King Victor and make it appear that the boy's uncle, Grand Duke Clement of Montego, was responsible for the crime. By disposing of the royal family in this way, General Aragas will make himself permanent ruler and embark on a course of international adventurism that would engulf the whole region in war. Your mission, Jim, should you decide to accept it, is to stop Aragas. As always, should you or any of your IM Force be caught or killed, the secretary will disavow any knowledge of your actions. This tape will self-destruct in five seconds. Good luck, Jim.

Clement, who has kidnapped Victor to save him from Aragas, has succeeded only in antagonizing the boy king, who idolizes Aragas. Reluctantly, Clement has security chief Moya drive Victor back to Aragas. He doesn't know that Moya will drive Victor into a death trap within the borders of Sardia, so Clement will be blamed.

Barney uses remote-controlled gas to put Moya, Victor, and the others in the car to sleep. As they pass out, they watch their car seem to lose control and crash into a breakaway IMF hay truck. Moya awakens in Dr. Phelps's office, where his accompanying officers lie "dead." Victor, he is told, has vanished. While both Clement and Aragas mount massive searches, Victor finds refuge in a gypsy camp, attended to by friendly *gitanos* Paris, Willy, and Zorka. Paris tries to sell the boy to Aragas, who arrests him and tracks the Gypsies to an abandoned warehouse where the mission's final scene is played.

GUEST CAST: Mark Richman (General Stefano Aragas), Rudy Solari (Colonel Moya), Barry Atwater (Grand Duke Clement), Barry Williams (King Victor), Margarita Cordova (Zorka Banat), Roberto Contreras (Captain Mestovo), Robert Carricart (Erdos), John Rayner (Captain Luis Serra), Leo G. Morrell (Major Forano), Richard Romanos (Guard). *Unbilled:* Jack Baker (Tourist), Ted White (Piqueros), James Turley (Brinadi)

Sardia's Captain Serra must rate as the IMF's most sinister accomplice. It is he who sweats confessions from Moya's "dead" soldiers and, with the IMF, brings them to Clement who, typically, cannot believe that his friend Moya has betrayed him. Serra is downright apologetic when he informs Clement that he promised the informers their lives in exchange for their confessions.

Gypsy dancer Zorka Banat, one of the most interesting IMF ladies, is played by Margarita Cordova, a flamenco dancer discovered by Marlon Brando for his film *One-Eyed Jacks* (1961). She worked frequently in series like *Gunsmoke*, *The High Chaparral*, and *Marcus Welby, M.D.* and was a member of Theatre West, Los Angeles's professional actor's workshop whose ranks included Martin Landau, Barbara Bain, Greg Morris, Leonard Nimoy and "Gitano" costar (Peter) Mark Richman. Coincidentally, she and Richman worked together years later on the daytime drama *Santa Barbara*. "It was like old home week working on *Mission: Impossible*," says Margarita, "and very easygoing."

259

95: PHANTOMS

Written by: Laurence Heath
Directed by: Marvin Chomsky

First Aired: 2/8/70

TEAM: Phelps, Paris, Barney, Willy, Nora Bennett, British television commentator Edmund Moore

Good morning, Mr. Phelps. Leo Vorka, the aging dictator, has assigned the notorious Georgi Kull to begin a purge which will decimate his country's younger artists. If carried out, such a bloodbath would crush all hope for the new generation that is friendly to the West. Your mission, Jim, should you decide to accept it, is to remove Vorka from power and ensure Deputy Premier Bartzin's succession to the premiership. As always, should you or any of your IM Force be caught or killed, the secretary will disavow any knowledge of your actions. This tape will self-destruct in five seconds. Good luck, Jim.

Vorka's main target is poet Stefan Zara who, despite a weak heart, is ruthlessly questioned to incriminate his colleagues.

While Moore and his English Broadcasting Company film an interview with Vorka in the dictator's office, crewman Barney switches the mantelpiece clock with a duplicate containing a speaker, takes a book from the shelf and leaves a duplicate containing a miniature television camera, and substitutes Vorka's eyeglasses for a pair designed to see infrared projections.

Vorka is shocked when the "ghost" of Lisa Ruger (Nora), a woman from his past who bore him a son, appears in his office. She tells Vorka that their son, who disappeared as a child, is still alive: "He is Zara, Stefan Zara, raised in the state orphanage!" The old man who brought the boy to the orphanage years ago (Paris) informs Vorka that the child had a weak heart. Vorka is skeptical but wistful, longing to meet the son he never knew. He orders Zara brought to him.

Willy liberates Zara from his captors and takes him to the IMF hideout, where the ghostly projections are produced. Guard Willy then delivers

"Zara" to Vorka, who questions him about his childhood before proclaiming, "Stefan, you're my son!" When "Zara" angrily denounces him, Vorka strikes the young man, who falls and suffers a "heart attack." To his horror, Vorka sees Zara's "ghost" emerge from the body and, with "Lisa," point accusing fingers at him. "Murderer," Nora cries. "You have killed your own son!" Vorka loses control and fires at the images, alerting the guards and Deputy Premier Bartzin. They find Vorka raving, pointing at ghosts only he can see. Bartzin assumes the premiership. Willy carries "Zara" to a waiting truck, where Paris rips off the face mask.

GUEST CAST: Antoinette Bower (Nora Bennett), Luther Adler (Leo Vorka), Jeff Pomerantz (Stefan Zara), Michael Baseleon (Georgi Kull), Ivor Barry (Edmund Moore), Ben Astar (Deputy Premier Bartzin), Gregory Sierra (Gomal), Jack Bernardi (Guard), Eli Behar (Secret Policeman), Walter Alzmann (Driver), Ralph Leabow (Jan Golni)

"Phantoms" was inspired, curiously enough, by the writings of renowned Soviet exile Alexander Solzhenitsyn. Laurence Heath's wife was reading a passage from one of the author's books which told of Joseph Stalin's claims of seeing ghosts during his days as leader of the Soviet Union. Heath saw irresistible possibilities and developed the idea into one of *Mission*'s more successful ghost stories.

Luther Adler, the highly regarded New York actor, makes a rare TV appearance as Vorka. "This script is meshuga," he told Heath. "I love it." Adler has some wonderful moments and makes the character come alive. In one scene, Lisa's "ghost" appears to him while his ghostwriter (no pun intended) Phelps is in the room. Jim feigns ignorance of the strange sights and sounds. Vorka thinks twice, then pompously declares, "Only a peasant would fear the

unknown." A second later, however, he's peering toward the vision again with the look of a scared little boy. At times the part was too much for an actor of Adler's advanced years. Before the end of one particularly strenuous day, Adler calmly announced that he was too tired to continue, and apologized. In deference, Adler's scenes were completed the following morning.

96: LOVER'S KNOT

First Aired: 2/22/70

Produced by: Bruce Lansbury
Written by: Laurence Heath
Directed by: Reza S. Badiyi
Directors of Photography: Robert F. Sparks and
  Keith C. Smith

TEAM: Phelps, Paris, Barney

"Lover's Knot" has no tape scene. Instead, as Phelps explains to American Embassy official Marvin Rogers in London, the IMF must uncover "K," head of all European espionage against the United States.

Snaring "K" requires using Lady Cora Weston, young, beautiful wife of an elderly British lord and a known enemy agent. The lure: an unscrambling device which permits monitoring of all telephone and radio transmissions entering London's U.S. embassy.

Lady Weston meets new communications officer Jim and protocol man Paris, both of whom seem attracted to her. Cora is partial to Paris, but is reminded by "K" that Jim, who has access to the unscrambler, is her target. Cora takes helpless gambler Phelps to Conway's, a rigged casino where he loses heavily. Unable to make good, Phelps is forced to deliver the unscrambler as payment. Meanwhile, all embassy communications are switched to a new wavelength and over the old one is piped, for Cora's benefit, taped conversations between Rogers and a Washington official.

Cora hears that Paris is not only in charge of all espionage activities in the area—he is also about to be arrested for allegedly stealing millions in payoff money during a recent Asian mission. She informs Paris of his trouble and induces him to come over to her side. They are interrupted by Phelps, drunk and hostile. He and Paris fight; Jim falls, hits his head, and "dies." Paris and Cora dispose of the "body" in a furnace. Tied together now, Cora takes Paris (tracked by the IMF) to "K."

An unforeseen disaster exposes the IMF plan, placing both Cora and Paris in danger. Paris risks his own life to save Cora, with whom he has fallen in love.

GUEST CAST: Jane Merrow (Lady Cora Weston), John Williams (Lord Richard Weston), Don Knight (Tim Rorke), Jerry Douglas (Marvin Rogers), Charles Macaulay (Conway), Peter Ashton (Blake), William Beckley (Diceman), Ford Lile (Ross), George Wilbur (Chauffeur), Tony Giorgio (First Man). *Unbilled:* Vic Perrin (Peter Stone voice)

One of the few things we'd ever learn about the Great Paris was his bad luck in love. More than any of the others, Paris seemed particularly vulnerable to beautiful ladies, most of whom were in some kind of distress. "Lover's Knot" is the first in a string of romances for the master illusionist, all of which end unhappily.

This episode features none of the standard *Mission* opening sequences: no tape, dossier, or apartment scenes (and no Willy!). While the story machinations are handled by Reza Badiyi with his usual aplomb, the love story doesn't work. Nimoy and Jane Merrow make no sparks together, and the shocked glances Jim and Barney exchange every time Paris shows signs of vulnerability (and there are *five* of them) are laughable. "Lover's Knot" signals a new direction for *Mission,* one which would experiment with the format and the characters and one which would see its full fruition in the following season.

97: ORPHEUS

Written by: Paul Playdon
Directed by: Gerald Mayer
Script Supervisor: H. Bud Otto

First Aired: 3/1/70

TEAM: Phelps, Paris, Barney, Willy, Valerie

Good morning, Mr. Phelps. All attempts to identify the enemy assassin known as Werner Stravos have failed. There are no photographs of him and his only contact is Eric Bergman, head of his country's internal security. Stravos's next victim is to be killed two days from now at four o'clock. Your mission, Jim, should you decide to accept it, is to stop Stravos and end his murderous career. As always, should you or any of your IM Force be caught or killed, the secretary will disavow any knowledge of your actions. This tape will self-destruct in five seconds. Good luck, Jim.

Stravos gets his orders not from Bergman but from an unknown member of the central committee. Although they've never met, Bergman can arrange a meeting with Stravos in an emergency.

Jim poses as a corrupt American agent and heroin addict in charge of paying Western agents in Europe. When Phelps "kills" US surveillance agent Willy, he is forced to go over to the other side. Bergman puts him through "withdrawal" and learns that the Americans have been paying a double agent called Orpheus.

Valerie, as a special class security agent, identifies Paris as one of Stravos's former victims, believed dead. She and Bergman deduce that the double agent Orpheus must be Stravos, who identifies his intended victims to US intelligence so they can relocate them. Bergman sets up a meeting with Stravos, but it is Paris, disguised as Bergman, who meets the killer. "Bergman" fools Stravos into revealing the location of his latest victim, who is saved from a death trap at the last minute.

GUEST CAST: Jessica Walter (Valerie), Albert Paulsen (Eric Bergman), Bruce Glover (Major Deiter), Booth Colman (Werner Stravos), Gene Benton (Dr. Mannerheim), Pitt Herbert (Desk Clerk), Allen Joseph (Dr. Tratzmer), Bart LaRue (Lieutenant Reikman), Pat Newby (Bergman's Secretary), Karl Bruck (Defense Minister), Donna Ashbrook (Tratzmer's Secretary), Dan Deitch (Security Guard)

Stan Kallis' final *Mission* takes us back to familiar territory in another unnamed European country with eastern and western zones. "Orpheus" was also Paul Playdon's last *Mission* for a while, "Time Bomb" having convinced him that he'd lost his touch. Still, "Orpheus" isn't bad, and the typically tight Playdon plot is enhanced by good acting. Jessica Walter, one of the best of the season's surrogate Cinnamons, has a large amount of screen time and somehow manages to make her bitchy security agent strangely sexy. "I wanted Jessica to stay," Peter Graves reveals, "because she was terrific. She had the class and versatility, just a wonderful actress."

"Orpheus" features some unusually wry lines. When US agent Phelps nervously prepares to sell out to Bergman's man Major Deiter, he explains his anxiety by noting, "It isn't something you do every week," to Deiter, who, unlike us, doesn't know what Jim really does each week. Later, when Valerie meets Bergman to conduct a top secret investigation she cannot tell him about, Bergman says, "I believe we spend more time hiding things from ourselves than from our enemies." Valerie, straight-faced, replies, "Sometimes it is wise to keep things hidden, Colonel. Sometimes you do not know who the enemy is." Bergman gives her a searching, suspicious look!

98: THE CHOICE

Produced by: Bruce Lansbury
Teleplay by: Ken Pettus
Story by: Henry Sharp
Directed by: Allan Greedy
Script Supervisor: H. Bud Otto

First Aired: 3/22/70

TEAM: Phelps, Paris, Barney, Willy

Good morning, Mr. Phelps. During the past six months, the Grandduchess Theresa of Trent has come under the domination of a self-proclaimed mystic, Emile Vautrain. Vautrain is a sadistic charlatan who plans to use his relationship with Theresa to make himself ruler of the duchy. If Vautrain succeeds, Trent will become a cruel dictatorship allied with our enemies. Your mission, should you choose to accept it, is to stop Vautrain. As always, should you or any member of your IM Force be caught or killed, the secretary will disavow any knowledge of your actions. This tape will self-destruct in five seconds. Good luck, Jim.

Using psychology and drugs, Vautrain (who bears a striking resemblance to Paris) has convinced Theresa that she is an invalid. First Minister Picard, who sees through Vautrain, cannot convince Theresa that she is being taken.

Vautrain attends a performance of Jim's Theater of Horror and Illusion, in which Paris is "killed" in an electric chair. Jim is later caught tampering with a wired podium Vautrain will use the next day. Paris and Jim are brought before Vautrain, who assumes that they are in Picard's employ. "I was to be kidnapped," Vautrain theorizes to Paris. "You were to appear in my place and survive an electrocution. Then, with the duch-ess in absolute awe of you, you were to suggest that Picard be named her successor." Vautrain allows them to continue the game, with a revision. "You will survive an electrocution," he tells Paris, "after which I will substitute myself for you backstage." Paris catches on: "You blame Picard for the attempted assassination and you execute him. The duchess, believing that you are immortal, names you as her successor." Paris and Jim are returned to their cells, then Vautrain orders their executions once they perform their trick.

After Paris's "miracle," assassin Barney shoots *Vautrain* with a tranquilizer gun. Vautrain awakens as a prisoner, presumably of Picard. He overtakes his guards, takes Barney's gun (loaded with blanks), and makes for the palace.

Vautrain bursts in on Theresa and "Vautrain," accuses Paris of being an imposter, and shoots him. Paris takes a "bullet" in the chest but straightens up, declaring, "I will not die!" Vautrain is shot trying to escape. Paris exposes his tricks to Teresa and informs her that, "Things are not always what they appear to be." Before departing to a monastery, "Vautrain" recommends Picard as Teresa's successor. Alone with Paris, Picard shakes his hand and says, "Whoever you are, I thank you."

GUEST CAST: Nan Martin (Grandduchess Teresa), Arthur Franz (First Minister André Picard), Alan Bergmann (Colonel Antoine Benet), Sid Haig (Goujon), Dick Poston (Cook), Josh Adams (House Guard), Kurt Grayson (Security Guard)

The evil Vautrain from "The Choice" bears a striking resemblance to Paris.

Like Paul Krasny and Barry Crane, script supervisor Allan Greedy had wanted to direct *Mission.* It was through director Stu Hagmann that Greedy finally got an assignment. Hagmann liked Greedy, and when he was preparing his feature *The Strawberry Statement* (1969) for MGM, Hagmann told Bruce Geller that unless Greedy got an assignment, he would leave the series and work on Hagmann's film. Geller didn't want to lose Greedy, so he reluctantly gave him his chance.

According to Greedy, "The show started on Christmas Eve and ended on New Year's Eve. This was nothing new to *Mission,* since we worked until midnight New Year's Eve the first year. But this was the fourth year, and now everybody wanted to get out of there by five thirty or six o'clock. I fell behind. Worse, it was dull film because I fell behind." There were other problems as well. "This was the end of the season," Greedy adds, "and the budget was so tight that I couldn't get an extra to push a wheelchair. They did not want to spend the money for an extra." Ultimately the show fell so far behind that Greedy was removed and Barry Crane finished the show. Some of the company, like Leonard Nimoy, believe that Greedy was deliberately given very little help. "I tried to be very supportive," says Nimoy, "and I thought there were some people around who didn't intend to help him. I felt they were just laying for him, like, 'Okay, you want to direct a show? Try *this!*' That was a painful experience. When a director's replaced it's a terrible thing, especially when he's still around as script supervisor. You can always nurse a director through an episode, it's not like you're making a twelve million dollar movie." Many felt that it was Barry Crane who eagerly watched and abetted Greedy's problems, giving him an opportunity to keep the script supervisor in his place and himself another directing assignment. It was a mistake to give "The Choice" to a novice director, if only because of the difficulty of filming one actor (Nimoy) playing two roles throughout the show. Geller later offered Greedy second unit work for the following season. But Greedy, angered by the lack of cooperation, had already decided to leave the series. It was the loss of another longtime crew member, a superb details man whose absence was felt. Greedy went on to other script jobs in TV and features, and his subsequent directing credits include *Night Gallery* and *Banacek.*

While not the finest of all *Mission: Impossible*s, the show is a good one, betraying no hint of the problems which dogged the production. Greedy's time with the Paris-Vautrain scenes was well spent, with a remarkably realistic double for Nimoy in shots requiring both characters. In his most entertaining role to date, Nimoy cuts loose as Vautrain. This Rasputin type is a complete departure from low-key Paris in mood, posture, and voice (Nimoy affects a low, raspy voice as Vautrain).

99: THE CRANE

Produced by: Bruce Lansbury
Written by: Ken Pettus
Directed by: Paul Krasny

First Aired: 3/8/70

TEAM: Phelps, Paris, Barney, Willy, driver Clay, Globe Repertory Company

Good morning, Mr. Phelps. This is a man known only as Constantine. He's the leader of the People's Republican Army, the guerrilla force which is fighting the brutal, dictatorial military junta that overthrew the Republic of Logosia five years ago. This junta is headed by General of the Army, Yuri Kozani. Second in command is Colonel Alex Strabo, chief of the elite National Security Force. Several days ago, the struggle against the military junta was dealt a heavy blow with the capture of Constantine. He is to be brought into the capital of Logosia within twenty-four hours for execution. Your mission, Jim, should you choose to accept it, is to prevent the execution of Constantine and pave the way for his guerrilla forces to smash the military junta and restore Logosia's democratic government. As always, should you or any of your IM Force be caught or killed, the secretary will disavow any knowledge of your actions. This tape will self-destruct in five seconds. Good luck, Jim.

Guerrilla Phelps tries to kill Kozani and Strabo over a "deal" they made with "turncoat" Constantine. Soldier Willy overpowers and overtakes Jim. While Kozani and Strabo wonder what Jim was talking about, the IMF ambush the armored truck carrying Constantine to his execution. They grab the drugged rebel leader, deposit him in a con-

struction site's cherry picker, and hoist him high into the air. Strabo bases his search for Constantine at the ambush site, never guessing that his quarry hangs literally overhead.

"Strabo" (Paris) radios Kozani that Constantine has offered to surrender. A Kozani aide visits the meeting place, survives a booby trap, and finds a secret room containing propaganda which suggests that Constantine and Strabo have joined forces to overthrow Kozani. Anxious to break up this "alliance," Kozani asks Phelps to lead him to Constantine. Jim agrees only after Kozani signs a document proposing a coalition government and amnesty for all rebels.

Strabo is drugged, disguised as Constantine, and placed behind a desk in a deserted building. Phelps introduces "Constantine" to Kozani, who hands over the document and states, "Our country will never be united until Strabo is eliminated." "Constantine" pulls off his face and shoots Kozani. Barney revives and releases the real Constantine. "My men and I can handle Strabo," he assures Phelps as the IMF drives off.

In "The Crane," the IMF hides a fugitive (Eric Mason) in a spot so obvious that nobody searches it.

GUEST CAST: Carl Betz (General Yuri Kozani), Felice Orlandi (Colonel Alex Strabo), Don Eitner (Rafik), Eric Mason (Constantine), George Fisher (Lieutenant), Ralph Ventura (Clay), Micil Murphy (First NSF Man), John Blower (Second NSF Man), Conrad Bachmann (Third NSF Man)

"I liked 'The Crane,' " Bruce Lansbury says. "It had a great pace and was very simple in concept. The escaped prisoner was right under their noses and they never realized it." While this version of Poe's "The Purloined Letter" isn't bad, it is too similar to episode 85, "Submarine," produced only three months earlier. "The Crane" utilizes the same producer, director, military uniforms, Paramount streets, stock music and basic premise, plus a very similar montage depicting the search for the missing prisoner. Even actor Vic Perrin lends his voice as in the earlier show, this time as the voice of Constantine.

The climax is great, if predictable, fun. After the Constantine mask has been fitted to Strabo's face, Paris warns him that he will die if he does anything to prevent what is about to happen. He points to an IMF man aiming a rifle from a two-way mirror behind Strabo. After Paris leaves, the disguised Strabo watches in mute fury as Kozani enters and betrays him. Strabo grabs a conveniently located pistol and fires at the mirror behind him, destroying the glass (the IMF man, of course, is long gone). The subsequent mask peel off is well done. Actor Eric Mason (Constantine), standing off-camera, is reflected in the remains of the mirror. As he raises his hand to tear off the "mask," the camera quickly pans to Felice Orlandi (Strabo) ripping off a latex face.

100: DEATH SQUAD

First Aired: 3/15/70

Produced by: Bruce Lansbury
Written by: Laurence Heath
Directed by: Barry Crane

TEAM: Phelps, Paris, Willy

In a departure from the series format, Barney is arrested in the Caribbean after saving his girlfriend from the advances of the police chief's brother.

Vacationing with Jim, Barney falls in love with Alma Ross, a beautiful artist. Luis Corba, jealous of Barney, attacks Alma with a knife. During a scuffle with Barney, Luis falls and fatally lands on his own knife. Luis's brother, Chief Manuel Corba, arrests Barney and places him in cell block number ten—the death cell. When Corba scares off Barney's lawyer, Phelps brings in the IMF.

Interpol agent Willy questions Corba about jewel thieves Barney and Phelps, and suggests that they and Guamore, one of Corba's victims, were responsible for a recent jewel robbery. Corba feigns innocence, then demands a share from Jim, who claims that Barney alone knows the location of the stolen gems. Corba's aide Jocaro learns through jewel fence Paris that the late Guamore had a gem hidden on his person when he "disap-

peared." Jim and Willy trail Jocaro to a warehouse where Corba lynches his captives and keeps their belongings. Jacaro finds no hidden emerald, but the IMF finds a gallows and acid tank with which Corba disposes of his victims.

The Force helps Barney survive his own hanging. They take evidence of Corba's brutality to the governor, and Barney takes Alma to the US with him.

GUEST CAST: Pernell Roberts (Chief Manuel Corba), Cicely Tyson (Alma Ross), Leon Askin (Riva), John Schuck (Lieutenant Jocaro), Richard Angarola (Tolima), Val De Vargas (Luis Corba), Natividad Vacio (Flower Man), Luanne Roberts (Louisa), Trish Mahoney (Maria)

One of the best off duty episodes, "Death Squad" is the first show to center around Barney and is a harbinger of the upcoming season. Pitting a supersophisticated spy force against a corrupt small town police chief could be contrived and lacking in suspense, but not when Laurence Heath is the writer. Corba is irredeemably sadistic and evil, just the type of figure needed in a series with no time for depth or character development. The fun stems from our knowledge that Corba doesn't know who he's bullying—but we do, and wait impatiently for the IMF to snare him.

The show has room for two unusually human figures: Alma, played with great feeling by Cicely Tyson; and Barney's cellmate Riva, played with a light touch by Leon Askin. As he watches the genius escape from his cell by unscrewing a light socket and channeling its current into the electronic cell door, Riva asks, "What do they have you in for? Are you guilty?!" Later, Barney's fearlessness on the gallows serves as an inspiration to Riva, who emulates him. Non-stick figures like these would appear more frequently in *Mission*'s next semester.

Year Four: 1969–1970

101: THE MARTYR

Produced by: Bruce Lansbury
Written by: Ken Pettus
Directed by: Virgil W. Vogel

First Aired: 3/29/70

TEAM: Phelps, Paris, Barney, Willy, Roxy, Dr. Valari

Good morning, Mr. Phelps. To counteract heavy pressure from their country's young people, Premier Anton Rojek and his special advisor Josef Czerny have summoned a special congress of the government-controlled Youth Organization. Its purpose: to endorse Rojek's repressive regime. Your mission, should you choose to accept it, is to stop the student congress from being used as a rubber stamp, and to expose Rojek and Czerny before the young people and the world. As always, should you or any member of your IM Force be caught or killed, the secretary will disavow any knowledge of your actions. This tape will self-destruct in five seconds. Good luck, Jim.

Rojek fears the growing youth cult, which idolizes the memory of President Eduard Malik, the late freedom fighter.

US agent Jim is caught plotting to smuggle pro-Rojek student Paris out of the country. Under truth serum, Jim admits that Paris is President Malik's child, long thought dead, and that the US dreads the embarrassment that would result should Paris learn his true lineage, publicly condemn his father, and support Rojek. When Jim tells Paris of his heritage, Paris refuses to let familial loyalty stand in the way of his beliefs. He agrees to denounce his father at the student congress's closing rally.

Rojek gets a call from Dr. Valari (working with the IMF) who takes him to the remains of the true Malik child. Deducing that Paris will double-cross him by endorsing *Malik* at the rally, Rojek plots a counterstrategy by freeing Malik's widow from

jail. "When the imposter starts to denounce me," he tells Czerny, "Madame Malik will undoubtedly acknowledge that he is really her son. Then I will use the skull of the real Peter Malik to discredit her as a liar and her son as an imposter."

At the rally, Paris doubly double-crosses Rojek by supporting him. Madame Malik angrily disavows Paris as a phony and is led away by police, prompting the students to boo and revile Rojek. Jim, Paris, and Madame Malik are put in a police van which is comandeered by the IMF.

GUEST CAST: John Larch (Premier Anton Rojek), Scott Marlowe (Josef Czerny), Anna Lee (Maria Malik), Ken Swofford (Florian Vaclav), Lynn Kellogg (Roxy), Peter Brocco (Dr. Valari), Ed Bakey (Dr. Kadar), Buck Holland (Security Guard)

"The Martyr" is a simpler remake of episode 52, "The Heir Apparent," combined with the topical (for 1970) youth theme. Although it makes good use of stock footage depicting European student protests, the show's credulity is strained by Paris's pose as a twenty-five-year-old student. A prehypnotic suggestion from Paris, and a transmitter implanted in Jim's ear, enables Jim to resist Rojek's truth drugs and repeat whatever Barney tells him via the transmitter. This misinformation impresses Rojek of the Americans' anxiety about Paris and convinces him of his own cleverness.

Folk singer Lynn Kellogg makes her TV dramatic debut as IMF student activist Roxy, an extraneous character. As part of the plot, she renders Bob Dylan's "The Times They Are A-Changin'." The song was well chosen, since Roxy's youth and hippie style pointed the way to what lay ahead for the series in the next season.

Wrap

"Forgetting about the performers," Douglas Cramer told *TV Guide* early in the season, "the viewer watching *Mission* this year will see a show in no way different from what he has seen in the past. There are no fewer sets, no fewer extras, no fewer cuts. If anything, there's more. . . . I think we'll get along very well without [the Landaus]."

Cramer was wrong.

Mission's ratings had dropped disastrously from last season's number 11 to number 53, its lowest average to date. Several reasons were offered for the drop in viewership. An outside one was the controversial cancellation of *Mission*'s lead-in, *The Smothers Brothers Comedy Hour,* in June 1969. "The Smothers Brothers had a young, hip audience which would also look at our show," said Bruce Geller. The Smothers' replacements were not as popular.

Despite the fact that *Mission* was a "concept" series, the loss of Martin Landau and Barbara Bain did hurt the show. Leonard Nimoy was effective, but many simply felt that *Mission* was spiceless without Cinnamon. Viewers accustomed to watching one actress playing a variety of roles every week saw little fun in watching several actresses playing different parts. But the most damaging aspect of all was the distressing sameness of look. Far too much was filmed on Paramount's backstreets this year: At least ten episodes were shot *entirely* on the lot, and it showed. The studio's Administration Building continued a visibility so constant that it almost deserved costar billing.

Leonard Nimoy was disappointed by the work he was given. "I was not extraordinarily impressed with the show, and felt that it did not have the edge that I admired during the first three seasons." Nimoy began to wonder how much the departure of Woodfield and Balter (whom he'd never met) had damaged the series. "I got to do what I had come on to do, a wide variety of characters and that was successful, but not to the extent I was hoping." Nimoy also felt unwanted by CBS. "I was in the middle of a political morass. I felt like the odd man out. I think the network was very upset with everybody involved with the letting go of Marty and Barbara and felt that the studio should have negotiated with them. So I came on and I think I was something that was forced down the network's throat in a sense. I felt that I didn't deserve the kind of treatment I got; I was literally ignored." His suspicions seemed proven on the evening of that season's Emmy Awards. "The head of the network was giving a private party. Other people on *Mission* had been invited, and I hadn't," Nimoy recalls with a laugh. "I think I just represented a bad incident."

In addition, Nimoy felt no personal involvement in the series. "I wasn't able to sit down with the guys and get a real interaction going, and that was one of the empty aspects for me. The show was what it was, and they were working very hard to make them the best they could. Since I came in as a replacement rather than as an organic part of the growth and experience, I felt like an implant. I was trying to work as an implant and was partially but not terribly successful." His dissatisfaction would become more acute during the following season.

If *Mission*'s audience and network were disappointed by year four, the exact opposite was true of Paramount. At last the show had a producer on *their* side, not Geller's, and although the quality of the show had dropped, so had the financial losses. Bruce Lansbury kept the budget under control, but *Mission* had become less than what it once was, and its glory days were over. Stanley Kallis hypothesizes: "Those first three years of sweating it out were spent trying to find the extraordinary answer, because there was no ordinary answer. We did not know what an ordinary answer was. By the time Bruce Lansbury did the show he had, I venture to say, the ordinary answer. He could pop them out of the mold with a fair amount of ease, made them for a price, and never said, 'Gee, we're empty.' Lansbury's ultimate contribution was a volume that made the package far more valuable than did the few great shows of the first three seasons.

Barbara Bain and Martin Landau continued their careers after leaving *Mission*. Landau remains one of Hollywood's most respected actors despite a string of credits which steadily grew unworthy of him until an Academy Award nomination for his supporting role in 1988's *Tucker: The Man and His Dream* revitalized his career. Paramount's lawsuit legally restrained Barbara from working until 1971. Apart from costarring with her husband in the two-season British series *Space: 1999,* her screen career consists of a few TV movies and guest appearances. In the mid 1980s she received exceptional notices for stage work.

"We were made to look like troublemakers," says Landau of their *Mission* exit, "but we weren't. We were and still are probably the most cooperative actors anyone will ever work with. It hurt Barbara's career and ultimately it hurt me too, I think."

"That dispute ruined her career," claims one of Barbara's *Mission* replacements. "Had she just stayed with the show she could have segued into a lot of wonderful things. She could have had two or three series after that, because she was really well liked by the public. It breaks my heart, because we really don't have enough classy ladies today."

Decades later, a certain bitterness lingers. "In the last few years, Barbara has spoken to me," Doug Cramer explains. "Martin still cuts me dead whenever I've seen him, twenty years later." Landau will always remember Cramer as a "one-man wrecking crew. He took something wonderful. . . . But he made a name for himself." Cramer's post-Paramount credits include some of television's most popular series. *"Love American Style, Love Boat, Hotel,"* Landau recites. "There's something very similar about all those shows, wouldn't you say? Wouldn't you say that they basically appealed to the lowest common denominator?" That question may best be answered by writer Bob Thompson, who once asked Cramer for his secret to success. Says Thompson, "This highly cultured and intelligent man said, 'If I hate it, then I know it'll work.' I think that he looked at *The Love Boat* and said, 'This is dreadful. Put it on.' " Decades after his exit from Paramount, Cramer remains one of TV's most successful and powerful executives.

In retrospect, it is obvious that everyone involved in the Landau-Paramount dispute suffered to varying degrees. Landau and Bain were labeled as difficult contract breakers, justified or not; Paramount angered television's dominant network; CBS helplessly stood by as one of its most outstanding shows was damaged; and *Mission*'s audience saw the series' delicate chemistry wrecked.

Mission garnered only six Emmy nominations this season, its lowest score to date: Greg Morris for Supporting Actor; Gibson Holley and Lucien Hafley for their work on "The Falcon" sets (originally built for *On a Clear Day You Can See Forever*); Al Francis for Cinematography (episode 91, "The Amnesiac"); Arthur Hilton for editing "The Falcon"; Jonnie Burke for Outstanding Special Effects (episode 90, "Time Bomb"); and Gordon Day and Nick Gaffey for Sound Mixing (episode 85, "Submarine"). The only winner was in the last category. Peter Graves got some good news, however: he won a Golden Globe for his work as Jim Phelps.

Mission: Impossible's fifth season offered a crowded roster.

Year Five

September 1970–April 1971

Production Credits

Starring: Peter Graves, Leonard Nimoy as Paris
Also Starring: Lesley Warren, Greg Morris, Peter Lupus, Sam Elliott
Executive Producer: Bruce Geller
Produced by: Bruce Lansbury
Associate Producer: Barry Crane
Story Consultant: Laurence Heath
In Charge of Postproduction: William Cairncross
Production Manager: Gordon A. Webb
Postproduction Supervisor: John A. Fegan, Jr.
Music Supervisors: Leith Stevens, Kenyon Hopkins
Theme Music by: Lalo Schifrin
Director of Photography: Ronald W. Browne
Art Director: Gibson Holley
Film Editors: David Wages, ACE; John Loeffler; Jerry Taylor; Larry Strong
Assistant Directors: Michael P. Schoenbrun; Harry F. Hogan, III; Charles E. Dismukes
Supervising Property Masters: Arthur Wasson, Robert O. Richards
Property Master: Art Lipschultz
Special Effects: Jonnie Burke
Set Decoration: Lucien Hafley
Supervising Costumer: Michael Tierney

Costume Supervisor (Women): Dodie Schaefer (nee Shepard)
Casting: Jim Merrick, Betty Martin
Makeup Artist: Bob Dawn
Hairstylist: Adele Taylor
Script Supervisor: Barbara Atkinson
Production Coordinators: Dale Tarter, Mike Jarvis
Vehicle Coordinator: Ed Chamey
Music Editor: Dan Carlin
Sound Editors: Michael Colgan, MPSE; Frank R. White
Editorial Coordinator: Larry Mills
Production Mixer: Dominick Gaffey
Rerecording Mixer: Joel Moss
Recorded by: Glen Glenn Sound
Wardrobe Furnished by: Worsted-Tex
Chrysler Vehicles Furnished by: Chrysler Corporation
Chevrolet Vehicles Furnished by: General Motors Corporation
Volvo Vehicles Furnished by: Volvo Western Distributors, Inc.
Executive Vice President in Charge of Production: Douglas S. Cramer

*"There was a youth movement and we
needed a fresh look."*
—BRUCE LANSBURY

*"There was a lot lost. You look at them and
you can see that the chemistry isn't the
same."*
—PAUL KRASNY

THE 1970–71 SEASON promised to be a bright one for Paramount Television. All of last season's series had been renewed and four new ones bought, making the studio second only to Universal as Hollywood's biggest television producer. Paramount TV occupied seventeen of the thirty-two stages on the Melrose lot, while ten more were rented to independents like Aaron Spelling Productions. This activity was a sharp contrast to Paramount's theatrical division which, in the spring of 1970, had nothing in production on the lot. Clearly, the company's television arm was keeping Paramount alive.

Those in the *Mission* offices did not share the sunny feeling of prosperity. The show had slipped for the first time, and although virtually everyone privately acknowledged that the reduced budgets and the loss of the Landaus were responsible for the drop in ratings, it was also understood that these weaknesses were here to stay. So, other reasons were found: the loss of *The Smothers Brothers* as a lead-in, or the lack of a female regular, for instance. CBS grew concerned over *Mission*'s repetition of plots. "Somebody said that the show had only three plots," relates Perry Lafferty, "and they did variations on them. We used to talk about it and say, 'Well, what else can they do?' It's got to be an impossible mission, and what does that entail? You've got to get something out of a safe or put someone in to do something or get someone out, and that's what it was. It's a limited form that doesn't lend itself to a lot of manipulation. You can have different tricks in each episode, but the structure was basically like skyscrapers: They all go up and they all have windows."

Laurence Heath, replacing Paul Playdon as story consultant, was well aware of the thinning of story material. "It was really hard coming up with them," he explains. "In the last couple of years it really got to be a burden coming up with new ideas." CBS's direct link to the series, Paul King, feels that *Mission,* "fell into a trap. The Broadcast Standards people wouldn't let you do stories that named names or dealt with the realities of those times, so you'd go the fiction route and very often some Iron Curtain country would have to be the culprit. That was the trap. Far too many of these stories had been done in the previous broadcast year, and it did hurt the series." To be precise, eighteen of last season's twenty-six hours took place in vaguely European settings; four in Latin America; two in the Middle East; and two in the United States. Whatever the reasons, it was clear to everyone in charge that *Mission* was growing stale. Something had to be done to lure back the program's old audience or find a

275

new one. With that in mind, CBS moved *Mission* from its traditional 10:00 P.M. Sunday spot to 7:30 P.M. Saturday in the hopes of finding a larger and younger viewership.

The time shift was one result of certain external forces making themselves felt at that time. Spearheaded by the youth movement of the late sixties, public antipathy towards American involvement in the Vietnam war had become intense and had led to a backlash against US foreign policy in general. It took years, but this point of view had at last reached entertainment executives, whose livelihoods depend on keeping the American public edified. "A segment of the public was saying that we should not meddle in foreign affairs," according to Peter Graves, "and that was a growing criticism of the show from some quarters." Bowing to this sensibility and in tandem with the network, Paramount made a decision which fundamentally changed *Mission: Impossible* once and for all.

This season the IMF would spend less time in foreign countries and more time in the USA. Gone were the Latin American strongmen and European monarchs; in their place as most frequent IMF target came that uniquely American type of royalty, the gangster. Beginning in year five and continuing through the rest of the series, Phelps and company concentrated almost all their attention on a battle with organized crime, most commonly referred to as "the Syndicate." This season served as a gradual changeover period, with fourteen foreign and nine domestic adventures.

The shift in program policy may have mollified some, but it also disappointed many loyal viewers. Mike Severeid, then a junior executive at CBS, tells how the change "put the show on a more mundane level, like any other cop show. It lost much of its style. I can remember being in graduate school in 1966 or 1968 where you just don't watch television. *Mission* was one of the only shows that we watched with regularity." Yet, as Severeid suggests, "What do you do with a show that's beginning to show signs of fatigue? How do you fix it?" Keeping the IMF at home was only the first step. Further alterations followed, not all of them successful.

In February 1970, while Heath and Bruce Lansbury were assigning scripts, Bruce Geller spoke with reporters of the coming changes. "The pattern of the show has probably become too established . . . the audience is getting ahead of us." He cited the celebrated tape, dossier, and apartment scenes as, "having brought the audience to the point where they know what they will see the first portion of the show. Because of this, next season, at least half of our shows will not have the tape messages—they make it a bit too pat structurally. And we will not use the dossier or apartment scenes."

"We are deliberately altering our structure," Geller continued. "We will come into a show with a mission already in progress and fill the audience in as the story dictates. There'll be more involvement with the characters, and the capers won't be pulled off always without a hitch. We will do more shows in which something unforeseen happens, and the team will have to improvise. There will be more suspense, we will deal with human fallibility. That doesn't mean that they will be stupid in planning, however."

Most of Geller's predictions came to pass, but the elimination of *Mission*'s three trademark opening scenes quickly proved itself a mistake. In a real sense, *Mission* was almost an anthology series featuring characters who took on different identities each week. The tape-dossier-apartment scenes were indeed familiar, but they were the *only* familiar and predictable elements in a show that was deliberately *unfamiliar*. Losing the plot's few expository scenes made the stories even more difficult to follow, especially in segments which began with the mission already underway. Lansbury and Heath recognized the problem early in the season

and corrected it: By midseason, the tape and apartment scenes were restored. The dossier scene, however, was never used again.

The plots did become more unpredictable. Series fans were surprised by the renewed sense of danger found in these new adventures. Things went wrong, and our heroes were frequently captured, injured, or victims of a variety of random elements that had never been encountered before. In one show, Paris takes the rap for a murder committed by the man he's impersonating; in another, an IMFer is abducted by a homicidal maniac. This return of the wild card, no matter how incongruous, pleased Geller, who'd wanted every episode to have one from the beginning. He was less pleased with the issue of deeper characterization, an issue attributable mainly to Bruce Lansbury. With plot options running low, Lansbury believed that an emphasis on the IMF *as people,* a tack so carefully avoided until now, could stimulate interest in the show and open it up to new writers. "We tried to do personal stories when we could and still obey the demands of the form," he says. This year we would go home with Jim Phelps, meet Barney's older brother, and share a nightmare from Paris's past. Romances abounded, two each for Barney and Paris, one for Phelps. The missions themselves, ranging from the search for a serial killer to the prevention of violence at a student demonstration, were certainly on a more personal level than ever before. "The fate of nations won't always be at stake," Geller had alluded. "The situation may be the redemption of an individual and not always important to the mission.

"I don't want anybody to think the show is becoming *My Three Sons,*" Bruce cracked to *Daily Variety*'s David Kaufman. "There will be changes in the pattern, but not the basic format of *Mission.*" One of the simpler changes was the addition of a brief teaser scene, usually preceding the main titles.* As Jerry Ludwig artfully elucidates, "The teaser showed how quickly producers wanted to get off to a flying start. The audience has a minimum of three shows they can start watching at the same time, so they'll switch channels if your show doesn't look interesting from the very start. The teaser was the best way to hook them, and the best teaser was usually to shoot a gun at somebody." *Mission*'s teasers were a departure for a supposedly nonviolent show. Six of this season's teasers depicted murders, and six more contained other acts of physical violence. Of course it was always the villains and never the IMF committing the mayhem, but it established a different feel to the series nonetheless. *Mission* was not the only series to present violent teasers. "People began to complain to the sponsors," Ludwig remembers. "So in order to eliminate violence in the teasers, the networks were persuaded that nobody should do teasers at all!" In fact, *Mission* retained the device for the remainder of its run, the violence level remaining more or less constant.

The accent on domestic plots with fuller characterizations drew a new group of writers to the show, many of them invited by Heath or Lansbury. Some would become series mainstays: Art Weiss, who wrote four episodes; Howard Browne (four); Ed Adamson (four); Jackson Gillis (three); Sam Roeca and James Henderson (seven); Harold Livingston (nine). All were TV veterans, yet their *Mission*s varied in quality. "I thought the stories in the first three or four years were the best," says Peter Graves. "I could never fault one. I would take them apart logically, from point *A* to *B* to *C* and they all worked. But now they started a little razzle-dazzle and the scripts, though still good, weren't nearly as tightly constructed." The main beneficiary of this new blood was Larry Heath, who actually had a script or two ready on the shelf when they were needed.

---

* A "hipper" orchestration of *Mission*'s main title was introduced this season.

One thing everybody agreed on was that *Mission* needed a regular heroine. Just who she would be was a matter of opinion. Many of the cast and crew had hoped that Lee Meriwether would still get her chance, while others liked Jessica Walter and Anne Francis. But Douglas Cramer and Bruce Lansbury had their own ideas, and the eventual choice surprised nearly everyone. In keeping with the show's fresh new look, and in an attempt to appeal to younger viewers, the job went to a wide-eyed, very pretty actress no more than twenty-three years old. Her name: Lesley Ann Warren.

Born in Manhattan to a former professional singer, Lesley Ann took her first dance lessons at age three. She was studying ballet by age six, a good indication of the unflagging determination she would apply to her future career. At fifteen, she was a veteran of television commercials and had appeared on the cover of *Look* magazine. Once out of high school, she won the lead in the Broadway show *110 in the Shade,* which led to her biggest break, the title role in *Cinderella,* Rodgers and Hammerstein's original musical for television. The reputation *Cinderella* established for Lesley as a promising young performer would follow her relentlessly through the years. "I have more 'rising star' awards than anybody in show business,' she joked in 1977. Two Disney films, *The Happiest Millionaire* (1967) and *The One and Only, Genuine, Original Family Band* (1968, directed by old *Mission* hand Michael O'Herlihy) followed. Then came *Mission: Impossible.*

"It was a big coup to get her," claims Doug Cramer, who was impressed by Lesley's work in a couple of unsold pilots, including a half-hour version of *Cat Ballou.* "At that point she could have had a feature or television career." Lesley Ann had initially been uncertain about taking the job. It was Jon Peters, her hairstylist and dress designer whom she married during *Family Band,* who convinced her that *Mission* would be a good career move, steering her away from the Cinderella-Disney image. "I didn't want to be America's ingenue," she once told a journalist. *Mission*'s promising new approach to characterization may have also tempted her. In the end she accepted the role of Dana Lambert, IMF—with reservations.

Almost instantly there were difficulties, beginning when Bruce Geller made his views on the casting decision known. "Bruce didn't like Lesley Ann at all, didn't think she was right," says Lansbury. "He thought she was too artificial." Geller had nothing against her as an actress or a person, according to his friend Jim Buchanan. "He just never thought she was right," Buchanan says. "Up to this point, Bruce had run *Mission* and it had been successful. All of a sudden somebody comes in and says, 'It's got to be this way and not that way.'" Honesty may indeed be the best policy, but Geller's straightforwardness didn't make the new member of the family feel particularly welcome. Bruce's direct and visible disapproval was fueled partially by anger over his ever-diminishing say in the show he created. Casting Lesley Ann Warren was just the latest example of his advice falling on deaf ears, and his status as mere figurehead infuriated him. "His concept of the show was at odds with what the studio wanted to do with it," Bruce Lansbury explains.

Like it or not, Lesley Warren (as she would now be credited) was in. Ironically, she brought with her some intriguing ideas concerning style and attitude that would sometimes have Cramer and Lansbury siding with Geller. The most startling was her reluctance to wear a bra—a decision in keeping with many women of the time who were burning their brassieres in symbolic public demonstrations of their newly found freedom, but one that shocked certain executives at the studio and the network. The ongoing debate spurred a certain amount of lighthearted banter around the lot. Since Lesley herself has stated, "I had big bosoms at

Lesley (Ann) Warren as Dana Lambert.

twelve," this was literally no small matter. Other obstacles quickly arose: extensive makeup and hair tests yielded results no one could agree upon.

Lesley was also having trouble in her marriage to Jon Peters, whose effect on her life and career was profound during this period. "For years . . . all the decisions had been made by Jon," she reminisced in 1982. "I was afraid to trust my own instincts so I left everything to him. He felt I should be more overtly sexy in the way I presented myself, so he'd pick out clothes for me and off I'd go to interviews in a tiny miniskirt wearing no bra. Inside, I wanted to die. It just wasn't me." Although her attention to her work never suffered, something was clearly wrong. "She wasn't emotionally happy on the show," says costumer Dodie Schaefer, who got along well with Lesley. "She was not having an easy personal life." Another crew member adds, "I found her very difficult, but in retrospect she was suffering at the time, like any woman would."

"She was being wrongly advised, too," another crewman believes. "She was going with a guy who didn't know anything about the business and was advising her what to do onstage. He was the wrong guy to listen to. He was an outsider and she was being swayed. Yet she was determined to be her own actress and do what she wanted to do. It led to some controversy." At least one cast member recalls his chagrin at the sight of Peters furtively whispering instructions in Lesley's ear between takes.

Some matters sorted themselves out in time. Lesley wore little makeup on-screen besides some gloss to cover her vast expanse of freckles, and her hair was usually done in a similarly natural manner. When it came to the brassiere issue (which could well have stemmed from Peters as much as from Lesley), a compromise was struck. Since she would be portraying a wide assortment of characters, Lesley would be allowed to go braless only when it was appropriate to the role she was playing.

As filming progressed, the actress became more dissatisfied. "It was too formatted," Bruce Lansbury insists. "Because of the very nature of the show, the characters in *Mission* were tools of the plot, and that wasn't what she was looking for in her career." Says director Sutton Roley, "Most of the actors were puppets on *Mission,* which is a thing an actor does not want to be." He speculates that Lesley's initial aversion to the show may have become a challenge. "Like a director, an actor will go in there saying, 'I'll be able to expand this and do so much more with this.' Then when they get into it they ask, 'Where do I move? *How* can I expand it?' " Lesley simply didn't have that much to do in the series that would enable her to make a difference.

"Lesley is one of the most versatile actresses around," says Gerald Mayer, who directed her first *Mission,* "but she sure wasn't right for *Mission.* The flat projection they wanted from the part was not her forte at all. She's an actress with a lot of expression; she becomes almost nothing when you flatten it out, and that didn't seem to work for her at all. She hated it because all of the directors, including myself, were trying to get something out of her that was not right for her. There was much more interest in the gimmicks than the characterizations, so the performances tended to be one-dimensional." Albert Paulsen, a friend from her New York days, states it simply: "She hated it. Hated it."

Lesley didn't mesh visually with her costars, all of whom looked at least ten years older than she. Greg Morris remembers an on-set concern that the "boys" not look like a bunch of old men around Lesley who, although twenty-three, could still look as young as sixteen. "She might have been too young to work with Peter Graves," cracks Peter Lupus, tongue definitely in cheek. "We thought she was totally wrong for the show," Graves remembers. "We had this

image of a cultured, sophisticated, mature leading lady, and even after Barbara left we tried to keep that. Lesley had a quality that was good for a couple of stories but I felt that overall, she was not the permanent member of the team that we should have. I wasn't alone in that feeling. She looked like a child." As the season progressed, Lesley grew closest to Leonard Nimoy. "I think that she was a misfit on the show," says Nimoy. "We never discussed it, but I knew what she'd been feeling, because I'd been through it the previous year."

All this may explain why Lesley Ann Warren so often looks self-conscious and out of place in *Mission*. She evidently felt just that way. "I wasn't very happy at that time," she readily admits. Watching her work in the series, one occasionally senses the feeling of untapped potential, but most often she seems miscast as an international trade diplomat (episode 107) or simply too young for a glamorous jet-setter (episode 115) or hardened bank robber (episode 122). Lesley may not have been right for *Mission,* but it is only fair to point out that the show never made genuine use of the skills which got her the job. According to studio press releases, Dana Lambert's talents include singing, but Lesley sings in only one episode. An accomplished dancer, Lesley's sole dance in *Mission* is a manic whirl while posing as an uncontrollable pill addict. A good opportunity to widen the scope of the show went unrealized.

Lesley verbalizes her feelings of that period in an understated way. "I found after participating after a while that I was happier acting in situations that required more demands of characterization in-depth, as opposed to the actors basically being involved in an action-suspense situation. I also enjoy creating a character and moving on then to a whole new situation and character as opposed to staying with the same character for twenty-four weeks out of a year.

"But I would most definitely like to add that the cast and crew of *Mission: Impossible* were lovely to work with, and there was generally a lot of laughter and good spirits accompanying the very difficult work." She even found herself the butt of a good-natured joke now and then, for whatever misgivings the *Mission* family had, the set remained as friendly as ever. Between scenes, Lesley would often use an exerciser to help firm up her breasts. There she would sit, inhaling and exhaling with the deadly seriousness which typified her work.

Propman Bob Richards describes what happened: "Just by looking at Graves and Greg, I could see that these jokers wanted to do *something*. I had a pretty good rapport with her, so while she was pumping away and Peter Graves was sitting next to her, I passed by and said, 'Lesley, I'd be very careful about using that thing.' She asked why, and I answered, 'Well, if you work too hard between shots, you won't match.' She never registered, but Peter Graves fell out of his chair laughing. He ran over to me and said, 'Keep it up! We've got to loosen her up.' Peter and Greg would give her some cues as to how and why certain things are done and they softened her a bit. They'd try to get her to laugh, but she was so tense and serious about everything that it was pretty hard to get to her sense of humor."

There would be one more, equally surprising cast change this season. Peter Lupus let it be known that he had grown dissatisfied with his salary and the scope of his duties. At the same time, it was known that Bruce Lansbury had never understood Lupus's function on the show, didn't see the actor's appeal, and saw little need for a strongman in the IMF lineup. "In the first three years he was something of an oddity," says Lansbury. "He was a strongman, he had a magnificent physique, and his acting ability wasn't up to the others'. He'd have been the first to admit it in those years." Sensing another chance to revitalize the series and stamp his own imprint on it, Lansbury opted to get rid of Willy Armitage and bring in a younger character with skills worthy of the Impossible Missions Force. Once again, Bruce Geller objected.

"Don't do this," he warned Laurence Heath. "Peter Lupus represents something important in the show." But, as Heath says, "We had felt the same way Kallis and Playdon felt two years before. We needed to expand our horizons because we were running out of story material." Partially heeding Geller's admonition, Lansbury arranged to have Lupus gradually eased out of the show over the course of the year and the new character, a physician, eased in. They would even work together on some missions. If the strategy worked, it would be evident by season's end that Peter Lupus would not be missed.

The role of Dr. Doug Robert* went to an untried twenty-five-year-old named Sam Elliott. A native Californian, Sam studied psychology and English literature in Oregon before deciding, in 1966, to move to Hollywood and become an actor. His good looks landed him a Twentieth Century-Fox contract and a minor role in *Butch Cassidy and the Sundance Kid* (1969), which starred his future wife, Katharine Ross. Other minor roles in Fox films followed, and after the studio's contract program was dissolved, Sam moved on to TV movies. One such film, *Assault on the Wayne* (1970), starred Leonard Nimoy and was produced by Bruce Lansbury, who took notice of Elliott and called him in for *Mission*.

Peter Graves remembers Sam as a "wonderful, big puppy dog" who got along well with the company. "He hadn't done much," Graves adds, "but he was this big, rugged, good-looking guy. I thought at the time that it might be a good idea to bring in somebody fresh, and this guy looked like a good bet. The idea was to have another male character to function as we needed him."

The only problem was that they never needed him.

Bringing in a doctor wasn't a bad idea; it was just unnecessary. The IMF had been using psychological and chemical means of stressing their adversaries from the beginning without requiring the regular presence of a physician. The character of Doug, like Dana, did little to widen the show's appeal or open up new story possibilities. In the thirteen episodes in which he appears, Doug rarely performs a function that couldn't have been handled by another IMF member. As the plots took care of themselves, Doug's role in the proceedings was every bit as minor as Willy's, and in fact Doug functioned most often as a surrogate Willy, driving the van or assisting Barney in typical feats of manual labor. "I used to see Sam watching intently," Leonard Nimoy remembers, "trying to pick up where he could fit into the scheme of things." The only story in which he was prominently featured, episode 117, "The Hostage," was finally rewritten to accommodate Paris. As a result, Doug's overall impact was minimal and as one writer phrased it, he was, "just another guy in a suit."

"They never found a way to use Sam properly," Graves says. "They couldn't write either for him or that part. It didn't work." Reviewing the affair years later, Lansbury acknowledges that, "We didn't exploit Sam as much as we could have or should have, not through any intention." Once more, Bruce Geller had been correct. "We thought we had another character that would play," says Larry Heath. "We were wrong." Heath later understood that the IMF was composed of specialists who were truly *special*. A master of disguise, an electronics genius, even a strongman, were special. In Heath's words, a doctor, "just wasn't special enough." The experiment did not succeed.

To the astonishment of many, Peter Lupus's absence hardly went unnoticed among *Mission*'s audience. His disappearance provoked a largely negative reaction, and pro-Lupus letters

---

* Doug's real last name is in doubt. Phelps refers to him in his first show as Dr. Robert. However, in later episodes Doug uses the name Lang, presumably an alias.

Sam Elliott as IMF physician Doug.

poured into the network and studio. The big man was asked to return to the series, but Lupus's feelings had been hurt and he considered making his exit permanent. "Everyone talked me out of it," he says. A friend, producer A. C. Lyles, had a long talk with him. "Stick with this show," he told Loop. "It's not that easy to find another hit. You don't realize while you're doing it that it's not that easy." "So I'm glad I stayed," Lupus concludes, "though I came very close to walking. And I'm glad that people liked the character so much, because Willy was probably the most dispensable character."

Typical of the pro-Lupus mail was a letter to Bruce Geller from a Minnesota college student and longtime *Mission* fan who wrote that the loss of Lupus was, "one of the gravest errors to ever strike a series" and "the most callous action I have seen on television since the loss of the Landaus, although it may not be visible until too late. Mr. Lupus and Mr. Greg Morris are the backbone of the show," he asserted. "Mr. Elliott generates as much excitement in the show as a soggy piece of cardboard."

By the time Geller got this letter, it was too late for him to intervene: The man behind the two series which put Paramount Television on the map drove to the front gate one day to learn that he had been barred from the lot. "They had two guards escort him to his office," Jonnie Burke recalls. "He took his personal belongings, and they escorted him off the lot." "I don't recall the specifics of what led to banning him," Doug Cramer claims. "There were two or three terrible situations that came up where he went around production, insisted on doing things that turned out to be costly and not worth it. It finally seemed we couldn't keep doing the show. It may have come down to the overall morale and the situation with Lesley. I just don't recall what led to something that extreme." The battle was over and, as was inevitable, Paramount had won. "The sad thing was that it wasn't really necessary," says Cramer. "As smart as Bruce was, if he had turned himself toward working with me . . ." Geller left, leaving nothing behind but his parking space. For months afterward, writer Eric Bercovici passed the empty space with Geller's name still stenciled on it and wondered, "Where the hell is he?" He was in fact at MGM, having accepted the invitation of that studio's vice president of motion picture and television production—Herbert F. Solow, who'd been so instrumental in getting *Mission* and *Mannix* off the ground.

"Bruce was barred off the lot because he was so far over budget," explains Stephen Kandel, writer-producer and friend of Geller's. "Paramount was always nervous with hour shows anyway. They're expensive, they're troublesome, they run over budget, they get out of control. They make them nervous. Bruce Geller, being very much his own man, made them even more nervous. He was executive producer, he had the title, he collected his fees, but he was not allowed to produce anymore because they felt he was uncontrollable."

Geller never moved back onto the lot, but he was not forgotten on the *Mission* set, a fact which occasionally frustrated the series' other Bruce. "I vividly remember Bruce Lansbury verbalizing his anger against Bruce Geller, who was not there," says Reza Badiyi. "Lansbury'd go on the set and say, 'Why is this like that?' and the crew would say, 'This is the way Geller wants it.' He couldn't shake that.

"He was fantasizing about changing the entire crew and bringing in another one but that was impossible, not because there was a special trick to doing the show, but because you needed a certain patience to do it, and a certain passion which was created by Bruce Geller to begin with."

For better or worse, *Mission: Impossible* forged ahead.

Year Five: 1970–1971

102: BUTTERFLY
(formerly POOR BUTTERFLY)

Teleplay by: Eric Bercovici and Jerry Ludwig
Story by: Sheldon Stark
Directed by: Gerald Mayer
Music Composed and Conducted by:
Robert Drasnin

First Aired: 10/31/70

TEAM: Phelps, Paris, Dana Lambert, Barney, Willy

Good afternoon, Mr. Phelps. Harry Kellem, an American businessman living in Japan and chairman of the new Economic Treaty Council, has been arrested for the murder of his wife. We have reason to believe that Kellem was framed and the murder actually committed by Mrs. Kellem's brother, Toshio Masaki, a powerful industrialist who is fanatically anti-American. In addition to personal hatred for Kellem, Masaki's motive is to discredit the Economic Council and shatter Japanese-American relations on the eve of the new treaty negotiations. Your mission, Jim, should you decide to accept it, is to stop Masaki's plan and vindicate Harry Kellem. As always, should you or any of your IM Force be caught or killed, the secretary will disavow any knowledge of your actions. Good luck, Jim.

Masaki stabbed his sister in the garden of his huge estate and arranged for Kellem to be found by the body, his fingerprints on the murder weapon. Now, to further humiliate the US government, Masaki schemes to have Kellem "commit suicide."

Renowned Kabuki artist Paris visits the Masaki estate for a short stay, while Barney and Dana sneak onto the grounds. Avoiding the private police, Barney films a painstaking recreation of the murder of "Mrs. Kellem" (Dana in a mask) by "Masaki" (Paris) at the site of the actual killing.

Dana uses the footage to try to blackmail first Masaki, then Kellem's distraught daughter, Nobu, whom Paris has befriended. On Paris's advice, Nobu informs police inspector Akita of the film. Akita follows Dana to Masaki, who has agreed to buy the film. She escapes just as Akita, Nobu, and Paris enter and demand to see the film. When the footage is screened and Masaki watches "himself" lead his sister to the murder site, he panics and rips the film off the projector before the moment of truth can be seen. "You killed my mother," cries Nobu. "Yes!" admits Masaki, who examines the remainder of the film and discovers it to be blank. Having admitted his guilt, Masaki is arrested and Harry Kellem is freed.

GUEST CAST: Khigh Dhiegh (Toshio Masaki), Benson Fong (Inspector Akita), Lisa Lu (Mioshi Kellem), James Shigeta (Shiki), Helen Funai (Nobu Kellem), Russ Conway (Harry Kellem), Dale Ishimoto (Saburi), Fuji (Osaki), Leonard Pronko (Speciality Dancer). *Unbilled:* Bill Sato, Roy Ogata (Fighters)

Sheldon Stark's name was on the list of authors Stan Kallis had hoped could write *Mission.* Stark's first try, a tale of diamond switching in apartheid Africa, was too similar to episode 18, "The Diamond." "Poor Butterfly," his second and final contribution, fared better, although Stark remembers rewriting it as many as four times, "and that practically never happens on other shows." The story was on the shelf when Bruce Lansbury replaced Kallis as producer. New story consultant Laurence Heath had a go at it before calling in Jerry Ludwig, who was working steadily on *Hawaii Five-O* with sometimes partner Eric Bercovici. "That was the year we did fifteen *Hawaii Five-O*s," says Bercovici. "I used to have dreams about Jack Lord. Not a happy way to spend the night." Ludwig found the idea of a faked,

Nimoy (top) performed a complex Kabuki dance in *one* take for "Butterfly." Dana applies a mask for a crucial disguise in the same episode (bottom).

incomplete film stimulating. After a fast meeting with Heath and Lansbury, Jerry and Eric wrote the script quickly and were soon back at CBS, grinding out more adventures for Steve McGarrett and his boys.

"Butterfly" is the first script to use the character of Dana Lambert, but Ludwig was given no instructions to introduce her. The procedure of changing actors and characters in television has always amused him. "The network and the studio just cross their fingers," he says with a smile, "and hope that the audience likes everyone who is there, and will still like the show with this new person. It's a case of, 'Pretend we haven't changed anything and maybe they won't notice. Don't make a big deal out of this, because how could we possibly gain by making a big deal out of this?' I only knew that we were writing for someone younger." For a look at an actual attempt to introduce Dana, see episode 106, "Flip Side."

Lesley Warren isn't the only element which makes "Butterfly" unique and fresh: The Japanese setting makes it perhaps the series' most visually charming segment. Although Masaki's estate is just a large indoor set, genuine exteriors were shot at the lovely Japanese village in Buena Park, California.

"Butterfly" presents new challenges for Paris, who must first become Japanese, then a Kabuki dancer. Nimoy's Japanese look, consisting mainly of slanted eyes and accentuated cheekbones, isn't very convincing, but needless to say, every character in the show buys it. Paris makes the masks used in the filming of the "murder" and truly does the impossible when, simply by donning the Masaki mask, he loses several inches in height.

For once, Willy figures prominently. In fact, the whole plan rests on his broad shoulders. As a distraction while the film is shot, Willy engages in a brutal jujitsu match with Masaki's bodyguard Osaki, a top martial artist. Since no one has ever lasted more than thirty seconds against Osaki and Willy will have to go at least three minutes, the strongman endures a crash course with a jujitsu master.* "We shot the jujitsu match over three days, and I was sore!" Peter Lupus exclaims. "No matter how great a shape you're in, your body has to get used to the shock of getting thrown to the mat. But I must say that my opponent, Fuji, was great to work with." Willy loses the match, but evens the score at the finale when he rescues Dana from Osaki's menacing clutches. In the first fight scene in years, Willy uses fast, nonclassical moves to send Osaki senseless to the ground.

"Butterfly" is enhanced by art director Gibson Holley, composer Robert Drasnin, and director Gerald Mayer. The acting is generally good despite the clichéd Japanese characters. It is not the purpose of this book to explore the sad waste of the Asian actor in Hollywood, but it must be noted that even *Mission,* one of the most progressively cast series of its time, hired Asians only when Asian characters were depicted. It is curious to note, however, that Khigh Dhiegh, who made a career of playing Asian characters (most notably archvillain Wo Fat in *Hawaii Five-O*) is in fact of Anglo-Egyptian Sudanese descent.

Bercovici and Ludwig went from writing to producing on the TV movie *Assignment: Munich* (1972, with Lesley Ann Warren) and the follow-up series *Assignment: Vienna* (1972–73). They wrote action features like *Three the Hard Way* (1974), and developed interesting projects separately. Bercovici had hits with miniseries like *Washington: Behind Closed Doors* (1977, for executive producer Stan Kallis) and *Shogun* (1980), which he wrote and produced. Jerry Ludwig kept busy producing, creating, or writing pilots and series like *Jessica Novak* (1974), *Today's F.B.I.* (1981–82), and *MacGyver* (1985–).

---

* In the apartment scene, Willy alludes to a knowledge of judo.

103: HOMECOMING

First Aired: 10/10/70

Written by: Laurence Heath
Directed by: Reza S. Badiyi
Music Composed and Conducted by:
    Robert Prince

TEAM: Phelps, Paris, Dana, Barney, Willy

In a departure from the series format, Phelps calls in the IMF to solve a string of murders in his home town.

In town to donate family property to the county, Jim finds the small community of Norville in a state of fear: three young townswomen have been fatally strangled, evidently at random. Phelps, his real occupation unknown to his childhood friends, sends for Barney, who poses as a criminologist to help.

Circumstantial evidence points to Seth Morley, an emotionally disturbed Vietnam vet. He is arrested, but Barney's findings suggest that Morley is not guilty. When Seth is to be transferred to a mental hospital, some locals, angered by what they consider a lack of justice, threaten to kill the suspect before he can be moved from the town jail. To keep Seth alive and root out the real killer, Phelps summons the rest of the IMF.

GUEST CAST: Jacqueline Scott (Cynthia Owens), Joe Maross (Sheriff Brad Owens), Fred Beir (Joe Keith), Frank Webb (Seth Morley), Patricia Smith (Julia Keith), Sharon Acker (Connie Hastings), Loretta Swit (Midge Larson), Larry Pennell (Karl Burroughs), Jack Donner (Stan Sherman), James Sikking (Corrigan), Owen Bush (Reynolds)

"One of the things Geller didn't want to do is to personalize the characters," Laurence Heath observes. "There was a lot of validity to this approach because they became other characters in every show, so it was better to keep their personal lives aside." Since this opinion wasn't shared by everyone, "Homecoming" was written to explore the background of *Mission*'s prime mover.

Back home for the first time in years, Jim stares wistfully at the old Phelps homestead and its aged sign advertising his father's boat and lakeside equipment business. His idyllic youthful flashbacks are shattered by the reality of the town's current crisis. Since Sheriff Owens is ill-equipped to find the killer, Jim takes matters in his own hands, and as discreetly as ever.

The mystery unfolds in a manner that has nothing to do with the established *Mission* formula. The rural setting, small town tensions, and nostalgic interludes are a deliberate flight in mood and style. Apart from the sequence in which Seth Morley is spirited out of jail, there is none of the customary derring-do. To explain his reasons for getting involved, Phelps actually espouses a genuine personal feeling to the sheriff:

PHELPS: I got involved when I was born in this town. What bothers me is how it's changed. Bitterness and guilt, people out there with guns ready to shoot down a kid who was one of them until they sent him off to war.

An even more intimate scene, in which old girlfriend Cynthia (now the sheriff's wife) declares her undying love for Jim and begs him to take her away with him, was jettisoned—probably for the best.

In a rare instance of network concern, CBS felt unsure that Reza Badiyi could direct a show so devoid of flashy visuals. They needn't have worried, for there is nothing wrong with the performances. One key scene required supporting player Loretta Swit to break down in

hysterics. In deference to the actress, Badiyi kept the set absolutely quiet, gave Swit all the time she needed, and had the crew make their cues in whispers instead of the usual shouts. Loretta played the scene well, and the take ended as silently as it began. Standing by was Lesley Warren who, as Greg Morris recalls, was "in awe."

The general consensus regarding "Homecoming" was not favorable. Series fans thought it was too much a departure, and critics who had previously cited the show's lack of personality were not happy with this first experiment. "We got a lot of criticism from people," says Heath, "including CBS executive Fred Silverman, who didn't think it should have been done." Some viewers felt that *Mission* was trying to prove that it could be just as mundane as any other show, and Reza Badiyi is not the only one to feel that the episode is much more typical of *Mannix* than *Mission*. "Homecoming" was the Lansbury regime's first step for a new, original *Mission*. Less drastic steps would follow.

A pose for "Homecoming."

104: THE REBEL

First Aired: 11/28/70

Teleplay by: Ken Pettus
Story by: Norman Katkov and Ken Pettus
Directed by: Barry Crane
Music Composed and Conducted by:
Hugo Montenegro

TEAM: Phelps, Paris, Dana, Barney, Dr. Doug Robert

In an episode with no tape scene, the mission is twofold: save three scientists from their government's hostile regime and prevent their notes from falling into enemy hands.

The IMF spirits two of the scientists out of the country, but the third, Dr. Khora, refuses to leave and is executed by the government. Phelps and Dana meet with Khora's son Alex, a guerrilla leader in the hills near the tiny village of Kefero, to obtain the late doctor's valuable notes on bacteriological warfare. The group is ambushed by the militia, led by Colonel Bakram. Dana, Alex's girlfriend Irina, and a rebel named Klos are captured and jailed in Kefero.

Regrouping, Jim learns from Alex that his father's notebook no longer exists: "Irina *is* the notebook. She has it memorized." Jim talks the rebels out of storming the jail and is given a few hours to free the prisoners, who are pressured to reveal the location of the notebook.

Barney and Doug parachute into the hills with special gear. Ministry of Information officer Paris meets with Bakram to strengthen his image with the people of Kefero, who hate him. Paris suggests a more lenient attitude toward the clergy in general and in particular one Father Sebastian, the popular local priest who has been openly critical of Bakram and the new regime.

A truck (driven by Barney and Doug) transporting a huge religious statue "breaks down" in Kefero's town square. The hollow statue, containing Phelps, Alex, and digging tools, is temporarily unloaded over a sewage grate, through which the pair tunnel toward the jail. Paris urges Bakram to keep the statue and appease the townspeople but Father Sebastian, aware of Bakram's motives, refuses to accept it. They argue long enough for Alex and Jim to crack the jail and rescue the prisoners, who follow them back into the statue.

Paris persuades Bakram to have Barney and Doug move the statue to an abandoned mountain monastery. When Bakram learns that his prisoners are gone and discovers how they escaped, he destroys the statue, expecting to find his quarry inside. But he is too late: They have fled, leaving Bakram with nothing but a pile of rubble and the even deeper hatred of the people of Kefero.

GUEST CAST: Mark Lenard (Colonel Bakram), Robert Purvey (Alex Khora), Davana Brown (Irina), Jonathan Lippe (Father Sebastian), David Roya (Klos), Richard Shelfo (Haratch), Diane Holly (Girl), Ralph Ventura (Soldier). *Unbilled:* Arthur Batanides (Lieutenant Kappelo)

This Trojan horse plot is beset by dull direction, a repetitive score, and surprisingly ineffective performances. Beginning in the penultimate moments of the mission, the background of "The Rebel" is explained too quickly via awkward expository dialogue in the first scene. Willy was written out of the script early and his customary duties as truck driver alongside Barney were performed by new semiregular Sam Elliott in his debut performance. To facilitate the need for physician Doug, Jim is shot in the shoulder during the opening attack.

In his only *Mission* score, Hugo Montenegro employs a Latin-flavored version of the series theme which plays endlessly throughout the show, although snippets from Schifrin's pilot and "Submarine" scores come to the rescue. There is an odd scene in which Jim demands that the rebels spare the lives of captured government soldiers, and a funny moment when Paris, alone in the local church, discreetly drops a coin in the collection box. But apart from that, "The Rebel" is a poor show and as empty as the hollow statue it prominently features.

105: THE KILLER

Written by: Arthur Weiss
Directed by: Paul Krasny
Music Composed and Conducted by:
  Lalo Schifrin

First Aired: 9/19/70

TEAM: Phelps, Paris, Dana, Barney, Willy, many others

Good morning, Mr. Phelps. A hired killer, Eddie Lorca, will arrive in this city on TransAmerica Flight number 1 on Friday. Lorca has a contract with the most powerful underworld leader in this part of the United States, a man we know only by his code name, Scorpio. Lorca's mission is to kill someone. We do not know whom he will kill, or where, when, or how he will do it. Your mission, Jim, should you decide to accept it, is to prevent the murder and discover the identity of Scorpio. This tape will self-destruct in five seconds. Good luck, Jim.

Operating totally at random and making last-second decisions have made Lorca too slippery for conventional law enforcement agencies to nab. Now it's the IMF's turn.

Lorca arrives in Los Angeles, arbitrarily chooses a hotel from the phone book, and hails an airport taxi. He tells the cabby (Paris) his destination: the Bower Hotel. Listening via transmitter, Phelps and a small army of agents swiftly turn an empty, unmarked building into the "Bower Hotel." Inside, Lorca randomly chooses a room; Barney, listening upstairs, sticks the proper room number on the door of the one room which has been thoroughly bugged.

Lorca calls Scorpio's "bag woman" and arranges to meet and receive his instructions. Paris intercepts the girl and gets the information: a photo of the target, his location, and the time at which the killing is to happen. As the IMF move the target to safety, bag woman Dana delivers the packet to Lorca with one change: The photo inside is of Barney.

Lorca evades the tight IMF surveillance, plants a death trap in Barney's hotel room, and exits. Only a last-moment hunch from Phelps gets Barney out of the room before it explodes.

Outside the hotel, Lorca sees an IMF man rush out and yell, "A man's been blown to pieces!" Lorca's meeting with Dana for his payoff is interrupted by gunfire from a passing (IMF) car which "mortally wounds" Dana. Before "dying," she informs Lorca that Scorpio's intention was to kill *him.* The killer angrily hails a cab (Willy) and, tailed by the Force, makes for Scorpio's home. When Phelps and crew enter, they find that Scorpio and Lorca have shot each other, Lorca's wound a fatal one.

GUEST CAST: Robert Conrad (Eddie Lorca), Davis Roberts (William Barton), Carole Carle (Flo), Byron Morrow (Alfred E. Chambers), Martin Ashe (Clerk), Helen Spring (Old Lady), Pegi Boucher (Girl), Victoria Hale (Maid), Tom Huff (Bellhop), Dick Karie (Man). *Unbilled:* Rachel English (Woman)

"The Killer" is the epitome of what the Lansbury regime wanted the series to be. It presents an extremely difficult assignment, eschews an important and traditional series conceit and, in terms of sheer suspense, is one of *Mission's* best.

As Laurence Heath explains, Eddie Lorca "did everything at random, so they (the IMF) couldn't get anything prepared ahead of time." The lack of exhaustive IMF preplanning is a welcome twist, forcing our heroes to think on their feet all the way through. It wasn't just the on-screen principals who were hard pressed. "Bruce Lansbury, Arthur Weiss, and I sat plotting for literally two full days," Heath adds. "It was Bruce's idea, his basic premise."

How can you stop, or even predict, the actions of a man when even *he* doesn't know what he will do? It's too tough a job for a mere five agents, even specialists like these, so Jim recruits a large retinue of operatives, most of whom are hidden away in the phony hotel. Once Lorca tells Paris the name of the hotel he's picked, everyone goes into action by turning the "blank" building into the Bower. Everything is labeled or initialed: key tabs, registers, towels, soap wrappers, stationery, ashtrays, and so on, and it all must be ready by the time Lorca arrives. To this end, every attempt is made to slow down Paris's taxi. Paris drives as slowly as he can; Willy jams a traffic light; IMF drivers block the cab route with slow-moving trucks. The intercutting between Lorca, sitting impatiently in the cab, and the rushing IMF artisans, makes for the first of several fine suspense sequences.

The hour's linchpin, and the main reason it is so successful, is Robert Conrad's performance as Lorca. Plotting his actions literally on the roll of the dice he carries with him, he is subtle, unpredictable, and very dangerous. Conrad and director Krasny had previously worked together on a *Mannix* in which the actor played a magnificently obnoxious movie star. On "The Killer" they reteam to bring off an hour just as good and even more memorable, the first hint that there may still be some life left in *Mission: Impossible*.

As the season's premiere, "The Killer" would be subject to the usual critical scrutiny; opening a season that promised to be progressive meant that the reviews were particularly important. By and large, the reaction was favorable. *Daily Variety*'s review of September 21 called the show, "a bristling suspenser which sustained throughout." *Variety* concurred, citing the show's fresh approach and singling out Conrad and Lesley Warren. "The Killer," "thrust the viewers into the situation and challenged them to turn away from the set," wrote *Mor*. "The tight writing, staccato direction, and expertly laconic thesping . . . are going to stand [*Mission*] in good stead in its move to early Saturday evening."

Subsequent episodes, and the all-important Nielsen ratings, would support this prediction.

Barney, marked for murder, uses a decoy in "The Killer."

Year Five: 1970–1971

106: FLIP SIDE

Written by: Jackson Gillis
Directed by: John Llewellyn Moxey
Music Composed and Conducted by:
  Benny Golson

First Aired: 9/26/70

TEAM: Phelps, Paris, Dana, Barney, Willy

Good morning, Mr. Phelps. Every year illegal, dangerous drugs cost the lives of thousands of Americans, mostly young people. The biggest distributor of these drugs on the Pacific coast is Mel Bracken. He is supplied from south of the border by businessman Diego Maximillian, who in turn gets his drugs legally from mid-western drug manufacturer C.W. Cameron. Your mission, should you decide to accept it, is to stop, to expose and destroy that vicious circle, including all three men who run it. Good luck, Jim.

There is nothing illegal in Cameron exporting his drugs to Maximillian in Mexico. The IMF can shut down the operation only by connecting manufacturer Cameron directly to Mel Bracken.

Barney follows a truckful of Cameron pills to Maximillian Enterprises in Mexico, and learns exactly how and when the drugs, packed in peanut cases, are sent to Bracken in Los Angeles.

Denver Syndicate man Phelps orders $500,000 worth of pills from Bracken, who eagerly awaits Maximillian's truck. When it arrives, he is stunned to find that the peanut cases contain . . . peanuts (Barney has overtaken and replaced the cargo). Jim gives Bracken six hours to deliver the pills—or else. Maximillian is picked up by Mexican authorities, forcing Bracken to go directly to Cameron for the shipment. Cameron reluctantly ships the pills to Bracken via air freight to meet the deadline. Phelps buys the drugs from Bracken; Barney photographs the sale, which leads to the arrest of both Bracken and Cameron.

GUEST CAST: Sal Mineo (Mel Bracken), Dana Elcar (C.W. Cameron), Robert Alda (Diego Maximillian), Jose DeVega (Freddie), Kasey Rogers (Bunny Cameron), Joy Bang (Girl), Ford Lile (Pusher), John Rivera (Tito). *Unbilled:* Bob Golden (Customs Man)

Considering the relative mediocrity of "Flip Side," it is surprising to learn that it is one of Bruce Lansbury's favorite episodes. The show is laced with then-hip references to the drug-soaked late sixties and has dated badly. It was, however, one of the first *Mission*s to deal with a topical American concern, which may explain the producer's pride in the show.

This is the first of three good scripts from veteran Jackson Gillis, whose many credits include shows as diverse as *Adventures of Superman, Lassie, Perry Mason,* and *Columbo.* Gillis had researched drug smuggling for another project and was fascinated by what he'd learned. According to him, the MO used by heavies in "Flip Side" actually works in real life. "American drug companies sell South American countries about five times the amount of pills that all the people in South America, if they were all addicts, could possibly consume. The American government has never done anything about controlling this because it would be interfering with American enterprise; it's good business." He was surprised when Lansbury bought the idea. "The whole point of the story was that it wasn't just the Mafia getting involved in the drug smuggling business. I thought the network's Program Practices was going to throw it out, but they never did."

The interesting plot is padded by adding Dana and Paris as struggling rock musicians who make a tenuous connection between Bracken (who uses a music company as front) and Cameron. Lesley Warren sings two songs and has fun with Nimoy in their scenes together.

293

Part of the plot requires Dana to fake a fatal overdose in Cameron's hotel room. When Paris finds her, he holds her to his chest, supposedly grief stricken. Eulogizing her, he faces us (but not Cameron) and pulls a wonderfully bogus expression of sorrow that only Leonard Nimoy could get away with.

The script originally included a scene which actually introduced Dana into the IMF and the series. Dana is singing a blues number in an empty rehearsal hall when Phelps walks in.

DANA: I didn't think I'd ever see you again.

PHELPS: Why not . . . You're young, tough, and your record with the other agencies proves you know your job.

DANA: Where do we start?

Jim shows her a news story about a young drug victim.

DANA: I've known so many kids in the theater who turned on—and then tuned out like that. Oh yes, Jim, I'd do anything to stop those vultures who—

Phelps interrupts her with a smile, taking her arm to lead her out.

PHELPS: Oh no, solid citizens! Good old American enterprise—*that's* where this begins!

This scene was filmed but ultimately cut, probably because no one could be certain that "Flip Side" would open the new season (in fact it didn't). It's an unfortunate omission, since having the audience meet Dana at the start of her IMF tenure would certainly have been unique and notable. It also told us a little about Dana, a character we never got to know.

"Flip Side" is brightened by the polished performances of three distinct villains: slimy Sal Mineo, nervous Dana Elcar, and seedily elegant Robert Alda.

107: MY FRIEND, MY ENEMY

Produced by: Laurence Heath
Teleplay by: Gene R. Kearney
Story by: William Wood and Gene R. Kearney
Directed by: Gerald Mayer
Music Composed and Conducted by:
　Robert Drasnin

First Aired: 10/25/70

TEAM: Phelps, Dana, Barney, Doug

In a departure from the series format, Paris falls into enemy hands and is brainwashed into killing his "Control"—Phelps.

Paris is spotted in Vienna by Communist agent Karl Maur, a former victim of Paris who runs the motorcycling spy off a deserted road, drugs him, and delivers him to brain specialist Dr. Tabor. Mentally stressed by Tabor, the drugged Paris reveals only minor data about himself, such as his deep aversion to murder. It is learned, however, that Paris has twice suffered the loss of women he loved to a father figure. Tabor concocts a plot to capitalize upon these psychological scars, then implants an electrode in Paris's brain (through the upper palate to avoid detection) which will manipulate him by remote control.

Unaware that he has been held captive, Paris is released and put through standard IMF clearance procedures by Phelps and Doug, who find nothing physically wrong with him. When Barney locates Paris's motorcycle and discovers Maur's fingerprints, it becomes clear that Paris's future is in jeopardy. Jim delays reporting these findings to the secretary and traces Maur to his current post at Vienna's East European Trade Commission. Dana creates a diversion while Doug and Barney break into the building's upper level, find Tabor's apparatus, and report to Jim.

Paris has meanwhile fallen in love with Enid Brugge, a Communist agent who claims to be defecting but is really working with Tabor. When Tabor murders Enid, Paris becomes convinced that his current authority figure, Phelps, is responsible.

In a murderous fury, Paris confronts Phelps and they engage in a physical struggle which is interrupted by Tabor and his aide Bandar. "This is the man we have been searching for," Tabor tells his accomplice, who holds the pair at gunpoint. "His Control. Kill him." Paris's abhorrence to murder comes to the fore: He reflexively wounds Bandar

before snapping out of his programmed state. Tabor is "taken care of," and Paris rejoins the IMF.

GUEST CAST: Mark Richman (Dr. Paul Tabor), Bruce Glover (Ernst Bandar), Wesley Lau (Karl Maur), Jill Haworth (Enid Brugge, aka Marla Kassel), Tony Giorgio (Meerghan), Chris Holter (Inga), Aaron Fletcher (Desk Clerk), Edward F. Bach (Guard #1), Bart LaRue (Guard #2), Walter Davis (Attendant)

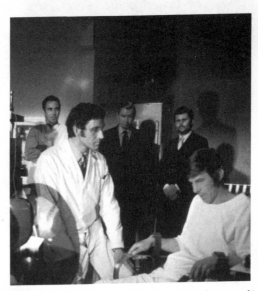

Paris is brainwashed by an evil enemy doctor (Peter Mark Richman) in "My Friend, My Enemy."

For four seasons the IMF was the hunter and never the hunted. Our globe-hopping spies were never recognized by the opposition. The law of averages finally catches up with our heroes in this episode, and another series conceit falls in the most intimate of all the "personal" shows.

In his debut as *Mission* producer, Laurence Heath (whose name appears on the final draft script) discloses a bit of the IMF's inner workings and offers a striking psychological profile of the Great Paris. In fact, we learn more about Paris in this hour than we learn about any regular before or since. During Tabor's hypnotic questioning, Paris reveals that his father drove away Paris's mother while Paris was still a boy . . . an incident he still resents. A more traumatic revelation follows, involving a key figure from Paris's past.

While wandering around Europe as a young man, Paris met a great magician named Meerghan and soon became his assistant. Things soured when Paris fell in love with Inga, Meerghan's beautiful co-assistant. Paris watched helplessly one night while Meerghan jealously shot and killed Inga during a performance.

TABOR: Twice, father figures, figures roughly like his Control, have taken away women he's loved.

Tabor has all he needs to come up with a seemingly infallible strategy.

After his release, Paris has nightmares about Inga and suffers searing head pains, the latter caused by Tabor and the electrode in Paris's head. There is something else, something much more subtle, which troubles Paris. It is never specifically stated but strongly suggested that should evidence reveal that he has been in enemy hands, more than his standing in the IMF will be taken from him. Early on, Paris pessimistically tells Jim, "You know what'll happen to me if you don't clear me." Later, Barney implies that Paris will be through if Jim reports their findings to the secretary. Paris's anxiety builds friction between himself and Jim and before long, when Paris looks at Jim, he sees Meerghan instead. He also confuses his new romance, Enid, with lost love Inga. When Phelps delicately suggests that Enid may be a plant, Paris bristles.

PARIS: Can't you understand real emotion, or have you become some kind of a machine? Now I understand. You made up all that stuff about me being captured because you want the girl for yourself. You're gonna send me home, aren't you? You're gonna let them destroy me so you can have her!

When Paris finds Enid's corpse and suffers another painful jolt from the electrode, he loses control and goes after Phelps. This leads to a startling scene in which Paris chases Jim, shooting at him and screaming, "You killed her, Meerghan!" The chase turns into a grappling match which ends when Tabor arrives. Luckily, the unspoken IMF rule against outright murder saves the day.

"My Friend, My Enemy" ends on a sweet note when Paris leaves the hospital to rejoin his friends and Max, Tabor's canine guinea pig who, like Paris, has had his brain electrode surgically removed.

108: THE INNOCENT

First Aired: 10/3/70

Teleplay by: Marc Norman and Laurence Heath
Story by: Marc Norman
Directed by: John Llewellyn Moxey
Music Composed and Conducted by: Harry Geller

TEAM: Phelps, Paris, Dana, Willy, Doug

In a departure from the series format, Barney is caught and poisoned during a mission, forcing the IMF to compel an unwilling outsider to take his place while they try to complete the mission and save Barney.

Somewhere in the Middle East, Barney and Willy penetrate the Interoco Chemical Plant where Dehominant-B, a lethal compound that kills in eight seconds, has been perfected. Attempting to gain access to the computer which synthesizes the drug, Barney is exposed to Dehominant-A, which instantly and painfully immobilizes him. Their presence discovered, Willy must abandon his teammate and escape. Barney is interrogated by security chief Orlov and the scientist responsible for the Dehominants, Dr. Vazan. Unless he confesses, Barney will die in four painful hours.

Washington relays data on the only other man in the area who can work the Interoco computer: Dr. Jerry Carlin, a near-genius dropout who happens to be in the same city. Dana makes an unsuccessful direct appeal to indifferent Jerry. Then narcotics agents Paris and Doug "uncover" heroin in Jerry's girlfriend's purse and arrest her. Paris tells Jerry that she will be released only if Jerry helps Dana's group and provides information on "them." Jerry has no choice but to agree.

Jerry and the boys enter Interoco via a conduit tunnel while journalist Dana interviews Dr. Vazan

and helps Paris "become" Vazan. "Vazan" questions Barney and plants a tiny speaker unit in Barney's ear. Jim feeds Barney a false confession which implicates the technicians currently manning the computer. Barney passes out, is declared dead by "Vazan," and is taken to an autopsy room, where Doug revives him, mere moments from death.

Jim and Jerry replace the technicians fingered by Barney. Despite Orlov's hawklike eye, Jerry ruins the Dehominant and erases the computer's memory of the formula. Making a narrow escape from the installation, the IMF takes Jerry—and the real Dr. Vazan—with them.

GUEST CAST: Christopher Connelly (Dr. Jerome Carlin), Robert Ellenstein (Dr. M. Vazan), Larry Linville (Colonel Leo Orlov), Than Wyenn (General Skolpin), Katherine Darc (Judy Moore), Victor Brandt (Doctor), Gene Tyburn (Technician Tirkin), Sy Prescott (Security Guard), Jorge Ben Hur (Waiter)

"The Innocent" isn't just one of the best *Mission*s; it is also one of the most arresting because it examines IMF ethics and by doing so, challenges the premise of the show.

Marc Norman, a young writer whose first break was the TV film *The Challenge* (1970, featuring Sam Elliott), had a droll attitude toward episodic television. "I always had trouble with series premises," he claims, "because it's a hard kind of writing to do. Once a series has a premise it becomes sacrosanct. You don't question it and you can't fool with it very much. But I would come up with ideas that would question the very premise of the series, just to see if the series would stand being questioned." With this attitude it isn't surprising that Norman turned to feature writing, with credits including *Oklahoma Crude* (1973) and *The Aviator* (1985).

Norman believed that *Mission*'s most notable element was the IMF's manipulation of

people, good guys *and* bad. "They did it in the name of national security," says Norman, "or stopping World War III or keeping the bad guys from getting the plans, and that seemed to be all the justification they needed to do what they did. What if someone says, 'Wait, you don't have the right to do this to me. I'm an individual, I have personal choices, and I don't like being manipulated'? What if they needed one guy to do a mission and when he got involved and found out who they were, he tries to pull out because he doesn't want to go along with it?"

Jerry Carlin symbolizes a growing philosophy of the time, especially among America's youth, who found the idea of meddling American spies distasteful. Certainly, the fact that the IMF forces Jerry at gunpoint to risk his life in the name of fair play is an intriguing one to ponder. "These days it's a lot easier to accept the premise of 'The Innocent,' " Norman feels. "We've come through a period when individual rights are more important. You can't assume that because you're a professional and he's an amateur that you can impose your professional needs and decisions on someone else. I don't think that's a radical concept now, but it was then." So Norman delivered a script with undeniably exciting elements, which undeniably required extensive revisions to conform to series style. As Norman explains, "Heath rewrote it. They didn't change the plot very much but they tried to backtrack on what they bought, which was the concept of a guy who stands up in the middle of a *Mission: Impossible* and says, 'This isn't right, I don't want to do it.' "

Heath softened the story's more sinister questions and slightly altered the basic thrust. "The idea," Heath says, "was to get somebody in there who didn't know what he was doing." In Heath's version, Jerry cooperates because he believes that his girlfriend's freedom is at stake. Midway through the mission, he recognizes "cops" Doug and Paris as part of the very team he is helping and becomes so disgusted at their duplicity that he refuses to complete the mission, thereby jeopardizing the entire crew. Heath didn't erase all the questions which Norman's script posed. Early on, Paris asks if they have the right to involve an innocent.

PHELPS: Do we have any right not to, Paris? Vazan's government intends to use the Dehominant against their neighbors immediately. They're already projecting fifty thousand casualties.

This is all the justification Phelps offers. By setting Jerry in the frame which forces him to spy on Dana and "her people," Jim effectively compromises Jerry's idealism. So when Jerry criticizes the team's morality, Phelps can counter.

PHELPS: What were you planning to do to us? You were ready to spy on us and, if necessary, to have us shot.

JERRY: Their stuff's no worse than what we've got. Weapons are all the same. They're meant to kill.

PHELPS: No arguments.

JERRY: Then why are you here?

PHELPS: Maybe to keep one more weapon from coming into the world.

As Jerry, Christopher Connelly provides much enjoyment as he watches the IMF go through their improbable paces. And though he may object morally, he develops a grudging respect for the team's skill. When Barney is recovered and the time comes to sabotage the computer, Jerry still refuses to act until Phelps, with fifty thousand lives on the line, volunteers to do it, even though he knows only an expert can succeed. More for self-preservation than patriotism, Jerry relents. "You're gonna get us all killed," he tells Jim.* He gets a quick

---

* In Norman's version, Jerry ridicules the very idea of Barney, a black man, even entering the obviously Russian command room.

briefing from Barney before heading to the computer room with Phelps.

After the mission is accomplished and the team makes its obligatory hairbreadth escape, Jerry asks what will become of the unconscious Vazan. Jim assures him that Vazan will be put someplace, "where he can't develop Dehominant-*C*." In Norman's draft, Jim's reply was much more specific.

PHELPS: We drop him off near the border. They'll capture him and blame him for all that's happened. He won't be producing any more Dehominant.

The original ending was also different. Jerry tells Jim:

JERRY: You said you wanted to destroy that formula, not use it, so I threw the (computer) readout away.

To Jerry's dismay, Jim reaches into his pocket and pulls out the discarded formula! Then, very deliberately, Phelps puts a match to the readout and the formula goes up in flames.

Because it is such a perilous and exciting outing in so many different ways, "The Innocent" easily rates as one of *Mission*'s finest hours.

109: DECOY

First Aired: 11/7/70

Written by: John D. F. Black
Directed by: Seymour Robbie

TEAM: Phelps, Paris, Dana, Barney, Willy

Good morning, Mr. Phelps. Before he died last year, Premier Kerkoska gave his daughter Anna a secret document containing the names of men within his government who privately favored friendly relations with the West. Word has reached us through diplomatic channels that Anna and her brother Alexi wish to defect. We know this is a plot devised by Alexi to acquire the document and at the same time capture American intelligence agents, thereby embarrassing the West. In spite of this trap, your mission, should you choose to accept it, is to get the document and bring Anna Kerkoska to safety. As always, should you or any member of your IM Force be caught or killed, the secretary will disavow any knowledge of your actions. This tape will self-destruct in five seconds. Good luck, Jim.

Anna, unaware of Alexi's plan, is closely watched by police chief Petrovitch, who is in league with Alexi. For Petrovitch's benefit, Jim plots a false rescue plot to hide the real one.

Publisher Phelps and his sister Dana enter the country on business. Dana is kidnapped by US agent Paris to force Phelps to cooperate with an "American plan" to take Anna out of the country. Petrovitch and Alexi carefully monitor the proceedings, hopeful that the Americans will trap themselves.

Jim and Anna become constant companions and fall in love. Petrovitch overhears Jim "confess" to Anna that US intelligence has ordered him to escort her and Alexi to a mortuary near the border for a fictitious funeral. Realizing that the Americans will make their move and that Anna will be carrying the document, Petrovitch rings the mortuary area with agents.

Despite Alexi's scheming, scores of secret police, and the country's mine-ridden border, Jim boldly spirits Anna and her father's list out of the country.

GUEST CAST: Julie Gregg (Anna Kerkoska), Michael Strong (Police Chief Petrovitch), Paul Stevens (Alexi Kerkoska), Sid Haig (Agent #1), Joshua Bryant (Stefan), Arthur Malet (Undertaker), Richard Eric Winter (Orishev), Bart LaRue (Agent #6), Rosanna Huffman (Guide), Tom McDonough (Agent #7), Victor Paul (Chauffeur)

Three plots propel "Decoy": the bogus plan which Petrovitch is meant to follow, the genuine IMF plan, and the romance between Phelps and lovely Anna Kerkoska. Does Jim woo her simply as incentive to defect, or are his feelings real? It's impossible to tell. When she learns that he is a spy, Anna breaks down and accuses him of lying to her just to get the list. He denies it and unconvincingly insists that he loves her.

The dual plots dovetail at the mortuary where a clever IMF ruse allows Jim and Anna to exit the parlor and board a hearse unnoticed. When the trick is discovered, Petrovitch and his squad give chase. Driver Barney stops the hearse and presses a dashboard button. The rear of the vehicle opens and out rolls not a coffin, but a compact, ultrafast hot rod carrying Phelps and Anna and heading for the border. Small and narrow, the speedster is so low to the ground that its occupants are virtually horizontal. At the border, the car darts under a mined steel gate and past the shocked guards who fire in vain after it.

"Jonnie Burke built that tiny little car," Peter Graves recalls. "God, that was real claustrophobia!" As usual, *Mission*'s special effects man had plenty of specifications to follow. He had

to create a car low enough to pass under a border gate, wide enough to carry Graves and guest star Julie Gregg, and narrow and short enough to fit in the rear of the hearse. "And as usual," Burke adds, "we built the thing from scratch in three or four days." Burke's prior work with car chassis served him well. "I had a beautiful little body for it," says Burke, "but Peter Graves has got such big feet that I had to cut the whole end off and reshape it. That's because he's lying down and he's so big that his feet are higher than his eye level. So we had to splay his feet and that's why the chasis had that double hump up front. Even then, he couldn't see the ground until about fifteen feet in front of him."

Outfitted with a Honda twin engine and the new chassis, Burke took a back lot test drive before shooting. "I knew it could go over 125 miles per hour, but I was worried about the handling ability." Once he got the feel of the car, Jonnie pushed it and was soon flashing past the soundstages at more than seventy miles per hour. "At about ninety, I realized that I hadn't tried the brakes yet. Now, all I'm laying in is a polished metal pan for the seat cushion to be mounted to. That thing handled as well as any chassis I ever worked on, but you couldn't turn it around—it had such a short wheel base that when you turned, the wheels would turn and the rear end would just push them straight ahead. It would skip. You couldn't turn it more than fifteen degrees at a slow speed.

"Now Dick Ziker, a pretty good stunt man, was the driver. Barry Crane was shooting the second unit and they went to the top of a winding, narrow road that hardly anybody uses. Barry's using a Chrysler limousine for the camera car and he told Ziker, 'Climb on it and we'll follow you.' Well, on the first turn they never saw Ziker again! But within fifteen minutes he had it down pat. He'd be going fifteen miles per hour, turn almost within the car's full length and go backwards, and have only lost a couple of miles per hour. And then he'd be going the other way!"

When the car was returned at the end of the first day, Burke discovered that the motor had been ruined. "They overwound it in one of the lower gears, kept driving it all day, and I saw that they had been running it on one cylinder. The head of the piston had worn down. We took it over to Honda where the guy took one look at it and gave us another motor off the shelf. We didn't have to buy it."

Honda, it so happened, was a *Mission* sponsor.

110: FLIGHT

Teleplay by: Harold Livingston
Story by: Leigh Vance
Directed by: Barry Crane

First Aired: 10/17/70

TEAM: Phelps, Paris, Dana, Barney, Doug, Stone, Butler, others

Good morning, Mr. Phelps. On Wednesday morning, Adolfo Rojas addresses a joint session of Congress. Before he enters the Congressional chambers Rojas will be dead, his government taken over by Manuel Ferrar, his chief of internal security. The murderer will be a professional assassin with the code name "Plato" whose true identity is known only to Ferrar. Although warned, Presidente Rojas refuses to cancel this vital appearance, and obviously our government cannot withdraw its invitation. Your mission, should you choose to accept it, is to learn Plato's identity and transmit the information to Washington before Presidente Rojas begins his speech. As always, should you or any of your IM Force be caught or killed, the secretary will disavow any knowledge of your actions. This tape will self-destruct in five seconds. Good luck, Jim.

Ferrar is to follow Rojas to Washington, leaving chief of police Diaz in charge of the takeover. Aboard a plane and awaiting takeoff, Ferrar is drugged, disguised, and hustled to an IMF replica of the plane. When he awakes, the "plane" develops engine trouble in mid flight. Seconds before the "crash," Ferrar is put to sleep again.

He awakens on a beach, and learns that he is on an uncharted island ruled by penal colony prisoners long thought lost at sea. Among the convicts is Paris, as a man Ferrar knew was a deep cover agent but had never met. Ferrar uncovers Paris's plot to escape from the island on a makeshift raft. Paris explains that his pose as a prisoner has uncovered the fact that Plato is a double agent whose true goal is to nail Ferrar. When the other prisoners "discover" the escape attempt, Ferrar identifies

himself to Paris and agrees to hold off the mob if Paris will inform their superiors that Plato is in fact journalist José Santos, who must be stopped. The message is radioed to Washington where Santos is apprehended seconds before Presidente Rojas enters the Congressional chambers.

GUEST CAST: John Colicos (Chief of Internal Security Manuel Ferrar), Lloyd Battista (Chief of Police Francisco Diaz), James Almanzar (Lieutenant Barata), Tol Avery (Stone), John Ragin (Butler), Shepard Sanders (Plato), Conrad Parham (Airline Clerk), Shirley Washington (Stewardess), Dom Tattoli (Presidente Adolfo Rojas), Ron Henriquez (Airport Guard), Bill Baldwin (Announcer)

One day in 1966, writer Harold Livingston was driving with his friend Bruce Geller, who'd mentioned that he'd just sold a spy series to CBS. Geller then diplomatically explained his belief that Livingston wouldn't be "right" for this show. His delicacy was unnecessary: Livingston was too busy with other projects to worry about this new program. Interestingly enough, Livingston was much closer to Laurence Heath than to Geller, and when Heath became *Mission*'s story consultant, Harold Livingston joined the stable of new *Mission* writers. Livingston, who'd ultimately write nine *Mission*s, was especially fond of the "big store," and took it to almost comical lengths in his later scripts. He considered *Mission: Impossible* an outright fantasy and saw no reason to pass up entertaining scams just because they were wildly unachievable. Perhaps he was right—his plots are often amusing and fun to watch. And although some series loyalists found his work too obvious and silly, Lansbury and Heath were glad to have him aboard. Livingston entered *Mission* at a time when the show was running low on inspiration and growing long in the tooth. If he had never arrived, it is quite possible

that someone else may have penned similar plots, and less skillfully. To survive, *Mission* would have to stretch, and by now there seemed to be no place else to go.

There is little in "Flight" to indicate the direction Livingston would later take. In early drafts, Paris and Barney's roles were reversed, and certain plot points, like a sadistic policeman who roughs up the captured Dana, were eliminated. Dana, caught when the authorities find the IMF pulling the old airplane-in-a-warehouse gag, makes a rotten attempt at playing innocent when she is grilled by Colonel Diaz at police headquarters. When this fails she drastically alters her strategy, informs Diaz that she is a US agent, and even tells him what the team is after. She persuades Diaz to release her so she can be followed to the IMF hotel rendezvous where Diaz can retrieve Ferrar and nab *all* the enemy agents.

Barney meets Dana at the hotel, blithely ignoring the plainclothesmen watching her room. Inside, they make small talk while Barney notices the light fixture in the center of the room's dropped ceiling. Unscrewing the fixture, he finds ample room inside to stow away with Dana. When the cops break in, they spot the room's open window and assume that the pair has escaped, never realizing that they are right under—or, *over* their noses. In an early draft, it is Paris who visits Dana and makes them up as an elderly bellhop and maid, respectively. They climb out the window and into an adjoining room. From there they exit into the corridor and past the plainclothesmen who pay no attention to them.

The rest of the team is busy fooling Ferrar into thinking he's on an island when in fact he's on the shoreline of his own country. In one diverting but pointless scene, the convicts must decide which of the crash survivors, Ferrar or Doug, shall live, since there is enough food for only one. After a vote which ends in a draw, Ferrar takes the initiative by grabbing the nearest pistol and "killing" Doug. "The deciding vote has been cast," he declares.

During the scene in which Ferrar is taken from the airplane, a copy of *Elite* magazine is clearly seen in the cabin's magazine rack. Since only the logo is visible, we can only wonder who the cover girl is.

111: HUNTED

First Aired: 11/21/70

Written by: Helen Hoblock Thompson
Directed by: Terry Becker

TEAM: Phelps, Paris, Dana, Barney, Doug, a helicopter pilot

Good morning, Mr. Phelps. For the past ten years the all-white government of African East Victoria has held Dr. Frederick Kolda prisoner. Now Kolda, black leader of a movement for the establishment of a biracial democracy, a symbol of freedom for all Africa, is seriously ill. Kolda has been transferred to a hospital in the capital where, according to our best information, he is receiving little or no treatment and is under intensive interrogation. Your mission, Jim, should you choose to accept it, is to go to Africa and rescue Kolda so he can establish a government in exile around which his people can rally. As always, should you or any member of your IM Force be caught or killed, the secretary will disavow any knowledge of your actions. This tape will self-destruct in five seconds. Good luck, Jim.

Medic Doug and an assistant enter Kolda's hospital room, burn through the window bars, and drop the patriot down a heavy canvas slide to the rest of the team, waiting outside. The pair are discovered: Doug slips out but his partner is shot in the leg while escaping. He staggers into the town's shabby black quarter nearby and passes out in a seamstress's shop. Maryana, a lovely deaf-mute dressmaker, tends to him and is intrigued by a loose flap of skin on his face. Peeling it away, she removes the Caucasian mask and finds Barney Collier underneath.

Kolda is flown out of the country but the IMF stays behind to locate Barney before the authorities can. By posing as the wounded fugitive in another neighborhood, Paris pulls the police out of the black area, enabling Jim and Doug to search that part of town. Policeman Phelps examines Maryana's shop but finds nothing (she has hidden Barney in a secret room).

Communicating with her, Barney learns that Maryana's father, one of Kolda's original freedom fighters, was shot by the government. He reasons that her disability may be a psychosomatic reaction to her father's death, and offers to take her to the US. When Barney sends her to the IMF rendezvous Maryana is frightened away by police, but not before Dana notices her and reports to Phelps. Jim returns to her shop and recovers Barney; then Maryana joins the rest of the team in a race to the border.

Paris, badly injured by two locals who try to capture him, is unable to join his cohorts. With the police in hot pursuit, Phelps and company race to a waiting helicopter and make a spectacular recovery of Paris while flying out of the country.

GUEST CAST: Ta Tanisha (Maryana "Gabby" Renfrow), Ivor Barry (Chief Inspector Banco), John Alderson (Follet), John Ragin (Pharmacist), Michael St. Clair (Blacksmith), Elaine Church (Pharmacist's Wife), Edgar Winston (Police Sergeant), Joseph Lancaster (Policeman), Joe Morton (Clerk), Kirk Scott (Guard), Herbert Jefferson Jr. (Luddy). *Unbilled*: Dick Dial (masked Barney)

If one hour fully justifies the risks taken this year, "Hunted" is it, a seamless mesh of rescue and romance. Chief among its assets is young Ta Tanisha as damsel in distress Maryana, toiling away in dingy surroundings and exploited by a greedy, freeloading cousin. Possessing a wonderfully expressive and beautiful face, the actress says visually what pages of dialogue would be hard pressed to convey. Her interplay with Greg Morris offers a rare insight into Barney's sensitivity and makes for some of *Mission*'s most touching moments.

As good as it is, "Hunted" has some questionable plot points. There is little practical reason

for Barney's participation in an apartheid Africa adventure—one can only speculate upon a personal motive for his part in Kolda's liberation. Whatever the reason, his guise as a white man and subsequent unmasking in the series' best teaser almost make the lapse in logic worthwhile. During the finale, the carful of IMFers are chased by a police car in radio contact with the rest of the squad. Jim fires a single shot that not only brings the car to a halt but also prevents the cops inside from responding to their radio! The show's biggest flaw is the use of a New York street as an African ghetto, an extreme example of location miscasting.

Mission: Impossible is often dubbed a badly dated, inescapable product of the sixties with little relevance to the contemporary issues of today. "Hunted" is an excellent counter to that claim, its apartheid theme and scenes of black townsfolk running from the sound of police sirens a sad testimony to the series' enduring topicality, decades after its production.

112: THE AMATEUR

First Aired: 11/14/70

Produced by: Laurence Heath
Written by: Ed Adamson
Directed by: Paul Krasny

TEAM: Phelps, Paris, Dana, Barney, Doug

In an episode which features no tape scene, the mission is to steal an Eastern bloc country's secret weapon, a rocket laser, and smuggle out Father Bernard and his list of Western operatives.

Parish priest Father Bernard puts the team in touch with Max Wittstock, who has access to the weapon. Through Dana in her cover as nightclub waitress, Max arranges a meeting with the IMF and delivers the weapon. Max is killed by pursuing police but the Force eludes capture. Police Colonel Eckert, frantic to retrieve the laser, seals up the country.

Phelps is unable to save Father Bernard, who dies of a sudden stroke, but he does obtain the list of agents. Dana's boss, ambitious nightclub owner Eric Schilling, saw Dana meet with Max. When the police ask questions about the late Wittstock, Schilling keeps his eyes open for any chance to profit. Eckert, suspicious of Schilling, taps his phone and puts him under surveillance.

Barney dismantles the laser into five essential units so each IMFer can take a piece out of the country. Schilling searches Dana's belongings, finds her laser component and steals it, hoping to sell it back to her.

Rejoining her teammates near the airport, Dana discovers the theft and realizes that Schilling is behind it. With no time to return to Schilling's town and retrieve it, Phelps formulates a plan to recover the component *and* board a plane at the intensely guarded airport.

GUEST CAST: Anthony Zerbe (Eric Schilling), Ronald Feinberg (Colonel Kurt Eckert), Lisa Pera (Clara Schram), Don Eitner (Zucker), Bert Kramer (Rausch), Joseph Breen (Danzig), Allen Joseph (Max Wittstock), Peter Brocco (Father Bernard), Biff Manard (Lieutenant Seelik), Al Roberts (Drunk)

Like "Hunted" and "The Innocent," this show pivots around an outsider who becomes entangled in an IMF adventure. This time, however, the interloper isn't an innocent or a conscientious objector; Eric Schilling is a meddler, played to perfection by Anthony Zerbe, who embodies writer Adamson's description: "wily, nasty, crafty, full of self-importance only thinly disguising a sense of futility and failure." Forever jabbing at his forehead to indicate his supposed brilliance, he really believes he can outsmart the police and the IMF. Dumb luck leads him to the component, but when he tries to put the squeeze on Dana and her boys, he gets in over his head.

Schilling's theft temporarily squelches a sly IMF maneuver to sneak onto a flight to Rome. Dana phones Schilling, neither one realizing that Eckert is listening. She asks him to make the long trip to the airport with the unit, but he wants sufficient incentive.

ERIC: I was thinking of kisses. Fifty thousand kisses.

DANA: You win, Eric. Be at the Dornberg Airport in two hours. My brother will meet you in the terminal building. . . . You'll give him a gift for me.

ERIC: But first he will give me a gift from you.

DANA: Eric, you think of everything, don't you?

ERIC: I have a computer for a mind!

Eckert saturates the terminal with secret police and surrounds the airstrip with a phalanx of soldiers, making it impossible for anyone to get from the terminal to the runway.

Did we say impossible?

The police watch Paris (repeating a disguise he used in episode 109, "Decoy") buy the unit from Schilling with counterfeit cash. Schilling is arrested but Paris avoids the cops by doffing his disguise and hiding the unit in an unlocked vending machine, where it is later picked up, unnoticed, by Phelps. Rendezvousing with the others in an airport maintenance truck, Paris calls the airport security chief. Posing as a high government official, Paris explains an impending matter of international importance. A plane lands and discharges passengers before preparing for its next destination, Rome. The IMF truck pulls up near the terminal entrance, out of sight of the soldiers who face the airstrip. Wearing matching blazers and carrying camera gear, the Force calmly exit the truck and stroll into the terminal, blending in with the arriving travelers. Once inside, they are met by the angry security chief. Is the jig up? Hardly. The security man informs this crew from the English Television Network that, upon orders from a high government official, their entry visas have been revoked and they must reboard at once. "You should have instructed your company not to insult our government," he snaps. After some protests, Jim huffily announces, "Very well, we'll leave!" He and his team turn tail, "reboard" the jet and in moments are safely on their way to Rome.

113: THE CATAFALQUE

Written by: Paul Playdon
Directed by: Barry Crane

First Aired: 2/6/71

TEAM: Phelps, Paris, Dana, Barney, Doug

Good morning, Mr. Phelps. Miguel Fuego, premier of San Pascal and his nephew Ramone Fuego, who will one day succeed him to power, have secretly signed a nuclear arms treaty with a hostile power, calling for the installation of nuclear missiles in San Pascal, aimed at the eastern United States. Such an act would trigger another Cuban crisis. Only public exposure of the treaty before the missiles are installed will avert a confrontation that could lead to war. Your mission, Jim, should you choose to accept it, is to get that treaty. As always, should you or any of your IM Force be caught or killed, the secretary will disavow any knowledge of your actions. This tape will self-destruct in five seconds. Good luck, Jim.

Paris, supposedly on the run from the secret police, informs Ramone that Ramone's late father Victorio was killed years ago by his brother Miguel, the country's current premier. Paris insists that *his* father, currently jailed in Madrena Prison, can verify this. Ramone finds this all hard to believe. First, Madrena has been closed for sixty years; second, he cannot believe that his uncle Miguel could have killed his own brother; third, it is common knowledge that Victorio, whose body lies on permanent public display, was killed by government soldiers during the revolution which brought the Fuegos to power. Paris is chased away by policeman Phelps but Ramone, who idolizes his late father, begins to wonder.

Dana lures Ramone into a tryst which is interrupted by her husband Doug. Ramone "kills" Doug, is "arrested" and thrown into Madrena Prison (secretly reopened by the IMF). Ramone knows he's been framed and suspects it has something to do with Paris's claims. He is shocked when an ancient, half-mad "old man" burrows into his cell. Ramone recognizes him as Paris's father, who says that Victorio was never killed and that a diary, which the old man hid prior to his arrest, will tell all. Unfortunately, he can't remember where the diary is hidden. Ramone "escapes" from the prison and abandons the old man, who removes his makeup to reveal himself as Paris.

Believing himself a fugitive, Ramone rejoins the "younger" Paris and tells him that his father died helping Ramone escape. When Paris mournfully relates stories of his dad, a wax sculptor, Ramone suddenly realizes where the old man's diary must be hidden. He and Paris go to Victorio Fuego's shrine, where the body lies in state. Ramone smashes Victorio's wax head, and inside finds the diary which claims that the real Victorio was lobotomized. The diary leads the pair to an asylum where Ramone finds his "father," under an assumed name, vegetating. The diary accuses Miguel Fuego of plotting it all.

Seething with rage, Ramone decides to ruin Miguel by exposing the treaty. He and Paris use a secret passage into Miguel's office, where Ramone removes the treaty from a safe. Paris quietly takes the treaty and steals away with it.

In "The Catafalque," Paris disguises himself as an old man.

GUEST CAST: John Vernon (Ramone Fuego), Will Kuluva (Premier Miguel Fuego), Ramon Bieri (Colonel Rodriguez), Sam Irvin ("Victorio Fuego"), Tony DeCosta (Operative #1), Miguel Riva (First Policeman), Arline Anderson (Nun), John Cardoza (Man #1), Johnny Bench (Captain of the Guards)

Less than a year after his abrupt departure from the show, Paul Playdon couldn't resist coming back and trying one more script, his first for Bruce Lansbury. Playdon was not happy with the end result, and "The Catafalque" would be his final *Mission* teleplay. The episode may not be a classic, but it does contain a visual caper that is one of the series' most outlandish.

In a dark public chamber, the body of Victorio Fuego reposes in a glass casket flanked at all times by four armed guards, their backs to the coffin and heads perpetually bowed in reverence. The guard is changed every hour. Somehow, the IMF must get the real body out of the casket, and the phony one (containing the diary) inside. But how?

Barney and Doug set up in the attic directly above Victorio's catafalque. Attaching handles onto a section of precut flooring, they remove the floor segment which allows them to look directly down on the glass coffin, and mount pulleys on either side of the gap in the floor. Wound onto the pulleys are thin, strong, and barely visible wire cables, with equally strong metal hooks attached to the end of each cable. Doug and Barney lower the cables down to the coffin until the hooks grip the casket. Using the pulleys, they then slowly, carefully lift the casket into the air, over the bowed heads of the guards, and into the attic. Victorio is removed and replaced by the waxwork, then the coffin is lowered back on to the catafalque, just as carefully and soundlessly. Describing the scene renders it as ludicrous as it would undoubtedly be if attempted in the real world. But on screen, backed by Schifrin's tense music and superbly cut by Jerry Taylor, it works perfectly and once again, the absurd seems possible.

"The Catafalque" offers Leonard Nimoy the enjoyable dual role of father and son. As the old man he is required to look as though he's been locked up for twenty years—be ghastly pale and wear a filthy prison uniform. Hairstylist Adele Taylor recalls that Nimoy's hair had to look like it hadn't been washed in years. To achieve the proper stomach-turning effect, Adele broke a cigarette into some styling gel. "Then I swept the makeup room floor and mixed it all together, then put it in the wig." Brought to life by Nimoy at his most inspired, it seemed all too realistic.* "The tobacco looked like little bugs in his hair," says Adele gleefully, "and that worked very well." It was effective enough to help win Bob Dawn an Emmy Award, the last one *Mission* would receive.

---

* Adele points out that since human hair grows at an average rate of a half-inch per month, Nimoy would have needed a wig the size of a lion's mane for the disguise to be 100 percent realistic.

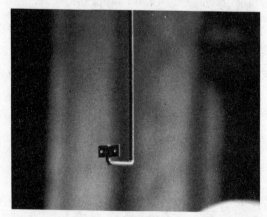

(Top to bottom): Despite armed guards
surrounding the coffin, Barney and
Doug lower thin cables . . .

. . . hook the coffin, and hoist it through the ceiling in this scene from "The Catafalque."

114: SQUEEZE PLAY
    (formerly SICILY)

First Aired: 12/12/70

TEAM: Phelps, Paris, Dana, Barney, Willy

Teleplay by: David Moessinger
Story by: Walter Brough and David Moessinger
Directed by: Virgil W. Vogel

Good morning, Mr. Phelps. Albert Zembra, the supreme boss of the Syndicate's Mediterranean branch which processes one-fourth of the world's illegal supply of heroin, is dying of cancer. Zembra will soon designate a successor to whom he will transfer his secret list of the opium farms, transportation routes, carriers, and corrupt officials through which he operates. Your mission, Jim, should you decide to accept it, is to obtain that secret list and prevent Zembra from perpetuating his empire. As always, should you or any of your IM Force be caught or killed, the secretary will disavow any knowledge of your actions. This tape will self-destruct in five seconds. Good luck, Jim.

Zembra will turn his operations over to his security chief Carlos Empori, who is engaged to Zembra's beautiful and sheltered granddaughter Eve.

Posing as a powerful American mobster who once spent an idyllic childhood summer with Eve at the Zembra estate, Paris visits Zembra and "renews" his friendship with Eve. Phelps, as a deadly rival of Zembra's, warns Carlos that the old man will hand his empire over to the American. He offers Carlos a large role in his organization if he will see to Zembra's demise. Carlos ignores him—at first.

Hired killer Barney penetrates the estate, nearly kills Zembra, and escapes, making a mockery of Carlos's security. Carlos then overhears a conversation between Paris and "Zembra" (Paris) in which the old man bequeathes the business to

Paris. Dejected, Carlos helps Jim kidnap Eve to force Zembra out in the open.

A meeting is held at a deserted factory. Paris enters first to "deal" with Phelps, but the plan stops dead when Eve reveals Paris as a fraud, having caught him in an earlier slipup. With the mission stalemated, Paris forces Eve to face the unpleasant fact that her grandfather is a murderer who must be stopped. He puts his life on the line by continuing the mission and counting upon her silence.

GUEST CAST: Albert Paulsen (Albert Zembra), Nico Minardos (Carlos Empori), Victoria Vetri (Eve Zembra), Nick Georgiade (Vito Nicola), Albert Carrier (Pierre Morat), Peter Kilman (Paul Corrigan)

"Squeeze Play" features one of the series' more credible romances and offers Leonard Nimoy his last substantial role, although the season was in fact only half over. In a typical reversal, the show's heavies seem much more sympathetic than our heroes. Zembra, a killer with an iron hand, is frail and often deceptively charming; Eve tries to ignore the family business by living in an artificial childlike innocence. Carlos the pawn is the most sympathetic. "Squeeze Play" violates a cardinal Woodfield and Balter rule: Never make it seem that the IMF is ganging up on some poor schnook. Actors Albert Paulsen (replacing Luther Adler, who fell ill at the last minute), Victoria Vetri, and Nico Minardos are so adept at shading their roles that when Paris levels with Eve at the end of the show, his words remind *us* as well as Eve just who the bad guys are.

PARIS: You've shut your eyes to it. Eve, he manufactures heroin. That destroys people by the thousands. Not quickly, not mercifully, but by slow degrees. . . . Your grandfather is a murderer.

Eve breaks down, knowing it to be true, and lets the game be played out. In a particularly

deft and speedy denouement, Carlos is exposed as a traitor, then eliminated by Zembra. Heartbroken, the old man gives Paris the secret information. Alone with Eve, Paris tries to comfort her.

PARIS: You're free now . . . I can help you.

EVE: I don't want your help. My grandpapa needs me. I'm not free until he dies.

PARIS: And then?

EVE: Then I try to forget.

She returns to her grandfather's limousine and drives off, as much a creature of duty as is Paris.

115: THE MERCHANT

Written by: Harold Livingston
Directed by: Leon Benson

First Aired: 3/17/71

TEAM: Phelps, Paris, Dana, Barney, Willy, others

Good evening, Mr. Phelps. For several years Armand Anderssarian has been one of the world's largest dealers in illegal arms. Now Anderssarian is about to complete his biggest deal, involving the purchase and resale of millions of dollars worth of American arms captured in Vietnam to guerrilla groups in key troubled areas of the world. If Anderssarian succeeds, new violence and bloodshed is inevitable. Your mission, should you choose to accept it, is to stop Anderssarian and put him out of business for good. This tape will self-destruct in five seconds. Good luck, Jim.

Anderssarian is set to hand over a balance of five million dollars for the arms upon delivery, which is imminent. When he discovers troubleshooter Phelps's scheme to steal a neighboring country's secret radar system, Anderssarian decides to sponsor the theft with five million dollars fronted by corrupt Minister of Defense Sartori. Anderssarian plans to sell the system for twenty million dollars.

Jim, Willy, and other IMF commandos stage an elaborate raid on the (IMF) radar station. They deliver the equipment and take the five million dollars—after which Sartori finds the material to be useless. He angrily demands reimbursement from Anderssarian, who has lost *his* five million to Paris in an electronically gimmicked poker game. Unable to purchase the arriving weaponry or repay Sartori, Anderssarian's fate is sealed.

GUEST CAST: George Sanders (Armand Anderssarian), Jo Morrow (Nicole Dubois), Jan Merlin (Leon), Ken Drake (Minister of Defence Karel Sartori), Todd Martin (Captain Ionescu), James Hong (Yin), Tony Giorgio (Croupier), Carmelo Manto (Manager), Noel DeSouza (Player #2), Riza Royce (Player #5)

This season's casino show was the final one aired this year and rightly so, as it is mostly a rehash of earlier plots, specifically episode 43, "The Emerald," in which another arms dealer was swindled by Barney's electronically sensitive poker tablecloth coupled with secret transmissions to an IMF player wearing mike-receiver eyeglasses. Writer Livingston freshens the bit by having Anderssarian uncover the scam (with IMF help). Anderssarian, who wears a hearing aid, adjusts the frequency so he can eavesdrop on Barney's bulletins to player Paris. He doesn't know that Barney is transmitting on *two* frequencies—one for Anderssarian's benefit, the other strictly for Paris. During the final game in which Paris must bankrupt the arms dealer, there is another twist: Anderssarian's girlfriend Nicole, sick of his terrible treatment of her and privy to the computer con, deliberately spills her drink across the table, shorting out the computer in the hopes of ruining Anderssarian. Barney cannot repair the damage, forcing Paris to rely on his own skills at poker to break Anderssarian. Guess who wins.

During the IMF radar station raid, Anderssarian's representative Leon watches our boys, dressed in Red Cross uniforms and gas masks, spray the compound with a "lethal" vapor in order to gain access. Had Leon seen the movie *Goldfinger* (1964), he'd have recognized the trick as a direct steal from the James Bond film, in which an attack on Fort Knox was faked in exactly the same way.

One of the show's most distressing aspects is the casting of George Sanders, once one of the screen's great rogues, as Anderssarian. "I remember him being a very depressed, sad man," says Leonard Nimoy. "He sat quietly by himself, did not interact with anybody." Says Peter

Graves, "It was sad, because this was near the end."* Greg Morris agrees. "Of all the guest stars that we had, he was probably the biggest shock. The man was a shell." Actor Tony Giorgio recalls Sanders cutting up his script and placing his lines in the palm of his hand or on tabletops. In his first scene with Graves, Sanders is seen in close-up, obviously reading his lines. When at the finale Anderssarian realizes his predicament and laughs helplessly, Sanders could not play the scene believably. As for Anderssarian, satisfaction over his downfall is largely negated since his supplier has already informed him that should Anderssarian default, the arms will simply go to the next highest bidder.

An important story point concerns Anderssarian's interest in card shill Dana who, according to the script, is to look exceptionally beautiful. This presented costumer Dodie Schaefer with quite a challenge: How to make Lesley Warren even more alluring than usual? "How can *anyone*," she wondered, "walk into a big colorful casino and make heads turn?" For the opening outfit, Lesley wore a Schaefer-fashioned, "handkerchief dress before its time, and a red head wrap. I was still making her shoes, by hand, the morning we went to camera." The footwear, never seen on-screen, indicates Dodie's attention to detail. All of Lesley's clothing in "The Merchant" mark a change in style: Dana's fresh, hip look was supplanted by a more mature, glamorous one for the only time. When she showed up for the final scene in a spectacular evening dress, Leonard Nimoy (himself spiffily attired in mod tux, tortoiseshell eyeglasses, and sideburns) reeled in mock horror at the thought of this gorgeous woman standing behind him and stealing the scene. "But that was the idea," says Dodie Schaefer. "It worked out great and everybody was happy with it—including Leonard."

---

* Sanders would commit suicide the following year.

315

116: CAT'S PAW

Produced by: Laurence Heath
Written by: Howard Browne
Directed by: Virgil W. Vogel

First Aired: 1/9/71

TEAM: Phelps, Paris, Dana, Barney, Willy

In a departure from the series format, the IMF assists Barney in his attempt to avenge the murder of his brother.

Newspaperman Larry Collier was murdered while trying to establish a link between corrupt police Captain Abbott and George Corley, head of a ghetto mob. Corley's insurance company fronts his illegal activities.

Barney meets Corley when he "rescues" his secretary Millie from a "mugger." Learning of Barney's past as a crooked accountant, Corley hires him to assist Goslin, a holdover from a mob Corley muscled out. Willy plants ten thousand dollars extra in the receipts which Barney "uncovers," putting Goslin in a bad light with Corley.

An IMF séance convinces Goslin to leave Corley and take incriminating evidence with him. He steals Corley's computer notebook and is promptly arrested by Detective Phelps, who makes him reveal a code which implicates Abbott.

Syndicate man Phelps uses the codebook to force Abbott into deserting Corley and backing Jim's new mob. Then Jim bribes Corley's gunsel Pod Hamp to kill Corley. Barney overpowers the killer and saves Corley's life. Corley runs but is picked up by Detective Phelps, who threatens to take him to Abbott's precinct. Knowing that Abbott would kill him, Corley agrees to talk to the district attorney, providing the case against himself and Abbott.

GUEST CAST: Hari Rhodes (George Corley), Abbey Lincoln (Millie Webster), William Wintersole (William Goslin), Kelly Thordsen (Captain Dave Abbott), Chuck Wood (Pod Hamp), Marc Hannibal (Larry Collier), Manuel Paul Thomas (District Attorney Scanlon), Morgan Farley (Wyatt), Dave Cass (Pinari)

Mystery novelist and screenwriter Howard Browne made his *Mission* debut when Bruce Lansbury called him in for an uncredited rewrite. Since Laurence Heath wanted another romance for Barney, and since Browne was a series fan whose favorite cast member was Greg Morris, Browne's first full *Mission* script was fairly easy work. It was so much to everyone's liking that Browne was invited to return to the show as often as he pleased. And although he would write only three more *Mission*s, Browne was a significant asset to the series, his snappy dialogue and tight plots a boon for a show suddenly emphasizing characterization and crime stories. As Browne describes it, "The challenge was to paint yourself into a corner that you cannot get out of. Then you get out of it." His characters, particularly in "Cat's Paw," seem more realistic than most of the people who populate the world of *Mission: Impossible*. "It's more interesting if you have human beings in an unsolvable problem rather than a bunch of sticks," he feels. Browne was busy on other series, but coming back to *Mission* was always a pleasure. "It was a relaxed show to work for. You do your best work when you're in a group that respects your work and you respect what they do. I admired Larry Heath tremendously. I've done quite a bit of story editing myself,* but Larry Heath was the best."

---

* Browne story edited many Twentieth Century-Fox series of the 1950s and 60s as well as Paramount's *Longstreet* (1971–72).

"Cat's Paw" seems the type of plot that could fit any cop show, but it makes a remarkably good *Mission.* Barney's brother, his violent death, and Barney's remorseless seduction of Corley's secretary Millie make the show memorable. The fun of seeing Barney with his big brother is shortlived, for soon Larry Collier is a victim of a firebomb, and Barney sobs over the body in the most emotional scene any series regular would play. His romance with Millie is driven by a ruthlessness all the more striking by the ease with which he hides it. Barney was not insensitive, according to Greg Morris, who ought to know. "It never came out, because that's not what the show was all about, but he was sensitive to the fact that he made this woman fall in love with him so he can get revenge for the death of his brother," Greg says. "While he's setting this whole thing up, he's not too crazy about what he's doing to her. But there's nothing he can do about it."

Millie Webster is the show's pivotal character. As written, she is classy, witty, vulnerable, and pretty—an unusually real character. Understanding how important the role was, Greg asked for Abbey Lincoln, the singer and occasional actress who garnered fine reviews for her work in the features *Nothing But a Man* (1964) and *For Love of Ivy* (1968). Ms. Lincoln, a selective actress, took the role because it was like none other she had ever been offered. Her finest moment comes at the finale, when she silently breaks down during Barney's confession. "At the end, I was supposed to look into Greg's eyes as if I wanted to fall into his arms," Abbey relates. "But I brought myself to the role, and my character did not want to fall into his arms. She wished him dead because he had betrayed her confidence." When Greg exits at the end of the scene, Abbey ad-libbed a bloodcurdling, "Drop dead!" Fifteen years later, Howard Browne still remembers the line and marvels. "I've never heard those two words said better!"

"I came to work angry that day," adds Abbey. "I had prepared for the scene and was really pleased when I got to the end of it. When I see the show, it always makes me feel good. So far I haven't appeared in anything that I don't really like; that's why I do so few things. This *Mission: Impossible* was something I could do, and I was glad to do it too."

117: THE HOSTAGE

Written by: Harold Livingston
Directed by: Barry Crane

First Aired: 12/19/70

TEAM: Phelps, Dana, Barney, Doug

In a departure from the series format, Paris is abducted by Latin American revolutionists who think he is an influential U.S. businessman.

Still in his cover after a completed mission, Paris is kidnapped by Robert Siomney, a notorious terrorist currently working with the Popular Revolutionary Front. Siomney demands the release of three PRF prisoners including Luis Cabal, son of PRF leader Jorge Cabal. If the rebels are not released within twenty-four hours, Paris will die.

By simulating symptoms of Hodgkin's disease, Paris forces his captors to radio the government and arrange to have medication air-dropped in an isolated location. Pilot Barney delivers a vial of "medication" with a transmitter in its cap, enabling the Force to pinpoint the hidden PRF base.

In direct response to Siomney's demands, government prosecutor Phelps condemns the three prisoners to death by firing squad unless Paris is freed. Incredulous, Siomney assures Cabal that the government is bluffing, but when the first two "executions" are televised, Cabal fears for the life of the remaining prisoner, his son Luis.

Posing as Luis's girlfriend, Dana enters the PRF compound and begs Cabal to spare Luis by freeing the American. Afraid that Dana will sway Cabal, Siomney quietly orders his assistant Frederico to kill her. Barney penetrates the base, overwhelms and "becomes" Frederico, and saves Dana.

While his father watches helplessly on television, Luis Cabal is brought before the firing squad. Siomney, with nothing left to lose, orders "Frederico" to shoot Paris. Luis gets an unexpected reprieve, one final chance for Cabal to free Paris. Before Cabal can act, there is a gunshot, and Paris is "dead." Furious that Siomney has defied him and surely doomed Luis, Cabal radios the government and agrees to a new trade: Siomney, "Frederico," and Paris's "corpse" are delivered to the government, and young Cabal's "death sentence" is commuted to a jail term.

GUEST CAST: Lou Antonio (Robert Siomney), Joe DeSantis (Jorge Cabal), Lee Duncan (Frederico), David Renard (Carlos Marchese), Pepe Callahan (Ortega), Conrad M. Parham (Roerca), Ron Castro (Luis Cabal)

One day while Laurence Heath and Harold Livingston were golfing, they discussed the latest turn of events in the endless Middle East conflict. Several Israeli soldiers had been captured, and the ransom demanded was the release of imprisoned opposition forces. Livingston said he'd enjoy seeing the Israeli government stalemate the kidnappers by charging *their* prisoners as accessories to the Israelis' murder. Heath, ever the story man, replied, "That would make a good *Mission.*" He was correct.

As originally written it is Doug who is grabbed, making the Hodgkin's ploy much more believable. Perhaps because Doug was too new a figure to engender sufficient audience concern, it is Paris who, before being jailed, discreetly grabs a handful of wild berries growing nearby. Alone in his cell, he eats the berries, which conveniently give him the look of a lymphomatosis sufferer. "Paris and I talked about Hodgkin's only a few weeks ago," Doug tells the rest of the IMF. "He must have found something that would give him a chill and a fever." A weak explanation to be sure, but the only one possible.

For his Frederico impersonation, Barney suddenly demonstrates talents for mask making, using a quick-set plastic liquid instead of a latex face. Leonard Nimoy, given less and less challenging roles in recent shows, began thinking "that the handwriting is on the wall. I

remember Bruce Geller being upset about such a crossover taking place. If something like that had happened on *Star Trek,* I'd have been picketing the studio." But since *Mission* gave Nimoy no emotional involvement, he had already decided that this season would be his last.

"The Hostage" addresses the subject of terrorism directed against Americans on foreign soil, a rare occurrence when the show was filmed but an all too common one in the decade to follow. The foreign setting allows the dubious ruse of a government sanctioning its own terrorism as a response against revolutionists. In an early script, hostage Doug goads his captors by explaining that the government has now learned to fight with their own weapons of terror. They are fully prepared to sacrifice him, he adds, because they will no longer submit to blackmail. To his chagrin, Siomney finds the government playing by *his* rules. In the finished episode, the prison *comandante* views Phelps's plan with skepticism. "The people you are dealing with are ruthless," he tells Jim. "They have nothing to lose. What can one do with such people?" Phelps says nothing, letting his plan speak for him. "The Hostage" offers a solution which, while too farfetched for reality, makes for a good show. Like episode 111, "Hunted," after two decades it has become more relevant than when it was produced.

118: TAKEOVER

Produced by: Laurence Heath
Teleplay by: Arthur Weiss
Story by: Jerry Thomas and Arthur Weiss
Directed by: Virgil W. Vogel
Music Composed and Conducted by:
   Lalo Schifrin

First Aired: 1/2/71

TEAM: Phelps, Paris, Dana, Barney, Doug

Good morning, Mr. Phelps. This man, boss Charles Peck, has determined to elevate his puppet, Mayor Steve Tallman, to the governorship of his state in the forthcoming election. Peck's plan calls for creating an image of Tallman as a strong man who knows how to deal with dissent, in contrast to his opponent, the incumbent governor, who is to be blamed for the violence which this young man, professional provocateur Billy Walsh, will provoke. Jim, this kind of disorder is severely damaging the prestige and influence of the United States throughout the free world. Your mission, should you decide to accept it, is to prevent bloodshed and to destroy Charles Peck for good. This tape will self-destruct in five seconds. Good luck, Jim.

Days before the local college's "protest week" is to commence, known provocateur Dana is arrested, and antiriot officer Barney arrives to oversee the demonstrations.

Walsh bails Dana out, and together they plot a violent protest which will culminate in the shooting of the governor's representative—Barney. Blackmailer Paris introduces Mayor Tallman to his illegitimate daughter—revolutionist Dana. When Peck hears of this, he fears that Dana's presence will weaken Tallman, so he orders Walsh to kill her, among others, during the demonstration.

As planned, Walsh, Dana, and other students seize the Municipal Building on the first day of protest week. When a student-police showdown seems inevitable, Dana pleads for more student input into educational affairs. Peck becomes enraged when "Tallman" (Paris) suddenly agrees with her. Peck orders Walsh to shoot the mayor, but Barney overpowers him and disarms a Walsh booby trap meant to kill police *and* demonstrators. "Tallman" exposes himself and Peck before the TV cameras, and Peck and Walsh are jailed.

GUEST CAST: Lloyd Bochner (Mayor Steve Tallman), Ken Swofford (Deputy Mayor Charles Peck), Richard Kelton (Billy Walsh), Todd Martin (Lieutenant Ross), Russel Thorson (Chief Danby), Byron Mabe (First Officer), Gordon DeVol (Alec), Tom McDonough (College Guard)

One of the odder year five shows, "Takeover" isn't really a *Mission: Impossible* literally or in concept. A strange segment back in 1971, its theme of campus unrest and storm-trooping police still belongs in the sixties. The mission sounds more suited to the Mod Squad than the IMF. "What we have to do," says Jim at the outset, "is to control the violence, so that *we're* the only ones in danger." To see our dirty tricksters going to such lengths to protect not only the local police and innocent bystanders but hippie students as well seems incongruous.

"Takeover" features good performances, including Graves's fascistic millionaire and villains Bochner and Swofford, but the show belongs to Lesley Warren, and is the only *Mission* to exhibit the promise she would later realize. Too young and all-American to convincingly portray a worldly secret agent, she is just right as a fervent college activist. When Paris introduces her to Tallman, the "father" who abandoned her, Dana must fake several conflicting emotions, all thinly veiled by a false bravado and a pair of tearful eyes. It is a perfectly realized insincerity and Lesley Warren's finest moment in the series.

119: THE MISSILE
(formerly TORPEDO)

First Aired: 1/16/71

TEAM: Phelps, Paris, Dana, Barney, Willy

Written by: Arthur Weiss
Directed by: Charles R. Rondeau

Good morning, Mr. Phelps. This is James Reed, a systems analyst with the Baltimore Corporation. He will arrive forty-eight hours from now at the Weapons Test Center to conduct an authorized survey of that facility. Reed is a foreign agent. His objective is to obtain the electronic guidance system of our latest missiles now being tested. His contact at the naval facility is Doris Gordon, a civilian secretary. Your mission, Jim, should you decide to accept it, is to allow Reed to steal a bogus guidance system in place of the real one, thereby short-stopping enemy weapons development in this vital field. This tape will self-destruct in five seconds. Good luck, Jim.

Dana replaces Doris Gordon and Jim becomes her boss, one of only two men with access to the missile lab. Reed photographs a tryst between lovers Dana and Phelps to blackmail family man Phelps. Reed tells Dana of his plan to kill Jim after the operation, but before she can warn Jim she is abducted by homicidal psychopath John Hecker, who believes Dana is a former girlfriend—a woman he killed.

While Jim allows Reed to photograph the phony missile guidance system, Barney and Paris try to find Dana. Meanwhile, Reed's accomplice tampers with Jim's car.

Paris and Barney locate Dana and subdue the killer. Dana calls Jim on his car phone just as Reed jams his brakes and steering by remote control. Jim jumps undetected from the car before it crashes. Reed, thinking Phelps dead, is convinced that his mission is a success.

GUEST CAST: David Sheiner (James Reed), John Beck (John Hecker), John Pickard (Commander Wardman), Gerald Hiken (Farrell), Karen Carlson (Doris Gordon), John Dennis (Duke), Barry Coe (Bob Willard), Percy Helton (Dailey), Jimmy Bracken (Bobby)

Charley Rondeau directed five year one *Mission*s before moving on to other Paramount properties like *The Odd Couple, Barefoot in the Park* and innumerable *Love, American Style*s. Now, to finish off a commitment he was back on *Mission,* and his four-year absence gave him a unique perspective of what had happened to the series. His mentor, Bruce Geller, was gone; so was the seemingly unlimited budget and freedom to reshoot he had enjoyed in earlier days. He found the script of "The Missile" unimpressive and the cast hardworking but tired. "It was terrible," he says. "No one liked the show and everyone seemed to want to get off it." His one nice experience was working with Lesley Warren, whom he put in one of his *Love, American Style* skits.

A minor sequence gives Peter Lupus a rare moment of glory. When Barney steps into a trap meant for Phelps, a heavy metal door closes behind him and he finds himself locked in a burning firetrap. Standing outside, Willy uses all his muscle to pry open the door and save Barney. The scene reminds us of Willy's original function as strongman, not chauffeur, but by now the plots called for this talent so infrequently that the character seemed virtually expendable—or so some believed.

120: KITARA
(formerly THE BIGOT)

Produced by: Laurence Heath
Written by: Mann Rubin
Directed by: Murray Golden
Music Composed and Conducted by:
  Richard Hazard

First Aired: 2/20/71

TEAM: Phelps, Paris, Dana, Barney, Doug

Good morning, Jim. This is John Darcy, code name Kitara, leader of a liberation movement in the African nation of Bocamo, which for over a century has been ruled by a colonial minority practicing severe racial segregation. Darcy has been captured by Colonel Alex Kohler, a provincial governor and a ruthless tyrant. If Kohler succeeds in torturing Darcy into revealing his true identity, the liberation movement, deprived of leadership and inspiration, will be destroyed. Your mission, should you choose to accept it, is to free Darcy and end Kohler's tyranny. As always, if you or any member of your IM Force is caught or killed, the secretary will disavow any knowledge of your actions. Good luck, Jim.

Darcy was caught in Kohler's province after stealing a truckful of government gold bullion. Kohler is determined to recover the gold and eliminate Darcy as soon as he can torture a confession from him.

Officers Phelps and Doug enter to verify Darcy's identity for headquarters. Barney, caught looting Kohler's home, is jailed—alongside Darcy. Via Morse code, Barney reveals himself to Darcy, learns the whereabouts of the hidden gold, and relays the information, via verbal code, to Phelps during an interrogation. Jim finds the gold in a deserted village hut—and leaves it there.

Doug tells Kohler of *"Lamposa hycondra,"* a rare ailment which causes blacks posing as white to abruptly revert to their "true" colors. That night Kohler takes a shower and goes to sleep. In the morning he is completely, utterly and inexplicably *black*. Despite his efforts to conceal himself, Kohler's dread "condition" is discovered by journalist Dana. Through her, Kohler meets local shopkeeper Paris, who happens to hold photographic "proof" that Kohler's grandfather was black. Kohler, an orphan, finds the evidence revolting but irrefutable.

His career over and his life in ruins, Kohler flees. Paris graciously takes him to a hiding place—the hut where the gold is hidden. The authorities find Kohler there, presume him to be the *real* Kitara (with IMF help), and arrest him. As Phelps and Doug prepare to return to headquarters with prisoners Barney and Darcy, a teletype arrives from "headquarters," ordering Phelps to take the gold with him. "Very well," Jim grumbles wearily, "but hurry it up, please."

GUEST CAST: Lawrence Dobkin (Colonel Alex Kohler), Rex Holman (Captain Maxfield), Robert Doqui (John Darcy), Jason Wingreen (Hawn), Ken Renard (Grandfather), Buck Holland (First Guard)

Mann Rubin's three *Mission* scripts center around racism. In the first two (episode 19, "The Legend" and episode 38, "Echo of Yesterday") the resurgence of Nazism is ironically quelled by party heroes Bormann and Hitler (both impersonated by Rollin Hand). In "Kitara" the backdrop is apartheid Africa, and the irony especially sweet when racist Kohler is led to think he's the very thing he's despised all his life. "Laurence Heath and I started talking about ideas," Rubin says, "and I think that he came up with the idea of turning Kohler black. I immediately said, 'Oh fantastic!' It was a great idea and we worked out of that structure."

An ultraviolet sterilizer lamp in Kohler's bathroom does the trick, aided by a pill dropped into his tea. When Kohler wakes up in the morning and looks in the mirror, he is as dark as Barney. Director Murray Golden remembers how potentially fatal the scene could have been.

"That could have been hilariously funny. I talked about it with Larry Dobkin, who played Kohler and is also a director. We tried to do everything to keep it serious, because a comic reaction would have been the end of this show." The look of horror and disbelief on Kohler's face is priceless and anything but comic.

Leonard Nimoy, by now eagerly awaiting the end of the season and his exit from the series, didn't let his impatience affect the quality of his work. In "Kitara" he is a local shopkeeper, a minor role. According to Golden, "We were having lunch together on location and he hadn't yet done his scenes. He said, 'I haven't got a bead on this character yet and I really don't know what the hell to do with him.'" With Golden, Nimoy worked out a meticulous, prissy, very neat gentleman, right down to his white gloves. By doing so, he made an unimportant character memorable.

In the finale, Kohler is chased through the jungle and arrested by his own troops. Author Rubin preferred another ending: "I had a scene where Kohler tried to seek refuge in a black home, and he begins to feel what it's like to be a black man after being such a rigid white supremacist. It could have been a very effective scene, but it was eliminated. They were on a very hurried schedule and I never got a chance to do a final polish." "Kitara" was indeed rushed. The earliest work draft, in effect the *first* draft, was completed November 1, 1970, only eight days before it would be filmed, and this before the inevitable rewrites (David Moessinger of "Squeeze Play" had an uncredited turn at the script).

At the wrap-up, Darcy asks Doug how long Kohler will remain black.

DOUG: About a week, after which both he and Maxfield* will probably turn very red.

---

* Kohler's immediate subordinate and eventual successor.

121: THE FIELD

Produced by: Laurence Heath
Teleplay by: Wesley Lau
Story by: Judy Burns and Wesley Lau
Directed by: Reza S. Badiyi

First Aired: 1/23/71

TEAM: Phelps, Paris, Dana, Barney, Doug

Good morning, Mr. Phelps. This satellite, launched this morning by a hostile power, contains several thermonuclear bombs, each large enough to destroy any capital city in the world. Controls for the weapon, which is designed for international blackmail, are situated on this fortified island in the Adriatic. The installation is protected by a sophisticated mine field designed by an American defector, Arthur Norris, and considered to be impenetrable. Your mission, should you choose to accept it, is to destroy the satellite. As always, should you or any member of your IM Force be caught or killed, the secretary will disavow any knowledge of your actions. This tape will self-destruct in five seconds. Good luck, Jim.

More than 1000 land mines surround the island stronghold's key installations: the Computer Center controlling the satellite, and the Command Center which controls the mine field.

Barney lands via submarine on the island. Outside the mine field, he fires projectiles to trigger some of the mines. Unable to find the source of these sudden blasts, the Command Center calls for Arthur Norris. No one on the island has ever seen Norris, so Paris, eschewing a disguise, arrives as Norris with the mine field plans (stolen earlier by Phelps). Paris shuts down part of the field so he can "work"—and so Barney can cross the field with the help of a meter which tells him when it's safe to move. In the Computer Center, Barney fouls the satellite's system, programming it to drop from orbit and burn up in the earth's atmosphere.

On the mainland, Norris is "taken out" by the IMF, but not before he murders his girlfriend, a government spy. When her body is found, "Norris" becomes the chief murder suspect. Paris is arrested and taken back to the mainland under police custody. The mine field is instantly reactivated—while Barney is crossing it to exit. He stops in his tracks to avoid being blown to bits. To save Barney, Jim must first somehow clear Paris of the murder charge before Police Inspector Koder, who knows Norris, can expose Paris as an imposter.

GUEST CAST: Michael Baseleon (Detective Lieutenant Rab), Denny Miller (Arthur Norris), Milton Selzer (Inspector Koder), Barry Atwater (General Marin), H. M. Wynant (Captain Strom), Patricia Priest (Kathrine Berat), Burt Nodella (General Bloch), Erik Holland (Lieutenant)

"The Field" offers much of what makes *Mission: Impossible* great—a tough assignment well worked out, a disastrous impediment, and an unexpected checkmate to save the day.

After they zap the real Norris in his apartment, Jim, Dana, and Doug are interrupted by Rab and Koder, two policemen looking for clues that will link Norris to the murder of his girl, Kathrine Berat. The IMFers hide themselves and the unconscious Norris, then listen as the detectives discuss the case. After they leave, Phelps kicks off his attempt to save Barney and Paris.

Doug injects Norris with a drug which simulates the symptoms of a heart attack. Norris awakens in pain, suffering from shortness of breath *and* hard-nosed Inspector Phelps, who grills him relentlessly about the murder. Doctor Doug arrives with medication—but Jim won't let it be administered until Norris confesses. In a terrified cold sweat, Norris explains the crime and reveals the hiding place of the murder weapon.

At police headquarters Paris is questioned by Rab, who calls for Koder. It's all over if Koder sees Paris, so the detective is tripped down a flight of stairs by Jim and quickly needled unconscious by Doug, who calls for an ambulance. Paris is no longer in danger of being exposed. Now all he has to do is wriggle out of a murder charge.

Rab informs Paris that a witness has come forth, and in walks Dana. Paris knows she is there to get him off the hook, but he doesn't know how she'll do it. In an artfully written, intensely played, and ingeniously thought out scene, Dana gives Paris enough subtle clues to enable him to force her to admit that, in a jealous fury, *she* killed Kathrine! Dana collapses, confesses, and even tells Rab where "she" hid the gun. Rab calls for a guard to take her away; officer Doug enters and drags her out. Paris, now exonerated, calls the Command Center and orders the field shut down until he "returns," allowing Barney to escape.

Because the confession scene was so crucial, two versions were written, one long and one short. Despite the fact that the longer version was picked, Leonard Nimoy wasn't convinced that the scene would play or that the audience would fully understand what was happening. But, says director Reza Badiyi, Nimoy, "put so much into it, he was wonderful and so was she. The acting elements in *Mission* were rare and very limited, unless they were built into the situation. Lenny would grab those moments and give a little bit more, and that scene was one of them." The scene serves not just as an example of the almost telepathic communication between IMFers, but also the diligence of Nimoy and Lesley Warren, both of whom couldn't wait to get out of the series at this point.

"The Field" is the last true international caper and marks the last time the "disavow any knowledge" disclaimer was used in the tape scene. In a way, it also stamped the end of *Mission*'s Bruce Geller era, although Geller had in fact already vacated the premises. Despite his absence and the series' changes, Geller's spirit and influence lingered. How did he engender such loyalty from cast and crew? Reza Badiyi tells a Geller story which took place during the making of "The Field," a story, "so unique that I'll never forget it. We were on location in Fort MacArthur near San Pedro and I was very worried because I was about to become a father. My wife was in Hollywood and about to go into labor. Bruce said, 'Don't worry, when the time comes you'll be in the hospital before Barbara.'" For two days, Geller had a helicopter standing by so his director wouldn't miss the blessed event. "People don't do those things anymore," sighs Badiyi. "He surmised that my full attention should be on my work. After all, the best producers shell themselves around the director. They let him be on the set and do his thing, they keep problems away from the set. He was that kind of person, an exceptional gentleman who was always there for you."

Little wonder that *Mission*'s family stayed so loyal to the missing man in charge.

122: BLAST

First Aired: 1/30/71

Written by: James L. Henderson and Sam Roeca
Directed by: Sutton Roley

TEAM: Phelps, Paris, Dana, Barney, Willy

Good morning, Mr. Phelps. This man, Gregory Tolan, is leader of an underground cell specializing in robberies designed to finance an American revolution. Tolan works for a man we know only as Jonathon Brace, who masterminds cells like Tolan's all over the country and whose eventual aim is the forcible overthrow of the United States government. Your mission, should you choose to accept it, is to apprehend and destroy Jonathon Brace. This tape will self-destruct in five seconds. Good luck, Jim.

Tolan's next target is Drake's Armored Transport Company. Demolitions expert Phelps and Drake's insider Dana are Tolan's latest recruits, joining hired guns Klinger and Sheels. The IMF must ensure the heist's success so they can trace Tolan to the mysterious Mr. Brace. Although Drake's cooperates with the team, for security reasons the police are not informed.

With Dana's help, the thieves "crack" Drake's and take over one million dollars. But when Jim deflects Klinger's attempt to shoot clerk Willy, the bullet breaks a window and alarms sound, alerting the police and wrecking the IMF plot. The crooks run, taking refuge in an empty suburban home. Theorizing that Brace will not pick up the cash personally, Phelps must provide Tolan with a safe way out of the house. Jim exits, supposedly to steal a car, and hatches a new scenario involving Paris. Jim returns with a (bugged) car. Paris and IMF operative Grace enter as the home's owners and are tied up by the criminals. Upon Brace's radioed instructions, Tolan and Dana take the money and run, leaving the others to kill the hostages and follow. When Dana and Tolan exit, Jim gets the drop on Sheels and Klinger. The IMF follows Tolan and Dana to Jonathon Brace.

GUEST CAST: Henry Darrow (Gregory Tolan), Kevin Hagen (Dave Klinger), Larry Haddon (Lee Sheels), Douglas Henderson (George Miller), Susan Odin (Grace), Pitt Herbert (Hendricks), Tamara Eliott (Monica Anderson), Charles Picerni (Juan Delgado), Tom McDonough (William Cabot), Dick Ziker (Finley), Don Edwards (Policeman). *Unbilled:* George Wilbur (double, Phelps), Tony Brubaker (double, Barney)

"Blast" introduces the writing team of Sam Roeca and Jim Henderson to the series, two journeymen with extensive TV and feature work, together and singly. "I really wasn't too fond of 'Blast,'" Roeca admits. Indeed, of the seven *Mission*s he and Henderson wrote, this is certainly a lesser entry. In the original story, Tolan's gang knocks over a bank and Doug is nominally involved as an armored truck guard. To save money, Doug was written out and the heist relocated to a counting house so it could be filmed entirely (yes, you guessed it) on the backlot. The Scenic Department Building makes a cameo appearance as Tolan's headquarters.

Sutton Roley was about to direct a *Movie of the Week* when a call from Bruce Lansbury lured him back for this, his first *Mission* since episode 64, "The Test Case." Roley is infamous within the industry as an extremely creative and excitable director. At times he has been so determined to shoot the images he visualizes that cameramen and crews have refused to work with him. Roley's contributions to "Blast" were minimal, however, as he was eager to begin his TV movie. "I really didn't spend that much time on 'Blast,'" he recalls. "It was over quickly and I did the *Movie of the Week*. I liked Lesley Ann Warren, though." The show does

contain some typically offbeat Roley touches. Kevin Hagen plays gunman Klinger as a psycho with dark glasses, a flat voice, and more than a touch of the young Richard Widmark. Also, a brief scene between Paris and the homeowner he impersonates is actually played for laughs and is something of a shock within the structure of the show.

Any oldtime TV writer or producer will tell you that a sure sign of a fading series is the appearance of a *Desperate Hours* episode, one which, like the 1956 Humphrey Bogart film, involves a group of people holed up in one location. It's an easy type of show to produce and is usually shot at the end of the season to save money. After five years, *The Desperate Hours* scene finally worked its way into *Mission: Impossible.* While "bottle shows" like this can be an absorbing change of pace for some series, it is ineffective within *Mission*'s format, mainly because the plot is so standard and a staple of every other "cop series" ever made. One can only hope that the studio saved a lot of money on it.

123: A GHOST STORY

First Aired: 2/27/71

Teleplay by: Ed Adamson and Ken Pettus
Story by: John D. F. Black and Ed Adamson
Directed by: Reza S. Badiyi
Music Composed and Conducted by:
    Benny Golson

TEAM: Phelps, Paris, Dana, Barney, Willy

Good morning, Mr. Phelps. This is Howard Bainbridge, noted specialist in chemical warfare who defected to the East, where he developed the lethal chemical TRA, a nerve gas formula known only to him. We believe that Bainbridge, contaminated by his own deadly chemical, escaped the Iron Curtain and returned to his father's estate, where the elder Bainbridge killed his son and concealed the corpse. Since Howard Bainbridge destroyed all his records before fleeing the East, the only existing trace of the chemical TRA is in his corpse. Your mission, Jim, should you choose to accept it, is to find Howard Bainbridge's body. This tape will self-destruct in five seconds. Good luck, Jim.

After attacking his son Howard during an argument, Justin Bainbridge hastily buried the body on his huge estate. He doesn't know that his chief of grounds security, Vincent Sandler, is an enemy agent intent on finding the corpse.

Jim enters as new tutor to Bainbridge's grandson. His comrades sneak into an abandoned air raid shelter with access to the main house. While Bainbridge sleeps that night, microspeakers are implanted in his ears, his ring is replaced by a duplicate containing a microphone, and Barney installs holographic projectors in his bedposts.

Soon Bainbridge is terrified by phenomena which only he can see and hear: an incessant heartbeat; the image of his dead son in a drinking glass; oboe music (Howard's late wife, Janette, whom Bainbridge had never met, played the instrument).

The "ghost" of Howard appears in his father's bedroom. "Fire can free me," the vision wails. "Burn me, father, destroy the poison in my bones!"

Bainbridge calls physician Paris, who diagnoses a psychological disturbance. The only remedy, he suggests, is the elimination of the old man's guilty conscience. When he sees the fiery "ghost" of Janette (Dana) begging him to burn Howard's body, Bainbridge panics and digs up his son's grave.

GUEST CAST: Andrew Duggan (Justin Bainbridge), Marion Ross (Mrs. Foster), William Smith (Vincent Sandler), Frank Farmer (Howard Bainbridge), Anthony Norwalk (Paul Bainbridge), John Winfield (Morgan)

This spook segment is hampered by an absolute lack of danger at every turn. Psychotic archconservative Bainbridge has his estate tightly patrolled by an army of stormtroopers, yet at the beginning of the show *four* IMFers cut through a fence and, in broad daylight, stroll toward the air raid shelter, large cases of equipment in their hands. Sandler, the greatest physical threat, is emasculated in his first scene by Jim, who knocks him down when he threatens Bainbridge's grandson Paul. It's not easy to make towering William Smith dramatically invalid, but "A Ghost Story" does. Bainbridge (well played by Andrew Duggan) also loses his credibility, for this paranoid fascist has allowed a houseful of enemies (Sandler, the IMF and others) to surround him.

The holographic projections of "Howard" (Paris) and Dana are dramatic, but it had been done before in episode 95, "Phantoms." Lesley Warren's ghostly charade is indistinguishable from Antoinette Bower's in the earlier episode, right down to the long white shroud. The ploy of bringing back the dead would be used even more frequently in *Mission*'s remaining years.

Year Five: 1970–1971

"The creation of the illusions in 'A Ghost Story' wasn't anything unique," Reza Badiyi admits, so he concentrated instead on the plot's classic gothic elements like young Paul's mysterious secret meetings in the attic, the fearsome thunderstorms, the voices, the whispers. "It was fun to do," says the director. Maybe so, but the dark corridors, ghostly apparitions, and secret passageways of "A Ghost Story" aren't enough to sustain this slow, strange hour.

124: THE PARTY

First Aired: 3/6/71

Written by: Harold Livingston
Directed by: Murray Golden

TEAM: Phelps, Paris, Dana, Barney, Willy, Doug, others

Good morning, Mr. Phelps. Alexander Vanin is now serving a twenty-year sentence for espionage. Immediately prior to his arrest, Colonel Vanin hid a list of EEPR agents operating in the United States. Gregor Mishenko, Vanin's control, has been ordered to locate the list but Vanin has thus far refused to reveal its whereabouts. He knows that once the list is found, his usefulness to his government is over and they will abandon him. Your mission, should you decide to accept it, is to find Vanin's list. This tape will self-destruct in five seconds. Good luck, Jim.

Jim has one clue to the list's location: a series of numbers which Vanin telephoned to his wife Olga moments before his capture. Vanin has since hypnotized himself to forget the numbers and their meaning. Olga Vanin is the only trigger that can unlock his memory.

EEPR agents Jim and Doug inform the imprisoned Vanin that he is going home as part of a trade to retrieve a downed US pilot. Paris enters the EEPR and, posing as a security agent, escorts Olga back to the US to rejoin her husband. Barney is "discovered" in the EEPR Consulate basement with a bomb that cannot be moved. Mishenko evacuates the building, leaving Barney to slowly, laboriously disarm the weapon. Dana and Willy use an underground tunnel to repopulate the empty Consulate with dozens of EEPR "natives."

Vanin and Olga are reunited at the Consulate "party" celebrating their country's anniversary.

While they talk in the study, the revelers quietly disappear. Mishenko reenters the building and is shocked to find the Vanins. Believing an American plot is afoot and that Vanin has divulged the list's location, Mishenko prepares to dispose of him. To save himself, the spy proves that he has been silent: He lets Olga trigger his memory by reciting the numbers which, he explains, is the serial number of a bus upon which he hid the list. The IMF, listening via a bug, take the list and arrest Vanin when he arrives to claim it.

GUEST CAST: Antoinette Bower (Olga Vanin), Alfred Ryder (Gregor Mishenko), Frank Marth (Alexander Vanin), Arthur Batanides (Valenkoff), Robert Sampson (Fitzgerald), Athena Lorde (Mme. Mishenko), Albert Szabo (Kovitch), Yuri Smaltzoff and Oleg Korbyn (Dancers)

"The Party" is a good, yet flawed, script. The first mistake is not the writer's: the tape scene's inserts don't match, and as a result the tape player has a disappearing dust cover. A bigger hole occurs at the climax when the brilliant Vanin blurts out the crucial data without realizing that the Americans would have certainly bugged the room. Otherwise the story moves along nicely, with all the classic elements in place.

To get the Vanins, who are arriving in separate cars, into the Consulate requires split-second timing, since Mishenko is across the street, waiting for Barney to disarm the bomb in the basement. IMF trucks, stopped at rigged traffic lights, block Mishenko's view long enough for the cars to stop and discharge their passengers, who calmly enter the Consulate.

The weight of "The Party" rests on guest stars Antoinette Bower, Frank Marth, and Alfred Ryder, the latter in a role identical to one he essayed in episode 53, "The Diplomat." Considering the somber performances of all involved, Ms. Bower's memories of the show are intriguing. "The thing I remember most about the show," she says, "is that Alfred Ryder wore this droopy mustache and had the most hilarious lines, like 'We will have a little talk later, but get this bomb out of here now!' He and Frank Marth and Nimoy and I got the giggles so badly we were hysterical, Ryder and I particularly." Antoinette and her costars were not the first

Mission: Impossible actors to find their dialogue amusing, but they may have set a record that week for most takes spoiled by uncontrollable laughter. According to the actress, they, "would stand there opposite each other with tears running down our faces, laughing hysterically. We could not restrain ourselves. My favorite line came at the end when Ryder said, 'What are you doing here?' For us that line had a double meaning: What *were* we doing here?! That whole show was the giggles. I look at it now and see exactly why, because the dialogue was so funny."

Except for the party scenes in which they are forced to act merry, "The Party" finds our heroes grimmer and more sober than ever, with the exception of Peter Lupus, who seems to be having a grand time. In light of the events his career underwent this season, it's no wonder he was in such a jovial mood. Leonard Nimoy seems especially withdrawn. "When an actor looks bored like that," opines Antoinette Bower, "especially a decent actor, you can be fairly sure that he's trying to restrain some terrible laugh." In fact Nimoy had reason to be happy, for he'd negotiated his way out of his five-year contract with the show and could not wait to pursue other, non-IMF assignments.

The possible reasons for the subdued behavior of the others are numerous. This was the final segment of a most challenging season, and there was talk of the series not returning for another (see Wrap). In any event, "The Party" marks the exit of Nimoy and Lesley Warren from *Mission*; Sam Elliott would last one more episode, the hapless victim of a failed experiment. Elliott's likable ruggedness and Warren's great flexibility were hardly evident during their tenure on *Mission* and their exit from the series surprised no one, including themselves.

Wrap

Mission's fifth season turned out to be its most daring. The risks taken by Lansbury and company didn't always succeed, but they did prove that the series parameters could be widened without destroying the show. *Mission*'s Nielsen ratings had improved respectably, finishing the season at number 33, with a 19.1 rating and 32 share. Such a comeback would ordinarily ensure another year for most series. But of course, *Mission: Impossible* wasn't ordinary.

The January 21, 1971 issue of *Variety* hinted that Paramount was planning to finally cash in on the series by canceling it and selling the reruns into syndication, where the show could at last show a huge profit. "A CBS executive said no decision has been made yet regarding *Mission,* but other sources said the figure called for in a pickup deal is so high it's doubtful the network will renew," read the article. *Mission*'s five-year contract with CBS had indeed expired, but a new deal had been drawn up which gave the network renewal options. So while Paramount may have been eager to wash its corporate hands of *Mission,* CBS had no intention of dropping an established program whose popularity had just rebounded. The network still wanted *Mission,* even if it meant paying Paramount a higher license fee than ever before. If only to keep the "Tiffany network" happy, Paramount reluctantly kept the series alive, one of the few times that a studio was hoping that one of their series would be canceled.

The end of year five signalled the end of Leonard Nimoy, Lesley Warren, and Sam Elliott in the show (although Sam would appear in the first year six episode). The enthusiasm Nimoy first felt for the series was gone by the middle of his second term. "I was finding it hard to be a successful implant," he says. "I'd done what I came in to do, and I felt that I was just there cashing in every week. I liked the people a lot; I admired Lesley. I hired her for the first thing I ever directed, a *Night Gallery* in 1972. But I sincerely wanted to get out of there. I felt in some ways not wanted, bored, and generally not good about myself."

Nimoy's boredom seems justified, considering the roles he was given this season—his year five functions weren't nearly as challenging as the ones during his first semester. Apart from the chance to play a Kabuki artist and a half-mad old man, Nimoy was wasted this year in filler parts like a surly drunk, a cab driver, or a bland government functionary. "I wasn't able to explore any character; I wasn't playing a real person. I was playing the people that Paris played and they were all an idea, not a person. A face to be ripped off. I had a good time with the makeup and wardrobe and dialects (some of which were successful, some weren't). I came to believe that I was so hidden in some of the makeup that people didn't know if it was me or someone else playing the role! I had some good times. I wasn't under stress and still, during the making of *Mission: Impossible* I had an ulcer attack. Obviously, my subconscious was trying to tell me something." He laughs. "I needed something else. Frankly, I didn't know what my options were. I was wondering who I was. I hadn't been out in the real world since *Star Trek* went on the air. I was on the same lot for five years."

It took weeks for Nimoy to convince his agent that he wanted to leave. "He thought I was crazy. Actors were fighting to get into series and here I was fighting to get out of one. Paramount thought it was a negotiation ploy and I said, 'No, I'm gonna *save* you money. You don't have to pay me a dime. I'm gone and this series will go on.' And I was right. I walked away from a lot of money, never regretted it, and never looked back." Nimoy calls the year following *Mission* a "perfect" one. "I did a low paid job in a western called *Catlow* in Spain; went on the road for eight weeks starring in *Fiddler on the Roof;* then flew immediately to London, did a TV movie called *Baffled* and had a great time doing that; and then I went to San Diego for three hundred dollars a week and acted in *The Man in the Glass Booth,* one of the great experiences in my life. Now *that's* a year! I accomplished everything I hoped to do in that year as an actor. I made a fraction of what I would have made if I'd stayed on *Mission* but I had enormous dividends from the work, and the *Mission* money made that possible." Leonard Nimoy went on to develop talents in still photography, writing, and directing and is bemused by the "lasting" effect *Mission* has had on his career. "I *never* get any questions about my years on *Mission: Impossible.* Never! I talk endlessly to the press and at conventions and colleges, and I can't remember the last time I had a question about *Mission.* People don't associate me with the series—it was a top secret experience! I was very grateful for the opportunity, I was excited, I did what I wanted to do, and it was over."

Lesley Warren and Sam Elliott, *Mission's* least effective actors, went on to become big stars. In the years directly following *Mission,* Lesley worked regularly and did another series, a short-lived situation comedy, *Snip* (1976). After splitting with her Svengali Jon Peters in the late 1970s, she began to make her own career moves and found herself more in demand than ever, earning an Oscar nomination for her comic turn in *Victor/Victoria* (1982) and ultimately becoming a reigning queen of TV movies and miniseries like *79 Park Avenue* (1979) and *Beulah Land* (1980), among many others. Sam Elliott's breakthrough came in 1976 as the lead in a sleeper film, *Lifeguard,* which in turn led to lots of television work, including the series *The Yellow Rose* (1983–84). By the mid 1980s he'd made the jump to genuine movie star in films like *Mask* (1984) and *Fatal Beauty* (1987). He seems most comfortable in westerns, exhibiting a quiet strength of character perfectly in tune with his Marlboro Man looks and Gary Cooper-ish mystique. "TV has allowed me to learn how to act," Elliott told a reporter in 1987. "When I got into the business I didn't know how to act. I knew I wanted to be an actor but I didn't know what it was about. I've still got a lot to learn, too—but it's a lot easier to watch the stuff I do now than it was to watch thirteen episodes of *Mission: Impossible.*" He considers *Mission* good experience, and it was the first major step in a successful career.

Mission's decreased impact at the annual Emmy Awards continued, with the series earning only two nominations. At the May 5 award banquet for technical nominations, the sound editing department failed to win for episode 122, "Blast," but Bob Dawn won a well-deserved Emmy for his work on Nimoy in episode 113, "The Catafalque." Bob's date that night was hairstylist Adele Taylor, a tacit acknowledgment of her great contribution both to Dawn's craft and the look of the show.

One of the presenters that evening was a young actress who'd play an important part in the future of *Mission: Impossible.* Her name was Lynda Day George.

Lynda Day George joined the series for Years Six and Seven.

Year Six
September 1971–April 1972

Production Credits

Starring: Peter Graves, Greg Morris
Also Starring: Lynda Day George, Peter Lupus
Executive Producer: Bruce Geller
Produced by: Bruce Lansbury (except where noted)
Associate Producer: Barry Crane
Story Consultant: Laurence Heath
In Charge of Postproduction: William Cairncross
Production Manager: Michael P. Schoenbrun
Postproduction Supervisor: John A. Fegan, Jr.
Theme Music by: Lalo Schifrin
Music Supervisor: Kenyon Hopkins
Director of Photography: Ronald W. Browne
Art Director: Gibson Holley
Film Editors: John Loeffler, Larry Strong, Jerry Taylor
Assistant Directors: Ray Taylor, Jr.; Bill Derwin; Bob White
Supervising Property Master: Arthur Wasson
Property Master: Robert O. Richards
Special Effects: Jonnie Burke

Makeup Artist: Bob Dawn
Hairstylist: Adele Taylor
Script Supervisor: Barbara Atkinson
Set Decorator: Lucien Hafley
Supervising Costumer: Michael Tierney
Costume Supervisor (Women): Dodie Schaefer
Casting: Jim Merrick, Betty Martin
Vehicle Coordinator: Ed Chamey
Production Coordinators: Dale Tarter, Mike Jarvis
Music Editor: Dan Carlin
Sound Effects Editor: William Andrews
Editorial Coordinator: Larry Mills
Production Mixer: Dominick Gaffey
Rerecording Mixer: Joel Moss
Recorded by: Glen Glenn Sound
Wardrobe Furnished by: Worsted-Tex
Chrysler Vehicles Furnished by: Chrysler Corporation
Chevrolet Vehicles Furnished by: General Motors Corporation

Lynda Day George as Casey, actress and disguise expert.

"We did stories in high rises rather than dungeons."
—BRUCE LANSBURY

"I don't think those were the best shows, but we had a few good ones."
—LAURENCE HEATH

ALTHOUGH YEAR FIVE had shown the path the series would take, year six officially ushered in *Mission*'s final phase, and the shift from international settings to strictly domestic locales. From now on, the IMF would stay home and fight "the Syndicate" in all but two segments (episodes 137, "Invasion" and 140, "Nerves"). To many, the change was inevitable. Peter Graves believes the show was, "getting tired. If we still had Geller really watching the store, things probably would have held up better. But all shows lose a certain amount of momentum after a period. So they decided to come back to this country and battle organized crime." Greg Morris was not enthusiastic over the change. "I'd have been happier if there had been an *expansion* in international intrigue. We *had* deposed every dictator in the world, but how many ways can you make one gangster get rid of another gangster? How many times can you do mob stories before the audience says, 'Enough already!'?"

Ironically, by narrowing its scope, *Mission* somehow *looked* better. It wasn't the increase in budget; that was mostly a result of union raises and inflation. The difference, says Bruce Lansbury, was that, "We got off the lot a good deal more. Because of the Iron Curtain stories, everything was a dull gray." Indeed, year five's last hours, including the U.S.-based episode 123, "A Ghost Story," are gloomy in the extreme. With the advantage of contemporary domestic plots, Lansbury feels, "We brightened it and made it crisper looking. We also had very good people in the art department like Gib Holley, who is excellent."

In an apparent attempt to lure back the series' older audience, CBS shifted *Mission* from 7:30 Saturday to 10:00. The cast also underwent an alteration. "The more people we had," says Lansbury, "the more difficulty we had in finding things for them to do." The departure of Leonard Nimoy and Lesley Warren was handled in a deft, economical manner by creating one character to fulfill the functions of both disguise expert *and* leading lady. After toying with the name Kit, Lansbury and Heath ultimately christened the new Rollin-Cinnamon character Casey. Then came the search for a suitable actress. "You get a list of names," Lansbury explains, "look at a lot of film of them, and see who is the most appropriate."

During the previous season, Aaron Spelling Productions had produced an ABC series called *The Silent Force* on the Paramount lot. The show, interestingly enough, centered around a trio of undercover agents who dealt exclusively with the dismantling of the American crime machine. The stars were Ed Nelson, Percy Rodriguez, and, as Amelia Cole, a twenty-five-year-old actress named Lynda Day.

Born in Texas to an Air Force daddy, Lynda spent much of her childhood traveling around

the American midwest. A desire to perform gradually overcame an interest in medicine, and she began modeling at age fifteen, eventually moving to New York City. Lynda spent five years as Dove Soap's commercial spokesperson and, after appearing opposite Jason Robards in *The Devils* on Broadway, landed the lead in a feature filmed in Brazil, *The Gentle Rain* (1966), opposite Christopher George. She made her Hollywood TV debut in an episode of *The Green Hornet* (1966). "I came out here with the idea that, 'If I can't do anything else, I want to do one *Mission: Impossible* and one *Star Trek*,'" says Lynda. "I never did do a *Star Trek* and I never guested on *Mission* either, but that was just fine with me," she laughs, "because I loved what I got to do there."

Lynda established herself as a proficient, reliable actress. Director Gerald Mayer remembers his experience with Lynda on an episode of *The Fugitive*. "At the last moment an actress who was to play a very strong emotional part bowed out, and they replaced her with Lynda Day, whom I'd never heard of. She was just marvelous in a very dramatic part, absolutely terrific," says Mayer. More TV work and a feature, *Chisum* (1969), led to *The Silent Force,* her biggest break.

Lynda's description of her *Silent Force* duties sounds familiar to anyone who has ever seen *Mission: Impossible.* "We are sent into a town where organized crime—we often call it the Syndicate—has taken over. We work undercover, probably for the federal government, although it isn't spelled out. The three of us rendezvous, plan the attack, capture the criminals, and turn them over to local authorities." *The Silent Force* bore many similarities to *Mission,* but there was one big difference: *The Silent Force* was a flop and lasted only half a season, despite airing directly after ABC's popular *Monday Night Football* broadcasts. "I always had the feeling we were just being made as a filler show to supplement football, and that someone was going to ask for the soundstage any minute," said Lynda, whose happiest memories of the series are of working at Paramount near her one-time costar Christopher George, now her husband and star of his own Paramount series, *The Immortal.*

When *The Silent Force* bit the dust, *Mission* borrowed its format *and* its leading lady. "I was very friendly with her and her husband Chris," says Doug Cramer, who oversaw the cast change before leaving Paramount for Screen Gems. "While watching her, it seemed that she had a warmth. When it didn't work as it should have with Lesley, this seemed like another way to humanize the show." Judging strictly from appearance, Lynda seemed a strange choice for *Mission* (which she called *"The Silent Force* for grown-ups.") Prior to *The Silent Force,* her honey-blonde hair and soft, delicate looks usually typecast her as a vulnerable waif in distress. Hairstylist Adele Taylor, who developed a rapport with her, recalls Lynda's versatility coming as a big surprise to many. "She looked like just another pretty face when she came in," Adele says. "You weren't aware that she was the drama student that Barbara (Bain) was. But when the cameras would roll, she was there, and she would pull it off beautifully." Bruce Lansbury agrees. "She was very good. She had acting ability, was glamorous, and really brightened up the screen." Barry Crane fairly gushed about her to *TV Guide.* "She is a fine actress," he said, "able to swing in a variety of parts. Speaking as a director—she gives you something, something unexpected and a little special." Although barely older than Lesley Warren, Lynda Day George (as she would now be billed) projected a much more mature presence and easily meshed with the crew and cast. "Now we finally had a regular girl who we thought was good," Peter Graves explains. "I thought Lynda fit in rather well and had that essential, classy look about her."

In addition to her talents of visual distraction and disguise, Casey would display other skills

when required by the scripts, including pick-pocketing, motorcycling, and card trickery. Unfortunately, as was the case with Lesley Warren, Lynda never had an opportunity to cut loose with a tour de force performance, but she was able to believably execute a wide range of characterizations in miniature. Unlike Barbara Bain, whose Cinnamon always kept a distance between herself and the part she was playing, or Lesley Warren's Dana, whose masquerades often seemed transparent, Lynda's Casey played her roles straight. If Casey was posing as a drug addict, Lynda played a drug addict, not someone pretending to be a drug addict. In this respect she lent to *Mission* an important sense of realism at a time when it was most needed. Yet it also made Lynda Day George the most underrated and unappreciated of the *Mission* ladies, an unfair tag considering the disparate parts she would play: murderess, showgirl, psychotic mental patient, amoral waitress, blackmailer, mail order bride, asthmatic socialite and, in two of the series' most desperate reaches, an alien from outer space and a 140-year-old woman.

The shrinking of the cast roster meant more work for series stalwarts Greg Morris and Peter Lupus. Greg was officially upped to costar, and episodes would continue to be written around Barney, whose tunnel-crawling days were mostly behind him. Unfortunately, starting with episode 135, "The Visitors" and continuing into the next season, he was too often cast as a mob hood and fell into a rut, relying more and more upon a laconic, irritating characterization and invariably ending every other line with a slow, "maaan." Greg still had his moments, though. When, in episode 127, "The Bride," he greets Casey (awakening from a heavy, drug-induced sleep) with a wink, it is a charming surprise. Peter Lupus likewise began to carry a heavier load and for once, not literally. Although his on-screen duties were never large, the final two seasons found him essaying roles which never would have come his way in years past. Lupus remained as likable as ever.

Midway through the season, Bruce Lansbury finally received his reward for the miracle work he did on *Mission*: he became Paramount Television's vice president in charge of creative affairs. "They wanted someone who understood production enough so that he could control costs," Lansbury suspects. Laurence Heath, having proven himself a capable producer last season, filled that function again when Lansbury made the move to management. In fact, Heath's episodes are the better ones this season. Whether because of Lansbury's preoccupation with the impending promotion or not, a slump occurred early in the semester. After three strong hours, *Mission* began missing the mark with uncommon regularity. Tedious entries like episodes 128, "Run for the Money," 130, "Mindbend," and 135, "The Visitors," indicate that the crime story requirements may have taken some getting used to. Happily, the series was back on track before long, making a strong comeback with shows like episodes 141, "Committed," 143, "Double Dead," and 145, "Casino."

Perhaps anticipating viewer resistance to the "new" *Mission,* the powers that be reinstated the original main title music over the credits, as if to assure fans that, despite the new changes, this was still *Mission: Impossible* (the later recording returned the following season). At the same time, one of the last traces of Gellerism disappeared when a *new* match-striking hand was introduced in the main titles, beginning with episode 137, "Invasion."

On April 29 and 30, 1971, Barry Crane put Peter Graves and the second unit through their customary paces for a new assortment of tape scenes, filmed in and around Griffith Park and Hollywood High School.

Year six was underway.

125: ENCORE

First Aired: 9/25/71

Written by: Harold Livingston
Directed by: Paul Krasny
Music Composed and Conducted by:
  Lalo Schifrin

TEAM: Phelps, Barney, Casey, Willy, Doug, Bill
Fisher, many others

Good morning, Mr. Phelps. These men, Frank Stevens and Thomas Kroll, preside over a criminal empire that threatens to take over the entire Northeast. Although they have been arrested many times, conventional law enforcement agencies have thus far been unable to provide the evidence necessary to convict them of any crime. Your mission, Jim, should you decide to accept it, is to put Kroll and Stevens out of business for good. This tape will self-destruct in five seconds. Good luck, Jim.

In 1937, Kroll and Stevens killed rival mobster Danny Ryan in New York, hid the body, and eliminated the witnesses, thereby avoiding arrest. It's up to Phelps to make Kroll lead the IMF to Ryan's remains.

Kroll, now past sixty, is intercepted, shot full of drugs and cosmetically altered to resemble his physical state in 1937. Then, on a Long Island movie lot which exactly duplicates his old neighborhood, Kroll is made to believe that he is back in 1937—the very day, in fact, that he and "Stevens" (IMF man Fisher) are to kill "Ryan" (Doug). Kroll reenacts the murder, and when he hides the "corpse" in a café basement, Barney and Willy locate the real café and unearth Ryan's skeleton—the necessary proof to send both Kroll and Stevens to jail.

GUEST CAST: William Shatner (Thomas Kroll), Michael Baseleon (Frank Stevens), Sam Elliott (Doug), Paul Mantee (Bill Fisher), James Daris (Arthur), Sam Edwards (Drunk), Janaire (Carol Swanson), Alex Gerry (Proprietor), Paul Bryar (David St. James), Martin Ashe (Doctor). *Unbilled:* William Benedict (Gate Guard), Charles Picerni ("Danny Ryan"), Frank Orsatti

William Shatner as elderly Kroll, who is transformed into a young man in "Encore."

The word "impossible" suits "Encore" better than any other *Mission*. This time it isn't the objective that is hopeless: It's the *scheme* that is totally absurd and preposterous, straining credibility way beyond the breaking point. Never before or since would Phelps lavish so much effort, expense, personnel, or attention to detail on one job, all to entrap two old men who hardly seem worth the trouble. Surely, there must be an easier way. The IMF shave thirty-five years off a man's life and body, albeit for only six hours; Kroll's barber shop is outfitted with swivel walls which pivot on cue to reveal 1930's decor on the reverse side; three full blocks of 1937 Manhattan are *perfectly* recreated on a movie backlot; Kroll's old apartment is also

340

completely reconstructed, right down to the half-empty bottle of buttermilk in the ice box, the unpaid electric bill, the used and imperfect furniture, and on and on and on . . .

How could anyone surrender to such foolishness and believe that he has gone back in time? The answer is obvious: All the ridiculous detail is exactly what sells it to Kroll. It's all so unbelievable, he reasons, that it must be real. Writer Livingston keeps Kroll in shocked disbelief through most of the show, desperately looking for some flaw in the illusion that will prove the whole thing a hoax. He finds nothing but overwhelming evidence to the contrary. Kroll listens to a 1937 Yankees baseball broadcast, reads about minor nuisance Adolf Hitler in the newspapers, spots an old-style propeller plane overhead, and hears vintage music everywhere. For this score, Lalo Schifrin reorchestrates "Cinnamon" and "Danger" from the *Mission* soundtrack LP, making him perhaps the only TV composer to release a series album and *then* weave its melodies into the series over the years. It's no wonder that Kroll writes off the second half of his life as some strange dream. His return to the present occurs at the climax, when he suddenly finds himself all alone in a "city" that moments ago was teeming with people. He runs through the streets looking for some sign of life as the IMF magic starts to wear off and his "youth" melts away. In seconds he is a gray and limping old man who keeps running until he inexplicably finds himself on an old-time western street! When partner Stevens, having traced Kroll, drives up and confronts him, they face each other like gunfighters of an earlier age.

It's all too much, even for *Mission: Impossible.* Yet "Encore" is very entertaining, and one of the series' most visually memorable segments. Some *Mission*s are fun despite their suspension of disbelief; "Encore" is fun *because* it is so far-fetched. Its epic magnitude is like an ever-expanding tall tale. Improbabilities abound, not the least of which is the fact that backlot "buildings" are always mere facades, making Kroll's eventual entry into them inconceivable. The insistence on thirties realism even sparks a gag. When Phelps spots one of his extras sporting a pair of mod sunglasses, Jim takes them and barks, "Squint!"

Director Paul Krasny was well aware of the script's pitfalls. "It was silly," he concedes, "but somehow, between Shatner and Mike Baseleon, *somehow* you believed it." The two guest stars are quite good in their dual roles as young and old heavies. "A number of *Mission*s were style over substance," Krasny points out, "and by that time they were stretching a little for ideas. I mean, when you start doing makeup on people to make them believe that they're thirty-five years younger . . .!"

Lynda Day George's debut is handled in characteristic *Mission* fashion. In other words, she is given no introduction and simply appears in the apartment scene. IMF agent Bill Fisher, who impersonates the young Stevens, is clearly a substitute for Paris in a plot which has all the earmarks of a year five script, including the participation of Sam Elliott as Doug who, in his final outing, "dies" gloriously as "Danny Ryan."

Although a fun show, "Encore" took the idea of the Great Con to new, stratospheric limits. It must have been obvious to Lansbury, Heath et al. that repeated use of such way-out ideas would result in a loss of series credibility, a substantial jump in the budget, and ultimately lead to a dead end. As a result, "Encore" was wisely passed over as the season premiere. To start off with such a wild flight of fancy would have disappointed many *Mission* viewers, most of whom appreciated the show's sometimes tenuous ties to reality. It was the next episode, just as engrossing but much more realistic, that was chosen to unveil the "new" *Mission: Impossible* to 1971 television audiences.

126: BLIND

First Aired: 9/18/71

Written by: Arthur Weiss
Directed by: Reza S. Badiyi
Music Composed and Conducted by:
  Benny Golson

TEAM: Phelps, Barney, Casey, Willy

Good morning, Mr. Phelps. Undercover agent Warren Hays, assigned to gather evidence against the underworld empire of John Lawson,* was recently blinded in the line of duty. Lawson's right-hand man, Carl Deetrich, and his chief business advisor, Henry Matula, are bitter rivals, each hoping to succeed Lawson. Henry Matula is our man, infiltrated into the Syndicate five years ago. Now he is in danger of being uncovered. Conventional law enforcement agencies are unable to protect him. Your mission, Jim, should you decide to accept it, is to preserve Matula's cover and to see that he is moved up in the organization. This tape will self-destruct in five seconds. Good luck, Jim.

Hays was blinded while tracing a Lawton saboteur who rigged an oil field explosion to discredit the petrol company's president. Lawton realizes that Hays's presence at the explosion indicates a leak in his organization. On Matula's advice, he sends hood Brown to keep an eye on Hays—now a broke, down-and-out drunk (Phelps) who was fired for not preventing the blast. Jim has been surgically blinded to impersonate Hays.

Brown takes a room at Casey's boarding house, where Jim resides. He befriends the blind man and bribes him to reveal the name of the agent who replaced him. When Jim provides the information, Lawton offers him a job: to uncover the informer. Phelps accepts.

Brown learns that Jim is leading Lawton on. He tells Deetrich, who pays Jim to finger Matula as

the fink. All parties (including Barney, who has penetrated the mob) meet in a Lawton warehouse, where Jim identifies Matula as the informer. Then Matula plays a tape of the conversation in which Deetrich and Phelps plot to frame him. A gunfight erupts, leaving Deetrich and Brown dead. Barney is ordered to kill Phelps as Lawton exits with his trusted aide, government agent Matula.

GUEST CAST: Jason Evers (Carl Deetrich), Tom Bosley (Henry Matula), Harold J. Stone (John Lawton), Peter Brown (Johnny Brown), Robert Patten (Dr. Warren), Dom Tattoli (Hood), Henry Slate (Bartender), Glen Wilder (Warren Hays), Calvin Chrane (Security Guard #1), Bob Golden (Security Guard #2)

The script's first draft has Barney and Willy performing the same job: keeping an eye on Phelps. Eventually, Barney was moved into Lawton's organization to ensure Jim's rescue at the climax. As originally written, Jim was to wander into a room of circuit breakers and nearly electrocute himself before scrambling out. Deetrich catches up to Jim near an elevator shaft. As Deetrich lunges to push him down the shaft, the blind man moves out of the way and it is Deetrich who falls to his death. The action was changed, but someone must have liked the elevator shaft idea, since it was used in the following episode.

In "Blind," Phelps fills Paris's vacated role of the actor, as Barney and Casey would do in subsequent shows. Peter Graves does some genuine emoting, and to see Mr. Phelps as a pathetic drunk in wrinkled suits and stubble is quite a shock. In his most challenging scene, he fakes delirium tremens for the benefit of Brown, who watches Jim writhing wide-eyed in terror. "I talked to my doctor and asked him about the specific emotional and physical

___
* Called Lawton throughout the rest of the show.

reactions," says Graves, who had to play it carefully and not make it *too* unsettling. "That's tough stuff. The line is so thin there, the danger of doing too much, going overboard and making it awful." Jim is medically blinded for the length of the mission because, as he tells his team, "A quick flash of light, a reflex reaction, and we're dead." Opaque contact lenses are implanted—evidently the eyedrops which blinded Cinnamon in episode 52, "The Heir Apparent" were discarded or forgotten! Phelps finds the masquerade physically grueling and painful, especially when he is hit by a cab—driven by Willy. "I had the green light," Willy tells onlooker Brown. At the denouement, Jim tumbles over a warehouse railing while trying to escape the gunfire, and lands on a concrete floor several feet below, unable to move until Barney assists him.

"Blind" was CBS's choice as year six premiere, and as an introduction to the new *Mission: Impossible,* a better show could not be found. The script is fast paced and features more physical action than usual for this series (Barney even shoots a man in the final scene). *Daily Variety*'s review of September 20, 1971 raved, proclaiming the series, "stronger than ever, zipping along at a fast pace. . . . All the changes have been for the better and there's new life in a show that was sagging from overuse of the same limited plots. . . . Arthur Weiss's script is topnotch and the direction by Reza S. Badiyi is excellent." The weekly edition of *Variety* had another opinion entirely. Noting the excellent guest cast, Graves's convincing portrayal, and the surprising lack of gimmickry, "Mor's" review of September 29, 1971 criticized the "slim" show and the wasting of Morris and Lupus. Lynda Day George was, "pretty in a dance hall girl sort of way, but lacks the necessary sophistication of some of her predecessors . . . . Sans a second string of regulars and minus the hardware, the series has a hard road ahead."

Hindsight proved this prediction to be partially correct. Despite "Blind," in which she has nothing of consequence to do except look pretty, Lynda Day George quickly became a valuable asset. But *Mission*'s "new look" and format did require some time before that hard road was crossed.

127: THE BRIDE

First Aired: 1/1/72

Written by: Jackson Gillis
Directed by: John Llewelyn Moxey
Music Composed and Conducted by:
  Benny Golson

TEAM: Phelps, Barney, Casey, Willy, Bob Roberts

Good morning, Mr. Phelps. This is Joe Corvin, one-time Syndicate killer and extortionist, and now an expert in handling illegal monies. Through Corvin, tens of millions of underworld dollars have been funneled out of this country and into Swiss banks, from there to be returned as "foreign investments" in American business. So far, conventional law enforcement agencies have been unable to stop Corvin's operations. Your mission, Jim, should you decide to accept it, is to put Corvin out of business for good. This tape will self-destruct in five seconds. Good luck, Jim.

Corvin uses courier Anders, whose diplomatic pouch is never searched, to smuggle Syndicate money out of the US. When he finds Anders embezzling from him, Corvin has him killed and must find a new way to ship eight million dollars—fast.

Casey, Corvin's mail-order bride, arrives from Europe but is soon exposed as a drug addict, supplied by airline employee-smuggler Phelps, whose luggage is never searched by customs. Corvin and Jim become partners to move the mob cash to Switzerland.

Airport security is "suddenly" tightened, making Jim unable to help Corvin. When Casey "dies" of an overdose, Corvin decides to ship the loot in her coffin, which is protected by a bogus embassy seal. Hidden in the hearse, Barney steals the cash en route to the airport. On the runway, the coffin "accidentally" breaks open, exposing Casey's corpse as a mannequin—and the money has vanished. Corvin is brought back to his apartment by agitated Syndicate man Mellinger, who wants the money back. Casey is there, alive and well and carrying *two* tickets to Miami. Mellinger chases her out and Corvin, unable to explain, is faced with his own favorite means of execution: an empty elevator shaft, ten stories deep.

GUEST CAST: James Gregory (Joe Corvin), Brad Dexter (Frank Mellinger), Charles Dierkop (Richie), Douglas Henderson (Anders), Harry Raybould (Thug), Gwil Richards (Harris/Bob Roberts), Larry Duran (Chief Loader), Rachel English (Girl at Party), Woodrow Parfrey (Collins)

What began as a Jackson Gillis "What if a Mafioso ordered a mail-order bride?" idea blossomed into the first segment to showcase the newest member of the cast. "The Bride" allows Lynda Day George a lot of screen time and the chance to display an assortment of emotions, from sweetness to irritability to desperation. She also sports an Irish brogue, as does guest star James Gregory, as her repulsive "fiance," Corvin. In retrospect, "The Bride" is one of very few episodes to headline Lynda, making this show so much more watchable.

The exterior of Collins's mortuary, where Corvin disposes of his victims, is in fact *Mission's* production offices. One can only assume that the casting of the show's headquarters as a funeral home was *not* an in-joke.

128: RUN FOR THE MONEY

First Aired: 12/11/71

Written by: Edward J. Lakso
Directed by: Marvin Chomsky
Music Composed and Conducted by:
   Robert Drasnin

TEAM: Phelps, Barney, Casey, Willy, jockey Nick Pressy

Good morning, Mr. Phelps. The two men you're looking at are Edward Trask and Frank Mason. Mason has recently been given control of the Syndicate's illegal betting parlors. He has modernized the operations with computerized tote boards and put tie lines between his parlors in cities all over the country. Trask has been assigned the job of removing the competition in these cities, which he is doing without regard for life or property. Conventional law enforcement agencies have been unable to gather sufficient evidence for the arrest of these men. Your mission, Jim, should you decide to accept it, is to break up this deadly alliance and thus prevent millions of dollars from being funneled into Syndicate coffers. This tape will self-destruct in five seconds. Good luck, Jim.

The goal: capitalize on Trask's jealousy of successful thoroughbred owner Mason.

Trask becomes interested in Phelps's mysterious but promising racehorse. When Casey desperately tries to buy the animal from Jim, Trask finds that the horse is actually a recently kidnapped, tremendously fast racer. Trask forces Casey to bow out, then buys the horse and enters it in an important upcoming stakes in which Mason's prize runner is also competing. Mason's booking computers report huge sums of money bet on Trask's new acquisition—money which Mason assumes was bet by Trask. Then he finds that his tote boards have been tampered with and deduces that Trask, ensuring an upset victory for himself, is responsible.

At the track, Mason orders a hit man to shoot Trask's entry before it can win the race. Barney subdues the hit man, and Trask's horse wins. The large bets apparently booked by Trask were actually placed by the IMF, who instantly collect four million dollars worth of Syndicate cash from Mason's parlors. Mason demands reimbursement from his "cheating" partner Trask who, unable to return "his" winnings, is taken for a ride.

GUEST CAST: Richard Jaeckel (Edward Trask), Herbert Edelman (Frank Mason), Val De Vargas (Miller), William Harmatz (Nick Pressy), Gene Otis (Jeffers), Charles Napier (Thug), Martin Golar (Technician), Walter Kelley (Operator). *Unbilled:* Ray Bianco (Carson)

Apart from a lively performance from Lynda Day George, "Run for the Money" has little going for it. The script's execution is interminable and far too talky, a slow buildup for the big race which comprises act four. Because this last act runs just seven minutes, the climactic race and subsequent resolution seem tremendously rushed in comparison to the rest of the show. The result is one of the dreariest episodes of the series and the first stumbling block of the season.

The brightest spot of the show was a history-making occasion which occurred off-camera. Since the days of Bain and Landau, *Mission's* crew shared a warm and friendly relationship with the show's stars. Propman Bob Richards has affectionate memories: "After an especially hard show, Peter Graves would often throw a party for the crew. He never took credit for it. Greg would do the same thing." For "Run for the Money," the company was shooting on location at Los Alamitos Racetrack on a sweltering June day, and the refreshment truck was quickly emptied. Since the budget wouldn't allow one more bottle of soda pop, it was up to the cast to chip in. "Peter Graves handed me twenty dollars," Richards remembers, "and Greg

gave me some money, too." Standing nearby was Peter Lupus. "Now he wasn't tight," Richards explains, "but he wasn't exactly generous, either." When Loop was asked to contribute, he responded with a typical, tongue-in-cheek reply. According to Richards, "He said, 'Well, I don't think I should give as much as you guys because I'm not in every episode.' Greg almost fell on the floor laughing!"

Ultimately, Lupus relented. "He turned his back to us," says Richards, "reached into his pocket, and handed me *one dollar*! Graves and Greg doubled up and went crazy. I took the dollar, mounted it, and had the sign shop put on top of it a little plaque: MILESTONES OF *Mission*—THE LUPUS DOLLAR. Underneath it, in quotes, I put, 'Throw the boys a party.' We presented it to Bruce Geller. It ended up somewhere in the office on a wall and Barry Crane had it in the end. Where it is now I don't know, but somebody somewhere has the Lupus dollar."

Rumors persist that the Lupus dollar soon found its way back to its original owner.

129: THE MIRACLE

Produced by: Laurence Heath
Written by: Dan Ullman
Directed by: Leonard J. Horn
Music Composed and Conducted by:
  Lalo Schifrin

First Aired: 10/23/71

TEAM: Phelps, Barney, Casey, Willy, Steve
Johnson, Manny, Sawyer, Nurse, others

Good morning, Jim. Seven weeks from now, on November tenth, eight million dollars worth of heroin will be landed at an unknown point along the coast. Undercover agent Milt Anderson lost his life trying to find out where. Only two men know the actual landing site—Alvin Taynor, biggest narcotics dealer in the Northwest, and Frank Kearney, his chief executioner. Conventional law enforcement agencies have been unable to develop any further information. Your mission, should you choose to accept it, is to intercept that heroin, and to get Taynor and Kearney. This tape will self-destruct in five seconds. Good luck, Jim.

To make this one work, Jim uses hedonist Kearney's violent hatred of the church and members of the clergy.

Taynor refuses a partnership deal from mobster Phelps. In retaliation, Willy "shoots" Kearney. At the hospital, surgeon Barney performs a "heart transplant" to save Kearney's life. During the recovery process, Barney drugs and hypnotizes Kearney, drastically altering his violent psyche into a passive, mild-mannered one. Kearney then checks out of the hospital one day before the heroin is to arrive.

Kearney is alarmed by his new, inexplicable temperament but tries to conduct business as usual. When Phelps becomes too meddlesome, Taynor sends Kearney to kill him. But when the time comes, Kearney is unable to pull the trigger.

Kearney hears an IMF radio report about organ recipients assuming the personality traits of the donors. With the help of new girlfriend Casey, he uncovers the identity of his anonymous donor: a priest! Filled with self-loathing, realizing that his career is over and that Taynor will try to eliminate him, Kearney decides to take the heroin and sell it to Phelps. He leads Casey (and her boys) to a beach where the drugs are delivered. Taynor confronts Kearney, whose life is saved by the timely arrival of the police.

GUEST CAST: Joe Don Baker (Frank Kearney), Ronald Feinberg (Alvin Taylor), Billy Dee Williams (Hank Benton), Lawrence Montaigne (Steve Johnson), Lee Delano (Milt Anderson), John Gilgreen (Sawyer), Ollie O'Toole (Manny), Leon Russom (Sam Evans), Rikki Stevens (Waitress), Francine Henderson (Nurse). *Unbilled:* Jim Malinda (Sailor), Charles Picerni (Jackson)

With Bruce Geller out of the picture and good story ideas becoming tougher to find, it's not hard to see why shows like "Encore" and this one were made. "The Miracle" has a silly, obvious premise, the kind that Geller probably would have rejected. After all, can even the IMF convince someone that the transplant of a priest's heart can turn a brute into a pacifist? "Yeah," admits producer Larry Heath, "it was reaching." As usual, however, once you *do* swallow the idea, the rest of the show is good fun.

The "attempt" on Kearney's life is outrageously nonchalant: Willy strolls up to the killer while he is dining and shoots him point blank in the chest (with a tranquilizer, of course). Awake during "surgery," Kearney is unable to see surgeon Barney and crew handing each other imaginary surgical instruments. Another Taynor hit man, Benton (creepily played by a young Billy Dee Williams), watches the operation on closed-circuit television. Naturally, he's really looking at stock footage of an actual transplant, interspersed with live close-ups of Kearney on the operating table.

Returning to *Mission* after a three-year absence to fulfill a studio commitment, director Lenny Horn's nimble touch is evident in technique and performance, making "The Miracle" a faster paced *Mission* than many this season. Dominating the show is Joe Don Baker's marvelous job as Kearney. By believably shifting from vicious killer to helpless patsy, he maneuvers himself perfectly through a less than perfect maze.

130: MINDBEND

Written by: James D. Buchanan and
Ronald Austin
Directed by: Marvin Chomsky
Music Composed and Conducted by:
Robert Prince

First Aired: 10/9/71

TEAM: Phelps, Barney, Casey, Willy

Good morning, Mr. Phelps. Alex Pierson, rising rapidly within the Syndicate, has formed an alliance with Thomas Burke, a psychopathic genius in the field of behavioral psychology. It is believed that Burke is enlisting fugitives from the underworld whom he first brainwashes, then programs to kill. These assassins have already committed three murders for Pierson and killed themselves immediately afterward. Since there has been no opportunity to question them, conventional law enforcement agencies have been unable to get any incriminating evidence against Burke and Pierson. Your mission, Jim, should you decide to accept it, is to stop these murders and to put Burke and Pierson out of action. This tape will self-destruct in five seconds. Good luck, Jim.

Burke lures his assassins with the promise of plastic surgery and freedom but instead uses mind drugs, stressful psychological techniques, and audiovisual stimuli to turn them into mindless psychotics bent on murdering their target, then themselves.

Petty hood Barney becomes Burke's next victim. He is brought to Burke's hidden lab headquarters, tailed by Phelps. Via a transmitter, Barney relates Burke's MO to the IMF. But when he is unable to take a pill designed to fight Burke's brainwashing, he is thoroughly programmed to kill a local politician, and then released. Zombielike, he heads for his rendezvous with murder.

Barney's failure to report doesn't alter the plan. Jim makes his way into Burke's lab and plants very damaging evidence. He then tells Casey to call Teague Williams, an agent who resembles Barney. Casey gets friendly with Pierson, and they meet at her high-rise apartment. They are interrupted by Teague who, wearing a Barney mask, fires several shots at Pierson, narrowly missing him. Teague then leaps out the high rise's window. Recognizing "Barney" as Burke's latest guinea pig, Pierson heads for Burke's lab with his henchmen.

Burke denies setting Pierson up, but to his amazement finds his lab loaded with evidence suggesting that Pierson was indeed Barney's target. Pierson has Burke tortured to learn who is behind this "conspiracy." Jim overpowers Burke's assistant and persuades him to divulge Barney's target and location. With seconds to spare, Willy stops Barney from carrying out his suicide mission. Burke provides enough information to send Pierson and himself away, while Barney recovers fully from his ordeal.

GUEST CAST: Leonard Frey (Dr. Thomas Burke), Donald Moffat (Alex Pierson), Dennis Cross (Pete), Rick Moses (Stambler), Ann Willis (Rita), Ivan Naranjo (Laborer), Bill Fletcher (Stan). *Unbilled:* Lee Duncan (Commissioner Charles Beresford), Don Gazzaniga (Deputy Mayor Harold Watson)

Seeing the world's coolest secret agent turned into a wide-eyed, screaming maniac is the fascination behind "Mindbend." Barney's brainwashing occurs during a forty-hour period, combining a theta-wave brain machine with a carefully constructed arrangement of slides projected endlessly on the bare lab walls. Soon, Barney cracks from the pressure, rips his bolted chair from the floor, and runs amok before finally collapsing in a frenzied heap.

This week's questionable story point: Pierson, who is supposed to have as little contact with Burke as possible, customarily receives large photo blowups of Burke's current assassins. So when Teague-as-Barney tries to shoot him, Pierson knows Burke must be responsible.

Teague's jump out Casey's window is not fatal: He falls several stories into Willy's canvas truck, cushioned with mattresses. The truck drives off, and beneath it lies a Barney mannequin amid shattered glass. Greg Morris calls the fall into the truck "the most dangerous stunt we ever did." It was performed by a young man named Tony Brubaker, whom Morris still respects greatly. "The stunt was so dangerous that half the crew couldn't watch it. They turned their backs. We looked up and there was Tony standing on the window ledge, rocking back and forth. I don't drink coffee, but I was so nervous that I went to get a cup, and couldn't hold the cup because my hands were shaking. The cameras roll, we hold our breath, and he took off, making the most beautiful landing in the padded truck. I told him that if production complains about whatever he charged them for the jump, tell them to see me about it! Later he came to me and said, 'I wouldn't have done that stunt for anyone but you.' That's the kind of stuntman he was."

The unassuming production of "Mindbend" is marred by two separate bloopers. Peter Graves makes one of his rare flubs when he radios Casey to call Teague. Instead of saying, "Make a mask for him," he says "Make a mask *of* him," further confusing the plot. This understandable gaffe is overshadowed by one that got past the director, cameraman, and script supervisor. Burke's lab is hidden in a building which also houses a large laundry operation called Superior Linen Supply. In one shot, a Superior truck pulls into the driveway. Above the truck is a huge billboard featuring the establishment's real-life name, the American Linen Supply on Highland Avenue in Hollywood.

131: THE TRAM

Teleplay by: James L. Henderson and
   Sam Roeca
Story by: Paul Playdon
Directed by: Paul Krasny

First Aired: 10/2/71

TEAM: Phelps, Barney, Casey, Willy

Good morning, Mr. Phelps. These two underworld leaders, Vic Hatcher and Johnny Thorne, have called a meeting of Syndicate leaders from around the country, at which Hatcher will propose the formation of a Syndicate holding company, the first step in the construction of an underworld financial empire with enormous power to corrupt American business and return huge profits to the Syndicate. So far, conventional law enforcement agencies have been unable to interfere with their operations. Your mission, Jim, should you decide to accept it, is to stop Hatcher and Thorne, and put them out of business for good. This tape will self-destruct in five seconds. Good luck, Jim.

Phelps can eliminate Hatcher and Thorne by learning the number of their Swiss bank account which contains over fifty million dollars. "A Swiss bank account is not inviolate," Jim tells the team. "Once an account number is known, it can be attached."

Mobster Phelps gains access to the meeting, which is held in a mountain lodge accessible only by a monitored aerial cable car. On his way up, Jim tampers with the car's wiring, requiring repairman Willy to be called. Upon Jim's arrival, Hatcher explains his financial proposal which requires a four million dollar investment to reap forty million dollars yearly. Casey phones Thorne and lures him into taking the tram down—accompanied by repairman Willy, who kayos him and stows him in the car's baggage department. Under the tram's landing platform, Barney opens the storage hatch and removes Thorne. He carries him to Willy's truck and they speed off.

Hatcher locks the four million dollar mob investment in his wall safe. Willy calls Hatcher and demands exactly *four million dollars* for the return of Johnny Thorne. Hatcher persuades his suspicious investors that he can buy Thorne's freedom, get the kidnappers, and keep the cash. As instructed, Hatcher brings the money to a warehouse, but is outsmarted by the IMF and winds up with neither Thorne nor the money. Barney sneaks into the lodge and plants four million dollars worth of counterfeit money in Hatcher's wall safe.

Thorne, held hostage by Casey and Willy, is told that Hatcher is behind the kidnapping. He escapes,

calls his man Jennings at the lodge, and tells him that Hatcher set up the abduction so he can keep the millions. Hatcher is forced to open the safe and is shocked to find four million dollars still in his possession. He is saved from death by Jim's associate Barney, who locks up the mobsters and boards the tram with Jim, Hatcher, and the "money."

The gangsters free themselves and order the tram guard on the ground to stop Hatcher at any cost. Hatcher, who has a weak heart, suffers an "attack," thanks to a gas which Jim sprays into the air. Jim then "discovers" that the cash is counterfeit. Certain that Thorne has framed him, and determined to keep Thorne from getting the Swiss money, Hatcher gives the account number to Phelps to forward to Hatcher's grandchildren. Willy stops the tram near an escape tower. Jim and Barney exit, but Hatcher feels too weak to move. The tram then continues toward the ground where Johnny Thorne and his men wait. Hatcher sets himself a final goal and shoots Thorne before he is killed during a gun battle. The IMF steal away with the account number and the genuine four million dollars.

GUEST CAST: Victor French (Vic Hatcher), Felice Orlandi (Johnny Thorne), Richard Karlan (Hinkle), Sidney Clute (Rudy Landers), J. Duke Russo (Cabot), Brett Parker (Roche), Allen Jaffe (Grossett), Tom Geas (Jennings Blaine). *Unbilled:* Barry Cahill (Arnold Gates), Jon Shank (Frank Colby), Pepper Martin (Batesly), Richard Shelfo (Grebbs)

After their first *Mission,* episode 122, "Blast," the writing team of Henderson and Roeca were assigned to do a story involving the Palm Springs Aerial Tramway, a beautifully pictur-esque location which transports its passengers hundreds of feet up to a mountaintop restau-rant. The writers spent a weekend getting some physical background. "We caught the tram," says Sam Roeca, "saw how it worked, and evaluated it for physical props and scenes. Visually, it was exciting and we liked it, so we tailored action around it." Heath and Lansbury added one minor sequence: the teaser, in which Thorne and Hatcher toss a troublesome rival off the tram to his death. "We had to keep that a secret from the Chamber of Commerce," says Roeca with a laugh. "They were most accommodating in allowing us to film that tram. It's good publicity, but they don't want somebody falling out of the tram!"

Location work amounted to just two days, a short time considering how much of the show takes place in and around the cable car. Director Krasny was assisted by Barry Crane, who shot most of the second unit work on this show. Besides battling time, the crew also had to contend with the erratic desert and mountain weather. "It was hot part of the time, freezing part of the time, and dusty," says Peter Lupus. "I thought going up on that tram was pretty dangerous. It was awfully windy up there that day, and the thing was swinging from side to side. That was a tough shooting day."

Veteran character actor Keenan Wynn was originally hired to portray Vic Hatcher. "That was the only time I fired an actor before we started," Paul Krasny states. The day before shooting began, Wynn met with Krasny and started changing the script and dialogue. Wynn was intractable, forcing Krasny to call Lansbury. On a day's notice, Victor French replaced Wynn. "We started shooting on the stage the next day," Krasny continues, "and I got this phone call: 'Keenan Wynn's coming down to see you.' I called the guards to catch him before he got onto the stage. I didn't know, maybe he was gonna shoot me because I fired him!" Wynn's visit turned out to be a pleasant surprise. "He came on the stage with a bouquet of flowers and started apologizing! It was very touching."

132: ENCOUNTER

Produced by: Laurence Heath
Written by: Howard Berk
Directed by: Barry Crane

First Aired: 10/30/71

TEAM: Phelps, Barney, Casey, Willy, Evie, Joe, Barbara, Paul

Good morning, Mr. Phelps. Conventional law enforcement agencies have been unable to prevent Frank Brady and his immediate subordinate Martin Stoner from successfully using terror tactics to force legitimate businessmen all over the Southwest into secret partnerships with the underworld. As a result, tens of millions of dollars are now flowing through Brady's organization into the Syndicate. Your mission, should you choose to accept it, is to prevent further violence and to get the evidence we need to stop Brady and Stoner for good. This tape will self-destruct in five seconds. Good luck, Jim.

Martin Stoner's corruption has helped turn his wife, Lois, into a hopeless alcoholic, hated by her husband and Brady.

Phelps picks up Lois in her favorite bar and brings her to his hotel room, where she passes out and is brought to a sanitarium to dry out. Casey dons a mask of Lois and tells Stoner that she is going to a woodland retreat for a cure. Brady sends along an assassin, Dekker, to watch her. If she starts talking about her husband's business affairs, Dekker is to kill her.

Saboteur Willy signs on with Brady and learns that his first job will occur Friday night at an unknown location. He relays this data to Casey who, as Lois, announces it during a relentless encounter group session moderated by Jim and attended by Dekker. Dekker's attempt to kill "Lois" almost succeeds: Casey takes a bullet in the shoulder, but resolves to continue the mission. Brady, wondering how Lois knew about Friday and how she survived the well-planned attack, begins to suspect Stoner of tipping off his wife.

On his sabotage run with other Brady goons, Willy makes sure his comrades are arrested, then tells Brady that they were set up. Brady sends Willy to kill Lois *and* Stoner. His attempt fails, but panics Stoner into taking Brady's records from a bank safety deposit box. Willy tells Brady that the Stoners are dead, but when the real Lois escapes from the sanitarium and calls Brady, looking for her husband, Brady sees he's been conned and races to the bank with Dekker. There they confront Stoner, whom Dekker kills. Jim and the authorities take the records, and Barney returns Lois to the sanitarium.

GUEST CAST: Elizabeth Ashley (Lois Stoner), Lawrence Dane (Martin Stoner), Val Avery (Frank Brady), William Smith (Dekker), Virginia Gregg (Smitty), Arline Anderson (Evie), Byron Mabe (Carey), Ken Scott (Krone), Renny Roker (Joe), Lauren Gilbert (Dr. Adams).

In an episode depending upon strong characterizations, the role of Lois Stoner (or, more accurately, Casey-as-Lois) was the most demanding of all. Luckily, and as Larry Heath so succinctly puts it, "We had a very good actress." At the time of "Encounter," Elizabeth Ashley had endured serious personal and professional setbacks, described in her frank autobiography *Actress* (M. Evans & Company, Inc., New York, 1978). Of the dual roles, drunken Lois was the easier one; the challenge was the encounter session scenes in which "Lois" undergoes a harrowing emotional workout for the benefit of Dekker, who watches warily. Ashley saw the part for what it was, "a huge acting assignment for me . . . it was the first time I had something that I could sink my teeth into, and I had to go for it." Director Crane, belying his background as production manager, allowed the actress as much prep time as was necessary. "He knew," Ashley says, "I wasn't putting up a front so he would think I was some kind of arty actress. . . .

He supported and encouraged me every way he could. So did everyone else on the show. Without my even realizing what was happening, they all began to rally around me.

"I was struck by the quality of quiet on the set when they called me back out. . . . It was just something in the air that came from the other actors. I needed them, and they were all right up for it." During one critical scene, she was allowed as many takes as she wanted to achieve the proper response. "You never get that on series television," she points out. That the extra time paid off was evident instantly when Ashley received a rare ovation from cast and crew when the take was over. "The boundless energy of that woman," Peter Graves marvels. "That was one of those 'acting' episodes when you get totally out of yourself to do something strange and different. That was fun." To Ashley it was more than that. She recalls it as a key turning point not only in her career, but also in terms of how she thought of herself as an actress: "It allowed me to start believing in myself as an actress. Not in a classroom exercise but on the line. In front of a camera . . . I went for the gusto and got it."

Ashley's versatility and utter lack of artificiality form the show's backbone, but there are other noteworthy moments. In a portent of things to come, Peter Lupus does quite well in an unusually large role for him. As a no-nonsense, brooding arsonist, he adds considerably to a part which was written simply as a cocky wise guy. In one scene he sits quietly while another Brady man sasses him. The man's attitude quickly changes when Willy stands up—Willy towers over him! Casey's wounding comes as a real surprise, even to her. "I guess I never really expected to get shot," she sheepishly tells Jim, who expresses some rarely seen concern.

Besides Elizabeth Ashley's bravura turn, "Encounter" is memorable for the demonstration of emotions, most of which are deliberately phony (like the encounter sessions). But genuine sympathy for Lois is expressed by Casey and, curiously enough, Barney, who drags Lois back to the clinic at the end of the show.

133: SHAPE-UP

First Aired: 10/16/71

Written by: Ed Adamson and Norman Katkov
Directed by: Paul Krasny

TEAM: Phelps, Barney, Casey, Willy

Good morning, Mr. Phelps. This man, Frank Delaney, controls the waterfront for the Syndicate. Despite the fact that the docks are public property, owned by the city, no ship can drop anchor, nothing can be unloaded without payment to the underworld. All efforts to dislodge Delaney and the Syndicate by conventional law enforcement means have failed. All potential witnesses against them have been killed. The current grand jury will end its session in seventy-two hours. Your mission, Jim, if you decide to accept it, is to get the evidence needed to break the underworld's stranglehold on the waterfront. This tape will self-destruct in five seconds. Good luck, Jim.

Dockworker Barney signs on with Delaney and proceeds to sabotage several warehouses full of goods, getting Delaney in trouble with his Syndicate bosses. *The Orion,* a ship on which Delaney once killed a man, reappears in port manned by Norse Captain Phelps, who cannot find a crew for this "ghost ship."

Posing as the daughter of the man Delaney killed on *The Orion,* Casey attempts to implicate Delaney in that murder. When Delaney sends his aide Saunders to kill her, Saunders is drugged and kept under wraps, while Casey's dockside "murder" makes noisy headlines, further angering Syndicate chief Mr. C.

Claiming to be employed by Syndicate liaison Morgan, Barney forces Saunders to arrange a meeting with Delaney on board *The Orion,* where Barney will kill Delaney for Morgan. Saunders

"escapes" from Barney, who then lures both Morgan and Mr. C. to *The Orion.*

On the ship, Delaney and Saunders conclude that Morgan will liquidate them. When Morgan arrives, he is killed by Saunders. Willy discreetly removes Saunders, and Mr. C. drives up to find Morgan's body and Delaney, ranting about conspiracies that he cannot prove. Mr. C. leaves Delaney with a hit man, but police lieutenant Orcott saves him by taking Delaney into custody so he can testify against the Syndicate.

GUEST CAST: Gerald S. O'Laughlin (Frank Delaney), Christopher Stone (Mike Saunders), Lonny Chapman (Lt. Bill Orcott), Anthony Caruso (Leonard Morgan), Grace Albertson (Jenny Delaney), Robert Mandan (Mr. C.), Larry Watson (Vic), Buddy Lewis (Bartender)

Veterans Ed Adamson and Norman Katkov wrote *Mission*s together and separately. Adamson, whom Katkov calls "the quintessential TV professional," had a long list of credits and before his death helmed the period private eye series *Banyon* (1972–73). Katkov, *Banyon's* story editor, was a New York City police reporter in the days when that city had fourteen daily newspapers. His first screenwriting credit was for *It Happened to Jane* (1959), a comedy based on a Katkov novelette. With credits ranging from *Ben Casey* to *I Spy,* Katkov, sick of TV writing, turned to novels, the most popular being *Blood and Orchids.* Ironically, when Lorimar Productions bought the miniseries rights to that book, the original screenwriter proved unsatisfactory and Katkov was called in to adapt his own book.

Katkov remains puzzled by his work on *Mission.* "To be honest," he says, "I've never been any good at that sort of thing. Eddie Adamson was excellent at intricacies. But Heath and Lansbury were marvelous to work for. In my experience Heath was very helpful, wanted you to have the story, wanted to give you the job. It was always a pleasant experience, and in fact I looked forward to it, which was goddamned rare in this town, even then."

134: UNDERWATER

First Aired: 11/6/71

Written by: Arthur Weiss
Directed by: Sutton Roley
Film Editor: Robert L. Swanson

TEAM: Phelps, Barney, Casey, Willy

Good morning, Mr. Phelps. Forty-eight hours from now, this man, George Berlinger, millionaire manufacturer and the country's largest dealer in stolen gems, is scheduled to transfer a huge shipment of diamonds to an underworld figure for seventy-five million dollars. At this moment, only one man in the world knows where those diamonds are and he is Berlinger's former lieutenant, Frederick Hoffman, who stole them, hid them, and is now being tortured by Berlinger to reveal their whereabouts. Conventional law enforcement agencies are unable to guarantee the recovery of the jewels. Your mission, Jim, if you decide to accept it, is to recover those diamonds, seize the seventy-five million dollars in cash, and put Berlinger out of business for good. This tape will self-destruct in five seconds. Good luck, Jim.

Hoffman hid the diamonds (and the body of their courier) at sea, but only he knows the exact location.

Barney springs Hoffman from Berlinger's headquarters and strikes a partnership, prompting Hoffman to dive for the jewels. At the same time Casey is seen showing off a stone which seems to be part of the missing cache. Casey leads Berlinger to scuba diver Phelps, who says he knows where the gems are located, and will retrieve them for five million dollars.

Using underwater homers, Willy follows Hoffman to the gems, monitored by Barney who electronically guides Jim (on Berlinger's yacht) to the spot. Hoffman uncovers the gems, is drugged and apprehended. Phelps submerges, helps Willy exit with the diamonds, and brings up *one* gem for

Berlinger. "I gave them to a friend of mine down there," says Jim. "When I see the five million dollars, I'll telephone my friend and he will bring the diamonds."

Berlinger, who must deliver the diamonds to stay alive, sets up a meeting between himself, the Syndicate buyer, and Phelps. When all parties have arrived, the police break in and arrest the crooks.

GUEST CAST: Fritz Weaver (George Berlinger), Jeremy Slate (Frederick Hoffman), Robert Yuro (Hawks), Demond Wilson (Simmons), Mark Tapscott (Captain), Ed Deemer (Dock Guard), John Lance (Stone), Allen Joseph (Bartender)

" 'Underwater' was a very difficult show to do," says Sutton Roley, "and I don't think it was very good. Underwater footage is always very slow, and it all starts to look the same." The actual underwater scenes were faked. "We did not shoot any of that underwater," the director points out. "We didn't use underwater cameras. I shot that in a tank at Marineland, right through the glass windows there." It was a convincing effect, one which Roley used fifteen years later in an episode of *Spenser: for Hire* on location in Boston. Two days at Marineland weren't as big a challenge to Roley as frequent disagreements with cinematographer Ronnie Browne and a physical upset: "Every time I go out on water I get seasick," he explains. To his credit, he keeps the underwater action lively and clear enough to follow.

In the main caper scene, Barney rescues Hoffman from Berlinger's clutches. Climbing an elevator shaft to the penthouse where Hoffman is held, Barney overpowers and "becomes" security man Simmons, Hoffman's torturer. In an early version of the script, Barney simply knocks on the door of the interrogation room and chops Simmons when he opens the door. The filmed version is more typical: Barney enters via the room's dropped ceiling and lowers

a tube near Simmons's head to gas him out. Then Barney drops in, speedily fashions a Simmons mask, and exits with his quarry.

The photo which introduces villain Fritz Weaver during the tape scene is the same one used in Weaver's year two segment, episode 36, "Charity." Also repeated: Barney's mask skills, first demonstrated in episode 117, "The Hostage." This time he also perfectly duplicates Simmons's voice during the disguise. Barney would display this new talent yet again this season (episode 144, "Bag Woman") in a perfect example of the series' blurring of characterizations and skills during the Lansbury years. Bad guy Simmons is played by Demond Wilson who, two months after the broadcast of "Underwater," began his run as costar of NBC's sitcom *Sanford and Son,* which aired opposite *Mission* during most of the following year and regularly pounded it in the Nielsen ratings.

135: THE VISITORS

First Aired: 11/27/71

Written by: Harold Livingston
Directed by: Reza S. Badiyi
Music Composed and Conducted by:
   George Romanis

TEAM: Phelps, Barney, Casey, Willy

Good evening, Mr. Phelps. Publisher and communications tycoon Edward Granger, the most influential man in his state, is controlled by a branch of the Syndicate which owns fifty-one percent of his newspaper, television, and radio empire. For a decade, Granger has supported Syndicate candidates and protected Syndicate politicians. He masterminded the murder of one of his own reporters who was getting too close to the truth. In the upcoming elections, the Syndicate slate is expected to sweep Granger's state and systematically loot it for the underworld. Conventional law enforcement agencies are unable to interfere. Your mission, Jim, if you decide to accept it, is to make certain the voters know the truth before they go to the polls seventy-two hours from now. This tape will self-destruct in five seconds. Good luck, Jim.

Fifty-five-year-old Edward Granger, a firm believer in extraterrestrial life, yearns for immortality.

Granger's new chauffeur Barney lets loose a mutant bee which stings Granger, causing paralysis. His physician is unable to help him until medics Phelps and Casey suddenly appear, cure Granger with futuristic equipment, then vanish as mysteriously as they arrived. When reports pour in that night of UFO sightings, Granger is sure that the strangers who saved him were aliens from another world. Casey returns and confirms his suspicions.

When she is "killed," then resurrected by Phelps, Granger begs for eternal life. Jim reluctantly agrees, provided Granger renounce his corrupt ways. Granger exposes the Syndicate candidates in a radio broadcast and is shot by his former aide, Syndicate man Kellog.

GUEST CAST: Steve Forrest (Edward Granger), Frank Hotchkiss (Kellog), Richard Bull (Dr. Laurence), Jack Donner (Leonard), Gene Tyburn (Ralph Robertson), James Gavin (Pilot), Tom McDonough (Guard)

"The Visitors" is the kind of script which seems to vindicate Bruce Geller's early judgment that writer Livingston was not "right" for this series. The story is like a *Mad* magazine spoof, the IMF strategy simpleminded and obvious, and Granger so gullible that he practically invites our people to flimflam him. Actor Steve Forrest, saddled with lines like, "The idea of my own death is thoroughly hateful to me," has the real impossible mission this time.

The show's science-fictiony elements are kept to a minimum. Barney sets up a pre-Spielberg light show outside paralyzed Granger's window to herald the arrival of visitors Casey and Phelps. After her "death" in the last act, Casey's makeup skills turn her into a hideously wrinkled and aged "corpse." Jim takes her and Granger to alien headquarters (the Paramount machine shop). Inside, Casey is placed in a plastic sarcophagus "resuscitator." Inside the cylinder and shielded by mist, she removes her mask and emerges fully "restored." By now of course, Granger is virtually drooling, but Jim sternly refuses to bestow the Gift, for Granger's evil ways have made him unworthy. Granger volunteers to make the broadcast and through the magic of his otherwordly console, Phelps patches him into the radio station which Granger owns. While Granger names names, the "aliens" exit. Kellog, who has somehow located his errant boss, walks in and shoots Granger who, in a bizarre finale, drags himself to the

resuscitator. The show ends on a close-up of his finger wavering at one of the cylinder's push buttons.

"The Visitors" was shot during a blistering August heat wave (Steve Forrest collapsed, in fact, during shooting). A sequence requiring the filming of a single bee caused more delays and headaches than did a similar scene involving hundreds of bees during episode 11, "Zubrovnik's Ghost." Barney scales Granger's roof, carrying a mutant bee in a small box equipped with a fan. Using the fan, Barney blows the bee down the chimney and into Granger's study, where it attacks its prey. Simple—on paper. But it was not as easy as it read, according to director Reza Badiyi. "I went for hours on that bee!" An upside-down crewman, his legs held by a colleague, was hidden inside the fireplace and instructed to let the bee loose on cue. "Every time he threw the bee the camera wasn't ready," says Reza, "and we had to do it again and again. Finally the guy who was holding the man's legs got tired and let his hands slip. The other man hit the floor headfirst." The director had to fake the shot with an out-of-focus "bee" dangling before a hand-held camera. Next, a real bee was to land on Forrest's neck. "We had thirty, forty bees," Badiyi points out, "and they would not cooperate. They were dying of the heat." Someone suggested covering Forrest's throat with sugar water to attract the bee, but it didn't work. Then bees were blown out a tube toward the actor, whose neck was now coated with honey to make the insect stick to his throat. This too was doomed to failure. Reza Badiyi: "When we shot the bee out fast, it hit Steve and died. If we did it softly, it got away. It looked awful, this man in a full suit with honey and sugar water all over him. He was such a patient, lovely man, but those bees would not stick, would not even go near him!"

Despite the difficulties, Badiyi says "I liked it. 'The Visitors' was very unique and I got such a kick out of doing it."

136: THE CONNECTION

First Aired: 12/18/71

Teleplay by: Edward Lakso and Ken Pettus
Story by: Edward Lakso
Directed by: Barry Crane

TEAM: Phelps, Barney, Casey, Willy, Simone, others

Good morning, Mr. Phelps. This is a photograph of Reese Dolan, who recently became the prime supplier of uncut heroin on the eastern seaboard. With an island base off the coast of Northwest Africa, Dolan plans to set up a unique and efficient new channel of manufacturing and distribution which will be virtually impossible to detect or prosecute through conventional law enforcement means. Your mission, Jim, if you decide to accept it, is to identify Dolan's overseas raw opium source and his US buyer, nullify Dolan's operation, and provide authorities with enough hard evidence to convict them all. This record will self-destruct in five seconds. Good luck, Jim.

Financed by distributor Clegg, Dolan has arranged to locate his business on the island of Malot at the chateau of French underworld figure Madame Renada, whom he has never met.

Renada's employees (Jim and Barney) fly Dolan and his men Page and Bates not to Malot, but to a similar-looking island off the coast of Georgia, where they meet Madame Renada (Casey). At the chateau, Dolan calls his supplier Hajii in Istanbul and orders a planeload of raw opium to be sent to Malot. Barney has the plane rerouted to Rome, where the pilot is held. An IMF flyer takes over and makes delivery to Dolan, who pays him $600,000. Dolan processes the opium into heroin and sends Bates to deliver it to Clegg in New York City. Before he can leave the island, Bates is quietly taken into custody.

When his pilot fails to return from Malot, Hajii calls Clegg and suggests that Dolan is double-crossing them. A stranger (Willy) walks into Clegg's office and tries to sell him a huge supply of heroin. Clegg forces Willy to admit the drugs stem from Renada and her new "American partner." Clegg and Willy are flown to "Malot" by Barney. Clegg confronts Dolan, who is aghast to find the heroin still in his possession. The local police surround the chateau and make arrests.

GUEST CAST: Anthony Zerbe (Reese Dolan), Joe Maross (Clegg), Jeff Morris (Page), Bruce Watson (Charles Finch), Michael Lane (Lew Bates), Françoise Ruggieri (Simone), Ed Bakey (Attendant), Nate Esformes (Turk). *Unbilled:* Richard Angarola (Atak Hajii), Dick Ziker (Hood).

The only episode of the season requiring our heroes to venture outside the United States, "The Connection" is also *Mission*'s most geographically encompassing story. The action takes place on three different continents, with many characters shifting location as events warrant. The transformation of the sleepy island of Morefield, Georgia, into "Malot" is accomplished mainly by replacing license plates and signposts, and making certain that Dolan and his men venture no further from the chateau than is necessary.

Casey, in short skirt and shorter wig, is an exceedingly cool Madame Renada. As her main assistant, Phelps comes on very strong. In one scene, Page and Bates try to force him to hand over his car keys for a night of carousing in town. Despite Page's gun, Jim makes short work of them both with a few precise strikes.

137: INVASION

Written by: James Henderson and Sam Roeca
Directed by: Leslie H. Martinson

First Aired: 11/13/71

TEAM: Phelps, Barney, Casey, Willy, many others

Good evening, Mr. Phelps. Because of recent earthquakes, our Distant Early Warning radar system has been severely crippled. The United States is now in danger of an undetectable preemptive nuclear strike. A few hours ago, this man, Defense Department advisor Whitmore Channing, murdered an Air Force official and stole top secret data specifying the exact areas where our warning system is no longer operative. He has placed this data in an unknown location for pickup at 5 P.M. tomorrow by an enemy agent. The identity of this other agent is unknown. Your mission, Jim, if you decide to accept it, is to prevent this information from falling into the hands of the enemy. This tape will self-destruct in five seconds. Good luck, Jim.

To kill the invasion, Jim needs the code name and flight number of the arriving enemy agent. Only Channing can provide it.

Channing's entire block is evacuated without his knowledge. When his oven gives Channing an (IMF) electric shock, Willy (through an electrical wall outlet) shoots him with a sleep dart. While he sleeps, his radio and TV are furnished with taped "bulletins," his clock adjusted, and his wristwatch advanced a day ahead. Channing comes to, assumes that a day has passed, and that his contact has already picked up the DEW material. He turns on his television and learns that the armies of the European People's Republic have already invaded, and that the US government is preparing to surrender. Channing's smugness is cut short when he is arrested by "EPR military" and tossed into a van. A loudspeaker atop the windowless van plays appropriate troop and tank sounds for the benefit of its passenger.

Channing is brought to a court building where an EPR military tribunal is summarily sentencing all US military personnel to death. He sees stoic Major Barney and hysterical secretary Casey condemned by tribunal chief Phelps, then executed by a firing squad. When called, Channing angrily declares that *he* was responsible for the invasion, and when questioned, tells Phelps only that the Distant Early Warning data was left at Drop B. With a small smile that Channing notices, Jim places him in a small holding room.

Growing wary, Channing notices that the area has suddenly become devoid of people. The courtroom is empty and the firing squad gone, along with the body bags which held its "victims." Fearing that he's been tricked into revealing the drop site of the DEW data, Channing hastily calls an airline, asks that a specific passenger, "Mr. Six," be paged, and gives the flight number. The call is intercepted by the IMF. Willy follows Mr. Six to a warehouse, where the DEW material is recovered.

GUEST CAST: Kevin McCarthy (Whitmore Channing), Scott Walker (Shewitt), Ted Gehring (Novak), Lee Paul (Gristin), Eric James (Operative), David Bond (Wounded Man), James Essex (Soldier), Conrad Bachmann (Second Soldier), Roy Rowan (TV Newsman)

This season's World War III outing is one of the best, told and presented in a fast, no-nonsense style. In an early draft, Phelps identifies the scores of IMF "soldiers" as volunteers from the L.A. Theater of Improvisation.

PHELPS: The separate elements of the plan have been proven in other situations. But remember that we have to rely on amateurs with a minimum of preparation. Our real enemy will be the unexpected.

Jim's fears are justified when Shewitt, a killer hired by Channing's control, penetrates the

IMF environment and takes a shot at Channing. Jim's mentioning of the "innocents" was jettisoned, but the Shewitt subplot remained.

"Invasion" features a novel tape scene: Jim is dining in a posh restaurant with a lovely young lady when a waiter informs him that he has a phone call. Waiting for Phelps in the phone booth is a tape player and photo of Channing. We next see Jim in the apartment scene with the rest of the team, their informal dress indicating that they have been called to action in very short order.

With this show Bruce Lansbury introduced a new director to the series. Boston-bred Leslie H. Martinson got his start at MGM during the 1940s before moving to Republic, the best possible training ground for anyone who'd one day direct *Mission: Impossible*. "At MGM, we'd sometimes go a whole day rehearsing and not shooting," says Martinson. "But at Republic, we'd do one hundred setups a day!" After TV work with Roy Rogers and Dale Evans, Martinson moved to Warner Brothers, where his reign as one of television's most prolific directors began. Twenty years later, he had racked up an enormous list of credits, including features like *Batman* (1966) and *Fathom* (1968), and series like *CHiPs* and the sitcom *Small Wonder*. "I've been going nonstop for thirty years," says the director, "and I've probably exposed more Eastman Kodak film than any five living directors. After all those years of directing, I learned a lot on *Mission* from Ronnie Browne. In addition to being a good lighting cameraman, he had a good sense of staging, which most cameramen were not concerned with then."

The success of "Invasion" was a harbinger of things to come: Martinson would direct eight more *Mission*s in the remaining season and a half.

Year Six: 1971–1972

138: IMAGE

Written by: Sam Roeca and James Henderson
Directed by: Don McDougall

First Aired: 1/15/71

TEAM: Phelps, Barney, Casey, Willy, Dave Scott, Dr. Charles Berk, Tom Hawkins

Good morning, Mr. Phelps. For years, this man, Emil Gadsen, has controlled the largest vice operation in the Northeast. Now Gadsen is about to flee the country to avoid a federal indictment, leaving his partner, Thor Coffin, in charge of the organization. The source of Gadsen's power is a secret list of public officials who are on his payroll. Gadsen plans to take the list with him and continue making payoffs from abroad. Conventional law enforcement agencies are unable to interfere. Your mission, Jim, if you decide to accept it, is to get that list so we can put Gadsen and Coffin out of business for good. This tape will self-destruct in five seconds. Good luck, Jim.

Willy eludes the sophisticated surveillance system of Thor Coffin's estate and steals his five million dollar stamp collection. Jim then tries to sell it to dealer Nate Ullstead, who knows Emil Gadsen.

Renowned psychic Barney holds a tarot card reading for devout believer Gadsen and warns him of impending doom involving a person "even closer than a brother." "I have no brother," insists Gadsen. Barney drugs him, shows him the tarot's death card, and tells him, "You will see this card again from time to time. . . . You will react to it in certain ways." He gives Gadsen very specific instructions before bringing him back to consciousness.

Gadsen and son Tony come upon a Professor Gadaradz, Emil's exact double, and his daughter Casey, both claiming to be from the "old country." Gadaradz is IMF operative Scott in an Emil mask. When the professor suffers an "attack," Casey discreetly holds a death card, which Emil sees. Gadsen immediately suffers a similar convulsion. The look-alikes agree to meet again but before they do, Tony sees the professor kidnapped by masked (IMF) men, who have evidently mistaken him for Gadsen. Emil consults Barney, who shows him the death card, causing Gadsen to feel the effects of torture.

IMF doctor Berk identifies a small scar on Gadsen's chest as a surgical mark left after a Siamese separation. Barney reminds Gadsen that Siamese twins separated at birth can still experience symbiotic reactions. Barney goes into a trance and explains that the professor's kidnapper is known and trusted by Gadsen. Barney "sees" a wine cellar and "men questioning." Knowing that Coffin has such a cellar, Gadsen sends Tony to check it out. Tony sneaks into Coffin's cellar and finds Willy "torturing" the professor, whom he believes is Gadsen, for the location of the list.

Gadsen is convinced that his life depends upon saving his "brother." Ullstead leads Gadsen to Jim, who is "forced" to reveal the tunnel which leads into Coffin's cellar. Gadsen, Tony, and Phelps find the professor "dead" in the cellar. Jim flashes the death card and Gadsen falls, unable to move. Certain that he is dying, Gadsen gives Tony his wristwatch, the list hidden inside. To his surprise, Gadsen recovers instantly and, with Tony, is arrested.

GUEST CAST: George Voskovec (Emil Gadsen), Warren Stevens (Thor Coffin), Dan Travanty (Tony Gadsen), Del Monroe (Hauser), Paul Marin (Dave Scott), David Frank (Dr. Charles Berk), Don Gazzaniga (Belkin), George McCallister, Jr. (Tom Hawkins), Walter Burke (Nate Ullstead). *Unbilled:* Dante Andreas (Alfredo)

The Corsican brothers plot falls prey to *Mission: Impossible* in a show that is less than successful thanks to plot contrivances big enough to drive Siamese trucks through. The large hole Willy leaves in the wine cellar wall is covered by a simulated brick facade *exactly* matching the hole he has haphazardly hammered open; Gadsen just happens to have a chest

scar of unknown origin which can pass as the sign of a Siamese operation; stamp dealer Ullstead, when confronted with Coffin's stamp collection, doesn't call Coffin because a Coffin hood once beat up Ullstead's son . . . but this doesn't explain how Ullstead knows Gadsen. The biggest problem is Gadsen's simple foolishness. He ought to be as suspicious as his son Tony, played by Daniel J. Travanti some years before he changed the spelling of his name and came into his own on *Hill Street Blues.* The older Gadsen, who has never experienced these psychic attacks until the day he meets Barney, believes the psychic's theory that close proximity to his "brother" is responsible for their shared symptoms. When Barney's nonsense gets especially silly, Tony turns to his dad with ill-concealed exasperation and exclaims, "He's suckering you! He tells you something, then you buy it!" If Gadsen is anyone's twin, he would have to be Edward Granger's (Steve Forrest in episode 135, "The Visitors")—their gullibility level is equally low.

To his credit, director Don McDougall keeps the show moving. His biggest triumph is his handling of the death card scenes, which he somehow keeps just short of laughable. "That was a very difficult show to do," Greg Morris recalls. "Graves and I expressed our displeasure to each other. George (Voskovec, in a dual role) was fine, but we were fully aware that we were skirting the credibility gap, which meant that we had to work harder. It was a challenge to us, one that was gladly accepted. It was competent. I don't know why Don (McDougall) didn't come back to the show, because he was good."

139: BLUES
   (formerly HARD ROCK)

Teleplay by: Howard Berk
Story by: Howard Berk and Orville H. Hampton
Directed by: Reza S. Badiyi
Music Composed and Conducted by:
   Benny Golson

First Aired: 11/20/71

TEAM: Phelps, Barney, Casey, Willy, actor Art Warner

Good morning, Mr. Phelps. This man, Stu Gorman, is a music industry figurehead for organized crime. His company, run for him by financial expert Joe Belker, has muscled into recording, booking, jukeboxes, record sales, and distribution—operations netting tens of millions of dollars annually for the Syndicate. Thus far, conventional law enforcement agencies have been unable to stop Gorman's illegal activities. Your mission, Jim, should you decide to accept it, is to put Gorman out of business for good. This tape will self-destruct in five seconds. Good luck, Jim.

Jim's approach centers upon Gorman's murder of singer Judy Saunders in her apartment after she threatened to talk to the authorities.

Into Gorman's recording studio walks arrogant singer Barney, who auditions with a song called, "Judy's Gone Now," shocking Gorman and Belker. Claiming that Judy had her tape recorder on while Gorman killed her, Barney blackmails Gorman for a big music contract. Belker bribes Casey in the police photographic library for the photos taken in Judy's apartment on that fateful night. Casey provides stills which show that Judy's recorder was switched on that night.

Willy is "caught" wiring Belker's car with a bomb, and Belker learns that Willy was employed by Gorman. Belker makes Barney admit that the incriminating tape is held by corrupt detective Phelps. Belker and Jim agree to squeeze Gorman dry, and Jim hands Belker the tape (featuring

Casey as Judy, and actor Art Warner as Gorman.)

That night in the studio, Belker plays the tape for Gorman who laughs, recognizing it as a phony. "The impersonations are good," he tells Belker, "but the words are all wrong." Belker threatens to go to the law, but Gorman pulls a gun on him. "You know I was in her apartment," he says, "you know I killed Judy. But without your statement, there's no case." The police burst in and arrest the pair, whose conversation has just been taped by Phelps in their own studio.

GUEST CAST: William Windom (Stu Gorman), Ed Flanders (Joe Belker), Vince Howard (Lt. Don Eckhart), Alex Rocco (Tanner), Robert Bralver (Pusher), John Crawford (Art Warner), Gwenn Mitchell (Judy Saunders)

Greg Morris's television singing debut seems to be the main reason for "Blues." In a voice certainly no worse than many recording stars of the time, he renders Otis Redding's "Dock of the Bay," but his first number, "Judy's Gone Now" (written by Benny Golson and Morris in an hour), really makes an impression—especially on Gorman and Belker, who understand the insinuation behind lyrics like,

> *Good-bye, Judy, it just don't*
> *   seem right*
> *That he's still here*
> *And you're gone forever*
> *Pushed into the night.*

Greg delivers one of his best performances in this show, creating a character so magnificently obnoxious and irritating that he is more unlikable than the villains of the piece. "The fun of acting is the latitude it gives you to create," says Greg, who got his first-ever ovation from the crew after a scene in which he fakes the symptoms of drug withdrawal. "I'd had many friends who were junkies," the actor points out, "and I called upon that experience to do it. The applause was a good feeling, because that crew had seen it all." Greg developed a memorable, swaggering walk for the character, which took the crew by surprise. He first used it in a street scene in which the camera was to track Greg on his way to a phony drug buy. "I got into my 'lean,' and waited for 'action.' Reza called action, and I started boppin' down the street. Well, some voice yelled, 'cut.' Ronnie Browne comes running up to me and asks, 'Greg, are you all right?' They'd never seen me walk that way before." The walk was infectious, and soon the technicians and electricians were bopping while they carried the lights and moved the equipment around!

The painstaking IMF recreation of Judy's murder, complete with background sounds and precise impersonations of Judy and Gorman, is typically flawless. Less perfect was the insert crew's work: Watch for an early scene in which Willy and Casey are working at a recording console. The medium shots show Lynda Day George using her left hand, as always, to write down information. But for the inserts, a woman's *right* hand is used.

140: NERVES

First Aired: 12/4/71

Teleplay by: Henry Sharp and Carrie Bateson
Story by: Henry Sharp
Directed by: Barry Crane
Music Composed and Conducted by:
   Robert Drasnin

TEAM: Phelps, Barney, Casey, Willy, Bill Williams

Good morning, Mr. Phelps. A cannister of deadly experimental nerve gas TX-222 ordered destroyed by the president has been stolen from an Army laboratory. The cannister was hijacked by this man, Wendell Hoyes, a fugitive Syndicate enforcer whose brother Cayman is serving a life sentence for the murder of a federal agent. Wendell Hoyes is threatening to release the gas in a heavily populated area unless authorities immediately surrender his brother. Obviously, the government cannot be party to any such deal. Your mission, Jim, should you decide to accept it, is to recover the cannister of TX-222. This tape will self-destruct in five seconds. Good luck, Jim.

The stolen cannister has a defective casing, and will begin to leak within forty-three hours.

Believing that Wendell's girl Saretta Lane, currently serving time for murder, knows where Wendell is hiding, Jim arranges to have her transferred via a police wagon, where she is handcuffed to fellow con Casey. The van is ambushed by Casey's pals Willy and Phelps, who "kill" the police before they too "die." Casey drags Saretta to a getaway car and the handcuffed pair speed off. Casey wants to head for the border, but Saretta guides her to an abandoned winery where Wendell and his friend Tully are secluded. The car is tracked by Barney. Meanwhile, the jailed Cayman Hoyes dies from heart disease. His death is covered up and IMF man Bill Williams, wearing a Cayman mask, takes his place.

Department of Corrections official Phelps delivers "Cayman" to a prearranged location, but is left empty-handed. At the winery, Hoyes reveals his plan to sell the TX-222 to a notorious terrorist.

Wendell is tracked to an observatory. Tully learns from a prison insider that Cayman Hoyes is dead and alerts Wendell, who unmasks Williams. Jim intervenes, forcing Wendell and Tully to run. The pair fall out during an argument and fatally shoot each other. Before dying, Wendell fires some shots toward the observatory roof, where the TX-222 is stowed. Army technicians bury the cannister in a cement block to neutralize the gas forever.

GUEST CAST: Christopher George (Wendell Hoyes), Paul Stevens (Cayman Hoyes), Tyne Daly (Saretta Lane), Rafer Johnson (Jack Tully), Charles Bateman (Brig. General Westerfield), Peter Kilman (Bill Williams), Robert Broyles (Mechanic), Russell Thorson (Warden), Shep Menken (Doctor), Ron Masak (Campbell). *Unbilled:* Dick Ziker (Policeman), Julie Ann Johnson (double, Casey), Hal Needham (double, Wendell), Tony Brubaker (double, Tully)

Domestic terrorism, a potentially good theme for the series, was rarely touched upon until *Mission*'s seventh and final season. As a result, this show, like episode 137, "Invasion," is a welcome departure in a year comprised almost entirely of gangster stories. Act four highlights good location work around the Griffith Observatory in the Hollywood hills, but the main attraction of "Nerves" is Christopher George's role opposite Mrs. George, the latter playing against type as a hardened criminal. Wendell Hoyes is as much a murderous little boy as an irrational, paranoid adult, given to sudden outbursts of joy or blinding anger. He is always on the edge of losing control.

"Nerves" offers three of the most physically threatening antagonists ever seen on the show: former Olympic decathalon champ Rafer Johnson as the quiet Tully, Tyne Daly as the immoral Saretta, and best of all, Chris George's Wendell Hoyes.

141: COMMITTED

Teleplay by: Arthur Weiss
Story by: Laurence Heath
Directed by: Reza S. Badiyi

First Aired: 1/22/72

TEAM: Phelps, Barney, Casey, Willy

Good morning, Mr. Phelps. Harve Harrison is the lieutenant governor of this state and the puppet of underworld boss Leon Chandler, now on trial for murder. Chandler's alibi has been provided by the lieutenant governor. The chief witness against Chandler is this woman, Nora Dawson, who is in a state mental hospital where she is being systematically driven insane in order to destroy her credibility as a witness. Conventional enforcement agencies have been unable to win Nora Dawson's release on legal grounds. Your mission, Jim, if you decide to accept it, is to deliver her in court in a mentally competent condition in time to testify against Chandler tomorrow. This tape will self-destruct in five seconds. Good luck, Jim.

Nora was committed by her husband, a state budget director who owes his career to Chandler. Nearly catatonic from psychosis-inducing medication, she is being held in one of two adjacent padded isolation cells at Dyer Bay Mental Hospital, an island prison installation.

Jim takes his emotionally disturbed niece Casey to Dyer. When she becomes violently uncontrollable during an examination, Casey is straitjacketed and placed in the isolation cell next to Nora's. Wracked by this turn of events, Jim "collapses" and is placed in the hospital infirmary. He sneaks out and picks his way into Casey's cell. Peeling away the padding from the wall separating the two cells, Jim blasts an opening in the wall. Casey dons a Nora mask, enters Nora's cell, and lures her nurse-guard in, knocking her out. When the nurse awakens she finds "Nora" sitting in a stupor, her apparent escape attempt a failure.

Jim calmly takes Nora out of the building and into a maintenance truck. In the bay, skipper Willy creates a diversion so scuba-suited Barney can climb into a large drainage pipe. Barney emerges in the prison boiler room, rigs a steam gauge, then waits as dangerous pressure seems to build up in the boiler. Repairman Phelps evacuates the area, takes Nora from the truck and passes her to Barney, who gets her to the shore via the pipe. Jim gasses the tower guard, allowing Willy to dock, pick up Barney and Nora, and sail off.

In court, witness "Nora" babbles incoherently and Chandler's attorney indicates her incompetence as a witness against his client. In a surprise move, Casey removes her mask and the real Nora Dawson, no longer suffering from the drugs, takes the stand and places Chandler and Harrison at the crime.

GUEST CAST: Susan Howard (Nora Dawson), Alan Bergmann (Lt. Governor Harve Harrison), Anne H. Francine (Maude Brophy, R.N.), Bert Freed (Leon Chandler), Robert Miller Driscoll (Dr. Carrick), Geoffrey Lewis (Kaye Lusk), James Sikking (Wilson), Dean Harens (Larkin), Jack Donner (John Dawson), John Howard (Foreman), Paul Sorensen (Tower Guard), Junero Jennings (Workman). *Unbilled:* Tom McDonough (Judge), Michael Regan (Baliff), Larry Watson (Contact)

The Rescue, that *Mission* mainstay, gets one of its last workouts in "Committed," filmed at Terminal Island, a genuine former prison. Director Reza Badiyi, perhaps the best choice for this perfectly clocked gambit, does his usual fine job with the visuals, but falls flat when handling his scowling villains, Bert Freed and Alan Bergmann, both of whom have surprisingly little screen time.

The best acting comes from Lynda Day George in her charade as the psychotic niece jealously in love with her Uncle Jim. A routine examination results in Casey's delegation to the general ward, which would kill the IMF plan. To ensure she is put in isolation next to Nora, Casey grabs a letter opener and tears the room apart, screaming, "Don't come near me. I'll cut your heart out!" She is quickly placed where she needs to be!

142: STONE PILLOW
  (formerly BIG HOUSE)

Written by: Howard Browne
Directed by: Leslie H. Martinson

First Aired: 1/8/72

TEAM: Phelps, Barney, Casey, Willy

Good morning, Mr. Phelps. The pictures are of Vincent Vochek, head of a powerful West Coast syndicate family, and Larry Edison, a former private detective who's been sentenced to prison. Vochek is suspected of murdering one Maurice Krohner, a police informer, six months ago. It is known that Edison holds a roll of film linking Vochek to Krohner's death, using it to blackmail Vochek. Conventional law enforcement agencies have been unable to locate this film and are helpless to proceed against the gang leader without it. Your mission, Jim, should you decide to accept it, is to learn where Edison's film is hidden and turn it over to the proper authorities. This tape will self-destruct in five seconds. Good luck, Jim.

Edison is unaware that Leona Prescott, his accomplice in the Vochek affair, has died.

Warden Barney welcomes Edison to prison. Guard Willy escorts him to his cell, which he shares with brainy con Phelps. Edison becomes frantic when someone seems to take a shot at him in the prison yard. Uncovering Jim's escape plan, Edison forces his way into it. Using prison psychiatrist Casey as hostage, Jim and Edison break out. Jim slugs Edison, then destroys their escape car to imply their deaths. Edison awakes hours later, sees the newspaper report of his death, and immediately calls "Leona" (Casey). She explains that, upon hearing of his death, she followed his instructions and sent the incriminating film to the district attorney. Jim hints that "Leona" may still have the film so she can bleed Vochek by herself. For Edi-

son's benefit, Jim makes a call which "reveals" that Vochek is currently in no danger of arrest.

Edison visits "Leona." She pulls a gun on him but is "shot" by the arriving Phelps. Before "dying," she calls a confederate and tells him to get to the film before Edison can. Edison uncovers a key from the leg of a swivel chair and speeds off to a warehouse, where the film is hidden. Phelps takes the film, leaving Edison in the hands of the police.

GUEST CAST: Bradford Dillman (Larry Edison), Robert Ellenstein (Vincent Vochek), Arthur Batanides (Joe Fort), Brooke Mills (Leona Prescott), Tom Stewart (Lawyer), Harold Jones (First Prisoner), Tom McDonough (Forest Ranger), Jock Gaynor (Cliff).
Unbilled: George Wilbur (First Henchman)

Howard Browne's dialogue and guest star Bradford Dillman are the chief joys of "Stone Pillow." The script is loaded with the fast-paced crime lingo Browne is so adept at, and Dillman rises to the occasion as Edison, uneducated but extremely shrewd. Sharing most of his scenes with old pal Peter Graves, his tough guy jargon makes a great contrast to Graves's erudite vocabulary. In their first jail cell scene together, Jim shows off a calculus textbook, which he claims to prefer over girly magazines. Edison eyes him warily and says, "I hope you're not gonna turn out to be one of those . . ." Jim looks him dead in the eye and replies, "Don't make the mistake of equating intelligence with a lack of masculinity." "I wouldn't think of it," is Edison's satisfied reply!

Actress Brooke Mills, playing Casey-as-Leona, has a voice similar to Lynda Day George's, which supports the credibility of the masquerade. A big plot hole occurs in the apartment scene when Casey notes that she has never heard Leona's voice. But, by using the proper regional Texas accent, she completely fools Edison! Much more convincing is the Leona face mask which Casey uses. It's an amazing reproduction of Ms. Mills's face.

According to the writer, the show's title stems from a line from the classic "Prisoners' Song" ("With my head on a pillow of stone").

369

143: DOUBLE DEAD

First Aired: 2/12/71

Produced by: Laurence Heath
Teleplay by: Jackson Gillis and Laurence Heath
Story by: Jackson Gillis
Directed by: Barry Crane

TEAM: Phelps, Barney, Casey, Willy

Good morning, Mr. Phelps. Conventional law enforcement agencies have been unable to interfere with the operations of these two men, Ollie Shanks and Rudy Blake, who run the loan shark racket in the Islands for the Syndicate. Now they are about to transfer almost ten million dollars in profits to the mainland, thereby motivating the organization to set up additional projects in this new territory. Your mission, Jim, should you choose to accept it, is to discourage the Syndicate from any further large scale expansion into the Islands by getting possession of that ten million dollars, and putting Shanks and Blake out of business for good. This tape will self-destruct in five seconds. Good luck, Jim.

Once in Hawaii, a simple IMF hit-and-run approach is ruined when Willy is caught stealing the cash from Blake and Shank's office safe. He is subdued and taken to corrupt Dr. Matier, who shoots him full of potentially fatal truth serum to learn who he is working for. Willy struggles manfully, but with each painful injection, he grows weaker.

As part of the new maneuver to complete the mission and retrieve Willy, Casey gets friendly with Shanks, while Blake meets with Syndicate liaison Phelps, who supposedly works for mainland chieftain Bolt. Casey drugs Shanks, who then helps the team steal the ten million dollars. When Shanks fails to appear at a meeting with Blake and Phelps, it is learned through "survivor" Casey that he was lost at sea while piloting his private plane. Blake finds his safe empty, and Jim plants the seed of doubt about Shanks's unproven "death." Blake must meanwhile reluctantly report the theft to Bolt, who flies out immediately.

Casey revives Shanks, who believes he passed out from too much drink, and takes him home.

They are confronted there by Phelps and Blake, the latter furious over Shanks's apparent treachery. Casey confesses that she helped Shanks steal the money. Suddenly, Syndicate man Barney enters and "kills" Phelps and Casey, exposing them as cops. Now Bolt arrives, demanding answers and the missing money. Unable to sort out the confusion and knowing that their lives are on the line, Shanks and Blake take Bolt—and Barney—to Willy, in the hopes that Dr. Matier has forced some information from him. Helped by the doctor's sympathetic nurse, Willy gets away and is rescued by the rest of the team. Bolt, ten million dollars poorer, deals with Blake and Shanks in time-honored fashion.

GUEST CAST: Lou Antonio (Rudy Blake), Paul Koslo (Ollie Shanks), Norman Alden (George Collins), Vincent Beck (Bolt), Irene Tsu (Penyo), Wesley Lau (Jim Thompson), Maurice Marsac (Dr. Matier), Hank Brandt (Steve Wells), Cynthia Lynn (Lucille), Fred Krone (Guard)

Author Jackson Gillis explains that "Double Dead" began as "a Damon and Pythias thing about splitting two partners apart. There was some emotional content in the story. It wouldn't have worked unless they really cared for one another. Damon wouldn't do this to Pythias, but of course you had to make it look like he did." Indeed, the Blake-Shanks relationship is warmer than most criminal partnerships seen in the series, and the partners (swinging Shanks, sober Blake) are strongly delineated.

Although he spends most of the show strapped to a table and in great pain, Willy Armitage for once has the spotlight and is the story's pivotal character. To see him bathed in sweat,

suffering from the body-wracking truth drug is disturbing. His only consolation is the presence of Penyo, a compassionate Eurasian nurse and indentured servant to Matier. She wants to let Willy go, but her sense of duty to Matier wins out—until the impatient doctor prescribes a heavy dosage which may kill Willy. Penyo administers distilled water instead of the drug, giving Willy time to regain his strength and stay alive. By the time Blake, Shanks, Bolt, and their goons arrive, Penyo has quietly cut Willy's bonds. Willy makes a daring breakout, literally carrying Penyo with him to the waiting IMF car and freedom.

"Peter (Lupus) always wanted to win the girl at the end," says Herb Solow. Six years later and long after Solow had vacated the premises, Lupus came as close as he ever would to getting his wish. Although there is no suggestion of a romantic attachment between Willy and Penyo, it's a satisfying turn nonetheless. Making Lupus's moment of glory so much sweeter is Irene Tsu, an accomplished actress whose exquisite, expressive face conveys all the delicacy, indecisiveness, and kindness required of Penyo.

144: BAG WOMAN

First Aired: 1/29/72

Written by: Ed Adamson and Norman Katkov
Produced by: Laurence Heath
Directed by: Paul Krasny

TEAM: Phelps, Barney, Casey, Willy, Dr. Bob Miller

Good morning, Mr. Phelps. For years, the Syndicate has been operating openly in a western state through enormous bribes to a highly placed political figure, known to us only by his underworld code name, C6. Conventional law enforcement agencies lost their only lead to his identity when special agent Jack Malloy was killed while on surveillance duty. We do know for certain that all organization payoffs for the area are handled by Syndicate veteran Harry Fife and his chief button man, Luke Jenkins. Your mission, should you choose to accept it, is to learn the identity of C6 and get the evidence that will put him behind bars. This tape will self-destruct in five seconds. Good luck, Jim.

Fearing that the late Malloy had uncovered his latest "bag man" (who delivers the cash to C6), Jenkins recommends a friend, Jean Royce, to make further deliveries to C6. Barney assumes the identity of Luke Jenkins, and Jean Royce arrives in the form of Casey, whom Willy will electronically follow to C6.

Fife, tiring of C6's ever-increasing payoff demands, gives Casey a bagful of explosives set to detonate upon opening. Barney discovers this, but is exposed and wounded while escaping. Barney alerts Jim, who calls Willy. But a traffic accident has destroyed Willy's tracer, making it impossible to warn—or even find—Casey.

Phelps allows Jenkins to escape from IMF confinement and return to Fife. Then, as a visiting Syndicate boss, Phelps reminds Fife that C6 is invaluable and well worth whatever price he demands. Fearing Syndicate retaliation for C6's murder, Fife has Jenkins call C6 seconds before he can open the bag. Jenkins also tells C6 that Casey is a cop. Jim traces the call and sends Willy, who saves Casey and busts C6.

GUEST CAST: Georg Stanford Brown (Luke Jenkins), Robert Colbert (Harry Fife), John Lasell (Winston Walding, aka C6), Russ Conway (Dr. Walter Manning), Joe E. Tata (Al), Lew Brown (Dr. Bob Miller), John Wheeler (Crowley), Glenn R. Wilder (Pete Walker). *Unbilled:* Todd Martin (Jack Malloy), Victoria Hale (Receptionist)

Luke Jenkins is devoted to Judd, his German shepherd, enabling Barney to make the switch with Jenkins at veterinarian Miller's office. Barney is uncovered when Judd manages to escape from his cage and returns to Fife's estate, where he attacks Barney and dislodges his Jenkins mask. Barney is grazed by a bullet, but gives Jim the bad news.

To save Casey, Jim repeats a ploy which worked in episode 133, "Shape-up," a show written and directed by the same trio behind this segment. Jenkins is drugged and tied to a chair in a shabby, abandoned room (the same room used to house actor Chris Stone in "Shape-up"). Phelps breaks a bottle against the wall, then revives Jenkins and leaves before the killer awakens. Jenkins sees the broken glass on the floor, and uses it to cut his bonds and exit, allowing Jim to follow through with his revised strategy.

One of Barney's secondary chores, discussed in the apartment scene, never occurs on-screen. During his guise as Jenkins, Barney is to crack Fife's safe and take his payoff records, but we never learn whether his exposure made this impossible.

For an example of Paul Krasny's flair at sequences requiring both a masked character and the person being replaced, watch for the scene in the vet's office when Barney replaces Jenkins. By cleverly timing the blocking of actors Greg Morris and Georg Stanford Brown, and panning the camera during one sustained take, Krasny makes it seem as if Brown is in two places at once—asleep on the floor as Jenkins, and standing nearby as the masked Barney.

Year Six: 1971–1972

145: CASINO
(formerly VACUUM, RUMBLE)

Written by: Walter Brough and Howard Berk
Produced by: Laurence Heath
Directed by: Reza S. Badiyi

First Aired: 2/19/72

TEAM: Phelps, Barney, Casey, Willy

Good morning, Mr. Phelps. This man, Orin Kerr, runs one of the west's most popular resort cities for the Syndicate, channeling millions of dollars into the underworld every year from unsuspecting tourists. Conventional law enforcement agencies could clean up the town, if a new bill presented by the governor ending county control of gambling passes. Undercover agent Mel Simpson was killed trying to gain evidence of Syndicate involvement to place before the state legislature. Your mission, if you decide to accept it, is to get that evidence in time to ensure passage of the bill. This tape will self-destruct in five seconds. Good luck, Jim.

Kerr's extravagant life-style has unsettled his superiors, who have assigned enforcer Cameron to bug Kerr's casino office. Phelps patches into the bug's wire and connects it to an IMF tape recorder.

Caribbean mobster Barney pays Kerr an innocent visit, but what Cameron hears over the bug is "Kerr" (a pretaped IMF actor) promising to buy his way into Barney's operation that very evening with $500,000. Next, Casey is ushered into Kerr's office for passing bad checks in the casino. While Kerr gives her scant time to make good, Cameron hears "Kerr" and Casey discuss a mysterious impending caper. Jim arrives to pay off Casey's debts, and Kerr recognizes him as the mastermind behind a twelve-year-old heist which netted more than $700,000—money that was never recovered. While Jim claims innocence of the theft, Cameron hears "Kerr" and Jim plot to rob the impregnable casino vault. Barney miraculously empties the vault and hides the money in a nearby ghost town. Anxious to steal Phelps's hidden fortune, Kerr

loans Jim $1000, then lets him go $5000 into debt, thanks to crooked blackjack dealer Willy. Kerr demands that Jim pay up, forcing him to unearth the money "he" stole "years ago." Kerr follows Jim and takes the money. Cameron learns of the vault theft and confronts Kerr, who is astonished to find himself carrying currency less than twelve years old—money stolen from the casino. Before Cameron can shoot Kerr, Barney intervenes, allowing Kerr to run—into the arms of the law. With little choice, Kerr happily volunteers to testify against the syndicate.

GUEST CAST: Jack Cassidy (Orin Kerr), Richard Devon (Steve Cameron), Frank Christi (Bill Wicks), Eddie Ryder (Joe Logan), Frank Farmer (Kelp), Dee Gardner (Blonde Showgirl), Biff Elliott (Mel Simpson), Walker Edmiston (Peter Wiley), Joseph La Cava (Wheelman), Ervin Richardson (First Patron)

"Casino" is a good rewrite of episode 51, "The Mercenaries," with three things going for it: the ruse of blocking Kerr's monitored conversations with faked, prerecorded ones; Jack Cassidy's smarmy performance as Kerr; and the vault heist sequence, which rates as one of *Mission*'s very best.

The Aquarius Casino vault is seemingly invulnerable to burglary. Only casino strongboxes filled with cash can enter the vault, via a conveyor belt. A magnetic arm picks up the box and opens it over a collator. The money spills out and is pressed and bound into small bundles which are placed on a wall shelf. What could possibly blow this tidy setup? A special IMF strongbox, of course, provided by dealer Willy while air-conditioning repairman Barney parks his van in the garage, just below the vault.

373

Once inside the vault, the IMF box opens on the conveyor belt, revealing a video camera and wheels. Controlling it remotely and using the camera as his eyes, Barney drives the box off the belt and onto the vault floor, where it lands upside down. Barney flips a switch, and a propping arm emerges from the top of the box to turn it right side up! Barney guides the box to a bank of batteries which control the vault alarm. A small drill protrudes from the strongbox and burrows into the batteries until they explode, shorting out the alarm. Barney climbs into an air duct with a laser and burns a huge hole into the vault floor. From the van he withdraws a large plastic hose, its other end attached to an extremely powerful vacuum machine in the van. He pushes the hose through the hole in the floor and locks it into place, then turns on the generator-powered vacuum. In moments, every piece of currency in the vault is sucked off the shelves, down the hose and into the van until the vault is empty. It's a beautifully done scene with a delightful string of toppers and a "star" who performed without the aide of a double. "We had just the one box," says its creator, Jonnie Burke, "and it had everything." Via radio control, small motors moved the box, turned its wheels, opened its doors for the camera lens and drill, and activated the drill and propping arm. "Practically everything we did on that show was an operating mechanism," adds Burke. "I had a great advantage because I had accumulated an awful lot of gear motors and hydraulics of various types. I didn't have to buy a thing for 'Casino,' outside of the explosives we used to blow up the batteries."

146: TRAPPED

Produced by: Laurence Heath
Teleplay by: Sam Roeca and James Henderson
Story by: Rick Husky
Directed by: Leslie H. Martinson

First Aired: 2/26/72

TEAM: Phelps, Barney, Casey, Willy

Good morning, Mr. Phelps. An army payroll equivalent to eight million dollars American has been stolen from a military base in Southeast Asia, and is now on its way to the United States. Although conventional law enforcement agencies have learned that the Stafford family—Joe, Arthur, and Doug—which controls a worldwide smuggling operation, is responsible, no information has been developed which might lead to a recovery of the money. Your mission, should you choose to accept it, is to get back that eight million dollars. This tape will self-destruct in five seconds. Good luck, Jim.

The Staffords are never directly connected to their smuggling activities—a routine which Jim plans to change.

The IMF comandeers a truckful of Stafford contraband. Jim and Barney offer it back to the Staffords on the condition that they pay "protection." Later, Phelps meets privately with ne'er-do-well brother Doug and claims that his brother Art will get rid of Doug unless he helps Jim to "hit" Art first. Unknown to Phelps, Art has already put out a contract on Jim. After failing to persuade Doug, Jim is ambushed by a Stafford killer. He survives, but is injured and loses his memory.

While Jim dazedly wanders the city streets, nightclub singer Casey beguiles Doug, who discovers Art's picture hidden in her apartment. Moments later, "Art" calls, asking for Casey. When he avoids a confrontation with hit man Willy, Doug figures that Jim was right and Art wants him dead. Doug makes a deal with Barney to provide "soldiers" for the war Doug will wage against his brother. Barney demands an immediate down payment of two million dollars. Doug agrees and leads Barney to the hidden loot. The mission is accomplished, but Jim, still suffering from amnesia, is unaware that Art Stafford's hit men are closing in on him.

GUEST CAST: Bert Convy (Doug Stafford), Jon Cypher (Art Stafford), Sharon Acker (Annette), Tom Tully (Joe Stafford), Rudy Solari (Broyles), Brigid O'Brien (Molly Stafford), Walter Barnes (Al), Arline Anderson (Middle-Aged Lady), Charles Picerni (Keller), X Brands (Barsi), Robert Ruth (Desk Clerk), Bob Golden (Ed Fenton)

In Roeca and Henderson's earliest draft, which takes place in Palm Springs, the Staffords steal ten million dollars worth of used American currency destined for destruction by the Treasury Department. Sexy Casey exacerbates the enmity between brothers Art and Doug, and Barney locates amnesiac Phelps in a hotel room. Phelps, who has escaped from a hospital and the police, does not know Barney. Believing himself a crook and Barney a cop, Jim brandishes a fireplace poker while Barney draws a tranquilizer gun. The pair scuffle before Jim puts it all together. The story ends on a deserted landing strip where Barney uses a rifle to blast the planeful of currency before it can take off.

In the filmed finale, Annette, a waitress at the club where Casey sings, shelters dazed Jim, who is a sitting duck for Art's approaching killers. Art is arrested and, intimidated by Willy, he clues the team to Jim's location. Barney calls Jim to warn him, but Phelps doesn't even recognize Barney's name. Finally, by dint of concentration and subliminal "memory" cuts, Jim remembers just as the hit men burst in. Phelps disarms them and sends them to the floor, then lamely thanks Annette, whose compassion has saved his life.

The amnesia plot device is an old one, and by the time "Trapped" was filmed seemingly half the characters on television, from Superman to Lassie, had fallen victim to the malady. Phelps's memory lapse lacks the impact it might carry if applied to a strongly defined, very distinctive personality. Since Jim Phelps has virtually no discernible character to begin with, this contrivance is merely a stumbling block within the plot.

As part of her guise to interest Doug Stafford, singer Casey performs in the style of Doug's lost love. Lynda Day George sings "The Gentle Rain," a song with special significance to her, as it was the title tune of the 1966 feature starring herself and husband Christopher George.

Wrap

The ratings for *Mission*'s sixth season came as a pleasant surprise: The series placed at number 31 in the Nielsens, a jump from year five's number 33 showing. *Mission* regularly beat ABC's *The Persuaders* and NBC's *Movies*. The show's share of the viewing audience had also increased, from 32 to 35 percent, suggesting that this season's relative stabilization appealed to more viewers than did the sometimes wildly erratic stories which made up year five. The addition of Lynda Day George, a more traditional *Mission* heroine than Lesley Ann Warren, was also undoubtedly responsible for the jump, as was the later time period, Saturday at 10.

The ratings increase meant an almost certain pickup by CBS, which put Paramount once more in the ironic position of renewing a series that the studio would rather have cancelled and syndicated.

The Emmy balloting yielded only two nominations for *Mission: Impossible* this season: Greg Morris for Supporting Actor, and Gibson Holley and Lou Hafley for episode 125, "Encore's" Art Direction and Scenic Design. For the first time, *Mission* failed to win a single Emmy.

With Lynda Day George on maternity leave, Barbara Anderson filled in as Mimi Davis.

Year Seven
September 1972–April 1973

Production Credits

Starring: Peter Graves, Greg Morris
Also Starring: Lynda Day George, Peter Lupus
Executive Producer: Bruce Geller
Produced by: Barry Crane (except where noted)
Story Consultant: Laurence Heath
Story Editor: Stephen Kandel
Postproduction Supervisor: Donald R. Rode
Theme Music by: Lalo Schifrin
Music Supervisor: Kenyon Hopkins
Director of Photography: Ronald W. Browne
Art Director: Gibson Holley
Film Editors: Larry Strong, John Loeffler, Jerry Taylor
Assistant Directors: Bob White, Bill Derwin, Ted Butcher, Max Stein
Set Decorator: Lucien Hafley
Assistant to the Producer: Dale Tarter
Casting: Betty Martin
Supervising Property Masters: Arthur Wasson, Bob Richards

Special Effects: Jonnie Burke
Makeup Artist: Bob Dawn
Hairstylist: Adele Taylor
Production Coordinator: Jack Clements
Script Supervisor: Barbara Atkinson
Supervising Costumer: Michael Tierney
Costume Supervisor (Women): Mina Mittelman
Vehicle Coordinator: Ed Chamey
Music Editors: Dan Carlin, Kenneth Hall
Sound Effects Editor: William Andrews
Editorial Coordinators: Larry Mills, Frederick Stafford
Production Mixer: Dominick Gaffey
Rerecording Mixer: Jay Harding, CAS
Recorded by: Glen Glenn Sound
Wardrobe Furnished by: Worsted-Tex
Chrysler Vehicles Furnished by: Chrysler Corporation
Chevrolet Vehicles Furnished by: General Motors Corporation

Producer Barry Crane directs Peter Graves in "Break!"

> *"That was the best time I had in the business."*
>
> —BARBARA ANDERSON

BRUCE LANSBURY'S move to management left the new season in the hands of continuing story consultant Laurence Heath and Barry Crane, now finally upgraded to producer. Faced with the perpetual difficulty of commissioning scripts for a series which seemed to have exhausted every possible variation, Heath was also writing pilots for Paramount like *The Magician* and a new version of *Call to Danger,* which had gotten Peter Graves into *Mission* many years earlier. On screen, the strain began to show. "The stories were less in the last year," opines Graves. "They were hauling out some of the first years' scripts and revamping." The most obvious examples are episodes 148, "Two Thousand" and 167, "The Fighter," based upon episode 4, "Operation Rogosh" and episode 138, "Blues," respectively.

Help arrived in the form of Stephen Kandel, one of the industry's most prolific writers and fastest rewriters. Unoffically on staff for *Mannix,* it was just a matter of time before he wandered down the hall to the *Mission* offices for some uncredited dialogue polishes. The next step, of course, was a story meeting. "I'd never seen *Mission,* never read a *Mission* script," Kandel admits. "I had no idea what *Mission* was about and didn't particularly care." He thought so little of the appointment that he forgot about it until the morning it was scheduled. "I zipped into the outer office and picked up a script from the pile they had there. I hastily read through it and came up with an idea." Kandel pitched the genesis of what would become episode 157, "The Question" and as he recalls, Lansbury and Heath "broke up. They said, 'Oh, you haven't seen the show in a while.' " In his haste, Kandel had read an obsolete Stanley Kallis script! Kandel's storyline "had nothing to do with *Mission: Impossible* and was absolutely different from the style. They said, 'Well, try it.' I wrote it and they did it. I did a rewrite, and the next thing I knew I was on staff."

Heath gave story editor Kandel a big responsibility. "One of my functions," Kandel says, "was to take an unusable script, unusable because of quality or size, and modify it without damaging it. They had accumulated a lot of scripts over the years which were unshootable because of cost or any number of reasons." In a sense, Kandel operated as a salvage expert. "No script is developed in a vacuum; it begins with an idea that everybody likes. Everybody wanted those scripts to work and usually there were several tries at them. If you revive and revise that script and make it viable, everybody's pleased because it proves they were right, that the idea does work."

Kandel shares "split credits" on several year seven scripts that were begun by other writers, then rewritten by Kandel. "I didn't meet the people, I just inherited the problems and made them work, which is what they hired me for." His primary contribution to these plots stemmed from his own perception of the *Mission* formula. "The show ran on a format which, like most shows, grew organically out of the first year. The formula was the 'wild card' at the end of the third act. To introduce it earlier and then *trump* it at the end of the third act was to give it a more interesting formula, I thought." Various wild cards can be found in the Kandel rewrites.

Some arrive as early as act one (Willy's shooting in episode 152, "The Deal"), while others (a close shave in number 167, "The Fighter") occur in the closing minutes of the episode.

New producer Barry Crane, unlike his predecessors, was not involved in story and script conferences. According to Kandel, "Barry had the creative capacity of a pound of lead. That's not a slur; it wasn't his strength. He was wonderful at taking an existing piece and carrying it out, and he was a very intelligent critic, but he had to have something to criticize. Larry Heath defined the show because he was in charge of the scripts. Barry Crane carried out the production process and did it extremely well." Crane's talent always amazed Kandel. "It was marvelous to watch Barry work. He read a production board the way you'd read a diagram. He then began reshuffling it in his mind, and the schedule would fall into a new and unusual configuration in about a minute and a half. He used to dazzle assistant directors."

Crane was adept at solving production problems, but even he couldn't solve a *reproduction* problem when, at the end of year six, Lynda Day George announced that she was pregnant. After reduced roles in the first four episodes of this season, she took a ten-week maternity leave. "I didn't actually leave until I was *very* pregnant," Lynda points out. The wardrobe and makeup departments "had a great time trying to camouflage me," she adds. "Sometimes I looked like a lamp shade," she jokes, "sometimes like the back of a very large chair." She was also "camouflaged" behind desks, consoles, moviolas, and anything else large enough to hide Lynda's delicate condition.

During her leave, Lynda was spelled by a variety of leading ladies (although she kept her billing in the main titles). For once the absence of a series character was explained on-screen: While Lynda awaited her baby, Casey was on special assignment in Europe. *Mission's* format provided a perfect mode of concealment: In some stories Casey dons a mask for plot purposes, and Lynda Day George disappears for the rest of the episode.

Women's costumer Mina Mittelman, new to *Mission,* had to keep the guest actresses and the ever expanding Ms. George in style. Mina, who'd worked on *They Shoot Horses, Don't They?* (1969), *The Great White Hope* (1969), *The Grasshopper* (1970), *Diamonds Are Forever* (1971), and the Paramount series *The Young Lawyers* (1970–71), believes the job of costuming an actress whose weight was changing weekly was a true learning experience. When Lynda returned, her gradual weight *loss* had to be hidden as well. "We had to be careful about how we dressed her until all the weight was lost. Lynda had a closetful of clothes. You couldn't continue to use them, but you could take pieces of them, although in her case you couldn't do much until after the baby was born." Like so many others, Mina was spurred by a company attitude which, from the beginning, never faltered. "These were people who cared about what they did. They cared about the show and the actors. It's called style. And though I met him only once, Bruce Geller was obviously the man who set the style and they kept to it and didn't make a mistake. This is what style, and integrity, mean." Later work took Mina into series like *The Magician* (1973–74), *The Barbary Coast* (1975–76), and features like *The Hindenburg* (1975), *Pretty Baby* (1978), *1941* (1979) and *Under the Rainbow* (1981).

Lynda's first replacement was Barbara Anderson, three-time Emmy nominee and one time winner for her role as Policewoman Eve Whitfield in *Ironside* (1967–71). Barbara left the series and the business for marriage and family. "The only reason why I went back to work," she explains, "was because we didn't have kids right away. So I said, 'I'll just free-lance until we have kids.' I hired an agent and two weeks later I was called in for *Mission: Impossible.*" After a quick interview, Crane hired her for episode 151, "Break!" as ex-con turned IMF operative Mimi Davis. "I looked right," she feels. "There was a special look for that show, and you had

to go a lot of ways with the look you had. I think I had an edginess, a toughness that would work. For *Mission,* the woman has to have something inherently strong about her, because she gets into these situations and you've got to believe that she can get out of them! Lynda was wonderful, and Barbara Bain was just perfectly cast."

Barbara was called back for another segment (episode 155, "TOD-5") and another, eventually guesting in seven of the ten episodes sans Lynda. "Barbara was good," says Peter Graves, "and she had that wonderfully classy look." She found *Mission* much more challenging than her previous series. "If I had started in that series I never would have left, because you had a different role every week. You never get stale like you do in other series. My character in *Ironside* never grew, she stayed a policewoman for four years and that was boring, unfortunately. The only change they ever made was my hair." She also found her *Mission* scripts the most daunting she'd ever seen. "I must have read that first script two or three times before I could piece together what my character was doing and why she was doing it. It was a crossword puzzle, and you had to work out the puzzle before you worked out the character. I had to read them twice. First for idea, second for continuity, because you couldn't read them once and know what was going on.

"You know what the hardest part was? Shooting those damned opening scenes when Mr. Phelps would explain it to us. Peter Graves was like a robot, you could not break his concentration and he could do it in one take. The rest of us were like, '. . . uh . . . uh . . .' It was horrible! That was also the glamour set. They wanted Mimi to be her most beautiful then. The hair, the makeup, the evening gowns, it was all very posh."

Since the season's first episode would be shot partially in San Francisco, Barry Crane took a second unit and Peter Graves up two days early to film tape scenes in spectacular locations like the San Francisco Civic Center, Maritime Park, and the Bay Cruise. Propman Bob Richards recalls a typical Crane magic act while on location. "He took a single unit to San Francisco, and we had enough work for twice the time we were supposed to be there, but they only gave him so much money and manpower. So he works it out that he's got just enough to split the unit in two, with cameras for both units. Then he splinters off another group from one of the units, and then sends a spare camera to get shots of something else. We were shooting with four units!

"One day the camera truck arrived on location and there weren't any cameras for the principal production unit because they were all out with the other units. We were delayed maybe forty-five minutes to an hour, and we made it up the next day."

With eleven tape scenes in the can, production on "Speed" commenced Thursday afternoon, April 13, 1972.

383

147: SPEED

First Aired: 2/16/73

Written by: Lou Shaw
Directed by: Virgil W. Vogel

TEAM: Phelps, Barney, Casey, Willy

Good morning, Mr. Phelps. Last night, the Stonehurst Chemical Plant was robbed of three tons of D-amphetamine sulfate, commonly known as speed. Conventional law enforcement agencies believe that Sam Hibbing, the west's largest dealer in illegal drugs, engineered the robbery and now has the drug hidden at a secret location where he plans to package it in pill form and sell it to the underworld at a huge profit. Your mission, should you decide to accept it, is to find and recover the speed before Hibbing can distribute it, and to put Hibbing out of business for good. This tape will self-destruct in five seconds. Good luck, Jim.

Sam Hibbing's speed-addicted daughter Margaret is intercepted and replaced by Casey. Hospitalized after a traffic "accident," she introduces a new friend, straitlaced Phelps, to Hibbing. Jim promises Hibbing that he will get "Margaret" off her pill habit. Checking on Phelps, Hibbing learns that Jim owns a charter plane and once served time for killing a man with his bare hands.

By pooling resources with regular Hibbing buyer Dayton, New Orleans mobster Barney is high bidder at Hibbing's drug auction, and buys the cache on the condition that Hibbing have it in New Orleans the following day. Hibbing, who relies upon Fred Snelling to make the delivery, agrees.

Jim checks on the recovering "Margaret" at home and, with Hibbing, is outraged to find her flying on speed. When she claims that Snelling gave her the pills, Phelps goes berserk and "fatally" beats Snelling. With no way to transport the drugs to New Orleans, Hibbing blackmails Phelps into flying the cargo to Barney on his charter plane.

Hibbing uncovers Casey's disguise. She escapes, but Hibbing, realizing he's been set up, stops Jim as he takes possession of the drugs. Barney and Willy disarm Hibbing, and Margaret is placed in a sanitarium to kick her habit.

GUEST CAST: Claude Akins (Sam Hibbing), Jenny Sullivan (Margaret Hibbing), Ron Soble (Phalen), Jesse Vint (Zinc), Dave Cass (Hugo), Tom Winston (Guard), Dick Ziker (Operative), George Wilbur (Driver), Russ Grieve (Shiner), Charles Bateman (Dayton). *Unbilled:* Ross Hagen (Fred Snelling)

San Francisco's mountainous streets are used to good advantage during a wild chase between Hibbing and his motorcycling "daughter," Casey. The scene began with an unexpected thrill, according to Ron Soble, who plays Hibbing's henchman Phalen. "Claude Akins (Hibbing) and I were to leap into our car and take off in pursuit of the motorcyclist. Virgil Vogel, the director, asked me to drive as swiftly as possible. I hit the accelerator and we were off 'as quickly as possible.'" But Soble hadn't noticed that just before him was a ridiculously steep road. "As a result, Claude and I found ourselves airborne almost immediately! It was the scariest ride of our lives, sad because most of it was off-camera."

For her first *Mission* assignment, new costumer Mina Mittelman was to provide a riding costume for "Margaret" that could accommodate, in various shots, lithe Jenny Sullivan (daughter of former *Mission* guest Barry Sullivan), expectant Lynda Day George, and a male stunt driver. This meant fashioning three copies of the same outfit which, for continuity reasons, had to cover the arms, legs, and torso. Mina's solution: a poncho, which effectively masked everything. "That was my entry to *Mission*," says Mina, "on location where I fit the stunt person before I could see Lynda, who was en route from visiting her husband. It was a good thing she was as wonderful as she was, because I could not have done it without her."

Setting the tone for the next three episodes, "Speed" requires little of Lynda's presence, although in this show she is the central character (albeit masked as Margaret). After the apartment scene, during which she is artfully blocked, she is barely seen until the end of the show.

Of somewhat more dubious interest is the first appearance of Greg Morris's mustache, which he decided to grow for no particular reason. "I grew my first mustache when I was thirteen or fourteen," Greg explains, "and wore one when I first started in the business." The actor shaved it off after his first *Ben Casey,* feeling it made him look older. The new mustache went over fairly well with the *Mission* crew, but when one tiny fan told him, "I think you're much handsomer without a mustache," Greg shaved it off once again. "Shows you how much a fan can affect you," he muses.

The San Francisco shooting was a pleasant way to begin the new semester, and everyone was delighted—except director Virgil Vogel, who found himself sharing the crew with Barry Crane. "Barry was trying to make it pay by breaking up my crew and sending them off to shoot other things for other shows," says Vogel. "He'd been such a terror about costs, but he was the guy who was going over all the time." Crane the director would have the crew for a certain amount of time before Vogel could begin. "Then you got the crew for the remainder of the day, which often was only two hours. By then of course, Barry was back as unit manager again, and complaining about why you haven't done your day's work," he says with a laugh.

148: TWO THOUSAND

First Aired: 9/23/72

Written by: Harold Livingston
Directed by: Leslie H. Martinson

TEAM: Phelps, Barney, Casey, Willy, White, Sergeant, Corporal, Admiral, Marshall, Soldier, Civilian, others

Good morning, Mr. Phelps. Joseph Collins, a brilliant nuclear physicist, has stolen fifty kilograms of plutonium from his former employer—enough to construct a dozen Hiroshima-strength bombs. Collins has sold the plutonium to an unidentified foreign interest whose representative, a man named Haig, is to take delivery of it at noon the day after tomorrow. Conventional law enforcement agencies have been unable to identify Haig or to locate the plutonium. Your mission, Jim, should you decide to accept it, is to recover that plutonium before it leaves this country. This tape will self-destruct in five seconds. Good luck, Jim.

On the day he is to leave the country, Collins hears reports of impending military action in the Middle East. Collins is arrested for murder by detective Willy and taken to police headquarters, where further radio bulletins and news paper headlines warn of an imminent global crisis. When air raid sirens suddenly blare, Collins watches helplessly out the window as the city is destroyed by an incoming missile. Collins is slap-needled, Phelps turns off the trick film Collins has been viewing, and Casey works cosmetic wonders on the sleeping target.

Collins awakens as a feeble old man in a military-run, badly damaged prison. Prisoner of war Barney tells Collins that this is the year 2000, and that the world has been ravaged by World War III. He then explains that the government exterminates people when they reach age sixty-five—and Collins's sixty-fifth birthday is two days away.

Collins escapes from his cell during an air raid and "happens" upon a meeting of the existing military heads of state, who are preparing to surrender because their nuclear supply has been exhausted. "I can show you how to win this war," cries Collins. In exchange for his life, he proceeds to explain how—and *where*—he hid the plutonium just before the "attack."

Hidden under the makeup is Vic Morrow in this scene from "Two Thousand."

GUEST CAST: Vic Morrow (Joseph Collins), David White (Max Bander), Mort Mills (Marshall), Marvin Miller (Smith), Russ Conway (Civilian), Harry Lauter (Admiral), Don Diamond (White), Ivor Barry (Haig), Mark Tapscott (Lt. C.A. Sager), Barry Cahill (Sergeant), Jim Beach (Young Policeman), Tom Pace (Corporal), Lee Raymond (Soldier), Dallas Mitchell (First Agent), Marian Nichols (Policewoman). *Unbilled:* Harold Jones (Second Agent), Charles MacArthur (Photographer), Joanna Cassidy (Model)

"Two Thousand" is fresh, audacious, and outrageous—unless of course you've already seen episode 4, "Operation Rogosh." This show is simply a more expensive-looking remake of the earlier classic. Just like in "Rogosh," there are futuristic dates inscribed in Collins's cell walls, and Barney repeats the Caribbean prisoner character he originated six years earlier.

This version adds the aging gag and a truly spectacular location. To turn Collins into an old man, Casey uses a variety of drugs, including an astringent ether compound and Acrostatin, which lowers the body temperature by five degrees. As usual, the illusion lasts but a few hours and when the mission has been accomplished, Collins watches his old age melt away. In a typical Livingston finale, Collins laughs insanely after realizing he's been deceived. An earthquake-ravaged hospital in Sylmar, California, was used as Collins's "prison." The crumbling exterior had just the right bombed-out look the script required, and was well used by director Martinson.

Guest Vic Morrow, an intense actor and very much his own man, caused some concern for Martinson. "Vic never gave you the same take," the director remembers. "He was endlessly searching, and always feeling for the character." The pairing of this volatile performer and the equally emotional Martinson (who has been known to beat his fists against walls and cry when things go wrong) could have been explosive. Martinson never knew how Morrow felt until the final day of shooting. "When it was all over, Vic said, 'I gotta tell ya Gadg, thanks.' " "Gadg" was the nickname for director Elia Kazan, whom Morrow respected enormously. It was the actor's way of saying he really enjoyed the week. "Coming from Vic," says Martinson, "it was the supreme compliment."

In the tape scene, filmed outside San Francisco's Palace of Fine Arts, Phelps contacts a photographer who is shooting a lovely, windswept young lady. This unbilled model is Joanna Cassidy, who'd make two more appearances this season before moving on to bigger things. Her main task in this scene was to keep the day's heavy wind from blowing her off the modeling platform. "I kept hoping," she cracks, "I would be blown off the platform and into Mr. Phelps's arms." Years later she would star in her own TV spy series, *Codename: Foxfire,* in which she played a sort of female Jim Phelps. Also appearing in this show (and also unbilled) is Harold Jones, the hands of Barney Collier for *Mission*'s inserts. He's one of the agents spying on Collins in the teaser.

149: UNDERGROUND

Written by: Leigh Vance
Directed by: David Lowell Rich
Music Composed and Conducted by:
  Lalo Schifrin

First Aired: 10/28/72

TEAM: Phelps, Barney, Casey, Willy

Good morning, Mr. Phelps. Yesterday, a gang specializing in smuggling criminals out of the country engineered the escape of this man, Gunther Schell, the brains behind the Syndicate's illegal money operations. Conventional law enforcement agencies are unable to locate either Schell or the millions in Syndicate gambling profits he concealed before his arrest. Your mission, should you choose to accept it, is to recapture Schell and recover that money. This tape will self-destruct in five seconds. Good luck, Jim.

Evidence suggests that the gang brainwashes their clients into revealing the whereabouts of their fortunes. Jim has a sender-receiver planted in his ear and is given a hypnotic suggestion from Barney which allows him to divulge only information which Barney radios to him.

Phelps makes headlines as a wealthy doctor wanted for murder. Private eye Barney arranges through an intermediary to have Jim taken out of the country. Jim meets a Mr. Clavering, pays the fifty thousand dollar fee, and (tracked by Willy and Barney) is taken to a warehouse. But when Jim is placed in a coffin as part of his alleged escape route, his transmitter is inhibited by the casket's lead lining, and his teammates are unable to follow him.

At Lotus Hills Mortuary, where Clavering's operations are headquartered, Jim sneaks a powder into the air-conditioning duct which provokes a violent physical reaction in diabetics such as Gunther Schell who, despite heavy stressing from psychiatrist Hargreaves, hasn't revealed the location of the Syndicate's hidden twenty-seven million dollars. Schell goes into a coma and is diagnosed

by Phelps as terminal unless an operation, which Phelps can perform, is arranged. Hargreaves provides the equipment and Jim, requiring an anesthetist, calls in Willy (followed by Barney and Casey). Willy releases a gas into the air which immobilizes everyone but himself and Jim, who wear tiny gas masks. Together, they get Schell out.

Schell's superior in the organization, Arnold Lutz, is under pressure to find Schell and the money. Barney sells Schell to Lutz, and they rush to the hidden cash. They uncover the money, are disarmed by the IMF, and arrested by the police.

GUEST CAST: Peter Mark Richman (Dr. Hargreaves), Robert Middleton (Clavering), Joseph Bernard (Karp), Jeff Morris (Smiler), Dennis Cross (Arnold Lutz), H. M. Wynant (Gunther Schell), John Stephenson (Director), Carl Byrd (Takis), Herman Poppe (Kales), Robert Rhodes (Barman). *Unbilled:* Bill McKeever (First Officer), Joey Hooker, Duffy Hamilton (Stunt Drivers), George Wilbur (double, Phelps), Ham Minn (Mioshi)

A show reminiscent of episode 130, "Mindbend" does not suffer from that episode's dark, claustrophobic look. Again, psychological torture forms the basis of the story. Schell (and ultimately Phelps) is strapped into a chair which is rooted into the floor and capable of tilting. The chair movement, combined with Hargreaves's powerful drugs, psychedelic light show, and wild noises, seems enough to break anyone. But Jim's hypnosis serves him well and despite the torture, he doesn't answer any of Hargreaves's questions. The puzzled doctor attributes this resistance to autohypnosis, since medical man Phelps is a fugitive with a "million dollar secret" and had probably anticipated great stress.

Lynda Day George, seen almost exclusively in close-ups, has nothing to do but hang around and pick up the boys at the finale. The sprawling Lotus Hills Mortuary estate is in fact Los Angeles's Brand Library, and mob boss Lutz's plush apartment is all too strikingly similar to Jim's domicile, although the sets were actually on different soundstages.

150: LEONA

First Aired: 10/7/72

Written by: Howard Browne
Directed by: Leslie H. Martinson

TEAM: Phelps, Barney, Casey, Willy

Good morning, Mr. Phelps. The photographs are of Mike Apollo, leader of one of the Syndicate's most powerful families, and Louis Parnell, an undercover federal agent who for the past year has been Apollo's trusted lieutenant. Parnell disappeared thirty-six hours ago when his cover was blown and is presently undergoing torture to force information from him. Conventional law enforcement agencies have so far been unable to learn where he's being held. Your job, Jim, should you decide to accept it, is to find Parnell and rescue him. This tape will self-destruct in five seconds. Good luck, Jim

The IMF strategy rests on one fact: that Leona Epic, wife of Apollo's fellow Syndicate boss Joe Epic, died under mysterious circumstances on St. Patrick's Day while, miles away, Apollo was traveling by air with Lou Parnell.

Insurance investigator Phelps reopens the Leona Epic case and informs Epic that he is the prime suspect in her "murder." When Jim tells Epic that he has learned of an illicit affair Leona was conducting, Epic does some investigating of his own. With the help of cabbie Willy and doorman Barney, Epic finds a plush apartment full of incriminating evidence: sexy ladies' nightwear, men's pajamas with a monogrammed *M,* and photos of Leona and Mike Apollo, the latter inscribed to his "darling." In keeping with Syndicate protocol, Epic demands a mob "sit-down" to air his grievances against Apollo. Meanwhile, Jim, on a date with Epic's secretary Edith (whom Phelps knows is on Apollo's payroll), drunkenly reveals that Epic is planning to get rid of Mike Apollo.

At the sit-down, which is attended by several underworld leaders, Epic accuses Apollo of seducing and murdering Leona, and recruits Willy and Barney as witnesses, the latter identifying Apollo as Leona's companion. Apollo countercharges that Epic is trying to eliminate him, and produces Phelps as a witness. Instead of adhering to the story he told Edith, Jim betrays Apollo by stating his new theory that Leona was killed either by her husband *or her lover.* Apollo, knowing that Parnell can substantiate his St. Patrick's Day alibi, sends for his captive. When Parnell is smuggled into the meeting, Jim cues a police raid, then impassively tells Epic, "Your wife had nothing to do with Mike Apollo."

GUEST CAST: Robert Goulet (Joe Epic), Pippa Scott (Edith Thatcher), Dewey Martin (Mike Apollo), Nate Esformes (Jules Cordova), William Boyett (Louis Parnell), Bruce Watson (Kelly), Beverly Ralston (Leona Epic), Dick Valentine (Plainclothesman). *Unbilled:* Will Kuluva (Anton Malta)

The name Leona appears often during *Mission*'s last two seasons, notably in episodes 134, "Underwater," 138, "Image," and 142, "Stone Pillow." This is undoubtedly traceable to Howard Browne, author of "Leona" and "Stone Pillow" and a familiar face around the *Mission* offices. The female leads in all of Browne's mystery novels have names starting with the letter *L,* including two Leonas *(Halo in Blood* and *Thin Air).* "A bit of superstition is involved," Browne confesses. "Since the first name of the female lead in my first detective novel started with the letter *L,* for good luck I stayed with it on the others. Seemed to work, too."

This is the last show to feature Casey for some time, although "feature" is hardly the correct word. In fact, she has nothing to do, so an IMF subplot involving the haunting of Joe Epic

is executed. Wearing a Leona mask, Casey appears in various places simply to spook Epic, including a city street and Epic's apartment (which happens to be identical to Arnold Lutz's pad from the previous show). Of course, these scenes required much less of the very pregnant Lynda Day George than they did of actress Beverly Ralston, who plays Casey-as-Leona.

"Leona" marks not only Lynda's temporary departure from the show, but also the final appearance of Greg Morris's mustache!

151: BREAK!

First Aired: 9/16/72

Written by: Sam Roeca and James L. Henderson
Directed by: Paul Krasny

TEAM: Phelps; Barney; Willy; parolee Mimi Davis, former girlfriend of Press Allen

Good morning, Mr. Phelps. This man, Dutch Krebbs, controls the largest illegal gambling empire in the southeast. Conventional law enforcement agencies are certain that undercover agent Fred Stenrock, known as Toledo, who was gathering information that would have led to a government indictment, was murdered by Krebbs and his longtime lieutenant, Press Allen. At the time of his death, Toledo was wearing a wristwatch-camera which we believe contained enough microfilmed information to smash Krebbs's empire. Your mission, should you decide to accept it, is to locate Toledo's body and recover that watch before the exposed film deteriorates. This tape will self-destruct in five seconds. Good luck, Jim.

To attract the attention of billiards buff Krebbs, Jim poses as a first-rate pool jockey, with a little help from Barney's computer-guided cueball and a two-way transmitter implanted in Jim's ear. Krebbs plans to pit Jim against rival racketeer Tim Sharkey's best pool shooter. Jim's girlfriend Mimi, "jealous" over his womanizing, exposes Jim and Barney's edge to Krebbs and Press, who are now convinced that Phelps can't possibly lose. Krebbs bets heavily on Jim.

Press is robbed—twice—of Dutch's collection money by the IMF. Krebbs furiously demands reimbursement from Press's own pocket, making Press receptive to Barney's suggestion that they make a lucrative deal with Sharkey. Barney guarantees Sharkey that Phelps will lose to Sharkey's man.

Barney double-crosses Sharkey and Press by letting Jim win the match. Sharkey accuses Krebbs of rigging the game; Krebbs, knowing that only Press could have tipped Sharkey off, puts out a contract on Press. Willy, having infiltrated Krebbs's organization, tells Press about Toledo's watch-camera. Press joins forces with Sharkey to retrieve the film which will ruin Krebbs. Press exhumes Toledo's corpse and delivers the watch to Sharkey who, at gunpoint, hands it to the IMF. With Casey away on assignment, Phelps asks Mimi to join the team on future missions. Now off parole, Mimi happily agrees.

GUEST CAST: Carl Betz (Dutch Krebbs), Barbara Anderson (Mimi Davis), Robert Conrad (Press Allen), Med Flory (Fred Stenrock, aka Toledo), Francine York (Waitress), Allen Joseph (Willard), Robert Mandan (Tim Sharkey). *Unbilled:* Robert Lee Woods (Stick Hudson), Eddie Robin (Endicott), James Michael (Jerry Cross), Hal Needham (Mork), Larry Watson (Colton), Gail Cameron (Artist)

Sometimes good ideas turn up at the least likely times. So it was with "Break!," which Roeca and Henderson halfheartedly tossed out during a story meeting after other ideas failed. "It appealed instantly to Lansbury and Heath," says Roeca, "because people like pool, it's good visually, and it's right down Barney's alley." Interestingly, Barney's computer-guidance system adds only a 5 percent edge to a game, so Jim relies on his own considerable skill to put the mission over.

"Break!" introduces Barbara Anderson as Mimi Davis. She is crucial to the plot because she was Press Allen's girl before being jailed for unspecified transgressions. Her motivation for joining the Force is never adequately explained, but Mimi is determined to ruin both Press and Krebbs. She turns out to be an astonishingly professional actress, and never once shows any weakness when reunited with her old boyfriend. The only anxiety Barbara Anderson confesses

to on "Break!" was, oddly enough, a simple kissing scene with Robert Conrad. "On *Ironside* I never kissed anybody, or maybe once in four years," she says.

Hal Needham, stuntman and later director *(Hooper, The Cannonball Run)* is seen as Press Allen's subordinate. When strongarm Willy applies for a job in Krebbs's outfit, he demonstrates his skill by knocking Needham flat. Krebbs hires Willy on the spot (Wouldn't you?). *Mission* trivia buffs will notice the reappearance of Robert Mandan and Larry Watson in roles identical to those they had in episode 133, "Shape-up," that of gangster and gunsel, respectively.

This episode's refreshing look, colorful performances led by the energetic Robert Conrad, and steady direction make the show probably the best of the series' many gaming segments. The final cut was so good it was chosen to open the season on CBS, and the hour falls flat only in the last scene when Mimi, her parole rescinded, joins her new friends outside a courthouse.

PHELPS: Listen Mimi, I just had word from the secretary. Casey's gonna be on some special assignments in Europe. Would you like to work with us from time to time?

MIMI: I'd love to.

PHELPS: That's great.

The scene, shot eight weeks later by Terry Becker during episode 159, "Movie," plays as blandly as it reads—and why does Jim so casually mention the secretary to a relative outsider like Mimi anyway? The script's work draft, in which Barney and policemen crash Krebbs's victory party for Jim (Barney nonchalantly swinging Toledo's watch on his finger), might have provided a more satisfying conclusion.

"Break!" was a good choice to open up the season, but by now, *Mission: Impossible* just wasn't getting the kind of attention it once did. *Variety* gave it an inconclusive pass, while *The Hollywood Reporter*'s (September 19, 1972) most telling comment was, "Lalo Schifrin's theme doesn't wear as quickly as this series' premise."

Krebbs (Carl Betz) doesn't know that pool-shark Phelps will ruin him in "Break!"

152: THE DEAL

Teleplay by: George F. Slavin and
   Stephen Kandel
Story by: George F. Slavin
Directed by: Leslie H. Martinson
Set Decorators: Anthony D. Nealis and
   Bill F. Calvert

First Aired: 9/30/72

TEAM: Phelps, Barney, Willy, Mimi Davis, Blair,
others

*Good afternoon, Mr. Phelps. General Oliver Hammond, British soldier of fortune who heads the
armed forces of the Republic of Camagua, is about to take over the government—aided by Syndicate
money. In return, Syndicate leader John Larson and his lieutenant Charles Rogan will control all
gambling and prostitution in Camagua. Rogan is bringing Hammond a five million dollar payoff—in
the form of a key to a safe deposit box. We have not been able to locate that bank. Your
assignment, should you accept it, is to get that key—which will identify the bank and lead to the
bank access card, signed by both Rogan and Hammond himself. Publication of the syndicate deal,
backed by the proof in that safe deposit box, will discredit Hammond and prevent syndicate takeover
of an entire nation. This tape will self-destruct in five seconds. Good luck, Jim.*

Rogan and three companions sail to Camagua to deliver the key to Hammond. Crewman Willy, searching for the key aboard Rogan's yacht, is discovered and shot while jumping overboard. He washes up on a Camaguan beach and is hospitalized.

Camaguan Navy officer Barney arrests Rogan's party and locks them up at an IMF-manned naval base. Colonel Phelps informs the prisoners that Hammond incriminated them in a written confession before abruptly dying. Meanwhile, a thorough IMF search fails to produce a key onboard the yacht, despite the use of metal detectors.

Jim sentences the prisoners to death by firing squad. When only Rogan and his girlfriend Marcy are left, they discover Barney preparing to free another prisoner: Mimi, posing as Hammond's girlfriend. Rogan buys their way into the break-out, and Barney springs them. Rogan takes Barney to the yacht and uncovers the *plastic* safe deposit key. Barney zaps him, takes the key and leaves, moments before Hammond and his militia arrive, searching for the overdue Rogan. Willy escapes from the hospital and swims out to rejoin the team.

GUEST CAST: Robert Webber (Charles Rogan), Barbara Anderson (Mimi Davis), Van Williams (Arnold Sanders), Lana Wood (Marcy Carpenter), Lloyd Bochner (General Oliver Benjamin Hammond), Robert Phillips (Lawrence Chalmers), Lee Paul (Schmidt), Peter Leeds (John Larson), Roberto Contreras (Fisherman), Paul Gleason (Blair). *Unbilled:* George Sawaya (Stunt Guard)

Location work at Port Hueneme's Naval Construction Center and at sea add a breath of fresh air to "The Deal," while the Caribbean locale returns us to some familiar territory. The script does have some questionable moments. For instance, Barney supplies the IMF firing squad with blood-tranquilizer bullets which simulate death—fine. But the first man to be "executed," Chalmers, is replaced by an IMF man in a Chalmers mask and it is *he,* not Chalmers, who is shot in view of the other prisoners. So why bother with tranquilizers if you're "shooting" your own people?

Viewers interested in *Mission* continuity will be amused by Phelps's casting of ex-con Mimi as the brutalized, tough cellmate of Rogan's girl (Lana Wood). "That was fun," Barbara Anderson admits, but adds, "I was a little *too* tough!"

The subplot involving Willy's shooting provided some peril for both Willy and the actor portraying him, as Peter Lupus was a near-fatality while out at sea. "They had Navy sharp-shooters with us in case of sharks," Loop remembers. Just before he was to dive off the yacht to avoid Rogan's gunfire, Lupus waved off stunt men who wanted to douse him with buckets of freezing water. "I had to dive in, stay deep, and get pretty far away from the boat. Well, I dove in too deep and the water was *freezing*! It was one of the most horrible experiences you'll ever know. It felt like somebody had a vice on my chest and I could not breathe. When I got my head above the surface I couldn't breathe in or out, and my muscles were frozen." Pete then realized that the bucket-toting stuntmen wanted to get him used to the shock of cold water before he plunged into the icy sea. A scuba-suited stuntman jumped in and saved Lupus's life. "When I got back on the boat," he adds, "I had a temperature and was seasick, and I'd never been seasick in my life. I'd already had a temperature and didn't know it. I just wasn't ready for it all, and thought I'd had it."

Almost immediately afterward, the sharpshooters spotted sharks nearby. Now nobody wanted to get back in the water, even Lupus's stuntman, but director Martinson still needed a shot of Willy swimming away from the boat, and wanted the stuntman to do it. Lupus recalls that when the stuntman balked, "the director 'accidentally' bumped him and he went into the water! He said, 'Now that you're in there, do you want to do the shot? We'll give you a bonus.'" The stuntman reluctantly obliged, and the shot was made. Les Martinson smiles and claims not to remember the incident but notes, "If Peter said that, it could very well be. Actually, for all the action I've shot, I'm proud to say that I've had not one casualty. I learned my lesson very early when I nearly lost Dale Evans many many years ago."

Whether or not Lupus's stuntman ever got his bonus remains a mystery.

153: IMITATION

First Aired: 3/30/73

Written by: Edward J. Lakso
Directed by: Paul Krasny

TEAM: Phelps, Barney, Willy, Duval

Good morning, Mr. Phelps. These are the Marnsburg crown jewels, brought to this country three days ago to be displayed at the United Nations Building. They were stolen yesterday, while being transported to the UN from their consulate. The jewels themselves are valued in excess of ten million dollars but the collection, because of its historic value, is priceless. Although conventional law enforcement agencies believe that Jena Cole is behind the theft, they have no leads to the location of the jewels themselves. So far, the government of Marnsburg has kept the theft secret. Your mission, should you choose to accept it, is to retrieve the jewels before they are scheduled to go on display in seventy-two hours. This tape will self-destruct in five seconds. Good luck, Jim.

Jena Cole will turn over the jewels to Syndicate man Stevens and his buyers, who financed the theft. Barney, as an ex-cellmate of Jena's brother, manages a loan from her, then returns and empties her safe. Jena finds him with sophisticated electronic equipment and blueprints of the Marnsburg consulate.

Marnsburg official Willy arrives at the consulate with the "real" jewels, explaining that since a robbery was expected, paste copies were sent instead. Jena's informant Dunson, a consulate insider, relays the bad news to her, which is confirmed by her diamond fence Carter (IMF man Duval in a mask). Now Jena must get the "real" jewels or face the Syndicate's wrath.

Jena and Barney become partners. He breaks into the consulate and steals the "real" jewels. Barney plans to turn them over to menacing creditor Phelps, so Jena distracts him while she substitutes her "fake" set for his "real" ones. Jena watches Barney walk out with the "imitations," assuming that Phelps will kill him. Stevens and the Syndicate buyers arrive and determine that Jena's set is counterfeit. Before mayhem erupts, the police take them all into custody—including Jena Cole.

GUEST CAST: Barbara McNair (Jena Cole), Pernell Roberts (Boomer), Charles McGraw (Stevens), Thalmus Rasulala (Eddie), Alfonso Williams (Honey), Olan Soule (Desk Clerk), Lew Brown (Dunson), Oscar Beregi (Mellon). *Unbilled:* Jack Bernardi (Gerald Carter), Ray Ballard (Duval)

The government of Marnsburg is hostile to the United States, so Barney must steal the phony jewels from the consulate vault without inside help. The theft is a complicated process which begins when security courier Willy deposits the jewel case in the vault. That night, Barney jumps the consulate fence, burns through a barred basement window, and confronts the vault door. He is well armed, this time with a device capable of creating an electromagnetic field within the vault door. Barney triggers a dish hidden inside the jewel case which rises and rotates, bouncing a signal around the vault which enables Barney to read the door's combination from the outside via a hand-held gauge.

As the hard-edged, unscrupulous Jena Cole, Barbara McNair plays against her beauty, despite a dazzling wardrobe. Her obligatory romance scenes with Greg Morris work, largely due to a natural rapport which developed between them. "I loved working with that wonderful cast," she recalls, "and I have remained very close friends with Greg and his wife, Lee, for all these years."

"Imitation" was the final first-run *Mission: Impossible* aired on CBS.

Barney woos Jena Cole (Barbara McNair) to retrieve a priceless jewel collection in "Imitation."

154: CRACK-UP

Teleplay by: Arthur Weiss
Story by: Robert and Phyllis White and
    Arthur Weiss
Directed by: Sutton Roley

First Aired: 12/9/72

TEAM: Phelps, Barney, Willy, Sandy, Dr. Adler, Orderly

Good morning, Mr. Phelps. Peter Cordel, a killer for hire, is a man of extraordinary intelligence. Although we are certain that he has murdered at least nine persons, conventional law enforcement agencies have never been able to obtain the evidence even to arrest him. More importantly, we have been unable to identify the Syndicate employer for whom all these murders are thought to have been committed. Your mission, Jim, if you decide to accept it, is to get Cordel and to learn the identity of his employer. This tape will self-destruct in five seconds. Good luck, Jim.

Using a hypnotic drug, posthypnotic suggestion, and the persuasive charms of Sandy who tempts him to join a competing mob, the IMF convinces Cordel that he is suffering from blackouts during which he mindlessly kills Dr. Adler, police lieutenant Barney, and his own brother and Syndicate man Harry Cordel.

Peter Cordel awakens in a mental hospital where he endures an unprovoked, near-fatal assault by a burly orderly. Assuming his boss has lost faith and wants him dead, Cordel has Sandy deliver a message, warning him to call off his hit men.

Sandy meets the Syndicate boss, who is promptly seized by the police.

GUEST CAST: Alex Cord (Peter Cordel), Marlyn Mason (Sandy), Peter Breck (Harry Cordel), Cathleen Cordell (Mrs. Taylor), John Pickard (Doctor), Edward Knight (Driver), Earl Ebi (Gentleman), Bob Kenneally (Bartender), Arthur Franz (Dr. Adler). *Unbilled:* Stephen Roberts (President), Bart LaRue (Goon), Britt Leach (Leslie Harper), Mike Masters (Orderly), Ralph Johns (Samuels)

"Sutton Roley was an excellent director," says Bruce Lansbury. "Sutton would take a flabby script and inject great visual excitement and pace. He'd paint a whole room red just to create something new. He always surprised you." Roley's flair is especially evident in "Crack-up," a childishly plotted show by *Mission* standards. Oddly enough, its simplicity is refreshing and makes the show enjoyable for viewers who normally hate *Mission*. It's another example of a simpleminded premise carried off with great panache. "I was very pleased with that show," the director recollects. "It was off-centered. It could have been deadly, but there was something about it. . . ."

Peter Cordel is a brilliant chess master. During a match, Phelps sprays one of Cordel's chess pieces with a drug which will make Cordel easily susceptible to suggestion. Later, Jim gives hypnotized Cordel specific orders, telling him to freeze each time he hears the phrase, "When in doubt, take a pawn." That line is uttered by various IMFers just before they fake Cordel's "murders." Each time Cordel comes to, he finds another corpse on the floor and the murder weapon in his hands! At times Cordel is so overwhelmed by the IMF offensive and his fear of impending insanity that he almost becomes sympathetic, a point which concerned producer Barry Crane. This problem was handled in the usual manner, by portraying the villain so nastily that his predicament is more satisfying than disturbing.

The show's pitfalls—the potentially dull chess sequences, the silliness of Cordel's zombielike blackouts and subsequent "killings," the plainness of the plot and the sympathy dilemma—are sidestepped with confidence, making Roley's final *Mission* a most accomplished one.

155: TOD-5
(formerly THE CARRIER)

First Aired: 10/14/72

TEAM: Phelps, Barney, Willy, Mimi Davis, others

Written by: James D. Buchanan and
Ronald Austin
Directed by: Lewis Allen

Good morning, Mr. Phelps. This man, Paul Morse, is a government scientist who intends to sell a top–secret biological weapon called TOD-5 to a terrorist ring called the Alpha Group. It is headed by this man, Dr. Victor Flory. We believe the Alpha Group intends to use chemical and biological weapons to terrorize the nation in a bid for power within the next few days. Ex-intelligence officer Gordon Holt is Alpha's contact with Morse and the one man who can lead us to Alpha headquarters. Conventional law enforcement agencies have not been able to locate the Alpha Group. Your mission, should you choose to accept it, is to find the Alpha Group and destroy their biowarfare operation. This record will self-destruct in five seconds. Good luck, Jim.

Holt schedules a meeting with Morse in a small town to buy the TOD-5 container, but when he arrives he finds that Morse has vanished, that a mysterious disease is killing the townspeople, and that the Army has sealed off the town.

When Holt contracts symptoms of the deadly sickness, he fears that the TOD-5 has leaked. He escapes to Alpha Group headquarters and infects the saboteurs to force them to develop an antidote and save themselves. The Force trails Holt, uncovers Alpha Group, and reveals that the plague was a hoax.

GUEST CAST: Peter Haskell (Gordon Holt), Barbara Anderson (Mimi Davis), Ray Walston (Dr. Victor Flory), Michael Conrad (Ralph Davies), Ross Elliott (Paul Morse), Susan Brown (Alpha Woman), James McCallion (Green), Owen Bush (Clerk), Peg Stewart (Screaming Woman)

To fake the spreading plague, the IMF utilizes a drug which, when injected, causes open sores to appear on the body. Getting it into Holt without his knowledge provides the show's cleverest bit. Holt has befriended Mimi, who is immune to the disease. While they talk in his hotel room, the radio broadcasts a news update which is, in fact, a prerecorded IMF tape. In mid sentence, Mimi slap-needles Holt. Jim quickly injects Holt with the drug while Mimi sets Holt's watch back by two minutes and Barney rewinds the tape in the radio. When Holt revives, Mimi completes the sentence she began when she zapped him. At first, Holt is dazed and confused. But since the radio newsbreak is continuing, Mimi is finishing the sentence she "just" started, and his watch shows no lapse in time, Holt shakes off his momentary bewilderment. Before long he too falls victim to the "plague."

When he is covered with lesions, Holt staggers into the Alpha lab with Mimi, whose immunity is essential to finding a cure. Holt passes out and appears to die. Before an autopsy can be performed, the place is invaded by the IMF. Holt comes to, amazed to be alive, and finds that his sores now crumble at his touch.

HOLT: Wh—what happened . . . I'm not dead.
BARNEY: You're not supposed to be.

156: COCAINE

Teleplay by: Harold Livingston
Story by: Norman Katkov and
    Harold Livingston
Directed by: Reza S. Badiyi

First Aired: 10/21/72

TEAM: Phelps, Barney, Willy, Mimi Davis

Good morning, Mr. Phelps. Carl Reid is the most important distributor of cocaine in the United States. Fernando Laroca is his chief supplier. These men have set up ingenious, undetectable pickup and payoff locations, and conventional law enforcement agencies have been unable to stop the flow of this dangerous drug. We've learned that within the next seventy-two hours, Laroca will deliver to Reid the largest shipment of cocaine ever to be smuggled into the United States. Your mission, should you accept, is to locate and seize this shipment. This tape will self-destruct in five seconds. Good luck, Jim.

Jim relies on Reid's ambitious lieutenant Joe Conrad to lead them to the cocaine—despite the fact that even Conrad doesn't know where the shipment is.

Reid, who completely controls the local cocaine distribution, is shocked when detective Barney makes headlines by busting a huge consignment of coke destined for Phelps's nightclub. Through Mimi, Conrad learns that Phelps and chemist Willy have devised a cheap way to produce synthetic, perfect cocaine. Eager to branch out on his own, Conrad forces his way into the deal. Barney uncovers their operation, but Conrad makes a deal with the cop: Three big buyers are coming to town to buy from Reid. Conrad will discreetly undersell Reid and split the five million dollar profit with Barney and Jim.

At the COD meeting with the buyers, Phelps and Mimi get the drop on everyone and take the cash. When the buyers find that the coke is in fact powdered sugar, they angrily grant Conrad and Barney a scant few hours to recover the drugs.

Barney blithely walks out on his deal with Conrad, forcing the latter to quickly come up with five million dollars worth of cocaine on his own. Desperate, he kills a mob intermediary to learn the whereabouts of Reid's shipment. Reid catches Conrad trying to take the drugs, but before violence can explode, the police enter and arrest the entire drug ring.

GUEST CAST: William Shatner (Joseph Conrad), Barbara Anderson (Mimi Davis), Stephen McNally (Carl Reid), Milton Selzer (Stanley), Gregory Sierra (Fernando Laroca), Tol Avery (Samuels), Miguel Landa (Rene Santoro), Annette Molen (Alice Chambers), King Moody (Detective Lieutenant Bruce Leonard), Barbara Darrow (Proprietress), Emile Beaucard (Steve). *Unbilled:* Charles Napier (Roland), Timothy Brown (Barret), James Essex (White), Bob Golden (Patrolman), Carol Henry (Clerk)

Jim gets some unseen help on this one from Casey, who, in Europe, relays important information about the nightclub owner whom Phelps impersonates. The government itself provides the exceptionally pure cocaine which assures Conrad that Willy's dream machine is too good to resist. In fact, it's too good to be true.

Apart from Barbara Anderson's role as a coke-addicted waitress, the show's main point of interest is the machine itself, which, as built by Jonnie Burke, was a huge, laser-generator affair almost the length of an entire room. "It was all Fairchild Aircraft camera cases, big fancy cast-aluminum electrical fittings, the motors that ran it were surplus," Burke says. "I bought practically everything for that machine in a surplus store. The total cost for building that thing was about twelve hundred dollars in those days."

William Shatner makes a second guest appearance in "Cocaine."

157: THE QUESTION

First Aired: 1/19/73

Written by: Stephen Kandel
Directed by: Leslie H. Martinson

TEAM: Phelps, Barney, Willy, Andrea

Good morning, Mr. Phelps. Nicholas Varsi, a top-grade assassin, was captured eight days ago. He claims to be a defector, but he's refused to reveal his mission to the Federal Intelligence Service—unless he is guaranteed safe asylum. But we cannot prove that he is a defector, that he's not here to feed us false intelligence. Unfortunately, we cannot trust the FIS in this affair. There's a strong possibility that they have been infiltrated by a deep agent. Your mission, should you agree to undertake it, will be to determine if Varsi is a genuine defector. You will have to kidnap Varsi from the FIS without their cooperation—and get the truth out of him. This tape will self-destruct in five seconds. Good luck, Jim.

Phelps and Willy spirit Varsi out of a guarded building and store him in an abandoned winery. Masquerading as a fellow agent, Jim demands to know why Varsi is defecting, but Varsi claims no intention of switching sides and, not trusting Jim, refuses to divulge his assignment. To prove his loyalty, Varsi is ordered to kill Andrea, supposedly an FIS agent abducted in the raid. Varsi pulls the trigger on an empty gun, and Phelps seems sufficiently convinced of Varsi's sincerity. He releases Varsi to carry out his mission. Varsi takes Andrea along as a potential hostage. Jim realizes that if Varsi is really a defector he'll return Andrea to FIS headquarters; if he is not, he will kill her.

Despite Varsi's precautions, he and Andrea are tracked to a hotel room where Varsi has arranged to meet his unknown superior, one Colonel Kemmer. When at last Phelps intervenes, he captures Kemmer, saves three lives, and learns the truth about Nicholas Varsi.

GUEST CAST: Gary Lockwood (Nicholas Varsi), Jason Evers (Ben Nelson), Elizabeth Ashley (Andrea), Richard Van Vleet (Coleman), George O'Hanlon (Captain Douglas), John Baer (Belden), Duke S. Stroud (Jameson), Paul Ryan (Attendant)

"The Question" is noteworthy for several reasons, especially in terms of series concept. Evidently, Nicholas Varsi is so canny that for once even Phelps's superiors are unable to render a moral verdict. The mission becomes a personal question for the IMF, which until now has never become involved in matters of guilt or innocence. This time Phelps cannot simply accept the mandate and charge off; the hatchet men have become the judge and jury. "I was emphasizing the emotional question of the story," says writer Stephen Kandel. "They liked it because it was different." The premise and resulting script were good enough to make Kandel the season's story editor and chief rewrite man.

The plot isn't the only thing which makes this show atypical: "The Question" looks and sounds different. It is undoubtedly one of the cheapest segments mounted. Most of the sets are abandoned interiors, and much of the show was shot on the streets of Hollywood as the Force tracks Varsi and Andrea down boulevards adjacent to Paramount Studios. The mechanical effects are kept to a minimum, even during the show's set piece, the Varsi kidnapping. Four tiny explosives help cops Armitage and Phelps enter the condemned hotel where Varsi is being grilled by the FIS. Amid the chaos, they slip into Varsi's room, zap him, clothe him in a police

uniform identical to theirs, and fit a Willy mask over his face. Willy climbs out a window, and Jim fakes a bullet wound on Varsi's chest, then calls for an (IMF) ambulance.

Predictable plot turns (like a Varsi-Andrea romance) and clichés (like foreign accents) are avoided. Stock music is sparingly used, with stretches of unaccustomed silence in its place. Ultimately, however, "The Question" relies upon delicately balanced performances from guests Gary Lockwood and Elizabeth Ashley. Her self-assured Andrea is a real turnaround from the helpless alcoholic she played in episode 132, "Encounter," while Lockwood's Varsi keeps us guessing right to the end. These elements all make "The Question" quite a neat change of pace, especially this late in the game.

158: HIT

First Aired: 11/11/72

Written by: Douglas Weir
Directed by: Reza S. Badiyi

TEAM: Phelps, Barney, Willy, Mimi Davis, Jack

Good morning, Mr. Phelps. The authorities suspect, but have been unable to prove, that crime syndicate chief Sam Dexter murdered his girlfriend Vicki Wells. Dexter is currently serving a prison sentence for tax evasion and because of the murder investigation, he has been kept under close surveillance. Nevertheless, his criminal organization continues to extort millions of dollars in illegal revenues, under the direction of Dexter's secret partner, known only as "the general." Your mission, should you choose to accept it, is to discover the identity of the general, and prove Dexter's guilt in the Vicki Wells murder, thereby smashing Dexter's crime syndicate. This tape will self-destruct in five seconds. Good luck, Jim.

Dexter killed Vicki upon learning, from corrupt assistant DA Reynolds, that she was responsible for Dexter's impending one-year prison stretch.

To Reynolds's dismay, special prosecutor Phelps produces eyewitness Mimi, who places Dexter at the scene of the murder. When he catches Mimi in a lie, Reynolds suspects that someone is trying to nail the imprisoned crime boss. Dexter's hood Murdock tries to force the truth from Mimi but is removed and replaced by IMF agent Jack. En route to Reynolds, "Murdock" is struck by a car driven by Willy. Before "dying," he gasps, "The general framed Sam and hit me." Phelps and Reynolds question Dexter, who feigns ignorance of any "general." Alone with Dexter, Reynolds incriminates himself by agreeing to put a hit on the general. The discussion is recorded and Reynolds is arrested, but Dexter still refuses to cooperate with the authorities.

Back in jail, Dexter muscles in on Barney's escape plan and offers him a fee to kill the general. The pair flee via drainage tunnels, and Dexter takes Barney to the general, intending to return to prison by morning so his absence won't be detected. About to kill both the general and Barney, Dexter is stopped by the IMF and can only lower his gaze when the general growls, "You idiot!"

GUEST CAST: Dane Clark (Sam Dexter), Barbara Anderson (Mimi Davis), Robert Reed (Assistant District Attorney Arthur Reynolds), Frank R. Christi (Ben Murdock), Tony Young (Gordon), Leonard Stone (Paul Lewis), Judson Pratt (Warden Lorimer), Stack Pierce (Barry), Jan Peters (The General), Barbara Rhoades (Vicki Wells)

"Hit" is a treat for Peter Lupus fans, since Willy turns up in a number of roles and with a good amount of screen time. First, he's a tattooed prison yard bully who taunts low-profile con Barney and ridicules Dexter and his clique of musclemen. "I'm Sam Dexter," the impatient crime boss announces, to which Willy responds, "That's your problem." Willy flattens Dexter's head goon and nearly incites a riot before Barney quietly steps in and sends the big man to the floor. As a result, Barney earns Dexter's respect. Willy is next seen behind the wheel of the car that apparently kills "Murdock." He *then* turns up in the hospital as his victim's attending physician!

159: MOVIE

First Aired: 11/4/72

Teleplay by: Anthony Bowers, Arthur Weiss, and Stephen Kandel
Story by: Anthony Bowers
Directed by: Terry Becker

TEAM: Phelps, Barney, Willy, Mimi Davis, Dave Waley

Good morning, Mr. Phelps. Norman Shields controls a major criminal operation which has been infiltrating the entertainment industry. Shields has been using illegal funds, supplied by the chief Syndicate money man: Benjamin Dane. Dane recently loaned Shields ten million dollars to take over Pantheon Studios. Theodore Dane, Benjamin's brother, will be flying to Los Angeles in the next few days, to head operations at Pantheon. Your mission, should you decide to accept it, will be to locate and seize the Syndicate financial records held by Norman Shields . . . records detailing exactly how criminal money is being funneled into the entertainment industry. With this information, the entire Syndicate can be smashed. This tape will self-destruct in five seconds. Good luck, Jim.

Shields and Theo Dane have never met, allowing Jim to remove Theo and take his place in Los Angeles. Jim angers Shields by backing a production called *Portrait of a Murder*. Directed by Barney and starring Mimi, it exactly chronicles a notorious murder Shields committed and barely avoided prosecution for years earlier. Phelps insists that the film will be a hit and make Mimi a star, but Shields dreads the adverse publicity the film would create.

Willy replaces Shields's gun with a duplicate, set to fire blanks by remote control. Late one night at the studio, Jim berates Shields and threatens to finish him. Shields pulls his gun which, to his astonishment, fires and "kills" Phelps. Unknown to Shields, who flees, the entire scene has been filmed by Barney, with Jim's back to the camera. The film is dubbed by IMF mimic Waley who, by impersonating the voice of Theo Dane, completely changes the circumstances of the "murder."

Shields blames the murder on a prowler but panics when Mimi comes forth as a witness and informs Benjamin Dane. Shields tells Dane that the killing was an accident. When Dane demands to see the *Portrait* footage to authenticate Shields's assertion that the movie would ruin him, he sees instead a film in which Shields, unprovoked, shoots an affable "Theo." Dane takes the syndicate records from Shields and leaves him with his goons. At gunpoint, Willy and Phelps take the records from Dane.

GUEST CAST: John Vernon (Norman Shields), Barbara Anderson (Mimi Davis), David Brian (Benjamin Dane), William Smith (John Brent), Rhodes Reason (Theodore Dane), Douglas Henderson (Henry Packard), James Whitworth (Heath), Lee Farr (Jack Welton), Ron Pinkard (Barr), Walker Edmiston (Dave Waley), Jerry Douglas (Daniel Moore). *Unbilled:* Eric Server (Reporter), Joanna Cassidy (Stewardess), Kahana (Trainer), Paul Factor (Mixer)

Anthony Bower's original story employed the bogus film gimmick, one of *Mission*'s cleverest and most infrequently used ideas. The plot was then retooled by *Mission* vet Art Weiss before finally undergoing the Kandel treatment, which added further complications. Kandel also eliminated the character of Karen Dane, a famous actress working with the IMF, and replaced her with the more familiar Mimi Davis.

Walker Edmiston, who appeared as a conventional law enforcement official in last season's episode 145, "Casino," is seen here as Rollin-Paris surrogate Waley who, in early drafts of the script, demonstrated his vocal dexterity by mimicking Phelps during a conversation with the

IMF leader! Edmiston returned to play an identical character (with a different name) in episode 167, "The Fighter."

Superobservant *Mission* fans will notice framed photos of Adele Taylor and Barry Crane adorning the offices of moguls Brent and Shields, respectively. One of the hour's highlights is Greg Morris's portrayal of an effete, pompous film director, a refreshing change from the endless mob hood types he was saddled with during this period.

The importance of the insert is evident in the last few seconds of "Movie." When Phelps and Willy flank Dane to demand the records, Dane glowers, then simply hands it over. It was decided afterward that Dane should have some extra incentive, so two inserts were added: one of Jim exposing the gun tucked in his waistband, and another of Willy's pistol leveled at Dane.

160: ULTIMATUM

Teleplay by: Harold Livingston
Story by: Shirl Hendryx and Harold Livingston
Directed by: Barry Crane
Music Composed and Conducted by:
   Duane Tatro
Director of Photography:
   Robert B. Hauser, ASC

First Aired: 11/18/72

TEAM: Phelps, Barney, Willy, Mimi Davis, Carl, Lisa, Jack, others

Good morning, Mr. Phelps. The brilliant nuclear physicist Dr. Jerome M. Cooper has informed the President of the United States that a fifty-megaton hydrogen bomb is located in an unnamed American city and will be detonated at noon tomorrow unless the following demands are met. First, eight congressmen and three senators and three members of the cabinet, whose names are listed here, are to resign their seats, to be replaced by men of Cooper's choosing. Second, certain United States foreign policy must be immediately and irrevocably reversed. The authorities are convinced that Dr. Cooper is telling the truth. He and his accomplices have placed millions of lives in jeopardy. Your mission, should you accept, is to locate and disarm the bomb. This tape will self-destruct in five seconds. Good luck, Jim.

The IMF has less than sixteen hours to locate the bomb (which is in one of seven Pacific coast cities) and identify Cooper's associates, who will disarm the weapon when they hear from Cooper that his demands have been met.

Cooper is instructed to meet the president at the western White House, but his car breaks down en route and he must stop at Willy's roadside station and café. Awaiting repairs, Cooper hears a radio "bulletin" which suggests that his demands will be met. Suddenly, killers Phelps and Mimi, on the run from the law, barge in and hold Willy and Cooper hostage until their teammate Barney arrives in a getaway helicopter.

Convinced that the president is acceding to his demands and frustrated by his inability to move, Cooper persuades Jim to let him call his accomplice Rogers, who will disarm the explosive (which, Cooper reveals, is right there in Los Angeles). However, before Rogers can deactivate the device, he is killed by Cooper's wife and aide Adele, who fears the collapse of their plan.

When he hears Rogers's death announced over the café radio, Cooper realizes that the weapon is still armed. When Barney arrives in the chopper, Jim and Mimi join Cooper's plan and fly off to neutralize the bomb. Cooper takes them beneath City Hall, where he shuts off the bomb with five seconds to spare and is instantly arrested, along with his wife.

GUEST CAST: Murray Hamilton (Dr. Jerome Cooper), Barbara Anderson (Mimi Davis), Madlyn Rhue (Adele Cooper), Donnelly Rhodes (Joel Morgan), Vince Howard (Patrolman Frank Dagget), Fred Holliday (Carl), Judy Brown (Lisa), Robert Legionnaire (Police Sergeant), Dale Tarter (Jack), Vic Vallaro (Frederick Rogers). *Unbilled:* Flip Mark (Delivery Boy), Scott Allen (Williams), Robert Nash (Police Sergeant)

Shirl Hendryx's original story involved Cooper, his hidden bomb, and the time element, but went in a different direction. Of Cooper, Hendryx explains, "He was a very egocentric character with great pride in his ability to develop this bomb." Fighting time, Phelps and company put Cooper to sleep. He awakens in a hospital bed, is told that he's been in a coma, and that many weeks have passed. "Then they turned him loose, knowing that this man was going nuts wondering why the bomb hadn't gone off. He then led them to it, because he could

not resist going to the bomb to find out what was wrong. Naturally, he got there just before it was going to really blow up." Perhaps due to story points similar to those in episode 137, "Invasion," the story was reworked. Harold Livingston added the irony of would-be bully Cooper himself being bullied by two-bit hoods Phelps and Mimi.

"Ultimatum" marks Barbara Anderson's final *Mission,* once again playing her tough girl character. Assistant to the producer Dale Tarter makes an on-screen appearance, this time in the IMF communications room peopled by anonymous agents. It is Tarter who calls Cooper on behalf of the president and arranges the meeting which starts the IMF strategy.

161: KIDNAP

First Aired: 12/2/72

Written by: Sam Roeca and James L. Henderson
Directed by: Peter Graves

TEAM: Barney, Casey, Willy, Dowager

In a departure from the series format, a crime boss abducts Jim Phelps and forces the IMF to steal an incriminating letter from a safety deposit box in exchange for Jim's life.

In exchange for federal immunity, Mitchell Connally, a former associate of Syndicate chief Andrew Metzger, will give authorities a letter which will certainly convict Metzger for murder. With less than six hours to get that letter out of Connally's bank deposit box, Barney hatches a plot to free Jim (held in Metzger's air raid shelter) *and* trap Metzger.

Inside the bank where Connally's letter is located, Casey uses a syringeful of quick-set plastic to forge a copy of the bank's master key which, with Connally's key, will open the box. Later, Casey and Willy become "trapped" in a stalled elevator with Connally and his two federal bodyguards. Casey lifts Connally's key, has Willy make a fast mold, and returns the key unnoticed. Using the two keys, Casey steals the letter, only to have

it stolen from her by Hawks, Metzger's scheming subordinate who plans to blackmail his boss.

Before Hawks can contact Metzger, Barney hastily forges a phony envelope and promises Metzger delivery of the letter upon proof of Phelps's safety. In the bomb shelter, the IMF rescues Jim and corners Metzger, Hawks, and their underlings.

GUEST CAST: John Ireland (Andrew Metzger), Charles Drake (Mitchell Connally), Jack Ging (Hawks), Geoffrey Lewis (Proctor), Marc Hannibal (Eckworth), Arline Anderson (Sandra), Monty Margetts (Dowager), Glen Wilder (Henzel), Chuck Hicks (Security Guard), Edmund Gilbert (Armsby). *Unbilled:* Gwil Richards (Parmel)

"Kidnap" is *Mission*'s only sequel, a follow-up to last season's "Casino." Jim and Barney are vacationing at a tennis resort when Metzger grabs Jim, introduces himself to Barney, and hands him enlargements of Phelps and Barney from the earlier show.

METZGER: You two headed the team that hit the Aquarius Casino about a year ago. We have automatic security cameras in the casino. It took me three weeks checking out film, eliminating possibilities. . . . I put the word out. It took a little while but we spotted your friend (Jim) two days ago. . . . I've been trying to check you people out, but I came up empty. No records, no traces. You're good. So I want you to do a job for me.

In an early draft, Metzger admits that a "hit" he put out on the team was nearly fulfilled until he found it necessary to employ his adversaries instead.

Although Barney acts as mastermind, the mission depends upon Casey's skills at deception and pick-pocketing. Lynda Day George, making her return to the series, carries most of the action and acting. Using her native Texan accent in the bank, she portrays a chronic asthmatic. By wheezing, asking for water, and dropping her jewelry, she preoccupies the bank clerk in the vault, giving herself time to copy the bank key. In the elevator scene she's an hysterical claustrophobe, clawing at the other passengers as a cover for her pick-pocketing of Connally's key.

Peter Graves, who had directed an episode of *Gunsmoke* prior to joining *Mission*, "wanted to direct one and have some fun." Phelps's unusual lack of screen time in "Kidnap" made this episode a good opportunity for Graves to indulge himself. "I'd watched all the other directors

and seen them get lost in the maze of production problems on the show," says Graves. "I said, 'Nobody knows the show better than I do. I will get the crew out every night by 6:00, we'll have a tidy little show, and that will be that.' " Naturally, it wasn't quite so simple, and the show fell behind schedule on day one. "It turned out to be a much more difficult show than I had realized as an actor," Graves admits. "It was fun, but I realized then what all our other directors had gone through."

Despite (or because of) the extra time, "Kidnap" is probably the best show of the season. Graves's direction and the uncommonly challenging script make it the last top-notch *Mission*. Atypical scenes are handled adroitly, like the fistfight denouement in the bomb shelter and the early vacation sequence in which Jim, true to form, analyzes his opponent's tennis game while easygoing Barney simply wants to enjoy his time off. The acting is better than usual, and the very nature of the story provides an exceptionally high amount of tension, capped by the team's loss of the letter at the end of act three.

"That wasn't a bad show," Graves believes. *Daily Variety* concurred in its review of December 5, 1972, referring to director Graves's work as "top calibre."

162: THE PUPPET

Written by: Leigh Vance
Directed by: Lewis Allen
Music by: Lalo Schifrin

First Aired: 12/22/72

TEAM: Phelps, Barney, Casey, Willy, Hank, Khalid

Good morning, Mr. Phelps. You are looking at a picture of Paul Ostro, head of the criminal family of that name, whose activities include narcotics, gambling, prostitution, and extortion. A few weeks ago he suffered severe facial injuries in a hunting accident and is confined to bed. He is using his younger brother Leo as his spokesman and contact for the outside world. Since the time of Paul's accident, there are rumors that the Ostro family is planning a new criminal enterprise involving over one hundred million dollars. Your mission, Jim, should you decide to accept it, is to discover the reason for the Ostro's change of policy and smash the new plan, whatever it is. This tape will self-destruct in five seconds. Good luck, Jim.

Unknown to all (but suspected by Jim), Leo killed his brother Paul and has substituted a bandaged "puppet" who endorses all of Leo's plans. Leo talks four crime bosses into each depositing one million dollars into a mysterious scenario which Leo won't explain—not even to rival Larry Gault, who reluctantly contributes his share.

Jim and Casey involve Leo in a huge oil deal with a corrupt Middle Eastern minister (IMF man Khalid). Ostro chef Barney drugs "Paul," who appears to suffer a heart attack. Doctor Willy clears the room and lowers unconscious "Paul" out the window as IMF agent Hank, in identical pajamas and bandages, replaces him. Willy steals the four million dollars from the Ostro safe and hides it in a secret compartment in Phelps's briefcase.

Gault, having Leo watched, learns from Casey that Leo plans to abscond with the Syndicate's four million dollars. Gault grabs Leo and Jim as they finalize the oil deal. Leo is shocked when he finds the four million dollars and a ticket to Zurich in his briefcase. Seeking support from "Paul," he is further amazed when his "brother" claims that Leo shot him and has kept him drugged. When the bandages are removed, Hank (disguised as a badly scarred Paul Ostro) convinces the mobsters of Leo's perfidy. His life on the line, Leo divulges his master plan to counterfeit huge amounts of South African currency. When he takes the hoods to the printing presses, Barney alerts the police, who raid the place.

GUEST CAST: Roddy McDowall (Leo Ostro), John Larch (Larry Gault), Val Avery (Augie Leach), Richard Devon (Hank), Joseph Ruskin (Khalid), John Crawford (Paul Ostro), Lewis Charles (Sam Zercos), Ken Scott (Fusco), Shirley Washington (Girl Travel Agent), Colin G. Male (Guard), Joe Haworth (Police Officer)

This show is like old home week, with familiar faces Larch, Avery, Crawford, Devon, and Ruskin. But it is Roddy McDowall who dominates the episode. His facial reactions at the climax, when his plans unravel and he comes perilously close to death, are exquisite.

In one of the best sequences, Leo forces chef Barney to drink a milk shake which Leo thinks may have induced the heart attack in his puppet (in fact it did). Barney takes a drink and shows no ill effects (the drug takes two minutes to work). He calmly exits, then runs like hell to the kitchen, where the antidote is hidden!

411

163: THE FOUNTAIN

First Aired: 1/26/73

Written by: Stephen Kandel
Directed by: Barry Crane

TEAM: Phelps, Barney, Casey, Willy, others

Good afternoon, Mr. Phelps. As the result of a power struggle between Syndicate executives Tom Bachman and Matthew Drake, Bachman stole the Syndicate's top secret computerized records: enough information to destroy their operations in eight midwestern states. In the process, Bachman killed two men and seriously wounded four others, including Matthew Drake, whose organization is now desperately hunting for Bachman and the records. Your mission, should you decide to accept it, is to get those records before Drake does. This tape will self-destruct in five seconds. Good luck, Jim.

The aging Bachman, about to be pushed out of the Syndicate, crippled Drake in an explosion. Now Drake, wanting revenge as much as the stolen records, has traced Bachman to a tiny village in Mexico where Bachman awaits a smuggler named Mallory to fly him to a hideout. Drake sends hoods Dawson and Perez to bring Backman back.

Bachman and Mallory (Barney) crashland in the wilderness, where they stumble across the Fellowship of the Golden Circle, a strange cult whose members include Phelps, Casey, and Willy. Bachman learns that this commune has discovered the fountain of youth in the form of an underground waterfall. When he drinks the water and has his youth restored, Bachman sees the commercial possibilities. Perez and Dawson find Bachman and take him to Drake along with Casey, whom Bachman uses as proof of his miraculous findings.

Bachman offers to return the records to Drake in return for mob backing to finance distribution of the water. When Casey, deprived of the water for two days, ages and "dies" before his eyes, Drake agrees to the deal, hoping the water will cure his crippled hand.

Bachman takes Drake (and the IMF) to an abandoned restaurant where the stolen computer tapes are buried. Jim enters and takes the tapes as policemen make the arrests.

GUEST CAST: George Maharis (Thomas Bachman), Cameron Mitchell (Matthew Drake), Luke Askew (Dawson), Pepe Callahan (Bartender), Charlita (Waitress), Carlos Rivas (Perez). *Unbilled:* Ed Connelly (Mallory)

Using the eternal youth ploy which has worked since year three, Jim snares another vain villain with an abundance of thinly-veiled tricks. "The Fountain" recalls last season's episode 125, "Encore" but, unlike the earlier show, doesn't require the outrageously detailed chicanery which conned poor William Shatner.

The fun is in watching the Fellowship of the Golden Circle completely hoodwink Bachman. The broken leg Barney suffers in the plane crash is instantly healed; a dying raccoon is restored (thanks to a drug surreptitiously administered by Casey); well placed photos and news clippings depict Casey as an Old West settler, Willy as a World War II pilot, and Phelps as an Indian fighter. Bachman gets his chance to sample the water and quickly passes out. By the time he awakens, Casey's makeup wizardry has made him look and feel twenty years younger.

For her death scene in Drake's office, Casey wears two masks, a horribly old and wrinkled one under another mask of her normal visage. Her hands are similarly covered. Swallowing a "death" pill, she then applies a solvent to her face, hands, and hair (which has been chemically treated to turn gray). In seconds, the normal Casey mask and hands disintegrate, exposing the aged disguise beneath. Then the pill takes effect and Casey "dies."

In a move designed, no doubt, to please the front office, the location of the hidden tapes is in fact the Paramount commissary kitchen, thus saving the cost of constructing another set.

164: BOOMERANG

Produced by: Laurence Heath
Written by: Howard Browne
Directed by: Leslie H. Martinson
Music by: Lalo Schifrin

First Aired: 1/12/73

TEAM: Phelps, Barney, Casey, Willy, Dorlan

Good morning, Mr. Phelps. Two days ago a private plane exploded while en route to Los Angeles, killing John Vayle, a member of an underworld family headed by Stanley Luchek. We have reason to believe Vayle's death was arranged by Vayle's wife, Eve, enabling her to obtain records he carried vital to the Luchek organization. In the proper hands those records would put an end to the mob's operation and place Luchek himself behind bars for life. Your mission, should you decide to accept it, is to locate those records and turn them over to the authorities. This tape will self-destruct in five seconds. Good luck, Jim.

Eve had her husband killed and hid his syndicate records to blackmail Luchek.

Police lieutenant Barney catches Phelps trying to kill Eve but must let him go when she refuses to press charges. Eve charms Jim into admitting that he doesn't know who his employer is; he only knows that he was paid by a pretty girl. Eve pays Jim to find the man who hired him.

When her safe is robbed and the only clue is a fresh Johnny Vayle fingerprint, Eve becomes worried. Can Johnny still be alive? Phelps and Eve locate Casey, the woman who paid Phelps. Jim "pressures" her into revealing that Johnny survived Eve's murder attempt and now wants Eve dead. That night, IMF agent Dorlan, disguised as Johnny, steals into Eve's bedroom and leaves a hypo mark on the sleeping woman's arm. Eve awakens to see a gloating "Johnny" climbing out a window.

Barney visits Eve the next day. He claims that Johnny—his cohort—injected her with truth serum to learn the whereabouts of the records. To prove it, Barney indicates the needle mark on Eve's arm. According to Barney, Johnny told *him* the location of the records at which point he killed Johnny and took the records. Barney then shows Eve "Johnny's" body and what seems to be the briefcase the data was stored in.

Eve demands that Phelps kill Barney, but when Jim hints that the cop may only be bluffing to muscle in on Eve's blackmail payments from Luchek, Eve is compelled to check the records—if they're still where she left them. She leads Jim (and, unknowingly, Luchek) to the records, whereupon both Eve and Luchek are apprehended by the IMF.

GUEST CAST: Laraine Stephens (Eve Vayle), Ronald Feinberg (Stanley Luchek), Walter Barnes (Homer Chill), Charlie Guardino (Johnny Vayle), Amzie Strickland (Mildred), Jerry Jones (Cabbie), Charles Picerni (Ollie Maybrick), Richard Reed (Dorlan)

Since both "Boomerang" and episode 150, "Leona" were written by Howard Browne, it's not surprising that they seem so similar. "That was a good idea," Browne says, "so we set it in two directions." In this version, the IMF must get Eve to believe her husband is still alive—no mean feat, since Eve *saw* Vayle bludgeoned, then placed in a plane that exploded seconds after killer Garth bails out. Eve saw the parachuting figure jump from the plane—but was it Garth or Johnny?

With longer dialogue scenes than usual, "Boomerang" has a strange feel to it. Director Les Martinson offsets the lack of standard *Mission* action by concentrating on the relationship between vulnerable tough guy Graves and (in a role originally slated for Stefanie Powers)

Laraine Stephens, decked out in some impressive outfits by award-winning designer John Anthony.

The idea of convincing the mark that she talked in her sleep was so good that it returned in the following episode. And Mr. Phelps must have enjoyed his charade as hit man Dave Ryker in this adventure because he plays the same character in the upcoming segment, 167, "The Fighter."

165: INCARNATE

Teleplay by: Buck Houghton and
    Stephen Kandel
Story by: Buck Houghton
Directed by: Barry Crane

First Aired: 1/5/73

TEAM: Phelps, Barney, Casey, Willy

Good morning, Mr. Phelps. Hannah O'Connel is the ruthless leader of a criminal gang that recently stole over a million dollars in gold bullion. Her lieutenants have been her two sons, Thomas and Robert. Recently Robert turned government witness, enabling the authorities to indict Hannah O'Connel for tax fraud. However, she escaped with Thomas, and Robert is presumed dead. Conventional law enforcement agencies have located Hannah and Thomas O'Connel on their way to the Caribbean island of Jamada, a nation with which we have no extradition treaty. We cannot kidnap her on foreign soil, of course. Your mission, should you decide to accept it, will be to induce Hannah O'Connel to return to the United States of her own free will, so that she can be captured and the gold recovered. This tape will self-destruct in five seconds. Good luck, Jim.

When Robert tried to hijack the gold, Hannah shot him and dumped the body at sea.

In Jamada, the O'Connels and their two gunsels stay in a house run by Casey, who hints that the place is haunted. That night, superstitious Hannah is visited by Robert's laughing "ghost." After her hoods are found "dead," Hannah has local shopkeeper Barney arrange a voodoo exorcism, during which Robert's "ghost" demands the location of the gold. Then Hannah blacks out, thanks to a drug administered by Barney.

When Thomas O'Connel "kills" Willy in a fight over Casey, he is forced to run. Casey tells Hannah that he has returned to America. Barney then confesses that the voodoo ceremony and the "ghost" were tricks concocted by Robert to get Hannah to divulge the location of the gold. Fearful that she talked during her blackout, Hannah frantically hires crooked pilot Phelps to sneak her back into the US. She leads him to the gold and is immediately arrested.

GUEST CAST: Kim Hunter (Hannah O'Connel), Robert Hogan (Thomas O'Connel), Alex Rocco (Dall), Solomon Sturges (Robert O'Connel), Bob Hoy (Kelso)

"I don't think that Bruce was pleased with the script I gave him," suspects writer-producer Buck Houghton, whose story was revamped by Kandel. "Incarnate" employs the old IMF spook tricks like Barney's hologram projections to scare Hannah into arranging the exorcism, during which she sees Robert superimposed over the ceremonial pyre. "The gold, mother," he cries, "My soul is weighed down with the gold. The hidden gold. Tell me where it is, Mother. Free me!" When she comes to the next day and deduces, from data provided separately by Barney and Casey, that Thomas has duped her, she has ample reason to return home—fast.

Series scholars will be amused to hear the name Jim drops to Hannah during his opening spiel to her. He claims Benjamin Dane (whom Jim put away in episode 159, "Movie") is his business associate!

Shooting in Arcadia, propman Bob Richards devised a little gag which inadvertently provoked a bigger one. To break the monotony of location shooting, Richards recorded a silly "Boom a laka" team song and played it for the crew, then forgot all about it. Later, director Crane was setting a scene in which Morris and Lupus were in the woods, manning speakers and a tape recorder, ostensibly playing jungle drum music (to be dubbed in later, of course). Just before the take, Richards realized that *his* nonsense chant was on the tape recorder, and turned the machine's volume knob all the way down. As Bob relates, "It was the last shot of the day, we were behind schedule again, and working hard to beat the dark. During the take, Barry says to Lupus, 'Reach over and turn some of the knobs on the recorder so it looks like you're adjusting the volume.'

"Lupus, who hardly ever hit the right switch in his life, turns the knob way up, and there's me yelling this team call! Greg's trying to keep a straight face but can't, because Lupus falls out of the shot laughing and the entire crew breaks up too. Barry screams, 'If I told you once, I told you a thousand times, I want only *clear* tapes on those machines!' He's turning red, and the crew, many of whom were afraid of Barry, start disappearing into the dark until it's just him and Greg Morris and me. Even Lupus walked away!"

Crane apologized to Richards the next day but later had a chance to even the score. For the scene in which Hannah finds her hood Dall hanging in her room, only Dall's feet were to be seen in the shot. To hold the actor, Richards rigged a parachute harness from the soundstage rafters. "How do I know that's gonna hold the guy's weight?" Crane asked Richards, who replied that the harness could hold five tons. Finally, to prove his point, Richards himself got into the harness and Crane seized the moment: The prop man was instantly hoisted thirty feet into the rafters and left hanging for almost half an hour.

166: THE WESTERN

Written by: Arnold and Lois Peyser
Directed by: Leslie H. Martinson

First Aired: 3/2/73

TEAM: Phelps, Barney, Casey, Willy, Walker, a Driver

Good morning, Mr. Phelps. The Azteca Museum was recently looted of over five million dollars worth of Pre-Columbian art by a brilliant thief, Van Cleve, and his partner Matthew Royce, now missing, presumed dead. In the process, a guard was murdered. Conventional law enforcement agencies have been unable to move against Van Cleve. We've determined that the stolen art has been brought into the United States and is hidden here. Our government is most anxious to return this national treasure to its rightful home. Your mission, should you decide to accept it, will be to locate the treasure and prove Van Cleve's guilt. This tape will self-destruct in five seconds. Good luck, Jim.

When Royce tried to end their partnership, Van Cleve lured him into a desert cave and sealed it off with an explosion.

Walking down a city street, Cleve sees a skull face on a man moments before he is "killed" in a traffic accident. Later, he meets Casey and spots a large sum of cash in her purse which then seems to vanish. When Casey suggests that he may be clairvoyant, Cleve scoffs, but his "vision" seems to come true when Casey is a big winner at a local casino.

At his desert ranch home, Cleve finds surveyors Barney and Jim working on a top secret project. Bribing Jim, Cleve learns that a nearby dam is ready to burst and flood the entire area. Cleve's next "vision" depicts his own corpse floating in his swimming pool. That night, Cleve's bedroom is rocked by an "earthquake." Expecting a fatal deluge, he flees into the desert and retrieves the stolen art, which is hidden in a remote canyon. When the IMF trace him they also nab Matthew Royce, who survived Cleve's death trap and has been attempting to kill his ex-partner.

GUEST CAST: Ed Nelson (Van Cleve), Michael Ansara (Ed Stoner), Barry Atwater (Matthew Royce), Frank Farmer (Driscoll), Don Gazzaniga (Walker), Joanna Cassidy (Stewardess), Troy Melton (Driver)

Larry Heath's neighbors, Arnold and Lois Peyser, had toyed with the notion of writing a *Mission* for some time but were unable to come up with a suitable premise. Then, at a party they overheard a discussion about a jacklike device strong enough to shake buildings and determine if structures were earthquake-proof. "Wouldn't that be great," Arnold thought, "to make somebody think there was an earthquake." The Peysers tied that idea into their hobby, Pre-Columbian art collecting, and went to see Heath and Stephen Kandel. "They were a great help in structuring it for us," Mr. Peyser explains. "We just had the theft of the art, and the device that could shake a building."

The explosion which supposedly kills Royce is stock footage from episode 69, "The Bunker," added to scenes with actors Ed Nelson and Barry Atwater filmed at the same location, Bronson Canyon. The show's most elaborate effect, the self-dissolving Van Cleve dummy in the pool, was Jonnie Burke's last major gag of the series. To achieve the effect of a melting "corpse" rising to the top of a violently churning pool, Burke first installed air lines of different sizes at the pool's bottom to get the water bubbling. Then, with the Ed Nelson mannequin, he dropped a weighted bucketful of dry ice and several handfuls of detergent to make the dummy seem to melt away.

Why is the show titled "The Western"? Because a small ghost town near Cleve's estate (actually Paramount's western street) is the setting for a frenzied gunfight between Royce and

the IMF, who saw him shooting at Cleve and gave chase. Reminiscent of the series' early action days, the sequence seems oddly out of place.

Arnold Peyser's fondest memory of the show concerns a call his youngest son received from his former college professor shortly after the episode was first aired. The educator asked if the young man's parents were the same Peysers who wrote this peculiar show. "He had seen it go on and started to go past it," Peyser says of the professor, "but started watching it despite himself. Then he said, 'Suddenly, I realized that it was a literate show! Is it always like this?' "

If only he'd seen some of the classics!

167: THE FIGHTER

First Aired: 2/9/73

Teleplay by: Stephen Kandel and
    Nicholas E. Baehr
Story by: Orville H. Hampton
Directed by: Paul Krasny
Music by: Lalo Schifrin

TEAM: Phelps, Barney, Casey, Willy, Dave Rawls

Good morning, Mr. Phelps. The Syndicate operation in the boxing game is handled by Jay Braddock. He has corrupted Paul Mitchell, once an honest promoter, now his partner. Braddock and Mitchell own a number of promising fighters whose careers they are manipulating for illegal profits at public expense. Middleweight James Loomis recently defied them and was brutally murdered in a phony "accident." Conventional law enforcement agencies have been unable to act. Your mission, should you decide to accept it, will be to expose Braddock and Mitchell and to destroy their criminal operation. This tape will self-destruct in five seconds. Good luck, Jim.

IMF intent: Sucker weak Mitchell into believing his ruthless partner Braddock plans to eradicate him.

Representing a powerful new mob, Barney coolly walks into Mitchell and Braddock's office and offers to buy their top contender, Pete Novick, for $37,800—exactly the sum stolen from the promoters' box office that evening by Phelps and Barney. When Barney proves intractable, Braddock (realizing that killing him could be dangerous) decides to solve the problem by having Pete Novick killed. Braddock calls a Syndicate contact for a hit man but is cut off by IMF mimic Rawls, who tells him that top man Phelps will be sent.

Mitchell and Braddock watch Jim plant a firebomb at Novick's house. Mitchell is horrified when his daughter Susan, Novick's girlfriend, drives up and goes inside. Before he can save her, Mitchell sees the house blown to bits. "Susan" is

Casey, who escapes with unconscious Novick through a back door.

Grief stricken and embittered, Mitchell wants out but Braddock won't allow it. When he overhears Phelps talking about another contract killing, Mitchell thinks he's next and considers special investigator Willy's offer to testify against the Syndicate. Then Braddock derails the IMF plan: To placate Mitchell, he will kill the killer—Phelps!

GUEST CAST: William Windom (Paul Mitchell), Joe Maross (Jay Braddock), Geoffrey Deuel (Pete Novick), Jenifer Shaw (Susan Mitchell), Herbert Jefferson, Jr. (James "Gunner" Loomis), Walker Edmiston (Dave Rawls), Conrad Bachmann (Cashier), Martin Ashe (Steve Lawson), William Benedict (Denver). *Unbilled:* Arline Anderson (Telephone Voice)

Last season's "Blues" underwent two rewrites before reemerging as "The Fighter." Both scripts center around the divide-and-conquer angle, and all that was changed was the setting, from the recording business to the fight game. For once, there are more coincidences *behind* the scenes than in front of the camera, namely in casting. William Windom, the more domineering of the two crooks in "Blues," this time plays the more passive role, his hair permanently skewed across his forehead. Joe Maross, the hard-nosed Braddock, played Windom's partner in crime way back in episode 33, "The Widow."

A script subplot involving a "fatal" accident for motorcyclist Willy spelled the second time this season that Peter Lupus was almost killed. Preparing to film some "drive-bys" on Griffith Park's winding mountain roads, Lupus at first refused to wear a cycle helmet. "I don't want to mess my hair," he remembers saying. When wardrobe assistant Wes Eckhart insisted, Peter donned a helmet and climbed aboard the cycle. Moments later, turning a curve at twenty-five

miles per hour, the front of the cycle twisted and sent Loop looping off the steep road and into space. "I went down about thirty feet," Lupus says, "hit a huge boulder, caved in the helmet, and thought I'd broken my neck. The last thing I said as I went over was, 'I can't believe it.'

"I rolled on, and was about to drop who knows how much further down the mountain when my feet got caught in some bushes. While I dangled there, the motorcycle landed about three feet away from my head. Finally, the police came down with ropes and pulled me up. I never lost consciousness, though." Lupus credits his strong back and neck with absorbing the impact of the boulder, but readily concedes that Wes Eckhart saved his life. "My head would have been splattered all over that rock if I didn't have the helmet."

168: THE PENDULUM

Written by: Calvin Clements, Jr.
Directed by: Lewis Allen
Director of Photography: J.J. Jones
Set Decorator: Bill F. Calvert

First Aired: 2/23/73

TEAM: Phelps, Barney, Casey, Willy, Arab, Benson, others

Good morning, Mr. Phelps. Gunnar Malstrom is one of the leaders of the Pendulum, a secret terrorist organization seeking to dominate the power centers of our country. We have been unable to identify any other members, but we have learned that the Pendulum group is putting into action a plan code-named Nightfall, involving a major attack on our government. Your mission, should you decide to accept it, will be to prevent this catastrophe by discovering what Nightfall is—and stopping it. This tape will self-destruct in five seconds. Good luck, Jim.

Casey dates Malstrom and takes him to the headquarters of World Resources Ltd., a huge international organization with which she is associated. Barney sits Malstrom in a chair outfitted with a hidden polygraph, and pressures him to leave Pendulum and join their ranks. Carefully worded questioning, combined with the polygraph results, indicate that Nightfall involves the assassination of Air Force General Weston. However, they do not learn that Weston has already been killed and replaced by a Pendulum double who is about to convene the heads of every major US military organization—and annihilate them with a bomb.

Malstrom meets Jim, the head of World Resources, who explains that Pendulum's sloppy plotting has jeopardized Jim's larger, more sinister goals. Malstrom is shocked when Jim casually mentions the Weston plan, but still refuses a plum role in World Resources in exchange for canceling Nightfall. He is then allowed to escape, carrying an IMF transmitter.

Phelps warns "Weston" of the assassination plot, and the false general graciously invites Jim to sit in on the targeted staff meeting. Barney electronically eavesdrops as Malstrom confronts Pendulum's leader and unsuccessfully urges the postponement of the bombing. Barney alerts Jim, who finds the bomb and heaves it out a window seconds before it explodes.

GUEST CAST: Dean Stockwell (Gunnar Malstrom), Scott Brady (Allen Bock), Frank Maxwell (General Weston), Jack Donner (Leader), Leon Lontoc (Houseman), Peter Mamakos (Arab), Jack Collins (Admiral), Beverly Moore (Telephone Operator), Don Reid (Manny)

"The Pendulum," the last *Mission: Impossible* to be made for over fifteen years, is not a stirring finale to the series. Despite an uncredited Kandel rewrite, a potentially involving story is crippled by comic book plotting, obvious contrivances (like a character named Malstrom conceiving a political maelstrom), and quite possibly the worst dialogue in the history of the series—which is really saying something. Only Peter Graves could get away with a line like, "Keep me briefed through the microreceiver."

The music editor, perhaps seeing the writing on the wall and feeling a little nostalgic, spices the show with choice *Mission* melodies, some dating back to the pilot. They are a welcome change from the more often used later selections.

The restaurant at which Casey and Malstrom dine is identified, via a stock shot, as Apollo's Golden Chariot. We can only hope that the place is under new management since we last saw it: It was owned by nasty Mike Apollo in episode 150, "Leona"!

 # Wrap

Another season had come and gone. And while nobody was certain, there were those who felt that *Mission* wouldn't be back for an eighth season. The ratings had slipped again, and after CBS was finished moving the series around (from Saturday at 10 to Friday at 8, then back to Saturday at 10 for reruns), *Mission* had averaged at number 57 with a 26 percent share, an all-time *Mission* low. Emmy night was another shutout, with nominees Lynda Day George and Gib Holley and Lou Hafley (for episode 166, "The Western" art direction) going home empty handed.

In the event that the series failed to return, Peter Graves found time to star in a revamped *Call to Danger* pilot (written and produced by Laurence Heath) as a backup. For Greg Morris it didn't matter: He had already let it be known that seven seasons were enough for him. "They were sorry to hear about it, but they understood," says Greg of his costars' reaction. The response of CBS programmer Fred Silverman was far more show-bizzy: According to Greg, he simply grinned and said, "We'll work together again."

Peter Graves, seen with Diana Muldaur, starred in a revamped *Call To Danger* pilot in 1973.

Until CBS made up its collective mind, Laurence Heath had to be prepared for another season. Among the more intriguing stories lined up for year eight were a Howard Browne plot involving a rigged ouija board, and "Phobia," by first season contributor Robert Lewin. To uncover an ingenious heroin pipeline hidden in an alcohol rehabilitation center, Jim has wife Casey admitted—roaring drunk, for her intoxication can't be faked. She exposes the setup and informs the team, which pick up the drugs. Casey is caught, and to make her talk, the villains inject alcohol into her bloodstream, giving her a horrifying case of delirium tremens. Her biggest phobia overcomes her as she imagines scorpions and ants invading her padded cell and swarming over her. Miraculously, she doesn't break, but when Phelps tries to retrieve her, the heavies use them both as hostages to get the heroin from Willy and Barney. To avoid a double cross, a device is attached to Jim's back which can cripple him by remote control. In a skillfully planned finale, of course, the IMF prevails.

On a more lighthearted level, writer Sam Roeca remembers a story he used to pitch only half seriously. "The Laundryman" centered around a bagman who picks up and delivers laundered Mafia money. "He was a thorough crook," says Roeca, "and as a cathartic he preached at a revivalist tent. He goes to a dentist's office one day and is put to sleep. He comes to in totally different surroundings. He calls for a nurse, and when an angelic creature comes in, he thinks he's dead! But he's in a halfway house between heaven and hell, in purgatory with an up elevator and a down elevator. In order to clear himself, he has to confess where he got the money!" "The Laundryman" was considered jokingly over the course of three years, but was never written.

Stephen Kandel had his own ideas for year eight, including one tale, "in which the team was infiltrated and set up for a mass execution." In another story, Kandel brought back Eddie Lorca, the hitman portrayed by Robert Conrad who supposedly died at the end of episode 105, "The Killer," one of Kandel's favorite *Mission*s. Lorca was once again an assassin operating by chance, but this time his target was the head of the IMF. "One of my stories involved the necessity of recruiting a real sleazeball for an absolutely essential mission." These plots might seem revolutionary in terms of *Mission* format, but that's exactly why Kandel wanted to try them. "After seven years, the premise gets a little weary. If the show had gone another year, I felt it would have needed a jab in the ass. But I guess the word got out," jokes the writer, "because they canceled the show instead."

"I guess we could have come up with another twenty if we had to," Heath speculates. "I think the stories were getting tired. Even though we all liked it, we were getting tired of it. Our minds were tired." The circumstances surrounding the show's actual demise on February 9, 1973 seem shrouded in mystery. Although Bruce Lansbury was present when Paramount president Frank Yablans told CBS's Robert Wood, "I'm pulling *Mission*," neither Lansbury nor anyone else can remember why *Mission* was sacrificed in a dispute between Wood and Yablans. "Bob and Frank were going at each other a little bit," Lansbury says. "It was *mano a mano* between two egotistical business types. Personality clashes. And Frank decided he would pull *Mission*. Whether it was going to get an eighth year or not is moot."

Killing *Mission: Impossible* was more than Paramount haughtily snapping its fingers at CBS. For the studio, it meant that *Mission* would at last begin to show a profit.

Peter Graves and Bruce Geller strategize over an ill-fated basket-ball game against the *Mannix* crew.

Mission: Accomplished

*"You know, you sit on the set all those years
and idly wonder who's ever gonna see them.
Then you go out in the world and find out
that everyone has seen them!"*
—PETER GRAVES

FOR THOSE WHO worked on the show, *Mission*'s cancellation ended a cycle of hard work, long hours, and good times—like a memorable basketball match between the *Mission* and *Mannix* companies preceding a Los Angeles Lakers game. Characteristically, the *Mission* crew brought trick basketballs filled with mercury, but even with former college players like Bruce Geller and Greg Morris, they were outclassed. "We wanted Lupus as center because he was big," says Greg, "but he was out there in the corner, shooting hook shots! Graves didn't want to play, because Peter loves basketball like Christ loves sin. I think the score ended up eight-six. *Mannix* beat us and we were glad to get off the court. It was embarrassing. Bruce was glaring at everyone, and Lupus was saying, 'I had fun!'"

The *Mission-Mannix* rivalry extended into the realm of practical jokes. A constant tit for tat was played each week when the Nielsen ratings were released. If *Mission* outrated its sister show, Greg Morris would thoughtfully cover Mike Connors's dressing room door with photocopies of the Nielsen list. When *Mannix* was ahead, a large cake, adorned by a stuffed crow, was sent to the *Mission* stage. The message—eat crow!—was understood by all. On other occasions, Greg, Lupus, and others invaded the *Mannix* stage with prop machine guns to kidnap Connors in the middle of a take; Greg was locked in his dressing room with a smoke bomb; and Lupus once found his dressing room furniture suspended from the soundstage grids. "It took us four hours to get all that stuff down," says Loop. "I never did pay them back for that!"

Most of the pranks *within* the *Mission* camp were instigated by Greg Morris. A pair of crossed eyes could break Peter Graves's iron concentration, and even Barbara Bain was targeted. "Barbara was joking with our junior makeup man Ronnie Schneider," says Greg, "and playfully hit him on the arm. Ronnie grabbed his arm and walked off the stage. Now when Barbara makes a fist, she could maybe break a wet Kleenex with it! Bob Dawn said to her, 'You really hurt Ronnie. Didn't you know he had a bad arm?' She was distraught! It took us a half hour to make her believe that she did not really hurt Ronnie Schneider." The most frequent victim was Peter Lupus, who (luckily) was a great sport. Morris was so skilled at breaking Loop up on camera that for the last four years of the series, Peter refused to look him in the eye. "When I heard Lupus say that he thought he was losing his hair, we made him

425

think he was going bald for two weeks," says Greg. "I should never have heard him tell Ronnie Schneider, 'Put a little rouge on me, I saw the show last week and I looked pale.' I would say, 'Gee, Loop, you look pale,' and he'd say, 'I told those guys!' He'd call makeup and Ronnie would curse me." By the time the gag was over, "We made Peter Lupus look like Cochise!" At times mastermind Morris found that turnabout was fair play. "Once the crew weighed down my tool case with lead. During the shot I walked over to pick it up and I couldn't lift it! The crew howled, because here was Mister Efficient not being very efficient!"

Scant months after CBS aired its last rerun, *Mission: Impossible* was syndicated in the fall of 1973. Metromedia TV had bought syndication rights just ten weeks after the show's 1966 debut (the executive in charge of the buy was, interestingly enough, a former Desilu executive), and international syndication would eventually encompass over ninety countries. Studio records concerning syndication profits are often top secret, along the lines of atomic formulae, but *Daily Variety* reported in its October 19, 1976 issue that *Mission* had already grossed between fourteen and fifteen million dollars in syndication. More well known within the industry was the lawsuit Bruce Geller threatened against Paramount over the syndication monies.

"Bruce demanded an accounting from Paramount," says Bruce's friend Austin "Rocky" Kalish. "He felt he wasn't getting a fair shake and was going to call in his lawyers. It's not uncommon." Bruce told Chris Knopf that the studio offered him half of what was actually due. Says Knopf, "They told him, 'Sue us. It'll take you ten years. Maybe you'll get it, maybe you won't.' It's not unusual." According to Bernie Kowalski, who owns a piece of the show, Bruce and Peter Graves (another profit participant) were going to sue together. "The audit would have been well over one hundred thousand dollars," Kowalski says, "and Bruce, being a wise man with a legal background, knew that their bookkeeping factors were very tough to beat." In the end, Geller settled. "He was very bitter about the deal," says another friend, Ron Austin. "He was intimidated by all the legal stuff, so he settled for far less than he should have gotten out of *Mission*." Geller wasn't the only one; Peter Graves recalls Bruce Lansbury telling him that *Mission* never went over budget after its fifth season. "I remember that every time I get a financial statement from Paramount concerning my percentage of the profits, because there are no profits! I've never pursued it," says the actor. "There's nothing to do about it."

Bruce Geller's post-*Mission* career was a curious one. After his banishment from Paramount Geller produced a feature, *Corky* (1972) at MGM; produced and directed another, *Harry in Your Pocket* (1973) for United Artists; and produced and directed a 1976 TV film, *The Savage Bees*. In 1975 he portrayed his father in *Fear on Trial,* a TV movie about a 1962 libel suit over which Judge Abraham Geller presided. For MGM he produced a TV movie, *Bronk* (1975), and its subsequent one-season series; and was an executive consultant on another short-lived show, *Jigsaw John* (1976). He was always busy filming pilots and had development deals with both NBC and CBS, but surprisingly, *Mannix* was the last hit he was associated with.

Bruce's friends had noticed a change in his work. "He lost his confidence as a writer," says friend Jim Buchanan, who cowrote *Harry in Your Pocket* and coproduced *Jigsaw John.* "He used to say he didn't write much anymore and he lost the talent for it, that he was a rewrite man and a producer." Bruce was far more interested in producing and directing, and some suspect that his later scripts and stories were mere conduits to a deal. "Bruce loved working with film," says Chris Knopf, who worked on two pilots with Bruce during this period, "and

426

I don't think he had quite the patience with a script that he had in the earlier days. The care and attention just weren't there."

Once regarded as a writer with a fine human touch, much of Bruce's later work was, like *Mission: Impossible,* surprisingly cold. "Bruce was a very nice man," says writer Steve Kandel, "warm, friendly, and loyal to a fault. But the work he created was mechanical, distanced in every way from simple human feeling. Why? I'll never know and he didn't know. I asked him, and he could not answer." Kandel worked with Bruce on a project about a man who took on the identity of other people.* The result was a total misunderstanding. "Bruce wanted somebody who, by use of plastic surgery, hypnotherapy, and computer training, takes on the persona of another person. Bruce wanted someone who took other people's identities and mastered, manipulated, and controlled them, and was secure while manipulating the false identity. What I wrote was somebody who immerses himself in the mind and soul of another human being, and then finds himself trapped by the man he doesn't know whose persona he has taken. Bruce's reaction was so visceral that it was staggering. It was personally alarming to him that somebody could become trapped in another person's mind. What I gave him apparently aroused very deep anxieties."

By 1978 Bruce Geller Unit productions was headquartered at Twentieth Century-Fox where he was considering producing a pilot (written by William Read Woodfield) based on the Fox film *Fantastic Voyage* (1966). On a foggy Sunday, May 21, 1978, Bruce and ABC's top programmer, Steve Gentry, took a pleasure trip from Santa Monica to Santa Barbara in a twin engine, dual propeller Cessna 237 Skymaster. About five miles from Santa Barbara the plane crashed into Buena Vista canyon, in the suburb of Montecito. Both men were killed instantly; Bruce was forty-seven, Gentry thirty-seven.

The accident shocked the Hollywood community. Geller's funeral brought out hundreds of mourners, quite a turnout for a supposedly remote man. He left behind his devoted wife, Jinny, daughters Lisa and Cathy, and many, many friends.

Bruce also left behind a series which, long after its cancellation, remained a part of popular American culture. Direct *Mission* references and parodies have appeared in media forms as diverse as feature films (*Blue Thunder, Revenge of the Nerds, 1969*), countless ad campaigns, and songs like Bruce Springsteen's "I'm a Rocker" (1980). *Mission*'s stars, who refused to spoof the show when it was being made, became more liberal once the series was over. A three-part episode of *The Jeffersons* (1983) featured Greg as an unnamed electronics genius who convinced a pair of con men that the world was coming to an end. In *Airplane II: The Sequel* (1982), pilot Peter Graves's attempt to shut down a computer results in the mechanism self-destructing amid a puff of smoke and the *Mission* theme music. A Hong Kong comedy, *Mad Mission 3* (1984), stars Graves as a secret agent who boards a rickshaw to get his taped instructions and photographs. When the tape announces its imminent self-destruction, the frightened rickshaw driver abandons the passenger and vehicle, which promptly career down a long sidewalk stairway to an explosive landing. In 1989 Graves appeared in a clever *Mission*-esque spot for Oldsmobile narrated by tape voice Bob Johnson, which also included a mask peel off!

The endless takeoffs indicate how *Mission* continues to shadow those associated with the show. "I was lecturing at the University of Michigan," says Max Hodge, who wrote one

---

* The story line echoes a Geller-produced TV movie from 1971 called *Hunter,* starring John Vernon.

episode. "When the professor mentioned *Mission: Impossible* among my credits, I got the biggest round of applause for that." Iranian director Reza Badiyi vividly remembers the impact *Mission* had back home. "It was the number-one show in Iran," he says. "On the nights that my shows ran, people shut down and went home to see it. They called me Mister *Mission: Impossible.* I became so famous that the government sent me first-class tickets for my family and the baby-sitter and the dog to go to Iran. The National Guard came to the airport, and there were maybe five hundred people there at one in the morning. When the jet arrived they played the *Mission: Impossible* music out of tune. It was fantastic. The people regarded it as much more than just a television show."

"The influence of the show was international and incredible," says Greg Morris. "I didn't realize it until I got to Monaco and saw my face on the cover of the local TV guide. I fell off the sofa when I saw *Mission* in Thailand and it was dubbed; then I understood why people all over the world thought that I spoke their language."

"I've heard every *Mission: Impossible* joke," Martin Landau claims, "every variable. People come over and generally as an opening gambit will say some self-destruct joke or try to pull their face off, and usually I'm their best audience." He recalls a Russian reporter who visited the *Mission* set. "He was a journalist living in New York and his son was going to an American school. He said, 'Mr. Landau, very nice meeting you, I like show very much. My son speaks like Yankee, no accent, but very embarrassing.' I said, 'Why?' He said, 'My son says, "Hey, Pop, why do all the bad guys talk like you?"' "

"It's an enormous hit all over the world," Graves points out. "It keeps playing in countries again and again. Watching yourself in all those languages is wild stuff. I've heard it in German, English, French, Spanish, Farsi, Mandarin, Japanese, Greek, Dutch, Norwegian. . . . The guy who dubbed my voice in Japan was short and bald, but he had a voice that matched my body. It was very good.

"Boy, there's nothing like having a hit television series. The one thing I had always wanted in my life was to walk down the Champs Élysées in Paris and be recognized as an actor. And I got it! *Mission* hit France like a rocket, and to stand in Paris and have rose petals strewn at your feet . . . ! How else in the world can you be treated like that, and meet kings and queens and princes and captains of industry and interesting people? A couple of them have since been deposed." Naturally, Graves disavows any knowledge of their actions.

If imitation is the sincerest form of flattery, then *Mission* is held in high regard indeed. The number of unsold TV pilots "inspired" by *Mission* could probably fill a book. "I can't stop it legally," said Geller in 1976, "so I may as well sit back and be flattered." One, *Inside O.U.T.* (1970), was directed by Reza S. Badiyi. In *Mission*'s wake appeared series with similar concepts. In *Charlie's Angels* (1976–81), three beautiful private detectives used confidence games to entrap villains. An unseen boss relayed their instructions not via a tape recorder, but an office telephone. The voice belonged to John Forsythe, who once turned down the lead in *Mission*. *Switch* (1975–78) was a Glen Larson production in which a former con man and former cop flimflammed bad guys. Both series used less complex plots than *Mission* and operated on a more lighthearted level.

Another successful *Mission* caricature was *The A-Team,* which premiered in 1983. Chronicling the adventures of a renegade group of Vietnam veterans who help the helpless, the accent was on comedy and gratuitous destruction (although in keeping with television standards of that time, no one was killed, no matter how many bullets were fired, cars crashed, or bodies assaulted). Some of the show's characters had familiar traits. The team leader was a master

of disguise; the mechanical expert was black; another member was an actor-con artist. A huge hit during its early seasons, *The A-Team* fizzled out quickly, proving Geller's theory that self-satire was terminal.

More ignominious fates awaited *High Performance* and *Masquerade,* which also appeared in 1983. *High Performance* was the name of an elite protection agency consisting of a stunt driver, a former military intelligence officer, a female martial artist, and, again, a black mechanical genius. It was a four-episode series. *Masquerade* was more interesting, centering around the National Intelligence Agency, which recruited nonprofessionals with special skills for hazardous spying missions. In fact, *Masquerade* borrowed as much from the old CBS pilot *Call to Danger* as it did from *Mission.* Despite the presence of William Read Woodfield as story consultant, *Masquerade* failed, lasting only eleven episodes.

In the meantime, an interesting trend was developing in television programming. Popular "dead" shows were returning to life as new TV movies, specials, pilots, and series: *The Beverly Hillbillies, The Andy Griffith Show, Leave It to Beaver, Perry Mason, The Twilight Zone, The Man from U.N.C.L.E., Get Smart, Gilligan's Island, I Dream of Jeannie, Father Knows Best, Gidget, The Monkees, Maverick, The Avengers, The Saint, The Munsters, Marcus Welby M.D., Kojak, The Six Million Dollar Man, The Bionic Woman, The Incredible Hulk, Bonanza, Gunsmoke, Kung Fu,* and more. Most of these productions were very successful, Nielsenwise. Paramount boarded the bandwagon with a vengeance, remaking or revising virtually every popular TV property the studio owned in series, TV movie, or feature form: *The Odd Couple, The Brady Bunch, Star Trek, Love American Style, The Untouchables...* everything, it seemed, but *Mission: Impossible.* It wasn't that the studio didn't *want* to bring back the show—they just weren't sure how. Unfortunately, the man best equipped to revive it wasn't available, although it is questionable whether Bruce Geller would have even been asked to helm the project had he lived.

In 1978 Paramount executives Arthur Fellows and Terry Keegan approached Gary Nardino, the president of Paramount Television, with the idea of a *Mission* "reunion" TV movie. By introducing new, younger characters to the IMF, the movie would also act as a pilot. CBS agreed to air the show as a two-hour movie, and a script was written for the "dream team" of Phelps, Rollin, Cinnamon, Barney, and Willy, plus new IMFers.

By the time the script was ready, CBS had dropped out of the project, and NBC entered. The resulting script, *Mission: Impossible 1980,* by George Schenck (based on a story by Schenck and Frank Cardea) was a shocker. In it, the law has caught up to the IMF, and the story opens with Phelps's release from a six-year prison sentence for conspiracy, burglary, wiretapping, and refusing to testify before a Congressional committee! When young TV newsman Rick Burns refers to him as "the last of the Watergate era," Jim takes offense, and, amazingly, explains himself.

PHELPS: It was different times. We did things for our country that, today, seem sort of radical. [pointedly] Everything I did ... everything the IMF did ... I believed was for the good of the country.

RICK: But you were violating people's civil rights and intervening in the domestic affairs of other countries.

PHELPS: I thought what I was doing had to be done ... for the good of the country.... If I was guilty of anything, it was of being naive and out of tune with the times.

Jim is surprised when John Victor, the taped voice himself, personally proposes a final mission: to retrieve a footlocker containing the remains of Peking man, the celebrated "miss-

ing link," which was stolen from the Smithsonian Institute by Rollin Hand and Cinnamon Carter! Victor explains that the artifact was sold to a Chinese tycoon and is hidden in San Francisco's Chinatown. Feeling partially responsible because of Rollin and Cinnamon, Jim reluctantly accepts the mission.

Barney is recruited from his teaching job, but Willy, now a gymnasium entrepreneur and star of his own TV show, *Workin' It Out with Willy,* refuses to go. A beautiful Amerasian IMFer and a Barney Collier protégé skulk through the secret passageways of Chinatown and recover Peking man, which is delivered to Victor.

When Jim learns from Cinnamon and Rollin that they had nothing to do with the theft, he realizes he's been deceived by Victor, who ransoms the treasure and threatens to destroy it, thus endangering Sino-American relations. Phelps hastily prepares a counterplot to undo Victor. "Hospitalized" after a "car crash," Victor panics when told that he's been unconscious for a week, fearing that his automated time device has already destroyed the fossil. He sees through the IMF ploy and rushes to Peking man's hideout—which is just what Jim had in mind. Peking man is delivered to the president, who returns it to Beijing.

Clearly, this script is not so much a continuation of the old series as a negation of it. The overall effect, to any *Mission* fan, is enormously depressing. Phelps in jail, a politically naive fall guy; Willy's adamant refusal to help; the IMF's hostility toward supposed crooks Rollin and Cinnamon; the treachery of the taped voice; it all undermines the series premise and the unswerving faith the IMF had in one another. Incidentally, the plot device of the taped voice sending the IMF on a criminal mission for his own evil purposes was one of *Mission*'s most often proposed and rejected story ideas and obviously so, since it impuned the validity of the entire series. Even Jim's dialogue rings false, as when he muses, "I preferred James Bond's romantic fantasies to the more ethical problems posed by John le Carré in his novels." Not very likely! In the prospective series, the IMF would have been "mavericks, Robin Hoods operating on their own," according to producer Keegan. "They had a rather substantial source of funding which Phelps put away over the years. Now they'd have the ability to pick and choose who to help. It was to repay his debt of having been a bad guy, but not knowing he was a bad guy."

NBC wisely rejected *Mission: Impossible 1980* and asked Keegan and Fellows to develop a more traditional *Mission* script. Oddly, none of *Mission*'s best writers (Woodfield and Balter, Laurence Heath,* Paul Playdon) were approached. The producers chose a man they'd worked with before—Harold Livingston, who'd written some of *Mission*'s most obvious plots.

In Livingston's *Mission: Impossible 1981* we learn that the IMF has been transformed into what Phelps contemptuously calls a "ponderous think tank" loaded with "accountants and attorneys and PhD candidates." Luckily, Phelps and Barney have been quietly training a new team reminiscent of the old squad. They are called to action when billionaire D. W. Snow threatens to explode a neutron bomb in an unknown location unless the president acceeds to his extremist, politically dangerous demands. Jim calls on Willy (again, a health magnate), Cinnamon (now a physician), and Rollin (an antique dealer), plus four new IMFers, younger versions of the prototypes.

En route to Las Vegas, Snow watches IMF news bulletins of impending international trouble. Gazing out his train window, Snow sees "Vegas" (an IMF movie) blown to bits, and

---

* "I went in for an interview with the head of development at Paramount," says Heath, "and talked to him about doing *Mission: Impossible 1980.* He said, 'Gee, I didn't know you had anything to do with *Mission.*'"

is rendered unconscious. He awakens "ten months later" as a prisoner of war, bearded and crippled (thanks to Cinnamon, who has inserted a surgical needle in the man's spine). The Russians have invaded the United States! Snow and fellow prisoner Barney escape to join the American resistance movement in a zoned-off area of Vegas which looks atomically devastated. A "Russian" attack led by Phelps "kills" Barney and others, and Snow, desperate to stay alive, reveals where the bomb is hidden just before it is set to detonate.

Livingston's script was certainly more traditional than Schenck's. In fact it's a remake of two episodes, 137, "Invasion" and 160, "Ultimatum"—neither of which Livingston originated—and his own 148, "Two Thousand." NBC was happy with the script, but the studio was not. "Paramount thought it was going to cost a fortune to make," says Keegan. "They perceived the production as being very, very expensive as opposed to how we perceived it being shot. It would have been two and a half million dollars tops. We also knew that it had a lot of value in terms of syndication overseas, but somebody at Paramount said to us, 'Don't mix your budgets and my bookkeeping!' We could have made it for a reasonable price." After minor rewrites, *Mission: Impossible 1982* (as it was then called) was ready to go when a new management moved into NBC and, as is often the case, jettisoned many of the old regime's deals—including *Mission: Impossible.* Because of its cost factor, Paramount let the script die.

In 1984, producer Ed Feldman thought "it was a very interesting idea to update *Mission: Impossible*" as a *theatrical feature* (*Star Trek* had already been reincarnated as three very profitable movies). Sy Salkowitz, writer of two *Missions* (episode 46, "The Town" and episode 49, "Trial by Fury") was assigned to write and produce the film. Says Feldman, "It was gonna be a very, very big movie. They were talking about it as one of their major summer pictures." For the next eighteen months, announcements to that effect never failed to make news (it made page 1 of the *Los Angeles Herald Examiner* of February 22, 1986). Most of the items asserted that Peter Graves would definitely be back as Jim Phelps, with cameos by Landau, Bain, Morris, and Lupus, plus a trio of new IMF agents. Actually, *none* of the original stars had been approached, not even Graves. "It's reared its head every year for the last five years," Graves said in 1985. "Nobody's approached me. I suppose I'd be the last one that they'd approach. This winter I got a call from Lupus, who asked what was going on. I said, 'Peter, you know more than I do.' My stunt man called me, then Wes Eckhart the wardrobe man, who said, 'We're breaking down the wardrobe for this new script right now!'" Leonard Nimoy *was* approached—not as an actor, but to direct the film (he had just helmed Paramount's *Star Trek III: The Search for Spock*). After an inconclusive meeting with Feldman and Salkowitz, Nimoy declined. "My heart wasn't in it," he says.

Salkowitz's script, *Good Morning, Mr. Phelps (Mission Impossible: The Movie)* took yet another approach. This time the mission is to rescue a kidnapped nuclear scientist and his family from the hands of Middle Eastern terrorists and prevent them from building enough reactors to melt the polar ice caps and raise the sea level, thus ruining every coastal city in the world. Jim chooses Willy, Barney, Rollin, and Cinnamon, plus a new crew: a handsome mimic; gorgeous expert on nuclear reactors; black strongman; and electronics genius. The action ranges from Istanbul, where the IMF liberate the scientist and his family from an underwater installation; to the jungles of Bangkok, where they destroy a reactor assembly camp; to the palace of the South American country of Montequiera where, from a guarded, full swimming pool, the IMF steal nuclear fuel cannisters from a vault! Distinguishing the script was an emphasis on witty dialogue among the team, a playful rivalry between Rollin and the younger mimic, a romance between the mimic and the female operative, and a series of

action-packed IMF escapes. "The studio requested big stunts," says Salkowitz, "to gather both ends of the audience spectrum. Those who remembered *Mission* would be turned on, as well as those who want to see the *Raiders of the Lost Ark* kind of thing." In the end Salkowitz may have succeeded too well: A projected budget of fifteen million dollars brought winces from Paramount executives, as did a proposal to shoot it in England for ten million dollars. This, plus the usual change of studio heads and policy (and an indecision over bringing back the original stars or hiring a younger, all-new cast) sent *Good Morning, Mr. Phelps* into "what we call 'development hell,'" says Ed Feldman.

As Graves, Morris, and Lupus knew all too well, there was still great public interest in a reunion. It seemed that wherever they went, the trio was besieged by questions about a "new" *Mission*. In 1984, Morris and Graves guest-starred in an episode of *Murder, She Wrote.* As Greg explains, "When we were shooting on location at the University of Washington, students saw the two of us together and asked, 'Is this *Mission: Impossible*? Is Peter Lupus coming?'" A few years prior to that, the three flew to New York to appear on *Good Morning America* as part of a *Mission* salute. After the show, says Greg, "We were to go on our separate ways, but we had time. I said, 'It's a great day, why don't we get a bite to eat outside?' *Wrong!* We did not get much chance to eat, because people were doing double takes and saying, 'They're together again!' Graves'll call me up and say he's been somewhere and people asked about me, and the same with me. For some reason, the audience always expects to see Lupus and Graves and Morris together. I've run into people who resent the fact that Graves and Lupus aren't with me!"

In 1988, Paramount, still reluctant to give up the concept, engaged veteran writer-producer Stirling Silliphant to write *another Mission* script. A strike by the Writers Guild of America neutralized the deal, but was also the catalyst for *Mission*'s eventual return.

Encore

"Time does march on."
—JIM PHELPS, 1988

THE 1988 WRITERS GUILD STRIKE lasted 150 days and paralyzed Hollywood. Faced with the prospect of no new product, some studio and network executives threatened (half seriously, it was believed) to reshoot *old* scripts. Paramount, which had spent eight years (and much money) trying to bring back *Mission: Impossible,* saw a golden opportunity.

"To offer viewers as much original programming as possible," ABC Entertainment president Brandon Stoddard announced in July that the network had signed with Paramount to remake thirteen of the best *Mission* scripts as new episodes to be filmed entirely in Australia with an all-new cast for fall 1988 airing. *"Mission: Impossible* was, and remains, a genuine 'evergreen' among television series," said Stoddard, "with new audiences still drawn to the old shows because of the unique casting and stories. With a new cast and a whole set of new locations to bring added sizzle to the best of the original scripts, we feel *Mission: Impossible* will deliver both originality and vitality to our fall program schedule." As a further sign of good faith, ABC scheduled the series for Sundays at 8:00, opposite big guns like CBS's *Murder, She Wrote* and NBC's *Family Ties.*

Not everyone was thrilled with the news. "I'm furious that my work is about to be used to prolong our strike," said *Mission* vet William Read Woodfield, noting "there's not a damn thing I can do about it. . . . The only consolation is it's going to cost (ABC) a fortune. Shooting the show here was almost impossible, but shooting it in Australia . . ." Both Woodfield and Laurence Heath had their names removed from the remade versions of their scripts.

Faced with the daunting task of remaking a classic were *Mission*'s new executive producers Jeffrey M. Hayes (formerly of *T.J. Hooker*) and Michael Fisher *(Strike Force, Spenser: For Hire).* One of their first decisions was to reconsider the all-new casting dictate: By mid July, Peter Graves was signed to return as Jim Phelps. While the original episodes were endlessly screened in an effort to find the thirteen "best" scripts, a quick but exhaustive search brought together an attractive new cast. Thaao Penghlis, an Australian actor of Greek descent and a popular daytime television performer *(Days of Our Lives, General Hospital)* was cast as Rollin Hand. The role of Barney Collier went to Greg Morris's son, Phil, who also made a splash in daytime television *(The Young and the Restless)* and had series roles in *Mr. Merlin* and *Marblehead Manor.* Pegged for Willy Armitage was English-born, Australian-raised Tony Hamilton, another daytime drama vet *(One Life to Live* and *The Guiding Light),* best known for his role in the short-lived spy series *Cover-Up.* The role of Cinnamon Carter went to Terry Markwell, an actress-model-designer living in Australia.

433

The four scripts eventually chosen for refilming were picked as much for their relatively apolitical leanings as their quality: episode 15, "The Legacy"; episode 44, "The Condemned"; episode 65, "The System"; and episode 105, "The Killer." The end of the Writers Guild strike in August allowed the producers to commission new scripts, some of which were reminiscent of old episodes: luring a drug kingpin onto American soil for extradition (as in episode 7, "Fakeout"); stopping an East German who profits from the existence of the Berlin Wall (episode 30, "The Bank"); using a circus to cover the rescue of an imprisoned priest (episode 2, "Old Man Out"); the brainwashing of a team member into a mindless assassin (episode 130, "Mindbend"); a team member stricken by amnesia during a mission (episode 146, "Trapped").

Despite the four recycled scripts, it was ultimately decided that the new series would be a sequel to the original, with a new IMF team. Phelps, of course, remained, but Rollin Hand became Nicholas Black, university drama teacher and expert in disguise, acting, and languages. Barney Collier was now *Grant* Collier, Barney's son, an MIT graduate at age sixteen and as brilliant as his father. Willy Armitage was changed to Max Harte, a muscular Australian who, while still in high school, rescued his brother from a Vietnamese prisoner of war camp. And Cinnamon was renamed Casey Randall, a top designer who entered the IMF by helping the team arrest the terrorist responsible for her fiancé's murder.

Chosen to open the series was "The Killer," its first act rewritten to show a retired Phelps returning to the IMF when its current leader, Tom Copperfield (Jim's friend and protégé) is murdered by an elusive assassin who, as in the original, operates unpredictably. At the end of the mission, Jim makes his return a permanent one.

Besides Jim Phelps, other *Mission* trademarks were retained to link the new series with the old. The tape and apartment scenes reappeared, with the taped voice once again Bob Johnson, whose old "Good morning, Mr. Phelps" has mellowed into the more informal "Good morning, Jim." Lalo Schifrin came back to score the premiere episode, and his *Mission* theme, reorchestrated for synthesizer, electric guitar, and heavy bass line, was as riveting as ever. Although the series didn't use a different main title montage for each episode, it did begin with the lighting of a match. This time, however, there was a face behind the flame: Jim Phelps.

Of course, there were other changes. Jim lives in a San Francisco apartment which is not black and white but gray, and outfitted not with an IMF dossier portfolio but a computer hidden in the coffee table which provides all necessary data. The self-destructing tapes were replaced by self-destructing laser disks enclosed in players which can be opened only by Jim's thumbprint and operated only after a three-digit code is pushed. In the old series, the phrase "IM Force" was never spoken except by the taped voice; here it's ubiquitous, with references to IM Computer Research, IM Laboratories, IMF Security, IMF files and more. The team's computer readouts and surveillance tapes frequently display the initials of this supposedly ultrasecret organization. In addition to familiars like face masks, needle rings, and transmitters, new IMF hardware included a hand-held "locator" to find hidden safes, eyeglasses with a liquid crystal display in the lens to receive messages, and a spray can or dart gun to induce unconsciousness. The old IMF card-cheating routine was spectacularly updated with playing cards covered with a liquid crystal screen that allows Grant to change the surface of the cards by remote control. Grant carries a laptop computer which has many uses, including data accessing and audiovisual monitoring; and an intriguing yellow camera which, when computer linked, can falsify documents, "matte" people into existing photographs, and design holographic projections. Some of Grant's equipment skirts the realm of credibility: a device that

recalls erased images from a videotape or a "developmental" headset that visually interprets a man's thoughts!

This IMF team shared a camaraderie not seen since the earliest days of the original series, and there was the definite presence of human feeling. Emotions have been displayed, with even Phelps expressing anger and frustration. The team skills were less strictly defined than before and acting assignments equally shared. Max had flashy roles like a homicidal maniac and a magician, and Grant was frequently a major participant in the cons. While a fine way to show off the entire cast, it weakened the role of Nicholas Black, who in days past would have gotten all the plum acting parts. Aside from his mimickry skills, poor Nicholas was just one performer among five. Even his cosmetic talents were superfluous: By episode 13, the face masks were designed and created by computer!

To justify a cast change during the first season, the producers took the unprecedented step of killing off a member of the Impossible Missions Force. In episode 12, "The Fortune," Casey Randall is sent on a surveillance mission by the secretary (why not Phelps?), and is caught chasing the estate of a deposed dictator, whose ruthless wife (played by Barbara Luna) injects her with a lethal chemical. When he hears a news report of Casey's body washing up on a beach, Jim is so stunned that he cannot tell the rest of the team for some time. When informed, the others are visibly affected and Max doubts that he can continue the mission.

PHELPS: I know how you all feel. She was like a daughter to me. We will nail whoever did this. That's a promise.

In short order they do, with the help of new IMF operative Shannon Reed, a former secret service agent and broadcast journalist played by new regular Jane Badler.

There were interesting references to the past. In episode 14, "Spy," Jim finds himself working with a Russian doctor—a former adversary whose life Phelps once spared. When Jim is wounded during their tandem mission, the Russian repays the favor. But the most fascinating segments were the ones that brought back old friends. In the remake of Laurence Heath's "The Condemned," the title character is none other than Barney Collier, wracked with guilt and grief over the death of his wife (who was buried before he even knew she had died) and laying low in Istanbul. Barney is framed for murder, jailed, and beaten so badly that he can hardly stand. He is amazed when Jim Phelps enters his filthy jail cell.

BARNEY: Jim, is that you? . . . Hell, you quit before I did!

PHELPS: Does any of us really quit for good?

In an improved rewrite of the original show, the IMF spring Barney from prison. Later, Barney tries to come to terms with his deep regret over the family he never had time for while Grant, who loves his father, comforts him. Well played by Greg and Phil Morris, the scene is, for *Mission: Impossible,* extraordinarily poignant. Barney later joined the team for episode 20, "The Golden Serpent," during which he suffers such brutal torture that the team believes him dead. Of course, Barney pulls through (Jim, at least, should have known better).

Even more revelatory is episode 17, "Reprisal," which recounts the story of Russell Acker, the genius behind many IMF tools and even the latex mixture for the face masks. Acker became unhinged after an auto injury, was let go by the IMF, and killed eight women before Phelps and three female IMFers apprehended him. In "Reprisal," Acker finds a way to revenge himself. Despite his confinement in a monitored cell, he escapes to kill two of the IMF women who trapped him—disguised as Phelps! Acker returns to his cell unnoticed, and Jim is sought for murder. Phelps warns the last lady on Acker's list—former IMF agent Casey, now a stage director. At the climax, the IMF sets a risky trap with Casey as bait. "Reprisal"

is one of the new series' best segments, highlighted by the sight of "Phelps" garotting women to death and the return of Lynda Day George as Casey, whose full name, we are told, is Lisa Casey. Jim refers to her as Lisa throughout the episode to avoid confusion with the late Casey Randall.

By filming in Australia, the show avoided the original series' greatest drawback. Australia's diverse geography (helped by matte shots) effectively passed for locales as diverse as Egypt, Paris, Africa, Greece, the Himalayas, Ireland, Hawaii . . . and Australia. For once, *Mission: Impossible* seemed to take place in the real world, not on a studio backlot, and the plots rarely occurred in the Latin American and East European settings that were so easy to duplicate in Hollywood. The series' lavish production values made the old *Mission* seem like a radio drama by comparison. Some episodes, like 18, "Submarine," and 26, "Target Earth," were almost handsome enough to pass as features. Bruce Geller would have liked that.

Unfortunately, all the effort was in vain. After a respectable start, averaging a 21 share in its first two weeks, the series dropped steadily down the Nielsens, even after being shifted to Saturdays at 8 P.M., opposite *Dolphin Cove* on CBS (which it usually bested) and NBC's popular comedies *227* and *Amen* (which regularly beat *Mission*). At seasons' end, *Mission* averaged a disappointing 64 (of 83), with a 9.5 rating and 16 share, prompting Paramount and ABC to cancel a vague plan to reunite the original cast in a TV movie. Nevertheless, ABC, which had increased the episode order from thirteen to nineteen, renewed *Mission* for the 1989–90 season.

For its second semester, the IMF faced its most dangerous mission when the show was moved to Thursdays at 8 P.M., opposite CBS's *48 Hours* and the number-one show in the country, NBC's *The Cosby Show*. Predictably, the ratings did not improve. *Mission* was soundly and consistently beaten in the Nielsen ratings. The show was rescheduled to its original Sunday 8:00 P.M. spot, but to no avail. *Mission* averaged a lowly 79 of the season's 96 series, with an 8.2 rating and 14 share. The show was pulled after fulfilling its 16-episode order, and on May 21, 1990, *Mission: Impossible* was canceled.

It is tempting to attribute the new *Mission*'s failure to develop an audience (or attract the old series' loyal following) to an overall lack of quality. Actually, with its superb production values, the show was a notch above most of its contemporaries. The series had flaws, of course, and its major one was fatal: the scripts.

"We never try to explain anything before it happens," Bruce Geller used to say. Alas, Bruce's rule was continually subverted by an overabundance of expository dialogue. This new IMF spent too much time explaining themselves or telegraphing the next scene's action with lines that began, "Time for . . ." With the attention span of the American public becoming shorter every year, it may have seemed wise for the team to repeat their intentions two or three times, as often happened. But fans of the original *Mission* who relished the visual unfolding of a plot were maddened by obvious, unnecessary lines like the following:

"Hamidou's responding perfectly."
"Good, it's working!"
"All right, the trap's been set. Let's spring it!"
"It worked; she's making the call."
"Right now Balzac and Laroux are getting a taste of their own medicine. Let's see just how desperate it makes them."
"Time to give Grant the time he needs."

"Our plan's working."
"Nicholas has done his job."
"Is the relay I planted working?"
"Now, to set the explosives."
"Everything's going according to plan."

An unfortunate holdover from the old series was a propensity for bad dialogue, with lines like "They're drug dealers. This wealth is at the expense of human misery" and "What kind of psychotic minds are at work here?" Even worse were the lame wisecracks uttered by Phelps at the end of many shows. It was a sorry comparison to the good old days when the team, with nothing clever to say and no reason to comment upon the obvious, simply boarded their van and drove off.

There were plot weaknesses as well. The new heavies were nastier than ever, but too often prone to stupidly fall into their own traps (as in episode 10, "The Lions") or blurt out confessions with little provocation (the villain in episode 33, "The Gunslinger," admits to murder before dozens of witnesses with virtually no prodding.)

The second season even saw errors within the *Mission* format. An agent murdered by the villains in the teaser of episode 20, "The Golden Serpent," is identified by the taped voice as the "leader of another IMF team," a claim which instantly destroys Phelps's longtime status. How many IM teams—and leaders—are there? In episode 34, "Church Bells in Bogota," a cardinal rule is broken when Phelps orders the team to rescue the imperiled Shannon at the expense of the mission!

It was no coincidence that some of the best scripts were by veterans Walter Brough and Stephen Kandel, both of whom wrote, however marginally, for the original series. In Brough's "War Games," an ambitious general plans to invade a neighboring country under the cover of war games. On his computerized war board, he watches what he thinks is the disposition of his forces as, according to plan, they obliterate the enemy's strategic targets. He has no idea that his battlefield display has been IMF rigged to show him what he *wants* to see; in fact, thanks to Grant's sabotage, the general is destroying his own army!

Kandel's "Target Earth" is an example of a preposterous concept beautifully executed. The IMF foil a terrorist takeover of a space launch, but not before Shannon, posing as the shuttle pilot, is launched into orbit, space-walks to repair a laser, and is set adrift before she can reenter the ship. Kandel manages to make all of it believable, then caps the show with Jim's call to an Air Force general about to eliminate the terrorist threat by destroying the shuttle base. Jim utters a government cryptonym to identify himself to the exasperated general, who cancels the attack, then yells at Jim, "How the hell did you get in there?" Phelps replies, "I'm sorry, general, we seem to be losing our connection," and hangs up!

The difference between this and an episode like episode 27, "The Fuehrer's Children," in which a group of boys raised as Nazis are converted by Grant *in one day,* is the difference between the ridiculous made plausible and the simply unbelievable. "It's amazing, isn't it," marvels Nicholas at Grant's success with the boys. It certainly was.

Unlike most shows, which depended upon characterization, *Mission: Impossible* always stood or fell upon its plots. The success of the original series was built upon imaginative, compelling stories, even when other production elements were lacking. The revival, conversely, had everything but the one factor essential to *Mission*—strong, well thought out plots. The writing standards seemed to completely collapse during the second season, and the hack

quality of the final few scripts was enough to sink the series, despite its spectacular look and capable cast.

Perhaps *Mission: Impossible* could never have succeeded again, no matter how well done. The uniqueness which helped make the original show a hit has been eroded by twenty years' worth of imitations; and in this age of sound bites and MTV, a series that requires an audience's attention may itself be an impossible mission. One matter, however, seems certain: As time goes on and further attempts are made to duplicate its formula, the original *Mission: Impossible* will only look better and better.

Mission: Impossible returned in 1988 with (left to right) Terry Markwell, Tony Hamilton, Peter Graves, Phil Morris, and Thaao Penghlis.

Year One:
1988–1989

Production Credits

Starring: Peter Graves, Thaao Penghlis, Tony Hamilton, Phil Morris, Terry Markwell (episodes 1 through 12), Jane Badler (episodes 12 through 19)
Created by: Bruce Geller
Executive Producers: Michael Fisher, Jeffrey M. Hayes
Producer: Ted Roberts
Coproducer: Walter Brough
Coordinating Producer: Barry Berg
Associate Producer: Dean Barnes
Executive Story Consultant: Ted Roberts
Directors of Photography: Ron Hagen, ASC; Stephen F. Windon
Production Designer: Stewart Burnside
Edited by: Roger Bondelli, Howard S. Deane, Pamela Malouf, Larry Mills, ACE
Australian Production Executive: Michael Lake
Script Editors: Stanley Walsh, Rick Maier
Unit Production Manager: Daryl Sheen
First Assistant Directors: Stuart Wood, Jamie Leslie, Brian Giddens, Charles Rotherham, Phil Jones
Art Directors: Dale Duguid, Richard Rooker, Philip Drake
Theme Music by: Lalo Schifrin
Australian Casting by: Liz Mullinar Consultants; Maura Fay & Associates
Casting: Helen Mossler, CSA

Production Services Supplied by: McMahon & Lake Pty., Ltd.
Production Coordinator: Sue Edwards
Costume Designers: Keely Ellis, Graham Purcell
Makeup Artists: Rozalina De Silva, Deborah Lanser
Hairstylist: Deborrah Tyson
Sound Mixer: Paul Clark
Script Supervisor: Joanne McClennan
Main Titles by: Betty Green
Postproduction Coordinators: Randy S. Nelson, Meryl Jackson (Australia)
Visual Effects Coordinator: Elan Soltes
Supervising Sound Editors: Doug Gray, Richard Corwin
Sound Editors: Ken Gladden, Mark Server, Richard Corwin, Gary Gelfand, Phil Jantaas, Craig Otte
Music Editor: James D. Young
Rerecording Mixers: Tom Huth, Sam Black, Tim Philben, George Groves, Scott Millan, Clark Conrad, Anthony Constantini
Sound by: Larson Sound Center
Electronic Laboratory™: Pacific Video Inc.
Special Video Effects by: The Post Group
Australian Telecine by: Hoyt's Videolab
Produced at: Village Roadshow Film Studios in Queensland, Australia

Grant uses an ultra-violet visor to help him open a laser-protected safe in "The System."

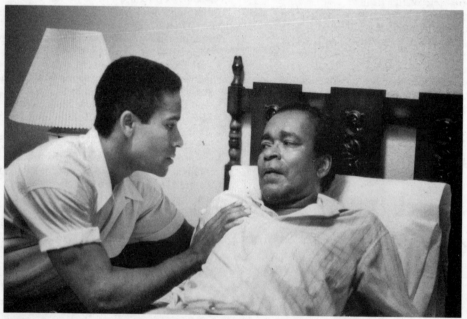

Greg Morris returned as Barney Collier in "The Condemned."

Year One: 1988–1989

1: THE KILLER
First Aired: 10/23/88
Written by: Arthur Weiss
Directed by: Cliff Bole
Music by: Lalo Schifrin
Mission: End the career of professional killer Matthew Drake and uncover his employer, known only as Scorpio (see original *Mission* episode 105, "The Killer").
Guest Cast: John de Lancie (Matthew Drake), Ted Hamilton (Alfred Chambers)

2: THE LEGACY
First Aired: 11/26/88
Written by: Michael Lynn and Allan Balter
Directed by: Kim Manners
Music by: Lalo Schifrin
Mission: Locate five billion dollars in gold before the grandsons of Hitler's highest officers use it to finance a Nazi resurgence (see original *Mission* episode 15, "The Legacy").
Guest Cast: Judson Scott (Ernst Graff), Steven Grives (Brucker)

3: THE SYSTEM
First Aired: 10/30/88
Written by: Robert Hamner
Directed by: Cliff Bole
Music by: Ron Jones
Mission: Get Bahamas casino head Frank Marley to testify against Bob Connors, head of the syndicate (see original *Mission* episode 65, "The System").
Guest Cast: James Sloyan (Frank Marley), Gus Mercurio (Bob Connors)

4: HOLOGRAMS
First Aired: 11/6/88
Written by: Robert Brennan
Directed by: Kim Manners
Music by: Lalo Schifrin
Mission: Lure a cocaine kingpin onto American-controlled soil for extradition and neutralize his successor.
Guest Cast: Gerard Kennedy (Colonel Gregory Usher)

5: THE CONDEMNED
First Aired: 11/20/88
Teleplay by: Ted Roberts and Michael Fisher
Story by: John Truman
Directed by: Cliff Bole
Music by: Ron Jones
Mission: Rescue an innocent American from certain death in a Turkish prison and eliminate the corrupt police officer behind the setup. The framed American is Grant's father, Barney Collier, former member of the IMF (see original *Mission* episode 44, "The Condemned").
Guest Cast: Greg Morris (Barney Collier), Adrian Wright (Captain Hamidou)

6: THE WALL
First Aired: 12/11/88
Written by: David Phillips
Directed by: Colin Budds
Music by: Ron Jones
Mission: Recover the kidnapped daughter of a West German negotiator from an East Berlin doctor and security colonel, both of whom have a financial interest in keeping the Berlin Wall standing.
Guest Cast: Alan Cassell (Dr. Gerstner), Peter Curtin (Colonel Batz)

7: THE CATTLE KING
First Aired: 12/18/88
Written by: Ted Roberts
Directed by: Mike Vejar
Music by: John Davis
Mission: Prevent an Australian arms dealer from completing a missile deal with a terrorist organization.
Guest Cast: David Bradshaw (Douglas Matthews), Warren Owens (Mulwarra), Sal Sharah (Terrorist)

8: THE PAWN
First Aired: 1/15/89
Written by: Billy Marshall-Stoneking
Directed by: Brian Trenchard-Smith
Music by: Ron Jones
Mission: Smuggle a heavily guarded Russian scientist and his daughter out of Czechoslovakia.
Guest Cast: Bryan Marshall (Antonov), Rowena Wallace (Major Natalia Zorbuskaya)

9: THE HAUNTING
First Aired: 1/28/89
Written by: Michael Fisher
Directed by: Mike Vejar
Music by: John Davis
Mission: Incriminate a serial killer whose latest victim may provoke an international incident.
Guest Cast: Parker Stevenson (Champ Foster), Janis Paige (Victoria Foster)

10: THE LIONS
First Aired: 2/4/89
Teleplay by: David Phillips
Story by: James Crown
Directed by: Rob Stewart
Music by: Ron Jones
Mission: Block a usurper's plot to kill the young heir apparent during the traditional test of kings.
Guest Cast: James Shigeta (Ki), Diane Craig (Lady Michelle Faulkner)

11: THE GREEK
First Aired: 2/11/89
Written by: Ted Roberts
Directed by: Colin Budds
Music by: John Davis
Mission: Stop a Greek tycoon from hijacking medical supplies intended for Third World countries.
Guest Cast: Cesare Danova (Socrates Colonnades), Nicholas Hammond (Woodward)

12: THE FORTUNE
First Aired: 2/18/89
Written by: Robert Brennan
Directed by: Rod Hardy
Music by: Ron Jones
Mission: Find and return the billions of dollars looted by a deposed dictator and his wife. This episode introduces Shannon Reed, who becomes a permanent member of the IMF when Casey Randall is killed during this assignment.
Guest Cast: Barbara Luna (Emilia Berezan), Michael Pate (Luis Berezan)

13: THE FIXER
First Aired: 2/25/89
Written by: Walter Brough
Directed by: Colin Budds
Music by: John E. Davis
Mission: Uncover and neutralize the blackmail files of an immensely powerful Washington journalist.
Guest Cast: Richard Romanus (Arthur Six), John Calvin (Doyle)

14: SPY
First Aired: 3/18/89
Teleplay by: Michael Fisher
Directed by: Rob Stewart
Music by: John E. Davis
Mission: Stop a renegade British agent and his chemical warfare plant in Africa.
Guest Cast: Tim Hughes (Christie)

15: THE DEVILS
First Aired: 3/25/89
Written by: Ted Roberts
Directed by: Arch Nicholson
Music by: John E. Davis
Mission: Establish guilt in a series of sacrificial murders in the English countryside.
Guest Cast: John Stanton (Lord Holman), Ron Graham (Challis)

16: THE PLAGUE
First Aired: 4/8/89
Written by: Rick Maier
Directed by: Colin Budds
Music by: John E. Davis
Mission: Retrieve a lethal chemical and eliminate the Parisian terrorist who stole it.
Guest Cast: Maud Adams (Catherine Balzac), Gary Day (Laroux)

17: REPRISAL
First Aired: 4/15/89
Written by: Walter Brough
Directed by: Rob Stewart
Music by: John E. Davis
Mission: Learn who is framing Phelps for the murders of former IMF members.
Guest Cast: Lynda Day George (Lisa Casey)

18: SUBMARINE
First Aired: 4/29/89
Written by: Dale Duguid
Directed by: Colin Budds
Music by: John E. Davis
Mission: Obtain the "antidote" to a computer "virus" capable of destroying the US Navy, and put its owners out of business.
Guest Cast: Mitchell Ryan (Admiral Sheppard)

19: BAYOU
First Aired: 5/6/89
Written by: Jeffrey M. Hayes
Directed by: Don Chaffey
Music by: John E. Davis
Mission: Rescue the victims of a Louisiana white slavery operation and bring its ringleader to justice.
Guest Cast: Paula Kelly (Pepper Leveau)

In the revival, Phelps received his orders on self-destructing optical laser discs.

Jane Badler replaced Terry Markwell midway through Year One of the revival.

Year Two:
1989–1990

Production Credits

Starring: Peter Graves, Thaao Penghlis, Tony Hamilton, Phil Morris, Jane Badler
Created by: Bruce Geller
Executive Producer: Jeffrey M. Hayes
Supervising Producer-Coexecutive Producer: Frank Abatemarco
Producer-Supervising Producer: Ted Roberts
Coordinating Producer: Dean Barnes
Line Producer: Darryl Sheen
Associate Producer: Randy S. Nelson
Staff Writer: Roger Dunn
Director of Photography: Barry M. Wilson, ACS
Production Designer: Stewart Burnside
Edited by: Howard S. Deane, Russell Denove, Jon Koslowski, Peter Basinski
Production Executive: Michael Lake
Visual Effects Designer: Dale Duguid
Unit Production Managers: Elizabeth Symes, Ray Hennessy
First Assistant Directors: Jamie Leslie, Phil Jones, Brian Giddens, Brendan Campbell
Art Directors: Phil Drake, Eugene Intas
Music by: John E. Davis
Theme by: Lalo Schifrin
Casting by: Helen Mossler, CSC
Australian Casting by: Maura Fay & Associates
Production Services by: McMahon & Lake Pty., Ltd.

Production Coordinator: Sue Edwards
Costume Designers: Graham Purcell, Sally Grigsby
Makeup Artists: Rozalina da Silva, Deborah Lanser, Karla O'Keefe
Sound Mixers: Paul Clark, Phil Stirling, Andrew Ramage
Script Supervisors: Joanne McLennan, Carmel Torcasio
Postproduction Supervisor: Randy S. Nelson
Visual Effects Supervisors: Elan Soltes, Jennifer Holstein
Main Titles by: Betty Green
Australian Postcoordinator: Claire Walsh
Postproduction Associates: Katherine Rager, Tim Muccillo
Supervising Sound Editor: Mark Server
Sound Editors: George Groves, Jr., Ken Gladden, Craig Otte, Joe Johnson
Music Editor: James D. Young
Rerecording Mixers: Tim Philben, Scott Millan, Clark Conrad
Sound by: Larson Sound Center
Electronic Laboratory™: Pacific Video Inc.
Special Video Effects by: The Post Group
Australian Telecine by: AAV
Filmed at: Australian Film Studios, Dallas, Australia

The new series retained the Apartment scene.

20/21: THE GOLDEN SERPENT (in two parts)
First Aired: 9/21/89; 9/28/89
Teleplay by: Michael Seims and Ted Roberts and Jeffrey M. Hayes
Story by: Michael Seims
Directed by: Don Chaffey
Mission: Identify, expose, and bring to justice the leaders of a worldwide drug smuggling triad.
Guest Cast: Greg Morris (Barney Collier), Patrick Bishop (Prince Selimun), Rod Mullinar (Conrad Drago)

22: THE PRINCESS
First Aired: 10/5/89
Written by: Ted Roberts
Directed by: Colin Budds
Mission: Thwart a Libyan-financed assassination attempt against an American-born European princess.
Guest Cast: Robert Coleby (Grigor Caron), Dale Stevens (Coyote)

23: COMMAND PERFORMANCE
First Aired: 10/12/89
Written by: Robert Brennan
Directed by: Arch Nicholson
Mission: Free an imprisoned priest who may know the location of an artifact containing information that will destroy a murderous Baltic defense minister.
Guest Cast: Grigor Taylor (Defense Minister Ivan Savitch), Ivar Kants (Father Thomas Vallis)

24: COUNTDOWN
First Aired: 10/26/89
Written by: Chip Hayes
Directed by: Brian Trenchard-Smith
Mission: Locate and disarm a hidden warhead before a fanatic and a military strongman destroy an Asian city.
Guest Cast: Julie Ow (Su Lin)

25: WAR GAMES
First Aired: 11/2/89
Written by: Walter Brough
Directed by: Rod Hardy
Mission: Undo a general's plan to invade a neighboring country during "war games."
Guest Cast: Kevin Miles (General Eli Szabo), Lewis Fiander (Colonel Garva)

26: TARGET EARTH
First Aired: 11/9/89
Written by: Stephen Kandel
Directed by: Colin Budds
Mission: Ensure that the world's first privately manned space flight isn't used in a terrorist plot to threaten the earth from space.
Guest Cast: Eli Danker (Robard), Lewis Fitz-Gerald (Rhine)

27: THE FUEHRER'S CHILDREN
First Aired: 11/16/89
Written by: Frank Abatemarco
Directed by: Don Chaffey
Mission: Discredit a powerful white supremacist before he is elected leader of a worldwide coalition of neo-Nazi organizations.
Guest Cast: Albert Salmi (Richard Kester), John Bell (Vogel), Nancy Black (Eva Kester)

28: BANSHEE
First Aired: 11/30/89
Written by: Ted Roberts
Directed by: Colin Budds
Mission: Finish an Irish arms dealer who uses violence to fuel his country's sectarian conflict.
Guest Cast: Peter Adams (Brian McCarron)

29: FOR ART'S SAKE
First Aired: 12/14/89
Written by: John Whelpley
Directed by: Colin Budds
Music by: John E. Davis
Mission: End the career of an art thief in the employ of Central American officials.
Guest Cast: Alex Cord (Travers), David Bradshaw (Ocha), Bill Ten Eyck (Danmeer)

30: DEADLY HARVEST
First Aired: 1/6/90
Written by: Jan Sardi
Directed by: Arch Nicholson
Mission: Quash a terrorist plot to ruin America's wheat harvest.
Guest Cast: Ritchie Singer (Jouseff K.), George Vidalis (Mukhta)

31: CARGO CULT
First Aired: 1/13/90
Written by: Dale Duguid
Directed by: Colin Budds
Mission: Prevent the genocide of Pacific island villagers by ruthless gold miners.
Guest Cast: Adrian Wright (Regehr), Larni John Tupu (Otagi)

32: THE ASSASSIN
First Aired: 1/20/90
Written by: Cliff Green
Directed by: Arch Nicholson
Mission: Trace the cause of a series of murder-suicides involving international government officials.
Guest Cast: Peter Curtin (Dr. Philip Westerly), Joe Gray (Chief Leopold Kombutu)

33: THE GUNSLINGER
First Aired: 2/3/90
Teleplay by: Ted Roberts
Story by: Dan Roberts
Directed by: Colin Budds
Mission: Determine whether an Old West theme park is a cover for a terrorist-arming operation.
Guest Cast: Michael Greene (Ian McClintock), Patrick Ward (Slade)

34: CHURCH BELLS IN BOGOTA
First Aired: 2/10/90
Written by: Frank Abatemarco
Directed by: Arch Nicholson
Mission: Foil a drug lord's plan to overthrow the Colombian government.
Guest Cast: Tony Kauet (Luis Magdelena), Henri Szeps (Esteban Magdelena), Michael Long (Sanchez), Bob Ruggerio (Dr. Romero)

35: THE SANDS OF SETH
First Aired: 2/24/90
Written by: Jeffrey M. Hayes
Directed by: Colin Budds
Mission: Confirm a museum curator's guilt in the murders of Egyptian politicians.
Guest Cast: Gerard Kennedy (Karnak), Tim Elliott (Horace Selim), Denzil Howson (Farthay), Michael Carman (Serapis)

HERE WE GO WITH MAD'S VERSION OF THE TV SERIES THAT STARTS OFF EACH WEEK LIKE THIS:

Good evening, Mr. Phelts. Thank you for pushing the **"message"** button. When you hear this week's **assignment,** you'll be sorry you didn't push the **"Coke"** button. Mainly because this is another—

MISSION:
RIDICULOUS

A valuable roll of **microfilm** has been stolen from the laboratory of **Dr. Demetrius Emo,** the famous microfilm-maker. Your job is to **recover** that film, rush it over to a drugstore to be **developed,** and then turn it over to the **U. S. I. A.** All we know is that the film is somewhere in the state of **Maine,** it is so **valuable** that you and your team will be **killed** the minute anyone learns you are trying to retrieve it, and that you have only **52 television minutes** left to do the job. So get going!

ARTIST: MORT DRUCKER   WRITER: DICK DE BARTOLO

As usual, at the end of this message, this recording will **discreetly destroy itself.** So, step back! Bye, now . . .

That Coke machine just **blew itself up!** Isn't that the most **suspicious** thing you've ever **seen!?**

Not really! They once got an assignment from a **hydrant** on **High St.** which **dissolved itself** immediately afterward!

This is the state of Maine—

How come it says "Texas"?

To confuse anyone watching!

It must work! I'm confused!

Now, we are all going to Maine for this assignment. But to avoid suspicion, we won't travel together. Bowling, you'll go by plane . . . Blarney by train . . . Synonym by bus . . . and I'll grab a cab. Synonym, did you get the tickets?

I got them, but the travel agent sure was suspicious about four friends going to one destination four different ways.

I'll have Billy, the fifth member of our team, take care of him and meet us here in El Paso . . .

Is that anywhere near Portland?

Idiot! That IS Portland! Now—in order not to attract attention, we will rendezvous in three days in the phone booth in the lobby of the Portland Hilton. Good luck!

Here we are . . . and the fare is $3,466.75. You know, this is the most suspicious thing I've ever heard of . . . taking a cab from Los Angeles to Maine! What are you, some kind of secret agent?

No, I'm some kind of secret nut!

Cigars . . . cigarettes . . . clues! Cigars . . . cigarettes . . . clues!

Why, Synonym! What a fantastic disguise!

You have no idea HOW fantastic . . . considering I'm not Synonym! I'm Billy, the strong man of this team! We couldn't find an empty phone booth, so sign the hotel register with a phony name and come up to room 1313 . . .

Welcome to the Portland Hilton, Mr. Smith . . . MR. SMITH!? You're the fourth person to sign "Mr. Smith" in the last ten minutes! That's the most suspicious thing I've ever seen!

What's so suspicious? It's a family reunion!

Yeah, but two of the four Mr. Smiths were women!

Glad you all made it. Now we can get down to business! Did you notice anything peculiar in the **hotel register**?

You mean all the "Mister Smiths"?

Besides that! A "Dr. Demetrius Emo" checked in today and listed his occupation as "top-secret micro-film-maker"!

Yes, but how can we be sure it's the **same** Dr. Demetrius Emo, top-secret micro-film-maker, **we're** looking for? There may be **hundreds** of them!

By checking his **room**! Only we've got to think of some clever way to find out **which** room he's in!

Leave that to me! Hello, **Room Service?** This is Dr. Demetrius Emo. If I told you to bring a bottle of **wine** to my room, **which** room would you **bring** it to? What do you **mean**, that's the most **suspicious** thing you've ever heard? That's a **perfectly legitimate question!!**

Uh-huh! Yes! I see— That's 1934! Thank you!

That was **brilliant!** So Dr. Emo is in room **1934!**

No, 1934 is the **year** of the **wine!** An **excellent** year! Dr. Emo, on the other hand, is in room **1963,** which may be a respectable enough room, but an **awful** year for **wine!**

There's **no answer!** Blarney, can you open this door?

Just watch! First, I take my **handerchief,** unfold it, and slip it under the door. Then, I take a pencil and push it through the keyhole—

The key inside falls onto the handkerchief and I pull them both from under the door! Easy, huh?

Great! Only there's a much **easier** way! First we try the door to see if it's **unlocked** . . . which it **is,** you idiot!

Look! It's **Dr. Emo!** And he's **dead!**

If he were just **sleeping,** he'd be on the **bed!**

Maybe he's just **sleeping!**

Listen! Somebody's coming down the **hall!** Quick! Get **inside!**

Who's there?

Room Service, Dr. Emo! I have your bottle of **wine!**

Good! Slip it under the door!

It won't fit under the door, sir!

Then **POUR** it under the door! Yes, sir!

But if you don't mind my saying so, sir—this is the **most suspicious** thing I've ever done in my life!

Don't **worry!** I have a **straw!**

A 📺 SCENE WE'D LIKE TO SEE

Good morning, Mr. Phelps! The man you are looking at has become a **serious threat** to the **Impossible Mission Force.**

He has squandered **millions of dollars of government funds** on such useless and extravagant contrivances as laser-beam fountain pens, radar wrist watches, closed-circuit mini-TV cameras embedded in belt buckles, and invisible sneakers . . .

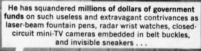

In addition, he has created an unusual **high-risk factor** by ordering his co-workers to perform **needlessly complex** and **dangerous tasks** in order to carry out assignments that could have been accomplished relatively safely and simply.

In other words, Mr. Phelps . . . **YOU'RE FIRED!!**

Good luck in your next TV series, Jim . . .

This sink will self-destruct in five seconds . . .

ARTIST: JOHN CULLEN MURPHY   WRITER: CHEVY CHASE

456